Hospitality
in Early
Modern England

FELICITY HEAL

CLARENDON PRESS · OXFORD
1990

Oxford University Press, Walton Street, Oxford OX2 6DP

Oxford New York Toronto
Delhi Bombay Calcutta Madras Karachi
Petaling Jaya Singapore Hong Kong Tokyo
Nairobi Dar es Salaam Cape Town
Melbourne Auckland
and associated companies in
Berlin Ibadan

Oxford is a trade mark of Oxford University Press

Published in the United States
by Oxford University Press, New York

British Library Cataloguing in Publication Data
Heal, Felicity
Hospitality in early modern England.—(Oxford studies in social history)
1. England. Hospitality, history
I. Title   395.30942
ISBN 0-19-821763-3

Library of Congress Cataloging in Publication Data
Heal, Felicity
Hospitality in early modern England/Felicity Heal.
p. cm.—(Oxford studies in social history)
Includes bibliographical references.
1. Hospitality – England – History. 2. England – Social life and
customs.   I. Title.   II. Series.
BJ2021.H42   1990   89-70937
177'.1'09420903 – dc20
ISBN 0-19-821763-3

Typeset by Dobbie Typesetting Limited, Plymouth, Devon.
Printed and bound in Great Britain by Biddles Ltd
Guildford and King's Lynn

To Clive

PREFACE AND ACKNOWLEDGEMENTS

> An housholdere, and that a greet, was he;
> Seint Julian he was in his contree.

Chaucer, *Prologue to the Canterbury Tales,*
The Franklin.

JULIAN the Hospitaller, patron saint of innkeepers, boatmen, and even travellers (in rivalry to St Christopher), is a fitting patron also for this study. His attributes commend him, but as an individual he is totally obscure, probably a construct of the medieval hagiographers, his good works veiled by time and the accretion of traditions. St Julian has his place in the *Golden Legend*, but lacks a country, a tomb, and a dedication feast. Nevertheless, his name was invoked with some frequency in England before the Reformation, and his image is to be found in several churches, especially in East Anglia. His qualities of charitable giving and selfless openness to the needs of others, were those constantly commended in late medieval and early modern England whenever hospitality was discussed. While the quest for the real saint would probably be a fruitless endeavour, the pursuit of the behaviour advocated in his legend can offer a compelling entry into the history of a society.

Over a decade ago labours among the archives of the Tudor Church left me with an abiding puzzle. The bishops, whose economic and social fortunes I was endeavouring to study, were apparently being assailed by both Catholic and Protestant commentators, and even by members of the government, for their failures as hosts. It was alleged that they 'kept no hospitality', and yet in the next breath often claimed that they misused the resources entrusted to them in entertaining their families and the wealthy and powerful. The tenor of the complaints varied somewhat according to the presuppositions of the authors, but the essential message was surprisingly unchanging: bishops must give hospitality, and they must give it in ways that embraced a wider circle of individuals than merely acknowledged friends and relatives. A part of my puzzle was easily resolved by reference back to the Scriptures and the canonists, where demands for good hospitality were essentially injunctions to care for the poor. And there, for the time, I chose to leave the problem, observing the struggles of the prelates to justify their position by reference to criteria that seemed to have little immediate relevance to sixteenth-century English society.

However, the issue still intrigued and challenged me, since much contemporary discourse on hospitality clearly did relate to the circumstances of Tudor England, and to the cultural suppositions it had inherited from the immediate past. Bishops were in one sense evidently a sub-group of the landed élite, and their lay peers were equally often enjoined to be good hosts. Preachers and moralists even made it clear that other social groups could not consider themselves exempt from this social duty, but should care for outsiders so far as their means permitted. Therefore, Tudor prelates temporarily abandoned, it seemed worth embarking upon a more serious attempt to understand the nature and meaning of hospitality in early modern England, and to ascertain how far the ideal formulations of the moralists were matched by social action. The quest has proved both exciting and frustrating: exciting because it has led to the examination of a great diversity of sources, and to the pursuit of heterogeneous ways of reading the society; frustrating because the very concept of hospitality is multi-faceted and elusive in this culture and because any comprehensive view of social practice inevitably proved an impossibility. Instead, what can be assembled is a *bricolage* of individual evidence, offering what I hope are telling signs of the behaviour of a variety of men. At the very least the quest leads in directions that provide a rather distinctive perspective on social activity in England between 1400 and 1700.

This study has been long in the making, and in the pursuit of its diverse byways I have accumulated extensive debts. I am grateful to the archivist of the Marquis of Bath for the provision of extensive access to the Longleat House archives, and to the Trustees of the Berkeley Castle estate for the opportunity to examine the Berkeley muniments. Staff in a variety of record offices have offered much assistance, but I must express particular thanks to those of Norfolk and Staffordshire Record Offices for help given over a period of years. A short stay at the Folger Library in Washington DC provided me with access not only to its excellent manuscript collection, but to the best subject index of early printed material I have encountered.

The following have kindly given permission to reproduce plans and diagrams: Yale University Press (Haddon Hall and the isometric drawing of Hardwick Hall), the Society of Antiquaries (Thornbury Castle), the Walpole Society (Lord Buckhurst's House at Withyham), and the Royal Commission for Historical Monuments (Charlton House, Greenwich and Minster Lovell Hall).

Among more personal debts I must first express gratitude to the Principal and Fellows of Jesus College, Oxford, for the periods of sabbatical leave that have made this study possible. It is also my college colleagues who have by their actions reminded me that the practice of hospitality, in its early modern sense, is not yet wholly dead. Many fellow-historians have contributed to the genesis of this volume, either with general advice and suggestions or with specific references: I am grateful to Patrick Collinson, Cliff Davies, Kevin Dillow, Ken Fincham, Ian Green, Andrew Hope, Malcolm Kitch, Judith Maltby, Diarmid MacCulloch, Victor Morgan, Mary Prior, Glyn Redworth, Conrad Russell, Hassell Smith, and David Starkey. Christine Carpenter, Gerald Harriss, and Carole Rawcliffe did much to aid my faltering footsteps among the late medieval household accounts, and I am grateful for comment from Jennifer Thurgood, to whose dissertation I have frequently turned. Professor R. S. Khare provided me with valuable assistance on anthropological studies of hospitality. Mark Byford and Dorothy Owen have been particularly generous in placing unpublished material at my disposal.

Local inspiration and encouragement in times of doubt have come from John Walsh and Jenny Wormald. Paul Seaver has offered the same support on his visits from the United States. Ged Martin has sustained a flow of references to remind me that hospitality was not unique to Tudor and Stuart England. Sears McGee kindly read Chapter 3 in an earlier draft and offered helpful suggestions on structure as well as many particular references: David Palliser has read Chapters 2 and 8, and throughout the slow growth of the volume has given constant support and encouragement. Keith Thomas has from the beginning offered ideas and critical insights and has played a crucial role in reading the entire text and detecting weaknesses of presentation and argument. I am much indebted to my mother, without whose domestic support in a difficult period this volume would certainly not have been completed. Above all, this study could not have been brought to fruition without the help and inspiration of Clive Holmes. My personal debt is expressed through the dedication: my academic one is equally extensive. His provision of detailed references, constant availability for discussion, sharp antagonism to sloppy thinking, and final critical reading of the completed text have informed the whole endeavour. He has helped to make the quest a challenging intellectual adventure and a rare pleasure.

F.H.

Jesus College, Oxford
February 1989.

CONTENTS

Lists of Illustrations and Figures   xii

Abbreviations   xiii

1. The Language and Symbolism of Hospitality   1

2. Hospitality in the Great Household   23

3. The Changing Vision of Hospitality   91

4. The Élite and Household Entertainment: From the
    Elizabethan Age to the Restoration   141

5. Visitors and Voyagers   192

6. The Duties of the Pre-Reformation Clergy   223

7. The Clergy after the Reformation   257

8. Urban Hospitality   300

·9. Hospitality among the Populace   352

10. Conclusion   389

Bibliography   404

Index   431

LIST OF ILLUSTRATIONS

Between pages 226 and 227

1. The hospitable works of mercy: giving drink to the thirsty (stained glass window: St Andrew, Chinnor, Oxon.; courtesy of RHMC).
2. The hospitable works of mercy: feeding the hungry (stained glass window: All Saints Church, North Street, York; courtesy of RHMC).
3. Pilgrims received into the household: from the fifteenth century poem 'The Pilgrim' (courtesy of the British Library).
4. Giving to the poor in the late seventeenth century: the Tichborne Dole, by Gillis van Tirborch (courtesy of the Bridgeman Art Library).
5. Monastic hospitality institutionalized: The George, or Pilgrim's Inn, Glastonbury (courtesy of RHMC).
6. Citizens feasting: the Fête at Bermondsey, *c.*1570, by J. Hofnaegel (courtesy of the Marquis of Salisbury).

LIST OF FIGURES

2.1.	Schematic diagram of the Great House.	28
2.2.	Haddon Hall.	38
2.3.	Minster Lovell Hall.	39
2.4.	Thornbury Castle.	45
2.5.	Principal residences of gentry visitors to the Le Strange household, Hunstanton: 1520–38.	60
4.1.	Plan for Lord Buckhurst's house at Withyham.	156
4.2.	Charlton House, Greenwich.	160
4.3.	Isometric drawing of Hardwick Hall.	161

ABBREVIATIONS

APC	*Acts of the Privy Council of England*, ed. J. R. Dasent
BRO	Bedfordshire Record Office, Bedford
Bodl.	The Bodleian Library, Oxford
BL	British Library
BIHR	*Bulletin of the Institute of Historical Research*
C. St. P. Dom.	*The Calendar of State Papers Domestic*
CUL	Cambridge University Library
CCCC	Corpus Christi College, Cambridge
EETS	*Early English Text Society*
EDR	Ely Diocesan Records, Cambridge University Library
ERO	Essex Record Office
Folger Lib.	Folger Library, Washington DC
GLRO	Greater London Record Office
GRO	Gloucester Record Office, Gloucester
HJ	*Historical Journal*
HMC	*Historical Manuscripts Commission*
JBS	*Journal of British Studies*
JEH	*Journal of Ecclesiastical History*
JWCI	*Journal of the Warburg and Courtauld Institutes*
LPL	Lambeth Palace Library, London
LP	*Letters and Papers Foreign and Domestic in the Reign of Henry VIII*, ed. J. S. Brewer, J. Gairdner, and R. H. Brodie
Li. RO	Lincolnshire Record Office, Lincoln
NRO	Norfolk and Norwich Record Office, Norwich
PP	*Past and Present*
PRO	Public Record Office
RHMC	*Royal Commission for Historical Monuments*
Staff. RO	Staffordshire Record Office, Stafford
TRHS	*Transactions of the Royal Historical Society*
VCH	*Victoria County History*
Wa. RO	Warwickshire Record Office, Warwick
Wi. RO	Wiltshire Record Office, Trowbridge

1
The Language and Symbolism of Hospitality

IN our pantheon of social virtues hospitality occupies a modest, though honourable, place. It is most valued as a private quality, involving the opening of some part of our domestic worlds to chosen others, to whom friendship can most effectively be expressed through forms of commensality. The public, more compulsory, façade of entertainment—the business lunch, the annual works dinner, or the modish offering of corporate hospitality at sports events—are also comprehended within our use of the term, though often with the mental reservation that they devalue a concept which should ideally express personal amity and connection. The American usage 'hospitality industry' suggests an immediate paradox between generosity and the exploitation of the market-place. For modern Western man hospitality is preponderantly a private form of behaviour, exercised as a matter of personal preference within a limited circle of friendship and connection. As such, it is also considered a social luxury, to be pursued when circumstances are favourable, but abandoned without serious loss of status when they prove adverse. Few would claim that it possesses any centrality in our value-systems, or that the obligation to entertain could be described as a moral imperative.

It is the purpose of this book to argue that this perception of hospitality is a relatively recent phenomenon, and that in other times and places the entertainment which groups and individuals gave to outsiders was of far greater cultural significance. Anthropologists and historians studying such societies as Homeric Greece, early Rome, medieval Provence, the Maori, and the Indian tribes of the North-West Pacific Coast of Canada, have already argued for the centrality of hospitality.[1] In these cultures generosity and good behaviour as a host were no mere matter of personal preference, but rested on fundamental beliefs about the nature of relationships, and about the effective functioning of the social universe, beliefs that enjoined certain patterns of behaviour, which could only be neglected at the cost of humiliation and perhaps loss of power. While hospitality was often expressed in a series of private actions, in the sense that it depended on an individual household and a particular host, it was integrated into a matrix of beliefs that were shared and articulated publicly. The present study, of English society in the period loosely described as early modern, that is to say approximately from 1400 to 1700, originated in an awareness that in these centuries domestic beneficence and good entertainment was often a matter of public concern. The duty of generosity was proclaimed from the pulpit, and urged in prescriptive literature. It was seen as one of the foundations of the moral economy, though a foundation that was constantly shaken by the failures of Englishmen as hosts.

The language of writers and moralists provides a first entry into a world that seems closer to the ancient world than our own in its understanding of hospitality. However, only a full investigation of the practice of Englishmen can offer insight into the cultural significance of this ideal. If we compare early modern England with classical Rome, we find in the latter the development of a powerful ideology of generosity, formulated as an elaborate *ius hospitii*. But the ideology emanated from a practical need to integrate outsiders, which was achieved through the acceptance of guest-friends as a necessary part of the clientage system.[2] Thus, in Roman society good entertainment proved a necessary part of everyday behaviour for leading citizens. Similarly, in early modern England we must expect to judge the significance of hospitality not so much by the rhetoric of the guardians of the

---

[1] M. Finley, *The World of Odysseus* (New York, 1954); L. Bolchazy, *Hospitality in Early Rome* (Chicago, 1977); M. T. Bruckner, *Narrative Invention in Early Twelfth-Century Romance* (Lexington, 1980); M. Mauss, *The Gift: Forms and Functions of Exchange in Archaic Societies* (London, 1970); R. Benedict, *Patterns of Culture* (New York, 1934), ch. 6; M. Sahlins, *Stone Age Economics* (Chicago, 1972); E. Best, *The Maori*, 2 vols. (Memoirs of the Polynesian Soc., v, London, 1924).

[2] Bolchazy, *Hospitality in Early Rome*, ch. 3.

social order as by the functional role it played in the lives of contemporaries.

I

Nevertheless, a beginning must be made from words, from an attempt to disinter the various meanings that the term 'hospitality' possessed in early modern culture. This exercise might be thought redundant, were it not that there are risks in assuming a congruence between our linguistic usage and that of the sixteenth and seventeenth centuries. When we turn to the formal definitions offered by contemporaries, it is interesting to discover both that there was broad agreement over a long period of time, and that they delineate a concept far more general than our own. The Dominican, John Bromyard, preaching at the end of the fourteenth century, stressed that feeding and harbouring of all sorts and conditions of men was the essential duty of the good housekeeper, and that the man who discharged these works of mercy was being guided towards the heavenly household.[3] George Wheler, who published *The Protestant Monastery* in the 1690s, was perhaps deliberately anachronistic in some of his definitions as he sought to persuade his fellow-countrymen of the virtues of monastic patterns of behaviour.[4] Nevertheless, he took it for granted that all good men agreed on the essential nature of hospitality: it was 'a Liberal Entertainment of all sorts of Men, at ones House, whether Neighbours or Strangers, with kindness, especially with Meat, Drink and Lodgings'.[5] In this short definition Wheler encapsulated both the range and the complexity of the idea that was available to his contemporaries. The location of generosity was the household, its elements primarily food, drink, and accommodation. These notions seem obvious enough: less expected is the insistence that the neighbour *and* the stranger, the rich *and* the poor, were all to have equal access to a host's generosity. This ideal, based above all on Christian perceptions

---

[3] Thomas Bromyard, *Summa predicantum*, 2 vols. (Venice, 1586), i, cap. 5, 362.
[4] George Wheler, *The Protestant Monastery: Or Christian Œconomicks* (London, 1698).
[5] Ibid. 173.

of beneficence, provided the key paradigm from which most discussions of hospitality took their departure. Even when the generality, and impracticality, of the ideal was challenged by contemporaries, they could not wholly free themselves from the obligation to discuss appropriate behaviour in the light of these premisses. The language of hospitality spoke of openness and giving, of according all men a temporary place within domestic society. Confronted with this trope of generosity, it was difficult for men to retreat into the private assumptions about entertainment that are commonplace in the modern world.

The existence of such a perdurable description is only the first element in a much more complex configuration of ideas. The detailed language of hospitality, and of related social values, reflects subtle changes in different times and circumstances, changes which may in their turn illuminate shifts in actual behaviour. The idea of a 'law of hospitality', that is, a clearly formulated series of conventions that dictated particular behaviour towards outsiders, is a late arrival in the writing of the early modern period. It seems to depend upon an awareness of the Roman *ius hospitii*, and of the Stoic tradition of natural law, and hence to be a humanist import.[6] Philip Sidney provided one of the earliest uses of the term when he wrote in *New Arcadia* of a law of hospitality that dictated good behaviour towards strangers.[7] Thereafter, it became common for men with classical knowledge to speak of good entertainment as natural and normative: Caleb Dalechamp, preaching in the 1630s, spoke of the binding obligation that men had to care for strangers as a law, and in the same decade Christopher Wandesford, Strafford's deputy in Ireland, advised his children to accept that there was a natural law that governed their dealings with outsiders.[8]

[6] The interest in Senecan ideas in the last decades of the 16th cent. is of relevance here; see below, ch. 3, sect. I. Anthropologists suggest that some 'law of hospitality', based on the logical need to entertain outsiders in a complex culture, is a feature of all advanced societies: J. Pitt-Rivers, 'The Law of Hospitality', in his *The Fate of Shechem* (Cambridge, 1977), 107–11.

[7] Philip Sidney, *The Countess of Pembroke's Arcadia*, ed. M. Evans (London, 1977), 385: 'if it be so that the law of hospitality (so long and holily observed among you) may not defend a stranger fled to your arms for succour . . .'

[8] Caleb Dalechamp, *Christian Hospitalitie: Handled Commonplace-wise in the Chappel of Trinity Colledge in Cambridge* (Cambridge, 1632), 68 ff; Christopher Wandesford, *A Book of Instructions to his Son*, ed. T. Comber (London, 1777), 83. Wandesford's language is particularly interesting: he refers to the 'common Rule of Hospitality' required by 'the Law of Nature'.

William Heale, writing against wife-beating in 1608, brought the concept into the heart of the family unit by arguing that husbands should accept the logic of the law by which 'None who entered into an others house, should for the time of his aboad there, suffer any kind of iniury upon any occasion'. Since a wife had left her own family and entered her husband's home, 'he takes her into his own hospitality; receives her into his own protection, and himself becomes her sole guardian'.[9] In such circumstances, it was an offence against nature to abuse a wife physically. The law constrained individuals to behave towards one another according to principles of reason and distributive justice, and was posited on the assumption that both guests and hosts consented in a relationship which would be made symmetrical by the reciprocal return of entertainment.

While this self-conscious language of law is a late arrival in English, it is in many ways no more than the abstract formulation of a notion that hospitality had a mandatory quality. This concept had a long medieval pedigree, both in the Christian idea of harbourousness and in the sense of obligation to give food and lodging that was part of knightly culture.[10] For the religious orders there was, of course, the very specific injunction of the rules that generosity must be shown to strangers: above all, the Benedictines placed this form of giving at the heart of their duties to society. The secular clergy were also bound by a series of requirements under canon law; requirements that often led parishioners to denounce absentee incumbents for a failure of hospitality.[11] But the laity were also constrained to domestic

---

[9] W. Heale, *An Apologie for Women, or an Opposition to Mr. Dr. G.[ager] His Assertion. That it was Lawfull for Husbands to Beate theire Wives* (Oxford, 1609), 23.

[10] There are hints that in the early Middle Ages hospitality was sometimes binding by custom in England, as it long remained in Ireland. The ballad 'King Arthur and King Cornwall', for example, mentions the duty to provide 'one ghesting [night's lodging] and two meales meate': F. J. Child (ed.), *English and Scottish Ballads*, 8 vols. (Boston, 1857), i. 284; K. Simms, 'Guesting and Feasting in Gaelic Ireland', *Journal of the Royal Society of Antiquaries for Ireland,* 108 (1978), 86 ff. I am grateful to Ged Martin for drawing my attention to this article. Long before the 16th cent. Bartholomaeus Anglicus had already formulated the properties of good entertainment in his *De Proprietatibus Rerum*, trans. John Trevisa, eds. M. C. Seymour *et al.* (Oxford, 1975), 330–1.

[11] A. H. Thompson (ed.), *Visitations in the Diocese of Lincoln, 1517–1531,* 3 vols. (Lincs. Rec. Soc., 33, 35, 37, 1940–7), i. 62–4, 78, 86.

giving, especially if they were heads of independent households.
This is suggested by the common conflation of the ideas of 'keeping
house' and 'keeping hospitality' which is found in sixteenth-
century sources. The connection is sometimes a matter of careful
rhetorical choice, as when George Abbot, the future Archbishop
of Canterbury, praised the Earl of Dorset in his funeral sermon for
'keeping a great house' and providing generous entertainment.[12]
But there are more artless examples which have greater utility in
evaluating contemporary assumptions: in the 1620s Thomas
Hawes, for instance, assured John Winthrop that he would be
pleased to welcome him to his house, as long as he dwelt there
and 'could keep any hospitality within it'.[13] Court records often
make a full identification of household and hospitality, the usual
linguistic form being that adopted in an anti-enclosure petition of
the reign of Charles I which complained that, when plots were
engrossed, 'noe hospitalitie ys kepte upon the same'.[14]

Other aspects of the rhetoric of hospitality connect this sense
of entertainment as duty with the idea that political advantage
was to be gained from these displays of virtue. The household
is sometimes described as an arena, in which the host can
dramatize his generosity, and thereby reveal his hegemony. The
household ordinances, regulating the behaviour of noble
establishments, frequently indicate the importance of social drama
in their insistence on ritualized behaviour. The house was no mere
assemblage of rooms: instead, it served to embody the qualities
of its owner. This is expressed with great clarity in a passage from
Henry Wotton's *Elements of Architecture* (1624):

Every mans proper Mansion house and home, being the theatre of his
Hospitality, the seat of self-fruition, the Comfortablest part of his own
life, the Noblest of his sons inheritance, a kind of private princedom;
Nay, to the Possessors thereof an Epitome of the whole World; may well
deserve by these Attributes, according to the degree of the master, to
be decently and delightfully adorned.[15]

[12] George Abbot, *A Sermon Preached . . . at the Funerall . . . of Thomas
[Sackville] Earle of Dorset* (London, 1608), 16.
[13] *Winthrop Papers*, 2 vols. (Massachusetts Hist. Soc., 1925), i. 371
[14] PRO, SP 16/307/2. Andrew Boorde argued that it was better not to set up
'a household or hospytalyte, than to set up household lackynge the performacyon
of it', *A Compendyous Regyment or a Dyetary of Helth* (1542), ed. F. J. Furnivall
(*EETS*, E.S. 10, London), 1870, 240. For other examples see below, p. 382.
[15] Henry Wotton, *The Elements of Architecture* (London, 1624), 82.

The social ritual of the great household, at its most effective when presented for a large audience, was a coded language, designed to articulate both power and magnanimity. This was not the mere manipulation of symbols, the acting-out of limited roles: since late medieval culture did not fully differentiate the person from the image, the household in some measure *was* its head, its behaviour the physical presentation of the attributes of the man.[16] It is with an awareness of this identity of symbol and thing symbolized that the paired ideas of 'keeping house' and 'keeping hospitality' should be read. The household possessed moral and active qualities, emanating from the good behaviour of its head: 'keeping hospitality' expressed the vital, ethical element in what would otherwise be merely a functional description of the domestic unit.

These concerns with the embodiment of the qualities of the head of household indicate that it is important to read the English pattern of hospitality primarily from an understanding of the domestic unit. Already in the sixteenth century, the Englishman's home was his castle in proverbial wisdom. One Henry Neville even tried to justify the resistance that he offered to the constables who tried to arrest his lodger, on the grounds that the integrity of the household was so powerful that it made it a sacred duty of the host to protect all under his roof, not only his family, 'but also . . . their friends sojourning or abyding with them by way of hospitality'.[17] This bedouin notion was unlikely to appeal to common lawyers who had to establish limits to the sanctuary offered by the household, but it does suggest that an elevated view of the duty of the host had a certain currency in the period.[18] The consequence of such a view was not necessarily hostility to

[16] On this role of the household see D. R. Starkey, 'The Age of the Household', in S. Medcalf (ed.), *The Background to English Literature: The Later Middle Ages* (London, 1981), 243–61. On the significance of coded messages in the display of early modern England see D. Norbrook, 'Panegyric of the Monarch and its Social Context under Elizabeth I and James I', Oxford D.Phil. thesis (1978), 5–18.

[17] PRO, STAC 8/21/7. On the use of the proverb, see G. Jacob, *A New Law-Dictionary* (London, 1736). English law acknowledged some of the sacrosanctity of the house: the doors were only to be broken when arrests were to be made for treason or felony: *Plowden, 5.*

[18] In bedouin culture the guest is protected with the same measure of sacrosanctity that the head of household accords to his womenfolk; A. H. Abou-Seid, 'Honour and Shame among the Bedouins of Egypt', in J. G. Peristiany (ed.), *Honour and Shame: The Values of Mediterranean Society* (London, 1965), 7–23.

the outside world: indeed, a pride in the bodying-forth of the qualities of a good host led rhetorically in the opposite direction, towards proud assertions of openness. This openness was symbolized for all (friendly) comers by the free passage allowed through gateway or door. Sir Thomas Sadler, for example, was described in his funeral sermon as having 'his doors allwayes open to rich and poore . . .'.[19] For Thomas Fuller, writing in the mid-seventeenth century, the test of good entertainment was still a buttery door constantly open for the poor. Another contemporary proverb made the point succinctly: 'noble housekeepers need no doors'.[20] In the golden age, claimed the author of *This World's Folly* (1615), men had a motto engraved above their gates: *porta patens esto, nulli clauderis honesto*.[21] The same sentiments were repeated *ad nauseam* in the literature of the later sixteenth and seventeenth centuries.

The obverse of this openness so beloved by writers was sometimes the closed gatehouse, vividly evoked in the image of Mock-Beggar's Hall. In this trope the wayfarer, or needy peasant, approached a magnificent house in the expectation of succour, only to find the entrance barred, no chimneys smoking, and an aged retainer at the wicket gate telling him no one was at home.[22] This became a favourite with the ballad makers of the Jacobean and Caroline periods, and was readily invoked whenever the flight of the élite to London was condemned. Yet the contrasting image that is of more significance for an understanding of hospitality is not closure opposed to openness, but enclosure. The gate or door was the transitional structure that stood between the general territory of the stranger and the particular environment of the household. To cross it was to undertake the crucial transmutation from stranger (even if known) into guest. To allow total openness would have been to deny the significance of this transition, and hence of the integrity of the household and its head. Therefore an accommodation had to be sought between two objectives: the desire of the householder to

---

[19]   Inner Temple Lib., Petyt MS 531 E, H2–23, fo. 7.
[20]   Thomas Fuller, *The Holy State and the Profane State* (Cambridge, 1642), 297; George Herbert. *Outlandish Proverbs* (London, 1640), no. 91.
[21]   I.H., *This World's Folly* (London, 1615), sig. B5.
[22]   *Roxburghe Ballads*, 9 vols. (London, 1871–97), ii. 132–6; Nicholas Breton, *A Merrie Dialogue betwixt the Taker and Mistaker* (London, 1603), 4–5.

maintain internal power, and his wish / obligation to display this through extroverted gestures of generosity. We can sometimes perceive in sources like the ordinances how this accommodation was achieved. For example, it was the usual practice to maintain an open gate, guarded by a porter, in the noble household, but at mealtimes and during prayers it was ordered that the doors should be closed.[23] Prudential considerations are probably a partial explanation—waste and dislocation were avoided by these actions—but the closed gate also reiterated the message that the household was an integral unit, and emphasized that the lord retained the crucial freedom to dictate the terms of his generosity. The symbolic meaning of such a gesture is revealed in an example from the Scottish Highlands at the end of the seventeenth century. There the Reverend James Kirkwood, travelling among a people still obsessed with hospitality, noticed that when a formal meal was prepared men would 'lay a white rod acrosse the door, and none who see it will come in'.[24]

The language and symbolism of early modern England, therefore, seem directed to an affirmation of the role of the host. It appears at times that the outsider exists merely as the necessary instrument permitting the head of household to perform in his proper function. This reading is afforced by the English use of the term 'stranger' in the period. It could already be employed in ways commensurate with our own usage, as a description of the alien who was unknown. However, it was used with equal regularity as a term of domestic art, to describe an individual who was not attached to a particular *familia*. Thus, when a clerk had to keep records of visitors to the great household, he would divide his categories not on the basis of known or unknown, but domestics and others. Friends, visiting kin, and even non-resident officials were placed in the latter group.[25] If there was a compelling need to differentiate aliens from the rest, the clerk

---

[23] 'A Breviate touching the Order and Government of a Nobleman's House', *Archaeologia*, 13 (1800), 337; 'Orders for the Household of Robert, Earl of Leicester', *HMC, De L'Isle and Dudley*, vi. 1–2.

[24] J. L. Campbell (ed.), *A Collection of Highland Rites and Customs* (London, 1975), 30.

[25] For example, the records kept by the clerks of kitchen to Elizabeth Berkeley, Countess of Warwick, for 1420, and William, Lord Paget, for 1551, show this division being maintained systematically: Longleat Misc. Bk. IX; Middx. RO, Acc. 446/4/13.

would be forced to resort to some circumlocution such as 'men unknown', but it is interesting that this was rarely done in domestic accounts. This conflation of language remained common until the early seventeenth century, but less so thereafter, until by the eighteenth century it vanished completely.[26] Several inferences might be drawn from this interesting piece of terminology, the most important being that it suggests a sharp division between insider and outsider, the latter apparently not being worthy of subtle differentiation according to status and connection with the household.

However, anthropologists, especially those studying Mediterranean societies, suggest that cultures with a strong belief in the integrity of the household give great honour to alien visitors as one way of articulating that belief.[27] On this issue our sources do not speak with a united voice. The most sustained evidence that there was pride in generosity to outsiders comes from the reiterated claim that the English were a uniquely generous nation, especially in their dealings with foreigners. Views on hospitality here became enmeshed with that self-assertiveness that led Englishmen to claim that they were peculiarly favoured by the Deity.[28] Comparisons were made with the French, the Dutch, the Spanish, and the Italians, all of whom were believed to be deficient in the matter of entertainment. The author of *The Institucion of a Gentleman* (1555), claimed that it was hospitality that differentiated the English from their neighbours: 'the drynk draweth the fleming to your friendship, good housekeping the Englishman and correction the peple of France.'[29] Henry Wotton asserted that the hospitality of England was natural, while Richard Fanshawe, the Caroline diplomat, insisted that good housekeeping was 'wholly essential for the constitution of England'.[30] Other commentators acknowledged that the élite were 'counted the chiefest honourers of strangers', and foreign

---

[26] Jacob's *Law Dictionary* firmly states that a stranger 'signifies generally in our Language, a man born out of the Realm, or unknown'.

[27] Abou-Seid, 'Honour and Shame', 21; Pitt-Rivers, 'Law of Hospitality', 100.

[28] J. W. McKenna, 'How God became an Englishman', in D. L. Guth and J. McKenna (eds.), *Tudor Rule and Revolution* (Cambridge, 1982), 25–44.

[29] *The Institucion of a Gentleman* (London, 1555), sig. G3r.

[30] Wotton, *Elements of Architecture*, 70–1; N. H. Nicolas (ed.), *Memoirs of Lady Fanshawe, Wife of . . . Sir Richard Fanshawe . . .* (London, 1829), 35.

observers, often the beneficiaries of this largess, usually allowed themselves to be impressed by the entertainment offered by the natives.[31] It is unlikely that the nobility and gentry were moved to generosity by any fear of aliens, but there was both a contractual sentiment, the hope that giving would be returned, and an awareness that the collective honour of the realm was at stake. Margaret Cavendish, Duchess of Newcastle, who pronounced herself rather unenthusiastic about the feasting habits of her countrymen, made an exception when foreigners needed to be entertained. They must see 'the Plenty, Riches and Magnificence' of the kingdom, so that they 'may not despise it when they return to their own Native Countrey, but give cause to renown it in their Relations'.[32]

This concern for the collective reputation of the realm, although sometimes expressed by the universities or by the Corporation of London, was primarily an aristocratic sentiment. Indeed, it can be seen merely as one aspect of the more general concern of the élite to show honour through the household and its good entertainment. At the beginning of our period, as in earlier feudal society, the existence of a community of honour was affirmed partly through the maintenance of appropriate *familia*. In the opinion of the influential *Book of Chyvalry*, one of the essential elements of true knighthood was the keeping of a good household.[33] While individual members of the community of honour could demonstrate their standing in isolation—the quest would be the obvious moment here—in normal circumstances a full display of honour required a suitable domestic establishment to personate the qualities of the knight. Even the individual contributed to this affirmation of community, gaining validation for his social identity by temporarily assuming the role of guest. It was often through the exchanges between members of the knightly class within the household that the full

---

[31] Laurence Humphrey, *The Nobles or Of Nobility* (London, 1563), bk. II; C. A. Sneyd (ed.), *A Relation . . . of the Island of England ca. 1500* (Camden Soc., O.S. 37, London, 1847), 15, 21; J. A. Cramer, (ed.), *The Travels of Nicander Nucius* (Camden Soc., O.S. 17, London, 1841), 14.

[32] Margaret Cavendish, Duchess of Newcastle, *The World's Olio* (London, 1671), 406.

[33] A. T. P. Byles (ed.), *The Book of the Ordre of Chyvalry*, trans. William Caxton (*EETS*, 168, London, 1926), 113.

virtues of courtesy and *franchise* were best displayed.[34] Moreover, it was hospitality that secured a reputation for good lordship extending beyond the immediate élite, enhancing power by asymmetrical acts of largess.

In the world of the great Tudor household, gestures and words used in entertainment continued to be judged by their contribution to the collective honour of the head. Each offering made to a stranger had to be evaluated so that, in the words of Jane, Lady Berkeley's, ordinances, it redounded to 'my lords honour and mine'.[35] Thus an environment was created in which the stranger could not be treated solely as the undifferentiated creature earlier encountered. While the integrity of the household made it necessary to see the outsider as the generic 'other', aristocratic honour demanded the obverse, the handling of strangers with a fine sense of the contribution they could make to reputation. Rules of domestic etiquette, already complex in the fifteenth century and becoming more so with the development of concepts of civility, demanded that the *amour propre* of both host and guest should at all times be preserved. Sometimes in the conduct literature this manifests itself in an almost ludicrous obsession with rank and degree: John Russell's *Book of Nurture*, written in the 1440s, paid minute attention to the seating of each social group at table; other ordinances give a similar attention to the reception of strangers.[36] But underlying the pointillist approach of the conduct authors is a sensitivity to the need to preserve reputation. While a certain value might accrue to the host from total openness, so that 'the more resort he hath, the more is the master of the house honoured', true influence depended on subtle management of the honour community.[37] The case of total strangers presented particular difficulties, best resolved by assuming that they should be treated with disproportionate courtesy, for 'they come but seldome, stay

---

[34] Bruckner, *Narrative Invention*, 102.

[35] John Smyth, *Lives of the Berkeleys*, ed. J. Maclean, 3 vols. (Gloucester, 1883–5), ii. 418.

[36] F. J. Furnivall (ed.), *Manners and Meals in Olden Time* (EETS, 32, London, 1868), 115–99.

[37] *Cyvile and Uncyvile Life* (London, 1579), in W. C. Hazlitt (ed.), *Inedited Tracts Illustrating the Manners of Englishmen during the Sixteenth and Seventeenth Centuries* (Roxburghe Club, 1868), 33.

not long, and have no emulation with persons of your own country'.[38] Thus, the acknowledgement of the otherness of outsiders had to be matched by an acceptance that, when those outsiders were known, they had in becoming guests to be treated in a way that secured the head of household correct standing in his wider community.

Honour and reputation attached to good lordship, generosity, and the appearance of an open household: these were sentiments generally expressed in early modern English culture. Their influence is perhaps best evaluated by considering their opposite: the degree of shame inhering in a failure to be generous. A classic example of this behaviour is to be found in the dispute between Sir Thomas Posthumous Hoby and members of the Eure clan, which erupted into Star Chamber and the Privy Council at the turn of the sixteenth century. Hoby was an intruder into the society of the North Riding of Yorkshire: marriage to the godly Lady Margaret gave him access to the manor of Hackness, good connections in London assured him of a place on the Bench and an influence in local politics.[39] A Puritan and man of intense ambition in a Catholic environment, he swiftly fell foul of a number of the local families. It was the Eures who decided to visit upon him the unusual punishment of an unbidden hunting-party, made up of the young bloods of the locality, which proceeded to humiliate him in his own home, finally insulting Lady Margaret and doing significant damage to his property. Hoby's subsequent suits in Star Chamber were intended to retrieve an honour which he claimed had been grievously damaged by the charivari.[40] The rhetoric of these cases is powerfully evocative of the shaming power inherent in the abuse of hospitality: Hoby claimed that the defendants sought to bring him into 'disgrace and contempt'; one of his senior servants lamented that 'the lawes of hospitalitye [were] by them [the defendants] so greatly vyolated . . .'. In their turn the Eures claimed that Hoby was already shamed before the local community for his

---

[38] Obadiah Walker, *Of Education, Especially of Young Gentlemen* (Oxford, 1673), 221.

[39] D. M. Meads (ed.), *The Diary of Lady Margaret Hoby* (London, 1930), intro.; J. T. Cliffe, *The Yorkshire Gentry from the Reformation to the Civil War* (London, 1969), 276.

[40] PRO, STAC 5, H16/2, H22/21, H50/4.

inhospitable and discourteous behaviour in the past, as well as his lack of generosity to the hunting-party. Each side sought to reclaim the high ground of honour in order to complete the humiliation of their adversaries.[41]

The weakness of these types of sentiments, in the context of a belief in open hospitality, is that they spoke primarily to those within the community of honour. A complete form of generosity might acknowledge status, but could scarcely overlook the needs of those whose standing was uncertain, or who were recognizably poor. In an interesting dialogue on the nature of civility, published in the mid-Elizabethan period, the countryman who was one of the protagonists argued that the good rural household welcomed all comers: 'I mean Noblemen, Gentlemen, Yeomen, our Neighbours and many others that either have occasion to come thither for business, or passe that way for their own affaires or pleasures.'[42] This certainly extended beyond the honour community, but, as his city friend noted, 'these mennes presence in your houses, do rather honor you, then shew that therby you be charitable'. Here a fundamental problem about the nature of English thinking on hospitality is encountered: should it be extended only to those who were in some sense part of the same social universe as the host, or did it comprehend those in need of generosity by virtue of their poverty?

The language of contemporaries once again provides some entry into this problem, although it is burdened with ambiguities. In the later Middle Ages the most common use of the term 'hospitality' linked it to clerical beneficence. The canonists, glossing Pauline injunctions, saw household giving as a primary duty of the bishops, and through them of the parochial clergy who had assumed their responsibilities. They argued, unequivocally, that hospitality was to be given first to the poor and needy.[43] This reading remained the norm throughout our period when it was the duties of the clergy that were under discussion. The translation of the concept 'hospitality' into the language of lay entertainment is a later, less complete, development. There are plenty of commentators who, by the

---

[41] *HMC, Salisbury MSS*, x. 303, 391; xi. 11–12.
[42] *Cyvile and Uncyvile Life*, 34.
[43] B. Tierney, *Medieval Poor Law* (Berkeley, Ca., 1959), 44 ff. For a more detailed discussion of the duties of the clergy see below, ch. 6.

early sixteenth century, identify the two: for example, Edmund Dudley in his *Tree of Commonwealth* urged the King to 'constrain the nobles . . . both spiritual and temporal, to keep good hospitality'.[44] Bishop Fisher, preaching the funeral sermon for Lady Margaret Beaufort, commended her 'godly hospitality and charitable dealing with her neighbours', making it clear from the context that he saw the two as synonymous.[45] We have already noted the identity between household and hospitality often found in sixteenth-century sources. Even in the next century, funeral sermons sometimes continued the convention, as when, for example, Sir Francis Pile was said to be hospitable in relieving the poor at his gates.[46] Thomas Fuller still felt that hospitality comprehended a full range of household entertainment when he wrote that it had three divisions: 'for ones familie, this is of necessity: for strangers, this is Courtesie: for the poore, this is Charity.'[47]

This suggests that it was accepted that the term 'hospitality', as applied to lay entertainment, could include the poor. However, the matter is complicated both by the changing nature of the language of charity itself, and by the divisions that were always perceptible between giving to different social groups. The idea of charity, as is well known, underwent a fundamental transition in the centuries between 1400 and 1700: at the earlier date the term was almost always used to describe mutual amity, an experience of shared love that might issue in giving to the needy, but was primarily directed towards the articulation of Christian community.[48] On the other hand, by the time Fuller was writing, 'charity' had moved inexorably towards its modern usage of giving to the needy and the deserving, hence to a narrowed reading in which it was something donated to another, that

---

[44] Edmund Dudley, *The Tree of the Commonwealth*, ed. D. M. Brodie (Cambridge, 1948), 42.

[45] John Fisher, *English Works*, ed. J. E. B. Mayor (*EETS*, E.S. 27, London, 1876), 296.

[46] Inner Temple Lib., Petyt MS 531 E, H2–23, fo. 7; Bartholemew Parsons, *A Christians Remembrance or Felicity by Hope. A Sermon Preached at the Burial of Sir Francis Pile, Bart of Collingborne Kingston, Wiltshire* (Oxford, 1635), 35.

[47] Fuller, *The Holy State*, 153.

[48] J. Bossy, *Christianity in the West, 1400–1700* (Oxford, 1985), 140 ff.; S. Brigden, 'Religion and Social Obligation in Early Sixteenth-Century London', *PP*, 103 (1984), 67–112.

something being readily articulated in monetary terms. In so far as charity had become linked with the idea of separation of giving, rather than with shared amity, it would seem to reflect a shift away from the species of integration that should have been characteristic of domestic hospitality.

Even before these changes occurred, it is possible to read a separation of the notions of entertainment and charitable giving in some of the texts. John Fitzherbert, in his *Boke of Husbandry* (1523), distinguished between the sort of feasting that promoted love and amity, and alms-giving, which could take various forms, but was not closely related to hospitality.[49] Similarly, Latimer, in his famous description of his yeoman father, differentiated the hospitality the latter offered to his poor neighbours from the alms he gave to other needy.[50] Funeral sermons and monuments of the later sixteenth and seventeenth centuries tend to follow this division, seeing hospitality as something offered to the peer group, to travellers, or to neighbours, charity as alms to the needy. The narrowing definition of charity obviously facilitated this development. It became conventional to have two divisions within the stereotyped biographies used in funeral sermons, one for hospitality and one for charity. Yet in the seventeenth century there still remained an awareness that the two were closely linked: Clement Ellis, for example, characterized his gentleman in *The Gentile Sinner* (1660) as one whose 'Table is moderate, that so his Charity and Hospitality may exceed'.[51]

These definitional complications may throw light on two substantive issues that must play important parts in an analysis of English hospitality. The first is the nature of charitable giving to the poor: giving within and from the household suggests an intimacy that brought donor and recipient into a direct relationship, even when that directness was tempered by the host's substitution of an almoner or usher to personate his generosity at the gate. Each move away from this form of directness was likely to emphasize the 'otherness' of the poor, and diminish the distinctive role of the household in articulating the generosity of its head. Money alms,

---

[49] John Fitzherbert, *Here Begynneth a Newe Tracte or Treatyse Moost Profytable for all Husbandemen*, 2nd. edn. (London, 1534), fos. 65ᵛ, 84ᵛ–86.
[50] Hugh Latimer, *Sermons*, ed. G. E. Corrie (Parker Soc., Cambridge, 1845), 101.
[51] Clement Ellis, *The Gentile Sinner* (Oxford, 1668), 170.

rather than the giving of food, drink, and lodging was one such distancing device, and it is noteworthy that Wheler's definition of hospitality excluded it. It has been suggested that when tokens, money equivalents, were introduced for the payment of the poor in fourteenth-century Florence this subverted the intimacy that had previously existed between donor and recipient based largely on food-gifts.[52] Some of the same process of separation obviously enters into English dealings with the poor in the course of the sixteenth century, both because of the rejection of casual almsgiving by some Reformers, and because of the need to manage the growing problem of poverty through the use of public agencies. However, the household remained an important source of giving, and the language of generosity reflects this in its oscillation between the idea of integration—hospitality and commensality—and that of distancing—monetary alms.

The second issue presented by the shifting language concerns the poor stranger, in the sense of alien. While giving to the known poor could be organized according to principles that were determined by recognized need and standing, the ambiguity of the alien lay in the fact that he or she could not be labelled according to these 'objective' standards. The outsider was in some measure self-defined, and the role assumed, especially if it was that of the petitioner, could only be rejected by the householder if he was willing directly to challenge the integrity of the stranger. The story of Abraham and the angels whom he entertained unawares was an ever-present reminder of the importance of not denying sustenance to outsiders.[53] The idea that the stranger might possess a peculiar sacrosanctity is not a common one in English writing of the period, but it was invoked from time to time, especially by bibliocentric Protestants who wished to maintain what they believed to be traditional Christian standards. Edward Topsell, writing in 1607, urged his readers not to 'forsake strangers, for the Lord loveth them and goeth with them'.[54] A few years earlier Robert Allen had been even more specific, persuading his readers that all good men must be received into

[52] P. Gavitt, 'Economy, Charity and Community in Florence, 1350–1450', in T. Riis (ed.), *Aspects of Poverty in Early Modern Europe* (Florence, 1981), 100–1.

[53] On the sacredness of the stranger see A. M. Hocart, 'Divinity and the Guest', in his *The Life-Giving Myth* (London, 1935).

[54] Edward Topsell, *The House-holder or Perfect Man* (London, 1610), 172.

the household, for 'who knoweth how great blessing God will grant at their holy suit and supplication . . .'.[55]

When the stranger appeared in the role of pilgrim or hermit before the Reformation, or of godly Protestant exiled for the sake of the gospel thereafter, it was an obvious folly to proffer cold charity rather than domestic hospitality. The stranger and the pilgrim were even one and the same linguistically, the term *peregrinus* standing for both, and expressions of generosity could deliberately play on this form of identity. When William Clopton was memorialized in Long Melford Church in the early fifteenth century, his epitaph spoke of his hospitality thus:

> *Pauperibus patuit semper sua ianua abivit*
> *Nullus ac hac vacuus indigna seu peregrinus.*[56]

Although the palmer vanished with the shrines he had sought at the Reformation, the metaphor of the pilgrimage, with its implication of shared travelling towards a spiritual goal, could still be used as an argument for material charity. 'We may', Dalechamp told his Cambridge congregation, 'become strangers as well as they, and adde a particular peregrination to our common and generall pilgrimage.'[57]

Any simple conflation of almsgiving and entertainment, even when both were offered from the household, therefore seems difficult. However, non-monetary alms were frequently described as though they were a part of that process of welcoming outsiders to which Scriptural precept and social convention bound contemporaries. It might perhaps be best to think of a continuum, in which food and other resources were offered to the peer group and chosen figures within the inner household, to lesser contacts in its outer circles, and to the needy at the gates. All were in some measure bound together in the consumption of shared commodities, best expressed in the notion that the poor were the residuary legatees of household generosity.[58] The same

---

[55] Robert Allen, *A Treatise of Christian Beneficence* (London, 1600), 88.

[56] D. MacCulloch (ed.), *The Chorography of Suffolk* (Suffolk Rec. Soc., 19, 1976), 98.

[57] Dalechamp, *Christian Hospitalitie*, 98.

[58] See e.g., the ordinances established for the household of Lionel Cranfield, Earl of Middlesex, which express this continuity very clearly; LPL, Fulham Papers 426.

concept of a continuum is to be found in the advice on giving
to which Englishmen frequently turned: the categories first
developed by St Ambrose and often quoted by Reformation
divines. Ambrose provided a model of giving that could be
conceived as a series of concentric circles: the innermost one
consisting of the household, since a man's first duty was to his
family, and then extending outwards to comprehend spiritual and
other kin, neighbours, friends, and finally strangers and
enemies.[59] This was a model well attuned to a social system
which accepted open hospitality but needed some method of
regulating its potential anarchy and costliness: the stranger was
placed upon the periphery, but was still included within the
circles of the generosity of the host. It seems logical for this
analysis to follow Ambrose, and include household giving to the
needy within the idea of hospitality, though with a due
acceptance of the ambiguities of which contemporaries were
themselves aware.

In all its varied forms the notion of hospitality in early modern
England seems to be bound to that of reciprocity, of the exchange
of gifts and rewards to which value not simply articulated in
money terms attaches. A willingness to consume in acts of largess
what otherwise might be turned to financial profit, seems to
characterize cultures that feast lavishly and provide grandiose
welcome to outsiders.[60] It is easy enough to demonstrate that,
when Englishmen wrote of hospitality, they used a language of
exchange in which reciprocities were not assigned a monetary
value. They were advised by the moralists from Ambrose onwards
that the reward for giving was in God's hands, and that it was
therefore 'sweet' to seek for grace, not lucre.[61] Rhetorically
early modern writers concurred, opposing hospitality as a frank
offering and free benefit to the greed of those who were a part
of the cash nexus. But in practice the English acknowledged a
system which traded in the less tangible assets of honour, loyalty,

[59] N. De Romestin (ed.), *Some of the Principal Works of St Ambrose*, in *The Nicene and Post-Nicene Fathers* (New York, 1976), x. 15; John Downame, *The Plea of the Poore. Or a Treatise of Beneficence and Almes-Deeds* (London, 1616), 130 ff.; William Gouge, *A Learned . . . Commentary on the Whole Epistle to the Hebrewes* (London, 1655), ch. 6, sect. 71.

[60] The classic study of the significance of such gestures is Mauss, *The Gift*, but see also B. Malinowski, *Argonauts of the Western Pacific* (London, 1922).

[61] De Romestin, *The Nicene Fathers*, x. 59.

alliance, and beneficence. Christopher Wandesford urged his son to 'let your entertainment of your neighbours be always cheerful and friendly: such as may persuade them to look upon you often, and at all Times with Contentment'.[62] The transaction might involve a measure of sentiment, but a rational calculation of self-interest was obviously also of significance. Dalechamp, whose main concern was to urge beneficence to needy outsiders, conceded that entertainment of equals was acceptable since it promoted gratitude, civility, and local harmony.[63] The cultivation of such friendships was scarcely altruistic, even though it eschewed monetary considerations. It could, suggested Edward Panton, be summed up in the maxim: 'do to your neighbour, what you would have him do to you, which comprehends all that can be said on this subject.'[64]

Reciprocity was designed to keep these qualities of liberality and civility in motion: to reify and fructify them by constant interchange.[65] Richard Carew described the Cornish gentry in the Elizabethan period as maintaining amity by progressive cycles of hospitality, visiting one another's houses in ever larger numbers, until, like a giant snowball, the group temporarily collapsed under its own weight.[66] When the English sought a particular term to describe this behaviour they often found it in 'neighbourliness', that ideal which was, in Mildred Campbell's words, 'first in the criteria by which the social and ethical standing of an individual in a country community was judged'.[67] The reciprocal entertainment of neighbours, even among those far below the élite, was a process accompanied by powerful messages about status and generosity. Sons who were the beneficiaries of advice writing by their fathers were routinely reminded of both the advantages and the burdens of being kind to neighbours: the

---

[62] Wandesford, *Instructions*, 82. On the exchange of such intangible goods, and their significance for the spirit of the society, see L. Hyde, *The Gift: Imagination and the Erotic Life of Property* (New York, 1979), 8–11; R. A. Sharp, 'Gift Exchange and the Economies of Spirit in *The Merchant of Venice*', *Modern Philology*, 83 (1986), 250.

[63] Dalechamp, *Christian Hospitalitie*, 7.

[64] Edward Panton, *Speculum Iuventatis: or, a True Mirror where Errors in Breeding Noble and Generous Youth . . . are Manifest* (London, 1671), 305.

[65] Sharp, 'Gift Exchange', 250–2.

[66] Richard Carew, *The Survey of Cornwall* (London, 1602), fo. 65.

[67] M. Campbell, *The English Yeoman* (London, 1967), 382.

advantages were always believed to outweigh the burdens, provided that prudential care was taken of costs.[68]

Trading in forms of generosity to peers and known friends is obviously to be differentiated from the forms of asymmetrical giving that were a necessary part of the behaviour of the élite. Here the theatre of hospitality offered the opportunity for the expression of political and economic loyalty, through such institutions as the tenant feast, or the visiting of a nobleman by his followers. Henry Peacham observed that one of the marks of nobility was that 'We must attend upon him, and come to his house, and not he to ours'.[69] Although Edward Panton was dismissive about peer-group entertainment, he was clear that the pursuit of superior gentry involved the duty to 'visit, honour and follow them, taking part in their Interests, esteeming them as your Master'.[70] This direct clientage relationship seems less easy to identify with a gift-economy than does peer-group hospitality. Nevertheless, the very obligation it created in the élite to act with beneficence can legitimately be described as part of such an economy. Largess was essential to the noble, and largess implies the giving of rewards without immediate return. When return was made, it would be in terms of an enhanced sentiment of loyalty, which issued in political action. Owen Feltham saw clearly that the gift-giving involved in patronage bound the recipient to an enhanced return: even a monarch, who put no apparent condition on his generosity, was usually more than rewarded in kind, 'for a petty benefit he often gets an inestimable friend'.[71]

Yet hospitality as a part of gift-giving, even at this level, involved rather more than the substitution of calculated reciprocity of self-interest for financial exchange. Entertainment was, and is, potentially burdensome to the spirit, whether in the role of host or of guest. Adequate performances in the theatre of hospitality were not easy in a culture like that of early modern

[68] Dudley, 4th Lord North, urged that householders should show their generosity above all by entertaining 'the poor neighbourhood', an idea of Christian beneficence that seems to have found much more general acceptance than giving to the poor alien; Dudley, 4th Lord North, *Observations and Advices Œconomical* (London, 1669), 78; Walter Mildmay, *A Memorial for a Son from His Father 1570* (London, 1893).

[69] Henry Peacham, *The Compleat Gentleman* (London, 1622), 13.

[70] Panton, *Speculum Iunventatis*, 306.

[71] Owen Feltham, *Resolves Divine, Morall, Politicall* (London, 1623), 169.

England: they are nicely encapsulated in the Duchess of Newcastle's aphorism that 'those who would be Honoured, must have Noble Civilities, Grateful Performances, Generous Liberalities and Charitable Compassions'.[72] They must, in other words, labour in the realms of affective relationships, if they were to secure success in their transactions. And, as the example of Sir Thomas Hoby has already shown, this was unlikely to be a matter of personal preference, since authority and power frequently rested on good social performance. Jean Gailhard noted that a full programme of visits could scarcely be avoided in the seventeenth-century countryside, since without these gestures 'there is a danger of discontents and quarrels'.[73]

Five interconnected themes can be extrapolated from this initial exploration of language and symbol. The 'naturalness' of the guest / host relationship is in part a feature of any society that seeks intercourse with strangers, but in one particularly concerned with good entertainment, like early modern England, specific rules and norms will emerge defining the parameters of proper behaviour.[74] Secondly, hosts have to reflect closely on the nature of the outsider, acknowledging his distinctive, or even sacred nature, and also calculating the reciprocal benefits that derive from his entertainment. One of these benefits that appears particularly important in England is the ability of the outsider to make the insider articulate his contribution to the collective interest of the unit offering hospitality. Thirdly, there is a strong connection between ideas of nobility and hospitality. Fourthly, altruistic giving, bred of a philosophy that refused to accept essential differences between individuals, was expected of householders. Lastly, acts of beneficence, linked together in a system of gift-exchange and reciprocity, were claimed to have a transactional value at least as significant as the market-place trading of possessions. With these initial readings in mind, it is now possible to turn to the closer investigation of behaviour among the various groups that exercised social influence in early modern England.

[72] Margaret Cavendish, Duchess of Newcastle, *The World's Olio*, 222.

[73] Jean Gailhard, *The Compleat Gentleman* (London, 1678), 28. Feltham lamented the imposition represented by these courtesies which are 'the most extreme extortions that can be' since men are bought out of liberty by being bound to reciprocate: *Resolves*, 168.

[74] Pitt-Rivers, 'Law of Hospitality', 109–10.

2
Hospitality in the Great Household

I

THE godly divines of the early seventeenth century were often at pains to remind their auditors that hospitality was a Christian duty which bound all men. Citing Matthew 10: 42 they argued that not even 'a cup of cold water given in His name, shall . . . be left unrewarded'.[1] Yet they were compelled to acknowledge that in practice household care was the prerogative of a limited group, those who possessed establishments large enough to absorb the rich and poor, neighbour and stranger. With the exception of the higher clergy, this meant most obviously the nobility and landed gentry. Not only did they have the resources to entertain, they also had the incentive. As long as honour and reputation were determined partially by the behaviour of a nobleman or gentleman within his household, it was wise of him to use his establishment as a stage on which his virtues were displayed. Hence, good housekeeping became identified as an attribute of true gentility, as embodying that quality of generosity which was a key distinguishing feature of the knight. *The Book of Chyvalry* had already in the fourteenth century marked out this aspect of noble behaviour, and it is a theme solemnly repeated in the prescriptive literature well into the seventeenth century. Most explicit is the observation of the *Institucion of a Gentleman*: 'good housekeeping is a thinge in all Gentlemen required.'

Even in the practical world of the law court hospitality could sometimes be accepted as a test of gentility. When, for example, the churchwardens of Great Burstead in Essex wished to deprive Edmund Blagg of the pew he had erected in 1613, they argued

---

[1] Richard Curteys, *The Care of a Christian Conscience* (London, 1600), sig. Fviir; Samuel Garey, *A Newe Yeares Gift for the Suole* (London, 1615), 8.

that they did so because, though he claimed the status of a gentleman, 'the gates of his house were not greasey with giving almes to the poore'. The vicar of Great Burstead was summoned in Blagg's defence, and claimed that, on the contrary, he had conducted himself in all ways as a gentleman, giving alms to the poor and keeping a good house and 'liberal hospitallytie'.[2]

Late sixteenth-century texts often reveal uncertainty about the standing of a gentleman detached from his household, whether by movement to London, by poverty, or by gentility based on a profession rather than on land. Although social mobility and changing circumstances, as well as the classical emphasis on nobility of virtue, enabled the close association between gentility and the great household to be challenged, the tradition that a man best exemplified his virtue through his domestic establishment was tenacious in early modern England.

While the whole community of honour was comprehended by these ideas, there were clear distinctions between the virtues of the greater nobility and those of mere gentlemen. The peculiar quality of the nobleman able to deploy large resources was thought to be magnificence: that contempt for moderation and any form of meanness which revealed itself in elaborate display and conspicuous consumption. 'Magnificence', according to William Vaughan at the end of the sixteenth century, 'is a virtue that consisteth in sumptuous and great expenses . . . so that . . . it is peculiar to Noblemen'.[3] It was the quality which marked out the royal household as well as that of the king's leading subjects: the introduction to Edward IV's *Black Book* is dominated by a concern for the splendour of the royal establishment.[4] Magnificence demonstrated the claims of king and noble to dominance in the social hierarchy and the household provided the stage on which this hegemony could most effectively be asserted. For gentlemen, on the other hand, the more modest quality of liberality was usually singled out as the

---

[2] *The Book of the Ordre of Chyvalry*, trans. William Caxton (*EETS*, 168, London, 1926), 113; *The Institucion of a Gentleman* (London, 1555), sig. G2; GLRO, DL / C / 220, fos. 553v–561. I am very grateful to Kevin Dillow for this last reference.

[3] William Vaughan, *The Golden Grove, Moralized in Three Books* (London, 1600), bk. 1, ch. 53.

[4] A. R. Myers (ed.), *The Household of Edward IV* (Manchester 1959), 86.

most appropriate mode of behaviour. Thomas Lever, writing in the Edwardian period, reminded his readers that 'the gentleman that kepeth a good house in his countrey, shall be better in credit with the people for his liberalitie, then the best oratour or lawyer in England, for all his eloquence'.[5] Liberality was not in any obvious way considered antithetical to magnificence, but it was cognisant of small things rather than large, according to Vaughan, and could certainly be applied to the generous behaviour of a man who could not hope to aspire to grandeur. Medieval discussions of the cardinal virtues often include some consideration of liberality: for example, Peter Idley's *Instructions to his Son*, based on the thirteenth-century text of Albertanus di Brescia, dwells specifically on the hospitable dimension of the virtue:

> Off thy mete and drynke be free algate;
> Daparte with suche as thou haste
> With good wille erly and late,
> And of thy frende be never agaste . . .[6]

In the latter half of the sixteenth century, interest in the idea of liberality as the virtue of gentlemen intensified, influenced in part by such classical texts as Cicero's *De Officiis* and Seneca's *De Beneficiis*.[7]

When liberality and magnificence were not separated from one another as the appropriate possession of distinct social subgroups, they might be linked under the even more traditional notion of largess, that 'queen of medieval noble virtues'. For Hoccleve, largess and liberality were still synonymous, although he drew a distinction between the 'fool largesse', roughly equivalent to the classical prodigality, and true generosity.[8] But by the end of the fifteenth century the term is rarely employed, even in descriptions of munificence such as the historical description of various royal courts that precedes the main sections of the *Black*

---

[5] **Thomas Lever,** *Sermons*, ed. E. Arber (London, 1870), 88.
[6] C. D. Evelyn (ed.), *Peter Idley's Instructions to his Son* [1445–50] (Boston, 1935), 84.
[7] See below, ch. 3, sect. I.
[8] M. P. Whitney, 'Largesse: Queen of Medieval Virtues', in C. Fiske (ed.), *Vassar Medieval Studies* (New Haven, Conn., 1923), 188 ff.; Thomas Hoccleve, *Works*, ed. F. J. Furnivall (*EETS*, E.S. 72, London, 1897), 165.

Book. Even the image of open-handed giving and indiscriminate feasting conjured by the word is more often to be found in the panegyrics of the Welsh and Irish bards than in English literary sources. In the Celtic traditions the tables of even minor chieftains and clerics still groan under the weight of venison and exotic meats, and their wine is still circulated without stint well into the sixteenth century.[9] This vision of largess neither distinguishes between magnificence and more common liberality, nor does it pay any heed to prudential calculations associated with cost or balance. There are examples of such praise in England, but they tend to be early, such as the observation in the thirteenth-century life of Fulk Fitz-Warenne that he diverted the king's highway through his manor of Alveston, the better to offer munificent hospitality.[10] The spirit in which the Neville feast, or Warham's enthronement, were recorded is fundamentally different: the purpose was to emphasize the magnificence and solemn ceremonial of these occasions, and perhaps to commit the detail to memory for reference when further ritual feastings demanded the reproduction of similar food and service.

One context for understanding the contrast between Celtic and English descriptions of feasting and household ceremonial is the preoccupation of the latter sources with ideas of prudence, moderation, and good order as well as munificence. Although late medieval discussions of the cardinal virtues certainly did not eschew magnificence, liberality, or generosity, they also invoked temperance as a guide to gentle behaviour. Building upon the Aristotelian belief that liberality was a mean between avarice and prodigality, householders were endlessly advised to exercise prudence in spending and giving. Peter Idley may again stand as an exemplar, when he warns his son to protect his estate:

> In mesure to spende, thus y meane
> Eche man after his astate;
> Not to take al the fatt fro the leene,
> But as he may contynue erly and late.[11]

---

[9] Simms, 'Guesting and Feasting in Gaelic Ireland', *Journal of the Royal Society of Antiquaries for Ireland*, 108 (1978), 67 ff.; G. Williams, *The Welsh Church from the Conquest to the Reformation* (Cardiff, 1976), 377–80.

[10] T. Wright (ed.), *The History of Fulk Warine* (Warton Club, London, 1855), 178.

[11] *Peter Idley's Instructions*, 84.

The leitmotiv of prudence and moderation, as a counterpoise to the extravagance and vaingloriousness of the external world, is indeed to be found as one of the most common images of late medieval literature, especially in such authors as Lydgate and in advice given to princes.[12] Although we cannot immediately assume an influence from these texts to social behaviour, we can at least observe that they provided an ethos which challenged notions of indiscriminate largess.

Such prodigality was also restrained by sources more relevant to daily domestic behaviour, the household ordinances. They were, of course, intended to sustain establishments of the nobility, and hence were dedicated to magnificent display and to operation upon a grand scale. Nevertheless, their objective was to combine order with magnificence, to limit and control waste, and to secure good discipline. The obsessive details of the Northumberland Household Book of 1512 probably bore only an imperfect relationship to the actual behaviour of the earl's servants, but its philosophy is clear.[13] It sought to combine the ostentation required of such a great noble with the precision of record-keeping that would reduce indiscriminate waste and keep a prudent check on all outgoings. The precision with which the *Black Book* describes the establishment appropriate to various social ranks is intended not only to reinforce hierarchy but to offer a model 'if the kinges hyghnesse plese to kepe a lesse household than the foresayde grete summe sheweth here . . .'.[14] The balance between magnificence and providence sought in these accounts was not easily achieved: Edward IV's later Household Ordinance of 1478 shows attempts to reduce the size of the royal establishment in order to save costs which were felt to be too high in the earlier reorganization. Nevertheless, the assumptions of ordinances which could begin from Aristotle's ethical argument for liberality as a mean, was far removed from the 'potlatch' mentality which can still be identified in Celtic

---

[12] John Lydgate, *The Fall of Princes*, ed. H. Bergen, 4 vols. (*EETS*, E.S. 121–4, London 1924–7), i. 11–12.

[13] T. Percy (ed.), *Regulations and Establishment of the Household of Henry Algernon Percy* (London, 1770). On the relationship between the ideals articulated in the ordinances and domestic reality, see G. R. Batho (ed.), *The Household Papers of Henry Percy, 9th Earl of Northumberland* (Camden Soc., 3rd ser. 93, London, 1962), xvii–xviii.

[14] *Household of Edward* IV, 89, 198–210.

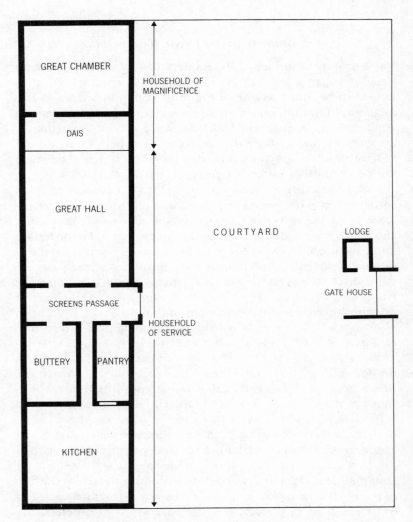

Fig. 2.1. Schematic diagram of the Great House

feasting, or at least in the descriptions of that feasting given by the bards.[15] In the late medieval English environment hospitality, like other attributes of the household, was integrated into this patterned world of hierarchy, order, and magnificence.

[15] Simms, 'Guesting and Feasting', 86–92.

To understand this process in operation we need first to consider the social geography of the great house. In simplified form the physical arrangement of most English houses of the late fifteenth and early sixteenth century were as in Figure 2.1: a gatehouse and courtyard, the latter usually enclosed by apartments, and a main structure comprising services at one end, the hall and screens passage as the middle block, and the rooms specifically allocated to the lord and his nuclear family at the other end. Actual variations on such a typology were, of course, almost in-numerable, but the essential organizational concepts underlying it were rarely breached before the middle of the sixteenth century.[16] Our interest in this configuration lies not in its architectural dispositions, but in its implications for the social behaviour of the lord and his household, especially in so far as they concerned strangers. By this period the house which had evolved from a simple hall structure was well arranged to express those hierarchical values that are so prominent in the ordinances. It contained a number of visible barriers restricting movement between one area of the establishment and another: barriers which were used as social as well as physical demarcators. For the household itself the most important of these was also one of the least obtrusive, the separation of the upper and lower parts of the establishment at the dais step in the hall. The dais, the chamber, and all the private rooms beyond were defined as part of the lord's side, or the household of magnificence; below the dais came the household of service. The sharpness of the divide can best be seen in the organization of the royal household, in which the two parts were wholly separated and treated as distinct in all the relevant ordinances from the fourteenth century onwards.[17] The smaller the establishment the less likely was it to create a total barrier between service and magnificence, but the nobility commonly had servants whose duties were confined to an upper set of chambers and who were sharply distinguished

[16] *A Collection of Ordinances and Regulations for the Government of the Royal Household* (London, 1790); Starkey, 'The Age of the Household', in S. Medcalf (ed.), *The Background to English Literature: The Later Middle Ages* (London, 1981), 244–5.

[17] D. A. L. Morgan, 'The House of Policy: the Political Role of the Late Plantagenet Household, 1422–85', in D. Starkey (ed.), *The English Court from the Wars of the Roses to the Civil War* (London, 1987), 26–34.

from the lesser figures in the hall and other services. In some cases these arrangements seem to have been becoming more complex at the end of the fifteenth century: the third Duke of Buckingham, for example, had a chamber staff of forty-six while his grandfather had been content with only a handful of attendants.[18] But even Buckingham does not seem to have followed the example of the royal household and developed an inner chamber, dividing the establishment into a tripartite structure. Or rather, if such division did occur, it was at a level of informality not visible in the surviving documents.

A second social barrier was the open division between the hall and the service rooms. For the household this had none of the symbolic significance of the dais step, and was merely a point of transition from the area of food preparation to that of its consumption. For strangers, however, the screens could represent the divide between those who were accepted to share in the lord's commensality and those who, if admitted at all, were only offered drink at the buttery bar.[19] Beyond the screens lay the door to the house, another obvious barrier, though one to which less social significance attached since admission to the gatehouse usually implied acceptance into the house. Finally there was the gatehouse, with its lodge and porter placed to filter into the courtyard only those outsiders who were considered of suitable status, or were on appropriate business. This was as critical a point of separation as the dais, marking as it did the immediate limit of the lord's territory. It is surely not only a matter of aesthetic choice that so many of the elaborate gatehouses built in this period were used to display the arms and heraldic devices of the family: marking the inanimate territory with the lord's badge in the same way that his retainers were marked with his livery.[20]

The household ordinances are rich in advice about the application of this social geography to the reception of strangers. Although fifteenth-century accounts, most notably Russell's *Book of Nurture*, elaborate the intricate rules of precedence and rank more fully than those of a century later, the essential messages

[18] K. A. Mertes, *The English Noble Household, 1250–1600* (Oxford, 1988), 43.
[19] *HMC, Middleton*, 540.
[20] See Starkey, 'Age of the Household', 272, for a valuable analysis of the importance of these labelling devices in the late Middle Ages; B. Harris, *Edward Stafford, 3rd Duke of Buckingham* (Stanford, Ca., 1986), 86.

remain the same. Guests must be cared for with a proper regard to their rank and degree, and not placed with those who would offend their social sensibilities. This meant that each great household had to maintain a chamber usher and an usher or marshal for the hall, whose principal duties were to place strangers properly and with due courtesy. In the particularly elaborate hierarchical pattern described in the fifteenth-century 'Orders of service belonging to the degrees of duke, marquis and earl', only those of at least the degree of the son of a baron might sit at the lord's board in his chamber, although esquires of ancient lineage might be permitted at the board's end.[21] Knights were also to be entertained in the chamber at a separate board. Men of worship, a term which the author very interestingly keeps distinct from that of honour, were to dine at the marshal's board in the hall. This was still within the penumbra of the household of magnificence, but all others such as servants or 'honest personages of the countrey' were required to feed in the body of the hall with the majority of the domestics. Even this precise advice seems general when compared with Russell's famous rhymed counsel on the seating of guests, supposedly born of his experience as usher to Humphrey, Duke of Gloucester, in the 1430s.[22] Russell is clear that there are certain men who can never cross the barrier between chamber and hall, still less descend below the dais:

> Pope, Emperowre, Kynge or Cardinalle,
> Prince with golden rodde Royalle,
> Archebischoppe, usyng to were the palle,
> Duke, all these dygnyte owt not kepe the hall.

Such individuals also had to be served at a separate mess, normally a portion allocated to up to four people. The next ranks such as bishops, marquises, earls, and barons, could sit in either hall or chamber, but were to be served only two or at most three to a mess. And thus the list continues, with an extraordinarily fine gradation of the social order, placing wives in relation to husbands, prelates in comparison with one another, former office-holders below the current occupants. It would be difficult to find

---

[21] BL, Harleian MS. 6815.
[22] F. J. Furnivall (ed.), *Manners and Meals in Olden Time* (*EETS*, 32, London, 1868), 115–99.

a more powerful evocation of what was meant by magnificence and order in the fifteenth century than this curious analysis of the minutiae of seating plans at table. But in modified form the insistence on careful ordering at meals survives in household ordinances well into the seventeenth century. And if the usher was not alert embarrassment and confusion could easily be the consequence: Nicholas Breton, in his *Fantasticks* (1626), has an amusing vignette of the dinner at which 'the meat will bee halfe cold, ere the Guests can agree on their places'.[23]

Russell's image is an essentially static one: the great feast at which all are seated, the living embodiment of that part of the chain of being that was relevant to the English élite. But the hierarchical system could also be presented dynamically as the guest moved from gate to hall to chamber, was escorted to his or her lodgings, and eventually took leave of the host. The 'Orders of Service' provide a particularly powerful description of the first acts in this social drama: the reception of guests.[24] Men of honour and title were always to be met at the gate by the senior officers, even if they appeared when a meal was in progress and the porter was denying general entrance. Most could simply be admitted through the half wicket gate, but if the visitor's status was as high as that of his host, or at least of the degree of baron, the great gateway should be opened for him. If he was the host's equal he could also claim the privilege of entering the courtyard on horseback, though 'after the old order of England [he] most comonlie would not onles he were earnestlie required by the head officers'. At the highest social level, a guest who was more exalted than the host had to be offered the staves of those officers, in a ritual of inversion designed to show that the hierarchical principle was retained intact, despite the natural authority of the householder over his own social territory. Hence the usual practice of surrendering control of the household to royal officials during the visit of a monarch. The man of honour then proceeded through the various realms of the establishment, sometimes pausing to be entertained by the lord's servants in the hall, and always accompanied by appropriate formal gestures from all the latter's representatives.

---

[23] J. O. Halliwell-Phillipps (ed.), *Books of Characters* (London, 1857), 15.
[24] BL, Harl. MS. 6815.

Lesser men, those whom the ordinances describe as 'of worship', were greeted with a truncated version of this ritual, still enacted by the head officers, but only in the hall. They did not share the experience of moving as equals through the hierarchy of the household with the lord's men, and they might be conveyed from the gate by an inferior officer such as the porter himself. Those strangers who were able to dine in the hall, but could claim no direct access to the household of magnificence, were required to demonstrate subordination by their gesture. Having eaten, they had to attend the chief officer's board on the hall dais, and 'do their reverence', before being permitted to retire to the buttery or cellar bar. Although the patterns of greeting and eating described in the ordinances show the greatest concern for the enactment of social drama, every stage of a guest's stay was governed by the same principles. A nice calculation of the distance a guest must be attended to his lodgings, and to the gate on departure, became part of the language of manners from the host; indeed, such rules of behaviour were if anything refined by the growth of courtesy literature in the early seventeenth century.[25] The essence of these gestures lay in their public acknowledgement of the demands of the honour code, in the continual reaffirmation of hierarchy, and in the contribution of the host to the maintenance of proper social order. Again the image of the household as the microcosm within which true principles of order could be articulated is obviously prominent in the minds of those constructing these elaborate codes.

The poor were also in some measure participants in the household drama, though their involvement was largely vicarious.[26] They remained beyond, or near, the gate, the passive recipients of food and other commodities conveyed to them with rituals as formal, if not as elaborate, as those associated with the reception of the nobility. The almoner, usually a cleric in the greatest households, played an interestingly ambivalent role, for he was both the lord's representative and the figure who reminded his master of the Christian imperative to care for the

---

[25] See e.g., Obadiah Walker, *Of Education, Especially of Young Gentlemen* (Oxford, 1673), 221–3.

[26] Though they might be more permanently involved as almsmen within the household; see below, pp. 69–70.

needy.[27] Since the physical isolation of the poor beyond the gates was sanctioned by long social usage, the almoner had to stand as their agent, ensuring that proper food was reserved for them, and that the household did not forget that in giving to them they were serving Christ. The duality of the almoner's obligations is well shown in some of the late medieval prescriptive texts: he was to appear as part of the procession of household servants at mealtimes, bearing the alms dish just as the carver carried in the meats.[28] However, in taking bread from the table, and accepting the first slices of carved meat, he was perceived as acting with the authority of his office, which bound the lord 'to serve God fyrst withouten lette'.[29] After the meal the almoner, or more likely his deputy in the hall, removed the contents of the alms dish and tub to the gate, where he presided over the distribution to the poor. At the gate the almoner's office was more clearly that of domestic servant, embodying the charitable instincts of his master. He retained his rod of office, and symbolically bound the needy into a brief involvement in household commensality by his affirmation of authority over the alms distributed. Such dignity of gesture, however, demanded an audience also willing to subscribe to its intended meaning: it may be presumed that the crowds at the gates were less interested in such symbolism than those being entertained within the household. A fifteenth-century satire offers a very different vision of household charity: the fool who is the interlocutor leaves his 'bauble' to an impatient almoner, who, beseiged by demanding beggars, beats them 'with hys staffe, that the Blode Ron Abowte there erys'.[30]

Even the critics of the hierarchical pattern of entertainment described in the ordinances remained influenced by its basic assumptions. One of the most powerful early attacks came from the Edwardian dean of Wells, William Turner, who, like many of

---

[27] This is made particularly clear in the description of the almoner's duties in 'A Generall Rule to Teche every man that is willynge for to lerne to serve a lorde or mayster in every thyng to his plesure', BL, Add. MS. 37969, printed in R. W. Chambers (ed.), *A Fifteenth-Century Courtesy Book* (*EETS*, 48, London, 1914).
[28] Ibid.
[29] J. O. Halliwell-Phillipps (ed.), *The Boke of Curtasye* (London, 1841), 30.
[30] F. J. Furnivall (ed.), *Early English Treatises and Poems on Education, Precedence and Manners in Olden Time* (*EETS*, E.S. 8, London, 1869), 78.

his reformist contemporaries, was bent upon indicting the nobility and gentry for their lack of true hospitality.[31] He was fiercely critical of the convention by which, 'yf a gentleman come to the house, whether he be knowen or not knowen, yet ether, for to receyve suche good chere againe of the stranger, or for good fames sake, that he maye be called a lyberal gentleman, and a good housekeeper, the maister of the house wyl byd him welcome, and make hym good chere'. Meanwhile the ordinary wayfarer was slighted and the poor were fed only 'slavered breade and noughtye drynke'. But Turner did not, like most others, rest content with excoriating the traditional system: he proposed reformation in its place. The master of a household should still feed all comers, but in an organized and disciplined manner. The poor would still eat outside or near the gates, in a dining-room served with specially prepared foods; there would be a second room within the house for 'honest plowmen, artificers and other strangers, under the degre of gentleman'. Finally, the lord might continue to receive his friends and equals in his chamber. Turner's ideal model is intriguing because, while criticizing what currently exists, he accepts the notions of hierarchy and separation which inform traditional descriptions of the household. Indeed, even the details of his model seem to have a precedent, in the behaviour of monasteries which established separate dining arrangements at least for his second and third categories.[32] If anything Turner seeks to harden the lines of division between his three social groups, isolating them physically and organizationally from one another within the overarching structure of the household.

This reformist vision of the open household should perhaps compel us to reflect further on the significance of the barriers in the traditional noble or gentle establishment described in the ordinances. Separation and division were certainly features of the system: indeed, the officers in charge of the crucial barriers were required to practise the subtle art of filtration in such a way that they excluded the unworthy without offending those who defined their claims to access as legitimate. In the case of the hall

---

[31] William Turner, *A New Book of Spirituall Physike for Dyverse Diseases of the Nobilitie and Gentlemen of Englande* (Emden, 1555), fo. 67-7ᵛ.

[32] See e.g., J. T. Fowler (ed.), *Rites of Durham* (Surtees Soc., 107, 1903), 89-92.

this meant, as the Elizabethan ordinances for the Willoughby household expressed it, 'that no rascall or unseemly person be suffer'd to tarry there'.[33] But the object was to filter, so that, with the exception of the really unworthy, everyone could be allocated a place within a subtly graded system. It therefore is as relevant to emphasize the permeability of these arrangements as their concern for separation. There is the sense of a *cursus honorum*, in which certain key status transitions existed, but in which the important feature was a graded ascent from gatehouse to inner chamber. An individual's place within this hierarchy was supposedly dependent on objective criteria, on status definitions readily apprehended and applied by responsible servants, but it was also no doubt contingent on perceptions of self-worth that allowed some modification of rigid categorization in practice.[34] Above all it was a system which in theory integrated all those who defined themselves or were defined as guests of the lord. The possibility of ascending movement through the generous household is given attractive expression in the character-sketch of a charitable gentleman by Richard Brathwait in the 1630s. 'Knocke at his gate, and you shall finde it not surely but civilly guarded; enter his Court, and you shall see the poore and needy charitably rewarded; Ascend up higher and steppe into his Hall, and you shall read this posie in Capitall Letters inscribed: A PILGRIMES SOLACE IS A CHRISTIANS OFFICE.'[35]

II

The actual houses of the fifteenth- and sixteenth-century English nobility and gentry often conformed closely to the ideal typology offered above. Haddon Hall in Derbyshire, for example, was one

---

[33] *HMC, Middleton*, 539.

[34] Hence the constant reminders to servants in the ordinances that they should endeavour at all costs to avoid offending strangers by evaluating their status wrongly.

[35] Richard Brathwait, *Whimzies: Or a New Cast of Characters* (London, 1631), 74–5. There is a fine description of the manner in which hospitality matched with the traditional house in Philip Sidney, *The Countess of Pembroke's Arcadia* ed. M. Evans (London, 1977), 71. Kalendar's house, usually taken to be an idealized description of Penshurst, was finely built, but favoured 'firm stateliness' over anything more extraordinary. 'The lights, the doors and the stairs rather directed to the use of the guest than to the eye of the artificer.'

of the many early Tudor homes that had evolved from an earlier core to manifest an essentially linear pattern in its main and service rooms, while employing both an outer and an inner courtyard for the provision of additional accommodation (Fig. 2.2). On a smaller scale Minster Lovell Hall in Oxfordshire reveals the same central features (Fig. 2.3). Occasionally, for practical reasons, builders in the fifteenth-century were already adding structures which undercut the neat progression from gate to porch and from hall to chamber. At South Wingfield, Derby, for example, the chamber was placed above the service rooms because the lie of the land prevented its construction behind the upper end of the hall.[36] More problematic for our purposes than these practical responses to architectural dilemmas are those unusual cases where a separate dining room or chamber was built at an early date at the lower end of the hall adjacent to the service rooms, so that the family could eat without food being carried ceremoniously through the hall. Margaret Wood identifies two such fifteenth-century dining rooms, at Great Chalfield in Wiltshire, and South Wraxall, Somerset, both medium-sized gentry households.[37] This is scarcely enough to indicate any general reaction against formal eating, though it may be a first hint at that flexibility of organization which permitted the middling establishment to move away from the traditional structure with some ease later in the sixteenth century. At a more exalted social level there are a number of examples of two separate halls in noble establishments, either ones designed specifically for the accommodation of retainers, as at Bodiam Castle, Sussex, or ones that are part of a second distinct suite of rooms, as in the tower-houses of Warkworth or Ashby-de-la-Zouch.[38] Two halls, as Girouard has pointed out, may more often mean two diachronous functions than a divided household, but may occasionally indicate the latter, as in the accommodation provided for estate labourers at the preceptory of the Knights Templar in South Witham, Lincolnshire.[39]

[36] M. Wood, *The English Medieval House* (London, 1965), 186.

[37] Ibid. 62–4.

[38] W. D. Simpson, '"Bastard Feudalism" and the Later Castles', *Antiquaries Journal*, 26 (1946), 170 ff.; M. Girouard, *Life in the English Country House* (New Haven, Conn., 1978), 63.

[39] Girouard, *Country House*, 60.

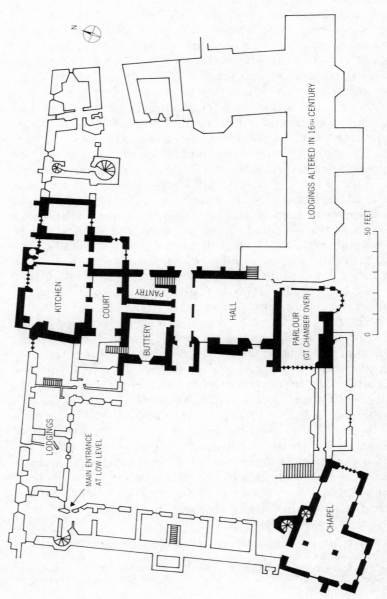

N

KITCHEN

COURT

PANTRY

BUTTERY

HALL

LODGINGS

MAIN ENTRANCE
AT LOW LEVEL

PARLOUR
(GT CHAMBER OVER)

LODGINGS ALTERED IN 16TH CENTURY

CHAPEL

0

50 FEET

Fig. 2.2.　Haddon Hall

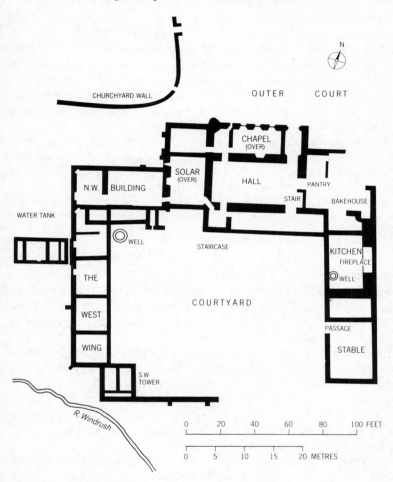

Fig. 2.3. Minster Lovell Hall

Although other architectural arrangements were equally varied, it is deviations from the fixed pattern of public and semi-public eating rooms that are of most interest in the context of hospitality. Since some form of public commensality, supported by the ritualized serving of meals, was essential to noble generosity as it was traditionally conceived, any alteration of rooms or of the groups occupying those rooms should reveal something of the changing nature of entertainment. The most fundamental change was already well advanced in the fifteenth century, and has so far simply been assumed in this chapter: that is the withdrawal of the lord and his immediate family and guests from dining in the great hall, and the growing use of the chamber. It is sometimes confidently asserted, on the basis of a Langland quotation so well known as to be almost hackneyed, that this change had taken place by the late fourteenth century.[40] Certainly the royal household, which is the only one adequately documented over long periods of time, had by then undergone the transition: Edward II was apparently already using his chamber for eating at the beginning of the century.[41] Other establishments no doubt began to follow suit before the 1370s, or Langland's moralistic lament:

> Elyng is the halle. uche daye in the wyke,
> There the lorde ne the ladye. liketh noughte to sytte.

would have made little sense.[42] Nevertheless, some caution is necessary in the face of late medieval evidence so fragmentary as to be almost non-existent. The series of ordinances called 'the service to the Baron-bishop of Yorke', which are appended to the description of the Neville feast of 1467, seem to date from the fourteenth century, and still assume that the prelate will be served in the hall.[43] Langland's own descriptions of meals elsewhere in *Piers Plowman* use the hall as the setting, as do those of *Sir Gawain and the Green Knight*.[44] On great occasions the nobility and even the king continued to dine in hall in the late fifteenth century and beyond: Edward IV's *Black Book* makes specific provision for this eventuality.[45]

Among the gentry it is probable that the habit of dining in the hall was retained longer. Even in the early sixteenth century there are indications in some regions that no retreat into the chamber had occurred. One of the most interesting pieces of evidence is

---

[40] See e.g., Wood, *Medieval House*, 91.

[41] T. F. Tout, *The Place of Edward II in English History* (Manchester, 1936), 257, 259.

[42] William Langland, *Piers Plowman: The B Text*, ed. W. W. Skeat (*EETS*, 28, London, 1869), 147.

[43] T. Hearne (ed.), *Johannis Lelandi . . . Collectanea*, 6 vols. (London, 1774), vi. 7.

[44] Langland, *Piers Plowman*, 199.   [45] *Household of Edward IV*, 92.

provided by the construction of elaborate dais canopies above the hall high table, designed no doubt in part to exclude draughts, but also as covers of honour analogous, it has been suggested, to the cellure over the high altar of a church.[46] The majority of the examples come from Cheshire and from north and central Wales, and some, such as the one at Adlington Hall, Cheshire, are spectacular works. It is difficult to believe that when this was erected at the very beginning of the sixteenth century it was intended only as a backcloth for the occasional feast, or for the regular dining of the steward and other household officers. Dais canopies were constructed from the fourteenth century onwards, but some of the finest examples belong to the early sixteenth. By then a process of cultural diffusion had occurred, at least in Wales, where yeomen, who certainly still dined in their halls, began to copy gentry canopies.[47] It may be that these late instances should be attributed to regional backwardness and traditionalism; however, they do raise intriguing problems about the extent to which we should infer gentry behaviour from that of the better-documented greater nobility. A little more information can be gleaned from inventories which survive for the northern ecclesiastical province in the fifteenth century. Of the seven inventories of gentry or senior clerics which provide a detailed description of the content of particular rooms, three show a great chamber equipped for eating as well as sleeping while the rest indicate that it was used only for sleeping and storage.[48] In the inventories pre-dating the 1440s only that of Henry Bowet, Archbishop of York, has clear evidence of tables and seating in the chamber: thereafter more variation occurs. The last example in which the chamber appears entirely as a bedroom is that of Elizabeth, widow of a minor gentleman, William Swydardby, whose possessions were appraised in 1468. From approximately the same social strata comes the example of Addington Hall, Buckinghamshire, whose owner still used the chamber for lodging at the end of the fifteenth century.[49]

---

[46] Wood, *Medieval House*, 134–6.
[47] P. Smith, *Houses of the Welsh Countryside* (RHMC, London, 1975), 427.
[48] J. Raine (ed.), *Testamenta Eboracensia*, 5 vols. (Surtees Soc., 4, 30, 45, 53, 79, 1836–84), iii. 3–4, 12–13, 44–5, 64, 69–72, 107–8, 134, 161.
[49] Girouard, *Country House*, 53.

Although the timing of the retreat of the nobility and gentry from their halls may not be as obvious as the Langland quotation implies, it had undoubtedly happened in most great houses by the early sixteenth century. In considering their motives for withdrawal the poet appears to hesitate between alternative explanations. On the one hand he saw it as a retreat into privacy;

> Now hath uche riche a reule to eten bi hym-selve
> In a pryve parlour . . .

On the other he hinted not so much at retreat, as at the pursuit of greater luxury by the élite:

> Or in a chambre with a chymneye and leve the chiefe halle
> That was made for meles, men to eten Inne.[50]

The two explanations are not, of course, incompatible, and both may have contributed to the choices made in great houses in the fourteenth and fifteenth centuries. But the difference in emphasis is important in the context of hospitality and magnificence: had the chamber become fully privatized, the territory of a gentleman and perhaps the most intimate of his friends, then even the claim that the household was sharing together in common meals, and entertaining outsiders as a unit, would have been difficult to sustain. It is the survival into the chamber of the semi-public forms of open dining that ensures continuity from the old traditions of commensality and permits the late medieval household still to be defined as a ritual unit. It is revealing that the ordinances, while making the separation of rooms clear, discuss the patterns of eating in communal terms. The habit of eating in separate chambers is vigorously opposed and it is always argued that the lord, his guests, and his whole household must sit down together, with the exception of those needed to serve at the main meal. No doubt the impulse to eat in more peaceful surroundings was present for some of the aristocracy, but the possibilities of luxury and magnificence offered by the chamber seem to have predominated. It is easier to envisage the ceremoniousness of the 'Orders for Service . . .', described at length by Girouard, being dramatically effective in a chamber with only two boards to serve, rather than in a hall full of activity.[51] There was the additional ceremonial advantage that the lord's food had to be transported

---

[50] Langland, *Piers Plowman*, 147.   [51] Girouard, *Country House*, 64.

through the hall, offering an ideal opportunity for displays of deference by those present. The ordinances of Henry, Earl of Huntingdon, dating from 1609, vividly evoke the ideal reception to be accorded to such a procession. The usher was to 'cause all men in the hall to come to the other side of the hall and be bare-headed whilst their Honnors' meate passeth through'.[52]

The semi-public nature of the great chamber therefore modified, but did not destroy, the concept of the integrated household collectively serving its master and his guest. Yet the growth of individual chambers in fourteenth- and fifteenth-century great houses is witness to an impulse towards privacy which did have the potential to challenge the values of the hierarchical household. When ceremonial achieved so important a place in these great establishments and became, if we can believe the ordinances, ever more refined, the inducement to create inner space free of ceremonial also grew. In practice this need was partially filled by the growth of rooms with specialist functions—not only sleeping chambers, but studies and parlours—that are to be found in early sixteenth-century inventories.[53] The creation of separate, inner dinning-rooms, however, breached much more significant conventions, and seems to have been delayed in many of even the greatest houses until the reign of Elizabeth. When the head of a household wished to withdraw from the elaboration of chamber dining it was often to eat alone, while his family and guests continued in his absence. In the Paget household books for 1551–2 it is several times noted that 'my lord supped in his chamber and the table furnished without', and the lists of those present then show Lady Paget taking his place at the head of the board.[54] Although breakfast, if it was served at all, might well be sent into individual chambers, this was unlikely at other meals, unless a traveller arrived at a time when no general eating was imminent. The Eltham Ordinances of 1526 sternly forbade members of the court to 'dyne in corners and secret places not repairing to the kinges chambers and hall ne to the hed officers of the householde'. The object was partly to

---

[52] *HMC, Middleton*, 539.
[53] See e.g., the Caister inventory, *Archaeologia*, 21 (1827), 232–80.
[54] GLRO, Acc 446/4/13, fo. 38ᵛ.

prevent waste, but the threat to 'good order' that came from private dining was also an avowed cause of concern.[55]

Even when a highly developed sense of privacy led to the creation of separate dining arrangements it need not necessarily be seen as a major threat to traditional hospitality. The best documented example of the quest for privacy is the third Duke of Buckingham's arrangement of the inner court of his spectacular mansion at Thornbury (Fig. 2.4). Buckingham left intact the hall of the older house which he inherited and used it as the focus for some of the most impressive Christmas festivities on record. At the same time he constructed a series of private apartments which included a dining-room separated from the main hall block by the great chamber. It is not known exactly when he used this room, but its existence does seem congruent with his elaborate device for reaching his chapel without passing through the public rooms of the house. A gallery was constructed from the great chamber to the chapel, and once there the duke worshipped in a small private area, though this latter arrangement was characteristic of chapels in great houses.[56] It does appear from the rather unusual architectural evidence in this case that Buckingham sought compensation for the lavish magnificence and external display of his public life in a private domain. However, there is not the slightest hint that this detracted from his pursuit of a reputation as 'bounteous Buckingham, the mirror of all courtesy',[57] The Duke's first royal master, Henry VII, achieved a similar blend of public magnificence and private withdrawal by developing the privy chamber as a separate department of the royal household, specifically designed as a refuge from the increasing ceremoniousness of the court.[58]

The size of the household establishment is of obvious relevance to its ability to maintain public hospitality, and numbers of servants offer at least a crude guide to the obligations which the nobility and gentry felt that they should undertake as hosts. It is possible here to start from an ideal typology which is not the

---

[55] Bodl. Laud MS. Misc. 597, fo. 22[v].

[56] Simpson, 'Bastard Feudalism', 169; Harris, *Buckingham*, 87–9.

[57] The quotation is from Shakespeare's *Henry VIII*, II. i, but is echoed in other contemporary views of the Duke. See K. B. McFarlane, *The Nobility of Later Medieval England* (Oxford, 1973), 208–9.

[58] D. R. Starkey, *The Reign of Henry VIII* (London, 1985), 24–6.

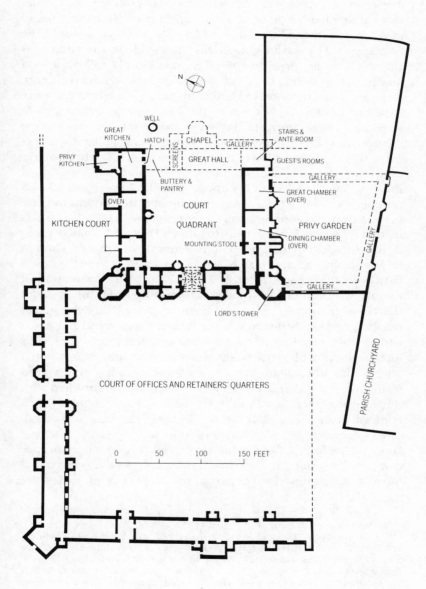

Fig. 2.4. Thornbury Castle

construct of the historian, but a statement of contemporary belief in what numbers of domestics were appropriate to various social ranks. According to Edward IV's *Black Book*, a duke should have as many as 240 servants, since his 'howsolde in the cuntrey is called a "garde corps du roy"'. He was closely followed by a marquis, who should have 200, and an earl, for whom the figure was 140. Then there was a significant gulf, for a baron was only expected to employ forty men, and a household knight a mere sixteen.[59] These contrasts may seem too dramatic to bear much relation to reality, but it is possible to document similar disparities from surviving lists of servants. The Duke of Clarence had an establishment of 332 in 1469, while Edward, Duke of Buckingham, had 187 in his household in 1503–4, and 225 on his check-roll in 1511. Thence the numbers descend to the 166 in the Earl of Northumberland's household in 1511–12, and 105 in that of John, Earl of Oxford, in 1507–8. It is much more difficult to document a small establishment, but that of Thomas Le Strange had approximately seventeen servants in the 1530s.[60] One problem in the greater households is the determination of exactly who can be classified as a domestic in the full sense of the term: it has, for example, been suggested that the actual Buckingham establishment was only about 150, after all additional and outside servitors had been discounted.[61] Most check-rolls listed some agricultural servants who cannot readily be numbered within the household proper, and some added those who maintained outlying manors and were rarely, if ever, resident with the lord. Moreover, although it is possible to cite examples which conform neatly to the *Black Book*'s image of the great household, others can be found which seem significantly smaller. The first Duke of Norfolk, whose domestic records reveal a very proper concern for order and style, had under 200 persons who could in any sense be described as part of his establishment, and under

---

[59] *Household of Edward IV*, 94–104.

[60] J. M. Thurgood, 'Diet and Domestic Households of the English Lay Nobility, 1265–1531', London M.Phil. dissertation (1982), 64–6; C. Rawcliffe, *The Staffords, Earls of Stafford and Dukes of Buckingham: 1394–1521* (Cambridge, 1978), 88; *Regulations . . . for Henry Percy*, 299 ff.; *Archaeologia*, 25 (1834), 493. Dr Mertes suggests that even minor gentry households needed twenty-odd domestic servants: Mertes, *The English Noble Household*, 103.

[61] Rawcliffe, *Staffords*, 88.

150 servitors proper. The Countess of Devon paid wages to between sixty-eight and seventy-three individuals in 1524, though here, of course, due allowance must be made for the somewhat different expectations that contemporaries might have of a widow rather than a male head of house.[62] On the other hand a baron or knight who was of consequence might well have far more men in his employ than the ideal notions of the *Black Book* suggest. Sir Thomas Lovell listed ninety-one persons as servants in 1537, including some agricultural and other out-workers: two years later his increasing status was reflected in a growth of his establishment to around 120 persons.[63]

A recent survey of surviving household accounts suggests that an 'average' size for the noble household at the end of the medieval period was around 150 persons, while about sixty-five was average for a gentry establishment.[64] Is it therefore conceivable that both could offer what contemporaries perceived as lavish hospitality, that both could effectively demonstrate their adherence to the ethos of generosity that was a part of the honour community? The evidence of the Le Strange household suggests that the answer must be a qualified yes. Although only seventeen servants were paid by Sir Thomas, they replicated in miniature the organization of much larger establishments. There were gentlemen and yeomen, those who served the hall, and those for the chamber, although it is not clear from the accounts that there was a full-time porter, and the duties of almoner would no doubt in so small a group have been discharged by the yeoman of the hall. As we shall see, the Le Stranges offered entertainment which, considering their standing and the relatively inaccessible location of their estate at Hunstanton on the Norfolk coast, compared favourably with that of the great nobility. Assumptions about the function and duties of the servants were probably more important than mere numbers once a certain basic size of establishment had been achieved. The so-called 'secret household' which the earls of Northumberland kept from time to time to avoid the pressure of public company included thirty-five servants, most of them

[62] J. Payne Collier (ed.), *Manners and Household Expenses of England in the Thirteenth and Fifteenth Centuries* (Roxburghe Club, London, 1844), 582; PRO, E36/223, fos. 59–60.   [63] *HMC, Rutland*, iv. 284, 296–8.

[64] Mertes, *The English Noble Household*, App. C.

presumably serving the needs of the nuclear family.[65] In contrast, even a yeoman aspiring to gentility could keep open port which deeply impressed his neighbourhood, provided that he surrounded himself with a few 'tall fellows'. This is what the Henrician ancestor of the yeoman farmer Robert Furse did when he had 'som viii tall fellowes in his leverye and . . . made grette waste'.[66]

What John Furse achieved on a small scale by having his tall men about him could be managed in the great household by the use of retainers as well as household servants proper. It is important to differentiate sharply between the ordinary members of the household, and those feed men who might be summoned into it on occasions by virtue of their possession of the lord's livery. However, when magnificence was required, especially on the occasions of a royal visit or that of a senior peer of the realm, it was possible to use these outsiders rather, one imagines, as a film director does his assemblage of extras. Bacon has a well-known story of Henry VII's visit to the Earl of Oxford at Castle Hedingham.[67] On his departure the King passed between the serried ranks of the Earl's servants, all clad in the de Vere livery, and commented: '"My lord, I have heard much of your hospitality, but I see it is greater than the speech. These handsome gentlemen and yeomen, which I see on both sides of me, are sure your menial servants".' When it transpired that they were largely retainers, the Earl supposedly became victim of a 15,000 mark fine for breach of the laws against retaining. Unproveable though the story is, it well evokes a contemporary sense that good hospitality required superfluous numbers of attendants, each providing the service of deference, rather than necessarily discharging any practical duty. In Bacon's account the Earl, replying to the King, makes a distinction between those servants who were present '"for mine ease"', and those who had come in '"to do me service"'.

[65] NRO, Le Strange P1,2: extensive extracts are printed in *Archaeologia*, 25, 411–569.

[66] H. Carpenter (ed.), 'A History of the Furse Family of Moreshead', *Trans. of the Devon Assoc.*, 26 (1894), 176.

[67] Francis Bacon, *Works*, ed. J. Spedding, 7 vols. (London, 1857–9), vi. 219–20. The Pastons were certainly impressed by the Earl's retainers: see N. Davis (ed.), *Paston Letters and Papers of the Fifteenth Century*, 2 vols. (Oxford, 1971, 1976), i. 245, 345. There is no surviving documentary support for Bacon's story: S. B. Chrimes, *Henry VII* (London, 1977), 190.

III

The traditional great house, therefore, provided both the stage-setting and the supporting cast for the exercise of lavish hospitality. It is, however, a difficult task to ascertain who actually appeared in the role of guests. The ordinances offer us generic categories of those who *should* be received, but to proceed beyond this to the social reality requires the equivalent of the nineteenth-century guest book. Fortunately, among the range of expenditure records kept by noble households in the medieval and early modern period is one type which does yield valuable information. One of the most important second-rank officials in these establishments was the clerk of the kitchen, whose principal duty was accounting for the daily expenditure on food and the flow of stock items from the demesne in and out of the kitchens.[68] In the relatively undifferentiated household of the thirteenth century these tasks might have been performed by the steward, who sometimes kept an informal tally of guests, but it was only from the fourteenth century, with the emergence of large and hierarchical structures, that it became essential to have a clerk who kept a daily record, or journal, of the movement of food, from which he could then account to the chief officers on a weekly or monthly basis. The clerk's interest in guests was logically confined to a calculation of how many extra messes of food had to be produced for strangers each day, a crude total which might usefully be recorded in the margin of his book. The Northumberland Household Book suggests that the main interest of the lord was also in the additional cost which outsiders generated: the chief officers were ordered to produce a precise record of additional expenditure on food purchases: 'as well at principal feasts double feast or festial days as in times that strangers come to his Lordship when his Lordship then doth cause his fare to exceed above the ordinary fare of the Service of the house accustomed'.[69] However, simple enumeration did not satisfy either the Earl of Northumberland, or apparently the heads of many other noble houses. The clerks of the kitchen were

---

[68] For some account of the functions and activity of the clerk of the kitchen, see Thurgood, 20–2.

[69] *Regulations . . . for Henry Percy*, 71.

ordered to 'breve every stranger by name that cometh to my lords house', and to be especially careful at the periods of open entertainment such as Christmas, Easter, and St George's Day. To understand the mechanisms by which such a detailed record was produced we have to turn to the much later orders for the household of Lionel Cranfield, Earl of Middlesex, where the clerk of the kitchen was instructed to keep a day book:

And in thee said day booke must sett downe thee names of all strangers and others, which sitt with my lord, my lady, or the daughters, and what meales they were from home, which the usher of the chamber shall every day give hym; also what strangers were in the hall, which hee shall have from the usher there.[70]

Since a principal objective of keeping guest lists was that it provided a prudential check on waste and corruption, its attraction was not confined to those great establishments which had separate kitchen organization and a complex hierarchy of bookkeepers. At least some gentry were noting their visitors as early as the fourteenth century, and by the later sixteenth century some of the most precise listings come from this social level.[71] It is the detail of the clerks' endeavours that make the journals an invaluble record for the study of hospitality, but a record which nevertheless must be evaluated very cautiously. The clerks were ordered to record guest-names, yet the only really practical incentive for so doing was, as the Montagu orders put it, 'that he may provide dyett and breakfast for them accordinge to their degrees'.[72] This was an invitation to specificity in the case of influential chamber guests, but hardly an encouragement to precise differentiation of the numbers in the body of the hall, most of whom would dine on similar fare. Thus it must be anticipated that the kitchen accounts will offer more information on powerful visitors than on the rest, and indeed some records do not even bother to note those present in the hall, or do so only to give a

[70] LPL, Fulham Papers 426, fo. 24.

[71] The best early example is that of the Le Strange household for the 1340s, NRO, Le Strange NH 3–8: extracts are printed in *Archaeologia*, 69 (1917–18), 111–120. For the later period, see the Bacon accounts NRO, Bradfer-Lawrence, VIIb (5) and the household books of Sir William Fairfax, extracted in *HMC Var. Coll. II*, 70–82.

[72] 'A Booke of Orders and Rules for Anthony, 2nd Viscount Montague', *Sussex Archaeological Coll.*, 7 (1854), 198.

numerical total. Beyond this there is an intriguing uncertainty among the clerks themselves about the purpose of their careful annotations. Journals which unhesitatingly record guests or numbers in a consistent manner over a year or more are the exception: the Beauchamp Household Book of 1431–2 and that for the Paget household in 1550–1 are among the best surviving examples.[73] More often listings begin purposefully, and then become less adequate over time, as do those of the Le Strange family, or they are kept fully only at times of festival, or when the family is in residence. Some clerks seemed to see guests as only intermittently intriguing and would jot their names in the margin rather as they might record some domestic tragedy or event of national importance. For example, the account-keeper for Elizabeth, Lady Berkeley, writing housekeeping records at the end of the 1620s, united notes about the comings and goings of the mistress and the entertainment of significant individuals with observations on sheep-shearing and household marriages and deaths.. Even the impeccable clerk to Lord Paget was capable of deviating from his task to note that, on 18 August 1551, 'was proclamyed a teaster to be but vid, A grote but 2d etc . . .'.[74]

It would be unreasonable to expect consistency from a series of records constructed under variant orders, which often seem of marginal importance even to their authors. And it is indeed irritating to see how even lists prepared for the same household, occasionally even by the same clerk, can change their form of presentation in a short space of time. The Le Strange accounts for 1527–8, for example, make no attempt to list servants or those dining in the hall; those for 1533 do.[75] The excellent Bacon / Townshend series, running from the 1590s to the later 1620s, change from recording guests at the end of each week to a more precise enumeration under a day, or at least a careful record of day of arrival and departure.[76] Sir John Thynne's clerk lost interest in noting the numbers present in Corsley Hall after the Christmas season 1569, although he had been doing so with

---

[73] Wa. RO, CR 1618/W19/6; Middx. RO, Acc. 446/4/13.
[74] GLRO, Acc. 530/H1; Acc. 446/4/13, fo. 103ᵛ.
[75] NRO, Le Strange P1,2.
[76] NRO, Bradfer-Lawrence VIIb/5; Raynham MS; Bacon Household Account Book, 1620–8.

great care since the previous September.[77] When the ephemeral
nature of the kitchen expenditure records is added to these
problems it may seem an almost irrelevant exercise to analyse
such notes of visitors as do survive. Nevertheless, this solemn
annotation of the margins of food journals does provide a crucial
insight into the actual behaviour of nobles and gentlemen as hosts
and at least some sense of the value which the household placed
upon various individuals and social groups bidden to share its
meals. The seasonality and periodicity of the domestic round are
also visible, as are the types of provision made by the traditional
household for the entertainment of its guests.

One of the most obvious features of the surviving lists of
'strangers' from the fifteenth- and sixteenth-century journals is
that, in listing all individuals not strictly of the household, the
zealous clerk included categories of visitor who cannot strictly
be described as guests. The easiest to identify are the craftsmen,
itinerant harvest labourers, and others, who had their diet in the
hall while performing services for the lord. Sir Hugh Hastings,
whose modest Norfolk household in the early 1530s rarely
included more than a handful of guests, often had several
workmen among them.[78] On a typical January day in 1531 he
had one stranger, unnamed, to dinner and four to supper, while
there were also three workmen at each meal. In May 1552, Sir
William Petre would normally have had more guests than this
on his Essex manor of Ingatestone, but often the largest group
of outsiders were the workmen who were undertaking alterations
in preparation for the marriage of his daughter in the following
month.[79] A group of workers particularly likely to be fed one or
two meals were the carters bringing firewood or other bulk goods
into the household: in the Duchess of Suffolk's accounts for 1564
there are several mentions of carters performing 'boon' work of
this kind, that is providing residual labour services to their
overlord.[80] When twenty-three appeared to perform this boon
work on Thursday, 8 June, presumably carting hay, they
outnumbered other strangers two to one. Later in the same month
there were two days when fourteen carriers bringing wheat were

---

[77] Longleat House, Wilts. Thynne Papers, Book 109.
[78] NRO, Le Strange, NH 15.
[79] ERO, D/DP/A12.   [80] LiRO, 1ANC, 7/A5.

fed in the hall. All this, as a part of the traditional economy of the household, can hardly be classified as hospitality, although in the case of tenants bringing rent in kind or performing services an element of reciprocity was surely a part of the food they were offered.

The second group of outsiders who cannot usefully be described as visitors were those agents of the lord who were not part of the household proper, but who, by virtue of their offices, spent much of their time in the establishment. Auditors, surveyors of land, receivers, bailiffs, and the like were rarely on the domestic staff, but constantly recur on guest lists, where, to add to the confusion, they are not usually designated by office. It has to be established from other sources that the most regular visitor to Sir Thomas Le Strange's table, Mr Banyard, was a rather distant kinsman who was also his auditor, or that William Knyvett, who routinely dined with the third Duke of Buckingham, was his chamberlain.[81] Such men might well spend a week or more dining with the master of the house while they were on official business and would reappear at frequent intervals. Although they cannot properly be described as guests they are much more difficult to isolate as a group than the labourers because they were often men of some standing, and therefore had some access to the social circle of the lord, as well as acting as his professional advisers. A common feature of the journals is the feeding of a group of such men, sometimes explicitly described as counsellors, as when the Countess of Devon's clerk noted under 29 May 1523: 'this day were dyvers of my lades counsellors.' Edward, Duke of Buckingham's council met for dinner with him in London on 4 February 1508, and were served with one quart of malmsey and a further three-and-a-half pitchers by the hands of the butler.[82] Such assemblies could undoubtedly have a social as well as a business dimension; when the Earl of Derby held a meeting for all his council at Knowsley in the 1580s they came in Whitsun week, stayed for four days, and had the benefit of hearing a couple of sermons as well as eating a number of meals.[83]

---

[81] Banyard is recorded as Le Strange's auditor in his general expenditure accounts. On Knyvett, see Rawcliffe, *Staffords*, 195.

[82] PRO, E36/223, fo. 109; Staff. RO, D1721/1/5, 85.

[83] F. R. Raines (ed.), *The Stanley Papers, pt. ii: The Derby Household Books* (Chetham Soc., o.s. 31, 1853), 29–30.

At other times the narrowness of the line between guest and servant is shown by the appearance of the wives of these professionals on festive occasions. In the Le Strange household, Mrs Banyard attended churchings, christenings, and the Christmas festivities, as the wife of a kinsman might have been expected to do, but it is less predictable that Mrs Maynard should have been one of Lady Paget's 'gossips' and a regular visitor on a Sunday when a species of open house was held in London or at Drayton.[84] Both because of the problems of identification, and because of the difficulty of separating guest from business adviser, it seems wise not to dismiss the latter as beyond the scope of a lord's hospitality.

The clerk of the kitchens' accounts reveal that much of the entertainment offered by the great establishments of the fifteenth and sixteenth centuries was of this composite character, part business, part sociability. But the bare enumerations also list figures who seem to be visitors in the conventional sense of that term, men and women appearing for a meal or staying for a few days, bringing with them their own attendants. In the greatest households, those of the Beauchamps in the 1420s and 1430s, of the Staffords in the 1470s and at the beginning of the sixteenth century, and of the Howards and Seymours in the reign of Henry VIII, a shared feature is the relative infrequency with which members of their peer group were entertained.[85] This is, of course, partly a function of the limited number of families at the apex of the social hierarchy, and hence the unlikelihood that they would intersect regularly with one another, especially in the localities. During the year 1420–1, the accounts of Elizabeth Berkeley, Countess of Warwick, show that the only entertainment offered to a great magnate was the feast she made for John, Duke of Bedford, in June 1421.[86] The same household, recorded in the Beauchamp book ten years later, was more lavish, but only because the Earl was resident at Rouen, where he did receive a steady flow of important English visitors.[87] Elizabeth, whose

---

[84] GLRO, Acc. 446/4/13, fos. 31ᵛ, 43, 44ᵛ, 77, 121, 133. Maynard was one of Paget's senior estate officials.

[85] Thurgood also notes that this is the common pattern in all the great fourteenth- and fifteenth-century households that she studied; Thurgood, 227.

[86] Longleat, Misc. Bk. IX, fo. 120ᵛ.

[87] Wa. RO, CR 1618/W19/6.

journeyings in England form part of the 1420/21 volume, confined herself largely to her social inferiors. Forty years later Lord Henry Stafford was equally modest in the company he chose, except on the occasion when he made a feast for the Duke of Somerset.[88] The third Duke of Buckingham had plenty of leading gentlemen, but no nobles, at his table, and the same was true of the Duke of Norfolk in the 1520s. Only Edward Seymour, among the householders studied, had peers of the realm by his side with any regularity: in the last two weeks of October 1538, for example, he received the Dukes of Norfolk and Suffolk, the Bishop of Winchester, the Earl of Sussex, and a host of senior courtiers.[89] But Seymour was exceptional in two ways: his position as a key courtier and politician made it essential that he entertain the other powerful men of the Henrician court, and he was in London when this extensive hospitality was given. Behaviour in London always contrasted with norms of entertainment in the localities and offered very different opportunities for conviviality. When Seymour returned to his family seat, Wolfs Hall, Wiltshire, or even when he retired to his Hampshire home at Elvetham, he adopted a very different pattern.

While circumstances provide much of the explanation for the limited visiting between great peers, it may be that sensitive issues about territoriality and good lordship also played their part. The very precision with which the household ordinances try to resolve issues of rank serves to remind us that in the 'lethally competitive world' of the fifteenth century dangers could arise from the encounter of equals. The riding household of a great noble could hardly expect to appear unbidden at the gates of another, not only because of the problems of provision, but because of the potential threat they presented. Thus it seems that alternatives were often sought: for example, when Elizabeth Berkeley travelled between London, Warwick, and the south-west she stayed with dependants, on her own estates, at inns, or at a convenient monastery.[90] The extended kin group might provide another option for the mighty, and by the sixteenth century inns were not a total impossiblity. When the Lovell and Seymour houses moved to and fro between London and the

[88] Thurgood, 227.   [89] Longleat, Misc. MS. XVIII.
[90] Longleat, Misc. Bk. IX, fos. 80^v–119^v.

country they seem on occasions to have stayed in paid accommodation like their inferiors.[91] None of this precluded the possibility of grand feasting of one's peers, nor of great formal moments of hospitality such as that which de Vere offered to Henry VII. These were times for the full display of competitive magnificence and largess, either to affirm solidarity with friends or to impress and threaten outsiders. In this context de Vere's only error seems to have been a misreading of the narrowness of the line between impression and threat; the third Duke of Buckingham's penchant for display could be seen as a similar error.

While the clerks' books only offer a few examples of these titanic encounters of the great, they are rich in evidence of entertainment given to the next ranks in society, gentlemen, knights, and esquires, and a variety of others who could be defined as worshipful. On a fairly typical day at Wolfs Hall in 1538, Edward Seymour had at his dinner table Lord Stourton, Sir John Bridges, Lady Darrell, Mr Wroughton, Mr Hungerford and his wife, and Mrs Cheke, all individuals belonging to the influential families of the county.[92] Edward, Duke of Buckingham's famous Epiphany feast of 1508 included ten of the local gentry of Gloucestershire, with a substantial following each, and he often had at least two or three such figures present at an ordinary meal.[93] When Sir William Petre was temporarily home from the court in September 1548 he tended to have local gentlemen and members of his extended kin at table each day: for example, on Tuesday, 18 September, he dined Sir John Mordaunt, Sir Henry Tyrell and his lady and Mr Tyrell, who were all relatives, and Mr Bridges from the locality.[94] In the same year Sir Francis Willoughby had a day in May when he entertained Sir Marmaduke Constable, Mr Burdet, and Mr Horton at Wollaton, in this case perhaps an example of entertainment being given to Yorkshiremen on a journey north or south through Nottinghamshire. Willoughby also received guests of higher status than himself, but apparently only members of the Grey family, who were related to him by marriage.[95] Individual examples

[91] *HMC, Rutland,* iv, 287, 320; Longleat, Misc. MS. XVIII, fos. 6ᵛ–8ᵛ.
[92] Longleat, Misc. MS. XVIII, fo. 3.   [93] Staff. RO, D1721/1/5.
[94] ERO, D/DP/A12.   [95] *HMC, Middleton,* 395.

could be multiplied, for all journals that list guests include some men of gentry status, and these are usually the most carefully recorded figures, with their servants and accompanying members of their family added. In the fifteenth-century lists few men are recorded as accompanied by their wives, although independent women as guests appear in those of the Beauchamp household and the much earlier example of the thirteenth-century accounts for the Countess of Leicester.[96] Even the Buckingham lists for 1507–8 have a distinctly masculine air. However, by the time journals become common in the 1530s and 1540s it is usual for the gentry to be entertained with their wives, at least at the festivals and on Sundays.

To proceed beyond the impressionistic notion that gentlemen, often from the locality, appeared on guest lists, it is necessary to analyse some particular journals in more depth. Although the Berkeley and Beauchamp books for the 1420s and 1430s are sufficiently detailed to lend themselves to such an analysis, it is perhaps more appropriate to turn to the early sixteenth century where comparisons between different sizes and styles of establishment becomes possible. Among the early sixteenth-century accounts two series of particular interest are the 1507–8 Household Book of Edward, Duke of Buckingham, which is the record of a house replete with all the attributes of late medieval magnificence, and those of 1520 and 1533–7 for Sir Thomas Le Strange of Hunstanton, Norfolk. The latter are unique, the product of obsessive book-keeping in a modest gentry home on a rather remote part of the east coast, and therefore an invaluable insight into the behaviour of a medium-sized household at an early date.[97]

A study of the origins and role of the gentry and men of standing who appear in Buckingham's book immediately indicates the breadth of his connection, and the extent to which his sociability was restricted to dependants. At his Christmas and Epiphany feasts gentry from Gloucestershire, Somerset, South

[96] Longleat Misc. Bk. IX, fos. 112–15; M. W. Labarge, *A Baronial Household of the Thirteenth Century* (London, 1980), 48–9.

[97] Staff. RO, D1721/1/5; *Archaeologia*, 25, 411–569. Although there are a few gaps in the printed Le Strange transcriptions, they provide a very full cover of the guest lists, though these have been checked against the originals in the Norwich Record Office.

Wales, Bedfordshire, and Staffordshire were entertained in his chamber, and in London men from East Anglia and mid-Wales were also prominent.[98] In almost all cases they came from areas of Stafford influence, where lands and lordships pulled the local gentry into the ambit of this great family. Moreover, most of them held, or had held, some office within the estate or legal administration of the Duke; for example, Sir Robert Poyntz, one of an important Gloucestershire family, had been surveyor-general in the 1490s, and Robert Partesoil was steward of Huntingdonshire. Hugh Boughey from Staffordshire and William Kemys from an important Welsh family, also held minor office in their respective areas. Indeed, of the gentlemen present at Thornbury that Christmas, only the three Berkeleys from Gloucestershire and Edmund Gorges and John Rodney from Somerset show no immediate evidence of being office-holders. Outside the festive season Buckingham was even more likely to have his dependants at table: on three occasions in London he did entertain Robert Radcliffe, Lord Fitzwalter and later Earl of Sussex, but a more common pattern was that shown on 4 February 1508, when the majority of those received were part of his council. William Knyvett, his chamberlain, and his two sons were present, as were Buckingham's younger brother Lord Henry Stafford who held several stewardships, the auditor William Walwyn, Robert Turberville the receiver-general, John Scott the attorney-general, and Humphrey Blount the receiver of Newport.[99] A full council meeting of this kind was by definition unusual, but the men who attended it were also those who came and went regularly at the Duke's board, supplying much of his social contact as well as his business needs. The Knyvetts, William Walwyn, and Humphrey Blount were sometimes joined in London by specialists such as sergeants-at-law, or by visiting clerics, but always there was a businesslike air about those who gathered around the Duke. Even those like the Berkeleys who did not hold particular posts under the Staffords and were not feed retainers, were part of a wider affinity and were presumably bidden to Thornbury at the Christmas season to affirm their loyalty to and support of the Stafford interest.[100]

[98] Harris, *Buckingham*, 92–3.   [99] Ibid. App. A.
[100] Rawcliffe, *Staffords*, App. B.

Although the Le Strange accounts post-date the Buckingham ones by only a few years, the first being for 1520, to move from Thornbury to Hunstanton is to enter a different world of hospitality. Gentry are still entertained, albeit on a smaller scale, but there is no evidence that the purpose was the affirmation of political loyalties, or in most cases the transaction of business relating to the estates. Instead, the listing of guests seems to indicate that Sir Thomas Le Strange received most of them either for reasons of pure conviviality, or because of his sense of social obligation to friends and kin. The two groups found most regularly at his table were his extended kin and local gentlemen, local that is in the sense of being drawn from his own county rather than beyond its borders. Although Sir Thomas was related to such families as the Vaux and Treshams of Northamptonshire and the Throckmortons of Warwickshire, his visitors were drawn almost entirely from Norfolk, or the immediate bordering area of Suffolk (Fig. 2.5).[101] They came for several days at a time, kin such as Roger Woodhouse and his wife, or Edmund Wymondham, often remaining at Hunstanton for a week or more. Wives very often came with their husbands, the exception being births and christenings, when they might come alone, or masculine gatherings either for business or hunting, when they were excluded.

In his turn Sir Thomas did the rounds of friends and kin, meeting them at their own houses, or taking part in pilgrimages to Walsingham or assize and sessions visits, all moments which he regarded as appropriate for conviviality, if the sums he spent on eating are any adequate guide. This gentry world was already one of mutual good cheer, where the honour of the individual depended on a continual accessibility to known men of similar status. The Le Stranges were not called upon in the four years covered by the kitchen accounts to receive many guests of higher status than themselves, the exceptions being Robert Ratcliffe, Earl of Sussex, a kinsman, and Lady Boleyn, the mother of Anne. When it was necessary to display deference Sir Thomas moved from his own house, visiting the home of the dukes of Norfolk

[101] *The Visitation of Norfolk 1563 and 1613*, ed. W. Rye (Harleian Soc., 32, 1891), 271–2; William Dugdale, *The Antiquities of Warwickshire*, 2 vols., 2nd edn. (London, 1730), ii. 749.

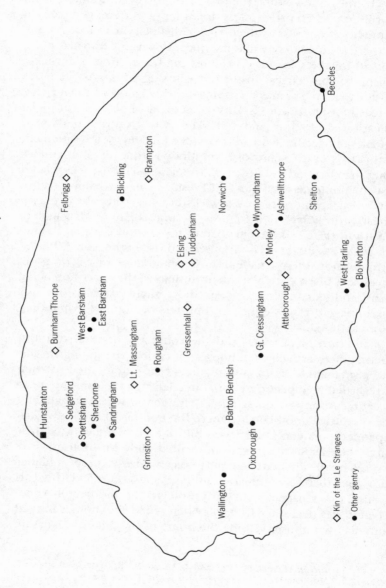

Fig. 2.5. Principal residences of gentry visitors to the Le Strange household, Hunstanton: 1520–38

at Kenninghall at least once a year, and riding with the other local gentry to attend any members of the royal family who visited the county.[102]

It is impossible to reconstruct the exact principles upon which the Le Strange gentry guests were chosen, or selected themselves. Kin seem to have had a claim to very generous hospitality even, in the case of one brother-in-law, Sir Hugh Hastings, to semi-permanent board within the household in time of difficulty.[103] Both young and old availed themselves freely of Sir Thomas's entertainment: among the older generation Roger Woodhouse and Mr Banyard, both married to aunts of Sir Thomas or Lady Le Strange, often stayed at Hunstanton for periods of a week or longer. Among the younger, Edmund Wymondham, John Cressener, one of Sir Thomas's wards, and Mr Calthorp, his son-in-law, appeared regularly. Beyond the family there were men and women apparently introduced by kin: John Robsart, a relative of the unfortunate Amy, first came with Edmund Wymondham, and Calthorp often brought with him a Mr Coningsby of Wallington. It is tempting to think that these were friendships among the younger gentry, able to travel easily from house to house in the manner later described disparagingly by the *Cyvile and Uncyvile Life* as daily visiting 'Gentlemens houses, with man and horse, hauke and dog, til the poore Maister of the house hath al his linnen foule, al his provision eaten'.[104] But the casualness, as well as the negative quality, of this vision, does not seem to accord with the well-defined networks of gentry connection that the Le Strange records reveal. Certain families, the Bedingfields, the Knyvetts, the Lovells, and the Robsarts, recur in the records, and suggest that there were mutual friendships involved in their entertainment. Other, equally notable, Norfolk gentry clans, such as the Gawdys and the Pastons, played no obvious role at all in this circle. Moreover, when Sir Thomas returned visits it was usually to the same group of extended kin and associates. He often met with, or visited the house of, Sir Thomas Wymondham, and other establishments that he visited more than once included

---

[102] *Archaeologia*, 25, 419–512, 549. [103] Ibid. 535.
[104] *Cyvile and Uncyvile Life* in W. C. Hazlitt, *Inedited Tracts Illustrating the Manners of Englishmen during the Sixteenth and Seventeenth Centuries* (Roxburghe Club, London, 1868), 64.

those of Sir Thomas Bedingfield, Roger Woodhouse, and Richard Southwell, another remote relative. The case of Southwell is interesting, for this was a kinsman who was never recorded as making the journey to Hunstanton, but who Sir Thomas travelled to Woodrising to see on at least three occasions; possibly to defer to a man of greater power and influence in East Anglian affairs and at the Henrician Court.

The zeal with which the clerks of the kitchen kept their books tended to diminish as the social status of the guest declined. However, one other group was deemed worthy of careful itemization: the clergy. In the case of bishops, abbots, and priors this interest was understandable, for such men ate in the chamber, travelled with trains of servants as large as their lay peers, and were even more likely to provide reciprocal entertainment for the host should the need arise. The Abbot of Kingswood was one of those at Buckingham's Epiphany feast, bringing with him a retinue of six, and the Prioress of Westwood was entertained in the household of Elizabeth Berkeley in 1421.[105] In the early Le Strange accounts there is more systematic evidence for the comings and goings of the higher clergy. One individual, the last head of Coxford Priory in East Rudham, seems to have been a friend of the family, for in the 1520s he was a frequent visitor, usually staying one or at most two days at Hunstanton. At various times other heads of houses passed through: the priors of Walsingham and Norwich and of the Austin Friars in Lynn, and the abbots of Ramsey and Sempringham, Lincolnshire. It was rare for such men to stay more than a day, although the Prior of Walsingham was sometimes persuaded to stay longer. In the absence of adequate comparative evidence it is difficult to be sure if the Le Stranges were demonstrating any unusual devotion to the Church in making their home so freely available to senior clerics. However, it seems probable that heads of monastic houses were able to claim such hospitality when they travelled on business precisely because they were bound to reciprocate. Even when such reciprocity did not take the form of offering accommodation, priors and abbots could offer generous gifts in the constant rituals of exchange which were so integral a part of élite behaviour. The Prior of Coxford was careful to remember

---

[105] *Archaeologia*, 25, 320; Longleat, Misc. Bk. IX, fo. 130ᵛ.

his hosts by sending fat pigeons and other food offerings at appropriate intervals.[106]

Since the mass of the clergy were neither bishops nor abbots it is to be expected that the majority of those noted in the journals would be monks, friars, or parochial clergy. In the precise listings for the great houses there are indeed frequent mentions of friars, priests, and chaplains, often with an identification of their place of origin, or of their attachment to a great household. In the Howard accounts for 1526–7 canons and friars, especially from Ipswich, are noted, and a few of the clerical proletariat are simply dismissed as priests of the country or of the town.[107] If the ordered listing of the clerks can be taken as describing some kind of hierarchy, then these priests do not seem to have ranked very high in the esteem of the host; though it is worth noting that the friar seated at Cardinal Morton's table in the first book of *Utopia* was accorded a place of dignity and that Langland presented his proud churchman as seated in the place of honour.[108] Beyond the strict ranks of the clergy came a category apparently much favoured by the Howard, Stafford, and Berkeley households— hermits. The Duke of Norfolk frequently permitted a hermit to dine in his hall, and on one remarkable occasion in the Christmas season had two hermits present on the same day.[109] This generosity to the clerical estate and the holy also extended to local incumbents. In the early 1420s Elizabeth, Lady Berkeley, made it her business to entertain the vicar of the local church when she was in residence at Berkeley Castle, and even to receive incumbents when she was travelling. Buckingham had the vicar of Christchurch, Bristol, at his Epiphany feast, and Archbishop Bourchier fed the rector of Lambeth and the vicar of Croydon, both livings in his gift.[110] The traditionalism of this pattern of behaviour is suggested by the Le Strange accounts. In the 1340s Sir Hamon Le Strange had the vicars of Thornham and Stanfield

---

[106] *Archaeologia*, 25, 495.

[107] CUL, Pembroke MS. 300, unpaginated: some extracts are printed in E. M. Richardson, *The Lion and the Rose*, 2 vols. (London, 1923), i. 69–82.

[108] Geoffrey Chaucer, *The Complete Works*, ed. F. N. Robinson (Oxford, 1957), 98–9; Thomas More, *Utopia*, ed. E. Surtz and J. H. Hexter (New Haven, Conn., 1965), 83; Langland, *Piers Plowman*, 26.

[109] CUL, Pembroke MS. 300. The Le Strange accounts list a hermit as one of those fed by the family.

[110] LPL, Estate Documents 1973.

to eat with him from time to time: two centuries later his descendant Sir Thomas was still inviting the vicar of Thornham along with other local priests from Snettisham, Newton, and Wolterton.[111] There does not appear to be any particular pattern about the visits of the clerics, simply perhaps an assumption that men of standing in the locality, and those whose livings were in the Le Strange gift, had some claim on the family.

In the case of Sir Thomas's brother-in-law, Sir Hugh Hastings, whose kitchen accounts survive for one month of 1531, generosity to the clergy seems to be more than the discharge of a traditional obligation. The parsons of Elsing and Swanton, adjacent parishes to his estate, ate with him regularly: indeed the vicar of Elsing dined on no less than twenty occasions in the six weeks recorded, and must have been a semi-permanent resident in the household.[112] Others came less frequently: on 1 January 1532 the parson of Lyng joined the others, making the majority of named strangers that day clerics. Sir Hugh seems to have had an unusual propensity for clerical company, possibly because his lay social circle was more limited than that of his Hunstanton cousins. He rarely received any gentry of importance other than his kin, and his groups of guests were predominantly from men of the area.

Later household books indicate that an impulse to entertain the clergy was associated either with proprietorial control of certain parishes, as in the case of the Petres, or with a growing interest among the gentry in the intellectual society of their parsons. The latter is well demonstrated in the Elizabethan diary of Richard Stonley, former servant of the Petres and holder of a modest estate in Doddinghurst, Essex, as well as an official of the Exchequer. In the country Stonley, whose inclinations were those of a godly Protestant, and whose writings abound with scriptural texts and meditation, always attended his parish church and noted the words of the preacher with care and meditation.[113] Though deeply disapproving of the minister's resistance to aspects of the Book of Common Prayer, he almost always had him to dinner

---

[111] NRO, Le Strange, NH3,7. The habit is probably as old as the concept of *Eigenkirche*, and is to be found in the entertainment offered by the Countess of Leicester in the thirteenth century: Labarge, *Baronial Household*, 194.

[112] NRO, Le Strange, NH15.

[113] Folger Lib., V.a.459, fos. 19, 25, 39^v, 40^v.

after morning service. Although Stonley's rather dry entries do not record their discussions over the meal, it must be presumed that the minister was bidden as much for the interest of his society as from a sense of duty to the cloth. No such enthusiasm for local clerical company apparently moved Edward Seymour, William Paget, or Sir Francis Willoughby, all of whose guest lists give scarcely a mention to them.[114] We should not, of course, conclude from this that ministers were never dined by the great: the case of Seymour is an example of the danger of argument from the partial and short-term evidence of the journals since as Lord Protector he was noted as a man who befriended godly divines. But his selective choice of reformers and his apparent lack of interest in patronage of the local clerics of Wiltshire are not necessarily incompatible. They may both be indications of a movement away from older assumptions which gave the clerical order automatic and easy access to the houses of the great.

Questions of access begin to become crucial as we move down the guest lists towards the mass of tenants, traders, workmen, servants, and travellers who were permitted to occupy the body of the lord's hall. It is important to be able to differentiate those who were invited in as an act of beneficence, to offer them support for their journey, for example, and the rest. Unfortunately, this is precisely where the clerk's list is most likely to fail the historian: only the most obsessive bureaucrat was willing consistently to note the names of those eating in the hall, and questions of status or the nature of business which drew them to the household were usually irrelevant. Hence there are only very intermittent glimpses of the poorer guests and there is no way of evaluating the typicality of the few pieces of evidence that can be adduced. The problem is further compounded by the use by some clerks of ambiguous language: for example, in Sir Hugh Hastings's house the clerk listed a number of visitors' names after each meal, then adding that there were two or three or some other number of messes for strangers. This may be the normal household usage to designate outsider, or it may really indicate that Sir Hugh was entertaining a group of unknown men, whose names and status his clerk could not be bothered to record. Since the evidence is both fragmentary and difficult to interpret the

---

[114] Longleat, Misc. MS. XVIII; GLRO, Acc. 446/4/13; *HMC, Middleton*, 333 ff.

most that can be done is to isolate a few examples from different houses, applying some crude principles of comparability to try to extract the greatest value from limited material.

First, we can make some comparison between four noble households, each entertaining in one of their rural seats on a Sunday, commonly the day of most general access. Elizabeth Berkeley had the following guest list at Berkeley Castle on the fourth Sunday in Lent 1420:

To dinner; the vicar of the Church with one clerk. Item, Bracebridge. Item, Gylbert. Item, Frankby. Item, Philpot Chamburleyn. Item, William Ferrore. Item, 2 charcoal burners. Item, 2 valets of Portbury. Item, 2 pilgrims at the gate. Item, Katherine Candelmaker.[115]

Moving forward a century to the accounts of the third Duke of Norfolk, on Sunday, 30 September 1526, there were nineteen strangers at supper at Framlingham, most of them kin or members of the Norfolk circle, but including a number of servants on errands and a priest of Oxford.[116] Moving forward again some distance in time, the next promising detail derives from the Bertie household in 1561.[117] There on Sunday, 13 July, the Duchess of Suffolk entertained Mr Wingfield and his eight attendants, Mr Hall and his four, Mr Hatcher and three, Mr Banyster and three, twelve men from the local town, four men from Bourne, and five players. Finally on a Sunday in February 1585, Lord Berkeley sat down to dinner at Berkeley Castle with Mr Berry, who had come with three men, Mr Miles and his wife and daughter, Edward Welles and his wife, Rogers, Bowyer, a messenger from Mr Dockery, Mr Shipward's boy, and unspecified others. Since only one of the six messes laid that day was in the hall, it must be presumed that there were a small number of 'others' at the Castle.[118] All these examples are for days when the master or mistress of the house was in residence and no spectacular entertainments were in progress. Only the first Berkeley case is, however, truly informative on the social diversity of the Countess's guests, and even then we are left to hazard guesses upon the status of the named individuals. Many of those named without the designation of 'Mr' were presumably

---

[115] Longleat, Misc. Bks. IX, fo. 72ᵛ.   [116] CUL, Pembroke MS. 300.
[117] Li. RO, 1ANC 7/A4.
[118] Berkeley Castle, Gloucs., MSS. Bound Bk. 32, fo. 87ᵛ.

tenants or local men with some connection with the household: perhaps in the Bertie case some of the townsmen may have been its suppliers, a pattern found in the Le Strange accounts and in those of Nathaniel Bacon late in the sixteenth century.[119] Edward Welles was a tenant of the Berkeley family, and Mr Shipward's boy was a servant of one of their retainers, but beyond this it is very difficult to identify named individuals in any of the examples.

Two of our four cases seem to indicate a rather generous attitude to hospitality, with meals being provided for a substantial number of men and women who were not of specific importance to the head of household. The Duchess of Suffolk was accessible to a large group of ordinary townsmen, and Elizabeth Berkeley performed her Christian duty by allowing the two pilgrims to dine. On the other hand, neither the Howard example, nor the second Berkeley case, suggest very broad general resort, merely the odd addition to those who would normally be engaged in the business of the household. If we proceed more systematically through the surviving evidence we can find plenty of examples of another type of record, perhaps best exemplified by the month's account for Archbishop Bourchier in 1459.[120] In this case large numbers of strangers were fed in the hall on ordinary days as well as at festivals. Bourchier's own count of 'others' varied from eight to twenty persons, while at Berkeley in the winter of 1420 as many as twenty 'unknowns' were recorded with some regularity. The Petre household account for 1548 shows strangers in the hall at Ingatestone almost every day, with an average of about six dining and rather fewer to supper. Three years later William Paget had much the same number in his hall at Drayton in Middlesex, though not apparently when he was resident in London.[121]

When any attempt is made to differentiate this body of 'others', clerks often refer to men 'of the country' or 'of the town' rather than offering a status division. The Le Strange accounts suddenly begin to include others after 1533, and almost always they are described as 'other of the country', with no attempt to calculate

---

[119] I owe the information on the Bacons to Professor Hassell Smith.
[120] LPL, Estate Docs. 1973.
[121] The Paget book is much less explicit in differentiating hall and chamber guests than some of the earlier records for the greater nobility.

numbers or length of stay. This is scarcely any more specific than the 'others, comers and goers' which is a favourite phrase in the Elizabethan Willoughby accounts, but it may perhaps be intended to indicate that the visitors were known men of the neighbourhood. They are certainly generically distinguished from the 'wives' of some of the local towns, who visited the household after the birth of a child. The Buckingham accounts use the language of town and country with rather more consistency and precision; at the feast of the Epiphany, forty-two of the guests were drawn from the town and ninety from the country, and even on an ordinary day the accountant bothered to make the distinction: for example on Friday, 10 December 1507, when two men of the town and one of the country were present. The interesting aspect of this last case is that ordinary visitors had already been differentiated with a precision comparable to that of the Berkeley account: two skinners, a tailor, the embroiderer and his assistants, a bondman, and one man from Bristol being listed ahead of the general categories. Is it possible that what is here being distinguished is the local tenantry, divided into two groups according to the nature of their estate of residence? Since the largest set of 'others' at the Christmas celebrations are listed as townsmen and countrymen it is tempting to impose the category of tenant on them, for tenants were often the most important beneficiaries of Christmas feasting.

The comers and goers itemized in the Buckingham household list seem to be explicable either as men with business to the Duke or as local tenants and similar figures. It is rare to find that these or any of the early sixteenth-century accounts offer positive evidence of acts of charity to poor travellers or the poor in general, beyond the donation of alms and food at the gate. However, in the Petre accounts for 1551–2 there is clear evidence of the feeding of the poor within the household. During the very difficult winter of 1552 a few poor folk were fed in the hall each day, most of them by implication the local poor, though on Sunday, 24 April, it was observed that they included 'ii wayfaring men'.[122] However, after the end of April entries mentioning the

---

[122] ERO, D/DP/A12. There is a detailed discussion of Petre's housekeeping in F. Emmison, *Tudor Secretary: Sir William Petre at Court and Home* (London, 1961), 123–59.

poor become very uncommon, only four examples being available for the rest of the summer and autumn. Here the evidence of emergency provision is clear, and is supported by the special purchases of wheat and herring which the Petres made for distribution to the poor during the late winter and early spring. In the week of 22 March, three of the nine bushels of wheat used in the household were given to the poor. Among the limited surviving sources the reaction of the Petres to the dearth of 1552 stands out as unique, but the notion of some special provision for the poor at difficult times of the year can also be found in the Bertie journals. On 6 March 1561, the comptroller of the household was allocated four red herrings and one salt fish for the poor at the gates, and two white herring and six red for the poor of the town: the next week he had sixteen herrings to give in alms.[123] The habit of feeding the poor on herring, and sometimes on specially baked inferior bread from the household, has a number of medieval precedents. In the fourteenth century Dame Catherine de Norwich was feeding a limited number of paupers daily on salted herring and bread, while in the next century Elizabeth de Burgh gave the poor two substantial bulk gifts of eighteen quarters of wheat and nearly 7,000 herrings.[124] Ale or beer were also produced specially on occasions: in 1482 the Howard household book recorded that beer to the value of 3s. 6d. had been delivered to the poor in half barrels.[125]

Fortunate individuals among the poor might benefit more directly from noble hospitality by becoming almsmen and women within the household. Lady Margaret Beaufort had such an almshouse under her roof, and she provided her dependants with much attention, 'comforting them and ministering unto them with her own hands'.[126] Such an arrangement was not uncommon in the great households of the fifteenth century: just as the majority of a lord's entourage personated his qualities as a man of honour, so the deserving poor wearing his livery personated his virtues as a man of charity.[127] William de Worcestre remarks

[123] Li. RO, 1ANC/7/A3.   [124] Thurgood, 227–8.
[125] Collier, *Manners and Household Expenses*, 26.
[126] John Fisher, *English Works*, ed. J. E. B Mayor (*EETS*, E.S. 27, London, 1876), 296.
[127] C. Dyer, *Standards of Living in the Later Middle Ages* (Cambridge, 1989), 248–9.

that Thomas Beaufort, Duke of Exeter, managed to combine these various forms of domestic giving: he supported household almsmen, but also paid his cook to produce twenty-six gallons of pottage daily for the poor, who were fed on this and on wine [*sic*] at his gate. Beaufort showed his charitable disposition also by his entertainment of wayfarers and by washing the feet of paupers on Maundy Thursday with as much ceremonial as his monarch.[128]

IV

The household books are an invaluable guide not only to the general pattern of guesting, but to the cycle of the year and the specific arrangements for feasting adopted by the landed classes. Prescriptive sources, such as Thomas Tusser's *Five Hundred Points of Good Husbandry*, often organize the household year around the agrarian cycle, with feasting designated at Christmas, sheep-shearing, and harvest.[129] The household ordinances rarely mention particular events of this kind, but the Northumberland Household Book does isolate the principal feasts of the year when the lord can expect 'great repaire of Straungers'. As might be expected, they follow the liturgical rather than the agrarian year, isolating Easter, St George's Day, Whitsun, All Hallows Eve, and Christmas as the chief moments of celebration.[130] Among these various high days and holidays a sharp distinction must be drawn between Christmas and the rest, for all sources point remorselessly to the significance of the former season as the prime occasion in the year for the provision of general entertainment. A crude measure of the importance of the Christmas season can be gained by a look at the numbers of men fed in various households, and at the changing level of expenditure on food. The third Duke of Buckingham had an average of twelve outsiders a day in his house between November 1507 and the later part

[128] J. Harvey (ed.), *Itineraries of William de Worcestre* (Oxford, 1969), 357. On the duty of the nobility to perform the Maundy ceremony, see 'The Booke . . . Concernynge an Erles hous', Bodl. MS, Eng. hist. b 208, fos. 45 ff.

[129] Thomas Tusser, *Five Hundred Pointes of Good Husbandrie*, ed. W. Payne and S. J. Heritage (London, 1878).

[130] *Regulations . . . for Henry Percy*, 71.

of March 1508. On Christmas Day he received 182 strangers to dinner and 176 to supper, while at the famous Epiphany feast which concluded his celebrations he had 319 strangers to dinner and 279 to supper. Numbers as large as these must surely have been unusual, though we may compare them with John Smyth's claim that Thomas, Lord Berkeley, kept a great and splendid feast for all the country at Christmas 1303, and the Howard Household Book shows that the Duke of Norfolk fed 580, including his own establishment, at Framlingham on 1 January 1527 and 399 on Twelfth Night.[131]

Lesser men felt an obligation to follow the style of the magnates to the best of their ability. Sir William Paget did not celebrate every day of the Christmas season, but on three occasions during the Twelve Days in 1550-1 he had between twenty and forty guests at special meals, this in contrast with an average of between three and four outsiders. In the following year the household of Sir William Petre kept the whole season with great solemnity, culminating in a grand dinner on Twelfth Night, for which twelve messes were set in the hall. In the Thynne household at Corsley in 1569-70 it was necessary to lay the hall at least twice every day between Christmas and 6 January, and on 26 and 27 December and 1 and 2 January three halls were needed. Finally there is Sir Hugh Hastings, who usually only had two or three visitors, but who gave a grand New Year's Eve dinner for ten named friends and four messes of strangers.[132]

When an increase in guests is not immediately evident, there is the alternative information from the records of weekly food costs. In the Le Strange household in 1520 the usual winter budget was 17*s*. to 22*s*., while in the Christmas season one week cost 31*s*. 7*d*. For the Willoughbys the second week of the festival in 1547-8 costs £5. 2*s*. 8*d*., as against £2. 10*s*. for an ordinary period of equivalent length. It is interesting to note that fifty years later the Christmas season cost Sir Francis Willoughby £92.[133] At the end of the sixteenth century Sir Nathaniel Bacon's beautifully itemized accounts show very clearly the pattern of expenditure

[131] *Archaeologia*, 25, 318-21; John Smyth, *The Lives of the Berkeleys*, ed. J. Maclean, 3 vols. (Gloucester, 1883-5), i. 305; CUL, Pembroke MS. 300.
[132] GLRO, Acc. 446/4/13, fos. 23-31ᵛ; ERO, D/DP/A13; Longleat, Thynne Papers, Bk. 109; NRO, Le Strange, NH 15.
[133] Nottingham Univ. Lib., Mi A/27, fos. 29-32; Mi A/76.

considered necessary for a gentleman at Christmas. In mid-December 1594 his weekly costs climbed sharply from their norm of between £7 and £9 in the winter months to £28. 3s. 11d. Then in the two weeks of actual festivities costs stood at £18. 5s. 5d. and £19. 6s. 8d., before falling away on 7 January to £8. 5s. 1d.[134] This clear pattern in the Bacon accounts, indicating extensive preparations before the main feasts, is particularly interesting in the house of a gentleman of puritanical inclination. It demonstrates the strength of the tradition of generous hospitality throughout the twelve days of the Christmas season. In the case of accounts for the first part of the sixteenth century and earlier there are no examples of Christmas being celebrated in modest style except in the Seymour household in 1538. There costs remained fairly steady, with no obvious increase in visitors or in the number of dishes served. However, this is the exception which seems to prove the rule: Seymour's household was resident in London during the winter months of 1538, and inevitably its head was often with the King. He was apparently absent for most of the Christmas season, participating in the elaborate festivities of the court. In these circumstances traditional celebration would have lacked any adequate focus and was presumably deliberately neglected.

This extensive financial evidence for the importance of Christmas can, of course, be supported by a wealth of literary sources. There is, for example, the letter in the Plumpton correspondence in which Edward Plumpton, secretary to Lord Strange, speaks with pride of the great Christmas which his master was keeping in 1489–90, 'as ever was in this country'.[135] Or there are the later biographical accounts of men of the Henrician period who kept magnificent Christmas cheer. One of the most vivid of these is Gervase Holles's description of the celebrations of his ancestor, Sir William, who 'alwais began his Christmas at All-Hallowtide and continued it untill Candlemas'.[136] During that time he allowed any man to stay for three days without questions asked, while during the actual twelve days of the festival

---

[134] NRO, Bradfer-Lawrence VII b (5).

[135] T. Stapleton, (ed.), *The Plumpton Correspondence* (Camden Soc., o.s. 4, London, 1839), 89.

[136] Gervase Holles, *Memorials of the Holles Family*, ed. A. C. Wood (Camden Soc., 3rd ser. 55, London, 1937), 45.

he used a fat ox each day in his kitchens and made other equivalent provision. Some of the accounts suggest a self-conscious pride in the maintenance of a lavish tradition by gentlemen and noblemen: Sir Thomas Palmer of Wingham, Kent, supposedly kept sixty Christmases in his manor houses without intermission in the second half of the sixteenth century, and all of them were conducted 'with great hospitality'.[137]

The multiplication of examples, however, does not much advance our understanding of who was entertained during these periods of festivity. In a case like that of Sir William Holles this might be thought an irrelevant question, since it was obviously believed that he held completely open house, taking in anyone who approached his doors. That this paradigm of total openness influenced gentry behaviour can be seen in examples like that of the Petre accounts, where the feast on Sunday, 27 December 1551, was celebrated with a host of known friends and 'ii messes yt cam unbydd', and on several other days there were 'as greet a numbre of boyes'. Some at least of those at the Buckingham festivities described as 'of the town' or 'of the country' may well have arrived unbidden, and merely been categorized, for it is difficult to believe that when such general junketing was in train a steward or usher questioned the guests too closely. But a more careful examination of the evidence suggests that this spontaneity, if and when it did occur, was not the crucial aspect of aristocratic entertainment. The probability is that most guests were bidden, collectively if not individually, and that the total outsider was merely an appendage to a precisely organized occasion. The first and most obvious point is that, while all Twelve Days might be kept as holidays, the grand feasts were confined to a few dinners within that span. Christmas Day itself might be one, as it was in the Buckingham household, though in a number of gentry records the main celebrations were deferred until 27 or 28 December, the Feast of the Innocents being a particularly popular day. Then New Year and Twelfth Night completed the main feasts, the latter being the most favoured of all for grand entertainment. The routines of specific great houses seem to have varied according to local tradition, but must have been well known in their own neighbourhoods, so that in practice

[137] E. Hasted, *History of Kent* 12 vols. (Canterbury, 1797–1801), ix. 235.

even the unbidden only appeared on days when the household was *en fête*.

Gentry and other influential guests were a common feature of most Christmas lists, and the extended kin seem to have been more than usually favoured companions at this time of year. In 1551 Paget had several of his family staying for the period of the twelve days, as well as Sir Edward and Lady Warner who came on Christmas Day and were present most of the time until after New Year. Other important visitors from the Paget circle called for the occasional meal: Sir Thomas and Lady Chaloner were there on 28 December, Sir Philip Hoby both on New Year's Eve and 2 January, and Sir Richard Southwell on Twelfth Night. This was in London where more society could be expected than in the country, but an equally good provincial example is to be found in the record of entertainment at Coventry in 1584. We know from Smyth that it was the habit of Lord Berkeley to keep a grand Christmas for the neighbourhood gentry among others, and that year almost every day except the Nativity itself saw the house crowded with local gentlemen and their wives, the Curzons, Pearsons, Bakers, Newports, and Dentons.[138] Mr Zouche, who seems to have been a relative, was present from New Year's Day onwards, as was Mrs Dudley, who also seems to have been a distant connection. Sometimes the nobility, at least, appear to have used the Christmas celebrations as a way of affirming good lordship. We have already noted the Buckingham example, and that of Sir Thomas Le Strange riding to Kenninghall each Twelfth Night. Later in the century Richard Stonley felt himself obliged to visit the Petres at Ingatestone at least once during the Christmas season, even though by the 1580s he had long ceased to be in their employ and organized his own elaborate festivities at Doddinghurst.[139]

But the openness of the great house during the Twelve Days was not primarily designed for gentry conviviality or for the convenience of visiting strangers. This was the time of year *par excellence* when tenants and poorer neighbours were given temporary access to the lord's generosity, usually of course in return for the enforced gifts that were the mark of their

---

[138] Berkeley Castle MSS., Bound Bk. 32, fos. 11–17^v.
[139] Folger MS., V.a.459, fos. 39^v, 41^v.

dependence. The origins of Christmas tenant feasting are to be found in the 'gestums' of the earlier Middle Ages, those agreements which gave the villein bringing his 'look' or gift the right to have food and drink at the lord's expense.[140] Custumals determined the exact return in beer, bread, and broth that could be expected for the 'look', and gradually the habit of a Christmas meal seems to have become ingrained.[141] Sir Christopher Heydon deeply impressed contemporaries in Henry VIII's reign not because he was generous enough to give a tenant feast at Christmas, but because he was wealthy enough to have thirty master shepherds in charge of his own flocks to sit under his eye at Baconsthorpe.[142] Although by the sixteenth century the transactional nature of this arrangement is not quite so clearly articulated, the tenant feast still retained much of its earlier form. Now the gift was usually described as a New Year gift, and one of the main reasons for the displacement of major junketing from Christmas Day itself may well be that tenants brought in their offerings slightly later in the season. There are some late examples of feasts of Christmas Day, as in the observation of the clerk of the Willoughby household in 1548 that 'thys day, beyng Chrystymas day, my mayster feastyd all the tenantes', but the more usual pattern was for them to be asked from 27 December onwards.[143] The cycle of entertainment is particularly clear in the Petre accounts for 1551–2. On Christmas Day there were nine outsiders who could well have been tenants, the next day seven, and then on the 27th twenty-one men of Ingatestone with their wives, plus three families from Mountnessing, where the Petres also had property. On 28 December tenants from Margaretting and Buttsbury were entertained, while on New Year's Day there was a large group from the 'the town' who brought presents. A final set of Ingatestone men and women were received on 3 January, while on Twelfth Night there appears to have been a complete open house with twelve messes in the hall at dinner. The elaborate care with which Sir William received his tenants is particularly interesting since the Petres were a new family,

---

[140] G. C. Homans, *English Villagers of the Thirteenth Century* (Cambridge, Mass., 1942), 357.

[141] See e.g., *HMC, Wells*, i. 332–5.

[142] W. Rye, *History of Norfolk* (London, 1885), 131.

[143] *HMC, Middleton*, 394.

and had been living at Ingatestone less than ten years when they celebrated this Christmas.[144]

Not all great households can have been quite as systematic as the Petres in working their way steadily through the tenants and structuring their visits over several days, but the feasting of this social group was very common practice. It offered an opportunity for ritual exchange not only of gifts but of gestures of courtesy designed to secure loyalty. The presence of lords of misrule no doubt encouraged an atmosphere in which hierarchy was temporarily modified or discarded in order ultimately to be reaffirmed. Smyth, in his description of Henry, Lord Berkeley's Christmas feast, shows how this could become an act of deliberation. Lord Henry would 'in the midst of their dinner rise from his own, and going on each of their tables in the hall, cheerfully bid them welcome', on this unusual occasion breaching the carefully constructed barriers of the household in order to affirm *communitas*.[145] In their turn the tenants seem to have felt entitled to demand adequate entertainment, perhaps because of the contractual nature of the original 'gestum'. Christmas ballads abound with threats of aggression, or at least claims for food and drink as of right, as in the north country carol that calls for: 'Some ayle or beare | gentill butlere | some lycour thou has showe | such as you mashe | our throtts to wishe | the best were that you brew'.[146]

While tenants were the prime beneficiaries of noble and gentle entertainment at the Twelve Days, there does seem to have been a general tendency to extend a welcome to any neighbours, poor or prosperous, who might have a relationship with the great house. At the New Year's Day dinner given by Sir William Paget in 1552, six men of the parish were present with their wives and were served in the parlour, presumably to differentiate them from the generality in the hall. A number of those at the Berkeley Christmas in 1584 were men of Coventry, probably ordinary townsfolk, as well as civic dignitaries like the mayor who appeared one day. And when a minor gentleman like Richard Stonley set out to emulate the hospitality of his old masters

[144] Emmison, *Sir William Petre*, 27.
[145] Smyth, *Lives of the Berkeleys*, ii. 381.
[146] P. J. King (ed.), *Tudor Songs and Ballads* (London, 1978), 110.

he did so by asking in a number of his Essex neighbours on each of the festive days.[147] In the case of the poor the Christmas period was perhaps the one time when they might hope to eat in the hall, rather than at or near the gates. Although most accounts do not bother to record their presence, there are hints in the Berkeley and Hastings records that they were present.[148] Above all we have the testimony of the Petre Christmas. At Ingatestone poor were mentioned as present at a number of the feasts, notably that on 27 December, when eight poor folks were recorded, and on 28 December, when there were six. Most intriguingly of all, on Christmas Day, when supper was served to a rather small number of people, three 'poor fellows from London' were fed in the hall, suggesting that even the wandering poor were treated with unusual charity at the festive season. This charity was also extended to local youths, who appeared in a group at three of the meals and were treated as a separate category of visitors, no doubt as the licensed leaders of misrule. In general the image of the noble Christmas which emerges from the accounts is one of licensed openness, of the breach of conventions which obtained in the giving of hospitality for most of the year, though not entirely of genial anarchy, since a careful structure was imposed upon this display of aristocratic largess.

When compared to the spectacular evidence for the Christmas season, the other festivals enumerated by the Northumberland Household Book have left faint trace upon the journals. No doubt Easter was the most significant of the other celebrations, and isolated pieces of evidence can be found to suggest that it was observed in some style. Although the Le Strange books do not make any particular mention of Easter, in both 1527 and 1533 the relevant week was marked by a doubling of household costs; indeed in 1533 Easter was more expensive than the first week of the Christmas season. Since it was another of the feasts at which tenants brought their gifts of capons or eggs it seems reasonable to infer that once again they benefited from some of the expenditure. This also fits with the evidence from the Berkeley book of the 1580s: Easter was celebrated without any evidence of particular inflow of gentry to the household, but with five

---

[147] Folger MS., V.a.459, fos. 38–39, 97ᵛ–98ᵛ·
[148] Berkeley Castle MSS., Bound Bk. 32, fo. 15.

messes set in the hall instead of the usual one or two. Elaborate general entertaining at the Easter festival is noted only once in the journals, when Sir Francis Willoughby gave a dinner in 1565 for a number of knights and their ladies, as well as 'the number of fortye other person, beynge straungers'.[149] In some books the day is noted with no evidence of increased company or expenditure: for example, the Duke of Norfolk's household failed to mark Easter 1527 with any increased hospitality, even though the Duchess had returned from London in the preceding week.

Whitsun festivities are even less easy to trace, except in the case of the household book of the Earl of Derby for the 1580s, which indicates that Whit Sunday was a day of very general access to the household. Already Whitsun had acquired a particular importance in the northern counties, which probably explains why the Earl not only had a tenant feast on the Sunday, but had a large company of gentlemen all the week, including the Bishop of Chester for a part of the time.[150] This is not, of course, to argue that these and other feasts of the Church were not marked in the great house: indeed a study of the Stonors, Luttrells, Staffords, de Veres, and Ralph, Lord Cromwell, in the late medieval period shows that feast days were scrupulously observed. These households even seem to have isolated certain additional feasts that were distinctive to the particular establishment: the Luttrells singled out the feast of St Lawrence for particular devotion, the Cromwell household those of St Winefride the Virgin, St Nicholas, and St Thomas, while the Stonors celebrated that of the Holy Trinity, to whom their chapel was dedicated.[151] But a complex cycle of feast and fast within the household is not necessarily identical with general hospitality on festive days. Dr Mertes has emphasized the *intensity* of the ritual life that is evidenced in some of the late medieval accounts, the enclosed nature of the world that moved the household from hall to chapel, and provided it internally with all that was necessary for the process of rejoicing. Guests might well, of course, be present on these occasions, but they are not essentially a case of the

---

[149] *HMC, Middleton*, 418.   [150] Raines (ed.), *Stanley Papers*, ii. 30.
[151] K. A. Mertes, 'The Secular Noble Household in Medieval England, 1350–1550', Edinburgh Ph.D. dissertation (1981), 301–3.

household reaching out into the wider community, as was the Christmas celebration.[152]

It is the cycle of the week, rather than a clear patterning of the sacred year, that emerges most visibly from the recording of guests in the household books. Most households observed Friday as a fast day, eating fish even after the Reformation, and usually not providing supper for the servants that evening. This did not necessarily preclude entertaining guests for dinner on a Friday: two of the examples of substantial dinners already used from the Buckingham book were for Friday dinners, and they are in no sense uncommon. Sunday, on the other hand, was commonly observed as a feast day, when the table was furnished with more exotic food than routinely, and when meat was always available.[153] It might therefore be anticipated that Sunday would be a particularly favoured day for the reception of visitors, and indeed a number of the household books do show that there was normally an increase as compared to the rest of the week. When the Pagets were at Drayton from July to October 1552 they entertained on average two or three named visitors and about six servants, workmen, or others in the hall. On Sundays, however, the average number was twelve, and in several weeks in high summer the figure reached over twenty. A similar pattern can be seen in the fifteenth-century Berkeley accounts, in those of the Petre household, and in the Elizabethan Thynne books.

But the interest of the Sunday arrangements lies not in the general increase in guest numbers; instead it is in the nature of the visitors. The tendency to entertain clerics on a Sunday has already been noted: Elizabeth, Countess of Warwick, did it routinely in the fifteenth century, so did Sir William Petre in the 1550s, and Sir Hugh Hastings a few years earlier. Neither Sir William Paget nor Sir John Thynne seem to have been moved to give their local parson a Sunday dinner, but in other ways they followed the conventions of the rest of the households. These were that ordinary folk, neighbours or tenants, were specifically invited to dine in the hall on a Sunday, almost always wives and husbands together. This arrangement is particularly clear in the Paget journal: although on some Sundays there were a number of gentry at dinner there was always an increase in numbers

---

[152] Ibid. 297   [153] Thurgood, 178–80.

listed for the hall, even when visiting servants had been discounted. In some weeks names are given: for example, on 23 August the 'extras' in the hall were listed as 'Parich Hill, William Hochen and wife, Richard Hockyn and wife, Andrew Urchyn and wife, Audriy wife and her husband and others'.[154] At other times a simple number sufficed, while at still others the visitors were described as 'neighbours and their wives'. Since names are not repeated it would appear that Paget was slowly bidding the worthies of Drayton parish to share in his Sunday dinner, though not, of course to sit at his table. The Petres and the Thynnes also entertained an unusual number of ordinary folk on a Sunday, and it is interesting to note that in all three cases this pattern of hall hospitality continued regardless of the presence or absence of the head of house. This image of neighbourhood reinforced by occasional dining in the great house can be illustrated fully only from a few examples, but they are examples of particular importance since they operate neither at the level of hospitality as peer group conviviality, nor hospitality as pure charity. They perform an integrative function for the household, binding the lord of the community, or rather the community to the lord, by acts of beneficence less spectacular than the great Christmas feasts but perhaps more symbolically powerful because more specifically directed to the individual. A holistic ideal of household and neighbourhood still lingers in the actions of an assertive courtier like Paget, incongruously surviving upheavals in land ownership and political power and transcending the entire *arriviste* experience of the Henrician bureaucrat.

V

The intermittent festivities that marked rites of passage and other solemn moments for the nobility and gentry can be dismissed rather more briefly. Celebrations of christenings and marriages were almost entirely confined to the peer group and kin and are important only in so far as they illustrate the enthusiasm of the landed orders for a good party, attended with the appropriate

---

[154] GLRO, Acc. 446/4/13, fo. 106ᵛ.

rituals of status.[155] They no doubt strained the organizational resources of the household more dramatically than even Christmas feastings: only a royal visit was more traumatic. To provide just one illustration: one of the Bertie children was married in July 1561, and for the duration of the festivities the number of resident guests was increased from an average of three or four to fourteen, not counting casual comers and goers.[156] This sounds a relatively small figure, but all the arrivals had at least two servants, and some as many as six, so the outsiders totalled over sixty. And this was a rather modest wedding compared to that which Sir William Petre organized for his stepdaughter Catherine Tyrell or William More for his daughter Elizabeth.[157]

Only two of the rites of passage are of interest because of their integrative hospitality. The first was the visiting that followed a birth, and particularly the visiting associated with the ceremony of churching. This could be a ceremony principally for the gentry and the kin, as it was when Lady Strange was churched in 1588 amid grand celebrations, attended by Lady Compton, Sir John Savage, the Bishop of Chester, and many others.[158] There were, however, aspects of birth celebrations that were essentially female rituals, in which the participants were drawn from a wide social spectrum and united by gender and biological experience. When Lady Le Strange gave birth in 1520, she was attended by some of the women of her own circle, but was afterwards brought offerings by 'the wives of Hecham', while those of Hunstanton produced similar gifts on a later occasion.[159] A particularly good, though late, example, is that of the Petre family in 1607, where the birth of John Petre was celebrated by a flood of wives from the local community, who visited Thorndon on four successive days in July.[160] It seems to have been difficult for any member of the élite to celebrate a birth without offering a general welcome to the respected female members of the local community.

---

[155] For a highly elaborated form of aristocratic christening ritual, which includes the provision of a 'void' of food and drink to the godparents in the church, see Bodl. MS., Eng. hist. b 208, fo. 15 ff.

[156] Li. RO, 1ANC/7/A4.

[157] ERO, D/DP/A13; J. Evans, 'The Wedding of Richard Posted and Elizabeth, Daughter of William More of Loseley, Surrey', *Archaeologia*, 36 (1855), 35–52.

[158] Raines (ed.), *Stanley Papers*, ii. 48.

[159] *Archaeologia*, 25, 425 ff.

[160] ERO, D/DP/A26.

Better known than the ceremonies of birth as occasions for hospitality are aristocratic funerals and subsequent commemorations at the month's mind. The great funeral wake differed little in its character before and after the Reformation, even though the purpose of the general doles to poor mourners was undercut by the new theology. The feeding and alms-giving that attended the burial of the great was an even more obvious occasion for the display of the household as cornucopia than the yearly Christmas feasts. Some sense of the elaboration and generosity of these events can be gained from two descriptions of Berkeley funerals: that of Isabel, wife of Maurice, Lord Berkeley in 1517, and John Smyth's own record of that of Lady Katherine Berkeley in 1596.[161] Isabel died at Coventry, so the mayor and corporation were the fortunate beneficiaries of some of the entertainment: they were given a 'drinking' with cakes, ale, claret, wafers, sweets, and 'Blanch powder' and, as the accountant noted with relief, 'noe plate ne spones was lost yet ther was xxti desyn spones'. The hearse had to be sent down into the West Country where it was met by the Abbot of Combe and others, 'to the nombre of v or vi thosand pepull'. At the feast that followed the boards had to be set several times over, although at each sitting there were at least 210 or 220 messes. All this, of course, did not include the casual doles to the poor who attended. Lady Katherine's wake was held at Caludon in Warwickshire, where Lord Berkeley provided for all the invited mourners 'and many hundreds more'. The excess, Smyth claims, was sufficient to feed more than 1,000 poor folk in the afternoon. Numbers of other examples of largess on this scale can be given for aristocratic funerals at any time between the fifteenth century and the Civil War, although as Stone has indicated there is evidence of some change after the late years of Elizabeth's reign.[162] Until then at least the hospitable aspect of the great funeral was one of the most visible ways in which the nobility signalled their social power, and thus was one of the most important moments *not* to discriminate between those who appeared as mourners.

In all these displays of noble generosity it has so far been assumed that an active head of house was an essential prerequisite

[161] Smyth, *Lives of the Berkeleys*, ii. 176, 391.
[162] L. Stone, *The Crisis of the Aristocracy* (Oxford, 1965), 577-9.

for the exercise of hospitality. Some of the surviving journals were kept by clerks who travelled with their lord; indeed, most of the early examples, and those from the greatest establishments, fall into this category. They therefore do not permit any insight into what happened at Berkeley Castle when the Countess of Warwick was travelling, or at Wolfs Hall when Edward Seymour was at court. In other cases, such as that of the Howard household, the clerks' books do record the continuity of housekeeping at one estate, regardless of the presence or absence of particular members of a noble family. In these circumstances it is possible to say something about the difference made by an active head of house to the pattern of entertainment. Hospitality as a charitable endeavour obviously demanded a sustained willingness to receive ordinary visitors in the hall and to feed the poor at the gates. It was the failure of some establishments to provide these basic services that gave rise at the end of the sixteenth century to the image of Mock Beggars Hall. When the main household was broken up, and only a skeleton staff remained in a particular manor, it seems likely that very little entertainment was offered to outsiders. This was the case, for example, at Tattershall in 1447 when Ralph, Lord Cromwell, had reduced his staff to only ten. Some strangers were received, but almost all of them were from the outer circles of Cromwell's dependants and presumably had business in the household. The servants 'commoned' together, that is they divided any supplies that were left at the end of the week between themselves, which can hardly have encouraged them to give generously to the poor.[163] It is therefore no particular surprise to find that Christmas was celebrated with no increase of costs, and only at the Annunciation of the Blessed Virgin does the household seem to have undertaken any entertaining.

By the next century it may have been more difficult for any nobleman concerned for his reputation to be quite so neglectful of his local obligations. It was certainly an issue that concerned William Cecil, for his biographer was at pains to show that he did not forget the poor on his great rural estate at Theobalds. Instead he kept almost thirty servants regularly in the country,

---

[163] E. M. Price, 'Ralph, Lord Cromwell and His Household', London MA dissertation (1948), 237–9.

'And also relieved there daiely, twenty or thirty poore People, at the Gate'.[164] Household accounts which show the main establishment retained in being during the absence of its master nevertheless sometimes show a sharp reduction in the number of guests received. At Framlingham, when neither the Duke nor the Duchess of Norfolk were in residence, the household would often be empty of guests for several days at a time. For a long period during 1552 Paget's household at Drayton received few visitors of any standing, except for the extended kin, who sometimes came for several weeks at a time. Reduced company in this case must owe something to the embarrassment of Paget's imprisonment in the Tower, yet it continued to be the general pattern even after he had been released and partially rehabilitated.

Since few of the journals are consistent in their notation of hall visitors it is difficult to be clear on the experience of the ordinary guest in these circumstances. What does emerge from the Paget journal is that his household continued the practice of entertaining on a Sunday, and of taking strangers into the hall, regardless of his presence or absence. The same was true of the Petre accounts in 1548, though there the issue is clouded by the continuing presence of Lady Petre at Ingatestone. In 1552, when Lady Petre was away at court for much of February and March, the entertainment of men of standing dwindled to almost nothing, but the charitable endeavours of the household were if anything intensified, for this was the period when special wheat was given to the poor. Much the same was true of the month in 1564 when the Duchess of Suffolk left her Lincolnshire home to go to Grimsthorpe, although in the Bertie household a number of visitors of standing continued to be recorded along with the carters and ordinary tenants. In all these examples the crucial point seems to be that the temporary departure of the head of the house or his spouse did not entail the breaking up of the household, or the placing of servants on board wages. Such changes did occur from time to time, especially among the nobility with their substantial number of manors: the Northumberland Household Book makes very detailed provision for the limitation of the establishment while 'my Lorde keepith his Secryt Hous', and leaving a skeleton staff on a country estate

---

[164] F. Peck (ed.), *Desiderata Curiosa*, 2 vols. (London, 1732–5), I. i. 29.

during a prolonged absence in London must have had much the same effect.[165] But as far as the majority of the lesser nobility and gentry were concerned such elaboration was unnecessary, since most of the year would have been passed on rural estates, and visits away from the main seat which involved the whole of the nuclear family would have been rare. No doubt the poor suffered from any diminution in the size of the household, which would have led to a corresponding reduction in the food available for gate doles, yet their interests do seem to have been afforded attention in some cases, even when there was no master or mistress present to direct the daily work of charity.

One of the most frequent reasons for noble absence from a country estate was the demands of business in London. Even in the fifteenth century it was likely that politics, litigation, or the need for other specialist services would draw a gentleman or noble up to the capital from time to time. In some cases this made little difference to the elaboration of the household or presumably to the scale of entertainment: the lavishness of the Earl of Warwick's provisions in the fifteenth century in the city were noted by Stow and a huge urban mansion such as John of Gaunt's Savoy Palace could discharge all the functions of a great rural estate. It was in London, according to John Stow, that Thomas Cromwell daily fed the poor in huge numbers at his gate.[166] Nevertheless, such behaviour was the prerogative of a much smaller group in the city than in the country: costs, pressures of space, and the intermittent nature of most visits to London made it more attractive to limit household size and maintain only a riding establishment for the duration of a stay. The habit of not organizing elaborate kitchens, but depending wholly or in part on the service provided by inns and taverns was widespread. Even John Howard, first Duke of Norfolk, dined out at inns when he was in the city, and such behaviour was commonplace for the gentry. When Sir Thomas Le Strange went up to London he stayed at 'the Harp' and on the whole avoided sociability, though he did receive Sir Thomas Woodhouse and a Mr Fielding to breakfast.

---

[165] Li. RO, 1ANC/7/A5; *Regulations . . . for Henry Percy*, 303–9.
[166] John Stow, *A Survey of London*, ed. C. L. Kingsford, 2 vols. (Oxford, 1908), i. 89.

Sir Francis Willoughby's accounts leave no evidence about where
he stayed in London in 1523, but do itemize the cost of meals,
which suggests that he was not maintaining a full establishment.[167] The arrangements made by such gentlemen when they
were in London can hardly have included the gate doles or
entertainment of numbers of ordinary men that were possible in
the country. Hence they were encouraged to think in terms of
an alternative model of behaviour.

The alternative is already faintly indicated in the fifteenth-
century accounts of the Countess of Warwick. When the Countess
was in the country she entertained a variety of groups and
individuals, more or less it would seem all comers to the
household. In London, on the other hand, her company was
primarily female, and seems to have included a number of personal
friends such as Matilda Salveyn and Elizabeth, Lady Harington.[168]
Great noblemen such as Edward, Duke of Buckingham, or
Edward Seymour, Viscount Beauchamp, could not concentrate
on personal friends in this way, but the move from the country
to the town does seem to have freed them from some part
of that indiscriminate entertainment that was associated with
rural authority. The pattern adopted by the Pagets showed
less variation between town and country: even in London
Christmas was celebrated with a number of parochial guests
present, and the rural manor of Drayton was near enough
to the city for friends and clients to find their way there as
well. Nevertheless, Paget seems less burdened by the need
to prove himself a good lord on his urban property, where
the tradition of Sunday dinners was not carefully maintained
and sociability focused on friends of the family and members
of the court. There is some risk of reading later developments
into these London lists, but at the very least they indicate
that there was a greater flexibility in the sociability of the
city than the country, perhaps a greater opportunity to consult
personal preference in the choice of guests.

A principal purpose of the openness hosts displayed in the
countryside must have been the exercise of good lordship.
The politicized household of a great magnate had moments

---

[167] *Archaeologia*, 25, 430; *HMC, Middleton*, 354-7.
[168] Longleat, Misc. Bk. IX, fos. 112-114ᵛ.

such as the Christmas season and the celebration of rites of passage when it might logically expect that retainers, clients, and neighbouring gentlemen would appear to affirm their loyalty. But there were other occasions when feasting such men could have a more overtly political purpose, as when de Vere summoned his retainers to meet with Henry VII and do him service. Here the element of hospitality is only one part of a complex pattern of behaviour designed to articulate the status of the noble. When the Neville kin assembled for the famous feast that celebrated the enthronement of the Archbishop of York, they engaged in elaborate competitive display which was intended as a complete manifestation of clan power.[169] Such naked articulation of sectional interest was still possible in the uncertain world of the 1460s, but rapidly became the unacceptable face of bastard feudalism as the monarchy reasserted its power. Instead, ostentation outside the normal conventions of noble entertainment had to be linked increasingly to displays of political loyalty, as in the reception of the king on progress, the feasting of the judges or the return of a noble to his locality to execute his and the king's business.[170] The feasts recorded in loving detail for posterity by contemporaries often involved the crown: the most notable exception being the elaborate entertainment provided by William Warham on his enthronement at Canterbury.[171]

Though the crown could object to too overt a manipulation of hospitality in the service of magnate power, it might be anticipated that it would be at one with its élite in seeing conviviality as a potential instrument of control in the localities. Noble establishments were ideally suited to offering bread and circuses as a part of the process of defusing local disturbances. Yet it is surprisingly difficult to find examples of the direct use of the household and its resources in riot situations: the

---

[169] Hearne, *Lelandi Collectanea*, vi. 2–6.

[170] Mertes, *English Noble Household*, 131–3. A good example of the feast that deferred to the royal interest, albeit one not directly involving the monarchy, is the elaborate dinner that Robert Sherburne, Bishop of Chichester, gave to the Crown commissioners before they began the preparation of the *Valor Ecclesiasticus* survey in 1535. Anthony Waite claimed that 700 people were fed: *LP*, VIII. 530.

[171] Hearne, *Lelandi Collectanea*, vi. 16–34.

impulse of the upper classes being to retreat and reach for their swords rather more often than employing the suasions of good lordship. There is, however, at least one example of the use of hospitality in these circumstances. When Henry, Earl of Arundel, was charged with the task of calming the disturbances in Sussex that were associated with Kett's Rebellion of 1549, he adopted a variety of traditional methods of dispute-resolution, above all assuring their leaders on his honour that he would do his best to see their grievances answered. As part of this process he invited all the aggrieved to Arundel Castle to talk to him in person, and while they were there fed them. 'During wch time', says his biographer, 'who had sene the aboundance of victualls that was theare spent, would have mused—yea, the greate courte was not voide oftentymes of tables to supply the want of roomes within the hall'.[172] Whether the throwing-open of the hall had as much effect as the promise to resolve the grievances associated with enclosure is debatable, but Arundel evidently regarded it as a necessary part of good lordship in these difficult circumstances. It would seem that he was following the logic of a tradition of the open house, which at rare moments of crisis could be activated as one of the varied methods of social control at the disposal of the nobility.

The entertainment offered by little more than half-a-dozen families who have been the focus of this chapter may not be typical of the English upper orders as a whole. Buckingham and Sir William Petre, for example, had a reputation among contemporaries for their generosity, which presumably indicated a separation from the majority of their fellows. Nevertheless, Buckingham seems to have been cultivating on the grand scale those qualities of openness and magnanimity that were expected of the greater nobility, and which can actually be seen on well-documented occasions like funerals. Our vagueness about the details of hospitality at this level of society should not lead to the conclusion that lavish generosity was at all untoward for the nobility under Henry VII or Henry VIII. Its total openness, at least as it related to the poor and the outsider, is questionable,

---

[172] J. Nichols (ed.), 'Life of the last Fitz-Alan, Earl of Arundel', *Gentleman's Magazine* (1833), ii. 14.

but the obligation to behave with magnificence did encourage an undiscriminating pattern of entertainment which sought to include all social groups in the beneficence which was the embodiment of aristocratic honour. The problem of typicality only becomes acute when one descends from the magnates to the lesser nobility and gentry, so poorly represented by household accounts and so much less obviously part of the cultural tradition of magnificence. We can observe that the social behaviour of the Le Stranges and of Sir Hugh Hastings differs in significant respects from that of Elizabeth Berkeley, Buckingham, or Seymour, and that they moved above all in a circle of gentry conviviality which seems to have little relevance to the values of good lordship or munificence to the poor. But it is much more difficult to allow our two Norfolk families to stand as paradigms than to permit the nobility to do so. The Petres and Pagets, on the margins of nobility, seem to combine elements of sociability with a concern for the charitable dimensions of good lordship, while in the early Willoughby accounts the former clearly predominates.

When men of the late sixteenth and seventeenth centuries looked back on their ancestors they sometimes chose to isolate men who had behaved with the sort of munificence seen in the Petre records as though they were untypical even of an age which they characterized as hospitable. Gervase Holles's praise of his ancestor, Sir William, focuses upon his generosity throughout the year, as well as at the Christmas season. Robert Furse, with far less approval, saw his ancestor's conspicuous consumption as sheer ostentation given his social station, while Sir Hugh Cholmley recalled his predecessor Sir Richard with affection because he kept 'great port', and such a lavish kitchen that his servants could deprive him of twenty-four pieces of beef in a day.[173] All these accounts have the advantage and disadvantage of hindsight, but they do suggest that there was a model of gentry liberality, to which, with varying degrees of sensibility, these particular predecessors subscribed. What they do not argue is that all gentlemen could, should, or did behave in the same way: even among their own families these

---

[173] Holles, *Memorials*, 45; 'Furse of Moreshead', 176; Hugh Cholmley, *Memoirs* (Malton, 1870), 6.

men are thought of as distinctive rather than the norm. Good housekeeping, following the prescriptive sources, might have been required of every gentleman, but the munificence associated with an open house and entertainment for all comers was not necessarily a shared behavioural feature of the early Tudor period.

3
The Changing Vision of Hospitality

WHEN William Harrison produced the first version of his *Description of England* in 1576 he presented the world of the noble household as though it had changed little from its late medieval pattern.[1] The plentiful meals provided by the great were not, he argued, a reflection of gluttony, but 'since they have daily much resort unto their tables (and many times looked for), and thereto retain great numbers of servants, it is very requisite for them to be somewhat plentiful in this behalf'. In the establishments of the nobility meals were still served with full ritual, with the 'reversion also being bestowed upon the poor', and both chamber and hall remained theatres of commensality. In the hall, 'there are commonly forty or three score persons fed . . . to the great relief of such (poor suitors) and strangers [also] as oft be partakers thereof (and otherwise like to dine hardily)'. The behaviour of the gentry was not given the same loving attention by Harrison, but he argued that they kept tables and hospitality proportionate with their rank. At the beginning of the next century Fynes Moryson believed that some of these traditions were in decline, but he also observed that groaning boards and a lavishness of provision for all comers were still features of the life of the English upper orders.[2] Abundance of food and low prices, when compared with those of other nations, and a long-established custom of generous entertainment, 'make our tables plentifully furnished, whereupon other Nations esteeme us gluttous and devourers of flesh, yet the English tables are not furnished with many dishes, all for one man's diet, but severally

---

[1] William Harrison, *The Description of England*, ed. F. J. Furnivall, 2 vols. (New Shakspere Soc., 6th ser. 1, 5, London, 1908), i. 145.
[2] Fynes Moryson, *An Itinerary Containing his Ten Years' Travel*, 4 vols. (Glasgow, 1907–8), i. 172–3.

for many mens appetite, and not only prepared for the family, but for strangers and relief of the poor'. The images of Harrison and Moryson are borne out by the surviving late Elizabethan and Jacobean household ordinances, which speak of a society just as hierarchical, formal, and elaborate as that of their predecessors. Moreover, as late as the eve of the Civil War, descriptions of household behaviour show that it could retain most of the features it had possessed in the late medieval period. A note of the Earl of Worcester's dining arrangements at Raglan in the 1630s reveals a pattern of commensality involving the whole household and its guests, eating exactly as the household ordinances stipulated that they should.[3]

The survival of this noble mode of existence can also be seen in the funeral pomp that still marked the death of a great man, or in the courtesies offered to a magnate by his circle of tenants, clients, and affines on such occasions as his return to his own territories after long absence. The Earl of Derby was greeted in 1597 by almost 500 Cheshire horsemen when he entered that county, and by 700 men of Lancashire when he reached Warrington, at which point an open-air banquet was held for all the participants.[4] Although the nature of the good lordship that Derby provided for his followers had been modified by the political circumstances of the sixteenth century, it remained necessary to articulate loyalties within his locality in these traditional forms. In mimetic form the continuity of these displays of deference can be observed even into the later part of the next century when Robert Paston, first Earl of Yarmouth, was escorted into Norwich in 1675 by 'Baronets, knights, Esquires, gentlemen and clergy, Aldermen and Town Clerk of the city . . .'.[5] This, of course, is a display of Tory political loyalty, rather than a reversion to older forms of clientage, but its external forms carefully echo the aristocratic past. It is therefore not surprising to find that a return to the good old patterns of hospitality was a part of the behaviour of the Earl

[3] Wi. RO, 88/1/156.
[4] *HMC, Salisbury MSS.*, vii. 327; see also, B. Coward, *The Stanleys, Lord Stanley and Earls of Derby, 1385-1672* (Chetham Soc., 3rd ser. 30, 1983), 95-6. For similar receptions given to the Berkeley family, see John Smyth, *The Lives of the Berkeleys*, ed. J. Maclean, 3 vols. (Gloucester, 1883-5), ii. 370.
[5] *HMC, Appendix to the 6th Report*, 373.

of Yarmouth.[6] His political objectives might differ from those of his predecessors, but in holding open house for the Norfolk worthies, for his tenants, and for anyone else who might be susceptible to influence, he was able to draw on a continuity of belief about how the nobility should behave as good hosts.

Yet these continuities existed coevally with a rising chorus of laments that hospitality was dead, or at the very least dying, among the nobility and gentry of late Tudor and early Stuart England. It is, of course, necessary to exercise some caution in evaluating these jeremiads, which are part of the stock-in-trade of the moralist.[7] In any society which valued entertainment both as a source of mutual charity and as a prime form of support for the needy, those required to provide it were all too often likely to offend the purists who guarded the collective conscience. The condemnation of niggardly hospitality is as integral a part of Homeric writing as of that of godly preachers at the end of the sixteenth century.[8] Troubadours and Irish bards were very prone to curse erstwhile patrons who had not shown appropriate generosity, and to attribute their failures to a general decline in social standards as well as to personal avarice.[9] When hosts were judged against high standards of Christian *caritas*, it was all too easy to find them wanting, and to respond with the species of lament for the sins of the world that is to be found in Bromyard's sermon on hospitality. It may well be only because of the limited nature of late medieval sources that we do not possess a dozen examples of sermons like that of Bromyard, or of poetic denunciations of failure to maintain 'the good old ways' such as Langland's or Hoccleve's.[10] Nevertheless, more than a bias in the surviving sources seems to lie behind the growth in expressions

[6] Ibid. 375–9.

[7] For more extended comment on this problem, see F. Heal, 'The Idea of Hospitality in Early Modern England', *PP*, 102 (1984), 79–82.

[8] On the Greek background see M. Finley, *The World of Odysseus* (New York, 1954), 101–4. For the medieval period there are some valuable comments in M. P. Whitney, 'Largesse: Queen of Medieval Virtues', in C. Fiske (ed.), *Vassar Medieval Studies* (New Haven, Conn., 1923), 210–12.

[9] Simms, 'Guesting and Feasting in Gaelic Ireland', *Journal of the Royal Society of Antiquaries for Ireland*, 108 (1978), 79–80.

[10] Bromyard, *Summa predicantum*, 2 vols. (Venice, 1586), i. cap. 5, 362; Thomas Hoccleve, 'Dialogue with a Beggar', in his *Works*, ed. F. J. Furnivall (*EETS*, E.S. 72, London, 1897), 19. For Langland, see above, pp. 40–2.

of anxiety about the failure of hospitality in the late sixteenth century. Sermons, tracts on ethics, conduct books, and government pronouncements all point in the same direction, as do proverbs and ballads at the level of popular literature. The last are particularly interesting, since there seems to be some shift from early ballad examples which, through dramatic narrative, condemn specific cases of inhospitable or uncharitable behaviour, to those of the seventeenth century which provide broad and generalized laments on the death of hospitality.[11] By the first decade of the seventeenth century it seems that any writer on society who did not allude, at least *en passant*, to the decay of hospitality, was failing to observe one of the conventions of his genre.

It seems reasonable to begin from an assumption that both ideological and social changes lie behind the decline in generosity that so many writers thought that they observed in Elizabethan England. Since ideological questioning is, in the nature of its evidence, easier to isolate and describe than social transition, it is appropriate to begin with the self-conscious and articulate challenges that were offered to tradition before investigating any comparable structural changes in behaviour. But such a method demands a continuous awareness of the dangers of assuming that new ideas were necessarily modifiers of behaviour; at the complex interface between ideas and action a variety of possible causal patterns can be discerned, and indeed any form of monocausal explanation for something as elusive as a decline in hospitality may well prove inappropriate. The problem is compounded by a peculiar difficulty in the sources, since those prescriptive sources which claim to approximate most closely to reality in the case of the great household, the ordinances, were committed to a description of social experience that was designed to exclude the notion of change almost completely. While in practice making constant minor adjustments in their orders, they became in the seventeenth century more self-consciously wedded

---

[11] Examples of the former type can be found in P. J. King (ed.), *Tudor Songs and Ballads* (London, 1978), 117–22, and in J. Kinsley (ed.), *The Oxford Book of Ballads* (Oxford, 1969), 5–7, 420 ff. The latter type, which did not, of course, wholly displace the dramatic narrative, are well represented by Martin Parker's 'Times Alteration' (1635?), or by 'Pity's Lamentation' (1615?), H. E. Rollins (ed.), *The Pepys Ballads*, 8 vols. (Cambridge, Mass., 1929–32), i. no. 17.

to the idea of tradition and continuity. As Morgan Coleman explained, when he sought to justify the elaboration of his ordinances for Cranfield, he had endeavoured to avoid partiality, 'having framed, and squared out, and sett everie thinge with the true levill of antiquitie, and honorable custome'.[12] This very preoccupation with the need for continuity may be revealing of the threats posed to the old order, but it is obviously necessary to look elsewhere for any reflective comment on the nature of those threats.

One of the most powerful and fully articulated challenges to traditional perceptions of the household is also one of the earliest. In Book I of *Utopia*, Thomas More furnishes one of the first of the attacks on that aspect of magnificence that was associated with the keeping of crowds of idle attendants.[13] This merely fostered indolence among those who had never bothered to learn a trade, and risked financial ruin for an heir who was unable to support the same size of household as his father. In Book II, the alternative vision of the household described as current among the Utopians is fundamentally opposed to that of More's England. The Utopians believed in hierarchy, but only in the 'natural' authority of the old over the young, husbands over wives, and parents over children. Since inferiors would wait on their superiors this would, according to More's marginal note, provide 'A Method for Eliminating the Idle Host of Servants'.[14] In the specific context of meals, which the Utopians take in public dining halls, some hierarchy is preserved by the existence of a high table for the priest and his wife, but elsewhere old and young sit mixed together so that the young can be restrained 'from mischievous freedom in word and gesture'. The old are served first and distribute to the young, thus blending respect for authority with a general equality. Since economic redistribution eliminates the problem of poverty, and outsiders are a rarity in *Utopia*, the issue of hospitality does not present itself in anything resembling its European form. However, it would be consistent with the argument for the supremacy of the public over the private, that

[12] LPL, Fulham Papers 426, fo. 46.
[13] Thomas More, *Utopia*, ed. E. Surtz and J. H. Hexter (New Haven, Conn., 1965), 63.
[14] Ibid. 137.

domestic hospitality should be seen as at best a poor substitute for collective action upon poverty and state provision for men of honour from abroad. It is not the detail of Utopian arrangements that is relevant here, but More's general articulation of an intense dislike for the irrational ordering of the English household, which serves neither a moral nor an efficient social purpose. Of course, his setting of the debate of the first book at the genial table of Cardinal Morton might be argued to indicate a greater affection for English habits. However, it is revealing that the introductory description of the Cardinal given by Hythlodaeus does not make any comment on his domestic virtues, but dwells instead on his rhetorical skills, his learning in the law, and his crucial role in the commonwealth. More makes no concessions to the conventions of praise which would normally have encouraged Hythlodaeus to comment on Morton's generosity before describing the debate over his dinner-table.[15]

If we read *Utopia* as a devastating critique of contemporary European social forms we are forced to conclude that More remained a voice crying in the wilderness, lacking the power not only to change practice, but even to influence his fellow-humanists at all profoundly. But on certain themes his thought did intersect with other writers of his own and the following generation, and began to erode fixed assumptions about the nature of domestic organization. The most obvious similarity is the attack on idle servitors, which was taken up by Thomas Starkey and by the so-called commonwealth men in the mid-century, and which eventually provided a justification for changes in social behaviour at the beginning of the Stuart period.[16] A pattern can be traced by which the ideas of the critics were assimilated into conventional thinking and argument, so that by Elizabeth's reign so orthodox a thinker as Harrison could complain that 'no nation cherisheth such store of them [serving-men] as wee doo here in England'.[17] At the next stage we encounter the advices of the end of the reign often specifically

---

[15] More, *Utopia*, 61.
[16] Thomas Starkey, *A Dialogue of Pole and Lupset*, ed. J. M. Cowper, 2 vols. (*EETS*, E.S. 12, 32, London, 1871, 1878), ii. 84. See also J. Guy, *Christopher St. German on Chancery and Statute* (Selden Soc., suppl. ser. 6, London, 1985), 25–31.
[17] Harrison, *Description of England*, i. 135.

recommending that nobles and gentlemen should be served by 'a fewe discreet civill men', and, by the early seventeenth century, actual decline in the number of attendants and servants in some great households can be documented.[18] This is not to suggest that the élite began to shed their trains of superfluous attendants purely because the humanists argued that they should do so; there were sound economic motives and other cultural influences at work as well. However, it was surprisingly difficult for authors by the end of the sixteenth century to stand against prevailing intellectual fashion which condemned 'the idle drones'. A specific literature in defence of the serving-man was able to plead a special case, but otherwise authors seemed uneasy about a romantic nostalgia that included a vision of 'tall men' as figures of value in the cultural landscape.[19]

While changing patterns of service ultimately influenced the nature of hospitality, the aspect of More's vision which touches most directly our central theme is his insistence on the primacy of the public good in Utopia. The Utopians espoused a life of collective virtue which, while not denying a significance to the family and the individual unit, concerned itself above all with the general weal. Here More was at one with his fellow-humanists who had imbibed from the classics a notion of civic activism that was in many ways at odds with the prevailing ethos of the English nobility. Within two decades of the writing of *Utopia* this activism was beginning to find an outlet in legislation, most notably in the 1536 poor law (27 Henry VIII, c. 25).[20] The genesis of the wide-ranging proposals made to Cromwell, and embodied in the first draft bill, and the problems that it encountered in parliament, have been discussed elsewhere and

---

[18] Li. RO, 2ANC 14/17. This is advice to the son of Lord Willoughby by his father's steward, John Guevara. See also Sir William Wentworth's advice to his son in J. P. Cooper (ed.), *Wentworth Papers, 1597–1628* (Camden Soc., 4th ser. 12, London, 1973), 14–15; Stone, *The Crisis of the Aristocracy* (Oxford, 1965), 212–13.

[19] *A Health to the Gentlemanly Profession of Servingmen* (London, 1598), repr. in W. C. Hazlitt (ed.), *Inedited Tracts Illustrating the Manners of Englishmen during the Sixteenth and Seventeenth Centuries* (Roxburghe Club, London, 1868); William Basse, *Sword and Buckler: Or a Serving-Man's Defence* (London, 1602). The rather poor press given to servants in late Elizabethan literature is also of interest.

[20] On the context of the 1536 Act see P. Slack, *Poverty and Policy in Tudor and Stuart England* (London, 1988), 115–19.

need not detain us here. Their major interest for our purposes is that they suggested a process for the integration of poor relief under the control of public authority, including the organization of funding via a tax on incomes. Such integration was to include 'broken meats and fragments' that had previously been given by individuals at their doors, but were now to be collected and distributed by some appropriate local figure.

Had these proposals passed directly into law they would have challenged very explicitly the old patterns of household charity which depended for much of their efficacy on the personal generosity of a master to the particular poor at his gate. And the significance of this change was not lost on members of parliament, for in the course of its stormy passage three clauses were added to the bill which undercut the centrist impulse for the organization of charity in the form of food. In the Commons an extra clause secured the right of parishioners to give either money or fragments to the local poor and to prisoners, while the Lords stipulated that the alms of noblemen should be protected and they should be permitted to give 'as well to poor and indigent people of other parishes as of the same parishes . . .'. The third additional clause protected the traditional rights of the monasteries and of secular clergy in the giving of alms.[21] It is perhaps unwise to dismiss these provisos as minor amendments, as one commentator has done. They were, no doubt, less dramatic than the attack on compulsory funding which seems to have moved critics of the bill most powerfully, but they do indicate an ideological conflict over the nature of alms-giving that is surely of importance. Lords and Commons, laity and clergy, shared a desire to maintain the customary patterns of domestic giving, especially the giving of food rather than money alms, which Cromwell's bill threatened to destroy. Like *Utopia*, and like Bucer's later proposals for the public organization of alms, it proved too radical a challenge to domestic authority to win acceptance from the élite represented in parliament.

Although the most radical proposals made in 1536 were for the moment stillborn, they provided one conceptual frame that was fundamentally to influence later Tudor thinking on the relief of the poor. By the mid-century English towns began to manifest

---

[21] G. R. Elton, *Reform and Renewal* (Cambridge, 1973), 122–5.

in their practical actions against poverty precisely that civic activism and concern for godly discipline of which More would have approved.[22] As the government itself slowly began to follow this urban initiative and legislate for a more structured system of relief, there is less evidence that the élite continued to feel an obligation to defend the old modes of care from the household. After 1536 the only legislative moment at which hospitality assumed any importance was in the mid-1590s, in the face of a major subsistence crisis. A variety of explanations could be adduced for this silence: in ideological terms the direct critique of the humanists may have contributed in some measure; though the influence of Protestantism, considered more closely below, was probably of greater significance. In both cases it was not necessarily the most explicit challenges to old modes of thought that proved most influential; rather the slow transmutation of value systems induced by these major intellectual implants eventually eroded existing perceptions. If we take the case of humanist advice first, it is difficult to argue that the critique of More's generation modified attitudes in fundamental ways, even though it eventually fed into a broad stream of commonwealth writing. On the other hand, humanist thought was also directed to two aspects of social behaviour that were to be of major significance into the late sixteenth century and beyond, the consideration of the nature of giving, of generosity and liberality, that emanated from the works of Cicero and Seneca, and of civility and the social role of the individual. In alliance with the functionalist challenge that civic humanism did offer to older norms, classicism and civility were eventually to offer the English élite a new way of perceiving social relationships.

In the previous chapter we noted that classical ideals of liberality, generosity, and prudence were important elements in descriptions of élite hospitality in the later medieval period as well as the sixteenth century. The overwhelming influence of Cicero's writings on ethics and society in the Tudor period, and the growing significance of Seneca from the 1580s onwards, in some ways merely reinforced a pre-existing impulse to discuss a social practice like hospitality in terms of the cardinal

[22] Slack, *Poverty and Policy*, 119–22.

virtues.[23] Liberality as a mean between prodigality and avarice was one of the most commonplace ethical descriptions in the moralistic tracts which proliferated in the later years of Elizabeth's reign. But the influence of Cicero did not reside solely in his transmission of Aristotelian categories into every Tudor schoolroom. In *De Officiis* in particular, he reflected very coolly on the advantages of certain modes of behaviour, including gift-giving and entertainment. Moderation in gift-giving was urged, though the bonds of society would be best maintained 'if kindness be shown to each individual in proportion to the closeness of his relationship'.[24] Although honouring of noble strangers was commended as a credit to one's own country, there was an expectation that there would be a return on this investment, as there would be even in defending the poor, since this would gain loyal adherents. Always Cicero emphasizes the prudential and calculative elements in the evaluation of social action, the need to reflect before taking any decision, and to be aware of its possible consequences. While the message differed little in substance from traditional accounts of generosity as right-doing, Cicero's insistence on self-awareness undercut at least some of the behaviour associated with magnificence and liberality.[25] A feature of the species of hospitality that characterized the Buckingham household, for example, was its easy acceptance of very diverse groups, each defined by its position in the social hierarchy, but each finding a niche without, one presumes, over-precise enquiry from the lord. Cicero did not deny that generosity was a social good, but enquired more precisely who was entertained, and what purpose was served by the reception of different individuals. When linked to a concern for prudent management he could be used to justify the destruction of the older, more lavish, ways of offering hospitality.

It is difficult, of course, to argue neatly from *De Officiis* to the limitation of entertainment on any one estate, but an intermediate level may be found in some of the advice literature that was so popular by the end of the sixteenth century. The guidance that

---

[23] For this amplified use of the cardinal virtues, see Thomas Elyot, *The Boke Named the Governor*, ed. S. E. Lehmberg (London, 1962), 159 ff.

[24] Cicero, *De Officiis*, ed. and trans. W. Miller (London, 1968), 50.

[25] Ibid. 237, 243.

Christopher Wandesford left for his children, speaks of the old aristocratic virtues of generosity and openness, but also urges prudential calculation about the effects of giving and of the utility of each gesture.[26] More overtly Ciceronian sentiments may be found in William Cornwallis's *Essays* (1600), when he insists that the only reasons for entertaining guests were love or business: 'I am readie . . . to entertaine all: but to keepe open house untill I shall be compelled to shut up my doores, must be pardoned me: I have a purse and a life, and all that I am for some fewe; but they are indeed but a fewe.'[27]

If Cicero is important because of the coolness of his social vision, the growing influence of Seneca is significant because his form of Stoicism married a concern for individual ethics to Ciceronian moral calculus. *De Beneficiis* weighed actions in terms of their ability to enhance the well-being of the doer.[28] Hence the significance of the gift lay in the attitude of the giver, rather than in the nature of the thing given, or in its effect on the recipient. External actions were not irrelevant, but were treated as instrumental means to the achievement of inner virtue and peace of mind. Even in the pseudo-Senecan works in circulation in the reign of Henry VIII the aphoristic wisdom was already directed towards consistency of moral purpose, especially to the ability to live honestly regardless of external circumstance. Readers of *The Glasse of Maners* (1547) were counselled to live alone as they would in the market-place and to accept that 'Thy countrey is, where so ever thou arte well, and lyvest honestly: it is nat in ye place, but in the man'.[29] Later in the century the Stoic vision of the pursuit of the life of wisdom becomes central to the ethical discussions of the Elizabethans. Among the texts that give serious consideration to the question of hospitality, for example, it informs *Cyvile and Uncyvile Life*, Cooper's *The Art of Giving*

[26] Christopher Wandesford, *A Book of Instructions to his Son*, ed. T. Comber (London, 1777), 78 ff.

[27] William Cornwallis, *Essays*, 2nd edn. (London, 1606), ch. 9, 'Of Entertainment'.

[28] Seneca, *'De Beneficiis'*, in *Moral Essays*, iii. ed. and trans. J. Basore (Cambridge, Mass., 1935), 43–5.

[29] *A Fruitfull Worke of Lucius Anneus Senecae Called the Myrrour or Glasse of Maners*, trans. R. Whyttynton (London, 1547). This is actually a translation of material adapted from Stoic sources in the sixth century.

(1615), and Vaughan's *Golden Grove* (1598).[30] The townsman in *Cyvile Life* gives eloquent expression to Senecan values when he argues that the virtuous man is honoured just as much if he 'walks alone' as if he is accompanied by the full panoply of an aristocratic following.[31] The importance of this vision in a society which was more fluid and more complex than that of the fifteenth century is self-evident. Among those who sought to enter the community of honour in the later sixteenth century were many men who could not depend upon an elaborate household to personate their virtues, and who therefore had need of an alternative model of ethics to buttress their social position. The Senecan movement at the turn of the sixteenth century owed its power to other, more overtly political, aspects of Stoic thought as well, but in the competitive environments of the court and of London its emphasis on the integrity of the individual was of great importance.[32]

A consideration of Senecan influence cannot readily be separated from the development of that ideology of conduct that is inextricably linked with the Elizabethan and Jacobean élites— civility. Castiglione, Guazzo, and della Casa provided the Italianate foundations for a new language of social interchange that became mandatory in court circles and was gradually diffused throughout the landed orders.[33] Such a code was needed, at the crudest level, to establish rules for the new modes of behaviour that were an inescapable part of political and cultural centralization, of the shift from the world of the household to that of the court. Detached from his own defined hierarchical world, the noble or gentleman who attended upon the king had some of the same social nakedness that a guest possessed in any alien establishment. Of course the analogy is not perfect, since

---

[30] *Cyvile and Uncyvile Life*, in W. C. Hazlitt (ed.), *Inedited Tracts*; Thomas Cooper, *The Art of Giving* (London, 1615); William Vaughan, *The Golden Grove, Moralized in Three Books* (London, 1600).

[31] *Cyvile and Uncyvile Life*, 45.

[32] On the significance of Senecan thought under late Elizabeth and James, see Seneca, *De remediis fortuitorum*, ed. and trans. R. G. Palmer (Chicago, 1953), intro.; W. L. Ustick, 'Changing Ideals of Aristocratic Character in Seventeenth-Century England', *Modern Philology* 30 (1932), 147 ff.

[33] Baldassare Castiglione, *The Courtier*, trans. T. Hoby (London, 1561); Stefano Guazzo, *The Civile Conversation*, trans. G. Pettie (London, 1581); Giovanni della Cassa, *Galateo . . . A Treatise of Manners*, trans. R. Peterson, (London, 1576).

traditionally the courtier had acquired identity not as guest, but as servant, as the possessor of the dependent yet defined status that derived from office. Those who held no obvious office, but were effectively guests of the crown when summoned to do service, were usually able to retain the essence of their honorific identity by bringing to court their trains of attendants. These patterns did not suddenly change in the early sixteenth century, but from the reign of Henry VIII onwards they proved inadequate in themselves to accommodate the growing complexity of social needs within an expanding centralized court.[34] The cultivation of the arts of civility offered an alternative, providing a method of handling regular interaction and competition with those who shared this difficult social space. Castiglione's principle of *sprezzatura*, the artfulness that concealed art, was designed to provide the courtier with his own identity emanating from his own abilities rather than the automatic claims of blood or office.[35] This is not to argue that the major theorists of civility sought to *substitute* native wit for the more traditional patterns of hierarchy: rather that gentility was usually assumed as the point of inception for the cultivation of those qualities which delineated the true courtier. The grace which was the final mark of refined behaviour was the consequence of self-conscious endeavour: a quality which must ultimately appear natural and easy although it was achieved and precarious.

Two aspects of the pursuit of civility which evolved from the Italian tradition seem of particular importance for the study of hospitality. The first is the idea that refinement separates those who possess it from the rest, and justifies them in seeking one another's company. The salon atmosphere in which the original *Courtier* debate was conducted offers the paradigm for later behaviour: the precise social standing of the participants is of far less importance than their ability to manipulate certain intellectual and cultural codes, to subscribe to the unwritten rules of their small coterie.[36] At times this ability to manipulate the correct language could permit quite dramatic challenges to traditional

---

[34] On the changing demands of court culture see D. Starkey, 'The Court; Castiglione's Ideal and Tudor Reality', *JWCI*, 40 (1982), 232–9.

[35] S. Greenblatt, *Renaissance Self-Fashioning* (Chicago, 1980), 162–4.

[36] A. C. Bryson, 'Concepts of Civility in England, c.1560–1685' Oxford D.Phil. thesis (1984), 146 ff.

hierarchies. For example, John Dee, the Elizabethan mathematician, was able not only to dine with the Archbishop of Canterbury, but to invite him in return to eat at his 'cottage', and on another occasion to entertain the Earl of Derby and his train, who arrived unexpectedly, to 'a scholar's collation', which 'was taken in good part'.[37] Ben Jonson's poem 'Inviting a Friend to Supper', although not directed across such a social gulf, addresses the same issue: the feast of the mind is given precedence over the gross feeding of the body, and the quality of the company, carefully selected by the poet, determines the success of the entertainment.[38] The author of *Cyvile and Uncyvile Life* had no doubts that the great merit of living in London was that one could choose one's own dinner guests, and have friends at your table, 'men of more civilitie, wisedome and worth, then your rude Countrey Gentlemen, or rusticall Neighboures'.[39] Here the attitude of the man of civility has spilled over from an enthusiasm for congenial company into a contempt for the uncultivated, an attitude which is also clear in George Whetstone's *A Heptameron of Civill Discourses* (1582). This is a courtly conversation-piece in the Castiglione manner, in which the theme in debate is the nature of marriage. The penalty for failure to conform to the rules of the debate, which was taking place in the Christmas season, was 'to bee turned into the great Hall, among the Countrie Trulles the whole Christmas'.[40]

Paradoxically, the second important aspect of the civility literature is its concern for the idea of accommodation.[41] Social versatility, and the ability to adjust to the needs of others for the avoidance of unpleasantness, became major themes in English writing from the mid-Elizabethan period onwards. The courtier who was well-versed in the arts of *politesse* was able to show a free and frank exterior to all whom he encountered, while not necessarily yielding his trust to any. This ease in exterior

---

[37] J. O. Halliwell-Phillips (ed.), *The Private Diary of John Dee* (Camden Soc. o.s. 19, London, 1842), 49, 55.

[38] Ben Jonson, *The Complete Poems*, ed. G. Parfitt (London, 1975), 70.

[39] *Cyvile and Uncyvile Life*, 80.

[40] George Whetstone, *A Heptameron of Civill Discourses* (London, 1582), sig. Biv[r].

[41] The following paragraphs are much indebted to the work of Anna Bryson on changing patterns of gentility, esp. 229 ff.

behaviour, and the ability to display a cultivated style in a wide range of social circumstances, could lead to charges of dissimulation and hypocrisy, to a tension between the inner and outer man; indeed, this is of course a common theme in the literature of the period. But at least in its ideal form it was a concept related to the Stoic notion of integrity, and was an emanation of an interior grace which had been made manifest by careful cultivation and education. The true gentleman, as the paradigm emerged in the early seventeenth century, was free and frank in his behaviour, not as a result of indiscriminate sociability or an unreflecting dependence on his birthright, but as a consequence of his training and his understanding of a variety of social milieux. When Richard Carew wrote of the Cornish gentry at the turn of the sixteenth century, and praised the 'frankness' of their entertainment, he still invested the word with a meaning of general amiability to all men, of casual *bonhomie*.[42] Sixty years later, Edward Waterhouse observed that 'a Free spirit and a Free port suit well, and nothing beneath it becomes Noblemen and Gentlemen', but it was a newer, more carefully nurtured frankness, and willingness to accommodate the needs of others, that he had in mind.[43] Between the two dates we can often find examples of the adjustment of the old traditions of social ease to the world of civil society, as when Gervase Holles praised the first Earl of Clare for his willingness to converse civilly with all his guests, talking to each one 'in his owne element', while making his table a *convivium philosophale* with his own discussions of divinity, philosophy, and history.[44] The funeral epitaph on the third Sir Thomas Lucy, who died in 1640, suggests a similar integration of the new and the old: he welcomed all men to his table, but especially those who could talk of theology or poetry.[45]

In cases such as these the problem of associating frankness of manners with the desire to consort with men of civility could be resolved along essentially traditional lines. However, authors sought to address all circumstances, especially those novel ones

[42] Carew, *The Survey of Cornwall* (London, 1602), fos. 144, 147[v].
[43] Edward Waterhouse, *The Gentleman's Monitor* (London, 1665), 62.
[44] Gervase Holles, *Memorials of the Holles Family, 1493–1656*, ed. A. C. Wood (Camden Soc. 3rd ser. 55, London, 1937), 112.
[45] Charlecote Church, Warwickshire.

in which the old models were of little value in determining correct behaviour. When tension between the old and the new did arise it could often be contained, if not resolved, by a clear separation between public and private spheres of activity. The gentleman was certainly required to be affable, frank, and at ease in his dealings with all men in public, but since the avoidance of stress was also an essential part of the cultivation of civility, he was wise to have a sphere of privacy into which he could legitimately withdraw accompanied only by a few like-minded men. This is the significance of the emphasis on private entertaining in *Cyvile and Uncyvile Life*: the gentleman, who can scarcely avoid having to be affable to many men in the city can, nevertheless, dine alone, or with a few carefully chosen friends.[46] Dining has here lost its quasi-public character and become part of private social space. For the courtier there were graver problems, since his role was essentially public, and the strain of honest behaviour could be overwhelming. The bitter power of Wyatt's poetry on the theme of 'doubleness' and the difficulty of maintaining integrity at court, summarizes the dilemma in a haunting manner.[47] In this situation the public and private had to be redefined so that the country, that is the retreat from the court, became the place of enclosure and of personal choice, where the demands of civility could be relaxed. For Wyatt the precarious civility of the court, cultivated at such a price, and yet essential to the new world of political competition, is sharply contrasted with the Arcadian and private environment of the Kentish countryside;

Among the muses where I sit and sing.

The perennial dialogue between *otium* and *negotium* is clearly present in Wyatt's vision, but it is of interest that he unhesitatingly identifies the countryside with the former quality, with philosophical retreat, leisure, and contemplation. The use of this classical paradigm was to generate a literature of the countryside that was at odds with the more traditional English image of rural sociability and of the politicized household.[48]

---

[46] *Cyvile and Uncyvile Life*, 80.
[47] Starkey, 'The Court . . . Ideal and Reality', 237–9.
[48] For a general discussion of the contrasting images, see R. Williams, *The Country and the City* (London, 1973), chs. 1–3.

It is no simple matter to identify the changes in thinking about hospitality which occurred as a consequence of the élite's growing preoccupation with civility. The texts do not speak with one voice: Italian and French sources, which were the major handbooks for much of Elizabeth's reign, usually gave only a limited space to the household, and were intensely preoccupied by behaviour appropriate to court and to city, though even here Tasso's *Householder's Philosophie* (translated in 1588) is an exception.[49] Once an English literature began to establish itself at the end of the century, some obvious divisions can be demonstrated between those texts which follow foreign precedent closely and those which seek to accommodate their key topoi to traditional circumstance. Henry Peacham's *The Compleat Gentleman* (1622) is the outstanding example of the former pattern, though James Cleland's *Hero-Paideia* (1607) is also important, while Richard Brathwait's *The English Gentleman* (1630) is the best-known work in the latter tradition.[50] Neither Peacham nor Cleland wholly ignored the problem of entertaining and visiting, but they addressed themselves to the issue only briefly, as part of the broader discussion of the correct mode in which an individual should conduct himself towards other individuals of honour, whether friends or strangers. Brathwait, on the other hand, continued to see the household, especially the household in the countryside, as an essential dimension of the experience of the élite, and to associate open entertainment with the honour of the landed classes. Although Brathwait followed a well-established courtesy text pattern by dividing his book into sections on youth, education, recreation, and so on, he gave particular attention to the social vocation of the gentleman, whose duty was to serve his monarch and his own country. For him the latter term was intended above all to denote the locality, for it was there that a gentleman found his natural sphere of action: 'Let your countrey (I say) enjoy you, who bred you, shewing there your hospitalitie, where God hath placed you, and with sufficient meanes blessed you.' At this moment

---

[49] Torquato Tasso, *The Housholder's Philosophie*, trans. T. Kyd (London, 1588).

[50] Other works which advise the gentleman about his traditional duties include Waterhouse, and Dudley, 4th Lord North, *Observations and Advices Œconomical* (London, 1669).

Brathwait seemed to be rejecting the artifice of self-fashioning, which was a part of the milieu of the court, in favour of natural patterns of behaviour that best suited the country.[51]

One way in which the old ideal of hospitality survived into the age of the complete courtier was, therefore, as part of a series of dichotomies: the natural against the artificial, the ordered against the competitive, the court against the country. It is not necessary to believe in the full reality of these images to see that they were important ordering devices and mental sets for many of the late Tudor and early Stuart élite. In the case of the connection between hospitality, nature, order, and the country this is nowhere better seen than in the minor genre of the country-house poem which has attracted so much critical attention in the last few years. Two major poems, Jonson's 'To Penshurst' and Marvell's 'Upon Appleton House', frame a small group of other pieces by Jonson, Carew, and Herrick, in which Martial and Horace are used as models for the praise of the country house and its contribution to the English rural scene.[52] Without exception, hospitality was seen as essential to the nature of the great house, and the paradigm of the open door is shared by most of the poems. For Jonson, Penshurst is the home:

> . . . whose liberall boord doth flow,
> With all, that hospitalitie doth know!
> Where comes no guest, but is allow'd to eate,
> Without his feare, and of thy lords owne meate . . .

At Saxham, Thomas Carew finds the same liberality:

> The Stranger's welcome, each man there
> Stamp'd on his chearfull brow doth wear;
> Nor doth this welcome, or his cheer
> Grow lesse, cause he stayes longer here.

The language of openness and generosity used by the poets is

[51] There are analogies here to the literature praising the simple country life, such as Nicholas Breton, *The Court and Country, or a Briefe Discourse between a Courtier and a Countryman* (London, 1618).

[52] The most useful secondary commentators on this literature are G. R. Hibbard, 'The Country-House poem of the Seventeenth Century', *JWCI*, 19 (1956), 159 ff.; J. Turner, *The Politics of Landscape* (London, 1979); W. McClung, *The Country-House Poem in English Renaissance Poetry* (Berkeley, Ca., 1977); M. A. McGuire, 'The Cavalier Country-House Poem: Mutations on a Jonsonian Tradition', *Studies in English Literature*, 19 (1979), 93–108.

closely identified with a traditional rhetoric: Saxham 'hast no
Porter at the door'; Robert Herrick's host, Sir Lewis Pemberton,
has a 'worn' threshold, porch, hall, parlour, and kitchen, in the
last of which mighty ribs of beef turn on 'laden' spits. Even the
more mannered images of Marvell follow a common pattern:

> A stately Frontispiece of Poor
> Adorns without the open Door;
> Nor less the Rooms within commends
> Daily new Furniture of Friends.[53]

Although the poems have different specific preoccupations and
themes, they share a concern to show the intimacy of the
relationship between the man-made environment of the country
house and nature. For Jonson, Penshurst is the embodiment of
that natural abundance which is the consequence of man's control
over the environment. So happy is the marriage between man
and his natural world in this Kentish garden that fishes run into
the nets of Robert Sidney's men as 'tribute'. In Carew's 'To
. . . G. N. from Wrest', the country house and garden is nature,
that is true nature with its 'fertile waters', 'balmie dew' and
'odours sweete', in contrast to the untamed wilderness through
which he has had to pass on his return from campaigning with
the king on the Scottish borders.[54] It is in this identification of
the natural and the social that the particular interest of the
country-house poem lies. Nature tamed and society tamed are
twin paradigms for these poets, whether they believe, as Jonson
affects to, that such processes can be spontaneous, or like Marvell,
that they are 'achieved and precarious'.[55] Their concern is not
with a return to some prelapsarian state of innocence, but with
the vision which the country house affords of a recaptured world
of social harmony existing outside the competitive and artificial
environment of the court in which they actually lived.

The results of this identification between nature and hospitality
are somewhat curious. For the poets, the generous entertainment

---

[53] Jonson, *Poems*, 97; Thomas Carew, *Poems*, ed. R. Dunlop (Oxford, 1949),
27–9; Robert Herrick, *Collected Verse*, ed. L. C. Martin (Oxford, 1956), 146.

[54] Carew, 86. On the importance of ideas of harmony and order in these
poems, see K. Sharpe, 'Cavalier Critic? The Ethics and Politics of Thomas Carew's
Poetry', in K. Sharpe and S. Zwicker (eds.), *The Politics of Discourse* (Berkeley,
Ca., 1987), 129–31.

[55] The phrase is taken from Williams, *Country and City*, 57.

offered by their hosts must not be seen as informed by artifice, even the artifice that was a necessary part of civility. Spontaneity was essential—at Saxham even the beasts are led willingly to the slaughter—and all social relationships had to be articulated in 'natural' terms. Since hierarchy was part of the natural order, it could readily enough be assimilated to such a vision, as in *Wrest* when the entertainment of various ranks by separate table is rather solemnly rehearsed. However, images of community, and of the shared experience of the 'little country commonwealth' understandably held a greater attraction for the poets. For Jonson, commensality was essentially part of the Penshurst ideal:

> Where the same beere, and bread, and self-same wine,
> That is his Lordships, shall be also mine.

In Herrick, this carefully modulated emphasis on *communitas* has been developed to a logical extreme. All seated at Pemberton's table enjoy 'equall freedome, equall fare', and Herrick proceeds to reinforce the point with an elaborate list of the animals on which all the guests were permitted to feast.[56] It is also Herrick who develops most powerfully the concept of openness, since Pemberton is claimed to give entertainment to 'the lanke Stranger, and the sowre Swain', bidding him to supper as well as dinner and feeding him on princely fare. The physicality of the poet's vision, shared to some extent by all the authors of country-house poetry, has prompted one commentator to observe that 'there is a peculiar and slightly grotesque heartiness about hospitality-poems, a smell of gravy that is absent from the usual decorous verse of the period'.[57] The observation is important, for the images of this poetry do frequently revolve around food, either as it is reared and produced on the estate or as it is consumed at the table. The economic significance of production and the dependent relationships it creates are obscured by the evocation of the household as a natural cornucopia. Jonson cannot ignore the walls of Penshurst, but he transmutes them to match his general image of benevolence:

> They are rear'd with no man's ruin, no mans grone,
> There's none, that dwell about them, wish them downe;

---

[56] On this anthropomorphic view see K. V. Thomas, *Man and the Natural World* (London, 1983).

[57] Turner, *Politics of Landscape*, 144.

It was essential, for the purposes of the poets, to evoke a community not only well ordered, but powerfully integrated in the shared ritual of eating, and so in harmony with itself and its environment.

It is relatively uncommon for this body of poetry to address itself directly to the dichotomy between court and country: only Jonson's 'To Sir Robert Wroth' makes rural retreat from city and court its major focus, and other themes, notably the contrast between 'rude nature' and the garden, often proved more attractive to the authors. Nevertheless, the contrast between civil and rural society is often implied. The country-house owner described by Jonson, Carew, and Herrick does not lack courtesy: Penshurst ends with a notable panegyric on the Sidneys, and epithets such as 'ancient honesty', 'reverent', and 'liberal' are easily to be found in the poetry.[58] But, like Richard Carew's Cornishmen, these hosts eschew the artifice of polite society, especially that impulse towards exclusion which was one characteristic of the growth of civility.

Herrick's choice of language, in particular, seems a deliberate challenge to conventions which threatened the casual *bonhomie* of the rural feast. In the specific context of the country house such rules were best set aside in the pursuit of community: indeed, for Jonson the great virtue of the Sidney ascendancy at Penshurst was that they had never been strictly applied. However, in lauding a particular tradition of hospitality the poets also delimited it. Although their intention was not necessarily to confine the ideal of open entertainment to the countryside and the great house, this is what they chose explicitly to do, thereby narrowing its focus. The court might not be actively hostile to the ideal portrayed in Penshurst, but Jonson was aware of its irrelevance to daily existence in London. Hence the very different tone of his verse inviting a friend to supper, in which the description of culinary delights is firmly subordinated to the promised freedom of discourse between like-minded friends. It is not necessary to see the country house evoked by the poets as a retreat from the 'real' world, though it has been suggested that Carew's impulses

---

[58] For Jonson's own experience of the Sidney family and Penshurst, see J. C. A. Rathmell, 'Jonson, Lord Lisle and Penshurst', *English Literary Rev.*, 1 (1971), 250–60.

were escapist. Rather, the rural estate is defined as autonomous, a microcosmic universe sufficient unto itself and open to its guests, but 'other' when compared to the routine urban experience of the poets.[59]

Of course, Jonson and his small group of imitators did not of themselves generate new attitudes to hospitality: rather they reflected and responded to assumptions which already had wide currency. Civility literature and the assumptions of Stoicism were enmeshed with the practical experience of a society which was more urban and centrist than that of the late Middle Ages. Thus, when we begin to examine the range of prescriptive comment on hospitality available by the early seventeenth century it is not surprising to find the Jonsonian images echoed in a variety of other forms. In particular, many sources demonstrate a tendency to think in terms of two dichotomies: those of country (hospitable) and city/court (inhospitable), and past (hospitable) and present (inhospitable). What both images have in common is the definition of customary hospitality as 'other', as belonging to some time, space, or social group that was not part of the centralist, modern paradigm from which most observers operated. To be defined as 'other' was not necessarily to be perceived as marginal: neither the country nor the English past were in any sense weak topoi at this period. It was, however, to separate social experience in ways which ultimately sanctioned the marginalization of the notion of hospitality.[60] The idea that the practice had existed in the past, or did exist in the countryside, could be an important critical weapon used to excoriate the attitudes of present-minded urban man. It could also develop into a paradigm in which *only* men in the past, and/or countryside, could be expected to be generous in entertaining all comers, so that the rhetoric was effective only as a plaint from that most marginal of groups, the poor.

The location of 'good old hospitality' in some distant era was, as already remarked, a part of the stock-in-trade of the moralist

---

[59] McGuire, 'Cavalier Country-House Poem', 97.

[60] For an extended discussion of this process see F. Heal, 'Hospitality and Honor in Early Modern England', *Food and Foodways*, 4 (1987), 321–50; also Williams, *Country and City*, 46 ff., and K. V. Thomas, *The Sense of the Past in Early Modern England* (Creighton Lecture, London, 1983), 11–14.

in an aristocratic society. For much of the time the English examples of the sixteenth and seventeenth centuries confine themselves to conventional laments and elegies for a vanished world, often, in the case of ballads and related sources, drawing on a very small stock of shared images. Yet the particular images are of interest, since they do represent a subset chosen from all possible concepts of hospitality with a degree of deliberation. The particular targets of the ballad-makers were the decay of Christmas celebration, the disappearance of the gentry to London, the craze for building which made no provision for the poor, and other forms of lavish expenditure, especially on clothing. In contrast, in the past:

> A man might then behold
> at Christmas in each Hall,
> Good fires, to curbe the Cold,
> and Meat for great and small.

Images of food and cooking abound in the ballads, Christmas fare especially being described with a sensuous pleasure that reaches far beyond that of poets such as Herrick. At the level of popular discourse, hospitality seems to be firmly associated with the giving of hot food, preferably meat, and especially good provision during the Twelve Days of the Christmas season.

Although both the past and the country were major locuses of a developing myth of hospitality, they must obviously be distinguished. The former could be used as a rhetorical weapon, to assail the greed, ambition, and extravagance of the present age, but it was self-evidently distanced from contemporary experience, the ideal ground for the development of myth. The English countryside, on the other hand, was an ever-present part of the environment of the élite, even of those men who had adopted London or court as the first sphere of their public life. Thus the myth of country hospitality was also an imperative call to action; a demand that the landed orders replicate the behaviour of their forebears. The power of 'To Penshurst' surely lies in its ability to evoke an ideal social world and to ground it firmly in the Kentish landscape and the life of the Sidney family. Even the more enclosed of the country-house poems, those of Carew, still argue that an order can be established in these microcosms that will be a model for the state. Saxham may be a retreat, but it is also open in its offer of hospitality.[61] This is not to argue that the seventeenth-century poets were directly didactic in their praise of rural life, though Jonson approaches didacticism when he concludes his poem with an attack on lavish building:

> Those proud, ambitious heaps, and nothing else,
> May say, their lords have built, but thy lord dwells.

More commonly they present an image of rural living that combines the pleasures of retreat and reintegration into the natural world with the equally 'natural' rewards of honour and reputation that accrue from the discharge of traditional duties. In the prescriptive writings of the early seventeenth century these same images are turned to a direct demand that the nobility and gentry leave London and take up their rural duties once again.[62]

In the countryside, the ideal of gentlemanly social behaviour offered by the poets could serve as a language of self-justification for the gentry. One of the most evocative examples is that cited by Cliffe of the Yorkshire gentleman, John Kaye of Woodsome, who chose to have the following verse inscribed on his portrait:

> I lyve at home in howsbandrye,
> Wythowte office or fee trulye,
> As servithe myne abylitie,
> I manteyne hosspitalytie.[63]

More commonly it was in funeral epitaphs that the gentry began, late in the sixteenth century, to use the language of country service and country hospitality in a conscious defence of their mode of living. Clement Paston, who died in 1600, was said to have lived long at Oxnead, Norfolk, 'with great renowne for feeding of the poore' and kindness to his neighbours.[64] Sir Henry Sidney of Walsingham, who died in 1612, but whose monument was not erected until the 1630s, was said to have settled in his mature years to the pursuit of hospitality and charity, to have been faithful to his friends and peaceable towards

[61] Sharpe, 'Cavalier Critic?', 132–4.

[62] See e.g., John Norden, *The Surveyor's Dialogue* (London, 1607), 85; I.H., *This World's Folly* (London, 1615).

[63] Cliffe, *The Yorkshire Gentry from the Reformation to the Civil War* (London, 1969), 97.

[64] *The Chorography of Norfolk*, ed. C. M. Hood (Norwich, 1938), 136.

his neighbours.[65] Examples could be multiplied both from epitaphs and funeral sermons of the power that the paradigm of good rural living possessed for the ruling orders. Just one more is worth specific mention, since it exemplifies the dichotomous urban / rural vision perfectly. Sir Thomas Rant died in Thorpe Market, Norfolk, in 1671, and had a suitably pompous epitaph inscribed on his tomb there. In it he was described as having pursued a career as a London lawyer until driven from the city because of his royalist sympathies at the beginning of the Civil war. Then, 'retireing into his Native Countrey he lived hospitably and honourably, spending his time successfully in composeing differences and preventing Suites between his Neighbours'.[66] It was only in the country, the epitaph implies, that such activities were a necessary part of good behaviour, and Rant is commended for his adaptibility in the face of ill-fortune. But he did more than adapt on the 'when in Rome . . .' principle: he was believed to have identified fully with the values of this different world, ending by founding an almshouse and remaining in the country even after the Restoration.[67] Retirement was not necessarily retreat, but translation from one pattern of social interchange to another.

Definitions of country behaviour no doubt developed dialectically, in response both to the actual growth of London and to the ideals of civility. Rusticity and simplicity, values which received negative treatment in the new world of the London playwrights and in the court, had to be analysed anew and reinvested with positive cultural power. An assertion that country living was 'natural' did something to advance this process, as did the abiding images of the country as a place of repose: the old dialectic of *otium* and *negotium* was of course important here. In the specific field of hospitality the new values were most clearly confronted by a renewed emphasis on plainness and on conviviality.[68] The plainness of English cooking, for example,

---

[65] F. Blomefield, *Topographical History of Norfolk*, 11 vols. (London, 1805–10), ix. 273.

[66] R. W. Ketton-Cremer, *Forty Norfolk Essays* (Norwich, 1961), 103.

[67] Ibid.; Blomefield, *Norfolk*, viii. 173.

[68] See e.g., Vaughan's emphasis on plain entertainment in *Golden Grove*, ch. 25. There is also a strong tradition in the ballad literature of satire on lavish banqueting, e.g. Martin Parker's *Bill of Fare*, in which the menu includes: 'Two paire of Elephants Pettitoes boyld, | A Greene Dragon Spitchcock (an excellent dish)'.

rarely remarked on as in any way distinctive in earlier periods, became a matter of cultural pride, and specifically of rural pride, in the later sixteenth century. The corrosive influence of foreign cooks was remarked from the mid-century onwards: the author of *Institucion of a Gentleman* thought that Flanders cooks were to be held responsible for the elaboration of dishes, and for their smallness.[69] Half a century later the blame had been firmly shifted to the French, where it remained for the rest of our period.[70] But in the early seventeenth century it was not just that French cooks were destroying the plainness of English cooking in London; they were spreading their malign influence into the countryside, where Sir Henry Slingsby thought they were destroying local tradition.[71]

For those who were fully committed to the 'Country myth', it became in certain instances a matter of pride to resist these incursions, as in the delightful story told of the Jacobean knight, Sir William Walter. Sir William was willing enough to follow the dictates of fashionable society to the extent of bringing a French cook into the country after his marriage, but was clear that his diet should continue to conform to tradition. Thus, after six months the cook asked leave to return to London with the remark: 'a peice of Beefe, a peice of Mutton and a pudding what needs that a French Cooke?'[72] A theme of Nicholas Breton's praise of the country against the court was that banqueting in the latter was no more than a dining on conceits, while the latter afforded the opportunity for good, plain housekeeping.[73] Among the various symbols which a gentleman could manipulate to demonstrate rural honesty and integrity, plain feeding could obviously occupy an important place. A marvellous vision of this rural pride at its height is given in Anthony Ashley Cooper's description of his eccentric neighbour, Henry Hastings, esquire. In the 1630s Hastings always had 'beef, pudding, and small beer'

[69] *Institucion of a Gentleman*, sig. G2.
[70] Sir Thomas Overbury, in his *Characters*, claims that the French chef is the reason 'why noblemen build their houses so great: for the smalnesse of their kitchin, makes the house the bigger'; S. Mennell, *All Manners of Food* (London, 1985), 102 ff.
[71] D. Parsons (ed.), *Diary of Sir Henry Slingsby* (London, 1836), 24.
[72] Folger Lib., V.a.180: this is from the merry tales included in the Fane Commonplace Book.
[73] Nicholas Breton, *The Court and Country*.

available in abundance, in a hall full of dogs and cats and strewn with marrow-bones. Hastings was inordinately proud of his good table and constantly generous, using the side chapel off his hall for storing the basic components of his meals: 'a cold chine of beef, venison-pasty, gammon of pasty, or a great apple-pye, with thick crust, extremely baked.'[74] No doubt Hastings was at ease with this mode of life, but it represented a deliberate challenge to the encroaching cult of gentility as well as a continuation of earlier tradition, and Hastings seems to have relished this as part of his reputation as an eccentric.

The cultivation of the ideal of conviviality could also represent an affirmation of country values. This is spelled out explicitly in *Cyvile and Uncyvile Life*, where the countryman defines the virtue of rural hospitality as permitting neighbours to 'meete often without ceremony, cheering and conversing one with another without disdayne or envie'.[75] It was this aspect of hospitality that the authors of the country-house poems chose to isolate: the ease of access to the great house and the comfort of the welcome it provided. Ease of approach and relaxed neighbourliness are certainly qualities that biographers and diarists considered important in the countryside. Hugh Cholmley described his dinner arrangements in Yorkshire in the 1630s as follows:

the gates . . . were ever shut up before dinner, when the bell rung to prayers, and not opened till one o'clock, except for strangers who came to dinner, which was ever fit to receive three or four besides my family, without any trouble; whatever their fare was, they were sure to have a hearty welcome.[76]

Informality and ease were also felt by Humphrey Mildmay to be hallmarks of Essex entertainment, although in this case it is revealing that he found no difficulty in transposing these relationships to London, where he spent as much of the year as possible.[77]

The image of the country as the focus of traditional hospitality was given a novel force in the early seventeenth century when

---

[74] J. Nichols, *History and Antiquities of the County of Leicester*, 4 vols. (London, 1795–1815), iii. pt ii., 592.
[75] *Cyvile and Uncyvile Life*, 31.
[76] Hugh Cholmley, *Memoirs* (Molton, 1870), 34.
[77] P. L. Ralph, *Sir Humphrey Mildmay, Royalist Gentleman* (New Brunswick, 1947), 25 ff.

it became associated with the attempts made by the Stuart
monarchy to contain the growth of London and to discourage the
landed élite from taking up residence there.[78] In a series of
proclamations, issued from the 1590s to the later 1630s, the
governments of Elizabeth, James, and Charles forbade the gentry
to live in or about the city outside the law terms, and specifically
required them to return to their country houses for the Christmas
period.[79] A variety of considerations moved the royal advisers:
in the 1590s the needs of defence, especially in the coastal
counties, predominated; thereafter, anxiety about the deficiencies
of local administration and about the problems created by the
explosive growth of London played an important part. But the
flurry of activity at times of dearth is also highly relevant:
proclamations in 1596, 1608, 1621, and 1622 were all issued in
years of harvest failure, and the crown's enthusiasm for the
enforcement of these acts seems to have owed much to anxieties
about supply and the dangers of disorder. It was in this context
that the notion of hospitality was invoked, as a specific against
dearth and as a means by which rural relationships might be
stabilized. For the Elizabethan government this appears to have
been a practical matter of employing any useful elements in
traditional thinking about poverty that might be of assistance at
a time of crisis.[80] Under James and Charles, however, other
ideological considerations were added to this practical impulse.
James, in particular, used the language of the 'country' and its
values with a passion that suggests conviction. The fourth and
fifth proclamations in the series speak with deep anxiety of the
decay of hospitality, and of the way in which the natural rulers
of England 'doe rather fall to a more private and delicate course
of life, after the manner of forreine Countreys', thereby neglecting
'that mutuall comfort between the Nobles and Gentlemen, and the

[78] For a full discussion of these endeavours, see F. Heal, 'The Crown,
the Gentry and London: the Enforcement of Proclamation, 1596–1640', in
C. Cross *et al.* (eds.), *Law and Government under the Tudors* (Cambridge, 1988),
211–26.

[79] *Tudor Royal Proclamations*, ed. P. L. Hughes and J. F. Larkin, 3 vols. (New
Haven, Conn., 1964–9), iii. 169–71; *Stuart Royal Proclamations*, ed. J. F. Larkin
and P. L. Hughes, 2 vols. (Oxford, 1973–82), i. 21–2, 356–8, 369–71, 561–2,
and ii. 170–2, 350–52.

[80] On the related attempts to use the clergy and preaching, see below,
pp. 128–9.

inferiour sort of Commons'.[81] That this distinctive argument is
James's own is suggested by Bacon's note on the warrant for the
1615 proclamation that the matter was 'signified to be yor Mātie
pleasure by Mr. Secretary Winwood'.[82]

From 1615 onwards James was increasingly determined to
compel the gentry to what he perceived to be a traditional
governmental role in the shires. He harangued them in a famous
Star Chamber speech in 1616, denouncing the creeping Italian
fashion which despised the countryside and depopulated it,
ensuring that soon 'England will onely be London'.[83] Linking
country residence firmly to Aristotelian notions of harmony and
balance in the commonwealth, he asserted that the English gentry
had moved out of their natural sphere, so that the old norms of
harmony had been destroyed. In a typical Jacobean figure, he
urged: 'as every fish lives in his own place, some in the fresh,
some in the salt, some in the mud: so let everyone live in his own
place, some at Court, some in the Citie, some in the Countrey.'
This Star Chamber speech was widely reported and recorded, and
was used later by several of the prescriptive writers on hospitality,
notably by Dalechamp, who took it as a prime text in his 1632
sermon.[84] What none of the writers seem to have grasped is the
energy with which James pursued his ideals, particularly in the
early 1620s when, for three successive Christmasses, he forced
the gentry to leave London for their country seats in a whirlwind
of confusion. Joseph Mead described the departure of 7,000
families and their 1,400 coaches just before Christmas 1622 as
a major crisis for the city, and there is evidence of individual crises
in the petitions addressed to the king for the right to remain as
a consequence of ill-health or pressing business.[85] Although
many of these petitions were successful, the King did not hesitate
on occasions to deny a request even from the nobility. When the
Countess of Lincoln sought permission to stay in town in the
winter of 1624, she was told directly by James that 'the countrey

[81] *Stuart Royal Proclamations*, i. 356–8.   [82] PRO, C82/1862/11.
[83] James I, *The Workes of James . . . King of Great Britain*, ed. James
Montague (London, 1616), 567.
[84] The relevant section of the speech is quoted in full by Caleb Dalechamp as
an appendix to *Christian Hospitalitie* (Cambridge, 1632), 125–7.
[85] *The Court and Times of James I*, ed. R. F. Williams, 2 vols. (London, 1848),
ii. 353; *APC, 1623–5*, 127, 383.

is the most fitting place for the ladies to live in, in the absence of their Lords', and that she must return and keep hospitality there.[86]

Although Charles did not display his father's rhetorical passion in upholding an ideal of country hospitality, he did continue the campaign against the urbanization of the gentry, using much the same language and assumptions. In the early 1630s this campaign reached its apogee in the prosecution of a large number of nobles and gentlemen for contravening the proclamations, especially that of 1632.[87] At this moment some of the most powerful legal and political machinery at the disposal of the crown was employed in the task of expelling the élite in order to realize a particular, and in some ways rather peculiar, vision of rural harmony. Charles's intention of recreating so many Penshursts or Saxhams was no doubt admirable in itself, though not untainted by concerns such as financial advantage for the Crown, and the need to restrict political interaction in London. Richard Fanshawe, one of those Caroline poets who, according to his wife's memoirs, believed passionately in the traditional values, was even moved to write a poem on the King's proclamation of 1630. In it Charles was praised for forcing upon the collective consciousness of the élite the happiness of English peace, when compared to the rage of war beyond England's shores and

> To roll themselves in envy'd leisure,
> He therefore sends the Landed Heirs,
> Whilst he proclaims not his own pleasure
> So much as theirs.[88]

But, when we examine both the Fanshawe poem and other views expressed on country life in Caroline court culture, it appears that the active vision of country service and country hospitality, from which James, and indeed Jonson, started, has been transmuted once again into the old dichotomy between *otium* and *negotium*. For Fanshawe there is no sense that duty beckoned in the shires:

---

[86] *C.St.P. Dom., 1623–5*, 378.

[87] Inner Temple Lib., Petyt MS. 538/43, fos. 178 ff.; J. Rushworth, *Historical Collections*, 7 vols. (London, 1659–1701), ii. 288–93.

[88] N. H. Nicolas (ed.), *Memoirs of Lady Fanshawe, wife of . . . Sir Richard Fanshawe . . .* (London, 1829), 35; H. J. C. Grierson and G. Bullough (eds.), *Oxford Book of Seventeenth Century Verse* (Oxford, 1934), 448–52.

instead the rhetoric of rural peace and plenty predominated. The country is here a retreat, even more obviously than in Carew's poems, and the benefits of that retreat accrue to the individual and his family rather than to the larger commonwealth. The same transmutation can be observed in one of the best of the Caroline poems praising country-house living: Richard Lovelace's 'Amyntor's Grove', probably written for Endymion Porter, Charles I's gentleman of the bedchamber.[89] For Lovelace, the country life is one in which relationships are of great importance, but are not the old relationships of lord and tenant, great house, servants, and community. Instead it is the sensibilities of the nuclear family, and the affinities between their harmony and that of nature that is hymned. Caroline Platonist sentiment is an acquired taste that scarcely commanded more general enthusiasm from the seventeenth-century élite than it has done from historians. However, it did in this instance speak to an aspect of that élite's experience in the years preceding the Civil War. Great Tew and Little Gidding could be cited as clear examples of desire for physical and intellectual retreat from the pressures of an urbanizing society.

The limitation of the ideal of hospitality essentially to a rural context in the early Stuart period can be interpreted as having a variety of consequences. In certain ways the narrowing of focus and definition proved a strength, since the élite was compelled by the intervention of the Crown, and by the constant haranguing of the moralists, to think and perhaps act more self-consciously than before in the management of rural relationships. Those who followed what they believed to be tradition were now able to affirm their behaviour in funeral epitaphs and sermons, and to cite King James as the chief maintainer of their views. It required a new degree of calculation and deliberation to live in the countryside and *not* make serious gestures of hospitality: it was, for example, one of the issues that Sir George Sondes felt compelled to address when he defended himself from a variety of charges of unneighbourly behaviour in the 1650s.[90] However,

---

[89] Richard Lovelace, *Poems*, ed. C. H. Wilkinson (Oxford, 1930), 71–4. For a discussion of the poem, see McGuire, 'Cavalier Country-House Poem', 101–3.

[90] Sir George Sondes, 'Narrative of the Death of his Two Sons', in *Harleian Miscellany*, 10, 49. For an account of Sondes see A. Everitt, *The Community of Kent and the Great Rebellion* (Leicester, 1966), 50–2, 299.

the narrowing and intensification of focus was also a weakness: not only did it implicitly, and sometimes explicitly, exempt the ruling orders from giving hospitality outside their own rural property, it also entangled traditional social duties of an onerous kind with that vision of the countryside as the place of retreat and lesiure that appealed to court writers. Since neither local administration nor a constant vigilance in caring for the poor were quite the easy and spontaneous activities that Jonson and others praised, there was a problem in persuading the élite to take positive action in the countryside. It must have been a tempting alternative to regard the country simply as a retreat, as the setting for hunting parties and the entertainment of fellow-gentlemen. Moreover, the notion of rusticity, attractive enough when applied purely to nature, was acquiring pejorative overtones when applied to men in nature's setting.[91] To identify the 'good old hospitality' with rustic values was to isolate it from the world of civility which held an increasing sway with the landed orders, and therefore to impoverish it.

II

While the changing secular values associated with civility and the growth of London did much both to fragment and focus the notion of hospitality, it might be more appropriate to see the fundamental challenge to the old integrative aristocratic ideal as arising from Protestant thought. If we take a very broad view of the impact of Protestantism from the break with Rome to the Restoration, it is difficult to deny that it contributed to a fundamental redefinition of charity, and hence of the nature of household giving and entertainment. The familiar focus of this change, as described by Jordan and others, is the new relationship between faith and works.[92] Since works were no longer efficacious for salvation, the need to offer personal charity, that is charity which was directed above all by a consideration of its value to the donor, in an indiscriminate manner, was

[91] Williams, *Country and City*, 32–4.
[92] W. K. Jordan, *Philanthropy in England, 1480–1660* (London, 1959), 151 ff.

removed. Allied to the new doctrine of the priesthood of all believers, and to a growing antipathy to idleness and waste which may or may not, according to the taste of the historian, be seen as peculiarly Protestant, this new perception of works as significant only as the fruits of faith, led to the institutionalization of charity at the hands of both the private benefactor and of the state. Once the general Christian duty of being charitable was separated from the urgent personal quest for the means to salvation that marked the late medieval period, it was then possible to take a much cooler look at the mechanisms of giving, to ask above all what purposes they served for the recipient and for the wider community, as well as for the donor. It was in this new intellectual climate that calculations of social utility, and the discrimination between the deserving and the undeserving poor, never wholly absent in the medieval period, achieved prominence, and were enshrined in legislation as well as effectively defended in the casuistry of the second and third generation of godly divines, such as Perkins and Sibbes.[93]

The broad vision of Protestant charity thus summarized has much to commend it. However, it rests on a dichotomy between faith and works which, though of great ideological significance, seems much less important when considered at the level of practice. The seven works of mercy were invoked as a model of charitable behaviour almost as often by Protestant authors of the early seventeenth century as by their Catholic predecessors. Sermons such as Richard Curteys's *The Care of a Christian Conscience* (1600) continued to model themselves directly on the seven works and to talk in very traditional terms of the duties of the Christian.[94] Even the Puritan casuists did not neglect models that would have been used before the Reformation: Downame and Allen, for example, wrote of household-giving in terms which differ little from those employed in the fifteenth-century homily *Dives and Pauper*, though they enlarged their view of Christian giving to include new patterns that would have

---

[93] On Puritan attitudes to poverty, see R. Greaves, *Society and Religion in Elizabethan England* (Minnesota, 1981), 554–68. A powerful exposition is given in Perkins, *The Whole Treatise of Cases of Conscience*, ed. T. F. Merrill (Nieuwkoop, Neths., 1966), 225–9.

[94] Richard Curteys, *The Care of a Christian Conscience* (London, 1600), 4th sermon.

been less familiar to an earlier audience.[95] If we seek a broad model for the impact of Protestantism it might be best to turn instead to the idea that both Renaissance and Reformation thinking on poverty involved a rejection of the personal, non-monetary aspects of giving, in favour of a more organized and activist attempt to define the poor as a separate group and to provide effective means for their relief and control. John Bossy has suggested that 'the state of enlarged sociability, which was what Augustine and the medieval Church had principally meant by charity, lost persuasiveness as a high object of Christian aspiration'.[96] The idea of *caritas*, as a Christian virtue to be practised in all kinds of neighbourly behaviour and in acts of social integration, gradually transmuted itself into a philanthropic concern for poverty which was distanced from the individual social act, and hence more readily expressed through monetary giving of an impersonal kind. This pattern was already gaining ground in England, as on the Continent, from at least the early sixteenth century onwards, and can be found in some of those assumptions of civic humanism considered earlier in this chapter.[97] Protestantism, with its denial of the efficacy of prayer for the dead, its preoccupation with justification by faith alone, and its commitment to Christian discipline, appropriated this social concern and gave it further ideological force.

It may be, however, that any generalization that seeks to comprehend the diversity of Protestant thinking on poverty and hospitality is inadequate. Time, circumstance, and variations of individual theological position guaranteed that there would be very different voices from within a supposedly monolithic reformed position. It is peculiarly difficult to think of the mid-Tudor generation of Protestant activists as sharing the same values as some of the Jacobean and Caroline godly: only the biblical texts provide a close link between the two. For the Edwardian divines who first raised the problem of poverty in a specifically Protestant context, the primary concern was the securing of traditional forms of distributive justice in a new doctrinal environment. They

---

[95] John Downame, *The Plea of the Poore. Or a Treatise of Beneficence and Almes-Deeds* (London, 1616); Robert Allen, *A Treatise of Christian Beneficence* (London, 1600).

[96] Bossy, *Christianity in the West, 1400–1700* (Oxford, 1986), 143.

[97] See above, pp. 97–9.

had to deflect the Catholic charge that reformed theology exonerated men from the need to perform good works, while also responding to the humanist concerns for the collective good of the commonwealth, to that social activism already considered in the context of *Utopia* and the 1536 Poor Law. Bucer's answer, that charity should be distributed centrally by public officials in order to ensure equity and to avoid hubris in the individual giver, found little response in the preaching of Latimer, Lever, Turner, or Becon.[98] There was, of course, a willingness to support public or municipal projects for poor relief: witness Ridley's role in the foundation of the London hospitals.[99] However, the reiterated message of the pulpit was that charitable behaviour was demanded of every Christian, that the obligation to do good could not be displaced onto some public body, and that the personal relationship between the rich and the poor was a necessary part of virtuous giving. In the context of domestic entertainment this meant that in many ways the reformers were willing to appeal to an idealized version of the past, and to argue that householders should perform their traditional roles, no longer as a matter of unreflecting sociability, or in the generalized hope of merit accruing from the prayers of the poor, but as a godly duty carefully undertaken. William Turner's precise construction of a model of hospitality, with the hierarchy of separate dining arrangements, is a characteristic, if elaborate, production of this generation.[100] The reformers sought to engage the élite in particular in a reaffirmation of the customary roles of good lordship, which would guarantee the continuation of the open house as a means of nurturing the poor.

Yet although the images might be traditional, they were used in a deliberately radical critique of existing patterns of behaviour. The rich had neglected their customary duties and, according to Lever, 'buyld many fayre houses, and kepe few good houses'.[101] The preachers identified with the poor, not because they sought to challenge basic beliefs in hierarchy and order, but

---

[98] Martin Bucer, *A Treatise How . . . Christian Mens Almose Ought to be Distributed* (1557?) 9–11.

[99] J. Ridley, *Nicholas Ridley* (London, 1957), 284–8.

[100] William Turner, *A New Book of Spirituall Physik for Dyverse Diseases of the Nobilitie and Gentlemen of Englande* (Emden, 1555), fo. 68ᵛ.

[101] Thomas Lever, *Sermons*, ed. E. Arber (London, 1870), 88.

because they were passionately convinced that the landed
orders and their rich allies were themselves destroying God-given
social harmony. Thus, William Turner acknowledged that there
were a few noblemen who kept 'honest and honorable houses',
but denounced the majority for failing to use their resources
properly for the domestic relief of the poor.[102] The rhetoric
of identification between the preacher and the poor is nowhere
more vividly displayed than in Becon's *The Pathway unto Prayer*
(1542), in which the lavishness of the rich is denounced and the
decay of hospitality mourned, a situation 'unto the grat
hinderance, yea, and almost the utter desolation of the
commonweal, as we poor wretches shall feel within these few
years'.[103] Apocalyptic urgency is the hallmark of much of this
writing, an urgency which permits of few fine distinctions
between the types of the needy, or much detailed consideration
of the precise means by which their material wants might be
relieved. The crucial concern, as an early Elizabethan text
expressed it, was to love thy neighbour, 'effectuously supporting
one an other', and through hospitality to 'eate thy bread with
the hungry and poore, and cover the naked with thy clothes'.[104]
Occasionally the preachers found it useful to employ the
aristocratic ethos of their audiences in support of this urgent
vision: Lever in particular reminded them that there was an
expectation that the gentry would maintain good houses, and
would thereby readily persuade others to good behaviour.[105]
But if great men could not be cajoled by appeals to their
customary activities, the reformers had no doubt that they must
be compelled into generosity by threats of the imminent decay
or collapse of the commonweal.

Thus, the Edwardian divines used traditional ideals of
household charity and of deep personal involvement with the
poor, to pose a radical challenge to existing behaviour. Their
reluctance to use the division of the poor into the deserving and
the undeserving is at one with their broad moral challenge: it

[102] Turner, *A New Book*, fo. 67.
[103] Thomas Becon, *Works*, ed. J. Ayre, 3 vols. (Parker Soc., Cambridge, 1843–4), i, 174.
[104] Stephen Bateman, *A Christall Glasse of Christian Reformation* (London, 1569), sig. m 1.
[105] Lever, *Sermons*, 88.

signifies little, and merely provides men with an excuse to escape a part of their social duties. Although this forceful evangelical message lost much of its power after the Marian crisis and the establishment of the Elizabethan Settlement, it remained one current of thinking about the poor throughout the period. The basic Christian message of *caritas* could never be wholly gainsaid by the godly, and even the most restricted view of charity had to admit that the really destitute must always be helped. William Perkins, whose narrowing definitions of alms-giving will be considered below, argued that when the godly man encountered extreme need it was his obligation to relieve it to the limit of his ability.[106] There were others who kept alive a far more extensive version of the old vision: Thomas Drant and William Bedel, for example, both preaching on the care of the poor in the early 1570s, argued that there should be no precise discrimination between persons in the giving of alms.[107] Both used the key text on the casting of bread upon the waters to support their plea for generosity. At the end of the century there are still echoes of this idea of catholicity in giving in the writings of Vaughan, Curteys, and Samuel Garey; indeed, in the 1590s it enjoyed a revival under the pressure of economic crisis and government concern for the poor.[108] The importance of this continuing emphasis on broad, and hence largely indiscriminate, Christian charity, was that it helped to perpetuate the links between alms-giving and household hospitality. The household remained the ideal theatre for the species of general giving that sought to imitate the seven works of mercy, and was also the most promising unit for emergency relief even after the establishment of urban and parochial rates had begun to address the chronic problem of poverty.

It must have been considerations of this order that prompted government interest in the idea of general hospitality in the 1590s. Since the 1530s the Crown had shown no overt legislative concern for hospitality as one of the social duties of the élite. Then in June 1595, in the first of the years of serious dearth

---

[106] Perkins, *Treatise*, 226.

[107] Henry Bedel, *A Sermon Exhortyng to Pitie the Poore* (London, 1572); Thomas Drant, *A Fruitfull and Necessary Sermon, Specially Concernyng Almesgeving* (London, 1572).

[108] Vaughan, *Golden Grove*, chs. 25, 28; Curteys, *Christian Conscience*, sig. Fvii r; Samuel Garey, *A Newe Yeares Gift for the Suole* (London, 1615), 7–9.

Elizabeth used the Star Chamber as the setting for a speech by
her Lord Keeper, ordering the gentry home to exercise their
role as JPs in regulating supply, and to give their customary
hospitality.[109] This was followed the next year by the proclamation already mentioned as part of the series elaborated by James
and Charles, and then in December 1596 the Privy Council
ordered the Lord Mayor of London to enforce fast days on
Wednesdays and Fridays and the Archbishop of Canterbury to
instigate a preaching campaign on the need for charity.[110] The
Lord Keeper's speech of 1595 was specifically said to have been
devised by Elizabeth herself; 'without any direction from her
Council', and it is perhaps characteristic of the Queen that she
should turn to old methods of undifferentiated charity in a time
of crisis. However, the methods used in 1595–6 to revitalize the
ideal of household giving also seem redolent of Burghley's
attitudes, which were in some measure shared by his son, Robert
Cecil.[111] The choice of an attack on consumption and the strict
enforcement of fast days echoes Burghley's earlier concern for
sumptuary legislation, and he is known to have taken a close
interest in hospitable provision both in his own household and
in relation to the bishops and clergy.[112] It may be that the Queen
and Burghley only saw the provision of indiscriminate household
charity by the élite as a temporary measure to counter an
immediate crisis, but there is probably also a preference for
voluntarism and for giving that emanated from the individual
establishment embedded in their behaviour.

The immediate consequence of the Privy Council's letter to
the Archbishop was the issue of three new homilies 'To move
Compassion towards the Poore and Needy'.[113] This was followed
by a preaching campaign, from which at least one sermon survives
in print: Richard Curteys's *Care of a Christian Conscience*.

[109] John Hawarde, *Les Reportes del Cases in Camera Stellata, 1593 to 1609*,
ed. W. P. Baildon (London, 1894), 19–21.

[110] *APC, 1596–7*, 293, 381, 384–5.

[111] On Robert Cecil's social policy, see J. R. Kent, 'Social Attitudes of Members
of Parliament, 1590–1624', London Ph.D. dissertation (1971), 64 ff.

[112] N. B. Harte, 'State Control of Dress and Social Change in Pre-Industrial
England', in D. C. Coleman and A. H. John (eds.), *Trade, Government and Economy
in Pre-Industrial England* (London, 1976); Peck, *Desiderata Curiosa*, I. i. 29.

[113] *Three Sermons, or Homelies to Moove Compassion towards the Poore*
(London, 1596), no fol.

Other works, such as Henry Arthington's *Provision for the Poore* (1597) and Samuel Bird's *Lectures on . . . 2nd Epistle to the Corinthians* (1598) show the influence of the renewed interest in hospitality, even though they were not a direct response to the preaching order.[114] The homilies represent a direct continuation of the Edwardian tradition: their emphasis is on the need for catholicity in giving, and on the essential brotherhood of the rich and poor. The household was still seen as the natural meeting-ground for all men; sociable entertainment of friends, 'whereby . . . neighbourhood and societie is maintayned', was not challenged, but the crucial importance of integrating the poor was stressed above all. The poor must be received in the house if necessary, since Christians must remember their common humanity. 'Why', the second homily asked rhetorically, 'shoulde wee thinke scorne to receive them into our houses, whom God has placed with us in the same house of the world?'[115] To this broad plea Curteys, and no doubt others, added the specific critique of the behaviour of the gentry required by the Council. The élite were charged with neglect of their country duties, with breaking up their household, and with escaping to London to avoid the cost of entertainment in time of dearth. Instead they must return to the countryside, 'to uphold that port, worship and credit, which their forefathers did', and share their bread with the poor.[116] In all the discussions on hospitality in the 1590s it is the affirmation of common humanity and neighbourhood with the poor through the sharing of bread that emerges as the dominant trope. Even Samuel Bird, who as one of the godly had grave doubts about indiscriminate charity, valued household giving and the sharing of a common meal with the poor, since 'it will helpe men also against that disdaine which is naturally in them'.[117]

After the immediate dearth crisis of the 1590s had passed, it is more difficult to trace pleas for the undifferentiated care of

---

[114] There is a section on fasting and giving food to the poor in Vaughan's *Golden Grove* that also suggests the direct influence of the Privy Council's initiative.

[115] *Three Sermons.*

[116] Curteys, *Christian Conscience*, sig. Fvii[r].

[117] Samuel Bird, *The Lectures . . . on the 8th and 9th Chapters of the Second Epistle to the Corinthians* (Cambridge, 1598), 79.

the poor within the household in the prescriptive writings of the major divines and moralists. To understand this transition it is necessary to return to the early years of Elizabeth's reign, and to the development of the alternative methods of considering the problem of poverty: differentiation between the categories of the poor, and emphasis on public rather than private provision. Separation of the needy into the deserving and the undeserving had, as already observed, a respectable history both in medieval theory and practice. It was also present as a part of the calculations of the humanist activists who framed the 1536 Poor Law, indeed in many ways it was already a commonplace of Tudor society, justifying harsh treatment of vagrancy. The intriguing juxtaposition of the harsh 1547 Act against Vagrancy with the beginnings of the preaching of the godly commonwealth men on the theme of social justice, has often been remarked.[118] Therefore, when Laurence Humphrey denounced 'vagabonds nedeless and vicious' at the beginning of Elizabeth's reign, he was not adopting any new perspective on the problem of poverty.[119] Even Thomas Becon, who could plead so eloquently for Christian *caritas*, saw no incongruity in denouncing 'idle lubbers and sturdy queanes' who were likely to take relief from the sick, the lame, and the blind.[120] The denunciation of beggars and vagrancy became, as is well known, a major aspect of Elizabeth legislation, although it was gradually balanced by a more systematic attempt to disentangle various groups of the deserving poor from the truly shiftless. The general development of the debate on the poor is not our concern here, but the specific issue of vagrancy is important because an attack on begging was very easily transmuted into a questioning of the traditional basis of household giving, the provision of alms at the gate. It is also important that hostility to begging, while shared by all sections of the Tudor élite, because identified with certain assumptions of the godly on discipline, labour, and the merits of the saints, assumptions which ultimately became divisive and sectional in the Stuart period.[121]

[118] W. R. D. Jones, *The Mid-Tudor Crisis, 1539–63* (London, 1973), 135–9.
[119] Laurence Humphrey, *The Nobles or Of Nobility* (London, 1563), bk. iii.
[120] Becon, *The Sicke Mans Salve* (London, 1561), 146.
[121] Greaves, *Society and Religion*, 383–91, though the divergence between Puritan and other Protestant attitudes is exaggerated here.

By the early 1570s the language of Protestantism could be used with powerful effect against vagrancy. The marginalia of the 1560 edition of the Geneva Bible had denounced the practice of giving to the wicked, while the later Beza–Tomson edition challenged that of giving to the idle.[122] In 1571, when parliament debated the problem of vagrancy, Thomas Wilson, the Master of Requests, invoked scripture to demonstrate '*ne sit mendicus inter vos*', and to argue that there should be no indiscriminate giving, and that beggars should be imprisoned.[123] It was only a short step from this position to that adopted by Perkins in his *Whole Treatise of Cases of Conscience* (1606). Since the vagrant and beggar were to be condemned not only as a threat to the order of the commonwealth, but as an offence against God's law, then begging itself, even by those unable to work or defend themselves, was reprehensible. 'They are not allowed', he argued, 'to gather their almost themselves by begging from doore to doore, but to be releeved at home in their houses'.[124] This is an extreme statement, but one which merely carries the general disapprobation of mendicancy to its logical conclusion. Samuel Bird provided a more sympathetic interpretation of the problem of poverty, albeit one equally hostile to the idle and vicious. He agreed with Perkins that pleading for alms was of itself to be reprehended, not so much because it was inherently sinful, as because of what it suggested about the behaviour of the giver. 'This forcing of men to aske is a shaming of them . . . That reliefe is most acceptable unto God, that is the most comfortable to the parties to be releeved: but giving without begging is most comfortable . . .'.[125] Both views challenged the casual assumptions on which the giving of gate doles were based, and both anticipated treating the impotent poor with humanity and dignity, though Perkins seems to see them more as a separated and isolated subgroup than Bird.

The poor laws which were finally completed in the Acts of 1598 and 1601 not only enshrined the general hostility to vagrancy, but acknowledged in some measure the idea that shame was attached to any form of request for casual alms. The 1598

---

[122] Ibid. 559–60.
[123] *Proceedings in the Parliaments of Elizabeth I, 1559–1581, ed. T. E. Hartley* (London, 1981), 219
[124] Perkins, *Whole Treatise*, 226.
[125] Bird, *Lectures on Corinthians*, 12.

law was the culmination of the movement of the earlier acts of 1572 and 1576 towards a compulsory poor-rate, the restriction of vagrants to their place of settlement, and the provision of work for the able poor. These moves not only affirmed the public nature of poor relief, but followed the direction of separation between the poor and the household, the former being seen as a subgroup to be disciplined and/or relieved by public arrangements, as a separate body within the community. After 1598, casual alms-giving was prohibited without licence, normally from a JP, although local begging could be sanctioned by the overseers. Robert Allen, in his paean of praise on the passing of the Act, claimed that it had suppressed those sturdy rogues 'by whom all mercy of alms-giving was so violently catched up and devoured'.[126] Michael Drayton, in an intriguing scene in his play about Sir John Oldcastle, the Lollard knight, has a group of poor men begging for alms at Lord Cobham's Kentish manor-house and lamenting that 'if a poore man come to a doore to aske for Gods sake, they aske him for a licence, or a certificate from a Justice'.[127] Cobham does not ask for these evidences, but expresses his doubts about giving by abusing his steward Haproole, who is a defender of the old ways. The beggars are eventually relieved, but not before Drayton has made a double point, about the restrictive attitudes of a Lollard knight towards charity, and about the excuse which Elizabethan legislation offered to those who did not wish to perform their traditional domestic duties. At least Cobham's poor had an easier experience than that of unfortunate travellers who appeared in the Suffolk parish of William Bedell in the Jacobean period. They were interrogated by the godly divine, 'mixing both wholsom instructions and severe reproofs', and were sent to the constable if they did not have adequate documents proving their right to travel and beg. Understandably Bedell's biographer was able to claim that the travelling people 'shun'd the town for the most part, to the no small quiet and security of him and all his neighbours'.[128]

---

[126] Allen, *Treatise of Christian Beneficence*, 1.
[127] Michael Drayton, *Works*, ed. J. W. Hebel, 5 vols. (Oxford, 1961), i. 405.
[128] *Two Biographies of William Bedell, Bishop of Kilmore*, ed. E. S. Shuckburgh (Cambridge, 1902), 19.

A number of reasons might be adduced for the direction of poor-relief legislation away from casual household alms and towards a disciplined and public approach to the problem of poverty. The one that is most relevant here is that this view conformed most closely with that of those 'active Calvinists' who had become the driving force behind schemes for the poor in many English towns and some villages during the 1580s and 1590s.[129] The city fathers of Norwich and Warwick wholeheartedly subscribed to the belief that there were idle and vagrant poor who must be disciplined, and impotent poor who must be given consistent and well-structured relief.[130] Moreover, such men had no close interest in the maintenance of the old world of domestic loyalties that were enshrined in the great house. They were able to sever their ties with the old, personalized view of poverty because they had other, more efficacious, methods at their disposal. The endowment of almshouses and the establishment of funds for the assistance of the able-bodied poor who could be set to work satisfied their sense of personal duty, while the daily regulation of the supply of food, or of outdoor relief, was undertaken by actions that were merely an extension of the old urban traditions of collective action. In some parts of the country village élites adopted much the same pattern, isolating the poor as a subgroup and wholeheartedly accepting the legislative view that they were best organized and disciplined on a parochial basis through the levying of a poor rate. Both urban and rural élites often came to regard the poor law as a part of that process of reformation of manners and social control which assumed an increased significance from the 1580s onwards.[131] It is tempting to associate these developments with a specifically 'godly' mind-set, in which poverty became the consequence of sin, and an indication of individual worthlessness, rather than merely of the general tragedy of man's postlapsarian

[129] See e.g., K. Wrightson and D. Levine, *Poverty and Piety in an English Village* (Cambridge, 1979), 157 ff.

[130] J. F. Pound, 'An Elizabethan Census of the Poor', *Univ. of Birmingham Historical Journal*, 8 (1962), 135–51; A. L. Beier, 'The Social Problems of an Elizabethan Country Town: Warwick 1580-90', in P. Clark (ed.), *Country Towns in Pre-Industrial England* (Leicester, 1981), 46–79.

[131] Slack, *Poverty and Policy*, 130–1.

state.[132] A 'collective paranoia' towards the poor, expressed in obsessive rhetoric about drunkenness, whoredom, and godlessness is one of the least attractive consequences of this concern with social discipline.

It would, however, be an unwarranted oversimplification to identify the retreat from household charity exclusively with Puritanism and social control. While most 'Puritan' authors of the Elizabethan and Jacobean periods spoke in hostile terms of undifferentiated giving, many were emphatic supporters of domestic care for the poor, and some at least expressed doubts about the rapid growth in the public organization of relief. They opposed precisely that sense of separation, of the needy as 'other', which has just been discussed. In 1572 Edward Dering, that early model of godly nonconformity, was in trouble with the authorities for questioning the appropriateness of the poor law, partly on the grounds that the rich had an obligation to provide, which his enemies read as a statement of communitarianism, and partly because the needy could be committed to the 'rich to be kept'.[133] Although Dering denied these statements, they are not incompatible with the godly radicalism of the mid-century, which found some echo in later writings. Dering himself argued that he had merely spoken of the 'mutual duty of poor and rich', but even this language suggests that he was interested in the direct and reciprocal relationship between social groups, a relationship that might be seen as threatened by the operation of an impersonal poor law.[134] Godly writers were certainly eager to argue that a Christian's duty did not end merely with the payment of monetary alms to a collector. Bird, introducing his argument on the merits of hospitality towards the poor, stated: 'we must bid the poore to our houses, notwithstanding our money collection'.[135] Thus far there would have been little dissent among Protestants about the basic duty to offer relief in as many forms as possible. If it proved difficult to reconcile hostility to

---

[132] A 'Puritan' caricature, or total embodiment of this attitude, can be seen in Phillip Stubbes, *The Anatomy of Abuses in England*, ed. F. J. Furnivall (New Shakspere Soc., 6th ser., London, 1877), pt. 1.

[133] J. Strype, *Annals of the Reformation*, 7 vols. (Oxford, 1824), II. i. 414.

[134] P. Collinson, *Godly People: Essays on English Protestantism and Puritanism* (London, 1983), 309–10.

[135] Bird, *Lectures on Corinthians*, 79.

begging with enthusiasm for the entertainment of the poor, the two themes might be left to coexist uneasily within the same text, as they did in William Vaughan's *Golden Grove*.[136] The one issue on the organization of giving that differentiated a few specifically Presbyterian authors from the rest was that of the office of deacon. Dering may have been reluctant to witness the extension of state-organized relief not only because of his concern for the intensely personal operation of Christian duty, but because he saw the deacon as the crucial agent of charity. This is probably what underlies Perkins's later comment that each church had an obligation to care for its own poor.[137]

This specifically Puritan view of restricted giving leads on towards the more general problem of the worthy recipients of charity. It always proved easier to exclude groups, the vagabond and shiftless persons, than to define precisely who should receive care. The biblical injunction to care for those who were of the 'household of faith' became the critical referent-point for such discussions. In most sixteenth-century texts, regardless of the precise persuasion of the author on other doctrinal issues, the injunction to care for the 'household of faith' was taken as a guide to the ordering of priorities in the giving of charity.[138] Although all men not specifically identifiable as worthless should potentially be the subject of Christian care, yet priority could and should be given to the godly, since this was compatible with the Pauline injunctions and with the teaching of Augustine and Ambrose. This selective attitude could encourage the godly to continue to provide for the poor via the household, for they were now required primarily to accept a congenial subgroup rather than all comers. It may be that Bird and Vaughan, in advocating the feeding of the poor at the table, had this division of the godly from the rest as their model. When Sir Thomas Hoby provided board and lodging for three widows in his household at Hackness, it must surely have been a condition of their residence that they acted as part of the 'fellowship of the saints'.[139] It was when the

---

[136] Vaughan, *Golden Grove*, ch. 25.
[137] Perkins, 'A Golden Chaine or the Description of Theology', in *Works* (London, 1626), i. 92.
[138] See e.g., Downame, *Plea of the Poore*, 128–38; Gouge, *A Learned . . . Commentary on the Whole Epistle to the Hebrews* (London, 1655), ch. 6, sect. 71.
[139] PRO, STAC 5, H22/21.

separation of the virtuous from the rest becomes specifically a separation of the saints that a general Protestant attitude to neighbourly charity acquires definably Puritan overtones. Ministering to the saints might well involve giving the best of household charity to a small group, like the widows whom the Hobys maintained.[140] Most writers and preachers were at pains to point out that charity could never be wholly exclusive, and that well-doing and right-giving were signs of sanctification. Nevertheless, close identification with the saints was an acceptable part of Christian stewardship. Samuel Hieron summarized the matter effectively in a 1612 funeral sermon: 'The principall and first respect must bee to the Household of Faith, and that the bowels of the poore Saints may bee comforted. To such, a man must give both more affectionately, and more liberally.'[141]

The fellowship of the saints was above all a spiritual brotherhood, in which charity was first perceived as a matter of doing good in the spirit, and only secondarily concerned with material welfare. But charity to the 'poor in spirit' was often a blend of Christian counsel to the afflicted and substantive aid. John Dethick of West Newton was said by the preacher of his funeral sermon to have poured out his material charity to the poor, especially of the household of faith, 'not so much out of the hand as heart', always considering the spiritual needs of the recipients.[142] It followed that, for the select company of the godly poor, there was little of that sense of separation, of the abstract doing of good, that became the mark of some Protestant dealings with the needy. This chosen group, who incidentally were often seen as including ministers of the gospel and exiles who were temporarily impoverished, were those who could really provide blessing on their benefactors. 'Who knoweth', asked Robert Allen, 'how great blessing God will grant at their holy suit and supplication, to those good householders and families, where they are at any time, for the Lord's sake, kindly and lovingly entertained?'[143] Spiritual brotherhood created social

---

[140] PRO, STAC 5, H22/21.

[141] Samuel Hieron, *The Life and Death of Dorcas* (London, 1612), sig. C3.

[142] William Knapp, *Abraham's Image in One of his Sonnes* [John Dethick, esq. of West Newton] (London, 1657), 33.

[143] Allen, *Treatise of Christian Beneficence*, 88.

connections which might well be vertical rather than horizontal: Mrs Dorothy Hanbury, the zealous wife of Edward Hanbury of Kelmarsh, Northamptonshire, was said to delight 'in the meanest Saints, as if they had been persons of the greatest rank; she esteemed their company as a corner of heaven . . .'[144] Numerous Puritan biographies emphasize the pleasure that the godly derived in the society of the like-minded, regardless of their social standing. For example, John Bruen, whose Cheshire home was on the main route to Ireland, used his home as 'the common Inne, or constant harbour of the Church and of Gods children, and himself as Gaius, a godly and good Hoste, to give them liberall and cheerfull entertainment as they came unto him'.[145] This stress on spiritual brotherhood, and limited interest in the discussion of material charity outside a chosen circle, could have curious consequences. Francis Russell, second Earl of Bedford, was one of those godly Elizabethan noblemen who was exceptionally generous to the poor, and won plaudits from the ballad-makers and the Queen for his behaviour. Yet his funeral sermon is silent on his charitable activities, except in so far as they involved the exercise of spiritual care towards his neighbours.[146] Although it is easier to find 'Puritan' discussions of material charity than is sometimes implied by historians, it is surely right to argue that the godly were more interested in discussing duties which were subsumed under the First Table of the Law, duties to God rather than to man.[147]

While it is possible to identify some characteristically 'godly' or 'Puritan' elements within the general Protestant perception of household charity, it would be unwise to isolate them as part of a wholly separate typology. Calvinist social theory, while it stressed the importance of First Table duties over those of the Second Table, nevertheless still concerned itself with the general Christian obligation of charity. Hostility to beggars was in some

---

[144] Samuel Ainsworth, *A Sermon Preached at the Funeral of Mrs. Dorothy Hanbury* (London, 1642).

[145] William Hinde, *A Faithfull Remonstrance of the Holy Life and Happy Death of John Bruen of Bruen Stapleford* (London, 1641), 185.

[146] Thomas Sparke, *A Sermon Preached at Chenies . . . at the Buriall of . . . the Earle of Bedford* (London, 1585); Greaves, *Religion and Society*, 592.

[147] S. McGee, *The Godly Man in Stuart England* (New Haven, Conn., 1976), 189 f.

measure countered by a deep concern for the local poor which could be revealed as readily in household entertainment as in the provision of almshouses. For Gouge, Sibbes, and Perkins it was always crucial that the godly man should perform his duties of material care to show the fruits of faith: they offered 'evidences' of that presence of grace within the soul that were constantly needed in the quest of assurance of salvation.[148] In seeking for a counter-ideology in developing 'Anglican' thought, we need to proceed equally cautiously, since so much of what has been described as hospitality to the poor was as acceptable to Henry Hammond or John Hales as to godly Puritans. It may be, as has often been argued, that conformists and Laudians stressed Second Table duties, and therefore material charity rather than spiritual brotherhood. The interest of a number of the divines of the 1630s and early 1640s in reason and in a rejection of predestinarian theology, meant that their interest in the passionate denunciation of poverty and vagrancy as the consequence of man's innate sinfulness lessened. Initially a preacher like Lancelot Andrewes continued to make the customary distinctions between the deserving and undeserving poor, and discussed the poor in spirit in language very similar to that of Perkins.[149] However, by the 1640s, when Hammond came to consider the poor in his *Practical Catechism* (1645), he was far more concerned with the excuses that men made for not assisting them—that they were vagabonds or sturdy beggars—than with arguing for any bounds to Christian charity.[150] Almsgiving became for Hammond 'the queen of heaven', while an extreme reaction against Perkins's attitude to beggary is to be found in Hales's Shrove Tuesday sermon in which he commented that when 'the hungry man begs at thy gate . . . thou art in debt to him for his dinner'.[151]

Yet even the Anglican apologists did not really revolt against the attitudes to poverty that had emerged as dominant at the end of the sixteenth century. Charity for them, as for their Puritan

[148] McGee, *The Godly Man*, 92–4, 189 f.
[149] Lancelot Andrewes, *Sermons*, ed. J. P. Wilson and J. Bliss, 5 vols. (Library of Anglo-Catholic Theology, Oxford, 1841–3), v. 43–7.
[150] Henry Hammond, *A Practical Catechism* (Library of Anglo-Catholic Theology, Oxford, 1847), 163–73.
[151] John Hales, *Works*, 3 vols. (Glasgow, 1765), ii. 160.

opponents, was in practice a matter of discriminating between the worthy and the unworthy, and of treating the worthy as a group to be helped in a variety of contexts, of which the household was only one, and no longer perhaps the most important. Moreover, the views of the divines, although favourably disposed towards sympathy with the poor and some measure of good fellowship, scarcely amounted to that passionate sense of identification with the needy that has been characteristic of the first generation of Protestants. The rewards for giving were described in what McGee calls 'rapturous terms', relating the giver to Christ rather than identifying him with the recipient.[152]

It may be in this context that we should see the growing divergence between the language of hospitality and the language of charity, which, as noted earlier, is to be found in many mid-seventeenth century funeral sermons and epitaphs. The virtues of conviviality and care of the helpless continued to be related, but were juxtaposed rather than integrated: good neighbourhood was increasingly separated from the active doing of Christian good. The authors of Anglican sermons certainly did not advocate spiritual or material pride; indeed, like their predecessors they on occasion insisted that true honour was to be sought in such rituals of inversion as the washing of the feet of the poor in the Maundy celebrations.[153] However, their language often expresses sentiment about the needy that is far more distanced than that of the Edwardians. When Hammond talked of the 'godlike quality' that was consequent upon the relief of the poor, it is difficult to believe that he had avoided the sin of spiritual pride completely.[154] It is also worth observing that the preachers had little to say directly of the household or its charity. Although this is partially a result of the rhetorical style of Anglican preaching, with its avoidance of the specific and the illustrative; it may also relate to an indifference towards the old forms of giving, or at least towards their importance as socially integrative acts.

[152] McGee, *Godly Man*, 230.
[153] Farindon, *The Sermons of the Reverend Anthony Farindon*, 4 vols. (London, 1849), i. 111, 248.
[154] Hammond, *Miscellaneous Theological Works*, 3 vols. (Library of Anglo-Catholic Theology, Oxford, 1850), iii. 43.

In the decades between the 1590s and the Civil War the fragmentation of the idea of hospitality generated lively debate upon its true nature. Yet this debate, with its construction of a mythic past, and its excoriation of the cold charity of present Christians, probably did little to avert changes in social behaviour among the English élite. The rhetoric of the country, and of the sense of *communitas* associated with it, was perhaps strengthened by the firm identification so often drawn between the open household and the good rural gentleman. But in the care of the poor and of the traveller, various routes to the discharge of Christian duty were now available beyond that of household giving. And, crucially, honour and reputation were now commodities as easily sought in the shifting world of city and court as in the fastnesses of the enclosed manor-house. Good hospitality was, in this world, more likely to become a matter of personal taste than of powerful social obligation.

4

The Élite and Household Entertainment: From the Elizabethan Age to the Restoration

THE routine domestic experience of the English landowning class in the seventeenth century remained in many aspects similar to that of preceding eras. Great households, with a superfluity of servants, and hierarchical structures, remained commonplace. The country estates still provided the theatre, or perhaps one should say the scenery, within which the social rituals of local power were enacted. Precise forms of magnificence and liberality might have been modified, but these were still fundamental forms of self-definition for an élite which depended as much on influence exercised over men as on wealth as the basis of its authority. Yet within these essential continuities, little challenged even by the experience of Civil War, important changes of behaviour and style were obviously in train. The moralists, as we have seen, tended to isolate several developments that were believed to have undermined the good old ways: the drift to London, or to the other cities, prodigy building, excessive law suits, immoderate feasting and spending on clothes, and other forms of conspicuous consumption were the favourite targets for their wrath.

I

Two of these themes offer some possibility of close analysis in the context of hospitality, and some opportunity to evaluate what the obligation to be good hosts meant in practice to nobles and gentlemen in the Stuart era. The first is the drift to London, which is well documented for individuals if not for the entire social group: the second, changes in architecture and the internal arrangements of households. Discussions of the lure of London, even when penned by gentlemen themselves involved were liable, of course, to be permeated by nostalgia for the past and the countryside. Seventeenth-century biographers like D'Ewes and Clarendon tended to romanticize the experience of earlier centuries when the landed order supposedly remained based in the country, little influenced by the corrosive charms of metropolitan life.[1] This myth is scarcely supported by the evidence of the behaviour of at least the county gentry and nobility, who were regular visitors to the capital throughout our period. However, the notion that London exercised an increasing pull upon the élite is not entirely mythic: its attractive force undoubtedly did affect a growing group of families from the Elizabethan period onwards, with the 1580s and 1590s apparently marking the beginnings of a significant change in their patterns of behaviour.[2]

Individual examples lack statistical weight, but are nevertheless cumulatively evocative. Among the gentry whose domestic accounts survive for the period before the 1590s there are few cases of families who passed significant parts of the year in the capital. Lesser gentry, such as the Penruddocks of Wiltshire, managed perfectly adequately without the head of house spending any time in London: greater families, like the Gawdys of Norfolk, or the Thynnes, needed more regular contact with the capital and the court, but achieved it either by placing a member of the family permanently in the capital, or by visits by the head of house during the law terms.[3] When Thynne left Longleat on business, as he did with some regularity in the 1570s, his wife rarely went with him, though she sometimes visited her family at Broadhinton.[4] Many of the greater gentry who did intermittently indulge in the pleasures of the capital remained

---

[1] J. O. Halliwell-Phillips (ed.), *Life of Sir Simonds D'Ewes* (London, 1845), 29, 37, 41; H. R. Trevor-Roper, ed., *Selections from the Writings of the Earl of Clarendon* (Oxford, 1978), 10.

[2] L. Stone, 'The Residential Development of the West End of London in the Seventeenth Century', in B. Malament (ed.), *After the Reformation: Essays in Honour of J. H. Hexter* (Manchester 1980), 175–6.

[3] Wi. RO, 549/31; A. Hassell Smith, *County and Court: Government and Politics in Norfolk, 1558–1603* (Oxford, 1974), 66–8.

[4] Longleat, Thynne MS., Bks. 109–14.

firmly wedded to a country identity: Nathaniel Bacon of Norfolk, for example, spent a month or two each year in London, but vigorously proclaimed his identity with his own locality.[5] The assumptions with which Bacon and many of his contemporaries operated did not suddenly vanish in the 1590s; indeed, as the popularity of the city grew, so did the counter-ideology of the merits of the countryside. Practical men such as Sir John Newdigate of Warwickshire denounced the great wen as a place of vanity and idleness which 'hath undone many, enriched none . . .'.[6] London residence encouraged, on this interpretation, only further expenses and self-concern, and led the gentry to escape from their true commitments in the countryside. The advice literature of the seventeenth century is replete with examples of warnings on the dangers of the capital. Thomas Wentworth, advising the young William Savile as executor to his father's estate, argued 'you should lay aside all Thoughts of going to *London* these four or five years', so that he could learn to order his estate, employ himself in the affairs of the county, and cultivate the friendship and respect of his neighbours.[7]

Nevertheless, a decreasing number of the greater gentry were willing to avoid the temptations of London permanently. The most crucial change was surely the one which caused James I such anxiety: the growing habit of bringing wives, or indeed whole families into the city for a part of the year.[8] James denounced this horrendous practice in vigorous verse in the 1622:

> You women that doe London love so well
> whome scarce a proclamacon can expell
>
> .   .   .   .
>
> you dreame on nought but vizitts maskes and toyes
> And thinke the cuntrey contributes noe ioyes[9]

[5] Hassell Smith, *County and Court*, 169 ff; NRO, Bradfer-Lawrence, VII b/ (5).

[6] V. Larminie, 'The Lifestyle and Attitudes of the Seventeenth-Century Gentry, with Special Reference to the Newdigates of Arbury Hall, Warwickshire', Birmingham Ph.D. dissertation (1980), 392.

[7] W. Knowler (ed.), *The Earl of Strafford's Letters and Despatches*, 2 vols. (London, 1739), i. 168–9.

[8] Heal, 'The Crown, the Gentry and London', in C. Cross *et al.* (eds.), *Law and Government under The Tudors* (Cambridge, 1988), 214–15.

[9] James I, *Poems*, ed. J. Craigie, 2 vols. (Scottish Text Soc., 3rd. ser., 12, 26, Edinburgh, 1955), ii. 178.

It is possible to explain this change mechanistically, as a consequence of the development of the private coach, but political stability and the increasing concentration of fashion and culture in the capital would seem to have offered the most powerful inducements to change.[10] Whatever the initial motivation, the result was the rapid growth of a London season that led, at least by the end of the Jacobean era, to a self-perpetuating cycle of movement into the city.

The effects on an individual family can best be seen from the evidence of household accounts and diaries for the early seventeenth century. The Petres of Essex are a particularly interesting example, since they were a Catholic family who retained a conscious pride in their local role, giving generous hospitality at Christmas, and concerning themselves with the well-being of their tenantry. This did not prevent them from spending a part of each season in London in the Jacobean period. Typically, they would visit the capital for part of March and April, spend the summer oscillating between their two rural estates, and then go to London again in the autumn. Christmas was almost always spent at West Horndon, but sometimes the tedium of winter in the country apparently seized the family and they departed for the city during January.[11] The Petres had the advantage of relative proximity to the capital, and could move to and fro freely, though they normally did so only two, or at most three, times a year. They certainly never engaged in the species of perpetual motion that afflicted Elizabeth, Lady Berkeley. Her movements over a six-year period between 1629 and 1635 can be traced very precisely from her accounts, and they reveal frequent short visits to London and her other country estates from her base at Cranford in Middlesex (Table 4.1).[12] Families who lived at a greater distance from the south-east could scarcely have oscillated in this manner; instead they tended to have to make a decision to migrate for a whole season or longer. Lord William Paget, whose main country residence was at Beaudesert in Staffordshire, lived in London for the first seven months covered by his

---

[10] F. J. Fisher, 'The Growth of London as a Centre of Conspicuous Consumption', *TRHS*, 4th ser. 30 (1948), 46–64.

[11] ERO, D/DP, A25–27, 31.

[12] GLRO, Acc. 530/H1.

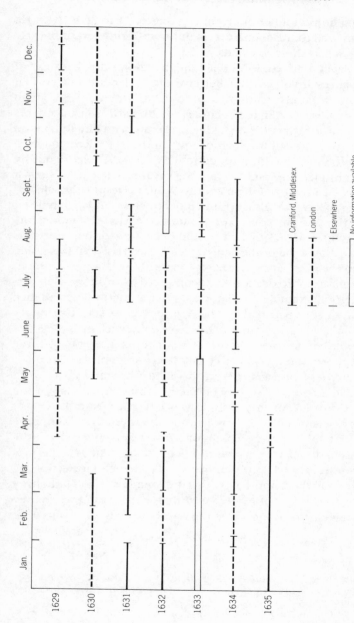

Table 4.1. Elizabeth, Lady Berkeley's places of residence, 1629–1635

surviving household book, from October 1611 to May 1612. He then removed to the country, remaining at Beaudesert until early in 1613 when the book ends.[13]

The Paget pattern is understandable not only because of the distances involved, but because of the labour and cost of removing a family from the country to the city. Sir Hugh Cholmley observed that his father, Sir Richard, ran into debts partly because he insisted on taking his family with him to London when he became MP for Scarborough in the 1621 Parliament.[14] 'Once in town they endeavoured to maximize the experience by staying until January 1622, when the royal proclamation against residence finally forced them back to Whitby. Despite the salutary warnings of royal displeasure and indebtedness, Sir Hugh himself several times went south for prolonged visits, including one for the winter of 1639 when he and his wife had their portraits painted.[15] For some of the gentry London exercised an increasing attraction as they grew older, the case of Sir Thomas Pelham, whose 'gradual intoxication' is documented by Anthony Fletcher, being a good example. Sir Thomas, after a youthful acceptance of rural Sussex, began from 1635 onwards to stay for longer periods in town, purchasing a house in Clerkenwell in 1637. Since the crown had by then almost abandoned its attempts to force out the gentry, he was able to enjoy his possession undisturbed, and from 1644 onwards began to spend Christmas away from Halland in Sussex.[16] For others, the youthful experience of the Inns of Court meant that London was never far from the centre of their consciousness, and no amount of grave advice about the need to establish housekeeping for a few years before facing the heady delights of the city would deter them. The true addicts might still return to their country seats for some months of the summer, but there must have been a number, like Humphrey Mildmay of Essex, who waited eagerly for the season when they could have 'much good company here that I wanted at Danbury'.[17]

---

[13] Folger MS., V. b.99.

[14] Hugh Cholmley, *Memoirs* (Malton, 1870), 15.   [15] Ibid. 36.

[16] A. Fletcher, *A County Community in Peace and War: Sussex 1600–1660* (London, 1975), 43–5.

[17] P. L. Ralph, *Sir Humphrey Mildmay, Royalist Gentleman* (New Brunswick, 1947), 25–6.

The only moments at which it is possible to quantify the arrival of the gentry in London are in 1622, 1632, and 1634, when the crown, in pursuit of its ambition to expel the élite, harried constables and JPs into making returns of illegal residents.[18] Unfortunately the figures can only be used to identify the tip of an iceberg: those for the Jacobean period are incomplete, and even the Caroline ones raise all the usual problems of the reliability of the recording officials. More significantly, they were only required to return delinquents, not those who had removed themselves from the city at the end of the law term, and not those who could claim court office or official business as a reason for staying.[19] Nevertheless, the counts are intriguing both for the crude totals that they offer, and for their evidence of the early settlement of families in the fashionable West End and the northern suburbs, as against the older areas of the city. In the most complete survey of 1632-3 nobles, clerics, and gentlemen of various ranks were found to be offenders against the proclamation, although only 248 were subpoenaed before Star Chamber in 1633.[20] Among the offenders were Sir Humphrey Mildmay, who was subpoenaed, and Lords Petre and Paget, who were not. It is incidentally of some interest that the great Catholic families are particularly well represented in the lists: among those present in London who would certainly not have contributed to county government were Sir John Gage, Sir Tobie Matthew, Sir John Shelley, Sir George Throckmorton, and Sir Lewis Tresham.[21]

It is not easy to evaluate the significance of the drift towards London for the exercise of traditional hospitality. The critical problem on which contemporaries usually focused was the provision of Christmas entertainment: a sensitive issue both because of the importance of the festival as an occasion for beneficence, and because it fell in the middle of the urban season. The popularity of London in midwinter was shared by some of the provincial capitals which, at least from the 1630s onwards, developed their own seasons for men who could not afford

---

[18] PRO, SP14/134/86; Bodl., Bankes MS., 14.

[19] *Stuart Royal Proclamations*, ed. J. F. Larkin and P. L. Hughes, 2 vols. (Oxford, 1973-82), i. 21-2, 44-5, 186-8.

[20] Inner Temple Lib., Petyt MS., 538/43, fo. 180 ff.

[21] At least two of those listed were under house-arrest, so unable to reside elsewhere.

the metropolis. In 1636 Anthony Mingay of Norwich complained to Framlingham Gawdy, 'we are pestered with you country knights this Christmas', men who did no good, except to raise the price of provisions.[22] The news-letter writers of London both under James and Charles were firmly of the opinion that a substantial section of the élite wished to stay in towns at Christmas, and were resentful of the crown's attempts to expel them.[23] Moralists shared the view that absenteeism at this critical time of year was on the increase as a result of greed and hubris. Samuel Garey, preaching an assize sermon at Norwich in 1619, criticized those 'many wandring Planets in some place who at Michaelmasse make the Countrie their Circumference, to gather in their Rents; but at Christmas . . . make the Citie, or their Cosens houses their Center . . .'.[24] Mingay observed to Gawdy in 1635 that, 'it is so dark this Christmas that our city gentlemen cannot see to keep good hospitality'.[25] This is not, of course, the whole story: we shall have occasion to note how seriously the Petre family, for example, took their Christmas duties, and even the city-loving Humphrey Mildmay was often to be found in Essex voluntarily entertaining visitors on the Twelve Days. In 1640 he noted that at New Year, 'to dinner came rascal upon rascal without sending for . . .', and each year he participated enthusiastically in the junketings of his rural neighbours.[26] Even retreat to the town at Christmas did not automatically mean the end of hospitality. When Sir Henry Slingsby and his family made an abrupt decision to travel to London in December 1639, they left behind 'all those provisions we had made for our accustomed keeping of Christmas . . .'.[27]

It may be that the crown and the moralists, in concentrating their attention on the duties of the gentry and nobility during the Twelve Days, were selecting an easy target but one which was only symptomatic of a deeper problem. Indeed, preachers

---

[22] *HMC, Gawdy*, 162.

[23] *The Court and Times of James I*, ed. R. F. Williams, 2 vols. (London, 1848), ii. 358, 383.

[24] S. Garey, *Ientaculum Iudicum or a Breake-fast for the Bench* (London, 1623), sig. A4.

[25] *HMC, Gawdy*, 156.

[26] Ralph, *Sir Humphrey Mildmay*, 107–8.

[27] D. Parsons (ed.), *Diary of Sir Henry Slingsby, of Scriven Bart* (London, 1836), 45.

and commentators sometimes assailed those who believed that a season of lavish entertainment was an adequate substitute for 'fixed and steady' care of the poor and tenants throughout the year.[28] It was this routine entertainment that was probably most threatened by the development of alternative foci of gentry activity, for the gradual transition from short visits to other gentlemen or the local capital, to longer business journeys to London and thence to the rental and final purchase of an urban residence, was a common experience for the greater gentry in the first half of the seventeenth century. Once detached from their main rural seat for some months of the year, it was likely that the household there would be broken up, or placed on board wages, thereby making the provision of general entertainment difficult. The change can be seen on a small scale in the Longleat household accounts for 1603. The Thynne family departed in the spring, leaving an active household of between sixteen and twenty people.[29] This continued to receive visitors, though not of course on the same scale as if the family had been in residence. At Whitsun, the servants substituted for their master in the traditional duty of entertaining the 'precessioners', in all about a hundred men, women, and children. The accounts for the later summer are missing, but when they start again in October Thynne was again absent, and obviously intended to spend the winter in London. The number of servants had been reduced to twelve and they received very few outsiders. Even in the Christmas season, two modest dinners on New Year's Day and 3 January were the only acknowledgements of the festivities.[30] Of course they may have continued to offer doles to the poor and refreshment to travellers, but in a household where no meals of any elaboration were being served, there can have been few offerings available for these hangers-on.

Longleat at least continued to function as a working household in Thynne's absence, an arrangement that is also to be found at Cranford under Lady Berkeley in the 1630s, and at Ashridge under the Earl of Bridgewater in 1652.[31] When the last-named added

---

[28] Downame, *The Plea of the Poore* (London, 1616), 66–7; Garey, *A New Yeares Gift for the Suole* (London, 1615), 8.
[29] Longleat, Thynne MS., Bk. 117.   [30] Ibid. Bk. 118.
[31] GLRO, Acc. 530; H. J. Todd, *The History of the College of Bonhommes at Ashridge* (London, 1823), 47 ff.

to his household orders in 1673, however, he made a careful distinction between times when he was present, and periods of absence 'when there is no house kept'. Although in these circumstances servants might still reside, they were not to take in visitors, 'for *I keepe house at London*; and strangers must not expect to be entertain'd while I am away'. Sunday, the most usual day for eating with the tenantry and other lesser men, was specifically isolated as the day of greatest expense and disorder, which should be reserved for prayer and meditation, 'not debauchery abroad, much lesse at home'.[32] The ferocity of Bridgewater's tone indicates the difficulty of preventing a household of servants from maintaining their own version of the hospitable tradition: indeed, the experiences of Lieutenant Hammond on his travels to the West in the 1630s suggest that entertainment by the servants was common, provided that there was some prior acquaintance with a member of the household.[33]

Logically, therefore, the next step was to close up the establishment completely, making it into the real Mock-Beggar's Hall of ballad fame, and leaving only a housekeeper and one or two servants to care for it. This seems to be the step that the Barrington family had taken by the 1670s on their Hatfield Priory manor. Earlier in the century, that formidable matriarch Lady Joan Barrington had been a central figure in the Essex Puritan community, and her son, Sir Thomas, despite his frequent absences in London, clearly defined himself as a man of his locality.[34] When he became deeply enmeshed in the Long Parliament, he delayed for eighteen months the decision to purchase an urban residence and move his family and possessions to it.[35] However, after the Restoration the family became identified with London, and their account book for the 1670s shows them spending only a few months of each year in the country.[36] A housekeeper left permanently at

[32] Todd, *Ashridge*, 55.

[33] L. G. W. Legg (ed.), *A Description of a Journie made into the Westerne Counties, 1635* (Camden Misc. 16, 3rd ser. 52, London, 1936), 30–1, 38.

[34] A. Searle (ed.), *Barrington Family Letters, 1628–32* (Camden Soc., 4th ser. 27, London, 1982).

[35] C. Russell, 'A Parliament in Early Stuart England', in H. Tomlinson (ed.), *Before the English Civil War* (London, 1983), 137.

[36] ERO, D/DBa, A20.

Hatfield faithfully recorded their comings and goings, usually receiving them in May or early June, and then attending their departure in September. Between these visits there would occasionally be one of a few days by some member of the extended kin, otherwise the house seems to have remained closed. It was matter of surprise and delight to the housekeeper when in 1677 John Barrington, his wife, and infant daughter chose to spend the Christmas season at the Priory. In these circumstances prohibitions on hospitality of the kind offered by Bridgewater can scarcely have been necessary, and indeed the household book offers no hint that outsiders were received.

The increasing mobility of at least a section of the élite bred, as the third Lord North suggested in his commonplace book, 'a great partiality to the equall conversation of Townes', even though life in the countryside might be 'most naturall, pleasant, setled, and profitable to the English breed and course'.[37] The sense of that 'equall conversation' is well conveyed in the kitchen book of Thomas Thynne, living in King Street, Covent Garden, in the 1670s.[38] His visitors were largely male, and included relatives and members of many of the great families, the Russells, Cliffords, Cavendishs, and the like. Many of them were younger sons, there was a sprinkling of military men, and the same names tend to recur: all of which suggests a circle of like-minded friends, dining, and perhaps gaming, together. The whole record is in sharp contrast with the Thynne series for Longleat that pre-dates the Civil War.

Even when towns were inaccessible, the society which was conditioned to look to civility as a prime good was likely to try to reconstruct urban conditions in the countryside. Conviviality among the gentry was, of course, nothing new: the Le Strange accounts provide a vivid illustration of its operation in the early sixteenth century, and no doubt if such documents survived from the fourteenth century there would be considerable similarities between them. But the construction of a polite society, based upon a combination of breeding and manners, and the increase of contacts among those members of the élite who were educated in a national system and who came together in its capital,

[37] Dudley, 3rd Lord North, *A Forest of Varieties* (London, 1645), 159.
[38] Longleat, Thynne MS., Bk. 133.

stimulated the expansion of sociability within this self-defining group.[39] Developments such as the elaboration of conventions for visiting, while they may have restricted the most casual forms of encounter, also fostered interchange between those who understood the new rules. The young and bachelors were perhaps particularly likely to exploit these developments, moving from country house to country house as a way of avoiding permanent settlement. James Master, a well-connected bachelor from Kent, was able to spend much of the period of the Interregnum trading on his connection with the Howards of Saffron Walden and the Pelhams of Halland to lead a comfortable existence.[40] The young Thomas Caesar was guilty of over-exploiting these social conventions while at university: the head of his college when he transferred from Oxford to Cambridge was warned that 'he often will ride abroad unto the bordering gent[ry]. He is with all acquainted and will carrie thether unruly company to the great trouble of the same gent[ry].'[41]

But it was not only the young or homeless who gyrated: the account book of Anna, Lady Burgoyne, from the 1680s, shows a widow in constant motion between London and the countryside and between her various friends in the localities.[42] She seems to have reserved each summer for an extended visit either to the capital, or to some part of the country where she could depend on several invitations. Celia Fiennes, whose constant peregrinations at the end of the century are such a delight to read, seems in these circumstances to have been merely an unusually energetic and curious child of her times. The pressures to avoid the ennui of rural living by visiting others, or London, or, increasingly in the latter half of the seventeenth century, Bath or some other spa, are well documented in contemporary literature. Dramatists seem to have agreed with James I that the main initiative came from the women, whose lives were more restricted in the countryside than in the more fluid society of the towns.[43]

---

[39] On the theme of gentry interaction, see C. Holmes, 'The County Community in Stuart Historiography', *JBS*, 19 (1980), 54–73.

[40] 'Expense Book of James Master, Esq., 1646–79', *Archaeologia Cantiana*, 16 (1886), 152 ff.

[41] BL Add. MS. 11406, fo. 201.

[42] BRO, X143/1.

[43] M. Butler, *Theatre and Crisis, 1632–42* (Cambridge, 1987), 162–4.

It is difficult to generalize about the impact on hospitality that such changes had, but the lack of settled households was not easy to reconcile with the old assumptions about sustained beneficence and the engagement of both lord and lady in the local community.

II

When in London, the nobility and gentry had ample opportunity to learn new modes of behaviour and to make contacts with those specialists who could transform their old ones. One such process was associated with architecture which, during the later sixteenth and seventeenth centuries, became an increasingly 'professional' activity, presided over by experts who could transmit new ideas into new buildings. The ideas themselves often emanated from the other activities of the élite, notably their formal classical education or the experience of the Grand Tour. The design of the country seat that was the result of these experiences was unlikely of itself to determine whether or not a gentleman entertained, but it could both reflect his priorities and influence the form of his sociability. This is why Henry Wotton was so anxious to stress that Italian architectural forms were not necessarily suitable for English hospitality.[44] He argued that the arrangement of the service rooms below ground-level in the Palladian mode was inappropriate since: 'by the natural hospitality of England, the Buttery must be more visible; and we need perchance for our ranges, a more spacious and luminous kitchen, than the aforesaid Compartition will bear.'[45]

It is perhaps worth beginning from a reiteration of those features of traditional building which lent themselves to a hierarchical, but integrated, practice of hospitality. The hall, although it had long since ceased to be the exclusive focus of eating and sociability, still provided the central stage on which the drama of commensality could be enacted. The twice-daily procession from kitchen to chamber, and the reverse movement of the almoner and his assistants from the chamber to the gate, both asserted the hegemony of the lord and served to confirm

[44] Henry Wotton, *The Elements of Architecture* (London, 1624), 70.
[45] Ibid. 71.

that all were accepted under the cloak of his generosity. Chamber or parlour, hall and services, were usually arranged in a linear configuration that assisted this vision: they represented the public or semi-public aspects of noble behaviour, in contrast with the private lodgings that often comprised much of the remaining area of a courtyard or similar house. However, in emphasizing the integrative functions of the traditional house we risk ignoring the degree to which separation had already occurred by the mid-sixteenth century; eating was separate, the barrier between hall and chamber was a very real one, not the less significant because it might still on rare occasions be removed when the lord chose to feast with his retainers and tenants. Moreover, daily eating was not always subject to the highest standards articulated by the household ordinances: meals were often taken in individual offices by members of the establishment, and a certain casualness usually made it possible to eat directly from the kitchen when senior officials did not provide close supervision. In addition, it has already been noted that meals were taken in individual chambers by the lord and lady and even their guests when it proved convenient to do so.

The domestic architecture of the later sixteenth and early seventeenth centuries facilitated the further development of this centrifugal tendency and, at least for a time, also circumscribed the visual expression of hierarchy which the linear house had encouraged. By the time that John Thorpe was recording his work and that of contemporaries in his book of architecture, the number of formal rooms in even moderately sized country houses had begun to increase and their individual functions, therefore, to become more specialist.[46] In addition to the great chamber and parlour there were now often separate dining-chambers in large establishments, with drawing-rooms, distinct winter and summer parlours, and small banqueting-houses which might or might not be part of the house itself. This diversity did not necessarily increase the total number of rooms within a country house; indeed, Girouard has suggested that by the seventeenth century there was actually a diminution in the number of lodgings required in many houses, a process which helps to explain the

---

[46] J. Summerson (ed.), *The Book of Architecture of John Thorpe* (Walpole Soc., 40, 1966).

decline of the courtyard model of building.[47] But while private lodgings might stay constant or even decline in number, the élite now developed a taste for diversity and specialization that led to movement through a series of different chambers during the course of a social day. Here the fashion was, of course, set by the court, and translated into a rural environment first by the series of prodigy houses designed to emphasize their owner's special connections with royalty.[48] Diversity and elaboration of the ceremonial parts of a house were also echoed by the growing complexity of the services, the household 'below stairs'. A number of Thorpe's plans show several larders and serving areas, surveying-rooms and the like, in addition to the usual buttery, pantry, and kitchens. One or two of the greatest houses apparently went further and had either a day room for servants, as at Holdenby, or a separate waiters' chamber, as in the plan for Lord Buckhurst's house at Withyham which was never constructed (Fig. 4.1).[49] Here we have the beginnings of that separation of servants from the ceremonial areas of the house which, by the eighteenth century, was to culminate in a total upstairs/downstairs distinction in most establishments.[50]

It is difficult to believe that even in the greater establishments diversification and the beginnings of the isolation of servants from the major rooms of the house were initially associated with any conscious shift in the attitudes of the élite towards hospitality. It was precisely men like Sir William Cecil and Sir Christopher Hatton, builders in the new style, who endeavoured to identify themselves with the old traditions of public generosity to all comers.[51] Cecil's biographer describes with approval the 'honorable table, for Noblemen and others to resort to . . .' which was constantly set in his parlour, and his hall, which, in a

[47] M. Girouard, *Life in the English Country House* (New Haven, Conn., 1978), 108.

[48] M. Girouard, *Robert Smythson and the Elizabethan Country House* (London, 1983).

[49] *John Thorpe*, T183, T19/20.

[50] Girouard, *Country House*, 136-40.

[51] On Cecil, see the anonymous *Life* in Peck (ed.), *Desiderata Curiosa*, 2 vols. (London, 1732-5), I. i. 29 ff.; on Hatton, E. St John Brooks, *Sir Christopher Hatton* (London, 1946), 159. Barnabe Rich gave a glowing account of entertainment at Holdenby, even when Hatton was not there: 'From whence should he come, be he rich be he poor, that should not there be entertained, if it please him to call in?'

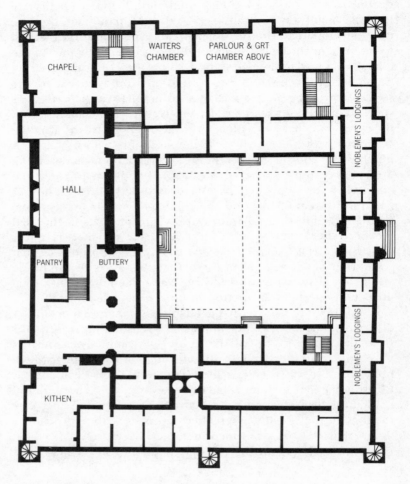

Fig. 4.1. Plan for Lord Buckhurst's house at Withyham

significant choice of language, he alleged 'was ever well furnished with Men, served with Meate, and kept in good Ordre'.[52] But he also reveals the change that could occur in the new, more diverse arrangement of the household if the circumstances of the

---

[52] Peck, *Desiderata Curiosa*, I. i. 31.

lord were altered. When Cecil was ageing and infirm he was forced to eat in his chamber, but was able to have 'as manie of his Friends and Children' to dine there as he had previously had strangers in his parlour.[53] The language of the biography does not make it entirely clear whether Cecil continued to maintain a ceremonial parlour in his absence, but the implication must be that he did not, and that age led him to retire into an intimate environment, leaving the hall as the only formal centre of hospitality.

A pattern which in Cecil's case was consequent on personal debility gradually became a common feature of élite dining. The great chamber, often, as Girouard has pointed out, a room as large and hence potentially as cold and uncomfortable as a medieval hall, was used on formal occasions or at certain times of the year, while an inner dining-room or chamber was employed for the family and their personal friends.[54] In April 1617, Lady Anne Clifford recorded in her diary that the family at Knole 'began to leave the little room and dine and sup in the Great Chamber'. On the 13th of that month her husband 'dined abroad in the great Chamber and supped privately with me in the Drawing Chamber'.[55]

These dispositions, which owed most initially to an increased interest in the comfort and convenience of the nuclear family, proved important in reducing the ceremony of dining among strangers, and hence in modifying assumptions about commensality and the importance of integrative hospitality. In the great chamber of a noble house, and indeed in the chambers of many gentlemen, it had usually been physically possible to set two or three boards, one for the master and his immediate guests, a 'knight's board', and sometimes a separate one for the gentlewomen.[56] Household accounts and ordinances show that

---

[53] Ibid. Cecil may not have been quite as generally generous as his biographer suggests: the diarist John Manningham repeats a London jest current at the end of the century that Burghley House gate in the Strand was called the Lord Treasurer's alms-gate, 'because it was seldome or never opened': R. P. Sorlien (ed.), *The Diary of John Manningham* (Hanover, NH, 1976), 46.

[54] Girouard, *Country House*, 99.

[55] V. Sackville-West, ed., *Diary of Lady Anne Clifford* (London, 1923), 62–3.

[56] Arrangements of this kind can be found in the household accounts for the Berkeleys, and for Sir William Fairfax, Berkeley Castle, Bound Bk. 32; *HMC, Var. Coll.*, II, 71 ff.

this continued to be done until at least the Civil War, though when a dining-chamber was used as the main semi-public place of eating one large table was increasingly substituted for the divided arrangement. In either case there was usually ample space to accommodate a large number of guests, which was not necessarily so when an inner chamber was employed for daily eating. When the Earl of Yarmouth attempted to regulate guests in Norfolk in the 1670s, the use of semi-public and more intimate dining arrangements provided a means of excluding the casual visitor, and of intimating that not every day was designed for general hospitality.[57] By the later seventeenth century it was an unusual household that maintained a pattern of general and daily access to the chamber. One such was that of Lady Anne Clifford, who in her old age at Brougham Castle, Westmorland, rarely sat publicly among her guests, but always insisted that 'her folk' maintain a formal table in 'the painted chamber'. There she was so rarely without guests that on one occasion she felt constrained to note the absence of visitors in her diary.[58]

When dining became, at least on a daily basis, more intimate and private than it had been in an earlier period, the grand ritual of the procession through the hall was no longer mandatory. It had probably only been conducted with full ceremonial in the greatest of houses, and, although the ordinances, as we have seen, continued to insist upon it in the early seventeenth century, it seems gradually to have been confined to unusual occasions.[59] Architectural developments of the early Stuart period would anyway have robbed it of some of its symbolic force. The linearity of traditional English domestic design gradually yielded to that passion for symmetry that compelled a modification of the internal configuration of buildings. The nobility and gentry did not abandon the hall completely as an eating and entertainment room: only after the construction of Coleshill by Sir Roger Pratt in the 1650s was this a serious option. However, the hall underwent all possible modifications short of losing its function as an eating-room completely. It was sometimes placed centrally across the line of the services and chamber, thereby surrendering the processional impact of a linear plan (Fig. 4.2).[60] Or the size of the room might be reduced to save space for other, more valued, apartments. In some of the prodigy houses the hall might be isolated from the more important ceremonial rooms of the house by one or more floors. This arrangement was used to most spectacular effect at Hardwick (Fig. 4.3).[61] Often, Jacobean buildings were designed to allow access from the kitchens to the rooms used for eating without the need to enter the hall at all.[62] Wotton approved of this arrangement, since otherwise 'perhaps some of the dishes may straggle by the way . . .'.[63] In even more cases the size of the hall was reduced until it became merely another chamber, suitable enough as a place for servants to wait and greet the individual guest, and adequate for one or two dining-tables, but hardly the dramatic focus of the house.[64]

Meanwhile, the development of more specialist rooms on the service side of the house might well encourage a tendency towards dining in individual offices that had already been criticized in some late medieval ordinances. The consequence was that the hall, although still in use as an eating-room, could contract in general importance as well as in size, and could cease, in Cecil's sense, to be well furnished with men. The Berkeley household accounts for the 1580s show this process at work in Coventry.[65] Although Maurice, Lord Berkeley had a high reputation for hospitality, he rarely had more than two messes served in his hall, out of the seven to ten messes distributed throughout the household. Two or three were provided for the parlour and the rest were sent to individual offices; these invariably included one for the gentlewomen, one for the laundry, and one for the kitchen, and also sometimes one for such out-servants as wainmen. When senior estate officials such as the auditor visited the Berkeleys they were also served separately when not

---

[60] See e.g., the Wollaton plan, Girouard, *Robert Smythson*, 98.
[61] Ibid. 155.
[62] See also Somerhill, Kent: J. Newman, *The Buildings of England: West Kent and the Weald* (London, 1969), 536–7.
[63] Wotton, *Elements of Architecture*, 71.
[64] See e.g., Blewhouse, Highgate, where the parlour was a larger room than the hall, *John Thorpe*, T62.
[65] Berkeley Castle, Bound Bk. 32.

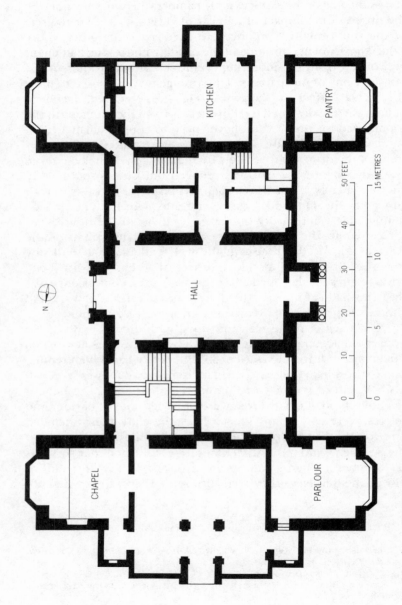

Fig. 4.2. Charlton House, Greenwich

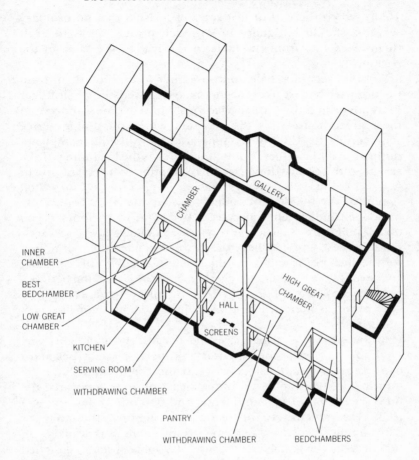

INNER
CHAMBER

BEST
BEDCHAMBER

LOW GREAT
CHAMBER

KITCHEN

SERVING ROOM

WITHDRAWING CHAMBER

PANTRY

WITHDRAWING CHAMBER

BEDCHAMBERS

CHAMBER

GALLERY

HIGH GREAT
CHAMBER

HALL

SCREENS

Fig. 4.3. Isometric drawing of Hardwick Hall

particularly invited into the parlour.[66] In other households
where the great chamber rather than the parlour was the place
of eating for the family, the parlour might be used for senior
servants and gentlewomen, leaving the hall only to the yeomen
and guests of their status. This was the arrangement at Knole in
Lady Anne Clifford's time, and it was also true at Ashridge in the

---

[66] Berkeley Castle, Bound Bk. 32, fos. 9, 29ᵛ, 34.

1650s, when the Earl of Bridgewater insisted that no ordinary servants should be 'guilty of so much pride . . . as to exalt themselves . . . from the table in the hall to the table in the parlour'.[67]

Separate servants' halls, purpose-built to exclude them from the ordinary hall, scarcely seem to have existed before Sir Roger Pratt advocated the idea so vigorously in the 1660s. Indeed, in most great households the servants were still dining above stairs until the Civil War, separation only being completed during the mid-century.[68] But at least from the beginning of the seventeenth century there was an assumption that servants might in practice dine elsewhere.[69] Bacon, in his essay *Of Building*, reminded the builders of country houses that they could only have open and elegant staircases between the main floors 'if you do not point any of the lower rooms for a dining place of servants. For otherwise you shall have the servants' dinner after your own; for the steam of it will come up as in a tunnel.'[70] This certainly anticipates Pratt's argument that there must be separation between upstairs and downstairs, 'in that no dirty servants may be seen passing to and fro by those who are above, nor ill scents smelt'.[71]

Bacon's essay is also interesting because he highlights one method by which contemporary property-owners began to express a sharper division between the ceremonious and the informal in their buildings. In his ideal house he advocated the total separation of the banqueting and domestic sides: the one to be reserved entirely for 'feasts and triumphs', the other for daily living.[72] Such an extreme arrangement was unlikely in practice, but the gradual emergence of 'rooms of state', designed

[67] Sackville-West, *Anne Clifford*, lvii–lxi; Todd, *Ashridge*, 55.

[68] The account of the Duke of Beaufort's household in the 1670s by Lord North suggests an arrangement in which the servants dined publicly and with some ceremony, but in a hall especially allocated to them: Roger North, *The Lives of . . . Francis North, Baron Guilford . . . Sir Dudley North . . . and . . . Dr. John North*, 3 vols. (London, 1826), i. 272–3.

[69] *John Thorpe*, T183, where the plan for Holdenby suggests the existence of a separate servants' room.

[70] Francis Bacon, 'Essays', in *Works*, ed. Spedding, 7 vols. (London, 1857–9). vi, 483.

[71] R. T. Gunther (ed.), *The Architecture of Sir Roger Pratt* (Oxford, 1928), 27.

[72] Bacon, *Works*, vi. 482, 484.

primarily to accommodate the King or great guests, and separated from the normal rooms of family existence, is a parallel development which did occur. Such elaborate provision for visits is an obvious affirmation of continuing noble commitment to one aspect of hospitality: but it emphasizes the great at the expense of the rest and, more significantly, feasting at the expense of routine guesting.[73] The architectural evidence of Hatfield with its series of royal chambers, Audley End with its separate formal entrances for the King and Queen, or Hardwick with its two ceremonial floors, is congruent with the perpetual moan of Elizabethan and Jacobean moralists that grand banqueting and elaboration of the new architecture had driven out true hospitality.[74] The crown here had much to answer for in its determination to seek accommodation from its subjects. The fashion for formal building would no doubt have grown without the intervention of Elizabeth and James, but their demands for country entertainment did much to create a convention of ceremonious hospitality which was inevitably at odds with the ideas of informal feeding of and generosity to the poor.

One related development in late seventeenth-century architecture also reflects on attitudes to entertainment: that is, the arrangement of the most formal rooms of the great house in a linear configuration once again. Here the pattern was usually that of a progression from the least to the most intimate of rooms, often along one side of a house that was by now rectangular in overall structure. The model was, as so often, provided by royal architecture, and can be seen at its clearest in the William-and-Mary buildings at Hampton Court.[75] It was a peculiarly appropriate form for the monarch, since it permitted the filtration of individuals, some being denied access to one room, some to another, until the few were admitted into the inner sanctum. It is the imitation of this form in many of the great houses of the nobility, and even some of those of the gentry, that is of relevance for our purposes. It

---

[73] Almost all the 'prodigy' houses have some state-room arrangement, designed largely for royal entertainment: Girouard, *Robert Smythson*, 104.

[74] See e.g., Thomas Adams's complaints of 'sumptuous parlours, for Owles and Bats to flie in': 'The White Devil', in *The Workes of Tho: Adams* (London, 1630), 40.

[75] Girouard, *Country House*, 144, for a schematized plan of the modes of access in the formal house.

allowed for that specialism of function already discussed as a feature of the period, but it also intensified the ceremoniousness of the process of access. There had, of course, always been filtration and restriction upon access to the great: a prime duty of the usher of the chamber was to guard the curtain of the great chamber and to deny entry to those of whom he had no knowledge.[76] But that process was now enhanced by the careful gradations of architecture. The enclosed inner chambers were intended to compliment a few guests with the sense that they had private access to the master of the house. And, conversely, these dispositions could be used to isolate the master from the importunate visitors. In Glamorgan at the beginning of the eighteenth century, Sir Edward Mansell denied access to ordinary men, keeping them waiting for several days for half an hour's conversation as one disgruntled suitor complained, and locking himself away 'by the multiplied formalities of attendance'.[77]

Changes in domestic architecture occurred simultaneously with some alterations in the organization of the great household and its dependants. The crucial difference between the late medieval household and that of the early eighteenth century was that the latter no longer contained many servants whose functions were primarily ceremonial; the 'tall fellows' who, in their tawny coats and other liveries, had existed largely to personate the power and status of their masters. Of course footmen who could be dressed with great ceremony for formal occasions were still a feature of the great establishment, but trains of mounted servants were no longer expected to follow even the greatest of nobility.[78] Household retainers, in the quasi-feudal sense of that term, had little place in the world of the nobility after the Restoration, and were in decline as a group at least from the middle years of Elizabeth's reign. Although the Armada campaigns probably for a time arrested their demise—Archbishop Whitgift for example, very deliberately reorganized his household servants for military

---

[76] See e.g., the order in the 'Breviate touching . . . a nobleman's household', that the yeoman usher was to let none into the chamber 'but such as in his discretion shall be thought meet': *Archaeologia*, 13 (1800), 333.

[77] P. Jenkins, *The Making of a Ruling Class* (Cambridge, 1983), 198; this seems to have caused offence particularly because many of the Glamorgan gentry had continued in the old informal ways.

[78] L. Stone, *The Crisis of the Aristocracy* (Oxford, 1965), 267.

service in the 1580s—they were sufficiently vulnerable to be the subject of a series of defensive pamphlets at the end of the century.[79] The best-known example, the anonymous *A Health to the Gentlemanly Profession of Servingmen* (1598), attributed the decline of the superior servant to the decay of liberality and hospitality, but also to the arrogance of many masters who would no longer tolerate the intimacy and companionship that should exist between a worthy dependent and his lord.[80] Shorn of its moralistic tone the latter argument is important: servants of some autonomous social standing were no longer so necessary a part of the seventeenth-century world, since they were no longer the potential military supports of their lords, nor did they personate him so regularly in polite society. Although the state did not intervene directly in the affairs of the great house, its consistent discouragement of any autonomy in military matters by the nobility provided a further disincentive to the traditional patterns of service in times of peace.

The custom of rearing children in the houses of the great was also in sharp decline, though it was not wholly dead even in the second decade of the seventeenth century. There is an interesting letter from the Earl of Arundel to his younger son, dated 1620, in which he offers detailed advice on how the latter should conduct himself in the household of the Bishop of Norwich, to whom he was being sent as a page.[81] There is, however, a defensiveness in the father's language, as he urges his son to accept that this form of education was 'a breeding which youths of my House far superior to you were accustomed to'. Elsewhere, even the younger sons of the gentry would have been far more likely to receive formal classical education than to undertake a period of service in the early seventeenth century. The household lists for the servants of Lord Howard of Naworth for the period between the 1610s and the 1640s, contain no obvious names of northern gentlemen

[79] George Paule, *The Life of the Most Reverend Prelate John Whitgift* (London, 1612), 73–4.

[80] *A Health* . . ., 140 ff.

[81] F. J. Furnivall (ed.), *Manners and Meals in Olden Times* (*EETS*, 32, 1868), ix. Fulke Greville remarks much earlier than this that Elizabeth 'did not suffer the nobility to be servants to one another': Greville, *The Life of Sir Philip Sidney* (Oxford, 1907), 189.

or their offspring among the servants.[82] Beyond the immediate household the demise of the retainer as a regular part of the noble entourage is even more obvious. In the 1580s, retainers of the Berkeley household appeared with some regularity at Coventry, and were usually entertained as a group in the chamber.[83] However, none of the household accounts thereafter makes any allusion to retainers of this kind, and by the end of the century the linguistic usage of the term was already shifting towards the more modern meaning of ordinary servant. Changes external to the household—greater political centralization, widening opportunities for formal education and professional employment, and the decline of the military role of the aristocracy—combined to discourage the maintenance of servants of independent standing.

Despite the observations of the author of *A Health* . . ., it seems reasonable to argue that changes in patterns of entertainment were more a consequence than a cause of the demise of the gentleman servant. Fewer men with a claim to autonomous status in the social hierarchy were now regularly employed in the great household, and at least one part of the clientage system which had brought important local men to a lord's table regularly was also in decline. Therefore a widening gulf between employers and employed facilitated those changes in arrangements for commensality which have already been noted. Servants became more definitely part of the lower household, only the few administrators such as stewards, auditors, and chaplains occupying a middle ground. Moreover, household servants were more likely to be female than in the past, since a more functionalist perception of service led to the recognition that they could perform tasks effectively that had previously been allocated to men.[84] Moralists complained, with some justification, that gentlemen turned their 'men into boyes and sometimes into women'.[85] This last transition can be seen dramatically in the series of household ordinances for the archbishops of Canterbury. Until at least Abbot's years in office,

[82] G. Ornsby (ed.), *Selections from the Houshold Books of the Lord William Howard, of Naworth Castle, 1612-40* (Surtees Soc., 68, 1877), 54 ff.
[83] Berkeley Castle, Bound Bk. 32, fos. 29ᵛ, 38, 96.
[84] Girouard, *Country House*, 142.
[85] William Parkes, *The Curtaine-Drawer of the World* (London, 1612), 38.

the household was overwhelmingly male; after the Restoration it seems that about a third of the smaller establishment was female.[86] The idea of service as demeaning also slowly emerged from these social upheavals, until by the end of the seventeenth century Celia Fiennes could find it incongruous that Lord Paget could still summon local gentlemen to wait on him on solemn feast days.[87] This represents an extraordinary transition in collective consciousness from the experience of much of the sixteenth century, when service can still be seen as the basis of personal connection and political influence. The customary form of entertainment in the 'open' household was one victim of the transition: it created a sharp division in what had previously been the graded hierarchy of sociability, and facilitated the banishment of both servants and inferior guests below stairs. Dudley, Lord North, complained in 1669 that when halls were built they no longer had fireplaces, which would 'draw Company together, and give chearfulnesse to a Family'.[88] His very language, with the use of the term 'family' to comprehend kin and servants, is evocative of a rapidly vanishing pattern of social behaviour.

The emergence of the formal house and a more sharply differentiated domestic structure tended to militate against ease of access for a wide range of guests. Many of those who would previously have been entertained in the hall were, by the late seventeenth century, fortunate if they were allowed any access at all to the household above stairs. Tenants, servants on business for their master, and casual visitors of some respectability, were more likely to be taken into the buttery and the servants' hall than permitted to venture into the house proper.[89] Readers of *Joseph Andrews* will recall that Parson Adams was faced with this denial of access when he ventured into the house of Sir Thomas Booby, the highest contact he was able to make being the curious Mrs Slipslop, Lady Booby's gentlewoman. Lady Booby and her husband embody, in exaggerated form, the assumptions of London society: all country neighbours are by definition 'brutes',

---

[86] LPL, MS. 884; MS. 684/6; TG 1.

[87] C. Morris, ed., *The Illustrated Journeys of Celia Fiennes* (London, 1982), 229.

[88] Dudley, 4th Lord North, *Observations and Advices Œconomical* (London, 1669), 92.

[89] LPL, MS. 884.

and the curate 'a kind of domestic only, belonging to the parson of the parish'.[90] While this is peculiarly insulting to the worthy and learned Mr Adams, it also has wider implications in its comment on the failure of a landed élite, insulated by the experience of London and their own peer group, to comprehend the behaviour of their servants and tenants. Both Fielding and Richardson in *Pamela* address themselves compellingly to this division of sensibility and to the sentimental education of the upper orders that was a necessary part of understanding the shared humanity of lord and dependant once again. Although in practice many rural households still offered opportunities to bridge the gulf between the two on occasions such as the Christmas feast or the Harvest Home, among the greater gentry even these celebrations seem to have been in decline after the Restoration. Sir John Reresby who, as we shall see, took the entertainment of his inferiors very seriously, noted in the 1670s that in his part of Yorkshire a grand Christmas, 'which it was formerly the custome to observe with great mirth and ceremony, . . . was much lessened, few keeping up the custome of it . . . but myselfe'.[91]

III

It is, however, far too simplistic to assume that there was a perfect inverse relationship between the development of a civil culture emanating from London and the court, and the decay of old English hospitality. First there is the evidence that hospitality had been limited by convention before and during the sixteenth century; only a ballad-maker, or a poet of Merrie England like Herrick, assumed that all great households had been constantly open, providing food and lodging as though they were cornucopias. Secondly, we have already encountered a number of examples that suggest that individual nobles and gentlemen still perceived themselves as hospitable, or that others believed them to be so. They may by the mid-seventeenth century have been a minority, singled out in part because they exposed the

---

[90] Henry Fielding, *The Adventures of Joseph Andrews* (London, 1910), 9.
[91] A. Browning (ed.), *The Memoirs of Sir John Reresby* (Glasgow, 1936), 285.

deficiencies of the rest of the élite, but they are nevertheless a minority worth careful consideration since they appear to stand against the prevailing pattern of decay identified by so many writers. It could be argued that there were as many reasons for their behaviour as there were landed families who retained a pride in good entertainment; nevertheless, it is possible to identify certain shared values and circumstances which encouraged the maintenance of tradition among groups of families. The most important of these was probably religious sentiment, but the aristocratic ethos, the nature of particular local societies, and, interestingly, gender, all seem to have influenced the chosen behaviour of individuals.

Strongly held religious beliefs, whether Catholic or Protestant, were likely to modify other cultural assumptions. Protestantism, as suggested in an earlier chapter, could lead to a narrowing of the focus of household entertainment and charity, but it still demanded a reflectiveness about social obligation that was not necessarily shared in the élite as a whole. The case of Catholicism is more evident: Catholics did not have any scruples about indiscriminate charity or about the traditional cycle of feast and fast to overcome and, at least by the later years of Elizabeth's reign, they were motivated by a conscious desire to maintain customary social patterns as a means of consolidating communal behaviours.[92] There are a number of individual examples of Catholic families who were thought by their contemporaries to be unusually assiduous in the maintenance of hospitality. Petitions against penal recusancy fines often include a plea that the gentleman concerned maintained a good household, giving generous entertainment to his neighbours, even when they were not Catholic.[93] Thomas Tankerd of Brampton, Yorkshire, petitioned against his extraordinary assessment in 1637, arguing that he would have to give over housekeeping to pay the fines, and was supported by seven local JPs, who swore that he had always been 'an honest neighbour and good housekeeper'.[94] John Vavasour of Hazlewood Castle, another Yorkshire recusant,

---

[92] J. Bossy, *The English Catholic Community, 1570–1850* (London, 1975), 110–21.
[93] J. T. Cliffe, *The Yorkshire Gentry from the Reformation to the Civil War* (London, 1969), 224.
[94] PRO, SP 16/368/66.

was known as 'the only great and bountiful housekeeper in the north'.[95] A few decades earlier, Michael Hare, one of the Suffolk recusant gentlemen, had a high reputation for hospitality among his neighbours, even though his fines were unusually high and he built on a generous scale.[96] In examples of this kind it is important to emphasize that it seems to have been the maintenance of a general tradition that impressed outsiders, rather than the support of an introverted community. Hare was 'attended with many servants in liveries', and Lord William Howard of Naworth was, according to his visitors, bountiful with his 'hospitality and fre entertainment [which] agrees with [his] generous and noble extraction'.[97] Howard's household accounts for the period from 1612 onwards certainly indicate that he maintained customary ways in matters such as giving to the poor.[98]

It is not necessarily true, however, that there was no distinctive quality to Catholic hospitality in the later sixteenth and seventeenth centuries. It is the hagiographical account of the life of Magdalen, Lady Montagu, that best evokes the specific dimension of customary generosity for a devout Catholic. Lady Montagu was said to have maintained a large household consisting almost entirely of believers, who thereby received not only material support, but 'the same benefit of the word of God and the sacraments that she herself enjoyed'.[99] She also gave crucial protection to the persecuted priests of the mission, and engaged in all the seven works of mercy towards Catholics, including various attempts to redeem priests from prison. Yet even Lady Montagu was not wholly introverted in her charitable endeavours: she was said to be particularly generous in distributing alms to the poor, offending some of her Protestant neighbours by failing to distinguish between the deserving and the undeserving.[100]

---

[95] Cliffe, *Yorkshire Gentry*, 224.

[96] D. MacCulloch, 'Catholic and Puritan in Elizabethan Suffolk', *Archiv für Reformationsgeschichte*, 72 (1981), 259.

[97] L. G. W. Legg (ed.), *A Relation of a Short Survey of Twenty-Six Counties Observed in a Seven Weeks Journey . . . from Norwich* (London, 1904), 39–41.

[98] *Household Books of Lord Howard*, 54 ff.

[99] Richard Smith, *An Elizabethan Recusant Household: Comprising the Life of the Lady Magdalen, Viscountess Montagu*, ed. A. C. Southern (London, 1954), 39.

[100] Ibid. 40.

Although the idealized picture must be treated with due caution, it does seem powerfully to evoke the compromises between the old teachings on charity and the new demands of the persecuted faith.

The importance of both general and communal entertainment for the Catholic peerage can be studied in close detail in the superb series of household books surviving for the Petre family in the late sixteenth and early seventeenth centuries.[101] These provide ample evidence that it was often other great Catholic families who formed the core of the Petres' social circle. They entertained the Earl and Countess of Worcester, Sir Thomas Somerset, Sir Robert Drury, and Sir William Cornwallis with some regularity at both Ingatestone and West Horndon, often for several days at a time. A typical visit by a Catholic group occurred in September 1606, when the Earl of Worcester, Sir Thomas Somerset, and the Countess of Southampton arrived on the 3rd and left again on the 5th. Other visitors in the same year included Sir Edward Tichborne, Sir Anthony Browne, and Sir Edward Sulyard, all representatives of the best recusant families. Among their peer group it seems that the Petres were most at ease with men and women of their own faith, although they did not confine their efforts exclusively to Catholics. Kinsmen such as Sir John Tyrell and local gentry such as Sir Thomas Mildmay and Sir Gamaliel Capel were sometimes entertained, despite their different religious attitudes, and the Petres from time to time received the judges of assize or the sheriff to dine, as evidence of their continued involvement in the local community. Among lesser men in their own locality they showed no exclusive preference for Catholics: they did receive the Southcotes of Witham, the Paschalls of Great Baddow, the Pounsetts of Barking, and the Appletons of Great Baddow, all devout Catholics, but they also entertained the Knightleys and Bradleys who were not. In the decade before the household books begin, we have the evidence of Richard Stonley's diary to show that a man who had served the Petre household, but had subsequently become a very devout Protestant, was still expected to appear regularly as a welcome guest in his old establishment.[102] The Petres even extended their hospitality to include members of

---

[101] ERO, D/DP, A24–27, 29, 31.   [102] Folger Lib. V. a. 459.

the establishment of the Church of England: in 1606 the Dean of Westminster and his entourage dined at Horndon, and it was relatively common for local clerics to eat at their table. On 7 April 1607, dinner guests included Dr Ware and his wife, Parson Fabbin and his wife, and Mr Holford, all Essex clerics.[103]

However, perhaps the most interesting feature of the Petre accounts is the evidence they provide of tenacious adherence to those traditions of hospitality established by the family in the earlier sixteenth century. The poor were still given herring and bread at the gates during the early spring, special bread being baked for this purpose at least as late as 1614.[104] On Sundays worthy neighbours were often entertained in the hall and, if the day was a festival, there were usually substantial numbers involved. On a typical Sunday that was not a festival, 6 October 1605, the company included Mr Bradley, Mr Greene and his wife, Marwood and his wife, the Widow Letton, the Widow Holland, Mary What, and Goodwives Neale and Wetham. At Easter or Whitsun the numbers for this type of meal often rose to twenty or thirty, mostly men and women of apparently humble standing. Above all, the Petres regarded their Christmas duties to the neighbourhood with the utmost seriousness. Although the family spent significant periods of time in London in the early years of James's reign, there was only one occasion in the fifteen Christmasses covered by the accounts when they seem to have remained in the capital for the festival. Often they returned in early or mid-December specifically to organize the holiday: this was an elaborate procedure since each year tenants and neighbours were bidden on different days of the festival season, and the poor were given alms in money and kind. At Christmas 1623, some member of the household kept a separate record of the tenants to be invited on each day, and who was to issue the invitations.[105] Men from East Horndon were bidden on 28 December, those from Ingrave the same day, those from Childerditch, Little Warley, and Bulphan on 29 December, those from Shenfield and Brentwood on 30 December, and finally those of Great Warley, Brookstreet, and Cranham on New Year's Eve. In each case there must have been a substantial core of Catholics among the guests, since a conservative estimate of the percentage

[103] ERO, D/DP, A25.   [104] Ibid. A 31.   [105] ERO, D/DP, F160.

of Catholic tenants on the Petre estates puts the figure at 40 per cent.[106] However, there was no attempt to exclude non-Catholics, as the invitations to the parsons of East Horndon and Ingrave demonstrate. The nature of the household record makes it impossible to speak with any confidence about the Petres' motives for maintaining such an elaborate pattern of traditional entertainment; it may be that a combination of family precedent and the desire to assert local influence in one of the few ways available to a recusant family offer adequate explanation. The Petres were certainly not alone in their Christmas celebrations: a Paget household book for 1579 shows equal elaboration of entertainment during the Twelve Days. At the Epiphany feast the family fed a huge company of invited guests, and 'fourtie messe of the neighbours and others not bidden'.[107]

The obvious question raised by the Petre accounts, and by other descriptions of Catholic generosity, is whether these traditions survived the Civil War. The introversion of the Catholic community was already an obvious feature of the late Elizabethan polity, but does not seem to have produced an exclusively enclosed form of entertainment. Hospitality by such magnates as the Earl of Worcester or Lord William Howard looks distinctly old-fashioned in the 1640s, and does not really seem to have survived into the next generation.[108] Nevertheless, there did remain in some Catholic families a self-conscious pride in the maintenance of good hospitality which was felt to set them apart from their Protestant neighbours. The household book of Sir Miles Stapleton, a Yorkshire recusant, shows Christmas being celebrated in the years after the Restoration with general conviviality and the entertainment of neighbours and tenants who were not necessarily Catholic.[109] The household of Nicholas Blundell gradually moved away from a riotous celebration of the festival itself towards more overtly pious behaviour, but it still continued

[106] M. O'Dwyer, 'Catholic Recusants in Essex, ca. 1580 to ca. 1600', London MA dissertation (1960), ch. 4.

[107] Staff. RO, D(W) 1734/3/3/280.

[108] Stone, *Crisis*, 213; Legg, *A Short Survey*, 39–41. Even Lord William Howard perceived the virtues of increased privacy: he partitioned the great hall at Naworth to create a dining-chamber, *Household Books of Lord Howard*, lxviii.

[109] J. C. Cox (ed.), 'The Household Book of Sir Miles Stapleton, Bt., 1656–1705', *The Ancestor* (October, 1902), 148.

the tradition of open house on other days of the season.[110] Catholic gentry also preserved some of the traditions of charitable giving common in an earlier age: it was a Catholic family, the Tichbornes, who preserved the ceremony of the Tichborne dole, and took such pride in this display of formal paternalism that they had it painted in the 1670s.[111] The value attached to the dole is particularly interesting, since it was at once an extremely personal and visibly hierarchical mode of giving. There is no doubt about the engagement of the family in the act of giving, but giving here affirms hierarchy: there is no sense of the poor as reciprocally conferring benefits upon them. Thus this piece of apparently traditional drama lacks an element that would have been present in such exchanges as the Maundy ceremonies or the feeding of poor men in the hall, in which mutuality was an essential aspect of the performance.[112]

There is evidence that some Catholic gentry families continued to take pride in their reputation for good hospitality into the eighteenth century, although the community itself gradually became more introverted in the same period. The ninth Duke of Norfolk, retired on his Worksop estate in the mid-century, was said to have kept up 'the ancient spirit of hospitality in its primitive greatness', being particularly generous to the needy of the area.[113] Even more revealing is the memorial to the Catholic squire of East Lulworth, Dorset. Edward Weld was said to have lived in great credit and hospitality, always being careful not to confine his generosity to those of his own persuasion, but making it universal, as part of the 'good correspondence and harmony' that he maintained with both neighbouring gentry and clergy.[114]

Puritan conviction was less likely to sit easily with a ready acceptance of the old ways; indeed, as we have seen, some aspects of Protestant thought represented a deliberate break with the old casual conviviality. Nevertheless, the godly were particularly

[110] J. J. Bagley (ed.), *The Great Diurnal of Nicholas Blundell,* 2 vols. (Lancs. and Cheshire Rec. Soc., 110, 112, 1968, 1970), i, 25, 48, 196.

[111] See plate 4.

[112] See e.g., the full description of the reciprocity involved in the giving of maundy by an earl, Bodl. MS Eng. hist b, 208, fo. 45 ff.

[113] John Thoroton, *History of Nottinghamshire, Republished with Large Additions,* 3 vols. (London, 1790), iii. 399.

[114] John Hutchins, *The History and Antiquities of Dorset*, 2 vols. (London, 1861–74), i. 371.

enjoined to care for those in need and a social conscience was the logical result of a belief in one's own election. The Puritan gentry, like their Catholic neighbours, emerged from a culture which approved acts of personal generosity as congruent with the honour of the individual and his family, and it should, therefore, be no great surprise that some of them sought to maintain the best in the old pattern of giving, as well as responding particularly warmly to the needs of the saints. An early example of a minor gentleman who felt obliged to maintain tradition and to justify it from the new perspective of committed Protestantism is that of Richard Stonley.[115] Stonley seems to have modelled his social behaviour on that of his Catholic patrons and former employees, the Petres, but in entertaining his tenants and the poor at Christmas, and in receiving the minister and local worthies at his table on a Sunday, he apparently saw an opportunity to cultivate godliness in the community. A major purpose of the Sunday dinner was to discuss the sermon that had preceded it.[116] Yet Stonley, with his concern for the rituals of the Christmas season and his continuing warmth towards the most powerful of the Essex Catholics, is a somewhat incongruous character to describe as a Puritan. By the standards of the seventeenth century he was scarcely fully one of the godly. To see what a true member of that self-defined band could offer for hospitality we can look at the biography of John Bruen, published in 1641, but describing a life lived largely in the Elizabethan and Jacobean periods.[117]

Bruen was a minor Cheshire gentleman who, because of the location of his seat on the main road from London into North Wales, was able to entertain many of the 'household of faith' on their travels. As William Hinde, his biographer, describes it, they visited him 'not so much . . . for the ease and refreshing of their bodies, as for the comfort and rejoycing of their hearts, in seeing his face, in hearing his voice, in conferring and advising with him'.[118] The network of godly ministers and associates that is characteristic of, for example, the Harley household, or that of the earls of Warwick, is here given a specifically communitarian

---

[115] Folger Lib., V.a.459.   [116] Ibid. fos. 19, 22ᵛ, 38.
[117] Hinde, *A Faithfull Remonstrance of the Holy Life and Happy Death of John Bruen of Bruen Stapleford* (London, 1641).
[118] Ibid. 185–6.

meaning, with hospitality very consciously used as a way of strengthening bonds between brethren who were widely separated.[119] Nearer home, Bruen took pleasure in entertaining 'good people', often the self-defined godly. On one famous occasion he arranged that the godly should spend three days in the local church, listening to sermons and praying, so that traditionalists could not celebrate their 'popish wakes'. A part of this exercise was the spending of lavish provisions 'upon godly, and well affected people'. However, Bruen never confined his attentions to a narrow community: since he sought converts to his mode of life, he used hospitality deliberately as a tool for the influencing of religious attitudes. Each Sunday a preacher would deliver a sermon in his private chapel to which all were welcome, and some came to feed their souls, even though others, says Hinde, were 'willing and ready to presse into the Hall to fill their bellies'.[120] In his treatment of the poor Bruen apparently combined a desire to proselytize with traditional belief in the duties of the gentry: in times of dearth he fed large numbers at his gate, and gave in food and other support far more than was required of him by the public collectors.[121] In all of this Bruen was clear that one must have no dealings with the ungodly: he reproved his cousin, Mr Wilbraham of Woodhay, for making his house 'a thorough-fare of profane persons'.[122] But within a broad definition of the godly he sought to maintain in very full form the hospitable customs of his ancestors, and to turn them to positive use in the furthering of the gospel.

Other members of the godly magistracy seem to have endeavoured to turn old customs to new ends in the late sixteenth and early seventeenth centuries. A well-known case is that of the Lewkenor family of Suffolk, who over three generations showed unusual generosity to the poor.[123] Most interesting is the activity of Sir Edward Lewkenor who died in 1618, and was considered so valuable a member of the community of the godly that he was memorialized in two separate funeral sermons. Like his peers, Sir Edward delighted 'in the companie of the Saints', and frequently

---

[119] T. T. Lewis (ed.), *Letters of the Lady Brilliana Harley* (Camden Soc., O.S. 58, 1854), xi.
[120] Hinde, *John Bruen*, 87.   [121] Ibid. 187.   [122] Ibid. 195.
[123] Collinson, 'Magistracy and Ministry: a Suffolk Miniature', in his *Godly People: Essays on English Protestantism and Puritanism* (London, 1983), 445–66.

received them at his table.[124] However, he was also deeply
conscious of his duties to the poor, and not only fed them
regularly at his gates but 'reard up one building near his own
house, furnished it with a large table to the onely use and releefe
of the poore, that thrice a weeke resorted thither'. One of the
preachers suggests that thirty to forty persons were fed in this
manner on each occasion, most of them presumably being local
poor, since they were categorized as orphans, widows, and
fatherless children.

The arrangement described is so similar to that advocated by
William Turner half a century earlier that it is tempting to posit
a direct connection between the two, though Lewkenor could
equally well have been borrowing from a monastic model in
establishing his guest-house for the poor. Although it is not easy
to trace other examples of such systematic activity by the Puritan
gentry, it may be that Lewkenor was not unique. Richard
Brownlow, a retired prothnotary of Common Pleas, recorded in
his account book for the mid-Jacobean period payments to 'the
guest house' in Belton near Grantham.[125] In the Lewkenor case,
perhaps more obviously than in that of the obsessive Bruen, it
is possible to observe the transmutation of general conviviality,
with the poor as the residuary legatees, into a serious redirection
of resources to the needy, though still in customary patterns of
giving. No doubt it required considerable social and moral
earnestness to take this path which, as Sir Edward's eulogizers
admitted, imposed a severe strain on his finances.[126] This may
be why so many of the godly magistracy did not apparently
consider traditional hospitality very important: it receives no
emphasis in the writings of Sir Richard Grosvenor or Sir John
Newdigate on the subject of the political and social duties of the
élite, nor did funeral sermons for Puritan gentlemen always allude
to it.[127] Sir Edward Montagu, whose advices to his son include
the suggestion that tenants should be treated kindly, felt no need

---

[124] Bezaleel Carter, *The Wise King and the Learned Judge . . . Sir Edward
Lewkenor* (Cambridge, 1618), 49; Timothy Oldmayne, *God's Rebuke in Taking
from us Sir E Lewkenor* (London, 1619).
[125] E. Cust, *Records of the Cust Family*, 2 vols. (London, 1909), ii. 54.
[126] Carter, *The Wise King*, 63.
[127] R. Cust and P. Lake, 'Sir Richard Grosvenor and the Rhetoric of Magistracy',
BIHR, 54 (1981), 40–53; Larminie, 'The Newdigates', 362 ff.

to say anything in detail about the poor or entertainment.[128] However, their lack of articulated concern for hospitality does not necessarily argue for neglect. Sir Edward Montagu's son was described by Fuller as a 'pious, peaceable and hospitable patriot', who seems to have modelled himself on his father's behaviour.[129]

IV

Religious ideology rarely acted as the sole variable determining social behaviour; indeed, it was likely to be most influential when combined with other external circumstances. This is particularly relevant in the case of women. There is a familiar argument that élite women were disproportionately infuential both among godly Protestants and Catholics, and that they used their position within the family to promote their chosen beliefs.[130] Their considerable control over the domestic economy could also give them an influence over forms of hospitality, and the association of religion and specific forms of entertainment logically followed. The generosity of the Catholic Lady Montagu has already been considered, but equally good works were undertaken by a number of her peers, such as Lady Vaux.[131] On the Puritan side there is the amusing story told by Thomas Raymond of his lawyer-master who married a second wife, who, while a rich widow, 'undid hir selfe by entertaynments, especially of Puritans'.[132] More seriously, there is active advocacy of good entertainment in the funeral sermon of Mrs Dorothy Hanbury, who entertained the meanest of the saints.[133]

[128] L. Stone (ed.), 'Sir Edward Montagu's Directions to his Son', *Northants. Past and Present*, 2 (1958), 221–3.
[129] Thomas Fuller, *The History of the Worthies of England*, ed. P. Nuttall, 3 vols. (London, 1840), ii. 520.
[130] See e.g., K. V. Thomas, 'Women and the Civil War Sects', *PP*, 13 (1958) 45; N. Z. Davis, *Society and Culture in Early Modern France* (London, 1965), 65–70; M. Rowlands, 'Recusant Women, 1560–1640', in M. Prior, *Women in English Society 1500–1800* (London, 1985), 149–80.
[131] Rowlands, 'Recusant Women', 156–66.
[132] G. Davies (ed.), *The Autobiography of Thomas Raymond* (Camden Soc., 3rd ser. 28, London, 1917), 24.
[133] Samuel Ainsworth, *A Sermon Preached at the Funeral of Mrs. Dorothy Hanbury* (London, 1642).

Women had other inducements beyond the narrowly sectarian to act hospitably. Some were a reflection of the advantages women possessed in using the household as their sphere of social action. Henry Percy, ninth Earl of Northumberland, who was something of a misogynist, nevertheless provided some valuable insights into this theme in his instructions to his son, written in 1609.[134] Women, he observed, exercised greater control over domestic affairs in England than elsewhere in Europe. The reason was the demands of English hospitality: since a man had to pursue his business elsewhere, his wife perforce had to manage the domestic establishment, 'entertayning all comers, conducting there guests to there chambers; carefull of there breakfasts, keeping them company at cards, with many more complements of this nature, whiche is not ordenary in other places and other nations'. As an explanation of the behavioural contrasts between English women and their continental counterparts this appears rather limited, but it is a perceptive enough comment about the autonomy that an upper-class woman could enjoy within her household. Margaret, Duchess of Newcastle's trenchant comments on the merits and demerits of traditional hospitality suggest that she had an important voice in its exercise in her own home.[135]

Women of a charitable disposition could provide a powerful alternative vision of domestic care, because they were more likely than their husbands to extend the charitable work of the household into the community. One of the paradigms of virtuous female behaviour, constantly employed in the writings of biographers and preachers of funeral sermons, is that of service to the community through the giving of alms and the ministration to the sick and needy in their own homes. Sir Hugh Cholmley remarked of his wife that she was, 'very courteous and affable to her neighbours of all ranks, . . . often going amongst them to visit'.[136] Lady Margaret Hoby's generosity to the poor and sick of Hackness is a recurrent, though understated, theme, in her diary: she, like many of her contemporaries, shared in the

---

[134] 'Instructions by Henry Percy, 9th Earl of Northumberland, to his Son', *Archaeologia*, 27 (1838), 341.

[135] Margaret Cavendish, Duchess of Newcastle, *The World's Olio* (London, 1671), 67–70.

[136] Cholmley, *Memoirs*, 51.

experiences of her female neighbours to an extent that would have been unthinkable for her husband.[137] Nor was this species of generosity necessarily confined to rural manors. Anne Fanshawe, who was born in St Olave's parish, London, provided an image of her mother's behaviour there in the late 1620s that is a valuable antidote to the view that London living necessarily turned the gentry from their traditional paths. She was 'very pious, and charitable to that degree, that she relieved, besides the offals of the table, which she constantly gave to the poor, many with her own hand daily out of her purse, and dressed many wounds of miserable people'.[138]

Although wives might well enjoy the freedom to offer this personal care to the poor both inside and outside the household, it was widows who were most frequently remarked for their sustained generosity. Funeral monuments of the first half of the seventeenth century often comment on the hospitable lives led by widows for many years after the death of their husbands. Lady Jane Fenner, buried in Hampton Gay church, Oxfordshire, in 1663, was 79 at her death and had survived her husband by some years: she was praised for her 'piety, charity and hospitality [which] made her honor'd whilest shee liv'd and promiseth a glorious resurrection'.[139] Lady Lucy maintained the family tradition of generosity at Charlecote during the difficult years of the Civil War, and was given lavish praise in consequence in her funeral sermon.[140] Lord Herbert of Cherbury prided himself on the generosity of both his mother and grandmother: the latter, as a widow, 'kept hospitality with that plenty and order as exceeded all either of her country or time'; the former was praised by John Donne in his funeral sermon as having a house which was 'a court, with conversation of the best, and an almshouse in feeding the poor'.[141] An extreme example of the charitable widow is that of Annabel, second wife of the tenth Earl of Kent,

[137] D. M. Meads (ed.), *The Diary of Lady Margaret Hoby* (London, 1930), 86, 91, 100, 136–7.

[138] N. H. Nicolas (ed.), *Memoir of Lady Fanshawe, wife of . . . Sir Richard Fanshawe . . .* (London, 1829), 52.

[139] Hampton Gay church, chancel monument.

[140] Thomas Dugard, *Death and the Grave Little Regarded: A Sermon Preached at the Funeral of . . . Lady Alice Lucie* (London, 1649), 49.

[141] S. Lee (ed.), *The Life of Edward, Lord Herbert of Cherbury* (London, 1886), 18–19, 319.

who died in 1698, and was supposed to have spent most of her annual fortune on the poor. According to tradition, she prepared an elaborate meal every other day for the needy, and often had sixty to eighty people there to consume it. Like her peeers, she also engaged in other female works of mercy, distributing sums of money and providing medical care.[142] Since she was in greater command of the resources of her household than a married woman, such generosity might be expected of the pious widow. Indeed, so committed to hospitality did some widows become, that they risked conflict with a new spouse on remarriage. Some years before memorial tablets began to praise virtuous widows, there is an interesting example of the tensions generated by a widow's charity in the case of Margaret Cranmer, the former wife of the Archbishop. Margaret remarried during Mary's reign, but when her second husband died she apparently resolved to remain single, maintaining the 'good hospytallyte' towards the poor on which she had always prided herself. However, she was inveigled into a third marriage by a younger man who professed profound respect for her works of mercy, only to seize control of her remaining assets when they were united.[143]

But it may be a mistake to see the interest of widows, and indeed of other women, in hospitality, largely in terms of their pious impulses to serve the community. Even the funeral monuments chose to identify affability to all ranks as a characteristic of virtuous matrons, and there are plenty of eulogies to women who maintained a generous table even in their widowhood.[144] Such women were often praised for their good governance of their household, their civility and constant entertainment, in terms that superficially seem very similar to those used for their spouses. However, the rhetoric is in fact distinct: gravity and sobriety as well as good order were the approved characteristics of female government, and women's

---

[142] C. Jackson (ed.), *The Diary of Abraham de la Pryme* (Surtees Soc., 54, 1870), 8.

[143] PRO, C3/217/30; I am grateful to Mary Prior for drawing my attention to this case.

[144] See e.g., the tomb of Jane Knyvett, twenty-three years a widow, who died in 1562: she always, claims the memorial, kept house 'where rich and poor were fedde': Hood (ed.), *The Chorography of Norfolk* (Norwich, 1938), 79.

distinctive contribution was usually seen as their ability to mitigate the divisive effects of hierarchy. Lady Elizabeth Capel, who died in 1661, was praised because 'she learnt her Spirit to stoop even to the lowest, and submit to an entertainment of friendship and courtesie with the meanest persons of all'.[145] A similar charm is remarked in the biography of Christiana, dowager Countess of Devon, whose grace and affability 'drew the poor to her gates, and strangers to her table, and the city and court to her conversations'.[146] The countess divided her year between town and country but, unlike many of her Caroline contemporaries, steered the same 'steady course' in both and gained love and respect by her openness. To embody this matriarchal power to the full it was necessary to be widowed, and it probably was advantageous to eschew London society. When Lady Anne Clifford, who had been unusually restricted in her control of her household during her first unhappy marriage to the Earl of Dorset, was able to come into her northern inheritance, she had no doubts about the social power that a widow could wield from her own properties. She resolutely resisted the lure of London and even the provincial captial of York, and ruled from her own household, dispensing hospitality to a wide range of visitors from the justices of the central courts to the lesser tenantry.[147]

None of this evidence is intended to suggest that women were routinely defenders of the old traditions of hospitality. We have already observed that they played a peculiar role in the breakdown of the old order, with the development of the town season which provided a means of lessening their rural 'ennui'. It was women who 'gadded', and this not only in the misogynist literature of the early seventeenth century. It was also women who developed many of the rules of visiting, founded upon assumptions about civility which were again some threat to the old order. What is being argued, however, is that there were role perceptions that countered these developments, that offered women, and especially widows, a positive incentive to appear charitable and hospitable. Some measure of self-definition, albeit

[145] Edmund Barker, *A Sermon Preached at the Funerall of . . . Lady Elizabeth Capell* (London, 1661), 35.
[146] J. Nichols, *The History and Antiquities of the County of Leicester*, 4 vols. (London, 1795–1815), i, pt. ii, 288.
[147] Williamson, *Anne Clifford*, 265 ff.

within the domestic sphere routinely assigned to them, was achieved by women who used good entertainment as a mode of demonstrating their authority. This, plus the charitable giving and mitigation of division undertaken by virtuous gentry wives, was perhaps one of the most 'public' ways in which they could acquire honour and maintain reputation.[148]

V

The rhetoric of 'the country' has already been considered as a potent influence on the maintenance of traditional patterns of hospitality. It provided a justification for those who wished to avoid London living, and a language in which the Crown could assail pleasure-loving gentlemen who 'lurked about the city'. It appeared in the most unlikely places, as in Sir George Sondes's defence of his behaviour after the murder of his elder son by his younger brother, or in the quarrelsome Gervase Markham's claim that he had been wronged by his neighbours because, *inter alia*, they had accused him of keeping 'noe house nor hospitality'.[149] Much of this can be dismissed as but lip-service to a convenient ideal, made more convenient by the curious interest of the Crown in the issue under James and Charles. For a section of the élite, especially for those gentry who saw their power and interest as focused primarily within their counties, appeals to return to tradition and conviviality must have resonated somewhat oddly, since they had not abandoned their rural role. Sir Hugh Cholmley, describing his regime on his Yorkshire estate in the 1630s, observed that his table 'was ever fit to receive three or four besides my family, without any trouble, whatever their fare was, they were sure to have a hearty welcome'.[150] The old model is that described by Thomas Fuller for Edward Bash of Hertfordshire, who 'was a hearty gentleman, and a good English housekeeper, keeping a full table with solid dishes on it, and welcome guests'.[151]

---

[148] This obviously contrasts with the most common gender stereotype, in which female honour is largely bound up in the modest maintenance of chastity.
[149] George Sondes, 'Narrative of the Death of his Two Sons', in *Harleian Miscellany*, 10 (London, 1813), 49; PRO STAC 8/208/31.
[150] Cholmley, *Memoirs*, 34.   [151] Fuller, *Worthies of England*, ii. 58.

The reality of a gentry community where the old ways mattered is well evoked in the notebook of Sir John Oglander.[152] Oglander describes the society of the Isle of Wight between the 1620s and the 1650s in garrulous and unreflective detail, mixing marriages and funerals with major political events and comments on his finances. The world of gentry sociability that he conjures up is similar to that of the sixteenth-century Le Strange accounts. Every event was marked by eating and drinking; visitors, such as Richard, first Earl of Portland, who became Captain of the Island in 1631, were attended by all the gentry of the county and were expected to reciprocate with lavish entertainment.[153] Friends were judged by the openness of their housekeeping, and not by refinement of London manners. Oglander's boon companion, Sir Richard Worsley, 'kept a very bountiful house, and gave great entertainment; lived in great repute in his country and very happily', but had no respect for good clothes.[154] The diarist himself was inordinately proud of the fact that he kept one of the best houses on the island, and was never more depressed than in 1647 when political crisis meant that there was 'no resort, no neighbours seeing one of the other'.[155] Care of the poor, or tenants, receives little mention in Oglander, but he hints even here at approval of the old ways, scraps at the gate and a general hierarchical benevolence.

Island society, to this day a distinctive phenomenon, may have intensified the gentry's adherence to old customs. Elsewhere, 'county' sentiment was likely to be determined by more complex variables. When Christopher Wandesford recommended his children to win the affection of their neighbourhood in his 1630s *Instructions*, he held up to them the example of their Yorkshire grandfather,

whose neighbourly and friendly Behaviour to his Equals, Mildness and Care to perform Offices of Love and Bounty towards his Inferiors; begot not only a singular Respect and Dependency in the whole Country, in a Manner, upon him while he lived; but in Virtue thereof, a far greater Estimation to me, than I could otherwise have meeted of my self.[156]

[152] Sir John Oglander, *A Royalist's Notebook: The Commonplace Book of Sir John Oglander, Knt*, ed. F. Bamford (London, 1936).
[153] Ibid. 65.   [154] Ibid. 187   [155] Ibid. 112.
[156] C. Wandesford, *A Book of Instructions to his Son*, ed. T. Comber (London, 1777), 82.

Good neighbourly behaviour was necessary for this family not only because they wished to maintain influence in the county, but because there was already a clear expectation that they were generous. Only a dramatic change in their locus of interests could have liberated them from a need to maintain honour through generosity. When Lady Wandesford was widowed in Ireland she felt it incumbent on her for the sake of the family honour to keep up a great household at her own charges, and even when she retired to England she continued to hold open house despite her frugal resources.[157] In a case such as this the perpetuation of a tradition could become a major burden to the heirs: Sir Thomas Sadler, who died in 1607 in some financial embarrassment, had apparently continued his father's lavish ways since 'he knew not well how to spend lesse'.[158] A society which still easily transmuted spontaneous individual actions into collective obligations was inevitably one in which the behaviour of fathers created a weighty responsibility for children.

The ethos of 'good country hospitality' could also be reified as a self-conscious statement of a political position. Aspects of the hospitality of the gentry, like the celebration of Christmas, must have been closely integrated with the customary cycles of feast and revel that were an important part of village society. When these were assailed by the godly in the great reformation of manners that became so divisive an issue in the localities from the 1590s onwards, there were some gentlemen who deliberately supported the continuity of tradition.[159] Sir John Parham of Poyntington, Somerset, a Catholic landowner, was accused in 1604 of encouraging riotous displays by men of Milbourne Port.[160] His response was that he was merely encouraging the local church feast, by giving those who came to bid him to it 'some entertaynment such as of a suddayne his howse did afford'. Even this, in the circumstances of early seventeenth-century Somerset, was a political statement that identified Parham with hostility to the godly. Thirty years later Sir Humphrey Mildmay,

[157] C. Jackson (ed.), *The Autobiography of Mrs. Alice Thornton* (Surtees Soc., 62, 1875), 28.
[158] Inner Temple Lib., Petyt MS 531 E/H2-23, fo. 7.
[159] D. Underdown, *Revel, Riot, and Rebellion: Popular Politics and Culture in England, 1603–1660* (Oxford, 1985), 63–6.
[160] PRO, STAC 8/291/12.

with his adherence to the custom of a drunken and riotous Christmas, would seem to be offering a more deliberate challenge to the Essex godly.[161] During the Interregnum, celebration was elevated to an act of rebellion, as in 1655, when the royalist rising in the West Country was preceded by cavaliers keeping 'great Christmasses after the usual time with sets of fiddlers'.[162]

After the Restoration it was less likely that hospitality would need to be used as a direct statement of political affinity. Nevertheless, adherence to country tradition could still retain political connotations. Sir John Reresby, governor of York under Charles II, offers a valuable example of this pattern in his management of social relationships in the locality. When not in post he spent much of his time in London, but was careful to return to his Yorkshire estate for the celebration of the Christmas season. His comments on the failure of most of his contemporaries in this respect have already been noted, but it is important to realize that Reresby was at odds with much of the local community, and was a pugnacious man who rarely took a charitable view of the behaviour of others. On the other hand, his Christmas arrangements, as he describes them for 1682, were certainly elaborate: tenants from his various properties were invited to a sequence of dinners beginning on Christmas Eve; St Stephen's Day was the busiest, when fifty-four were present. From 30 December onwards he began to entertain the local gentry, and then on 4 January twelve of the neighbouring clergy came, followed two days later by the tradesmen of Rotherham and other towns.[163]

Outside the Christmas season Reresby received his extended kin and made efforts to cultivate the friendship of those of his gentry neighbours whose political standing might serve his local ambitions.[164] This form of entertainment, along with his oleaginous pleasure in receiving and being received by the Duke of Newcastle, belongs easily to the world of late seventeenth-century influence and patronage. But Reresby's Christmasses were also in their own way political statements. He made the matter explicit in a letter to Blathwayt about a mutiny in his company at the end of 1687. 'Hospitality', he remarked, 'being much laid

---

[161] Ralph, *Sir Humphrey Mildmay*, 101 ff.
[162] Quoted in Underdown, 261.
[163] A. Browning (ed.), *The Memoirs of Sir John Reresby* (Glasgow, 1936), 285–6.
[164] Ibid. 106–7, 129.

aside of late in thes parts of this time of the year, which dissatisfyeth the common sort of people and makes them apt to dispond, I left Yorke very lately to observe my constant custome of keeping an opon Christmas here'.[165] Social harmony, or perhaps one should say a modified form of social control, was the objective Reresby sought, and he wished to demonstrate that it was best achieved through an active paternalism. We may also legitimately infer that for the governor, and men who thought like him, village paternalism was in microcosm what royal paternalism should be in the realm at large.

It is, however, worth noting that active paternalism of Reresby's kind did not have to be identified wholly with an intense traditionalism. Gentlemen could associate newer, discriminating forms of care for the poor with the old ways. Sir Thomas Lucy, who died in 1640, was claimed to have cared for the poor both within doors and without, to have provided suitable light work for the elderly, to have given food at the Christmas season 'in the bordering towns', and to have followed tradition by feeding the neighbouring poor at the gates of Charlecote weekly.[166] The combination of charitable activity in which he engaged, and indeed the very order in which it is discussed, is significant. The Lucy family were forceful adherents of traditional behaviour, but their very knowledge of, and engagement in, the local community meant that they saw giving as a diverse process, conditioned by need, and not necessarily exclusively focused on the household. The quality praised in those early seventeenth-century gentlemen who were believed by their eulogists to be particularly charitable was an active and discerning pursuit of real need in the neighbourhood, and a willingness to respond vigorously to significant crises such as dearth.[167] Although doles and meals remained a part of this process, they were often demoted in favour of alternative approaches. George Abbot, for example, praised the first Earl of Dorset, who sent rye to six of the Sussex parishes in which he

---

[165] Ibid. 480.
[166] Robert Harris, *Abner's Funerall: Preached at the Burial of Sir Thomas Lucie* (2nd. edn., London, 1653), 240.
[167] See e.g., William Walker's praise of William, Lord Russell, who 'would enter into the poore mens houses and learne of them what they got by their weekely labour' in order to relieve them better: William Walker, *A Sermon Preached at the Funerall of William, Lord Russell* (London, 1613), 47–8.

held land as a free gift in 1597, and who again in 1608 arranged for 'certaine quarters of Wheat, to be carried from his own Granary at Lewes in Sussex and to be sold in the market to the poor at a farre lower rate than the price which commonly men did take'.[168] When no immediate crisis threatened, the élite often chose those more institutionalized forms of charity that would secure long-term benefits to the community: almshouses, or land endowed for various schemes to aid particular sections of the poor.[169]

VI

Finally, among the general inducements to remain hospitable, it is worth including the survival of the noble ethos of magnificence. The scale, and the public quality, of the entertainment expected of the very greatest men in the realm, imposed upon them greater obligations than those experienced by the mere gentry. Although the demands of interest and honour might not compel a nobleman to act quite as formally as did the Earl of Worcester at Raglan, they made it very difficult for him simply to neglect the concept of open hospitality.[170] Great houses like Hatfield, Petworth, Badminton, and Alnwick Castle were places of semi-public resort, a situation little changed by the upheavals of the seventeenth century. When Joan Flower was accused of witchcraft in 1618, it was remarked that she had haunted Belvoir Castle, where the Earl and Countess of Rutland ensured that the 'castle was a continual pallace of entertainment, and a daily receptacle for all sorts both rich and poore, especially such auncient people as neighboured the same'.[171] Margaret, Duchess of Newcastle, described how her husband spent his time during the Jacobean period living in the country, pleasing himself and his neighbours

---

[168] George Abbot, *A Sermon preached . . . at the Funerall . . . of Thomas [Sackville] Earle of Dorset* (London, 1608), 16; others, including William Cecil, were praised for similar behaviour.

[169] W. K. Jordan, *Philanthrophy in England, 1480–1660* (London, 1959), 147, 253 f.

[170] Stone, *Crisis*, 581–4.

[171] *The Wonderful Discoverie of the Witchcrafts of Margaret and Phillip Flower . . . Executed at Lincolne, March 11th, 1618* (London, 1619).

with 'Noble Housekeeping and Hospitality', and but rarely visiting court to wait on the king.[172]

The *Instructions to a Son* that Archibald, Marquis of Argyll, drew up on the eve of his execution in 1651, offer valuable insight into the assumptions that underlay this abiding generosity.[173] Argyll did not share the general view that Scottish hospitality was preferable to that of England; instead he argued that the English élite were still appropriately aware that niggardliness could lead to contempt from one's peers. His son was advised, as far as his resources allowed, to imitate English manners, to keep his own house, and be open to all guests, even the 'ruder sort' who, greeted with all courtesy, 'will soon abstain or soon be civilised'.[174] Good order was essential in a household, but especially in that of a nobleman, since 'Every ordinary mans house is his Castle, but a Noblemans is that and a Palace both, where there is reverence due to you as well as a bare power and command'. This also obliged the nobleman to celebrate public anniversaries, especially state occasions, with all solemnity, since his 'magnificence at those times are the most forcible impressions to make the people remember . . . the mercys and favours of such days'.[175] Argyll's sensitivity to the public visibility of the nobleman no doubt owed something to his own parlous situation, but it also reflected an essential image that survived the crises of the mid-seventeenth century.

The need for public display often made it difficult for noblemen to subscribe wholeheartedly to changing perceptions of the poor in this period. The later household ordinances remain suspended uneasily between the view that shiftless beggars must not be fed, and a continuing determination to issue bounty at the gates. The Huntingdon household regulations are typical in ordering that alms at the gate should be given 'to suche as are aged, poore and in want, and not to stout rouges and idle persons'.[176] Several other ordinances make only brief and passing reference to the feeding of the poor at the gates, stressing instead the duty of the porter in keeping beggars and other undesirables away from the

---

[172] Margaret Cavendish, Duchess of Newcastle, *The Life of William, Duke of Newcastle* (London, 1675), 5, 177.

[173] Archibald Campbell, Marquis of Argyll, *Instructions to a Son* (London, 1661).

[174] Ibid. 83.   [175] Ibid. 87.   [176] Nichols, *Leicester*, iii. pt. ii, 596.

entrance area. However, the second Duke of Buckingham was unique when, in the 1630s, he made no mention of feeding of the poor when talking of the duties of his porter and hall usher.[177] General doles continued in many households: Cranfield's ordinances, for example, separate them carefully from the feeding of the deserving poor with special food, and John, Earl of Bridgewater, still assumed that they were a necessary part of the behaviour of a nobleman in 1652.[178] Argyll argued in his *Instructions* that, though the condition of the poor meant that they could not be entertained within doors, yet 'a constant care and provision [must] be made for them'.[179] While it is difficult to prove that the care offered through gate dole was 'constant' in late-seventeenth century noble households, it does seem to be expected that something would still be done when the household was in residence. Only in the early eighteenth century do we encounter orders such as that for the establishments of the Duke of Newcastle at Halland and Bishopstone, Sussex, insisting on an end to the tradition of giving beer and doles to all comers into the lower household 'without stint or limitation'.[180]

Public magnificence remained an essential part of the vision of nobility; indeed, the trauma of civil war and revolution may have made it all the more crucial after the Restoration. Perhaps the most that the aristocracy could do was to modify the old ways: first and foremost the could absent themselves from their country properties, thereby using their resources on the rather different group of dependants who attended them in town. Secondly, they could employ the new codes of civility to restrict access to certain occasions. When William Hutchinson visited Alnwick Castle in the 1770s, he arrived on a 'public day', the first held by the Duke and Duchess of Northumberland since their return to the country. Hospitality on this occasion was carefully ordered, but there was general access and visitors of all ranks were welcomed. In a pompous flight of rhetoric Hutchinson asserted that: 'Hospitality cloathed in princely array, sits in the hall, dispensing with a brow of benignity, mixed with features of the

---

[177] Wi. RO 865/389, 28–30.
[178] LPL Fulham Papers, 426, fo. 31; Todd, *Ashridge*, 53.
[179] Argyll, *Instructions*, 88.   [180] Girouard, *Country House*, 189.

highest magnificence, gifts worthy of her hand.'[181] At the bottom of the social hierarchy, the poor were still being fed at the gates, though on a ticket system which suggests that only local men were beneficiaries. At Alnwick, Hutchinson seems to be observing the full working of traditional entertainment, but as a system extracted from mothballs a few times during the year, a way of affirming continuity with the past on a carefully circumscribed number of occasions. Much the same might be remarked of the lavish 'treats' given by eighteenth-century noblemen to celebrate national or familial events in the old style. By then Argyll's notions that the noble should keep himself at home, and keep constant and open hospitality, would have appeared very dated, but the obligation to display magnificence and munificence in public still compelled the greatest in the land.[182]

[181] W. Hutchinson, *The View of Northumberland*, 2 vols. (Newcastle, 1778), 195.

[182] For an example of eighteenth-century noble 'treating', see the birthday party of the Duke of Rutland in the 1790s: F. Heal, 'The Idea of Hospitality in Early Modern England', *PP*, 102, 89–90.

5

Visitors and Voyagers

GOOD hosts need good guests in order to display their talents to the full. Or, to put it another way, the social interchange that is the guest/host relationship demands that both parties behave according to learned conventions about their roles. In some senses the guest's role may be the more difficult: as the outsider he has obligations to accept the customary parameters of his host's establishment, functioning as a passive recipient of the goods and services defined by the latter as part of his hospitality. Often his very security must depend upon a belief that his host will obey the laws of hospitality and protect him in a potentially hostile environment.[1] Yet his role is not one of pure passivity: the very act of, for example, accepting or refusing food is one which affirms or challenges his host's generosity. And, even though the relationship is by definition asymmetrical in the short term, it will normally demand of him some gesture that restores social symmetry. This may merely be thanks, expressed by word or gift, or in many cultures by 'prayers and praise'. The eighteenth-century French writer, Grimod de la Reyniere, put this neatly when he urged guests to 'pay our share in happy speeches, fine words, erotic verses, witty repartee, amusing and short anecdotes'.[2] In early modern Britain this tradition of praise was most obviously sustained by the bards of Ireland and Wales, who still perpetuated great feasts in return for their sustenance. The Christmas feast of O'Ruaric, a Celtic chieftain who died in 1591, was enthusiastically sung:

---

[1] J. Pitt-Rivers, 'The Law of Hospitality', in his *The Fate of Schechem* (Cambridge, 1977), 108–11; L. Bolchazy, *Hospitality in Early Rome* (Chicago, 1977), 28–30; M. M. Wood, *The Stranger* (New York, 1934), 83.

[2] Quoted in I. de Garine, 'Food, Tradition and Prestige', in D. N. Walcher *et al.* (eds.), *Food, Man and Society* (International Organization for Human Development, 1976), 153.

By those who were there
Or those who were not.
His revels to keep,
We sup and we dine
On seven score sheep
Fat bullocks and swine.[3]

Or symmetry may be restored by the return of entertainment, and the reversal of roles: a point illustrated again by French usage, where *l'hôte* can only be translated as 'host' or 'guest' when the context is understood. Yet despite this need for reciprocity, the role of the guest remains largely reactive: if his trust in his host is abused by maltreatment the only resort open to him is normally that of the curse, a full threat only in cultures which still attached some idea of the sacred to the visiting stranger.[4]

It is no doubt the reactive quality of guestly behaviour that ensured it was less often discussed in the prescriptive literature of early modern England. There is, of course, a rich literature on proper table manners, which gradually extends into analyses of proper modes of visiting and exchanging other courtesies. But the notion that there should be a more sustained attempt to understand the role of the outsider rarely occurred to Englishmen, and when it did it was usually confined to advice literature on foreign travel—the dos and don'ts of living with the Italians.[5] An exception is to be found in the sermon Caleb Dalechamp preached on *Christian Hospitalitie* in the 1630s. Dalechamp, perhaps reflecting his own experience as an outsider, reminded his auditors that 'we may become strangers . . . and adde a particular peregrination to our common and generall pilgrimage'.[6] Men must, therefore, understand how to behave both as hosts and as aliens. In the latter role they must first recognize the importance of returning courtesies wherever possible, for 'Is not beneficence

---

[3] K. Simms, 'Guesting and Feasting in Gaelic Ireland', *Journal of the Royal Society of Antiquaries for Ireland*, 108 (1978), 93; the translation from the Irish is by Swift. On the bardic tradition in Wales, see G. Williams, *The Welsh Church from the Conquest to the Reformation* (Cardiff, 1976), 380–4.

[4] J. Du Boulay, *Portrait of a Greek Mountain Community* (London, 1973), 38–9.

[5] On the growth of this literature, see J. Stoye, *English Travellers Abroad; 1604–67: Their Influence in English Society and Politics* (London, 1952).

[6] Dalechamp, *Christian Hospitalitie: Handled Commonplace-wise in the Chappel of Trinity Colledge in Cambridge* (Cambridge, 1632), 98.

a binder and courtesie received a strong obligation to requitall
in one kinde or other?' The stranger must display discretion,
avoid meddling, show humility and patience, and accept 'an
offered entertainment. For the rude and churlish refusall of a
well-proffered courtesie argues plainly either ignorance or
immodestie.'[7] Perhaps the greatest virtue that a guest could
display was, for Dalechamp, that of thankfulness; this would be
expressed to a private host in a cheerful willingness to do him
favours in return, and to a public host, in the case of an alien
received by the commonwealth, in observation of the laws and
a willingness to accept any obligations laid upon him. It was,
Dalechamp concluded, partly the gracelessness of guests,
especially of aliens, that had led to the decay of hospitality and
to English xenophobic distaste for foreigners.[8]

As befits one of the few reflective treatments of the ethics of
hospitality, Dalechamp avoids much discussion of particular rules
for good visiting. He does, however, remind his auditors of the
old proverb that:

> At three dayes end a fish and guest
> Are often-tymes out of request

suggesting that it offers a general warning that no one should 'take
too much of a free house'.[9] Here the ethical standards of good
Christian and classical behaviour intersect with the idea of
accommodation to the sensibilities of others. The growth of the
literature of civility may be read as evidence of the attempt, first
to establish fixed rules of social conduct that facilitated adjustment
to the needs of others, and later to integrate these into a more
flexible perception of modes of good living in which
accommodation became internalized and habitual for the man
of breeding.[10] The notion was that the civil man adjusted
himself to the needs of his acquaintance in order to secure
ease of intercourse, and there can have been few social contexts
in which there can have been more opportunity to put these
learned skills to good use than in one's host's household. This
may serve to explain the anxiety displayed by travellers in
their determination not to intrude upon gentry hosts unless

---

[7] Dalechamp, *Christian Hospitalitie*, 109   [8] Ibid. 113 ff.   [9] Ibid. 110.
[10] A. Bryson, 'Concepts of Civility in England, *c.*1560–1685', Oxford D.Phil.
thesis (1984), 175 ff.

emphatically bidden.[11] Not only was awaiting an invitation the most appropriate mode of fitting oneself to the needs of one's host, but showing initially a becoming modesty about personal worth was a suitable posture.

The rhetorical elaboration of some written invitations from as early as the Elizabethan period is a part of this process: John Bourne, writing to Francis Yaxley in 1560, insisted on offering an extensive panegyric on the pleasures of country life before urging, 'come for goddes saak therfore, and make us mery with your presence'.[12] But this sort of conceit was as nothing when compared to the exaggerated invitations of the next century: by the 1620s, Thomas Meautys saw nothing curious about bidding his cousin Lady Cornwallis with the sentiment: 'I shall wish my own house on fier every time I see you passe by it to sleep in any other.'[13] Guests, according to this perception, had to be wooed as fully as a lover before they could venture to intrude on the hospitality of a friend. Proper adjustment to the needs of others was a delicate process: Thomas Knyvett found himself embarrassed in 1627 because he had failed to see Sir Roger Townshend at home. He therefore, 'did excuse our neglecte with the best complements I had, promisinge a suddaine visitt, which we must of necessitye performe'.[14] In fact, the Knyvetts were regular guests of the Townshends, and related to them, so the solemnity of Thomas's social gaffe should not be exaggerated, but if close friends had to exercise this type of prudential accommodation to one another's needs, the reticence of the total outsider becomes more comprehensible. It serves to explain the elaborate language in which three Norwich travellers in 1634 described their dinner with a mere gentleman at Coventry. They were 'curteously, and earnestly invited' by the man, who was an acquaintance of one of the three, 'whom wee would not deny upon any termes, and if we had, wee had beene much to blame', for both he and his wife did everything in their power 'to give us a free and reall welcome'.[15] Lieutenant Hammond, the most

---

[11] See below, pp. 205–7.   [12] PRO, SP12/11/14.
[13] [Lord Braybrooke (ed.)], *The Private Correspondence of Jane Lady Cornwallis, 1613–44* (London, 1842), 160.
[14] B. Schofield (ed.), *The Knyvett Letters, 1620–44* (Norfolk Rec. Soc., 20, 1949), 74.
[15] Legg (ed.), *A Relation of a Short Survey of Twenty-Six Counties Observed in a Seven Weeks Journey . . . from Norwich* (London, 1904), 69.

important of the three Norwich men, was equally careful when he travelled alone to the west in the subsequent year. He stayed to eat a meal with the parson of Havant and some of his friends from Arundel Castle despite his desire to make progress in his journey, since 'I had past the bounds of good Manners to have gone without his free leave, . . . and had lost a hearty and generous welcome at all hands'.[16]

The courtesy literature sometimes gave explicit help to those who feared offending by a failure to behave as proper guests. This was a particularly urgent need in an urban context, where rules of neighbourly sociability were not well defined, and where the social structure was itself fluid. Conventions for visiting within set routines were known in London at least from the early Elizabethan period onwards. One of the 'merry tales' told of William Hobson, the London haberdasher who died in 1581, shows him challenging the polite convention by which a host could deny access to guests by announcing that he was not at home. William Fleetwood, the Recorder of London, did this to Hobson, who responded when Fleetwood visited him by appearing in person to announce that he was not at home.[17] The interesting point here is that Hobson, or the story-teller, saw an important change in guest–host relationships being articulated by this new convention. Shame no longer attached to a fictive denial of access: it is instructive to note the contrast with the case of Sir Thomas Hoby, where only Lady Margaret was able to deny access by pleading indisposition, and even she was not wholly successful.[18]

Later elaboration of the pattern of visiting, diffused gradually from town to country in the first half of the seventeenth century, led to the establishment of days and times of entertainment which it was the duty of the good guest to master. Alice Thornton, daughter of Sir Christopher Wandesford, settled in Newton, Yorkshire, with her husband in 1662, and it was one of her first duties to announce a principal day on which she could be visited. At the appointed moment, 'all the best of the gentry and

---

[16] Legg (ed.), *Description of a Journie made into the Westerne Counties, 1635* (Camden Misc. 16, 3rd ser. 52, London, 1936), 39.

[17] J. O. Halliwell-Phillips (ed.), *The Pleasant Conceits of Old Hobson* (Percy Soc., 9, London, 1843), 36.

[18] D. M. Meads (ed.), *The Diary of Lady Margaret Hoby* (London, 1930), 141.

neighbourhood . . . made there several visits to me, although but a stranger amongst them'.[19] Similarly, the Earl of Yarmouth, when on his country estate of Oxnead, Norfolk, in the 1670s, announced that he was 'at home' on Tuesdays and Fridays only, though he found that all too many of his guests were insensitive to this rule.[20] He was also offended by the local gentry's casual disregard of another convention which he found easier to operate in London: several men, including a political enemy, Sir John Hobart, had the temerity to visit Oxnead twice, before he had had time to return their call.[21] By this time John Evelyn had already wittily denounced the tedium of visits in his satire *A Character of England* (1659). He particularly blamed women for the establishment of a series of rituals of excruciating tedium, which involved either long periods of silence or bitter censure and gossip, 'so difficult it is to entertain with grace, or to observe a mediocrity'.[22]

But these rituals were becoming an integral part of the culture of the élite by the mid-seventeenth century, and to assist laggards like Hobart, the courtesy writers tried to advise on good visiting behaviour. Obadiah Walker, writing in 1673, insisted that it was 'fitting to know how to entertain a Stranger; or how we are entertained by him'.[23] To do so he was forced to draw on Italian courtesy rules, which offered a fully-elaborated code of behaviour. According to this, women were not usually visited in the morning, and always had the upper hand in their own households; equals had to be attended to the door, superiors to coach or horse; and greater civility and freedom were to be expected if you were a stranger than if a known neighbour whose status was well defined. If a superior visitor followed an inferior, then the latter had to wait before being given attention. The main duty of the visitor, apart from the general notion that he must accept the status to which he was assigned, was to terminate the

---

[19] C. Jackson (ed.), *The Autobiography of Mrs. Alice Thornton* (Surtees Soc., 62, 1875), 138. Sir Nicholas le Strange gradually trained his country neighbours out of the habit of visiting the same house for both dinner and supper in Norfolk in the 1680s: NRO, Le Strange NE2, 9.

[20] *HMC, App. to 6th Rep.*, 377.

[21] Ibid. 378.

[22] John Evelyn, 'A Character of England', in *Harleian Miscellany*, 10 (London, 1813), 198.

[23] Obadiah Walker, *Of Education, Especially of Young Gentlemen* (Oxford, 1673), 216.

visit, making sure that he did not 'stay as long as the visited seems glad to receive him'.[24] Others, such as Henry Peacham, had earlier advised on the correct postures of gratitude for a guest, but few of the civility writers seem to have endorsed the full ritualism of the Italian approach. Rather, there was a concern not to challenge the spontaneity of hospitality by 'multiplied formalities of access'. As Walker suggested, all that was really needed in a guest was sensitivity, coupled to a willingness not to take offence at minor insults. William Cornwallis grumbled that the worst type of guest was he who stayed 'today and tomorrow and the next day, on purpose to say he loveth'.[25] And, as Simon Robson had earlier argued, a guest who felt himself diminished by his placing at table should not complain publicly, but should take an even lower seat in order to remind the host diplomatically of his true worth.[26]

Hosts in their turn were supposed to be able to manage their guests in such a way that no legitimate grounds for offence were given, and the household ordinances were, of course, partly directed to achieving this objective. But the guest who moved from an exaggerated sensitivity about his own honour to direct insult was stepping over a boundary far more fundamental than our own perceptions would suggest. Here the Thomas Hoby case is important, because the Eure clan seem deliberately to have parodied or inverted each of the activities of Hoby's household in a direct challenge to his honour. The holding of some crude form of a 'black mass' while the godly household was at its prayers, and the drinking of toasts that were normally banned in the establishment are but two examples of a sustained campaign that broke every cultural norm of good behaviour as a guest.[27] Though Hoby's Star Chamber suits may seem a foolish reaction, it is difficult to exaggerate the quasi-public humiliation that had been visited upon him. The behaviour of a Barnsley bailiff, seeking to arrest William Hinchcliff, gent., for debt in 1666, could

---

[24] Walker, *Of Education*, 220–4. Other important texts that discussed the rules of visiting were Jean Gailhard, *The Compleat Gentleman* (London, 1678) and Antoine de Courtin, *The Rules of Civility* (London, 1678), 118–19.

[25] William Cornwallis, *Essays*, 2nd edn. (London, 1606), essay 9.

[26] Simon Robson, *A New Yeeres Gift: The Courte of Civill Courtesie* (London, 1577), sig. A3ᵛ.

[27] PRO, STAC 5/H 22/21.

be read as an equally calculated insult, since he called for a quart of ale and drank to the householder before trying to arrest him.[28] A similar case involved one Henry Skipwith of Leicestershire who, in 1624, attempted the arrest of Sir Brian Cave of Bagworth Park in a novel manner. Skipwith allegedly arranged his allies in an ambush outside Bagworth Park, and then, 'under a counterfeite and seeminge frendly manner [did] repaire and come unto yor said subjects mansion howse where hee was kindly entertayned and welcomed as a guest and neighbour'.[29] After dining, Skipwith persuaded Cave outside, where he was set upon and nearly arrested, only being rescued by the opportune arrival of his servants. All of this, Cave piously argued, was a breach of royal law but was, above all, a breach of the laws of hospitality which, he or his lawyer implied, were even more binding because natural. The guest, by abusing his role, could reverse the power relationship that was implicit in the giving of hospitality, and could reveal the weakness of the host who exposed himself through his generosity and openness.

II

The most effective way of approaching an understanding of the culturally determined expectations that society had of guests, and the degree to which they were fulfilled, is to examine the evidence of travellers in early modern England. Under the Yorkists and Tudors this means largely the comments available from foreign visitors to the realm, supplemented by occasional English notes on journeys. By the early seventeenth century the habit of diary-keeping had extended itself to travel notes both for English and foreign journeys, the former offering rich insights into patterns of entertainment.[30]

---

[28] J. Raine (ed.), *Depositions from the Castle of York, Relating to Offences Committed in the Northern Counties* (Surtees Soc., 40, 1861), 142–3.

[29] PRO, STAC 8/111/19.

[30] R. E. Palmer, *French Travellers in England* (London, 1960); W. D. Robson-Scott, *German Travellers in England, 1400–1800* (Oxford, 1953); E. Moir, *The Discovery of Britain* (London, 1964); J. Parkes, *Travel in England in the Seventeenth Century* (Oxford, 1925).

We have already observed that, even in the late medieval period, the great were often dependent on either their own property, or that of their adherents, for the provision of accommodation when travelling, perhaps wishing to avoid the complex rituals that were a necessary part of social exchange among the élite.[31] If they chose to behave as guests, it was usually to the monasteries that they turned, sometimes, as in the case of St Alban's in the fifteenth century, making the monastery an alternative residence for an extensive time.[32] The Statute of Westminster (3 Edward I, c. 1), which attempted to curtail this lavish entertainment, seems to have been more honoured in the breach than the observance. The great probably sometimes paid for a part of their keep in these circumstances, as, for example, the Bishop of Hereford did when staying at Reading Abbey in the late thirteenth century, but if they exercised sufficient influence no doubt the monasteries accepted the costs in the hope of other benefits.[33]

For an understanding of appropriate behaviour for those below the narrow ranks of the nobility, it is possible to turn to the well-known *Itineraries* of William de Worcestre.[34] William travelled extensively in England both on business for others and for his own interest, and kept a journal which is an attractive jumble of architectural description, moralizing, and practical recording of everyday events. Since he was a cleric and a man of some standing, having served as Sir John Fastolf's secretary in the 1450s, he should have been reasonably certain of acceptance in any great house while on his travels. One would anticipate a steady progression from monastery to noble home as he moved down into the West Country or around his primary area of residence in East Anglia. The diaries show that he did indeed stay at a number of monasteries. He denounced one of them, St Benet's Holme in Norfolk, for its 'stingy hospitality', moved by righteous indignation that the monks had failed to honour the memory of

[31] See above, ch. 2.

[32] H. T. Riley (ed.), *Johannes Amundesham Annales Monasterii St. Albani* (Rolls Ser., 1870), 4 ff.

[33] J. Webb (ed.), *A Roll of Household Expenses of Richard de Swinfield, Bishop of Hereford . . . 1289 and 1290*, abstract and appendices (Camden Soc, O.S. 62, London, 1855), 60.

[34] J. H. Harvey (ed.), *The Itineraries of William de Worcestre* (Oxford, 1969).

their benefactor, John Fastolf.[35] However, he rarely seems to have stayed with the nobility or gentry: on only three occasions does he clearly state that he was accommodated by laymen who were not self-evidently friends or connections. Once he stayed overnight with the Earl of Devon at Oakhampton, once with Otys Phelip, a groom of the King's Chamber, and once with one Philip Pure near Devizes. The last case is the most interesting, since William remarks that Pure entertained him 'of his courtesy', conveying by his language something of the same surprise and pleasure that travellers of the seventeenth century were to experience when they encountered the hospitality of the bishop or the dean of Durham.[36] At other times he often stayed in inns, not only in large towns such as Exeter or Bristol, but in much smaller centres such as Castle Combe. Although William is not always specific about where he stayed, it seems that his expectations were to think first of a convenient monastery or other clerical residence, secondly of inns, and unusually of secular households as places to stay.[37]

Other fifteenth-century sources tell much the same tale. The record of the journey made by the bursar of Merton College to collect the rents of the northern properties of the college in the 1460s shows his depending largely upon public accommodation during his travels. Only at Cambridge, to which he deliberately diverted on his outward journey, was he given lodging that might be described under the heading of hospitality.[38] When Aeneas Sylvius, the future Pius II, was on his return journey through England from embassy to Scotland in the 1440s, he stayed at a private farmhouse in Northumberland.[39] It was this visit that prompted his famous description of the barbarousness of the border inhabitants, who had never seen either white bread or wine, and who treated this great emissary of the Pope as though he were one of the women. It would be difficult to argue that Aeneas Sylvius had any expectations of the proper behaviour of a guest in these circumstances; he was simply clear that Northumberland men had no idea how to act as hosts.

---

[35] Ibid. 3.   [36] Ibid. 37, 39.   [37] Ibid. 41, 117, 265.
[38] E. Bateson, 'Notes of a Journey from Oxford to Embleton and Back in 1464', *Archaeologia Aeliana*, 16 (1893–4), 113–20.
[39] L. C. Gabel (ed.), *Memoirs of a Renaissance Pope* (New York, 1962), 34–6.

The scattering of fifteenth- and early sixteenth-century evidence could perhaps be interpreted as an indication that travellers already expected to pay for their entertainment, even though they were willing to exploit the plurality of other opportunities available to them. Possession of a particular role—ambassador, pilgrim, cleric—no doubt facilitated access to private hospitality in clerical and lay households, but it was necessary to have some alternative in the form of inns and alehouses. Even the greatest in the land resorted to inns on their travels: the Berkeleys, Howards, and Seymours all stayed in such accommodation at times on their journeys to and from London.[40] Robert Hungerford, second Lord Moleyns, stayed at the George Inn, Salisbury, in 1449 and again in 1454, *en route* with his retinue to France.[41] On both occasions the behaviour of his followers provoked local riots, one of which had to be dispersed by the cathedral precentor processing with the Host. The list of guests at the Angel Inn in Leicester's Cheapside in the next century included the Earl of Huntingdon, the Earl of Derby, and Henry, Marquis of Dorset.[42] A number of old inns have rooms called the earl's or lord's chamber, suggesting that great visitors were their anticipated residents.

It is difficult to exaggerate the importance of the acceptance of the inn or alehouse by all social groups as the primary grid of accommodation for travellers in England by the later fifteenth century. An increasingly London-dominated economy, and the expansion of internal trade in the later medieval period had presumably provided the main forcing-ground for organized accommodation. Social groups other than traders then took advantage of arrangements that involved none of the reciprocal pressures of private, or even monastic, residence.[43] Causes and consequences are not easily disentangled, but what is evident is that a social pattern was emerging that was in marked contrast to

---

[40] Longleat Misc., Bk. IX, fo. 108; Collier, *Manners and Household Expenses of England in the Thirteenth and Fifteenth Centuries* (Roxburghe Club, London, 1844), 250; Longleat Misc., MS. XVIII, fo. 174.

[41] C. Haskins, *The Ancient Trade Guilds and Companies of Salisbury* (Salisbury, 1912), 292–3.

[42] C. J. Billson, *Medieval Leicester* (Leicester, 1920), 26.

[43] P. Clark, *The English Alehouse: A Social History, 1200–1830* (London, 1983), 8–9.

that of some other European realms, including England's northern neighbour. The situation in Scotland is suggested by the Act of 1425, by which James I sought to protect the modest inns in 'borowis or throuchfares' by forbidding travellers to lodge privately with their friends and contacts, or, if they did so, at least insisting they stabled their horses at the inn.[44] A later act of James V showed that the Scots were still struggling to erect inns in all burghs. Throughout our period the Scots continued to value private hospitality above the public entertainment offered by inns, though much of the private accommodation probably occupied the half-way position of paying lodgings.[45] The Scots, of course, subsequently made a virtue of what may at first have been necessity: inns remained uncommon outside the large towns, and a tradition of private hospitality was fully sustained, at least in the Highlands. Even at the end of the seventeenth century, James Kirkwood noted that the stranger could 'travail amongst them gratis', a commoning system being customary if the press of strangers became too great.[46]

Another indication of the importance of public accommodation is that a number of the early foreign visitors to England commented favourably on the standard of the inns. When the English enthusiasm for feasting was remarked, as it frequently was, inns as well as private homes were seen as the venue for entertainment. According to Etienne Perlin, a French surgeon who visited England in 1558, the country was full of rich inns and innkeepers, because of the passion the natives had for banqueting.[47] The conventions of English innkeeping suggest that in some measure landlords perceived themselves as analogous to private hosts, with the same duties performed for money rather than love. William Harrison emphasized that innkeepers believed they had to offer courteous entertainment, providing guests with private meals and sitting with them if they so

---

[44] *Acts of the Parliament of Scotland*, ii. 10.

[45] Ibid. 346. Fynes Moryson argued that public inns did not advertise themselves, but that citizens who brewed ale 'will entertaine passengers upon acquaintance or entreaty': P. H. Brown (ed.), *Early Travellers in Scotland* (Edinburgh, 1891), 89.

[46] J. L. Campbell (ed.), *A Collection of Highland Rites and Customs* (London, 1975), 45.

[47] Etienne Perlin, *Description des Royaulmes d'Angleterre et d'Escosse, 1558* (London, 1775), 22.

desired.[48] The Norwich tourists to the north in the 1630s spoke as warmly of their York hostess as they did of the great men who received them. She 'cheerfully extended her bounteous Entertainment to us; . . . and likewise tooke suche care of us . . . as if she had beene a Mother, rather than an Hostesse'.[49]

When it is possible to disentangle details of the journeys made by foreigners in the century-and-a-half after Aeneas Sylvius, it usually emerges that they stayed in inns, though they were frequently bidden to dine as guests by the Lord Mayor of London, by other towns, by colleges at Oxford and Cambridge, or by members of the lay élite. A typical case is that of Friedrich Gerschow, who visited England in the train of the Duke of Stettin-Pomerania in 1602. Part of the time he travelled separately from the main party, hampered by a lack of English, so that when he arrived at a Bicester inn and wished to eat he had to be assisted by the local parson who communicated in Latin. The parson had left his own guests to help, but, despite his kindness, obviously felt no sense of duty to offer hospitality to the stranger.[50] When the English élite did entertain foreigners, they tended to expend more effort and interest upon feeding than accommodating them. Since the English had a reputation for good entertainment, foreign visitors of high social standing came to expect that they would be wined and dined as they toured the country. Some, like the Duke of Wurtemberg, who travelled to see the two universities and a number of the major towns of England in 1608, was accompanied by royal letters asking that he be received with due honour, and pointing out that each corporation should ask him 'either to dinner or a banckett'.[51]

Englishmen who travelled through their own land in the seventeenth century offer even more valuable insight into patterns of hospitality than do foreigners. Unlike overseas visitors, who, if sufficiently distinguished or exotic, could be virtually assured of general welcome, the English tourist or traveller on business was not an automatic recipient of private

---

[48] W. Harrison, *The Description of England*, ed. F. J. Furnivall, 2 vols. (New Shakspere Soc., ser. 6: 1, 5, London, 1908), ii. 107–8.

[49] *A Survey . . . of Twenty-Six Counties*, 14–15.

[50] G. Von Bulow (ed.), 'Diary of the Journey of Philip Julius, Duke of Stettin-Pomerania, through England in the Year 1602', *TRHS*, N.S. 6 (1892), 40.

[51] R. Davies, *Walks through the City of York* (London, 1880), 272.

hospitality. Alternative accommodation in the form of inns and alehouses was available almost everywhere by the end of the sixteenth century, and therefore a decision to provide private entertainment was very much a reflection of the personal preferences of host and potential guest, rather than a matter of urgent physical need. Even in the seventeenth century there were moments when benighted travellers were given private shelter in adverse circumstances; for example, the three Norwich worthies who toured the northern counties in 1634 were given a meal in a poor cottage on the Howard estates, and Lady Anne Clifford recalled a traumatic journey across the Pennines in 1616, during which she stayed at the house of the poor parson of Penistone.[52] Even at the end of the century, Celia Fiennes found no public house in a village outside Beverley, and had to depend on the kindness of the tenants of the Hall House.[53] On another occasion she was benighted at Lower Shuckburgh, near Daventry, and was rescued by Lady Shuckburgh while enquiring fruitlessly for lodging.[54] But these cases, especially the Midlands one, were seen by the authors as exceptional. The remote corners of the realm, especially the north-west and Cornwall, were somewhat less predictable: there were areas of the Lakes and of the Border country where it was still easy to lose routes, and alehouses, at the end of the seventeenth century.[55] Carew had no illusions about the quality of Cornish inns when he commented on 'the bad drinke, course lodging and slack attendance' to be found there.[56] His countrymen defended themselves by claiming that there were few visitors to 'such an outcomer' anyway. The generosity and warmth of welcome offered by the Cornish gentry, on which Anne Fanshawe as well as Carew remarks, may have been intended to compensate for some of the deficiencies of their

---

[52] *A Survey . . . of Twenty-Six Counties*, 35; G. C. Williamson, *Lady Anne Clifford* (Kendal, 1922), 277.

[53] C. Morris (ed.), *The Illustrated Journeys of Celia Fiennes* (London, 1982), 100.

[54] Ibid. 116; on another occasion Celia stayed with a clergyman outside Rotherham: ibid. 102.

[55] R. Davies (ed.), *The Life of Marmaduke Rawdon of York* (Camden Soc., o.s. 85, London, 1863), 152. Rawdon remarks that upland Yorkshire inns were like those of Scotland, which he had found abominable.

[56] Richard Carew, *The Survey of Cornwall* (London, 1602), fo. 66.

fellow-countrymen.[57] On the whole, however, the authors of travel diaries were neither so impoverished that they had to ask for accommodation, nor so far from paying lodging that they could not find an alternative to the gentry household. And, to confirm an earlier argument, it is instructive to see that they paid for their residence in the overwhelming majority of cases.

The one general and predictable exception to the rule that travellers stayed in inns was the case of kinship or friendship. Even remote cousinage seemed to legitimate, indeed to necessitate, a few days' visit. Laurence Bostock, who recorded his journeying from London to Cheshire to see his family in the 1580s, managed to travel from cousin to cousin from the time he left Ashby-de-la-Zouch to the time he set out south once more.[58] In all he stayed with thirteen individuals named as cousins, and a few others who were mere friends. Celia Fiennes, whose gentry family did indeed have wide connections, stayed with kin in several parts of the realm, often making a relative's house the focus of one of her journeys.[59] To fail to stay with a relative or friend when one was nearby would have been to derogate from his honour. When personal connections failed, the individual who wished to travel cheaply might find an alternative in the letter of introduction. Access to gentlemen's houses normally depended on some personal or professional acquaintance, or on the availability of introductions. When young Nicholas Le Strange wished to wander far from his Norfolk homeland and travel in the West Country in 1680, he armed himself with a series of letters from the Bishop of Oxford to the Bishops of Bath and Wells and Exeter, and to the Dean of Hereford, and from a friend, Mr Trelawny, to his Cornish family.[60] In consequence he found a very warm welcome in a variety of places, and was able to acquire further letters from his new contacts which carried him around the entire area at little cost and effort. The same effect *might* be achieved by the mere cultivation of polite external behaviour, which, observed one advice text, 'wilbe like perpetuall letters

[57] N. H. Nicolas (ed.), *Memoirs of Lady Fanshawe, wife of . . . Sir Richard Fanshawe . . .* (London, 1829), 71.
[58] BL, Harl. MS. 2113, fo. 117^v.
[59] *Celia Fiennes*, 48, 189, 231.
[60] NRO, Le Strange NE2, 5–6.

commendatory and procure you good offices wherever you come'.[61] Mere manners, while an increasingly necessary condition for admission to appropriate entertainment, could not, however, be guaranteed to be quite sufficient to open all doors, and letters of introduction remained popular throughout the century.[62]

When hospitality was offered beyond the anticipated welcome extended by kin, friends, and connections, it was usually made the subject of detailed, and sometimes surprised, comment by the author. Bostock, on his journey from London into Cheshire, was accommodated one night by Sir Christopher Hatton at Holdenby and found the experience worth lingering over, even though he was bound northwards on pressing business.[63] Lieutenant Hammond, on his journey to the west, was greatly delighted to be entertained by the parson of Wareham, 'both at his owne house, and in the Towne'.[64] Three tourists from the Thames valley, *en route* to Cornwall in 1637, dined and spent the day with the Marquis of Winchester at Hackwood, the only occasion on the whole of the journey on which they visited a private home.[65] The 'ancients' of Norwich were overwhelmed by the entertainment of William, Lord Howard of Naworth, and dwelt upon it in loving detail in their narrative, though the connection between the Howards and Norfolk seems to have contributed to the graciousness of their reception.[66] They were also rapturous about the disinterested invitation to dine given them by the Dean of Durham: the details of his welcome occupied several pages in their account. Sir William Brereton, travelling through the north in 1635, also praised the Durham clergy highly: he was accommodated by Bishop Morton at Auckland for one night and wrote in glowing terms of his reception.[67] However, the only occasions on which Brereton seems to have been entertained by gentlemen with whom he had no personal connection were on

[61] Nathaniel Bladon, 'Advice to his Son' [1694], Folger Lib. Va/346.
[62] *HMC, Portland*, ii. 263 ff. Both John Taylor and Lieutenant Hammond made use of letters of introduction in their travels.
[63] BL, Harl. MS. 2113, fo. 117ᵛ.
[64] *Journie into the Westerne Counties*, 70–1.
[65] BL, Harl MS. 6494, fo. 129.
[66] *Survey . . . of Twenty-Six Counties*, 39–41.
[67] Ibid. 28–30; William Brereton, *Notes of a Journey through Durham and Northumberland* (Newcastle, 1844), 11–12.

his subsequent visit to Ireland, where he twice remarked on the
generosity of private hosts, rather than innkeepers.[68]

For the rest of the time, contacts between these earnest
travellers and the local élite seems to have been confined to
the process of drinking healths: one judges, for example, that
the governor of Holy Island must have spent much of his time
in drinking to the well-being of a series of guests.[69] This gesture
of hospitality, unlike the provision of a good meal or
accommodation, does seem to have been part of the welcome
anticipated by our travellers. Even if they, rather than the
hosts, provided the alcohol at a local inn, they still welcomed
the opportunity to drink with the 'better sort' of inhabitants
as a way of achieving temporary incorporation into the
community.[70] When hosts were reluctant to make this gesture
it was still the subject of adverse comment after the Restoration.
Thomas Kirk of Cookridge, Yorkshire, travelling to Scotland
in 1677, stopped at Alnwick Abbey in the hope of drinking
a toast to its owner.[71] The host did eventually appear and drink
with Kirk, but only after an hour's delay, the clearest possible
indication of distaste for his duty. This gracelessness in the
performance of a modest gesture of hospitality Kirk took as
evidence of social superiority, and resented. It certainly offended
against the ethos of accommodation to the needs of others
by the host. On the other hand, it may also be an indication
that some gentlemen were now wishing to signal that their
guests were failing to be socially accommodating by intruding
upon their privacy.

Travellers who were reluctant to risk even this species of rebuff
might still in a very limited form define themselves as guests by
viewing the houses of the nobility and gentry, often in the
owner's absence. The habit of country-house viewing can already
be discerned in the late sixteenth century, and by the 1630s was

---

[68] William Brereton, *Travels in Holland, the United Provinces, England,
Scotland and Ireland*, ed. E. Hawkins (Chetham Soc., o.s. 1, 1844), 189 ff.

[69] Brereton, *Notes of a Journey*, 32–3; Thomas Kirk, *Journeyings through
Northumberland and Durham Anno Dom. mdclxxvii* (Newcastle, 1845), 14.

[70] Kirk, *Journeyings*, 9, has an incident in which the travellers treat the
deputy-governor of Tynemouth in his lodgings with their own wine. See also
Journie into the Westerne Counties, 33.

[71] Kirk, *Journeyings*, 11: Kirk referred to the contemptuous owner as Sir
Fopling.

so commonplace as to be noted without surprise.[72] The work of escorting groups usually devolved either upon one of the ordinary servants, or on some intermediary figure such as the household chaplain. Lord North was guided around the Lewes home of the Earl of Dorset in 1607 by a woman who was presumably one of the resident servants, while at Longleat it fell to the chaplain to take round two ministers, Mr Hollewman and Mr Gregory, who came to view the house in 1603.[73] The ministers were unusually fortunate in being invited to dine in the absence of the family; it was more usual to offer something from the buttery as an adequate token of hospitality. Casual visitors who were given personal attention by senior servants or equivalent figures were duly flattered. In 1662 Edward Browne, visiting Warwick on a journey from Norwich, was delighted with the attentions that Lord Brooke's chaplain offered to him and his companion, 'though mere strangers'.[74] No doubt for lesser servants a guided tour of the great house was a useful means of supplementing income: Lord North paid the Lewes servant two shillings for her services, and several travellers' accounts remark on rewards paid for viewing a mansion.[75] Or servants might regard this gesture as their own form of hospitality: Lieutenant Hammond's contacts who showed him around Arundel Castle and Petworth House were peculiarly generous—at Petworth he was detained for a day and a night in their company.[76] The guided tour, which assumes the absence of the host, and yet still offers a welcome sealed with drink through his servants, is but the faintest echo of that care for wayfarers and strangers that was supposed to be binding upon the rich. Yet, like the public inn, it had its charms for the traveller, since it allowed him the pleasures of voyeurism without imposing any significant reciprocal burdens. Variations on these arrangements prevailed, apparently with satisfaction on both sides, until the twentieth century, when entrance charges and the market economy finally destroyed the residual aristocratic ethos of openness.

[72] Peter Mundy, *A Petty Progresse through Some Part of England and Wales, 1639* (Hakluyt Soc., 55, 1925), 29–30; *Journie into the Westerne Counties*, 30–1, 38, 66.
[73] Bodl., North MSS., b 12, fo. 123; Longleat, Thynne MS. Bk. 117.
[74] BL, Sloane MS. 1900, fo. 38ᵛ.
[75] Bodl., North MSS., b 12, fo. 123.
[76] *Journie into the Westerne Counties*, 30–1, 38.

III

The observations of English travellers are valuable evidence for forms of sociability but, until we reach Celia Fiennes and Defoe, they are not sufficiently detailed to offer much comparison between regions or between social groups. There is, however, one curious source that does much to remedy this deficiency. John Taylor, the so-called 'water-poet', was an inveterate traveller who, during the first half of the seventeenth century, undertook journeys to Scotland, Wales, the West Country, and the North, as well as more modest trips around the south-east of the realm.[77] This was in itself ambitious, but the interest of Taylor lies not only in his journeys and his publications from them, but in the fact that he sought to earn his living partly as a travel writer. He was one of those early authors for the commercial press, who lacking other means of support beyond his original employment as a Thames waterman, sought to gain influence and patronage through his prolific output. Journeying became his distinctive 'line', although he was prepared to turn his hand to almost any form of pamphleteering. This may have been because of a real interest in travel, but his writings suggest that Taylor was not a close observer of his environment in the tradition of Tudor topographers. Instead, he seems to have stumbled upon a gap in the market: descriptions of the realm were popular, and there was the additional advantage that Taylor could support himself by flattering those with whom he had had contact on his journeys with the promise of fame. With this inducement, he hoped to open doors on his travels, and benefit from the supposed desire of the gentry and others to be hospitable and to win honour through generosity to a stranger. His reputation and motives make Taylor a somewhat awkward witness for a study of routine hospitality in seventeenth-century England, but the range and detail of his travels, and his ability to test the goodwill of his hosts to the limit, make him an invaluable commentator on comparative behaviour.

The first and best known of the water-poet's journeys, and the one that provided inspiration for the rest, was his penniless

---

[77] John Taylor, *Works* (London, 1630), republished by the Spenser Soc., 2 (London, 1869).

pilgrimage to Scotland.[78] Taylor undertook this journey in 1617 as a demonstration that it was possible to travel without money and without begging. His reputation carried him some distance, as more practically did a series of direct or indirect connections with southern innkeepers. Until he reached Coventry he made no attempt to stay with individual gentlemen, and even then his first host was apparently a friend, a Master Doctor Holland.[79] From Coventry northwards Taylor relied partly on a contact of Holland's, but then found that his luck ran out in the North Midlands, where he was forced to sleep in the fields. Only when he was in Cheshire did he begin to be able to depend on a network of gentry who had no obvious connection with him, but were intrigued by his story. From Sir Urian Legh's at Adlington Hall, near Macclesfield, he was passed to Edmund Prestwich at Manchester, who paid all his charges, though accommodating him at an inn. His guide from Manchester took him on to Preston, where the mayor assumed responsibility for him, and then he was taken in by the under-sheriff of Lancashire, though this last was no chance associate for he was;

> A Gentleman that lov'd, and knew me well,
> And one whose bounteous minde doth beare the bell.[80]

The sheriff provided a warm welcome for Taylor at Lancaster, and ensured that on the next stages of the journey he was received either by gentlemen or by clerics. It seems that on this last part of the route into Scotland no official pressure was necessary to ensure that the doors of homes were open to a glib southerner.

Once in Scotland, the water-poet encountered more difficulty once again, but was soon able to depend on the combination of Scottish generosity and his associations with the Scots at the English court to secure a good reception.[81] On his return journey down the Great North Road he initially travelled with a group of Scots returning to London, but left them at Topcliffe to travel penniless once again. At York, Doncaster, and Newark he relied on gentlemen and clerics: George Atkinson of Newark 'made me as welcome as if I had been a French Lord'.[82]

---

[78] Taylor, *Penniless Pilgrimage*, in *Works*. Originally published in 1618.
[79] Ibid. 124.
[80] Ibid. 125–7.
[81] Ibid. 129–33.
[82] Ibid. 140.

Thereafter he was once again at the mercy of innkeepers, his own wits, and a letter of introduction from one of the Scottish lords. Even this combination scarcely saved him when he had an encounter with a landlord of a Huntingdon inn who expected payment for services rendered—a scene very similar to something out of *Joseph Andrews*. John Taylor had a vivid imagination, and *Penniless Pilgrimage* is no doubt elaborated far more than the journey was worth; nevertheless, the powerful sense of contrast between north and south carries conviction. Although letters of introduction were very useful even in the Highland zone, a fluent tongue and interesting cause could apparently open doors which were not readily accessible in the southern half of the realm.

Taylor's picaresque adventures were not resumed for another two decades, but in 1639 he bestirred himself once again and took a long summer journey into Yorkshire.[83] Once again he lodged at inns as far north as Leicester and Nottingham, no doubt aided by the fact that on this occasion he travelled with some money. At Nottingham he was entertained by Sir Thomas Hutchinson, and given money as well as food, and at Boston in Lincolnshire dined with Sir Anthony Thomas. Only in Yorkshire, however, did he really have good fortune. He dined with Archbishop Neile at Cawood, basing his claim to be a guest on a very tenuous contact from Neile's Winchester days.[84] There he met another slight acquaintance, Sir Francis Wortley, who insisted that he come and stay. Nothing hesitant, Taylor stayed with Wortley for two days, and was taken on a sightseeing trip to the Peaks, one of the few moments in his writings when he waxed lyrical about scenery. He also expressed himself grateful to Sir Francis with a rhetorical effusion that appears embarrassing even by the standards of contemporary discourse.

Two years later, in the last summer before the Civil War, the water-poet combined his love of journeying and socializing with his navigational skills and took some companions in a sculler-boat up the Thames, across the watershed to the Severn system as far as Hereford, and back across the Cotswolds.[85] It is tempting here to dwell on his technical feat, which was not inconsiderable, since

[83] John Taylor, *Part of this Summer's Travels, Or news from Hell, Hull and Halifax* (Spenser Soc., 7, London, 1870).   [84] Ibid. 20, 24.
[85] *John Taylor's Last Voyage and Adventure, 1641* (Spenser Soc., 14, London, 1873).

the boat had to be transported from the Thames to Stroud, and from Evesham to the Windrush on the return trip. Moreover, parts of the river system, notably the Wye, lacked any locks, and obstacles had to be negotiated by hauling the boat. However, Taylor remained alert to the possibilities of accommodation and free entertainment wherever he went. No one took much interest in his boat on the Thames, but its sudden appearance above Stroud caused a mild sensation. At Froombridge Mill, Mistress Bowser fed and accommodated the group for a very modest sum, 'though she were not acustomed to victuall or lodge Travellers, yet the rarety of our boate, and strangenes of my adventure moved her'.[86] Downstream they turned to the minor gentry, who provided food, and as they worked their way through Shropshire and Hereford they were entertained both by gentlemen and towns. The culmination of the trip came at Hereford, where the mayor, vicars choral, and local gentlemen all competed to bid Taylor to dinner: with the result that he had to miss a meal rather than offend any group. There are, however, occasional hints that hospitality was not always immediately forthcoming: the major of Shrewsbury welcomed him '(but had no leasure to bid me drinke)', and near Bewdley the party seem to have been denied access by Sir William Whitmore or his servants.[87]

In Taylor's late group of journeys—to the west in 1649, to Sussex in the early part of 1653, and to Wales later that year— these hints about failure of generosity assume a larger place. Although Cornwall was praised for its 'affable courteous people and . . . bountiffull housekeepers', the alehouses matched Carew's earlier strictures, and only the friendship of Mr Godolphin secured many entertainments for Taylor.[88] Yet Cornwall was a more welcoming environment for the traveller than the other counties of southern England, through which Taylor passed, describing a sad tale of ruined churches and ungenerous behaviour. When he travelled to Kent and Sussex four years later, the most he was able to record were a few payments by gentlemen for him to reside at inns and meals at Petworth and with the sheriff of the county.[89]

[86] Ibid. 14. [87] Ibid. 16.

[88] *John Taylor's Wandering, to see the Wonders of the West* [*1649*] (Spenser Soc., 7, London, 1870), 10, 12–14.

[89] John Taylor, *The Certain Travailes of an uncertain Journey* (Spenser Soc., 14, London, 1873), 13–16.

It is difficult to separate the various elements in this change of
behaviour; Taylor was travelling through the Home Counties which
had never offered him quite the abundance of the west and north.
He was also a known and vociferous royalist, which cannot have
made him a welcome guest in all houses. It did, of course,
sometimes ensure a warm welcome: John Carew, who rescued
him from the clutches of the Cornish innkeepers, insisted that he
stay for two days, 'where I found more Protestant Religion in 2
dayes than I had in 5 yeers before'.[90] But 1649, or even 1653,
cannot have been ideal times to engage in casual travel, even for
one with views less well known than the water-poet's. Casual
hospitality must have been disturbed by the experiences of war and
of continuing troop movements, and that 'free and frank discourse'
which was considered so essential a part of good entertainment
was less easily proffered in time of civil disturbance. Finally, many
of Taylor's potential hosts and acquaintances suffered various
forms of disablement for their royalism and must have shown
little interest in the costly business of open entertainment.

The final Welsh journey is perhaps more interesting than the
other two just discussed, since Taylor travelled extensively in
areas traditionally wedded to ideas of gentry generosity that had
suffered little physical devastation in the Civil Wars. Not that he
was able to escape the new politics completely: at Caernarvon
he was eventually treated well by the governor, but only after
his business had been carefully scrutinized.[91] Elsewhere in North
Wales he was treated with polite caution: he lodged in alehouses,
or with postmasters, or paid for his board in private homes, only
occasionally getting a free meal. He was particularly offended by
the treatment he received at Beaumaris, where he intended to
pay his addresses to Lord Bulkeley:

> But he to speak with me had no intent,
> Dry I came into's house, dry out I went.[92]

Like Kirk at Alnwick Abbey, Taylor was clear that this constituted
a breach of the norms of hospitality. From Aberystwyth south-

---

[90] *John Taylor's Wandering*, 17. Taylor's extensive royalist writings from the
Civil War period are collected in the Spenser Soc. edition of his works.

[91] John Taylor, *A Short Relation of a Long Journey . . . into Wales, 1653*
(Spenser Soc., 7, London, 1870), 14.

[92] Ibid. 13.

wards he fared rather better: there appeared to be a network of gentlemen's houses, beginning with that of Sir Richard Price, where the traveller was readily accepted. One focus was Golden Grove, near Carmarthen, where the Earl and Countess of Carbery entertained him to a generous supper. He was able to stay with gentlemen, or at inns at the expense of friends, almost all the way to Monmouth.[93]

The Welsh journey also produced one major incident that is unusually revealing about Taylor's perceptions of his rights as a guest. He stayed at Swansea with Walter Thomas, esquire, who sent him on the next stage of his journey with letters to his son. The son and his wife were both away and, unusually, the household servants refused him entry or any sustenance. Taylor argued with the waiting-woman, pointing out not only that he came from her master's father's house, but that he had letters of introduction from a gentleman of his acquaintance. Even if a mere stranger, a man 'endowed with all affability and courtesie to strangers as is every way accommodating to a Gentleman of Worth and Quality' would not allow him to pass unentertained, and how much more so when he came with all appropriate identification. This impassioned speech was met with utter indifference, and the water-poet was forced to beat a humiliating retreat.[94] The encounter is presumably recorded because he was filled by the righteous conviction that he had behaved correctly as a potential guest and that the laws of hospitality had been violated. It was his duty to arrive as well identified as possible, to deal courteously even with the servants, and to express gratitude for what he was offered. When all these conditions had been met, and hostility was still the response, then he felt free to excoriate the household. It is, of course, impossible to understand the other side of the story from this account, but at the very least it suggests a household not trained in making civil gestures to outsiders. This seems to be the only occasion in all his travels when Taylor felt wholly discommoded by a conception of politeness so different from his own.

What general observations, if any, can be drawn from John Taylor's half-century of acting as unsolicited guest? The first impression is of a certain shamelessness, a willingness to insinuate

[93] Ibid. 16–26   [94] Ibid. 23.

himself into the company of the gentry and to accept greedily any beneficence, including cash, that they were prepared to offer him. This, combined with his oleaginous praise of his hosts, makes one sympathize with William Cornwallis's complaints about those who took up residence for several days merely to express love. Taylor lived unashamedly by his wits, and seized every opportunity that fortune offered: when at his lowest ebb after the Civil War he financed his western journey partly through subscription.[95] On the other hand, he was careful to recognize the unwritten codes of good behaviour as a guest, especially in his willingness to render thanks and to reciprocate generosity with praise. These responses were not confined to his gentry contacts: praise was given where praise was due, as with the two Plymouth stationers who gave him tobacco and drink 'for which I requite them in Paper and Inke at London'.[96] Observing these rules, the water-poet hoped to travel the farther corners of the realm at little cost; there does seem to be an inverse correlation between the distance from London and the amount of free entertainment he expected. The north, in particular, proved fertile ground for his style of travel for, as the antiquarians and county historians often proudly remarked, it was there that the gentry still perceived themselves as preserving 'the true old English hospitality', which was no longer planted in the south.[97] In these 'far corners' Taylor seems to have proceeded with two implicit assumptions: that men welcomed news and stimulus and were willing to pay for it in giving hospitality, and that there was a stronger convention of open houses in the highland than in the lowland zone. These assumptions were frequently vindicated in practice: despite changes wrought by the Civil War, Taylor's letters and wit usually continued to open doors for him in the 1650s as they had done in the 1610s.

[95] *John Taylor's Wandering*, 1–2.
[96] Ibid. 19.
[97] *HMC, Salisbury MSS.*, xi. 11, in which Lord Eure criticizes Sir Thomas Hoby for not giving hospitality in ways considered appropriate in the North; Fuller, *The History of the Worthies of England*, ed. P. A. Nuttall, 3 vols. (London, 1840), i. 289, on Cheshire hospitality; William Camden, *Britannia*, ed. and trans. E. Gibson (London, 1695), 874, on that of Northumberland.

IV

The visitors and voyagers so far considered have all shared the characteristic of respectability, even if their position, like that of Taylor, was somewhat ambiguous. The stranger who lacked wealth or connection was altogether less likely to be welcomed as a guest. The poor traveller was, as we have seen, always a marginal figure, and the more so once the Reformation had destroyed some of the guises which might have legitimized his or her earlier claims to be an acceptable guest. Pilgrimage, and other forms of godly asceticism such as being a hermit, no longer existed to justify the sort of beneficence offered in the fifteenth century by Elizabeth Berkeley, or in the early sixteenth by the Duke of Norfolk. Prayers for the good of the host in return for alms given were also officially outlawed, though their residual influence could still be found as late as the seventeenth century. Anthony Wood has an interesting passage in which he notes that prayers for alms had superseded prayers for the soul, and had continued in living memory. However, 'in the broken times the fanaticks would not suffer them to say prayers at their dores', so the habit decayed, and by the time of his writing in 1670 the last two Oxford beggars to do this had died.[98]

Even a legitimating identity that might have survived the Reformation, that of the poor wandering scholar, was singled out for severe censure in the legislation of the 1590s.[99] However, it remained a relatively popular persona, despite the obvious risks. Arthur Sackfield, one of the vagrants interrogated by Warwick justices in the 1580s, had worked his way around the local gentry, claiming to be a scholar of Magdalen College, Oxford, and apparently had a particularly successful method of appealing to the godly and to preachers.[100] He extracted enough from a group at Coventry to buy cloth for new breeches, although the alehouse occupied much of his time and, presumably, income. When ordered to return to Oxford he wandered to Sir Thomas Lucy's house at Charlecote, where he got five shillings to renew

[98] Anthony Wood, *Life and Times*, ed. A. Clark, 5 vols. (Oxford Hist. Soc., 19, 21, 26, 30, 40, 1891–1900), ii. 212.

[99] 39 Eliz. I, c. 4.

[100] T. Kemp (ed.), *The Book of John Fisher, Town Clerk and Deputy Recorder of Warwick (1550–88)* (Warwick, 1900), 3.

his store. John Stephens, in his 'character' of a begging scholar, vividly evokes a man whose limited education allows him to act as adviser to a band of vagrants, but who, 'being admitted (for Hospitality's sake) to receive lodging', abuses his privilege by removing the silver spoons.[101] An even less likely figure seeking traditional forms of legitimation was the harpist, arrested at Maldon, Essex, in 1643, who was once employed in a noble household, and subsequently made his living 'at diver's men's houses of worth . . . by his harping'.[102]

The example of the wandering student highlights a more general problem of the perception of the stranger poor. Other claims to legitimate forms of mobility, such as those of professional entertainers or healers, those seeking employment or engaged in long-distance trade, were all increasingly treated as potentially subversive, and all came to be controlled by the vagrancy laws in the sixteenth century. From the perspective of travellers of this kind, it was often safest to depend on the alehouse, lest householders complained of harassment and the constable was alerted.[103] Like their more prosperous counterparts, they were not always willing to be drawn into the nexus of obligation and reciprocity that was an inevitable part of private hospitality. However, glimpses of the behaviour of those arrested as vagrants suggests that there was still a tenacious belief that seeking relief from the householder was a legitimate mode of behaviour for the indigent, and not a matter of shame. The best evidence for this comes from the well-known survey of the Warwick vagrants which the town recorder, John Fisher, and other magistrates undertook in the 1580s.[104] Fisher's informants had apparently been assisted on their travels by a number of gentlemen and other private individuals. Sometimes they had arrived in Warwick via a succession of houses: William

---

[101] John Stephens, 'Essays and Characters Ironical and Instructive', in J. O. Halliwell-Phillipps (ed.), *Books of Characters* (London, 1857), 187.

[102] P. A. Slack, *Poverty and Policy in Tudor and Stuart England* (London, 1988), 96.

[103] J. Kent, *The English Village Constable, 1580–1642* (Oxford, 1986), 200–5; A. L. Beier, *Masterless Men: The Vagrancy Problem in England, 1560–1640* (London, 1985), 223, shows that in the nine groups of arrests of vagrants where place of last entertainment can be determined, 41.2 per cent of those questioned had been at inns or alehouses.

[104] *Book of John Fisher.*

Ward, for example, who gave his place of origin as Northallerton, had been at the house of a Mr Sacheverell near Ratcliffe-on-Sower, and also at the home of a Mr Campion somewhere in Yorkshire. Thomas Corket claimed that he and his travelling-companion Richard Bonye 'had bene together at many gentlemens and honest mens houses to have their charytie'.[105] The most detailed circumstantial account came from William Laycon, a Warwick labourer, and interestingly shows the combined use of private hospitality and public alehouses:

On All Hallows day he dyned at Mrs. Belgraves and came to William Boughton . . . he saith that on wensday was a moneth he went from Warwick to seke for sovice and ment to goo to Sir Fulke Grevills house at Beauchamps court and supped that wensday night with one Mr. Fulwood who gave him his supper and afterward he went to an Alehouse . . .[106]

In all, the Warwick vagrants had been entertained by twenty-two men described as gentlemen or 'masters', and a further thirty-six persons with no status attribution, forming approximately 60 per cent of the places at which they claimed to have stopped.[107] Other investigations for the late sixteenth and early seventeenth centuries show lower figures for visits to the gentry: none of the eight cited by Beier having more than 10 per cent of this type of hospitality, though non-gentry usually account for upwards of 20 per cent of the examples.[108] The large groups of ordinary householders apparently emerging as open hosts in these surveys may well, as he suggests, be an illusion, since they may represent unlicensed alehouse keepers, or those who received travellers informally in paid lodgings. Yet behind even these figures lies some assumption that voyagers *could* at times still turn to private giving for relief, and no doubt if it were possible to analyse them more precisely they would reveal circumstances in which limited hospitality was still acceptable. The woman examined by the Isle of Ely justices in 1617 on a charge of theft may not be atypical. She had spent the Christmas season based in the Stilton area, but she visited five gentry houses between Christmas Eve and New Year's Day, receiving some sort of entertainment at each.[109]

It is, of course, well-nigh impossible to assess how the poor traveller or vagrant perceived hospitality. Contemporary accounts

---

[105] Ibid. 125, 29.   [106] Ibid. 174.   [107] Beier, *Masterless Men*, 223.
[108] Ibid.   [109] CUL, EDR E7/2, fo. 22.

are always coloured by the belief that the poor intended to
be disruptive and threatening; that within every beggar lurked
a thief. While the entertainment of tenants and of the local
poor might on occasions be understood by the gentry as their
customary and prescriptive duty, no such reading of the stranger
seems to have presented itself. Extreme need might on occasion
create its own justification, and gentry memorials such as
that of Clement Paston claim with pride that the hungry traveller
was never turned from the door, but this was a minimal provision
binding upon the Christian.[110] Those who asked for a meal,
or a space in a barn to sleep, may have conceived the matter
rather differently. It was the boldness of beggars that contemporaries so often condemned, and boldness could have been
nurtured as much by a sense of the rightness of their requests as
by sheer aggression. Sermons and popular literature continued
to remind hosts of their Christian duty well into the seventeenth
century, and although the chorus condemning begging grew
mightily, there still remained the assumption that the rich must
share their goods with the needy. There may also have been some
awareness that, at the dissolution of the monasteries, the new
owners had been required to assume the duties of the monks in
providing hospitality.[111] So those beggars whom Robert Allen
described in 1600 as 'very sturdy and shameles' as they stood
before the door of the great may have possessed some residual
feelings that their actions were legitimate, feelings that paralleled
those of tenants defending a Harvest Home or villagers' Rogation
entertainment.[112] When a Lancashire man was arrested in
Warwick in 1581 for entering a house and demanding drink 'for
God's sake', there was surely the echo of right as well as
desperation in his words.[113] Such behaviour, of course, merely
intensified the hostility of householders and underlined the plight
of a social group who were marginalized by fear in the latter half
of our period.

---

[110] D. MacCulloch (ed.), *The Chorography of Suffolk* (Suffolk Rec. Soc., 19,
1976), 88.

[111] The issue was occasionally mentioned in sermons: see e.g., Chedsey's
sermon of 1545 quoted in J. Haweis, *Sketches of the Reformation* (London, 1844),
269.

[112] Robert Allen, *A Treatise of Christian Beneficence* (London, 1600), 1.

[113] Beier, *Masterless Men*, 119.

V

One of the modest moralistic dialogues published early in the seventeenth century was Nicholas Breton's *A Merrie Dialogue betwixt the Taker and Mistaker* (1603). The piece begins with a parable in which the key actor is an impoverished traveller named Dorindo. On returning to his native land, Dorindo, hoping for employment, or at least 'a good dinner scot-free', came to a great house, only to find the door shut against him and the servants at dinner. The servant who finally came to the gate named it as the famous Mock-Beggar's Hall. Defeated there, Dorindo was rescued by a fellow-countryman who took him to an inn but did not pay for food or lodging, content only to offer a cup of wine and empty sentiment. Thus, he says, 'was I mistaken both in kin and countrey'. A country divine did no better, complaining of his limited resources which prevented him from doing 'anything for our poore brethren'. Finally, Dorindo encountered an honest yokel whom he at first despised, but who subsequently asked him home, where 'the doore [was] open, as unfearefull of theeves, or unprovided for strangers', yet there the table was furnished 'for both the host and a good guest', and all the weary traveller's needs were met.[114]

This salutary tale, with its resonances of late medieval 'estates' criticism, is of interest only because it returns us to the Christian argument that all men must act as hosts according to their means. Since the means of the nobility and gentry and, before the Reformation, the monasteries, were the greatest, their failures were also the most reprehensible and most clearly manifest to the weary voyager or needy dependant. But others were also bound by the laws of hospitality and could in some measure atone for the sins of the proud possessioners. The experience of English travellers suggests that this moralistic argument bears some relationship to social reality. When inns and gentlemen failed, they turned to ordinary countrymen or clerics to find hospitality: Anne Clifford and John Taylor did so in the Pennines and the mountains of the Scottish border, and the three Norwich worthies on their journey south from Naworth Castle. When Taylor failed

---

[114] Breton, *A Merrie Dialogue betwixt the Taker and Mistaker* (London, 1603), 4–18.

to gain accommodation at the house of Sir William Whitmore on his river journey, he was offered a roof by a poor man nearby which, 'necessity having no law, I accepted willingly'.[115]

It would, however, be an inaccurate reading of the literature of travelling to argue that clerics, townsmen, and ordinary villagers became hosts only as a last resort, as Breton suggests. Poor wanderers seem to have turned to non-gentry far more often than to their betters. Clerics were often perceived as more accessible targets than the élite because they were routinely resident within the community. In the absence of the constable, it was sometimes the local minister who was expected to organize accommodation for the needy or merely benighted.[116] And townsmen, at least in their corporate capacity, obviously had a more grandiose role in providing civic entertainment for the worthy. Taylor was particularly sensitive to this last obligation, since he believed that his exploits merited the full elaboration of mayoral receptions.

No analysis of the hospitality of early modern Englishmen can, therefore, rest on the assertion that it was to be found exclusively among the landed élite. At the very least, those supposed models of Christian generosity, the monasteries and the bishops, must be considered. However, much of the fascination of the subject must lie in an attempt to penetrate the motives and actions of the ordinary clergy, of townsmen, and of plain country-dwellers. How did they perceive the Christian imperative to give to the needy and deserving outsider, and did the honour culture that served to motivate the élite have any relevance to daily action in this wider community? It is to these issues that subsequent chapters attempt to return some answer.

---

[115] Taylor, *Last Voyage*, 16.
[116] George Herbert, 'A Priest to the Temple, or The Country Parson', in *Works*, ed. F. E. Hutchinson (Oxford, 1941), 245.

6
The Duties of the Pre-Reformation Clergy

I

THOUGH hospitality was a virtuous mode of behaviour constantly commended to the gentleman, for his clerical contemporary it possessed an even more mandatory character. All Christians were bound to follow the teaching of Christ, and to practise the seven works of mercy, but the clergy were constrained to do so both as individuals and as examples to their flocks. The dominical injunction to Peter to feed the faithful also made nurturing one of their primary duties, and nurturing was inclusive, embracing bodies as well as souls. Care of the poor, and material support of the community became part of the threefold sustenance that was expected of all those chosen to follow in the steps of the Apostles. According to Thomas Becon, adapting the basic Catholic message to the needs of Protestantism, 'spiritual ministers are bound to feed the flock of Christ three manner of ways: first, with the word of God and with true administration of the sacraments; secondly, with virtuous examples of life; thirdly, with hospitality, or provision-making for the poor'.[1] Since the organization of poor-relief in the apostolic Church had devolved upon its spiritual leaders, with bishops supervising the work of the deacons, the Epistles further underlined the basic message of the Gospels on the responsibilities of the clergy. St Paul spoke of the bishop as having a duty to maintain open house, in a passage from Timothy that was to cause some embarrassment to Reformation prelates.[2] The cumulative result of biblical precept and example was thus to provide a powerful foundation for the charitable behaviour

[1] Thomas Becon, *Works*, ed. J. Ayre, 3 vols. (Parker Soc., Cambridge, 1843–4) i. 3.
[2] 1 Timothy 3: 5.

of the clergy, especially for the episcopate, and for those possessing cure of souls.

By the time that canon law received its codification in Gratian's *Decretum*, biblical injunction had been elaborated both by the Fathers and by the practice of the Western Church.[3] Gratian, drawing principally on the works of Augustine, Ambrose, and St John Chrysostom, formulated a series of *Distinctiones* that were to remain central to the Church's teaching on the poor.[4] In *Distinctio* 82, the bishop was ordered to be generous to the poor though, following St Ambrose, it was argued that 'due measure is to be applied both of things and persons', allowing for a hierarchy of care to be erected. Chrysostom's insistence that 'in hospitality there is to be no regard for persons' was not rejected, but was counterbalanced by a careful insistence that the Church must address itself both to extreme need and to the worthiness of recipients.[5] In other parts of the collection bishops were specifically enjoined to defend the needy and oppressed, to care for those who could not work with their hands, and to assist widows and orphans. *Distinctio* 85 underlined the importance of these injunctions by arguing that 'hospitality is so necessary in bishops that if any are found lacking in it the law forbids them to be ordained'.[6] Although the texts cited appear to have a particular relevance to the episcopate, the intention of the canonists was clearly that holders of parochial benefices should be assumed to have inherited the obligations of ordinaries within their own territories. This is stated explicitly in *Distinctio* 42, where hospitality is said to be the peculiar duty of the priesthood, since they are bound to provide an example for their flocks, and must not be found wanting on the day of judgement.[7] William Lyndwood, in his important attempt to integrate English provincial decrees with the general canons of the Church, restated the point even more explicitly: 'The laws require that vicars and prelates be hospitable . . . and although the laws mentioned speak specially of bishops, nevertheless you understand the same of other clerics.'[8]

---

[3] B. Tierney, *The Medieval Poor Law* (Berkeley, Ca., 1959), 44 ff.
[4] Ibid. 52 ff.
[5] *Decretum magistri Gratiani*, dist. 82, ante c. i.
[6] Ibid. dist. 85.   [7] Ibid. dist. 42.
[8] William Lyndwood, *Provinciale seu constitutiones Angliae* (London, 1679), 132–3.

The regulars were even more forcefully enjoined to be charitable and hospitable. Here St Benedict provided the crucial initiative by his insistence in the *Rule* that his monks follow the command of Christ to harbour men in his name, or, as a fifteenth-century English version puts it:

> For god until [us] thus sal say
> In dome, upon the dredful day:
> 'Hospes eram et colligistis me—
> I was a gest in my degre,
> And in your hous ye herberd me.[9]

Thus, from the very origins of Western monasticism, the need to offer care to strangers and visitors became important; so much so that monasteries were the most visible centres of hospitality for much of the medieval period. Although other orders never accorded the guest quite so critical a role, even the most enclosed and isolated regulars were compelled to acknowledge some sense of obligation to the outsider.

It is obviously of considerable importance for any study of clerical hospitality to disentangle the language of charitable provision used by the canonists. They were entirely capable of distinguishing household entertainment from almsgiving, and on occasions chose to use this contrast to lend clarity to their analyses. This was especially true when it was necessary to consider the division of clerical income. The classical division made was into four parts, the bishop retaining one for himself and his household, giving one to his clergy, another for the repair and construction of churches and the last to the relief of the poor.[10] When Pope Gregory advised Augustine on the funding of the English mission, he advised that there should be one category of provision for the cleric, his household and hospitality, another for almsgiving to the poor.[11] At a later date parochial financing of the Church made a threefold division more logical, and once again commentators often included hospitality as a part of the first category, almsgiving

---

[9] A. de Vogue, *La Règle de St. Benoit*, 6 vols. (Sources Chrétiennes, 181–6, Paris, 1971–2), ii. c. 53, 610–16; E. A. Kock (ed.), *Three Middle-English Versions of the Rule of St. Benet* (*EETS*, 120, London, 1902), 102.

[10] Tierney, *Medieval Poor Law*, 67–89, 125–7.

[11] J. Johnson (ed.), *A Collection of the Laws and Canons of the Church of England*, 2 vols. (Oxford, 1850), i. 66.

as the third. The differentiation between forms of giving is also shown in Lyndwood's glosses on provincial decrees of Archbishops Pecham and Stratford. By these, non-resident rectors were required to provide sufficient hospitality through their deputies, but when a monastery was the appropriator it was 'not obliged to provide this kind of hospitality, but to distribute alms in money'.[12] Nevertheless, it was common practice throughout the medieval period for the lawyers to discuss hospitality as though it subsumed all forms of domestic giving. Gratian used his notion of lack of discrimination between individuals in hospitality to comprehend all giving, and later canonists commenting on *Distinctio* 85 saw it as a consideration of the virtue of hospitality.[13] Since the charitable provision made by the Church emanated from the household of the individual cleric or from a monastic establishment, the differentiation of entertainment and almsgiving was of little practical significance when the end and purpose was relief of material need. For those who formulated the general precepts of the Church the integration of all giving under one heading had some obvious advantages. It reminded the clergy that their daily possessions were in trust for the general care of the Christian community. It also integrated the local and the stranger poor: for example, an English provincial decree of 1281 insisted on the provision of hospitality, 'so that at least extreme necessity among poor parishioners is relieved', while accepting that the stranger was also a beneficiary from such giving.[14]

It is probable, however, that the integrative approach of the canonists did not resolve the ambiguities inherent in the nature of domestic giving. In 1240 the Berkshire clergy petitioned for exemption from taxation because they were so burdened by the duty of entertainment of the rich and poor, of clergy and laity; all performed *secundum suas facultates*.[15] Discrimination in the reception of outsiders was almost as difficult in theory as in practice; indeed, the basis of Chrysostom's pleas for general giving

---

[12] Lyndwood, *Provinciale*, 132–3; See also M. Rubin, *Charity and Community in Medieval Cambridge* (Cambridge, 1987), 238–9.
[13] Tierney, *Medieval Poor Law*, 69, n. 2.
[14] M. Powicke and C. R. Cheney (eds.), *Councils and Synods, with Other Documents Relating to the English Church (1205–1313)* (Oxford, 1964), 906–7.
[15] Ibid. i, 290.

1. The hospitable works of mercy: giving drink to the thirsty.

2. The hospitable works of mercy: feeding the hungry.

Of pylgrymes in goodly wyfe·
Sche dyde mofte trewely the fervyfe·
With chere benygne and glad vyfage·
Sche brought hem to ther herbergage·

3. The Entertainment of Pilgrims, from the MS. of the Fifteenth-Century Poem "The Pilgrim".

4. Giving to the poor in the late seventeenth century: the Tichborne Dole, by Gillis van Tirborch.

5. Monastic hospitality institutionalized: The George, or Pilgrim's Inn, Glastonbury.

6. Citizens feasting: the Fete at Bermondsey, c.1570, by J. Hofnaegel.

was that there should be no precise enquiry into need—an ordinary man should be welcomed without inquisition. It was but a short step from this to St Benedict's position in the *Rule*: all men should be welcomed under the monastic roof, especially all travellers, a regulation which positively encouraged the provision of hospitality for the rich and influential. Of course the poor were still intended as the primary beneficiaries of Benedictine giving: poor men and pilgrims were supposed to have priority as the visible members of Christ, while 'the fear which the rich inspire is enough of itself to secure them honour'.[16] Nevertheless, an absence of differentiation, and a lack of specificity in the language of giving provided an obvious opportunity to extend hospitality to all men regardless of need.

Although the existence of a body of canon law on hospitality and charitable giving placed the clergy under firmer imperatives than the laity, it would be a mistake to see its demands as rigidly inflexible. The later canonists took great pleasure in spinning subtle glosses on the work of their predecessors, but they continued to emphasize the importance of local circumstance and income in determining patterns of behaviour among the clergy. The tripartite division of resources advocated for the parochial clergy was not seen as a fixed equal apportionment; rather as a general guide to patterns of expenditure. In an interesting gloss on Archbishop Pecham's decree, Lyndwood contrasted the resources needed by a priest living on a frequented highway with those required in a remote or woodland area.[17] When some justification was sought for the appropriation of benefices to monasteries this was often the model employed: the regulars lived in an area much used by travellers, while by implication the parish concerned did not need all its resources for hospitality.[18] In this last example the dangers of flexibility are obvious, and it may be that the determination of the canonists not to offer precise guidance was a weakness when it became necessary to enforce giving.

---

[16] *La Règle de St. Benoît*, ii. 614.

[17] Lyndwood, *Provinciale*, 133: Lyndwood is here quoting the fourteenth-century canonist Johannes Andreas.

[18] I. Kershaw, *Bolton Priory: 1286–1325* (Oxford, 1973), 138. A variation on this was the Ely case, in which the Priory was allowed to appropriate Melbourn and Swaffham churches for the provision of hospitality, presumably to pilgrims: CUL, EDR, Reg. Arundel, fo. 63ᵛ.

Nevertheless, the clergy were provided with a forceful injunction to care for the needy, associated with a lack of specificity that allowed individual priests and ordinaries to respond to the demands of their own localities and times. It seems more appropriate to regard the decrees of the canonists and the rules of the monastic orders as normative codes rather than as narrowly legalistic rules intended to dictate the conduct of the local church. Provincial decrees, formulaic collections of case law such as that of Lyndwood, and episcopal visitation orders all sought to adapt the codes to the needs of late medieval England, but much was inevitably left to the initiative of communities and individuals.[19]

II

Monastic hospitality should, in theory, have been less subject to the vagaries of time and place than that of the secular clergy. Not only did the Benedictine *Rule* prescribe that all guests should be received, it offered some detail on the manner of their entertainment and on the limits of giving. There was already an assumption in the original *Rule* that an abbot or prior might have an obligation to entertain, and should have the resources to do so. Other rules also offered some detailed guidance on entertainment: for example, the Cistercians, while not excluding the possibility of care for outsiders, were explicit on the duty of the abbot to act with the body of his monks, not to have the independence of a separate table.[20] In practice, the rules permitted and legitimated exactly the wide variation of practice mentioned above. At the end of the fifteenth century it appeared that English monasteries could justify by reference to the words of the founder either the elaborate organization that made a house like St Albans almost an alternative home for some of the greater nobility and members of the royal family, or the provision of a few modest guest-beds and some food at the gate, which was all that was required at Bolton Priory.[21] It was even possible to

[19] Tierney emphasizes the need to see the words of the canonists as general guides to action.
[20] *La Règle de St. Benoit*, ii. 612–14.
[21] H. T. Riley (ed.), *Johannes Amundesham Annales Monasterii St. Albani* (Rolls Series, 1870), 4 ff; Kershaw, 138; *VCH Yorkshire*, iii. 198.

justify a total absence of hospitality on the grounds that the need did not exist, though such a position is implicit rather than explicit, and has (with some risk of circularity) to be read from the record of behaviour. When inns and alehouses became common, the obligation which the regulars owed to travellers might be argued to be correspondingly diminished, and the same was true of provision for the local poor who, at least in the fifteenth century, were less numerous than in the great days of English monasticism.[22] It is worth remembering that the Benedictine *Rule* insisted on a welcome for strangers, not on the deliberate cultivation of outsiders: that was more likely to be the task of those who sought honour and reputation in the lay world. An acknowledgement at the outset that this 'passive' element in monastic behaviour was perfectly congruent with the word, if not the spirit, of the *Rule* may help us to circumvent some of the heated, but essentially unreflective, controversy about the social utility of the regulars on the eve of the dissolution. The interesting issue is not whether the monasteries were cornucopias of generosity in the fifteenth and sixteenth centuries, but whether they adapted the basic ideals of the founders successfully to the circumstances of their own society.[23]

Those ideals, at least in the case of the Benedictines, demanded a willingness to receive both rich and poor, which was not radically different from the lay vision of an open household. Some of this vision can indeed be traced in the great rebuilding which occurred in many of the wealthier monasteries in the century before the dissolution. It is most explicit in the remodelled gatehouse of Cleeve Abbey, Somerset, a Cistercian rather than a Benedictine house, where Abbot Dovell introduced a new almonry and placed over the gates an inscription we have already encountered as a topos of openness: *Porta patens esto / nulli claudaris honesto.*[24] At Glastonbury Abbot Beere, who died in

---

[22] See below, p. 238.

[23] For the debate on monastic almsgiving, see A. Savine, 'The English Monasteries on the Eve of the Dissolution', in P. Vinogradoff (ed.), *Oxford Studies in Social and Legal History*, i. (Oxford, 1909); R. H. Snape, *English Monastic Finances in the Later Middle Ages* (Cambridge, 1926), 110–17; D. Knowles, *The Religious Orders in England*, 3 vols. (Cambridge, 1959), iii. 264–6; C. Haigh, *The Last Days of the Lancashire Monasteries* (Chetham Soc., 3rd ser. 17, 1969), 55–8.

[24] R. Gilyard-Beer, *Cleeve Abbey* (HMSO, London, 1960), 18.

1524, added a new wing to the guest quarters known as the King's Lodging, but he also built the church of St Benignus on the west side of the abbey specifically for the use of the poor who came to Glastonbury for alms.[25] Less immediately conformist to the Benedictine ideal are the rebuildings of guest-quarters at Basingwerk Priory, Flintshire, and the construction of lodgings fit for the king and the nobility at Carmarthen Priory.[26] Here the primary purpose was presumably to impress the powerful, but this was not necessarily detached from a desire to appear generous to the poor as well. Carmarthen was reported as feeding eighty poor persons a week at the time of the dissolution, and Abbot Dafydd of Valle Crucis cultivated a reputation with his bard both for groaning, well-stocked boards and for maintaining 'a whole township at the door'.[27] Rebuilding at Durham Priory in the time of John Wessington in the early fifteenth century produced a fine set of apartments for the prior, in which he entertained great men of the realm and region as well as his own monks.[28] But we know from the very precise description of hospitality at Durham in the *Rites of Durham*, written late in the sixteenth century, that feasting in the prior's hall continued alongside the feeding of ordinary travellers and pilgrims in the guest hall, and of generous giving to the local poor inside and outside the gates. the prior of Durham was said to be willing to receive all strangers of 'all staites both noble, gentle and what degree soever', and to encourage them to stay, 'not willing or commanding any man to departe upon his honest and good behaviour'.[29]

Few monasteries can have been quite so ideally attuned to general hospitality on the eve of the dissolution as Durham. Even the founders had hardly expected entertainment to be so open-ended: it was usual to suggest that guests should be allowed to stay for two days and two nights without question, but to remain longer only in unusual circumstances.[30] Archbishop Winchelsea regarded one night as an appropriate length of residence at

[25] *VCH Somerset*, ii. 93.
[26] G. Williams, *The Welsh Church from the Conquest to the Reformation* (Cardiff, 1976), 379.
[27] Ibid. 383–4.
[28] R. B. Dobson, *Durham Priory: 1400–1450* (Cambridge, 1973), 102–3.
[29] J. T. Fowler (ed.), *Rites of Durham* (Surtees Soc., 107, 1903), 89–90.
[30] F. A. Gasquet, *English Monastic Life* (London, 1904), 32.

Canterbury, where the demands of pilgrims imposed severe strain on the priory.[31] Yet it is not sufficient to dismiss the Durham description as nostalgic yearning for the world that had been lost. Robert Aske, deposing on the role of the monasteries in the aftermath of the Pilgrimage of Grace, also had some cause to romanticize, but his language is in fact explicit and unsentimental, and his view of the contribution of the monasteries to the local economy is hard-headed. He noted that the northern houses had discharged their duty towards wayfarers, and had served the needs of both the poor and men of some substance:

strangers and baggers of corn betwixt Yorkshire, Lancashire, Kendal and Westmorland and the bishoprick [were] greatly helped both horse and men by the said abbeys; for never was in these parts denied either horse meat or man's meat, so that the people were greatly refreshed by the said abbeys, where now they have no such succour.[32]

Others even less disposed towards a sentimental view of monks at times spoke of the survival of ideals of the founders in corners of the English realm. The dissolution commissioners in 1536 gave a number of honourable mentions to the generosity of particular houses. The Hampshire commissioners praised Netley Abbey and Quarr on the Isle of Wight for supporting both the local poor and seafarers.[33] Two Somerset houses, Cleeve and the Carthusian Priory of Hinton, were said to be honest establishments which offered good entertainment.[34] In Norfolk the Prior of Pentney, denounced by Cromwell's visitors as incontinent, was presented by Richard Southwell and Robert Hogen as a man of blameless life and extreme charity in the local community, while in Yorkshire the Hull Charterhouse was amongst those singled out for comment.[35] Houses of Austin Canons were not often remarked, but Ulverscroft in Leicestershire and the urban monastery in Northampton were both thought to be important for the relief of travellers and the poor.[36] Even nunneries were occasionally mentioned: Catesby in

---

[31] G. H. Cook, *English Monasteries in the Middle Ages* (London, 1961), 19.
[32] *LP*, XII, i. 901 (2).   [33] PRO, SC12/33/27, M.I.
[34] *VCH, Somerset*, ii. 117, 122.
[35] *VCH, Norfolk*, ii. 390; J. S. Purvis (ed.), 'Yorkshire Dissolution Documents', in *Miscellanea* (Yorks. Archaeol. Soc. Rec. Ser. 80, 1931), 28-9.
[36] PRO, E36/154/51; *LP*, XIII, i. 932.

Northamptonshire and Polesworth in Warwickshire both attracted comments from the commissioners.[37] Of course the men of 1536 were usually from the locality, and thus had some interest in displaying sympathy towards popular houses, but even Cromwell's visitors were not wholly immune from the charms of a well-regulated system of entertainment. Layton, for example, interceded with Cromwell for the Prior of Boxgrove in Sussex, for 'he is a great husband and keepeth great hospitality'.[38] Most surprising of all is Bishop Latimer's intervention on behalf of the Benedictine house of Great Malvern, which he attempted to protect, 'not in monkery . . . but to maintain teaching, preaching, study with prayeing, and . . . good housekeeping, for to the virtue of hospitality he [the prior] hath been greatly inclined from his beginning'.[39]

One should not presume that all the government's corre-spondents were seized with an overwhelming enthusiasm for the godly entertainment of the monasteries. Few events in English history can have produced so much self-serving argument and action as the dissolution, and the actual concerns of Cromwell's contacts were predictably diverse. At the one extreme is the example of the Abbot of Evesham, trying to preserve his house by converting it into a mixture of school and hostel, with care of the local poor thrown in for good measure. These admirable causes sit rather curiously with his insistence that Evesham was necessary as a superior lodging for the upper classes, since there was no other suitable accommodation in the area.[40] Rather more dubious is the attempt made by Sir William Parr to save the Cistercian house of Pipewell, 'being of very small revenue, keeping continual hospitality, relieving the poor, maintaining divine service in as virtuous and laudable a manner as any I know'.[41] This sounds admirable, but in the third letter sent by Parr to Cromwell it emerges that the reward for his protection had been a convent lease sealed, though not taken up, the previous Easter. For all Parr's disclaimers on exploitation, and insistence that he was moved primarily by the 'great relief and

---

[37] *VCH, Northants*, ii. 124; *LP*, X, 1166.
[38] *LP*, IX, 509. See also John Tregonwell on Wroxton, Oxon, where the prior is described as a 'good husband', though 'rude and unlearned': *LP*, IX, 457.
[39] *LP*, XIII, ii. 1036.   [40] *LP*, XIII, ii. 866.   [41] *LP*, IX, 822.

succour which the poor people have daily' from the house, it is difficult to believe that his judgement was not influenced by the Abbot's generosity.[42] But the interest of the many comments on hospitality lies not so much in the motives of the writers, as in their sense that the word was a shibboleth which was believed to possess some power to alter the attitudes of the government. In the absence of any better recourse, hospitality could be made the symbol of the social purposes of the monasteries; purposes to which the Henrician government itself paid some lip-service, when it insisted that any farmers or purchasers of former monastic property should maintain households and offer hospitality as their predecessors had done.[43] It may be that in particular, as well as in general, this appeal to the government did not fall entirely on deaf ears: Ulverscroft was spared for three years after 1536, Polesworth for three, and Pentney for two.[44] No doubt in each case the privilege of remission was also purchased for cash, but the appeal to good housekeeping was still felt to be a necessary ideological justification for survival.

What then did monks and sympathetic laymen claim they were trying to preserve when they spoke of good hospitality and expected Henry VIII to listen? The commonest argument was that the monks were necessary for the relief of local need, and that it was in supporting the local poor that they found their most obvious *raison d'être*. Hull Charterhouse fed 'men of the town', and Quarr Abbey offered 'by reaporte great refuge and comforte to all thinhabitants of the same yle [of Wight]'.[45] The Prior of Pentney 'relieved those quarters wondrously where he dwells', while Latimer's plea for Great Malvern took as its main theme his concern for the surrounding countryside, which was 'poor and full of penury'.[46] Although almsgiving to the local poor was, not hospitality in its narrowest sense, the correspondents of the 1530s obviously saw it as an integral part of household care, and

[42] *LP*, XIII, i. 1384. The unsavoury history of Parr's subsequent dealings is told briefly in *VCH Northants*, ii. 120-1.

[43] 27 Henry VIII, c. 28, clause xvii. For the problems associated with this clause, which appears on a separate sheet to the main Act, see J. Youings, *The Dissolution of the Monasteries* (London, 1971), 46.

[44] L. Butler and C. Given-Wilson, *Medieval Monasteries of Great Britain* (London, 1979), 358.

[45] PRO, SC 12/33/27, M.I.; *LP*, X, 980.

[46] *VCH, Norfolk*, ii. 390; *LP*, XIII, ii. 1036.

therefore comprehended under the name. The dispensing of almonry bread and the table remains under the eye of the almoner or his deputy must have remained one of the most visible manifestations of monastic giving even on the eve of the dissolution.[47] The assignment of a special room or area in or near the gate for the feeding of the local poor is an easily identifiable aspect of some monastic sites, and is described in such literary sources as the *Rites of Durham* and in Hooker's account of Exeter. Hooker gives a vivid picture of the provision made at St Nicholas's Priory, where there was a special Poor Men's Parlour to which:

There repaired daily seven poor men before dinner-time, and to every one of them was delivered on the flesh days a two-penny loaf, a pottle of ale, and a piece of fish, and on the Fridays likewise at afternoon, as soon as dinner was done, all such poor as were tenants came, and every one of them should have also a two-penny loaf, a pottle of ale, a piece of fish and a penny in money.[48]

This highly organized form of dole, probably a part of the obligatory alms of the priory, was presumably additional to the giving of general 'maundy' alms on a daily or weekly basis. At Worcester Priory a clear distinction was drawn between the giving of mandatory alms within the house and the casual doles which were issued at the hatch of the gate. It seems that many houses had abandoned the daily giving of the latter form of doles long before the sixteenth century: at Westminster, for example, they were no longer issued in this form from the mid-thirteenth century onwards.[49]

The rhythm of almsgiving, as it became more intermittent, may also have favoured the local poor who knew the obligations and anniversaries which bound each house to a specific pattern of giving. A commemoration feast, at which the anniversaries of all the deceased monks were celebrated together, was a common feature of Benedictine houses in the later Middle Ages.

---

[47] See P. I. King (ed.), *The Book of William Morton, Almoner of Peterborough, 1448–67* (Northants. Rec. Soc., 16, 1954), intro. xxvii.

[48] *Rites of Durham*, 91; G. Oliver, *Monasticon Diocesis Exoniensis*, 2 vols. (London, 1846–54), ii. 116.

[49] J. H. Bloom (ed.), *Liber Elemosinarii: The Almoner's Book of the Priory of Worcester* (Worcester Hist. Soc., 27, 1911), 5. The information on Westminster is derived from Miss Barbara Harvey's 1989 Ford Lectures.

Then portions for each of the deceased would be distributed. Maundy Thursday alms were common to most monasteries, and distributions might also reasonably be expected at the major feasts such as Christmas and Whitsuntide. Maundy Thursday giving was usually peculiarly generous: at Selby Abbey, Yorkshire, herrings were given to all the poor by the kitchener's office, while the almoner of Worcester had to distribute to twelve poor men for each monk in the house.[50] Other moments of giving were less predictable: the anniversary of the founder, or the obit of an individual benefactor, was often celebrated, or mandatory alms might be associated with a festival favoured by the community. Rochester Priory commemorated its founder with bread for the poor, and also marked the festival of Gundulph, one of the early occupants of the see. It was common to single out twelve or thirteen poor men to be the beneficiaries of these alms, especially if a meal was associated with the commemoration, although sometimes a dinner for a larger group of the poor was offered. St Gregory's Priory, Canterbury, spent £10 per annum on a dinner for its saint's day, and all the local needy were apparently bidden.[51] In such mandatory giving to the poor there is a clear notion of reciprocity: the chosen beneficiaries were to pray for those who had been founders and benefactors of the house or, in the case of the Maundy Thursday doles, to perform a symbolic role in permitting the ritual overturning of hierarchy as their feet were washed. The more practical consequence was that the local poor were bound into a cycle of feast and fast which might, in the best of cases, provide frequent relief, or at worst an annual treat to relieve the sufferings often associated with the end of the winter season.[52]

It is revealing that there should be a concentration on the needs of the locality in the attempts to defend monasticism, since the *Rule* of St Benedict charged monks principally with the duty of being harborous to outsiders, especially the pilgrim and the poor traveller. Much has already been said about English suspicions of the outsider, especially if he could be labelled a vagrant,

[50] G. S. Haslop (ed.), *A Selby Kitchener's Roll of the Early Fifteenth Century* (Yorks. Arch. Soc., 48, 1976), 122; *Almoner's Book of Worcester*, 5.

[51] *Valor Ecclesiasticus*, 6 vols. (London, 1825–34), i. 102, 25.

[52] Snape, *Monastic Finances*, 116.

but it might be expected that the monasteries would have
attempted to transcend these suspicions in accordance with the
letter and spirit of the *Rule*. Early patterns of hospitality do indeed
comprehend a concern for the poor traveller, often issuing in the
establishment of hospitals under the aegis of the monasteries.[53]
Appropriations of benefices in the thirteenth and early fourteenth
centuries make much of the demands of hospitality, especially
if the house concerned was on a highway and in a frequented
part of the realm. Despite the formulaic nature of these documents,
specific problems do sometimes emerge, as in the appropriation
of St Andrew's, Pershore, to the abbey in 1327. This was claimed
to be necessary because the abbey had lost some manors, because
of sheep murrain, because of fire in some of the conventual
buildings, but above all because of the increased traffic of both
rich and poor through the town and the demands that this placed
on monastic entertainment.[54] A little of this attitude survives
in the documents associated with the dissolution: the two
Hampshire abbeys already mentioned were praised for their care
of seafarers, and Carmarthen Priory prided itself on offering a
refuge to ordinary merchants. But it is rare to find any praise of
help offered to the common wayfarer. This is why a comment
by the commissioners on Ulverscroft is so arresting. Since,
they wrote, it was in the isolated forest of Charnwood, it
refreshed 'many pore people and waye faryng people'.[55] When
monasteries and their advocates did seek to defend their reputation
as welcomers of strangers, they usually spoke of those who
had sufficient resources to finance their own travel: Aske's
middlemen, the merchants visiting Carmarthen, or the nobles at
Evesham.

Perhaps the most important test of the attitude adopted by the
monasteries to the stranger poor is their response to pilgrimage.
The pilgrim was especially designated as deserving care by St
Benedict, and the abiding popularity of pilgrimage ensured that
this form of charity was as relevant at the end of the Middle Ages
as in the sixth century. The existence of individuals and groups
who claimed hospitality because they were pilgrims is attested

[53] Rubin, *Charity in Medieval Cambridge*, 102–3.
[54] *VCH, Worcester*, ii. 129.
[55] PRO, SC12/33/27, M.I.; *LP*, X, 1246; PRO, E36/154/51.

by some of the lay household books of the fifteenth and early sixteenth centuries.[56] Some evidence survives that the shrines of greatest resort still offered simple accommodation to their visitors: at Canterbury, for example, the Chequers Inn, built in the 1390s, was apparently conceived as an overflow dormitory for the monastic hospice. Although it fairly rapidly acquired a higher social standing, the major rooms of the hospice seem to have been used for ordinary pilgrims until the dissolution.[57] Smaller centres that established themselves as shrines, such as Castle Acre in Norfolk, also made some attempt to provide lodging for poorer visitors, though like most houses Castle Acre saw its relics as a valuable investment with which to attract the offerings of the wealthy and influential.[58] In some cases not even this level of charity was displayed to the ordinary pilgrim: the rapid growth in the popularity of the Walsingham shrine was not matched by adequate provision of accommodation, and the gap was filled by private enterprise. In the 1420s there were a series of major fires in the inns, started, one of the St Albans chroniclers gleefully surmised, by visitors who had been over-charged by the proprietors.[59]

The issue of the pilgrim raises the more general problem of monastic attitudes to the entertainment of those who had some resources, who could not plead poverty as title to food and accommodation. The evidence for particular behaviour is painfully thin, but there are indications that from a relatively early date some reciprocal gesture was expected of visitors. This might take the form of direct payment for food consumed: when Richard de Swinfield, Bishop of Hereford, stayed at Reading Abbey *en route* to London in 1290, he was at first entertained, but thereafter seems to have purchased his own food, as did Bishop Giffard of Worcester at Osney on his diocesan perambulation in 1284.[60] On the whole, however, houses probably expected rewards of a less commercial kind. When Humphrey, Duke of

---

[56] Longleat MS., Misc. Bk. IX, fos. 35ᵛ, 37ᵛ, 49.
[57] R. A. L. Smith, *Canterbury Cathedral Priory* (Cambridge, 1943), 200.
[58] Butler and Given-Smith, *Medieval Monasteries*, 185.
[59] *Johannes Amundesham*, i. 62.
[60] J. Webb (ed.), *A Roll of Household Expenses of Richard de Swinfield* (Camden Soc., o.s. 62, London, 1855), 60; H. E. Salter (ed.), *Chapters of the Augustinian Canons* (Oxford Hist. Soc., 74, 1922), 4.

Gloucester, recovered from an illness at St Albans in 1427, he made shrine offerings in thanksgiving.[61] Or rewards might be given to individuals, such as the gifts that Henry VIII's sister gave to the canons of Butley Priory after a prolonged visit in 1527.[62] Even these offerings were overt and explicit when compared with the benefit that must often have been anticipated: patronage and political support. It was presumably in the pursuit of these interests that many abbots and priors cheerfully ignored the implications of the statute 3 Edward I, c. 1, which had prohibited the visits of unwanted notables to monasteries. St Albans showed no inhibitions about its constant entertainment of members of the royal family in the 1420s; indeed, the descent of the Duke of Gloucester to spend Christmas in the abbey with 300 followers was recorded in loving detail.[63] The bursar of Durham complained in the 1440s that compulsory entertainment of magnates visiting the north on Scottish business had cost the Priory over £400 in the previous thirty years, but this piece of special pleading was made in the context of laments about taxation.[64]

Further down the social scale reciprocity was more likely to involve some form of money transaction. Here it is particularly pertinent to look at the development of distinct hostels or inns for travellers, which were a feature of monastic building programmes in the fifteenth century. Between the 1380s and the dissolution at least ten of the greater houses constructed inns, usually near the monastic site and often at considerable initial cost to the foundation.[65] It cost Prior Chillenden the extraordinary sum of £877 to erect the Chequers at Canterbury,

[61] *Johannes Amundesham*, i. 12–13.

[62] A. G. Dickens (ed.), *The Register of Butley Priory Suffolk: 1510–1535* (Winchester, 1951), 51.

[63] *Johannes Amundesham*, i. 4. Henry VI spent Christmas 1433 at Bury St Edmunds, and was so pleased with his entertainment that he stayed four months: Butler and Given-Wilson, *Medieval Monasteries*, 162.

[64] Dobson, *Durham Priory*, 108.

[65] W. A. Pantin, 'Medieval Inns', in E. M. Jope (ed.), *Studies in Building History* (London, 1961), 169–90; A. E. Richardson and H. D. Eberlein, *The English Inn Past and Present* (London, 1925). The ten are the Chequers, Canterbury; The New Inn, Gloucester; The George, St Albans; The George, Winchcombe; The Pilgrim's Hostel, Battle; The Pilgrim's Inn, Glastonbury; The Star, Oxford; The George, Norton St Philip; The New Inn, Sherborne; and an inn at Bedford; but the list is not exhaustive, cf. Buildwas below.

and it was noted with pride that the New Inn at Gloucester had been built at great expense from its foundations upwards in the early 1450s.[66] It is difficult to penetrate the motives of the builders with precision, since there are few explicit statements about the inns. However, there was probably most commonly a mixture of objectives, in which profit played a significant part. In the case of the New Inn at Gloucester there survives a clear statement that the property was built by John Twynning, 'to the great profit of the monks and their successors'.[67] Osney Abbey's construction of the Star Inn in the centre of Oxford seems clearly designed as a way of profiting from the burgeoning university, and Abbot Selwood described the George Inn, Glastonbury, as an endowment for the office of the chamberlain.[68] On the other hand, the duty of the regulars to ordinary travellers and pilgrims was not necessarily neglected. The original purpose of the Chequers has already been mentioned, and when the Cistercian house of Buildwas in Shropshire established an inn for travellers by Buildwas Bridge, they seem to have been intent on protecting those within their territories from commercial exploitation.[69] The existence of an inn did not, in this last case at least, prevent the commissioners in 1536 from commenting favourably on the intramural hospitality offered by the monastery.[70] It seems probable that the inns did represent a displacement of the duties of entertainment from the abbey or priory to the associated community, perhaps the logical extension of earlier arrangements by which those who could afford to pay and stayed for any period of time offered return of some kind for their lodgings. There are obvious parallels here with what has already been observed in the case of lay households: that the ideal of openness was in practice restricted, and that inns were considered the most usual place of resort for ordinary wayfarers. The monasteries were probably less restrictive than their lay counterparts even in the early sixteenth century, but the assumptions by which they proceeded were not very different.

The case of the monastic inns indicates a displacement of the ideals of hospitality adumbrated by the various orders, but it is less easy to call it an abandonment of those ideals. A similar

---

[66] Cook, *English Monasteries*, 20.   [67] Pantin, 'Medieval Inns', 190.
[68] Ibid. 190   [69] Ibid. 169, 181.   [70] *VCH, Shropshire*, ii. 58.

process of displacement might be said to have operated in the decline of communal entertainment within the conventual walls in favour of a more individuated pattern. Many of the examples of lavish entertainment recorded in the last century of monasticism focus on the household of the abbot or prior, rather than involving the community at large. The construction of lodgings for guests was most commonly undertaken in association with the quarters of the head of house, which, from at least the fourteenth century onwards, were scarcely distinguishable from the manor-houses of the nobility and gentry. When Prior More, the penultimate Prior of Worcester, entertained, he rarely did so in his lodgings in the priory, preferring instead one of the several rural estates at some distance from the cathedral city.[71] His household of ten yeomen and approximately twenty other servants went about its business of receiving local gentlemen, judges, the city burghers, and so on in precisely the same manner as a lay establishment. More did on occasions entertain monks of his own house, but they do not seem to have assumed any more significant place than secular clerics might have done in an episcopal household. Among his lesser visitors, the Prior included some of his tenants, especially at the Christmas season, and he gave fairly generously to the poor.[72] His easy life as a member of the landed élite did attract some adverse comment, especially some malicious gossip from a monk he had affronted. John Musard, the monk in question, claimed in 1536 that More's hospitality was directed to his kindred and servants, not to the poor, and that he was consuming the substance of his office in bribes associated with law-suits.[73] There seems to have been little specific substance in the charges, and they were ignored by Cromwell to whom they were addressed. However, the degree of separation of More's life from any traditional view of monasticism obviously made him an easy target for this kind of complaint.

In More's case the displacement of communal hospitality had reached the point at which his behaviour must be described as purely personal. However, the separation of the head of house

---

[71] E. S. Fegan (ed.), *The Journal of Prior William More* (Worcester Hist. Soc., 32, 1914), 76, 84, 123.
[72] Ibid. 77, 79, 97, 145.   [73] *LP*, X, 216.

from his monks could have effects that served to reinforce old values rather than undermine them. Prior Wessington of Durham, who was the dominant figure in his community in the first half of the fifteenth century, offers a good example of the positive advantages of a separate establishment. Wessington utilized two houses outside the walls of the monastery, but this in itself was fewer than those maintained by his predecessors, since many of the outer estates were placed in farm.[74] When visiting these two manors of Beaurepaire and Pittington, the Prior was often accompanied by some of his monks, and four times a year the monastic 'ludi' or retreats were held at Beaurepaire. Wessington also reconstructed the lodgings within Durham and came to regard them as his main place of residence. The importance they assumed in the collective life of the priory is indicated by the frequent references to them as the *hospicium*.[75] The lodgings were treated as an integral part of the house in the sense that they provided a focus for the entertainment of all guests except the poorest. The Prior was careful to receive not only the great, but also to feast his own monks from time to time, seeking to use commensality as a means of bridging the divide that had become common in Benedictine houses. The chance survival of the guest list for one feast indicates that Wessington sought a delicate balance between his role as head of house and his duty to the wider Durham community. A group of monks were included, very properly seated at a separate table under the eye of the subprior. The guests of honour were the suffragan Bishop and the Abbots of Newminster and Blanchland; the majority of the others present were ordinary clerics of the diocese. Since this was primarily a clerical occasion, only four laymen were included: the Prior's steward, and the sheriff, steward, and receiver-general of the bishopric. If this sounds a rather cosy and oligarchical gathering, it is nevertheless indicative of the serious purposes to which a successful head of house could put his hospitality.[76]

---

[74] Dobson, *Durham Priory*, 93, 97.

[75] Ibid. 97; the pattern of 'ludi' was maintained into the early sixteenth century, by then providing an occasion for general entertainment of the local populace: J. Raine (ed.), *The Durham Household Book . . . 1530–34* (Surtees Soc., 18, 1844), 9, 339; Dobson, *Durham Priory*, 103.

[76] Ibid. 107.

In a majority of the examples so far considered there is a sense that the counsel of St Benedict was retained in the letter rather than the spirit. Some participants in the historiographical debate about the monks and almsgiving have gone further and suggested that the duties of the regulars were, by the early sixteenth century, either completely abandoned or performed in the most limited way possible. The figures worked by Savine from the *Valor Ecclesiasticus* have often been invoked to demonstrate that only a tiny proportion of monastic income was directed to the relief of poverty.[77] They showed that in two hundred monasteries with an aggregate income of more than half the total for all houses, 'allowed' alms, that is, those believed by the commissioners to be mandatory, represented about 3 per cent of total income. The national figure was even lower, at less than 2 per cent.[78] A subsequent study of monastic finances, which looked in detail at six establishments, concluded that at most only 5 per cent of revenue was spent on alms and hospitality, and a few of those who have considered individual houses have arrived at similar figures.[79]

There are moments when the monks do seem to have abandoned all sense of responsibility for the poor, even to those whose needs were immediately visible to them. When the chronicler of Butley Priory observed the sufferings of the poor in the hard year 1527, he ejaculated piously: 'the Lord Jesus avert this for the better', but gave no hint that he or his brethren were aiding the Lord's work.[80] It may be that the praise that was heaped upon some houses in 1536 reflects badly on the rest, and that many were negligent or gave assistance in a grudging spirit. William de Worcestre excoriated St Benet's, Holme, because, despite the noble benefactions of his patron Fastolf, it provided: 'Filthy linen . . . stony bedding, a filthy stable, sword-like Hay, Stingy hospitality, A chilly fire in the chimney . . . Therefore the guests will leave without farewell.'[81] Since a later visitation complained that dogs in the cloisters were eating the food intended

---

[77] Savine, 'English Monasteries', 235–40.   [78] Ibid. 238–9.
[79] Snape, *Monastic Finances*, 116. Smith, *Canterbury Cathedral Priory*, 47; Kershaw, *Bolton Priory*, 141–2; however, both examples long pre-date the Dissolution.
[80] Dickens, *Butley Priory*, 14.
[81] J. Harvey (ed.), *The Itineraries of William de Worcestre* (Oxford, 1969), 3.

for the poor, it would seem that Worcestre's witticisms were justified.[82] Crowland Abbey was also abused in a contemporary rhyme for its stony beds, though some concession was made here, since the monks were believed to be 'courteous of their meat and drink'.[83]

There have been a number of attempts to counter the charge of failure of hospitality conveyed by the above figures. Regional exceptions can be demonstrated, most notably that of Lancashire, where average spending on alms has been calculated at 7.6 per cent, with Whalley Abbey spending no less than 21 per cent of gross income in this way.[84] Alternatively, it has been suggested that even modest proportions of income could represent considerable sums for daily food relief, as at Coventry, where the Carthusians spent £14. 0s. 10d. on thirty quarters of rye and thirty of malt, or at Worcester, where the total alms bill was estimated in 1535 to be £47. 9s. 5d.[85] More generally, it has been argued that the figures for compulsory giving are only a part of a more complex picture. They do not include any estimate of the value either of intramural entertainment of the needy or of the doles from the monastic table that had to be given regularly to the poor. Even in the case of money doles, the limited definitions of the ecclesiastical commission exclude many of the alms regularly given. David Knowles estimated that these and related sums might well have increased the value of almsgiving by 50 per cent, and that they represented a significant part of the activity of many monasteries.[86] The problem is that such calculations are extraordinarily tenuous, and depend upon an unproveable assumption that the basic duties of the monks were being discharged. The circularity of the argument obviously

[82] *VCH Norfolk*, ii. 335; the complaint was made in 1526 and repeated in 1532.

[83] Cook, *English Monasteries*, 18.

[84] Haigh, *Lancashire Monasteries*, 53–4.

[85] C. Phythian-Adams, *Desolation of a City: Coventry and the Urban Crisis of the Late Middle Ages* (Cambridge, 1979), 136; *Almoner's Book of Worcester*, 8. The generosity of the Carthusians, in this case the London Charterhouse, which, despite dearth, would still give 'as large livery of bread and ale to all their servants and to vagabonds at the gate', was adversely remarked upon by Jaspar Fylolle to Cromwell in 1535; *LP*, IX, 283. Thomas More, defending the generosity of the monastic orders, claimed that on occasions it was impossible to reach Westminster because of the throng of poor being fed at the Abbey gates.

[86] Knowles, *The Religious Orders*, iii. 265.

weakens it, though we should not, therefore, necessarily leap to the opposite conclusion that the critics of monastic generosity are correct.

Two rather more promising approaches are suggested by Brian Tierney in his work on the medieval poor law.[87] One is to ask whether there were widespread complaints of neglect at episcopal or other visitations. When this evidence is sifted for the century before the dissolution, it produces surprisingly few grumbles about almsgiving or hospitality. Bishop Nykke's Norwich visitations in the early sixteenth century yield little more than the St Benet's, Holme, case already mentioned, and the extensive Lincoln investigations of Bishops Atwater and Longland, which offer important evidence on the giving of parish priests, are almost silent on the monasteries.[88] Occasionally a surviving set of injunctions addresses the problem of what care should be given by the regulars. Those of Bishop Gray for Ely Priory in 1466 include a very detailed order on the entertainment of the family and friends of the monks, who were to be treated with respect, but not to be taken into the town.[89] Such injunctions seem more concerned to ensure that monks and nuns behaved with moral and social probity than that they were generous in the spirit of the founder. Convents were sometimes ordered to see that guest-quarters were adequately provided in order to avert any hint of impropriety.[90] Neither the monks themselves nor their visitors seem to have been much preoccupied with standards of giving and domestic care. It may be that such indifference indicates that all was well, that the charitable duties of the regulars, as perceived by contemporaries were well discharged, and that attention was therefore given to more pressing problems of neglect of the *Rule*. Such arguments *ex*

---

[87] Tierney, *Medieval Poor Law*, 106–8.

[88] A. Jessopp (ed.), *Visitations of the Diocese of Norwich, A.D. 1492–1532* (Camden·Soc., N.S. 43, London, 1888). Thompson (ed.), *Visitations in the Diocese of Lincoln, 1517–1531*, 3 vols. (Lincs. Rec. Soc., 33, 35, 37, 1940–7). A rare complaint about failure to distribute to the poor by monks, who gave instead to their relatives, comes from Faversham Abbey, Kent, in 1511: K. Wood-Legh (ed.), *Kentish Visitations of Archbishop Warham* (Kent Rec. Soc., 24, 1984), 34.

[89] J. A. Evans (ed.), *Ely Chapter Visitations and Ordinances* (Camden Soc. Misc. 17, 3rd ser. 64, London, 1940), 63.

[90] M. Bowker, *The Henrician Reformation: The Diocese of Lincoln under Bishop Longland* (Cambridge, 1981), 26–7.

silencio are obviously dangerous: it may be that no complaints were made because no visitation questions were asked about hospitality, and that this reflects the indifference of the inquisitors rather than the adequacy of the regulars.[91]

The second, and related, way of interrogating the evidence on charity is to turn to other sources on the perceptions of contemporaries. If few questions were asked and few complaints made in monastic visitations this may be because a limited generosity to outsiders and the needy could be assumed, and that by the early sixteenth century any greater effort would have been considered a work of supererogation. The monasteries were not primarily eleemosynary institutions, and it was their principal religious purpose of corporate worship that had to be given first attention.[92] Recent study of wills and benefactions on the eve of the Reformation has challenged the traditional view that the laity had ceased to value the spiritual functions of the regulars; instead, the image now presented is one of willing acceptance of their intercessory prayers until the very moment at which Cromwell's visitors began their rounds.[93] It is obviously no accident that most of the detailed evidence we can invoke on hospitality dates from the period of the dissolution: when praise of the prime function of the monks no longer availed, then their activity in and for the community became one of the few ways of defending their utility. It simply appears that almoners whose main income was spent on the organization of their office, and inns that were run as a business proposition by some senior obedientiary, were accepted features of late medieval monasticism, evoking little public criticism.[94] Even those humanists who began the assault on the regulars had little

---

[91] Ibid. 17–18. Longland in his sermon to the monks of Westminster concentrates on their spiritual morale.

[92] Tierney, *Medieval Poor Law*, 81.

[93] J. J. Scarisbrick, *The Reformation and the English People* (Oxford, 1984), 1–19.

[94] *Book of William Morton*, xxvii ff. Miss Harvey, in her Ford Lectures, suggests that the monks may have come to give their discretionary alms in discriminating ways in the later Middle Ages, largely excluding the begging poor. Since such a process of discrimination was compatible with contemporary secular behaviour, it is perhaps not surprising that the monks did not attract general criticism of their eleemosynary activities.

to say about their social role, beyond the mandatory attack on luxurious living within the walls.[95] The *Rule* of St Benedict was sometimes modified by the monks in curious directions, but the cumulative effect may not have been so horrifying as sixteenth-century Protestants and twentieth-century historians have often suggested.

II

The secular clergy faced problems rather distinct from those of the regulars in the discharge of the duty of hospitality. While the regulars had to balance the needs of strangers and the local poor, being guided, if anything, towards a preoccupation with the former, the bishops and parish clergy were indubitably expected to cater first and mainly for their own flocks. Much of the canonist discussion of hospitality concentrated on explicating the local duties of a cleric, moving from the premisses of the early church that a bishop would have direct comand of charitable resources, to one in which they were assumed to be organized at parochial level. While this narrowing of focus might be thought to simplify the task of entertainment and care, it placed burdens on the seculars that they were not necessarily well-equipped to meet. The monastic organization of entertainment evolved along sophisticated administrative lines that were appropriate in a large, fixed organization with an architecture that matched the offices. Such elaboration was beyond most English bishops, with their peripatetic life-style and limited tenure of office, and certainly far beyond the reach of the parochial clergy, including those with adequate endowments. Even a restricted definition of charitable obligations presented enormous practical difficulties for an ordinary incumbent with his small house (if he were fortunate) and his dependence on a few servants to support domestic activity.

In the case of the bishops, the obvious model to follow must always have been that of the great lay household rather than that of the monastery. Mobility between estates, and between London and the localities, had always been an essential part of the

---

[95] See especially D. Erasmus, *The Praise of Folly* (Oxford, 1913), 128 ff.

behaviour of the spiritual peers, and their role as great lords was often imperfectly differentiated from that of their lay counterparts.[96] The same hierarchy of officers served Archbishop Stratford, or Bourchier, or Cranmer, as served their ducal and baronial colleagues. The Canterbury household, which is by far the best documented throughout our period, had in the early stages of the Reformation a comptroller at its head, presiding over an inner coterie of senior officers who were required to maintain a tight discipline over a household that was probably about a hundred strong.[97] Even this seems small when compared with Wolsey's grandiose establishment, which may at the height of his power have included 500 men.[98] These servants of the great prelates performed tasks that were little differentiated from those of other magnates': providing a riding household and an appropriate company of 'tall fellows', as well as undertaking all the usual domestic chores. In the few surviving household accounts which record guests, one for Archbishop Stratford from the 1340s, another for Bourchier from the 1450s, and one for John Hals, Bishop of Coventry and Lichfield, for 1461, the clerk of the kitchen is to be found annotating visitors not unlike those already discussed for the laity.[99] Bishops seem to have visited one another rather more than peers did: in Bourchier's month of accounts he was host to three prelates and one dean. They also tended to welcome the clergy, as was to be expected: the Lichfield accounts show that the cathedral establishment could routinely anticipate dining at the episcopal table while the household was in the cathedral city.[100] In all other respects they conform to our earlier images of the late medieval establishment: the archiepiscopal household suggesting the magnificence of

[96] On the social role of the bishops before the Reformation, see F. Heal, *Of Prelates and Princes* (Cambridge, 1980), chs. 2. and 4.

[97] F. Heal, 'The Archbishops of Canterbury and the Practice of Hospitality', *JEH*, 33 (1982), 554 ff; LPL, MS. 884.

[98] George Cavendish, *Life of Wolsey*, ed. R. S. Sylvester and D. P. Harding (New Haven, Conn., 1962), 22.

[99] LPL, Estate Doc. 1973; Staff. RO, D(W) 1734/3/3/264.

[100] In Lichfield the bishop usually had the vicars-choral and choristers to dine with him, and sometimes his suffragans plus three or four other clerics. On his country estates of Beaudesert and Heywood he rarely entertained clerics, and indeed was often without guests for a week at a time.

the nobility, that of Coventry and Lichfield the liberality of a
country gentleman.

Is it therefore possible to identify the household of the
late medieval prelate as in any way distinctive from those
discussed in previous chapters? There seems to have been some
expectation that a bishop would preside over a sober and
disciplined establishment, for as Edmund Dudley wrote in 1510,
'it is not unfitting that there were a plain diversity between their
servants and the servants of other temporal men as well in
the honesty of their demeanours as in the sadness of their
vesture'.[101] Such an expectation must frequently have been
disappointed: early in the fifteenth century, Margery Kempe had
been appalled to find Archbishop Arundel's servants playing dice,
and had reproved him for it.[102] The deliberate showiness that
Wolsey encouraged in the clergy certainly militated against
sobriety in the years before the Reformation. Indeed, it often led
to behaviour that made the bishops easy targets for critical
radicals, such as George Joye, who denounced Stephen Gardiner
for the pomposity of his household, and for his feeding of a host
of 'idle bellies'.[103] The personnel of an episcopal household also
tended to be more clerical than that of the common run of
establishments, but even here cases like that of Canterbury show
that by the fifteenth century many of the senior offices were held
by laymen.[104]

Some form of hospitality towards the poor was no doubt still
considered mandatory: Bourchier's account, for example, shows
the provision of special issues of ale and bread as alms on a
regular basis, more obviously paralleling monastic behaviour
than that of the laity.[105] Several of the bishops in the generation
immediately preceding the Reformation had a reputation for great
generosity: Nicholas West of Ely was supposed to have fed
up to 200 men daily at his gates, and Richard Foxe won the
approval of Nicholas Harpsfield for providing the destitute of the

---

[101] Dudley, *The Tree of the Commonwealth*, ed. D. M. Brodie (Cambridge, 1948), 43.
[102] W. Butler-Bowden (ed.), *The Book of Margery Kempe* (London, 1936), 64.
[103] Quoted in L. B. Smith, *Tudor Prelates and Politics* (Princeton, 1953), 58.
[104] F. R. Du Boulay, *The Lordship of Canterbury* (London, 1966), 263.
[105] LPL, Estate Doc. 1973.

Winchester area with food and clothing.[106] Here the traditional perception of the duties of a good bishop may have been reinforced by humanist charitable concerns and a consciousness that the prelates had to justify their great wealth more actively than in the past. Already there were laymen who were prepared to criticize the prelates for not giving liberally from their great resources. Edmund Dudley, in his *Tree of Commonwealth*, alleged that they no longer gave one part of their income to charity and one to the household for hospitality but instead purchased lands for their heirs or 'for marriages of their kinsfolks'.[107]

A consciousness of the importance of playing the role of a good bishop as host and giver of alms is most powerfully revealed in the activities of Thomas Wolsey, so effectively described by Cavendish. Once Wolsey was compelled to retire from London in 1529 and to reside in his diocese, he obviously decided to use all his dramatic talents to present the vision of a perfect prelate. When he reached Southwell he 'kept a noble house and plenty both of meat and drink for all comers, both for rich and poor, and much alms given at his gate'.[108] Much time was passed in trying to reconcile differences between the local laity, and in winning friends by his sociability. When the Cardinal travelled further into his diocese, visiting a variety of the parishes around Scroby, he made it his practice to 'dine in some honest house of that town, where would be distributed to the poor a great alms as well of meat and drink as of money to supply the want of sufficient meat'.[109] At each of the main residences of the archbishops he assiduously cultivated the image of a loving prelate, keeping open house, and so won the love 'of both the worshipful and of the simple men of that country'. Cavendish was not so blinded by loyalty to his master as to underestimate the cool calculation that guided Wolsey's actions, but the success of this very belated attempt to live a life of godly generosity clearly impressed him. The Cardinal for a few months played the social role of a prelate for all it was worth, and in so doing

---

[106] F. Godwin, *A Catalogue of the Bishops of England* (London, 1601), 279; Nicholas Harpsfield, *Historia Anglicana Ecclesiastica* (London, 1622), xv, c. 20.
[107] Dudley, *Tree of Commonwealth*, 42–3.
[108] Cavendish, *Life of Wolsey*, 142.   [109] Ibid. 147.

demonstrated the power that resided in this sort of exercise of episcopal good lordship.[110]

It could, of course, still be argued that there was nothing very distinctive about this pattern of behaviour: magnates too returned to their localities to be greeted by effusive support from their dependants, which in turn demanded a lavish show of hospitality and general giving which extended to the very beggars at the gate. Perhaps it is useful to distinguish the prelates only by observing that their performance was likely to be more closely observed and criticized than that of their contemporaries, if only because there was always the authority of canon law as an ideal standard of comparison with actual behaviour. Even before the Reformation the bishops were also vulnerable because they were at once autonomous landowners and representatives of the crown and of the political centre.[111] They were, therefore, compelled to be Janus-faced, always conscious of the centripetal influence of the monarchy even in the far corners of the realm. When, for example, Thomas Ruthal undertook the first of his rare tours into the diocese of Durham, he found himself inundated with suitors and clients so that, as he wrote to Wolsey, what 'I spend here would make many towns and refresh my ruinous houses'.[112] The eight tuns of wine which he had brought from London had dwindled to two in less than eight weeks. This pattern by which the local gentry, followed by their dependants all the way down the social scale, flocked to greet a new bishop, created both financial and political problems. A prelate like Ruthal had to reassure Wolsey that he was not seeking a power base in the localities: rather he was sacrificing his immediate interests in order to perform the duties expected of a loyal Henrician bishop.[113]

What does emerge in a number of surviving sets of accounts is that housekeeping was the most important item in an episcopal budget. Robert Sherburne of Chichester, who had a reputation for good hospitality, spent £350 on housekeeping in 1522 out of

---

[110] Cavendish, *Life of Wolsey*, 148.
[111] Heal, *Prelates and Princes*, ch. 2.   [112] *LP*, I, ii. 2394.
[113] It was rumoured that Ruthal failed badly in this endeavour, since he accidently gave Wolsey a schedule of his own wealth, rather than the official document that was required of him as the King's secretary: Godwin, *Catalogue of the Bishops*, 530–1.

a gross income of about £590. Hugh Oldham, during his tenure of Exeter, averaged a household expenditure of £844 out of a total of just under £1,600, while at Canterbury there seems some justice in Archbishop Warham's complaint that he spent all his substance on housekeeping, since in the years immediately before 1531 about £2,800 out of a net income of £3,000 seems to have been expended under this head.[114] Such figures are not necessarily very illuminating in relation to hospitality, since they include a wide range of expenditures which had nothing to do with guests or the immediate food provisions for the establishment. However, they do indicate that lavish households were being maintained, and it can be inferred that visitors must often have been the beneficiaries.

It is impossible to abandon the theme of bishops and hospitality without mentioning the best-known account of an episcopal dinner-party: the description of Morton's dinner in the first book of More's *Utopia*.[115] The vivid portrayal of the conversation of a group of chamber guests is interesting precisely because they are such a heterogeneous bunch. Hythlodaeus has his experience as a traveller and a humanist to commend him to the Cardinal, and his fellow-guests seem chosen more for their interests than for their individual social standing. The lawyer and the friar both emerge from the dialogue with little credit, yet they are able to speak with a freedom and challenge that is indicative of the shared status of the community of the learned. We have already encountered the humanist perception that education and ability to converse were more important commendations in guests than mere social position, and here More seems to suggest that Morton already held that view under Henry VII. 'Fruitful converse' as the main focus of the episcopal table is an image encountered both before and after the Reformation, no doubt as one of the ways in which those writing of the prelates found they could justify their lavish provision.[116]

---

[114] Heal, *Prelates and Princes*, 83–6.

[115] Thomas More, *Utopia,* ed. E. Surtz and J. H. Hexter (New Haven, Conn., 1965), 61 ff.

[116] See particularly the description of Archbishop Warham's table by Erasmus: the Archbishop is alleged often to have sat at his board solely for the pleasure of conversing with others: Desiderius Erasmus, *Ecclesiastiae sive de ratione concionandi* (Antwerp, 1535), 71.

The experience of the ordinary parish clergy as hosts must have been a world apart from that of the bishops and the greater monasteries. Not only were their resources strictly limited, but they had few of the assistants necessary to offer good entertainment. Even the comparatively simple task of producing bread and ale for the local poor demanded an adequate number of hands to prepare the food. The Welsh clergy, who petitioned Cromwell's visitors against the outlawry of concubinage, on the grounds that it would force them to 'give up hospitality to the utter undoing of such servants and families as we daily keep, to the great loss of the poor people who are by us relieved', were being delightfully disingenuous, but in terms of domestic provision there was no doubt some force in their argument.[117] William Harrison, praising the reformed clergy for their improved provision for the poor, suggested that before the Reformation only a few 'double and treble beneficed men did make good cheer at Christmas only'.[118] Harrison was convinced that the support of a wife, rather than any significant improvement in income, had made it possible for the ordinary incumbent to do his duty to his parishioners. But income was also of importance if any adequate hospitality was to be offered, and there are plenty of examples of ecclesiastical revenues that barely met the basic needs of the cleric. Even a benefice that appears adequately endowed might not be so once the various charges for taxation, pensions, and ordinary living had been met. Thus, Hornsea would not have been identified as poor from the usual sources such as the *Valor Ecclesiasticus*, yet the incumbent found it difficult to manage within his income.[119] Indeed, the vicar pleaded to be exempted from residence precisely because he could not meet the costs of

---

[117] *LP*, X, 215.

[118] Harrison, *The Description of England*, ed. F. J. Furnivall, 2 vols. (New Shakspere Soc., ser. 6: 1, 5, London, 1908), i. 33.

[119] P. Heath, *Medieval Clerical Accounts* (St Anthony's Hall Public., York, 1964), 14. Moreover, changing circumstances might reduce an apparently prosperous cleric to a point at which he could no longer maintain hospitality. Thus the declining fortunes of the market town of Baldock meant that by 1462 the rector could barely support himself, let alone provide good entertainment, and the parishioners therefore acquired a papal licence to establish a guild to remedy the deficiency: G. Rosser, 'Communities of parish and guild in the late Middle Ages', in S. J. Wright (ed.), *Parish, Church and People: Local Studies in Lay Religion, 1350–1750* (London, 1988), 29.

hospitality. A detailed example of this kind may mean that we should give serious heed to the laments of the clergy in 1525 that high taxation would prevent them from offering hospitality.[120]

Yet in spite of these obvious problems it would seem that both church and people retained a belief in the value of clerical hospitality on the eve of the Reformation. What was expected can best be determined from the surviving visitation returns, most notably from the excellent series from Lincoln, from the episcopate of William Atwater (1517–20).[121] Unlike Bishop Nykke of Norwich, who in 1532 apparently failed to ask any questions about hospitality in his articles, and his successor Longland, who only asked about proper distributions to the poor, Atwater showed a particular interest in the problem of hospitality. In the archdeaconries of Lincoln, Stow, and Oxford the commissaries seem to have been very assiduous in questioning on this theme, and most of the returns come from those three jurisdictions. The most regularly voiced complaint was that monastic or collegiate appropriators had not done as required by Stratford's provincial decree and distributed money or grain to the poor. Grumbles on this score came from all over the diocese, though the spread was very thin: there were, for example, five cases for the 298 parishes of the archdeaconry of Leicester in 1518.[122] It is less easy to characterize complaints about hospitality proper, but behind the presentations seem to lie at least three distinct types of clerical delinquency. In some instances the failure of the incumbent was obviously associated with non-residence: at Sotby in Lincoln archdeaconry the rector was an absentee and did not keep hospitality.[123] In this case the diocesan authorities took a stern view of his behaviour, and ordered him back into residence to give entertainment appropriate to the value of his living. Yet, in contrast with post-Reformation visitations, the failure to be hospitable does not seem to have been associated overwhelmingly with absenteeism. Two other allegations were often made: that the incumbent did not live in the vicarage house, or sometimes that no such house

---

[120] G. Bernard, *War, Taxation and Rebellion . . . the Amicable Grant* (Hassocks, 1986), 102.

[121] *Visitations of Lincoln*, i. All information on hospitality comes from this period, rather than from Longland's 1530 survey.

[122] Ibid. i. 14–15, 16, 25.   [123] Ibid. i. 64.

existed, and that the rectory or vicarage was leased to a layman, who gave no entertainment.[124] No doubt the two grievances were often coterminous, though those clerics who lived outside their designated homes sometimes alleged that poverty and the decay of their property made it impossible to do otherwise. Lay farmers had a theoretical obligation to maintain hospitality in the absence of a cleric—or at least this was one reading of Pecham's decree—but the Lincoln commissaries showed no interest in trying to enforce this duty.

In addition to these groups of derelicts there were a number of other persons who were not fulfilling their duties in the eyes of their parishioners. At Friskney in 1519 the vicar was resident and had a household, but was informed against by his parishioners, and the same was true of the vicar of Offley and a handful of others.[125] Just under one-third of the thirty-five complaints involve incumbents who were not obviously absent from their parishes or their residences, but who had in some other way violated community norms. It is very difficult to judge from the returns exactly how they had offended: the vicar of Wendover was in trouble for failing to provide an Easter feast in the preceding two years, and the vicar of Stonesfield had not built the kitchen he should have provided in the church-house, but these are solitary examples of specific charges.[126] They do, however, suggest that when men of a parish complained about the absence of hospitality it was not the truly poor that were in their minds. Perhaps the expectation was rather that a cleric would be an active participant in the social life of his community, offering on occasions a focus for general good neighbourliness and fellowship; that he should be *in publico hilaritas*. The vicar of Kirmington apparently so pleased his parishioners by conforming to this image that they singled out his entertainment for praise; his merits were all the more worthy of remark because he was a regular and yet chose to keep his own household.[127] Both Peter Heath and Margaret Bowker have shown that this general accommodation into the commuity was seen as a central

---

[124] The last arrangement contravened Pecham's decree of 1281 that hospitality should be exercised by farmers if a cleric was non-resident: Powicke and Cheney, *Councils and Synods*, ii. 906.

[125] *Visitations of Lincoln*, i. 79, 97, 112.   [126] Ibid. 40, 129.

[127] Ibid. 91.

duty of the parish priest before the Reformation.[128] Such identity with the community would not, of course, have precluded care of the local poor, but above all it probably required a conviviality and accessibility which would have involved generosity at times of feast, and almsgiving in time of dearth.

It is just such an image that is evoked by one of the earliest funeral monuments to praise the personal qualities of a cleric. The master of the college of Great Ilford, Essex, who died in 1475, was recorded as 'A good householder, a fyne man, large in almys, he did worship to alle hys kynne, all the felasship was the meryer that Sir John Smith was inne'.[129] Almost a century earlier Nicholas of Louth, rector of Cottingham in Yorkshire, was rather more soberly commended as one who fed the hungry, helped the poor, and reconciled contending neighbours.[130] The model of the seven works of mercy was here, of course, held up as that which it was appropriate for clerics to follow. This ideal standard was obviously difficult to attain, but much could be done by a man generally conscious of his social duties, like the parson revealed in a small set of clerical accounts discovered on the flyleaves of a Cambridge University Library manuscript.[131] Richard Gosmore, incumbent of Basingstoke from 1499 to 1540, was one of the fortunate minority of clerics who was relatively prosperous: the vicarage was valued at £31. 7s. 1d. in 1535, and he farmed the rectory for Magdalen College, of which he had been fellow. The accounts reveal something about his household, though more about his activities as a farmer of an extensive glebe. Gosmore had the organizational resources to entertain, but even so his hospitality to the bishop's commissary was organized through the local inn, which provided soup, chicken, sucking pig, rabbits, and other delicacies at his expense.[132] On the other

---

[128] Bowker, *The Secular Clergy*, 110–12; P. Heath, *The English Parish Clergy on the Eve of the Reformation* (London, 1969), 4–8.

[129] T. F. Ravenshaw, *Antiente Epitaphes* (London, 1878), 14.

[130] I owe this reference to the kindess of David Palliser. Nicholas de Louth was prebendary of Beverley and of Salisbury, and is unlikely to have been regularly within his parish. However, his concern for the church is indicated by the fact that he erected the chancel: the Latin inscription describes him as 'factor et erector'.

[131] CUL, MS. L1.2.2. I am very grateful to Dorothy Owen for drawing my attention to this material and showing me an unpublished paper on the accounts.

[132] Ibid. fo. 2.

hand, he did spend regularly on bread, ale, and wine for his own hall, and at Christmas and Rogationtide discharged very explicit duties to his parishioners. At Rogation he provided bread and other foods for twelve, and at Christmas 1506 he and his servant prepared a meal of bread, meat, and leeks *et placebat bene omnibus*. Only the poor received no mention in the accounts, but they may well have benefited from Gosmore's giving at festival times.

By the early sixteenth century it was long since parish poor relief had rested solely, or even primarily, in the hands of the local cleric. Even the pious hopes of the preamble to the Pluralities Act of 1529, which limited the holding of multiple benefices for the maintenance of divine service, the proper preaching of God's word, 'the mayntenaunce of Hospitalitie [and] the relefe of poore people', seem anachronistic by the middle of Henry VIII's reign.[133] Alternatives such as guilds and fraternities, the benefactions of prosperous laymen, and the mutual self-help of the networks of family and neighbourhood were the logical choices of the needy.[134] This no doubt led to some resentment: More repeats a proverbial saying current in the early sixteenth century among beggars that nothing could be expected of a secular priest.[135] But the seculars had never assumed a very explicit responsibility for the begging outsider, and if their giving to local men came to focus upon festivals and moments of celebration on the one hand, or of desperate need on the other, then they were merely following in the direction of much contemporary charitable giving. Like the gentry, who gave doles at funerals and food at Christmas, the clergy may well have felt that they had thereby discharged much of their Christian obligation to the poor.[136]

[133] 21 Henry VIII, c. 13.

[134] C. Dyer, *Lords and Peasants in a Changing Society* (Cambridge, 1980), 349–51.

[135] More, *Utopia*, 83.

[136] For the narrowing of the pattern of medieval charity see Rubin, *Charity in Medieval Cambridge*, 292–9.

7

The Clergy After the Reformation

I

IN one of his lucubrations on the state of the English realm, William Cecil observed that 'the bishops and clergy that shuld by ther teachyng and devotion and speciallye by hospitallyte and releyvng of the poore men wyn creditt amyngst the people, ar rather despised than reverenced and beloved'. At the root of their behaviour, he believed, was the sin of covetousness, and especially that passionate pursuit of the interest of their wives and children that led them to hoard up wealth. This led them to deny even the Queen herself her legitimate requests for church lands and leases.[1] The unfortunate prelates of the post-Reformation Church were impaled on the horns of a peculiarly uncomfortable dilemma. They could defend their possessions against an assertive laity only by demonstrating that they were employing them for the collective good of church and community, by playing to the full the role of pastors to their flocks. Yet they were also expected to play traditional roles as leaders of the commonwealth, which involved behaving with much of the formality and ostentation that had been demanded of their predecessors. In this already difficult situation, the licence given to the clergy to marry was an additional complication, since provision for a family now became a matter of necessity, and the natural predilection of prelates for their children made them reluctant to invest their accumulated wealth in traditional ways.[2]

Thus it was a relatively simple matter to cause acute embarrassment to the leaders of Protestantism by the mere mention of

---

[1] PRO, SP 12/184/50.
[2] For a full discussion on this dilemma see Heal, *Of Prelates and Princes* (Cambridge, 1980), ch. 7.

clerical wealth, and almost equally easy for the laity to construct justifications for the alienation of ecclesiastical property. The great benefited from valuable episcopal and chapter lands and leases: lesser men pursued much the same goals by resisting the payment of contentious tithes or by gaining rectorial leases. These actions were underpinned by a powerful, if simple, series of moral assertions. *The Discourse of the Commonweal* exemplifies this language of righteous indignation when it enquires:

Yea, what better hospitalitie, residens, or minstrations, either of the worde or of other dewties, doe oure prelates and Bishoppes now then they did before? Doe they not lurke in theire mansions and manerplaces far from their Cathedrall churches, as they weare wonte? and skante once in a yeare will se theire principall churche, wheare they ought continuallye to be resident?[3]

Clerics in general, and bishops in particular, now had to justify their wealth by the quality of their pastoral care and by a standard of behaviour far higher than that of their predecessors.

In the new circumstances that followed on the breach with Rome, and more particularly on the dissolution of the monasteries, an appeal to the ideal of hospitality became a useful tool in the armoury of both the opponents and the supporters of clerical wealth. Both groups were acutely aware that it was no longer possible to defend the lands and incomes of the secular clergy merely by reference to the good old ways, since even the most generous of the monasteries and the most bonhomous of the prelates had been tainted by false doctrine and by an erroneous perception of the role of works in the process of salvation. Although Frotestant writers, such as Henry Brinkelow or the great Laurence Chaderton, were compelled to admire the giving of the monks, they nevertheless inveighed against the assumptions which underlay it. Mors condemned the monks as unlearned, but pointed out that 'thei kept hospytalyte, and helpyd their poor fryndes'.[4] For Chaderton these 'great and costly workes wherein we must confesse they [the papists] do exceede us' must be replaced with a willingness to perform charitable works suitable to the clerical calling, both to show the fruits of

[3] E. Lamond (ed.), *The Discourse of the Commonweal* (Cambridge, 1954), 133.
[4] Henry Brinkelow, *The Complaynt of Roderick Mors*, ed. J. M. Cowper (*EETS*, E.S. 22, London, 1874), ch. 14.

a lively faith and to fulfil Christ's explicit command to feed the flock.[5]

This sense that dominical injunction and the need to display a lively faith went hand in hand is to be found as a constant refrain of the Protestant writers, and helped to ensure that the idea of hospitality was revitalized in the mid-sixteenth century. The threefold Petrine feeding, with the word of God, with good example of life, and with material assistance, was considered a binding obligation upon the clergy by the evangelistic generation of preachers who led the Edwardian Reformation. The true and sincere preaching of the Word was at the heart of their conception of the Christian faith, but many of them also shared in some measure in the belief that they were moralists obliged to excoriate their audiences for their temporal failures. In the case of the clergy, those failings could readily be reduced to the second and third elements in the trope of threefold feeding: their lives did not provide good examples to their flocks, and their material charity had grown cold. The rhetorical skills of Latimer, Crowley, and Lever were used to flail prelates and double-beneficed men alike, inadvertently providing in the process much of that critique that was used against clerical possessioners by self-interested laymen.[6] Only slowly did it occur to these reformers that loss to the Church did not necessarily mean gain to the poor, to learning, or to the other projects close to their hearts.

The basic position espoused by the Edwardian reformers was a simple one founded in scriptural precepts. Christ had ordained that his flock should be fed by his chosen ministers, whether bishops or ordinary parochial clergy. Most were content simply to repeat Christ's injunctions to Peter, arguing that the clergy must eschew worldliness and regard their goods as held in trust for the service of Christ. However, there were those who singled out the prelates for especial comment, using Paul's images of the true bishop as the basis of their judgement. None was more committed to a concern for episcopal hospitality and charity than Somerset's chaplain Thomas Becon, who on several occasions used texts on

[5] Laurence Chaderton, *An Excellent and Godly Sermon, Preached at Paules Cross the xxvi Daye of October, 1578* (London, 1578?), sig. ci[v].

[6] On this theme see G. R. Elton, 'Reform and the "Commonwealth Men" of Edward VI's Reign', in his *Studies in Tudor and Stuart Politics and Government*, 3 vols. (Cambridge 1974–83), iii. 238–48.

material charity as the basis for extended expositions of prelatical duties. In his *General Preface* (1560), he glossed the Pauline insistence on the hospitality of prelates in detail for a Protestant audience: 'A bishop's house without hospitality is like a tavern without wine . . . Bare, naked and unhanged walls bring not such and so great a deformity to a spiritual pastor's house, as the lack of hospitality doth.'[7] For Becon even the Catholic models offered by the canonists, suitably modified, were acceptable props for the argument that feeding the body of Christ's flock was as vital as feeding its soul. So important was the idea among 'the father's of Christ's church, that if any spiritual pastor that were of ability, did not nourish and succour the poor, it was counted a sufficient cause to deprive him of his spiritual promotions'.[8] Few others were quite as emphatic, but the desire to relate all behaviour to the Word, and to resuscitate true charity as a feature of clerical living, was common among this evangelical generation.

When it did not emerge as a general form of precept based on scriptural models, this view was sometimes to be found in descriptions of particular godly clerics. Perhaps the most vivid of these is Peter Martyr's image of Bucer's household at Strasburg, given in a letter carefully constructed to strengthen the faithful congregation at Lucca. To Martyr, in flight from persecution in Italy, Bucer's establishment seemed 'a house of hospitality—such usual entertainment giveth he towards strangers, who are constrained to travel for the Gospel and for Christ's cause'. The essence of this entertainment was that it refreshed the spirit and the body together, but did so in an atmosphere of sobriety and moderation which contrasted sharply with that of contemporary episcopal households. 'This', Martyr claimed, 'is the office of a pastor—this is that bishop-like dignity described by Paul in the Epistles unto Timothy and Titus.' Not only had Bucer reverted to the true image of the bishop in the primitive Church, but he had taken seriously that belief which pervaded the writings of the canonists, yet very infrequently the practice of the Church, that all wealth

---

[7] Thomas Becon, *Works,* ed. J. Ayre, 3 vols. (Parker Soc., Cambridge, 1843–4), i. 24.
[8] Ibid. 23.

was custodial, to be employed for the poor and needy members of Christ.[9]

These typologies were clearly little more than the reworking of basic scriptural and canonistic themes in the light of Protestant theology and circumstance. Yet they are worth careful consideration both because they provided a modified image of the pastor as host and because they offered hostages to fortune, new ways in which the laity might assail the leaders of the reformed Church. The Edwardians were deeply concerned to avoid any charge of antinomianism, and found in works of material charity an ideal way of arguing for the visible godliness of the new order. They sought to defend the Church functionally, by placing its wealth firmly in the service of the commonwealth, but most of them stopped short of justifying an outright appropriation of that wealth by the state. Instead, they hoped that wealth would be employed for its proper purposes by clerics infused with new spiritual values. Since the dissolution of the monasteries eliminated that group whose role as possessioners was least justified, ordinary clerics would now be able to discharge their duties more fully. Ideally this would involve a return of appropriations to the parishes so that, to quote Francis Bigod, no longer would the parson be 'a theefe and thabbot another', but the priest would keep hospitality as Paul had commanded.[10] When the Henrician regime insisted in 1536 that the new owners of monastic property must maintain households and hospitality, it must have offered some faint hope to the reformers that their views were shared by those in power.

Most of the actual disputes between laymen and prelates about the failure of hospitality were, however, far removed from these earnest concerns for virtuous clerical behaviour. The bishops had been placed on the defensive by the beginnings of the appropriation of church wealth in the 1530s, and there were plenty of men at the Henrician court who assumed that, with a little pressure, their land would follow that of the monasteries. In these circumstances, complaints about episcopal inadequacy

---

[9] G. C. Gorham (ed.), *Gleanings of a Few Scattered Ears During the Reformation* (London, 1857), 21-2.

[10] Francis Bygod, *A Treatise Concernynge Impropriations of Benefices* (London, 1535?), sig. ciii.

were a very thin covering for naked greed. In 1541 Thomas Seymour, the brother of the later Lord Protector, endeavoured to trap Archbishop Cranmer with a charge of failure of hospitality, the notion apparently being that he could then urge Henry that some of the property of the archbishopric would be put to better use in the hands of the nobility.[11] Cranmer, according to Seymour, was wasting his lands for the benefit of his family, and keeping no household 'correspondent with his revenues and dignities'. Henry, ever-willing in the 1540s to play off one court grouping against another, forewarned the Archbishop, who provided a dignified display of traditional hospitality for the accusing courtier. In consequence Seymour was forced to withdraw his charge, and Henry seized the opportunity to lecture his followers, arguing that so long as the prelates maintained hospitality he would not allow them to be despoiled. The story is a valuable reminder that Henry could express serious commitment to the idea of hospitality. One may hazard, however, that the assumptions of the monarch were not identical with those of godly Protestants. When Henry spoke of hospitality he referred to a very traditional pattern of prelatical behaviour, one in which clerical households continued to act with the old ceremoniousness and grandeur of the preceding age, rather than as defenders of the needs of the poor or the humble visiting reformer.[12]

Although in circumstances such as these the shibboleth of hospitality was apparently of some relevance to Henry, this concern was not universally shared. When Cromwell issued the crucial royal injunctions of 1536 and 1538, for example, he appeared deliberately to eschew the traditions of the medieval Church on this subject. The only charitable obligation that the parochial clergy specifically incurred under these orders was that non-residents able to spend more than £20 per annum were compelled to give at least the fortieth part of their revenue publicly to the poor.[13] Indeed, the only moment at which legislation drafted by Cromwell referred to hospitality was in the

---

[11] *Narratives of the Days of the Reformation*, ed. J. G. Nichols (Camden Soc., o.s. 77, London, 1859), 260–1.

[12] For a detailed discussion of the Seymour incident, see Heal, 'The Archbishops of Canterbury and the Practice of Hospitality', *JEH*, 33 (1982), 544–5.

[13] D. Wilkins, *Concilia Magnae Britanniae*, 4 vols. (Oxford, 1761), iii. 814.

1536 Act of Dissolution. It would be consistent with the attitudes articulated in the Poor Law of that same year that he should show less concern for the old traditions of giving than for the structured organization of money alms in the parishes. On the other hand, the old assumptions were still alive in the statutes drafted by Nicholas Heath, George Day, and Richard Cox for the cathedrals founded or refounded at the beginning of the 1540s.[14] There the obligation to 'keep hospitality' was accorded a major place, with residentiaries being required to feed all comers, especially at their first entry into their stalls. The solemn detail of the cathedral statutes, which descended to such particularity that residentiaries were told how many times a year they had to entertain other members of the foundation, suggests that the senior clerics responsible for their drafting were wholly convinced of the value of good entertainment in the service of the Church. The 1548 royal injunctions for Lincoln Cathedral, one of the old foundations, show the same concern more specifically directed to charitable behaviour. The prebendaries were bound by their statutes to give hospitality, and should 'releve therwith the pore wayfaryng men, honest and nedy persons, and specially such as be poore Mynisters of this churche'.[15]

Had the assumptions of the royal injunctions of the 1530s prevailed for the parochial clergy, the issue of hospitality would probably have ceased to be a serious one for the leaders of the Church. Cromwell's concern for the organized giving of the fortieth part did indeed play an important part in many subsequent injunctions, and became the principal medium through which the charitable disposition of the clergy was evaluated. In the Edwardian injunctions of 1547 there was once again no mention of hospitality, and many of the episcopal visitation articles and injunctions of the same period take their cue from the government, and simply enquire into the giving of the fortieth part.[16] The desire to impose a more coherent structure on the old casual systems of almsgiving which is evident in secular poor-law legislation had by this time also

---

[14] *The Statutes of the Cathedral Church of Durham*, ed. A. H. Thompson (Surtees Soc., 143, 1929), xxxix, 111–13.
[15] *Lincoln Cathedral Statutes*, ed. H. Bradshaw and C. Wordsworth, 3 vols. (Cambridge, 1897), iii. 586.
[16] Wilkins, *Concilia*, iv. 3–8.

penetrated into the field of clerical giving. There were those among Edwardians, notably Bucer and William Turner, who saw this as the best way to guarantee the care of the poor in the future. Turner might seek to persuade the nobility that they should still be charitable in a modified version of the old tradition, but he was increasingly convinced that continental reformed methods of organizing relief through an established group of parochial elders were to be preferred to the old casual ways.[17] There were also those who recognized the dangers of continuity with a Catholic past that was both doctrinally corrupt, and that had possessed a false sense of values about the true obligations of the Church. Thus, in the eyes of Crowley and Turner, the popish clergy had misread fundamentally their priestly duties, and their successors were little better, defending their deficiencies as preachers of the word by claims of generosity. Crowley's double-beneficed man prided himself because he could:

> . . . kepe hospitalitye
> And geve as much unto the pore,
> In one yere, as thou dost in thre,
> And wyl performe it wyth the more.[18]

This, in the eyes of the reformers, was little better than the justification offered by the alehouse priest who argued that he drank with his parishioners because it was necessary to maintain community and good-fellowship. If hospitality and material charity were thus made excuses for failure to provide crucial nurture for the soul in the form of preaching, then the godly would have none of it.

However, there were influential men who continued to believe that the traditional modes of care should not be swallowed up entirely by the new. In 1547 Thomas Cranmer issued his own visitation articles for the see of Canterbury, and asked his wardens to comment on the behaviour of their incumbents in terms that associated old ways with Cromwell's ideas: 'Whether they be resident upon their benefices, and keep hospitality or no; and if they be absent, or keep no hospitality, whether they do make due distributions among the poor parishioners

---

[17] William Turner, *The Huntyng of the Romyshe Wolfe* (Emden, 1555?), sig. ei–ii.

[18] Robert Crowley, *Select Works*, ed. J. M. Cowper (*EETS*, E.S. 15, 1872), 77.

or not.'[19] It is difficult to be sure that the Archbishop attached great significance to his enquiry, which appeared low on the visitation agenda, after his questions on preaching, catechizing, and saint-worship. Yet he reopened a line of interrogation that was subsequently pursued by several prelates of impeccably reformed credentials, notably John Hooper, who showed an interest in hospitality in his very detailed enquiries for the diocese of Worcester in 1550.[20]

More explicit evidence about the Archbishop's attitudes can, however, be drawn from other sources. Cranmer, indeed, is probably the key figure in the preservation and redefinition of the ideal of the clergy as a charitable and generous estate, concerned for the bodies as well as the souls of their flock. His ambiguous status as the leader of a reforming church which nevertheless adhered to the structure and social role of its Catholic predecessor, forced upon him modes of behaviour that integrated the old and the new. The prestige of the hierarchy had to be maintained in the face of the species of hostile criticism offered by Seymour, and the Archbishop was always, therefore, a great housekeeper in the tradition of earlier primates. His surviving household ordinances show an establishment wholly in the late medieval mould, formal and hierarchical in its structure, carefully integrated and disciplined by a body of senior servants who would have been equally at home in a ducal train. Strangers of all rank were to be accorded a proper welcome by the Archbishop's servants. The poor were to benefit from the scraps at the gate, though Cranmer showed more than usual generosity to the needy by giving tenants hot dishes from his own table, and by allowing the almoner to lead them into the body of the hall to eat on occasions.[21] In order to maintain this elaborate establishment it is likely that he had to follow the practice of his predecessor, William Warham, who regularly spent most of the £3,000 income of the see on housekeeping.[22] Such ostentation might win friends, but it also attracted envy, and the obvious charge that this mode of living was inappropriate for a man of

---

[19] Wilkins, *Concilia*, iv. 24.
[20] W. H. Frere and W. M. Kennedy (eds.), *Visitation Articles and Injunctions of the Period of the Reformation*, 3 vols. (Alcuin Club, London, 1910), ii. 305.
[21] LPL, MS. 884.　　　　　　　　　　　　　　[22] PRO, E101/518.

the cloth. To counter such criticism Cranmer employed very traditional devices: in particular, says his biographer, he displayed a conscious asceticism in personal behaviour, and frugality amid the grandeur of his surroundings. Warham had earlier been described by Erasmus as delighting in the company of strangers, rather than in the food and drink at his board, so much so that sometimes he ate and drank nothing.[23] This topos of worldly asceticism was translated to Cranmer: he was said often to have sat at table with his gloves still on his hands, as a signal to his household servants that he would eat nothing.[24]

This behaviour still left godly reformers somewhat uneasy. Even Morice, Cranmer's biographer and secretary, felt the need to apologize for the richness of the archiepiscopal household, and when John Foxe incorporated the account in his *Book of Martyrs* he felt obliged to add further explanations. According to Foxe, the purpose of such solemn ceremonial at meals, when the Archbishop himself did not relish it, was that 'the alms-chest [was] well-maintained for the relief of the poor'.[25] The difficulty here is to differentiate Cranmer's own preferences from those of his godly biographers: his own desire to compromise between the old and the new led him, as is well known, to be a generous host to many foreigners of the reformed faith, and also to many of those engaged in the internal work of reformation. It is, however, difficult to be sure that he experienced any real unease about the more social use of his wealth. There is certainly an air of special pleading about Foxe's references to Cranmer's charity towards those wounded in the French wars of the 1540s. This would scarcely have explained lavish hospitality, although biographer and prelate were probably closer on the importance of the other particular beneficiaries: foreign reformers and 'learned men and commissioners, from time to time appointed for deciding of ecclesiastical affairs'. It seems likely that the martyrologist was still happier with the more radical use of hospitality by Bishop Hooper of Gloucester, who fed the needy at his table, but in return insisted that they accept instruction in

[23] Desiderius Erasmus, *Ecclesiastiae sive de ratione concionandi* (Antwerp, 1535), 72.
[24] John Foxe, *Acts and Monuments*, ed. S. R. Cattley and G. Townsend, 8 vols. (London, 1837–41), viii. 13, 20–2.
[25] Ibid. viii. 20–2.

the Lord's Prayer and the elements of faith. This was indeed to use the clerical household as the centre of reformation in the manner advocated by Becon and others: Hooper seems to demonstrate Lever's argument that persuasion through one meal could ensure more influence than could a dozen earnest sermons without such advocacy.[26]

It follows logically from Cranmer's management of his own household and revenues, that he should seek to employ traditional rules of behaviour in a reformed environment when disciplining the rest of the Church. In 1541 he took the unusual step of issuing a dietary regulation for the whole body of the English clergy, basing it on an original directed at the laity in the reign of Edward II. Sumptuary legislation was, of course, relatively common both locally and nationally under the Tudors, but it rarely concerned itself with diet rather than clothing, and this application to the clergy was unique.[27] What it shared with related orders was a deep concern for the preservation of hierarchy: archbishops were to restrict themselves to six kinds of meat at table, bishops to five, archdeacons to four, and so on. The purpose was traditionally moral, the avoidance of the sin of pride and of the arrogance of lavish display, but Cranmer added a characteristic justification: that the income spared should not be 'pocketed up, but laid out and spent in plain meats for the relief of poor people'. The timing of the dietary is of some interest: coming as it does after a period when the clergy had been the subject of intense literary and political criticism, it may be seen as part of a campaign to disarm and weaken hostile laymen. It seems to speak directly, for example, to the sort of challenge that Thomas Starkey had offered in his *Dialogue of Pole and Lupset*, that the bishops and prelates nourished idle serving-men and had lavish tables, 'spending their possessions and goods, which were to them given to be distributed among them which were oppressed

---

[26] Ibid. vi. 644–5.

[27] Wilkins, *Concilia*, iii. 862. The dietary was originally published by Matthew Parker: see Corpus Christi Cambridge MS. 106, no. 348. On sumptuary legislation in the sixteenth century, see F. E. Baldwin, *Sumptuary Legislation and Personal Regulation in England* (Johns Hopkins Studies in History and Political Science, 44, Baltimore, 1926), 167 ff.

with poverty and necessity'.[28] Cranmer no doubt hoped to forestall any further action on ecclesiastical wealth by winning approval for the cultivation of sober hospitality. The issue was certainly of interest to the government, for in his opening speech to the 1542 Parliament, Lord Chancellor Audley informed the members that it was convened *inter alia* to discuss '*quarundam legum regalium, que mandant sinceram predicationem evangelii, hospitalitatem sacerdotum, que vetant beneficiorum multitudinem etc.*'[29] But Cranmer's dietary should also be linked to his belief in the efficacy of traditional good works, not, of course, as contributory to salvation, but as the necessary fruits of faith.[30]

It might be expected that the Marians would seek to reverse the experience of the preceding decades by asserting the significance of material works of charity, and by emphatic rearticulation of the traditions of the Church in the area of hospitality. There is indeed some evidence in the visitation articles of the period that the bishops wished to re-establish confidence in the social and religious duties of the clergy. This is most clearly manifest in Bishop Bonner's enquiries for London diocese in 1554: the question on hospitality and residence appears very early in his listing, and is based upon the notion of threefold feeding: 'Item . . . whether you have your parson or vicar resident continually with you upon his benefice, doing his duty in serving of the cure? and whether, being able to do, he keep hospitality upon the same, feeding his flock with his good living, with his teaching and his relieving of them to his power?'[31] Archbishop Pole's visitation of Canterbury in 1555 also pursued the problem of non-residence and hospitality as an important issue, and in this case the survival of returns from the parishes enables us to see that action was taken against a number of defaulters.[32] In his Legatine Decrees Pole did not address himself specifically to hospitality, but he argued that good living was as critical as

---

[28] Thomas Starkey, *A Dialogue of Pole and Lupset*, ed. J. M. Cowper, 2 vols. (*EETS*, E.S. 12, 32, London, 1871, 1878), ii. 77.

[29] *Journal of the House of Lords*, i. 165. I am grateful to Glyn Redworth for bringing this document to my attention.

[30] Thomas Cranmer, *Remains*, ed. H. Jenkyns, 4 vols. (Oxford, 1833), ii. 164–8.

[31] Wilkins, *Concilia*, iv. 105.   [32] LPL, VG4/2.

preaching in the witness of the clergy, and hence that households should be sober, pious, and charitable. Prelates should abstain from luxury, but should keep an honest household, distributing as much as possible to the poor. Hence the concern with tradition, and the maintenance of customary obligations, were linked by the idea of sobriety which had acquired greater significance after the Reformation.[33] Pole himself apparently conformed closely to the model he suggested for his clergy: his household was large, and like his predecessors he spent most of his archiepiscopal revenues upon it, but he behaved with that same asceticism that had characterized the description of Cranmer. In Pole's case this appears even more likely to be accurate observation rather than the mere consequence of a rhetorical tradition: he had an aversion to company, except for that of like-minded scholars, and the lavish entertainment required of an archbishop seems to have been genuinely burdensome to his spirit.[34] He and his bishops also had the benefit of being able to adopt a more sympathetic attitude to the defence of their property than the Henricians and Edwardians: it was no longer constantly necessary to prove episcopal worth through lavish entertainment of the powerful, since the principle that surviving property must be defended was readily accepted by the Crown. Only once in the later stages of the reign was the virtue of hospitality adduced as a justification for property transactions, and that was when the bishops were made custodians of the revenue from first fruits and tenths so that they might use it to augment the livings of the poorest parochial clergy. The preamble to the *Act Extinguishing First Fruits* stated that a part of its purpose was to ensure that the realm would be provided with good incumbents able 'tinstructe the people with good and sincere Doctrine, and to bee hable to mayntayne Hospitalitee'.[35]

II

The Elizabethan Settlement inevitably meant a reversion to the *status quo ante*, with the bishops bearing the brunt of the

[33] E. Cardwell, *Documentary Annals of the Reformed Church of England*, 2 vols. (Oxford, 1839), i. 152–3.
[34] W. Schenk, *Reginald Pole, Cardinal of England* (London, 1950), 155.
[35] 2 & 3, Philip & Mary, c. 4.

challenge to ecclesiastical wealth and having to excavate all possible justifications for the preservation of their property. In less heady circumstances than those of the 1530s and 1540s, they were more reluctant to discuss alternative models of clerical behaviour than their Edwardian predecessors, and little was now heard from the clerical establishment of any reversion to primitive or scriptural models of behaviour. This did not, however, diminish the need to find some objective justification for wealth that would appeal to the laity, and once again hospitality proved a useful concept. It had a particular utility precisely because it was at once functional, idealistic, and conservative. Matthew Parker, Elizabeth's first archbishop, who was more instinctively conservative than Cranmer, pointed out in one of his early letters that it was essential to preserve goodwill via entertainment: 'the world looketh for port agreeable'.[36] Bishop Berkeley of Bath and Wells concurred rather bitterly, when surveying his badly depleted bishopric: 'the world expecteth and our vocation is to be hospitales.'[37] These were very much the expectations of the aristocratic society in which the bishops moved, but further down the social scale it was assumed to be as relevant for ordinary clerics within their own localities. Even the Crown acknowledged that the clergy should be assisted to be hospitable. The Act, 1 Elizabeth, c. 19, which allowed the bishops to exchange lands with the Queen, and to give long leases exclusively to the Crown, deliberately exempted estates that were in regular use for the supply of the household and were therefore necessary for the maintenance of 'port'. Opposition to the Elizabethan act took up this clause, and argued that it needed to be extended if the prelates were to have any hope of meeting their obligations.[38]

Since hospitality was supposedly so useful in influencing the laity, Parker was eager to practise what he preached. His household ordinances, based upon, but extending, those of Cranmer, show an even greater self-consciousness about the value of good entertainment as an aid to the maintenance of reputation.[39] The Archbishop was an instinctive antiquarian, and

[36] Matthew Parker, *Correspondence*, ed. J. Bruce and T. T. Perowne (Parker Soc., Cambridge, 1853), 208.
[37] PRO, SP 12/16/27.
[38] Heal, 'The Bishops and the Act of Exchange of 1559', *HJ*, 17 (1974), 236–8.
[39] LPL, MS 884.

he derived solemn pleasure from the collection and editing of great examples of past Canterbury feasting, and of documents such as the dietary already discussed. It was he who published the scroll containing particulars of the Neville and Warham feasts, and he also seems to have used them as some guide to his own activities as host. His assize feast at Canterbury in 1565, his celebration of the consecration of Grindal as Archbishop of York in 1570, and his two major moments of entertainment for the Queen, were strongly conditioned by his awareness of past ecclesiastical ceremonial.[40] His biographer follows the appropriate paradigm by describing the Archbishop as 'a mortified man to the world', much given to complaining that Cardinal Wolsey had ruined the clergy by 'first the wearing of silk, as that which brought in the Asiatic luxury'. Nevertheless, even he was compelled to admit that Parker took some pleasure in doing his duty as primate: 'yet his disposition led him to do things agreeable to his quality and condition, wherein God had placed him. And therefore, though he was above all affection of magnificence, yet he used magnificent hospitality, and great housekeeping, befitting his rank.'[41] His choice of guests, which can be traced for his various *convivia*, is also revealing. The Queen was obviously the prime target: arrangements for royal visits were discussed at great length in his correspondence, with a touching solicitude for the royal welfare. Parker's assize feast gave him a valuable opportunity to receive the county élite of Kent, while Grindal's consecration brought together the higher clergy of the realm. The importance which he attached to hospitality in the context of his diocese is also indicated by a Whitsun feast in 1566, at which the local gentry and members of the Canterbury corporation were present in the refurbished hall of the palace.[42] Although Parker's son was forced to defend his father's reputation after his death, and refute the charge that he was acquisitive, his works spoke for themselves: even the grudging Elizabeth expressed her admiration for the welcome offered to her at Canterbury.[43]

---

[40] J. Strype, *The Life and Acts of Matthew Parker*, 3 vols. (London, 1821), iii, 287–91; the information is derived from Parker's anonymous biography, the *Historiola*, printed by Strype in his Appendix.

[41] Ibid. 444.

[42] Parker, *Correspondence*, 494; Strype, *Matthew Parker*, 289.

[43] PRO, SP 12/137/54; Parker, *Correspondence*, 475–6.

Renewed interest in the concept of hospitality also connected it very deliberately to the care of the poor, and here again Parker seems to have been the moving spirit. The royal injunctions of 1559 reverted to the form of enquiry about residence and giving already encountered in Cranmer's 1547 series, and Parker then followed this in 1560–1 by making the issue of hospitality one of those raised in his investigation into the state of the clergy.[44] With that deliberate antiquarianism that was such a feature of his governance of the Church, he returned to Pecham's Provincial Decree and asked if farmers kept open house for incumbents in their absence. However, Parker was not the only one to believe that the preservation of household giving to the poor by the clergy was important: in the Convocation of 1562–3 one of the documents presented argued powerfully for the limitation of leases of rectories, since clerics should reside and dispense hospitality.[45] Some of the most committed of the reforming bishops made an enquiry about residence and hospitality an important feature of their visitation articles. For example, Parkhurst of Norwich asked in his 1569 visitation about the combined duties, and ensured that his deputies pursued the answer with some vigour.[46] Grindal made hospitality a part of his articles on his primary visitation of his northern see of York in 1571, and Freke did the same at Rochester in the following year. In the Canons of 1571, prepared under the leadership of Parker, the parish clergy were ordered to preach the Word in their cures and give hospitality to the poor for at least sixty days in the year, even if they were otherwise non-residents.[47]

Throughout the 1560s, 1570s, and early 1580s it is possible to discern in episcopal articles and injunctions a lively verbal commitment to clerical hospitality as a part of the charitable provision of the Church. Not only were enquiries common: the variation in their form suggests that at least some of the prelates were taking an immediate interest in the problem. While most articles followed the pattern of 1559, and were therefore ultimately dependent on Cranmer's enquiry about residence and

---

[44] Cardwell, *Documentary Annals*, i. 210; CCCC, MS 122.
[45] E. Cardwell, *Synodalia*, 2 vols. (Oxford, 1842), ii. 507.
[46] NRO, VIS/1.
[47] Frere and Kennedy, *Visitation Articles*, iii. 262, 340; Cardwell, *Synodalia*, i. 116.

the giving of entertainment, there were a number of prelates who worked to different formulae. In 1577 Bishop Barnes asked the wardens of Durham if their parsons settled themselves 'to the uttermost of their ability to keep good hospitalities, and do not let out, lease out, or tavern out, their livings . . .'?[48] A year later, Archbishop Sandys's elaborate enquiries for the Northern Province produced a portmanteau question on residence, hospitality, relief in money alms, the number of benefices held, and the keeping of alehouses in rectories or vicarages.[49] In some of the later investigations of the 1580s the formula of 1571 was employed: for example, in 1586 Westfaling asked at Hereford: 'Whether he [the minister] doth not at the least for one month in the year keep hospitality at his living, and also give, if his benefice be above twenty pounds a year, the fortieth part thereof to the poor?'[50] The early years of Whitgift's archiepiscopate seem to have witnessed just as much episcopal enthusiasm for the pursuit of clerical hospitality as had those of Parker and Grindal. But the visitation enquiries do suggest an important change towards the end of the 1580s. From 1589 onwards, the Archbishop himself adopted an almost standardized set of enquiries to be used at metropolitical visitations, and these inevitably came to exercise much influence on the form of other episcopal interrogations.[51] Whitgift did *not* choose to ask about hospitality in 1589 and, although the issue was by no means dead until well into the seventeenth century, never again did it form a common part of the enquiries about the behaviour of parish priests.

It is not easy to offer explanations for the rise and fall of concern for hospitality manifested in the visitation articles and injunctions of the Elizabethan bishops. Parker's personal anxiety to demonstrate that there was continuity between the reformed Church and its Catholic past in the matter of parochial care clearly

---

[48] W. P. M. Kennedy, *Elizabethan Episcopal Administration*, 3 vols. (Alcuin Club, London, 1924), ii. 73.

[49] Ibid., ii. 92. [50] Ibid., iii. 226.

[51] Ibid., iii. 248 ff; the only early seventeenth-century Articles that show specific interest in hospitality are those of Bridges for Oxford in 1604, Howson for Oxford in 1619, Overall for Norwich in 1619, Davenant for Salisbury in 1628, Montagu for Norwich in 1638, and Thornburgh for the archdeaconry of Worcester in 1638. Only Thornburgh asks anything more than whether the minister is resident and gives hospitality: *Appendix to the Second Report of the Royal Commission on Ritual* (London, 1867), 437 ff.

provides some reason for the initial interest, but this does seem unique to the Archbishop. In the case of Whitgift it may be important to emphasize the tactical relevance of hospitality to his campaign to defend ecclesiastical livings in the early 1580s. In the Parliament of 1584 the archbishop had to fend off the fiercest assault on pluralities and non-residence that the Commons had conducted since 1529.[52] In these circumstances it may have seemed that there was still advantage in an appeal to the old shibboleths. Deans and prebendaries who were pluralists were therefore defended, not only because of the need of the Church for learned men,—always the first protective line—but because they had extensive duties as hosts at a time when everything was to be 'required at double and treble prices'. In the case of the ordinary clergy, it was argued that they would be doubly disadvantaged if pluralities were taken away, since this would limit 'all ability in the ministry either of keeping hospitality, or of contributing to the state in case of necessity'.[53]

The difficulty for Whitgift and the bishops is that this argument may well have come to the end of its effective political life before the time of the 1584 Parliament. Although it still had some relevance when used by the bishops about their own entertainment, it was ceasing to carry much persuasive force in the context of the parishes. The slow development over the Elizabethan period of a national system of poor-relief based on the parish rendered much less central the idea that the clergy must be able to display liberality to the poor for the sake of the commonwealth. The only moment at which Archbishop Whitgift seems to have been able to employ it again with genuine authority was during the famine years of the 1590s, when he was under the direct orders of the Privy Council to compel his clergy to preach hospitality.[54] This he did, with the rider that they should themselves set an example to the laity, by giving generously to the poor. Even so, as Bishop Howson reflected sourly the next year, many of them could do little, given the simoniacal transactions by which some had acquired their benefices, and the

---

[52] C. Hill, *Economic Problems of the Church from Archbishop Whitgift to the Long Parliament* (Oxford, 1956), 232–3.
[53] Cardwell, *Synodalia*, ii. 557.
[54] Id., *Documentary Annals*, ii. 36.

poverty in which they found themselves.[55] A few years later Dr Crompton was again noting that, having lost any chance of the restored impropriations, the clergy 'cannot keep that hospitality which is required, for which one small benefice of cure, especially with wife and children, sufficeth not'.[56] Since it seemed hopeless to expect too much of the ordinary parish clergy, the bishops by and large lost interest in the attempt to enforce the duty of hospitality which Parker had undertaken with such initial enthusiasm.

However, even though the appeal to the ideal of good entertainment seems to have lost some of its force by the end of the sixteenth century, the bishops were never averse to disinterring it when the well-tried issues of non-residence, pluralities, and impropriations re-emerged. In the early Stuart parliaments there is an extensive history of attempts by the Commons to pass measures against non-residence, all of them blocked at some stage of their passage through the two houses. The liveliest conflict occurred in 1610, when the Commons passed a bill against non-residence, only to see it quashed in the Lords after vigorous debate.[57] There the bishops threw all the old arguments into the arena: Bancroft, in a particularly powerful speech, misquoted scripture, and invoked every possible argument, including the need for hospitality, in defence of the ministers' cause, Later, in the Committee of the Whole House, he returned to the original Commons legislation against pluralities of 1529, pointing out that the claimed objective was to ensure that ministers should have the resources to keep hospitality.[58]

By this period the virtues of clerical hospitality had become part of the rhetorical armoury of Puritan preachers as well: they also used the threefold model of ministerial behaviour when it suited their purposes, as when Robert Johnson used a fast sermon preached before the Long Parliament in 1647 to argue that there must be provision for hospitality.[59] But the idea was never

---

[55] John Howson, *A Sermon Preached at Paul's Cross: 24th December 1597* (London, 1597), 36–7.

[56] Quoted in Hill, *Economic Problems*, 160.

[57] E. R. Foster (ed.), *Proceedings in the Parliament of 1610,* 2 vols. (New Haven, Conn, 1966), i. 111–13.

[58] Ibid., i. 220.

[59] Robert Johnson, *Lux et Lex, or the Light and Laws of Jacobs House* (London, 1647), 35–6.

central to the perceptions of a godly ministry, and was perhaps too tainted by its associations with Bancroft's other causes, to exercise much influence in the mid-seventeenth century.

In the case of the bishops, interest in the ideal of hospitality seems to have survived rather longer. Whenever controversy about the role of the bishops surfaced in the public domain it was likely to be linked to complaints that they gave no good entertainment. John Harington, sympathetic to the hierarchy and deeply suspicious of Puritan motives, wrote his biographical account of the Elizabethan prelates largely to defend the order against the charge of covetousness. However, in the process, he provided some clever and stinging denunciations of precisely this vice—the first Elizabethan Bishop of Llandaff was so called, in his opinion, because all his lands were 'Aff'—and praised disproportionately those prelates who were hospitable. Martin Heaton, the last Elizabethan Bishop of Ely and a weak and ineffective character, won golden opinions from Harington merely because he was a good host.[60] The Queen continued to judge her bishops by their style and by their reputation for generosity until her dying day, a fact that Whitgift exploited to some political effect in his lavish entertainments of the Queen. Lesser laymen might well judge harshly those prelates who failed to be convivial at traditional times: when Richard Neile was Bishop of Durham, for example, it was claimed that he 'seldom entertained the gentry, *no not even at the Quarter Sessions*', and that he kept no household at all in his absence.[61] The local authority of a bishop could easily be undermined by this failure to sustain affability, especially if he was at the same time endeavouring to enforce religious policies which did not command universal support.

Even in the early Stuart period this weapon remained a sensitive one in the hands of the laity. In George Abbot's quarrel with the Duke of Buckingham in 1628, all the old issues about generosity and the openness of the archiepiscopal establishment were raised. Abbot was charged with exclusion of Buckingham's friends

[60] John Harington, *Nugae Antiquae*, ed. T. Park, 2 vols. (London, 1804), ii. 221, 108.
[61] J. Surtees, *History and Antiquities of the County Palatine of Durham*, 4 vols. (London, 1816–40), ii. 41.

and, worse, with being intimate with his enemies. The Archbishop angrily invoked the Pauline injunctions on the giving of hospitality by bishops, claiming that 'by nature I have been given to keep a house according to my proportion, since I have had any means, and God hath blessed me in it'. He reminded the favourite that when King James had given him the primacy he had insisted that 'I should carry my house nobly . . . and live like an Archbishop', and so he had endeavoured to do.[62] Whatever his behaviour towards the Court, we do have positive evidence from his accounts and from the description of Heylyn that Abbot lived up to his word in his entertainment of the gentry of Kent. On visitation he spent freely on the household, almost doubling the costs of his periods of residence in London. When at Lambeth, it was his habit to invite in all the Kentish gentry at the end of the law term, even hunting them out in Westminster Hall, St Paul's, the Exchange, and other general meeting-places.[63] His successor, Laud, proved something of an embarrassment because he derived no pleasure from this type of entertainment, and was the first archbishop since the Reformation to be widely criticized for his lack of generosity. What Laud lacked was apparently that general affability and openness, that almost public acceptance of access, that was expected of the archbishops. The occasional lavish entertainment of the Court was not a sufficient political substitute.[64]

III

The issue of hospitality therefore plays a significant, if diminishing, part in the ecclesiastical politics of the later sixteenth and early seventeenth centuries. Its importance derives from its scriptural foundation, and from the knowledge that the clergy were in theory only custodians for the distribution of their wealth within the community. When this knowledge was combined with an ideological challenge to the episcopate in its existing form, it could obviously form the basis of a forceful critique of the church

[62] T. B. Howell (ed.), *Howell's State Trials*, ii. cols. 1470–1.
[63] Peter Heylyn, *Cyprianus Anglicus, or the History of the Life and Death [of Laud]* (London, 1668), 244.
[64] See e.g., Laud's entertainment of the Court at St John's College, Oxford.

hierarchy. We have already seen that various archbishops of Canterbury endeavoured to refute this critique, not only by their verbal pronouncements, but by the formality and generosity of their own housekeeping. It is obviously necessary, however, to ask in more general terms whether the bishops and the rest of the clergy deserved the strictures that were produced by their enemies, and indeed what they believed their duties as good hosts to be. In the case of the higher clergy, and especially the prelates, it is possible to answer the questions from two distinct sources: the evidence of daily behaviour recorded in correspondence and accounts, and the growing number of biographies, especially those of Jacobean and Caroline divines. The first sources have the advantage of immediacy, but are difficult to render cohesive; the second obviously suffer from the disadvantage of self-conscious construction and model-building, but are ultimately more useful in their detailed insight.

Elizabethan and Jacobean prelates collectively struggled in adverse financial circumstances to maintain adequate households and families. Many, especially under Elizabeth, became indebted and fell into arrears with their taxes, so much so in some cases that they had to live in quiet retirement and dissolve their large households. Bishop Parkhurst of Norwich was defrauded by his deputy tax-collector, one George Thimbelthorpe, and, in order to repay his debts, had to live with a small group of servants on the rural manor of Ludham for the rest of his days.[65] He still apparently managed to be generous to the poor of nearby Acle, but can scarcely have sustained the usual range of public sociability that would have made him an important presence in Norfolk society. One of his successors, John Jegon, who suffered a major fire at Ludham, apparently abandoned the unequal struggle to live as a bishop, for according to a contemporary satire:

> Our short, fat Lord Bishop of Norfolk, 'twas he
> That caused that great fire at Ludham to be
> He could not abide the poor at his gate
> Nor yet to see them early or late.[66]

[65] R. Houlbrooke (ed.), *The Letter-Book of John Parkhurst* (Norfolk Rec. Soc., 43, 1974–5), 111.
[66] F. Blomefield, *Topographical History of Norfolk*, 11 vols. (London, 1805–10), iii. 563.

Jegon's secretary, Antony Harison, admitted the retired and limited life-style of his master, though he naturally attributed it to financial prudence rather than parsimony.[67] Even those who were not encumbered by debts and other immediate difficulties found it a struggle to perform at anything like the standards set by scriptural precepts, or by the behaviour of the archbishops of Canterbury. Bishop Young of Rochester took great pride in the 1590s in having a table 'as good . . . as any in England, excepting that which is prodigal', but he was aware that he did so at the cost of other obligations, because of the poor endowment of the see.[68] Others were less than generous hosts in part because they were at odds with many of the leading men of the locality: Sandys at Worcester, Scory at Hereford, and Cox at Ely seem to have come into this category.[69] The issue of wives and children was always a live one here: it does seem possible, for the Elizabethan period at least, to make some tentative correlation between the existence of large families and reputations for parsimony. Certainly, if one can judge the concern for giving casual households alms by a comparison with the giving of more structured charity, the major bequests of the Elizabethan period came from those prelates who were bachelors, or who had only one or two children, rather than those like Aylmer, Sandys, and Fletcher who were blessed with a quiverful.[70]

There were, however, always those who managed to transcend the secular pressures and perform the roles of good host and good pastor effectively. Some of the first Elizabethan generation were still profoundly influenced by the ideals of the godly bishop developed under Edward by Becon and others. Parkhurst, despite his poverty, maintained a rural household that was the centre of a 'little rural commonwealth', and John Jewel at Salisbury combined very generous entertainment with the sobriety of establishment and austerity of personal life that made him a model prelate to his foreign reformed visitors.[71] Later this particular paradigm proved more difficult to sustain, as the bishops

---

[67] Anthony Harison, *Registrum Vagum*, ed. T. F. Barton, 2 vols. (Norfolk Rec. Soc., 32, 33, 1963–4), ii. 238.

[68] BL, Lans. MS. 79/42.

[69] See Heal, *Prelates and Princes*, 237 ff.   [70] Ibid. 247–8.

[71] H. Robinson (ed.), *The Zurich Letters*, 2 vols. (Parker Soc., Cambridge, 1842–5), ii. 86.

reasserted their worldly authority, but instead prelates who were serious about their hospitable duties used traditional models of behaviour well-understood by the lay community. We have already noted that several of the travel diaries of the 1630s singled out for praise either the Bishop or the Dean of Durham, both of whom seem to have taken seriously the injunction to receive strangers.[72]

Some prelates seem to have been particularly anxious to show generosity through Christmas entertainment that rivalled that of the laity. In the 1630s John Warine, Bishop of Rochester, was famed for his generous feeding of the poor, especially at the Christmas season.[73] George Paule, Whitgift's biographer, made much of his habit of holding completely open house at Christmas, having his hall set several times over in order to manage the influx of guests.[74] A fortunate survival among the Lansdowne manuscripts allows us to see exactly what such a Christmas was like. Tobie Matthew, Archbishop of York, kept the feast in 1624 at his manor of Bishopthorpe, close to the cathedral city. On St Stephen's Day he had 103 unspecified persons at dinner: the following day there were ninety-three from Middlethorpe and elsewhere. The Feast of the Innocents saw the appearance of all the local ecclesiastical court officials with their wives, followed next day by some of the gentry and local professionals such as the apothecaries. On Thursday, 29 December, the county gentry appeared in some numbers, led by Sir Henry Slingsby and the rest of the Archbishop's council. There was then a brief pause, but on 2 January Matthew was hard at work again, receiving some of the lesser gentry of the area, and he completed his festivities the following day by giving dinner to all members of the Minster. The next year much the same pattern was repeated, though his tenant guests seem to have been spread over several days, rather than concentrated on 26 December.[75] The extremely self-conscious structuring of the festivities is, of course, reminiscent of the behaviour of the Petres decades

---

[72] See above, ch. 5.

[73] Thomas Fuller, *The History of the Worthies of England*, ed. P. A. Nuttall, 3 vols. (London, 1840) ii. 421.

[74] George Paule, *The Life of the Most Revered Prelate John Whitgift* (London, 1612), 77.

[75] BL, Lans. MS. 973/80.

earlier, or of Sir John Reresby after the Restoration, but Matthew's activities are distinctive in that he gave attention in rotation not only to tenants and gentry neighbours, but to all those who had a formal connection with the diocese and its administration.

This emphasis on the needs of the clergy points to a future of episcopal hospitality that has roots in the pre-Reformation period, but also a marked continuity into the late seventeenth century. The Bishop of Coventry and Lichfield had constantly entertained his cathedral establishment and other local clerics in the fifteenth century. Over two centuries later, the biographer of Seth Ward, Restoration Bishop of Salisbury, felt that it was particularly important to emphasize the openness of the episcopal table to clergy of all degrees, 'He used to say', claimed Pope, 'that he expected all his brethren of the Clergy, who upon any business came to Salisbury, should make use of his Table.'[76] In the intervening period there are many examples of episcopal generosity to their diocesan clergy, both in formal contexts like visitation and informally in routine sociability. The perception underlying this behaviour was well expressed by Stephen Gardiner when he welcomed two royal chaplains appointed to Winchester canonries in 1548. He held a dinner in their honour at the palace of Wolvesey, telling them, 'ye are now of my church, and you must take this house as your own, as others of the church do'.[77] In this case the ideological confrontation between Gardiner and the new prebendaries added a piquancy to the traditional gesture: here, as elsewhere, hospitality could be used as a political weapon in the sixteenth century.

While something can be gleaned of the successes and failures of episcopal hospitality from these sources, for more detailed insight it is necessary to turn to the tradition of biography which was developing rapidly in the later sixteenth century. Some of the conventions of the clerical biography have already been mentioned: it is likely that a scriptural text or texts will supply the biographer with his frame of reference, the most obvious choices being the seven works of mercy, or St Paul's account of the duties of a bishop. Certain tropes, such as the mortification of

---

[76] W. Pope, *The Life of the Right Reverend Seth, Lord Bishop of Salisbury* (London, 1697), 70.
[77] Foxe, *Acts and Monuments*, vi. 253.

the flesh and worldly asceticism, are almost mandatory, as are images of learning, piety, and general charity. Within these constraints religious preference dictated some differences: writings by, or about, Calvinist divines of Puritan sentiment are, for example, more likely to emphasize the ideas of calling, conversion experience, and an austere image of the pastorate than their 'Anglican' equivalent. But the saving merit of the biographies as evidence is that they are frequently the work of friends or students of the cleric, and as such usually manage to transcend the highly conventionalized paradigms from which they begin.

   When we look at the biographies for evidence of hospitality and charitable giving, it is initially surprising to find that there is no particular unanimity of view on its importance. Although all the early studies of the archbishops of Canterbury emphasize household giving and conviviality, by the time Heylyn's writings on Laud are reached the issue is dismissed in a few lines.[78] Abbot, of whom Heylyn deeply disapproved, was indeed praised for his generosity, but it was with no hesitation that Laud was said to have failed to entertain the gentry of Kent. Heylyn explained that the Archbishop was thought to be retired and inhospitable 'out of a dislike of that Popularity, which was too much affected by his Predecessor'. Although he makes no direct judgement on the matter, his text clearly implies that Laud made a wiser choice in spending his income on permanent endowments, rather than in the pursuit of evanescent popularity. Bishop Hall, writing his own autobiography, showed the marks of a true Calvinist conscience by passing over the external circumstances of his life as a bishop with great rapidity, deliberately presenting his study as an investigation of the providences which had shaped his experience.[79] Some biographers of the post-Restoration period, such as Walton on Sanderson, seem almost to have forgotten that it was a duty of the good bishop to be hospitable, according it at most a passing mention.[80]

   There is, however, a core of seventeenth-century texts that do concern themselves with the exercise of material charity and

---

[78] Heylyn, *Cyprianus Anglicus*, 539–40.
[79] Joseph Hall, *Works*, 12 vols. (Oxford, 1837), i. xxxix–xlvi.
[80] C. Wordsworth (ed.), *Ecclesiastical Biographies*, 6 vols. (London, 1810), iv. 473.

hospitality. Most post-date the Civil War, and were written in the knowledge that the bishops were blamed in that crisis for their failures of charity, as well as for their general authoritarianism. The defence of episcopal generosity was therefore a political as well as a spiritual duty. For Isaacson, Lancelot Andrewes's charity and hospitality existed as very distinct categories: he gave money-relief to the poor, and freed a number of prisoners; he entertained 'people of quality and worthy of respect, especially scholars and strangers'. Despite the usual worldly asceticism of his own behaviour, his table was lavish, so that his guests believed 'that his Lordship kept Christmas all the year'.[81] John Williams's life at his rural manor of Buckden was portrayed in much the same terms by Hacket: noble and gentle guests travelling from north to south were guaranteed a warm welcome and were fed at a sumptuous table, and others as humble as the yeomanry of the neighbouring towns were also invited. Only in one respect were these two great houses differentiated from their lay counterparts: conversation was sober, and a meal was accompanied by reading in the monastic style. According to Hacket, at Buckden 'a Chorister read a chapter in the English translation at Dinner, and one of his Gentlemen another in the *Latin* translation at Supper'.[82]

Baddiley's study of Morton follows in many essentials the two already discussed, emphasizing the charitable disposition of the Bishop, his interest in learning, and his indifference to the detail of household management.[83] There is, however a much clearer undertow of anxiety about the worldly prosperity of the Bishop, rather than the ready acceptance that characterizes Isaacson and Hacket. Baddiley seems most assured in his discussion of the modest circumstances in which the Bishop found himself during the Civil War, when he continued to engage in acts of charity regardless of his own comfort. Morton's generosity in his see is passed over with a brief comment on his bounty. The main emphasis of the narrative is upon the notion of stewardship: Morton, like a famous bishop of Orleans, 'never esteemed any thing properly his own, but what he either gave in private to poor

---

[81] Henry Isaacson, *The Life of the Reverend Father in God Lancelot Andrewes*, ed. S. Isaacson (London, 1829), 47.
[82] John Hacket, *Scrinia Reserata: A Memoriall Offered to the Great Deservings of John Williams D.D.* (London, 1693), 29, 32.
[83] John Baddiley, *The Life of Thomas Morton* (London, 1668), 123–4.

indigent persons; or els in Publique to pious uses'.[84] Here the Reformed conception of the bishop not merely as a man mortified in the flesh, but as the humble steward to his flock is more clearly visible than in any of the biographies so far discussed: again and again in Baddiley's account there are echoes of the language of Becon and his contemporaries. One consequence is a shift of emphasis in the discussion of hospitality and charity: it is made clear that Morton did his duty to those who passed his door on important business, but that his primary interest was in the poor and the needy. The same was claimed to be true of Miles Smith, the Jacobean Bishop of Gloucester, whose published sermons of 1632 were prefaced with a brief account of his life. Smith 'shewed himselfe most ready to minister to the necessity of the indigent and needy, having a tender touch even naturally that way'. He provided daily relief at his door in the old style, 'and was ever forward in succouring and releeving poore strangers and travellers that came unto him'.[85] Like Morton, Smith was one of the most committed Calvinist bishops of the early seventeenth-century Church, and therefore perhaps more disposed to present a modest view of the episcopal office than Andrewes or Williams.

The two biographies of William Bedell, Bishop of the Irish see of Kilmore, merit separate treatment, since they relate to a man who was not only a Calvinist in belief, but was very close to non-conformity in some of his behaviour. His chaplain, Alexander Clogie, who wrote one of the texts, entitled his piece *Speculum Episcoporum, or The Apostolick Bishop*, and directed it to a demonstration that it was possible to hold high office within the Church, while behaving as a true successor to the apostles.[86] One might expect that this Calvinist saint would take an austere and limited view of hospitality, but in fact both his biographers were at pains to argue that works of material charity were of great importance to him. Bedell's son, who wrote the other life, discussed his father's behaviour as a parochial incumbent in Suffolk. In his living Bedell took a solemn view of the need to entertain despite his own very sober disposition: he insisted on

[84] Baddiley, *Life of Morton*, 127.

[85] Miles Smith, *Sermons* (London, 1632), preface.

[86] E. S. Shuckburgh (ed.), *Two Biographies of William Bedell, Bishop of Kilmore* (Cambridge, 1902), 1 ff.

feeding all worthy parishioners once a year, while relieving the poor, presumably with money and food alms. On the other hand, he took a firm view upon the limits of his obligations: visiting strangers who came begging were likely to be treated critically: 'These he would not fail to examine, mixing both wholsom instructions and severe reproofs. Nor rested he there; but if they had any passes to travel by, he would be sure to scan them thoroughly, and finding them false or counterfeit, his way was to send for the constable.'[87] The severity of the Puritan saint, tempered by kindness to the souls directly in his care, was obviously Bedell's paradigm. His difficulty must have been to translate this model to the episcopal office, for the Bishop had responsibility for such a broad flock. This was compounded by the fact that at Kilmore most of Bedell's flock was Irish, heretic, and in English eyes scarcely human. It is therefore a mark of the seriousness with which the Bishop took his duties as described by St Paul that in Ireland he accepted the need to hold some species of open house. At the Christmas season he even 'had the poor Irish to feast and sit about him, both men and women that dwelt next unto him, that scarce had any whole cloathes on their backs, or could understand a word of English.'[88] A variant edition of Clogie's text indicates that the Bishop used at least half an Irish beef a week, much of it being distributed to poor Irish families. This depiction of the model Puritan bishop is intriguing because it is in practice so heavily dependent on earlier conventional notions of godly behaviour being fully assimilated into the reformed polity. What Thomas Lever and Thomas Becon had preached, William Bedell sought to execute in one of the most hostile environments an English cleric could encounter.

It is, however, difficult to argue that the style of Morton and Bedell prevailed in the post-Restoration Church. The model of hospitality that proved most enduring was that of Andrewes: prudently charitable and sensitive to the nuances of social rank. Seth Ward of Salisbury not only entertained his clergy, affecting not to concern himself with their status, but received 'Persons of Quality [who] pas'd betwixt London and Exeter', and was

---

[87] Ibid. 19. [88] Ibid. 160.

always extraordinarily deferential to those 'of greater quality than himself' who often passed *en route* to Ireland. The latter were not accommodated by the bishop, but he always made a point of visiting their lodgings and asking them to dine with him. Ward adhered to the old image of a good bishop by feeding the poor daily at his gate, but they were kept at a prudent distance from the Bishop: the only humble men with whom he apparently had contact were the curates of his own diocese.[89]

IV

There was general agreement among the post-Reformation commentators that the bishops had an extraordinary responsibility for good entertainment and the care of the poor. This had always been recognized by the Christian community, and was reinforced by the bibliocentric literalism of the reformed faith. Public provision for the needy might alleviate their burden, but did not fully meet the complex notion of good entertainment still accepted by contemporaries. The case of the parish and other clergy was a little different: they were, of course, the inheritors of a generalized responsibility for the care of the poor in their communities, and of a concern for good parochial relationships that made them obvious foci for conviviality, but as we have seen, they do not appear to have been the subject of any great expectations on the eve of the Reformation. In some ways the developments of the sixteenth century diminished their charitable role still further: public provision for the poor displaced the burden from cleric to parish, and the religion of the Word placed preaching, not social practice, at the centre of good ministerial behaviour. Yet, as we have seen, some prelates of impeccably reformed credentials continued to attach importance to the duty of hospitality in the parishes, and to ask about it at visitation. Some homiletic authors also made it their business to advise on the best modes of giving and entertainment, and when ordinary clerical biographies begin to appear in parallel with those of the

[89] Pope, *Life of Seth Ward*, 70–2.

bishops, they also often emphasized the importance of generous behaviour.[90]

The difficulty in studying any more than the handful of clerics who attracted full biographies, is that the practice of hospitality remains extraordinarily elusive. It rarely assumes a major place in the disciplinary records of the post-Reformation Church, even when the bishops themselves chose to make it a focus of attention at visitation. When questions were asked of the churchwardens, they often seem to have ignored them in favour of more tangible grievances about non-residence or the absence of sermons. However, something can be established from two particularly thorough sets of enquiry: those for Cardinal Pole's visitation of Canterbury in 1555, and those for Parkhurst's visit to Norwich in 1569.[91] The former yields sixteen complaints that hospitality was not kept; the latter thirty. As in the earlier evidence for Lincoln, failure to give entertainment was often associated with non-residence: seven examples in Canterbury and no less than twenty-three in Norwich can be linked to absenteeism. Other examples involve ruined parsonages, which compelled the incumbent to live elsewhere, general poverty which prevented adequate housekeeping, and broad dereliction of duty. In Norwich in particular the wardens sometimes seem to have added a complaint about hospitality almost as an afterthought to a series of grumbles. The Rector of Cawston, for example, read divine worship service inadequately, failed to preach or pray for the Queen, was a fornicator, a frequenter of suspicious houses, and a player of dishonest games.[92] In the circumstances he would have been an unlikely figure to act as a social focus for the community or to give generously to the poor. In this case, as in others, the episcopal authorities found it easier to take action on the Rector's other sins than on his failure to entertain. Indeed, one of the problems for Parkhurst, if he was serious about hospitality, was that his officials seemed to have no well-ordered

---

[90] Leonard Wright, *A Summon for Sleepers . . . Hereunto is Annexed a Pattern for Pastors* (London, 1589); Richard Curteys, *The Care of a Christian Conscience* (London, 1600); P. Gerard, *A Preparation . . . to the Most Holie Ministerie*, trans. N. Becket (London, 1598), 98–106. The last, a French Huguenot author, is particularly explicit on the duty of all clerics to entertain the poor in their households. I am grateful to Ian Green for this reference.

[91] LPL, VG4/2; NRO, VIS/1. [92] NRO, VIS/1, fo. 13.

response to a parochial complaint under this heading, unless it could be resolved coincidentally by ordering the incumbent back into residence.

One growing element in the post-Reformation complaints is that the leasing of parsonages, rather than just their decay, was often adduced as the reason for the failure of hospitality. Although in theory this issue was covered by Pecham's decree ordering farmers to give entertainment in the absence of the rector, it seems to have been recognized that the long rectorial leases of the sixteenth century made this desideratum difficult to enforce.[93] The wardens at Pole's visitation complained of the impediment of leases in seven cases: those of Stourmouth were so irritated by the complications involved that they gave the entire history of the lease, which had passed through four hands in a very short space of time.[94] Although in theory limited by law to three years' duration, rectorial leases tended after the Reformation to acquire a life and momentum of their own, often effectively preventing an incumbent from residing for years on end. That web of interest associated with non-residence and plurality, which the bishops were never able and willing fully to engage, must have proved one of the major discouragements to giving a reasonable level of hospitality in many parishes. The other disincentive was obviously poverty: the bishops' argument in 1584 that plurality was necessary to ensure that those who did have benefices could keep adequate house in their place of residence, has at least an element of truth about it. Complaints at both Canterbury and Norwich show a few examples of benefices so poor that it is difficult to imagine the incumbent could have had any hope of giving food, shelter, or other entertainment to outsiders. The problem is that much plurality was directed not at the supplementation of the inadequate income of the parochial clergy but at the augmentation of the revenues of the ecclesiastical élite.[95]

One other issue associated with hospitality that is fitfully illuminated by some of the visitation returns is the illegal sale of ale in vicarages and parsonages. Under 21 Henry VIII, c. 13, it was ordered that no incumbent should engage in any trade for profit, and the bishops took seriously the notion that this was

---

[93] Hill, *Economic Problems*, 114–17.   [94] LPL, VG4/2, fo. 81.
[95] Ibid. fos. 34ᵛ; 55, 69ᵛ; NRO, VIS/1, fos. 14ᵛ, 19.

particularly pertinent in the case of alcohol. Again and again enquiries were made about priests who either sold their own ale, or permitted others to do so in their houses, and sometimes returns reveal a number of cases where a farmer or even an incumbent had indeed been brewing for public consumption.[96] Some of these examples were no doubt simple abuses of the rectory and of the spiritual authority of the parson, who was able to establish himself at the centre of local conviviality while making a modest profit on the side. But it seems likely that the margins between pure exploitation and entertainment were narrow, and that some of the cases were consequential on an over-liberal interpretation of the duty of giving hospitality. Archbishop Grindal's investigations at York in 1575 suggest this latter situation: comments on the keeping of alehouses tend to focus on the scattered upland parishes of Yorkshire, especially those of the Deanery of Craven, where parishioners often had to travel some miles to reach the parish church.[97] In these circumstances the provision of ale by the parson must have been a kindly relief for a thirsty congregation, though if payment were involved the transaction was evidently more dubious. It certainly seems that some wardens themselves recognized the social value of the parsonical alehouse: for example, those of Kettlewell admitted to Grindal's visitors that an inn was kept in the vicarage, but insisted that it was only for 'honest resort'.[98] In the following century the importance of this use of the cleric's house as the hospitable focus of a scattered congregation can be elegantly demonstrated in the lives and diaries of such non-conformist divines as John Angier and Oliver Heywood. They inevitably ministered to a diffuse body of believers, who were expected to attend two services on a Sunday: in consequence their homes became the centre of congregational feeding; the better sort participating in the ministerial roast, the poorer having bread, broth, and ale or beer.[99]

[96] Kennedy, *Elizabethan Episcopal Administration*, ii. 54, 73, 92, 111; iii. 155, 183, 192.
[97] W. J. Sheils (ed.), *Archbishop Grindal's Visitation of the Diocese of York 1575* (York, 1977), 13–20.
[98] Ibid. 19.
[99] Oliver Heywood, *Autobiography and Diaries,* ed. J. H. Turner, 4 vols. (Brighouse and Bingley, 1881–5), iii. 276–7.

As for the overwhelming majority of parochial clergy against whom no complaints were made by the laity, it is well-nigh impossible to judge if they were dispensing hospitality and, if so, what form it assumed. William Harrison's observation on the pre-Reformation clergy has already been mentioned: he was convinced that the arrival of wives and families ensured that '[the clergy's] meat and drink is more orderly and frugally dressed, their furniture of household more convenient and better looked unto; and the poor oftener fed generally than heretofore they have been'.[100] It certainly seems to be true that there was some expectation that a minister's house could provide shelter and sustenance to travellers since, if other established premises failed, the constables often brought the needy to the door of the parsonage. This is presumably how William Bedell came to be interrogating poor travellers about their papers, a process which his biographer justified on the grounds that it protected his own parishioners from being troubled by the importunate.[101] There is also a scattering of evidence to indicate that even in relatively poor parishes something would be expected of the cleric at Christmas, and possibly also at the time of the Rogationtide processions. Non-residents were occasionally sufficiently conscious of the importance of conviviality at Christmas to appear just for that season: in 1531, for example, Latimer told Sir Edward Baynton that he intended to make merry with his West Kington parishioners, 'lest perchance I never return to them'.[102] The 1571 Injunctions on partial residence may well have encouraged this pattern of seasonal hospitality.

Local traditions might dictate other moments at which the incumbent had to make provision for at least some of his parishioners. In 1562 the Rector of Sandy, Bedfordshire, found himself engaged in complex litigation about the lease of his parsonage, and charged among other things by his parishioners with failing to provide a breakfast for all his choirmen on Easter Monday morning and at Christmas. It seems that the breakfasts were a custom rather than a contractual obligation, and had been discontinued because the incumbent was at odds with his choir,

---

[100] Harrison, *The Description of England*, ed. F. J. Furnivall, 2 vols. (New Shakspere Soc., ser. 6: 1, 5, London, 1908), i. 33.
[101] *Two Biographies*, 19.   [102] *LP*, V, 607.

but the issue caused great offence in the parish.[103] Brief glimpses such as these into the working of parochial routine can perhaps lead us to hazard two guesses about clerical hospitality in the sixteenth century. First, it was governed by conventions that led local men to know there were a few specified occasions on which they might dine at the cleric's expense. Secondly, that, except in the case of the provision of bedding and food for the truly benighted traveller, an incumbent saw his hospitable duty as directed to his own flock, just as he had done before the Reformation.

This, however, is the casual and traditional form of care of the community that even the least reflective Protestant cleric might assimilate as part of his parochial duty. At worst it was the type of care satirized by Ben Jonson in *The Magnetick Lady*, where Parson Palate, the prelate of the parish, is described as foremost in all the entertainments of the parish,

> top still, at the public mess;
> Comforts the widow and the fatherless,
> In funeral sack . . .[104]

At best it was the behaviour that George Gifford satirized in his *Briefe Discourse of Certaine Pointes of Religion* (1581) in which a country-dweller, Atheos, defends his curate against the righteous indignation of Zelot, for he was 'content with his living: many of your spirituall men are never satissfied; for with that poore lyving he hath, he doth keepe a good house, and doeth feede the poore'.[105] No doubt this was a start, even though Zelot would have none of it unless the pure Word was preached. However, even in the field of material charity more was ideally expected of those who had means and any sense of calling.

Perhaps the best-known image of the ideal parson is that offered by George Herbert who, in *The Country Parson* (1633), gave

---

[103] PRO, C24/102, no. 3. A similar case is recorded for Great Yarmouth, where the Dean and Chapter of Norwich was responsible for a Christmas breakfast, given by the farmer for all parishioners: Henry Manship, *A Booke of the Foundation and Antiquity of Great Yarmouth*, ed. C. Palmer, 2 vols. (Great Yarmouth, 1854–6), i. app. 132.

[104] Ben Jonson, *The Magnetick Lady*, in *Works*, ed. C. H. Herford, P. and E. Simpson, 12 vols. (Oxford, 1925–52), vi. 516.

[105] George Gifford, *A Briefe Discourse of Certaine Points of Religion* . . . (London, 1581), fo. 5v.

detailed advice for the discharge of the duty of hospitality. His cleric owed 'a debt of Charity to the poor, and of courtesie to his other parishioners'.[106] The former, Herbert was interestingly inclined to argue, was best discharged with money gifts 'which they [the poor] can better employ to their own advantages and sutably to their needs'. The latter group, on the other hand, should be entertained, preferably on a Sunday, since this was 'both suitable to the joy of the day and without hindrance to public duty', and it was best to receive on a strictly rotational basis, 'because countrey people are very observant of such things, and will not be perswaded but being not invited they are hated'. Like Bishop Hooper, Herbert firmly believed that the winning of souls could be linked closely to the giving of dinner. He suggested that those who were invited most frequently should be those 'whom he sees take best courses, that so both they may be encouraged to persevere, and others be spurred to do well'. With the possible exception of Herbert's enthusiasm for Sunday sociability, about which at least some of the godly had doubts, there was nothing in his advice that was not suitable to an incumbent of any persuasion, even though his detailed preoccupation with social duty is indicative of an Anglican sensitivity to Second Table obligations.[107] This sensitivity, it is worth remarking, still did not extend far beyond the bounds of the parish. It is true that Herbert advised the warm welcome of any minister, however humble, 'as if he [the parson] were to entertain some great lord', but in the case of other outsiders he was a child of his generation in urging that they should only receive assistance in overwhelming need or with 'some testimony'.[108] Such testimonies should not be subject to too intense a scrutiny, in the conviction that they might be forged, but prudence and obedience to authority should in practice govern the parson's attitude towards outsiders.

It is now possible to see more clearly the nearly perfect match between what Herbert preached and what William Bedell supposedly practised: Sunday entertainment, care of the basic needs of the poor, and a cautious response to vagrant outsiders. The same parallels can be found between Herbert's concerns and

---

[106] Herbert, 'A Priest to the Temple', in *Works*, ed. F. E. Hutchinson (Oxford, 1941), 243.
[107] Ibid. 244 ff.   [108] Ibid. 245.

those of Godfrey Goodman, later Bishop of Gloucester, who noted in the front of one of his own books that, when he was parson of Stapleford Abbots in Essex and of West Ilsley in Berkshire, he had no beggars, alehouses, law suits, unemployment, or quarrelling, and that 'on the Sunday noe poore man dined at his owne howse, but was ever invited'.[109] Other clerical biographies show a similar, if not identical, pattern. In his great Durham parish of Houghton, Bernard Gilpin, the so-called 'apostle of the north', was said to have entertained his parishioners steadily each Sunday, during the period between Michaelmas and Easter, and his barn was constantly stocked with the necessities for receiving guests. In the case of the poor, Gilpin was inclined to give food alms, especially to send hot food at least once a week to the poor of one particular area of Houghton.[110] The two Willets, father and son, who were memorialized by Peter Smith in the 1630s, both sought to use the surplus revenues of their parishes on the provision of hospitality and alms. The father, who held the benefice of Barley in Hertfordshire, was also incumbent of Thurlarston in Leicestershire, where he maintained a curate and visited himself twice a year. When in Leicestershire he held completely open house, but in his main benefice he also appears to have practised a rotating species of entertainment, with money alms reserved to the poor. His son, who became Rector of Barley in his turn, was equally generous, giving alms and gleaning-rights to the poor, and entertainment to all his neighbours at the Christmas season, though his biographer emphasized his enthusiasm for strangers, especially learned men, when specifically discussing his hospitality.[111]

Henry Hammond was also seen by his biographer, John Fell, as a model of generosity: perhaps appropriately for one who was a leading Arminian divine. At Penshurst, where he held the cure in the 1630s, Hammond gave fixed alms to the poor, as well as continuing the old tradition of feeding them daily at the door. He received all 'the better parishioners' at his table on a Sunday as commended by Herbert, and was exceptionally generous at the

---

[109] G. I. Soden, *Godfrey Goodman, Bishop of Gloucester, 1583–1656* (London, 1953), 64.

[110] Thomas Fuller, *Abel Redevivus*, 2 vols. (London, 1867), ii. 61–2.

[111] Andrew Willet, *Synopsis Papismi*, ed. P. Smith (5th edn., London, 1634), appendix.

Christmas season. He knew, remarks Fell, 'how effectual the loaves were to the procuring of disciples'.[112] Finally, lest this should appear to be an analysis too heavily weighted towards leading conformists, there are some examples of godly parochial care in Samuel Clarke's *Lives of Eminent Divines* (1662). John Dod, for example, was not one of those who disapproved of too much company-keeping on the Sabbath: in his parish of Hanwell, Oxfordshire, he was 'given to hospitality', and took a particular delight in having his table filled on a Sunday and after the Wednesday lecture.[113] Admittedly Dod addressed himself to a slightly different group to the parish worthies: he fed those who came to hear him from near and far, and made a particular point of including the poor at his table. By implication there must also have been exclusions, since he delighted in entertaining 'godly people', but nevertheless, Clarke's image is of one who took pleasure in the openness of his household, and in the spiritual ministry that could be conducted at his table.

Most of these models of clerical propriety were by definition prosperous members of the élite ranks of the ministry. After the Reformation, as before, poverty no doubt prevented the majority of clerics from offering lavish hospitality, and families had to be supported as a first claim on even comfortable revenues. Occasionally, however, we can glimpse an 'ordinary' parish minister who took great pride in his generosity and chose to describe it in his parish registers. William Sheppard of Heydon in Essex is one of the most interesting cases: during the 1560s and 1570s he noted year by year the improvements he had made in his church, the money he had allocated to charitable purposes, and provision he had made for the needy.[114] He often gave money to the local poor, and in a dearth year sold his grain at the previous year's rate. Substantial sums were given to the needy members of the parish at their marriages, and in 1567 Sheppard gave all his glebe lands, rent-free, to 'my power neyghbors of this parysch'. His concern for his parish was overwhelming: charity rarely extended outwards, except in the hospitable gesture of

---

[112] Wordsworth, *Ecclesiastical Biographies*, iv. 337.

[113] Samuel Clarke, *Lives of Eminent Divines* (London, 1660), 199 ff.

[114] Sheppard's 'Epitome', parish records of Heydon, Essex: I am very grateful to Mark Byford for allowing me to use a transcript of this document which he has made.

re-roofing the market cross for his neighbours but also 'for the releff of the wayfayryng and power folks'. Since the list is concerned with monies expended on particular projects, it is not surprising to find little mention of entertainment, but two items do suggest that Sheppard believed he had an obligation in this area. In 1567 he built a new kitchen for the town-house, and repaired the old hall with new thatch and pargeting, and ten years later he bought six dozen vessels, plates, and dishes, for the 'yeld haull'. Such a stewardship must have been extraordinary, especially in the troubled first decades of Elizabeth's reign, but another example of similar preoccupations can be found in the parish register of Womburne in Staffordshire in the early seventeenth century.[115] They are important reminders that clerical beneficence was not the monopoly of an élite, or confined to the more comfortable and prosperous period that began for the Church after the Restoration.

Although it would be a mistake to assume that Puritan ministers were less likely to be generous than others, the clerical biographies do suggest that in the late sixteenth and early seventeenth centuries, 'Anglicans' were more frequently praised for material charity than 'Puritans'. Among Clarke's studies, for example, only two other godly ministers were said to show the same concern for giving as Dod. Moreover, the funeral sermons for Puritan divines, which begin to appear in large numbers from the 1620s onwards, are rather less likely to address themselves to charitable activities than were those of their lay counter-parts.[116] Given their preoccupation with Second Table duties, it is not surprising that Anglican memorialists were more inclined to dilate on the social virtues of their subjects than were Puritans, for whom the issue of spiritual charity usually remained preponderantly important. Much the same is true of the clerical diaries that have survived. The most famous of all, that of Ralph

---

[115] Stebbing Shaw, *The History and Antiquities of Staffordshire,* 2 vols. (London, 1801), ii. 216, for a record kept by Ithiel Smart, incumbent of Womburne in the 1630s.

[116] Clarke, *Lives of Eminent Divines*; Mainwaring and Hildersham were the two others praised. It is tempting to think of William Whately, the great Banbury pastor, as more typical of the godly divines; he was said by Fuller to be 'judiciously charitable to such as showed the power of godliness in their lives', Fuller, *Abel Redevivus*, ii. 34.

Josselin, the Rector of Earl's Colne, Essex, in the mid-seventeenth
century, does allude to visiting and being visited, but not in a
spirit that would suggest that any importance beyond the merely
social was attached to these occasions. At one point in 1648 when
Josselin was feeling particularly impoverished—a usual state for
him—he lamented that an incumbent was still expected to
provide for his family and to be liberal to the poor, although in
his case he had a net income of only £50 with which to undertake
this.[117] He seems to have thought of hospitality largely as it was
directed to the poor: in November 1649, he and his wife resolved
to fast themselves for a meal or two each week, and to 'give away
a meales provision in meate broth, or money to the poore'.[118]
A slightly later entry suggests that this gesture may not have been
accepted by the recipients in the appropriate spirit, since poor
people 'were never more regardless of god then nowadayes'.
Since Josselin was uncomfortably at odds with many of his leading
parishioners in these years, it is not perhaps surprising that he
found the duty of providing general hospitality uncongenial, and
resorted instead to the social company of a small group of the
godly.

The crisis of separation from the established Church legitimized
this process for men such as John Angier and Oliver Heywood,
who refused to conform after the Restoration. They no longer
felt any duty to the community at large, except to the really
needy, and therefore directed most of their efforts to caring for
their own flocks. Yet the topos of the minister who fed the body
as well as the soul survived with them in these new circumstances,
as can be seen in Heywood's description of his father-in-law's
entertainment:

He was given to hospitality, a Bishop indeed, a Gaius, that freely
entertained Gods Servants, Ministers and Christians, so that he seemed
to be an host to the Church; it is incredible to relate what variety of
strangers and friends came Weekly, almost daily to his house, and were
handsomely treated, tho not with varieties, yet with sufficiency: he had
a standing Table of wholsom fresh meat, Noon and Night. Upon Lords-
days his Table was always well furnish'd with guests . . .[119]

---

[117] A. Macfarlane (ed.), *The Diary of Ralph Josselin* (London, 1976), 135.
[118] Ibid. 184–5.
[119] Heywood, *The Life of John Angier of Denton*, ed. E. Axon (Chetham Soc.,
N.S. 97, 1937), 84.

In the changed circumstances of the nonconformist congregations in the later seventeenth century, clerical hospitality could evidently retain some vitality as an integrative force.

At best this was no doubt still a possibility in the cohesive Anglican community governed by a hierarchy of squire and parson. But, just as the truly poor had already been separated from this arrangement by the time that Herbert wrote his vade-mecum, so by the end of the century the assumptions of polite society made it less necessary for a cleric to entertain the common run of the parish with any regularity. In the 1670s the Rector of Clayworth, Nottinghamshire, Richard Willis, still fed his parishioners at Christmas, and provided some kind of 'treat' when the Rogationtide procession took place. However, he undertook these duties without much enthusiasm, and at the end of his long incumbency, in 1701, complained that he was unduly burdened by the perambulation costs. They had arisen after the Restoration, and should have been shared between the substantial members of the parish, but gradually 'charity began to wax cold . . . but on ye Parsons shoulders it still rested, and was expected as a Right'.[120] Since the total cost of Willis's 'treat' this year was only 10*s*. 6*d*., it might be argued that it was in the parson himself that the spirit of charity had grown cold. In the 1690s White Kennett, when Vicar of Piddington, Oxfordshire, complained bitterly that the pleasure of receiving his tithe money and corn was disturbed by the need to provide entertainment for 'five or six men and Horses' who brought the levies.[121] Again, it was the enforced nature of the hospitality made binding by custom to which he objected; since it compelled vicars who had 'neither the gay humour, nor perhaps the good ability, of the first Authors of such a sociable practise'. This outburst is peculiarly interesting since it comes from a man who was deeply interested in folk custom, and who often wrote with some sympathy about the behaviour of his parishioners. It suggests an important conviction that such actions by ordinary villagers should no longer have any binding force on the élite. Had White Kennett been writing in the next century

---

[120] H. Gill and E. C. Guilford (eds.), *The Rector's Book: Clayworth Nottinghamshire* (Nottingham, 1910), 143.
[121] White Kennett, *Parochial Antiquities . . . in the Counties of Oxford and Bucks* (Oxford, 1695), 606–7.

it seems unlikely that he would have felt constrained by the quaint remains of enforced hospitality. By the time one reaches the famous clerical diaries of the eighteenth century, such as that of Parson Woodforde, Herbert's injunctions about the use of good hospitality as a means of curing souls seem entirely outdated. The good parson revelled in entertainment, and was on easy terms with most of his parish, but would have seen no purpose in providing them with general hospitality of any kind.[122] There were still voices raised in defence of the old apostolic ideal of general and open care, but they were not normally the voices of mainstream Anglicanism: the greatest exponents of open hospitality were William Law, the non-juror, and John Wesley.[123]

If there was any objective to be served in giving entertainment in this world, beyond mere desire to indulge in conviviality, it was perhaps to be found in disposing 'persons of quality' favourably towards the established Church, since many clerics could now aspire to entertain the great, at whose tables they had in the past been gratified to be humble guests. Changes in the social standing of the clergy, which had begun before Herbert wrote, but were accelerated by the re-establishment of the Church after 1660, enabled them to aspire to a greater social dignity than had previously been possible.[124] The advantages of this were interestingly declared publicly in the very last of the visitation articles and injunctions that addressed itself to the question of hospitality. Scarcely any of the post-Restoration enquiries mentioned the issue, and then in 1688 Archbishop Sancroft chose once again to give it prominence in his metropolitical enquiries. He gave the very traditional order about residence and the keeping of hospitality, and then followed by insisting that the clergy: 'maintain fair Correspondence (full of the kindest Respects of all sorts) with Gentry and Persons of Quality in the

---

[122] James Woodforde, *The Diary of a Country Parson 1758–1802*, ed. J. Beresford (Oxford, 1978).

[123] J. H. Overton, *William Law, Non-Juror and Mystic* (London, 1881), 226–8, 243–5. I am grateful to John Walsh for information on Wesley's attitude to hospitality.

[124] The language of sharp social differentiation was often used by biographers after the Restoration; e.g. Sanderson was described by Walton as behaving with 'condescension and obligingness' to the meanest of his clergy: Wordsworth, *Ecclesiastical Biographies*, iv. 473.

Neighbourhood, as deeply sensible what reasonable Assistance and Countenance this poor Church hath received from them in her Necessities'.[125] Admirable sentiments no doubt, cast in the elegant language of establishment enlightenment. They suggest, however, that the Church had moved far both from the canonists' insistence that hospitality was the serious answer to the problem of poverty, and from the moral earnestness with which the first generations of Protestant divines had endeavoured to persuade the clergy that they must model their social behaviour on that of the Apostles and the primitive Church. When, in a later age, faint echoes of this moral earnestness were heard, it was a matter of amazement for social commentators. In 1831 William Cobbett, no great friend of prelates, remarked on an extraordinary incident in which Bishop Sumner of Winchester was stopped by a begging band a mile from his palace at Farnham. Instead of prosecuting the offenders when he had the opportunity, Sumner 'set twenty-four labourers to constant work, opened his Castle to the distressed of all ages, and supplied all with food and other necessaries who stood in need of them'.[126] Cobbett commented, with a certain irony, 'this was becoming a Christian teacher'. It might be fairer to observe that Sumner's action was distinctive not because of a total failure of charity within the establishment, but because by then no one expected that it would come in the form of open and public hospitality to the needy. That was part of a world that the Victorian Church had lost.

[125] *Appendix to the Second Ritual Report*, 657.
[126] W. Cobbett, *Political Register:* January 15th 1831.

8

Urban Hospitality

I

THE experience of the early modern town appears superficially very different from that of the nobility, gentry, or clergy. While the nobility and gentry subscribed to a value-system in which ideas of individual honour predominated, and the clergy were supposedly motivated by charitable concerns, the towns were corporatist and economic units in which social duties were conceived rather narrowly and the profit motive legitimized. Practical constraints of space and circumstance also pointed out contrasts with the rest of the élite. City merchants, even the most prosperous among them, lacked the obvious resources for entertainment that were readily available in the countryside. Houses were rarely as large, or numbers of servants as great, as those of the nobility or greater monasteries. Open access was therefore less easy, and the inevitable difficulty and cost of lavish provisioning in the greater cities also imposed limitations on generosity. On the other hand, the role of the towns as foci of economic and social activity ensured the early growth of inns and alehouses, so that public provision of care for the outsider was already well developed in most English towns by the fifteenth century.

It was perhaps the combination of these circumstances that made the reluctant hospitality of townsmen proverbial in Elizabethan England. William Harrison cites a current jest against urban dwellers in general and Londoners in particular: 'The old country clerks have framed this saying . . . *Primus iucundus, tollerabilis estque secundus, Tertius est vanus, sed fetet quadrinuanus.*' Moreover, he added that in the countryside men could expect a fat capon or plenty of beef for welcome, while in the town a cup of beer or wine and 'an "You are heartily welcome" is thought to be great entertainment'.[1]

The image of the city encountered in earlier chapters tends to reinforce the idea that it was inimical to the old rural values of open entertainment. Both the conventional *rus/urbs* dichotomy, and the evolving role of London and other provincial capitals in the experience of the English élite, suggest that the town was commonly identified with the breakup of households and the failure of hospitality. As Dudley, Lord North, professed to a friend in 1639, he regretted his return to London because he would not 'buy ill ayre, strait lodging, ill drinke and little company so deare'.[2] Its anonymity protected many of those who found their rural role tedious or financially burdensome, and its social possibilities led men to question traditional conviviality. The aristocracy learned civility and exclusiveness, in part at least, from living among urban dwellers.

If, however, we look more closely at English towns in these three centuries, it becomes clear that the concerns of the urban élites were not necessarily in stark contrast with those of their rural counterparts. The same assumptions about order, hierarchy, and social control existed, though they were mediated through a different set of institutions and articulated with a slightly variant rhetoric.[3] Among the ideas relevant to hospitality considered at the beginning of this study at least three can be identified with the interests of the town. The first is a concern for honour and reputation, which proved such a motive force in gentle behaviour. This could be manifest individually by the mercantile class, whose feasting, Harrison claims, was just as elaborate as that of the gentry, even if it occurred less frequently.[4] Members of the oligarchy had to show an appropriate face to the outside world:

[1] William Harrison, *The Description of England*, ed. F. J. Furnivall, 2 vols. (New Shakspere Soc., ser. 6: 1, 5, London, 1908), i. 152. Caleb Dalechamp, *Christian Hospitalitie: Handled Commonplace-wise in the Chappel of Trinity College in Cambridge* (Cambridge, 1632), 110; and Edward Waterhouse, *The Gentleman's Monitor* (London, 1665), 297, use the same Latin tag.

[2] Dudley, 3rd Lord North, *A Forest of Varieties* (London, 1645), 68. It is interesting that North added that it was often necessary in town to be civil and charitable to every stranger.

[3] On the importance of the public expression of these ideals see C. Phythian-Adams, *Desolation of a City: Coventry and the Urban Crisis of the Late Middle Ages* (Cambridge, 1979); M. E. James, 'Ritual, Drama and the Social Body in the Late Medieval English Town', *PP*, 98 (1983), 3–29.

[4] Harrison, *Description of England*, i. 148.

one mayor of Lincoln was strongly criticized in the 1540s because he and his wife 'did not use such housekeeping nor wear such apparell as they ought'.[5]

But it was more clearly shown in collective behaviour, especially in ceremonial organization and display. Honour was sought in the rituals that marked the sacred and secular year, most vividly perhaps in the celebration of Corpus Christi, with its affirmation of the wholeness of the urban community.[6] The great guild marchings in London and Coventry, in which each craft was assigned a processional place commensurate with its local prestige, were an obvious opportunity to articulate both collective reputation and the honour due to particular sectors of the society. In the context of feasting, the formality of the Lord Mayor's inaugural dinner is similar. Sensitivity to the collective honour of the corporation is nicely revealed in a London incident from the reign of Edward IV. The Mayor and aldermen had been bidden, as was customary, to the great feast given by the new sergeants-at-law. However, the Earl of Worcester was given precedence over the Mayor at table, in breach of established custom. Like an affronted modern diplomat, the Mayor recognized that the prestige of his office, and hence of his city, had been questioned, and withdrew with the aldermen to a feast in his own house.[7] The quest for honour was also revealed in the elaborate welcome offered to eminent outsiders, and in the solemn interchange of gifts that was an essential part of their visit. These activities were as necessary an aspect of the behaviour of urban oligarchies as was a display of good lordship for the great nobleman. Since the status of the town was less secure than that of the landed magnate it may even be that reputation-enhancing gestures were even more mandatory in a civic context than in the countryside.[8]

---

[5] Quoted in J. H. Thomas, *Town Government in the Sixteenth Century* (London, 1933), 36.

[6] James, 'Ritual', 3–29; C. Phythian-Adams, 'Ceremony and the Citizen', in P. Slack and P. Clark (eds.), *Crisis and Order in English Towns, 1500–1700* (London, 1972), 58–60.

[7] On the liverymen and the civic calendar in London, see I. Archer, 'Governors and Governed in Late Sixteenth-Century London, c.1560–1603: Studies in the Achievement of Stability', Oxford D.Phil. thesis (1988), 60; B. R. Masters, 'The Lord Mayor's Household before 1600', in A. E. J. Hollaender and W. Kellaway (eds.), *Studies in London History* (London, 1969), 108.

[8] See below, pp. 312–14.

A second resemblance between town and country is to be found in the shared belief that neighbourliness was central to the community. Here hospitality could be employed as a means to reduce social conflict and enhance solidarity internally, but also to promote a vision of the generosity of the town externally. When the corporation of York was confronted by the severe economic crisis of 1557–8 it responded by reducing drastically the number of feasts that it held. However, some were retained because 'meeting of neighbours at the said feasts and dinners and there making merry together was a good occasion of continuing and renewing of amity and neighbourly love one with another'.[9] The godly corporation of Hull argued in much the same way in 1573. Despite its distaste for general feasting, it retained its midsummer drinking for the relief of the poor, since it provided circumstances for 'mutual society and good neighbourhood among the rest [to be] nourished and maintained.[10] Through commensality the sharp boundaries between social groups could temporarily be abolished, a process that was even more necessary in the enclosed environment of the fifteenth- or sixteenth-century town than elsewhere. When the internecine struggles separated men who had to live in such close daily proximity, and whose collective interests demanded the presentation of unity to outside economic and political pressures, the restoration of harmony in the corporate body was an urgent necessity. Thus, Maldon re-established its Sessions feasts in 1598 after a series of local disputes: 'for a means of the better enjoyinge and contynyinge of common Amytie and brotherlie kyndnes and amytie in and with the whole Companie, societie, bodye of this house, one membre with another.[11]

Although the need for neighbourly amity was primarily an internal concern for the town, it could also become a justification for generous entertainment of outsiders, especially of the local gentry. An occasion such as mayor-making at Coventry, or the guild feast at Ipswich, could be used to extend welcome to strangers 'of the town and country alike', and to offer them

[9] A. Raine (ed.), *York Civic Records*, 8 vols. (Yorks. Arch. Soc., Record Ser., 98–119, 1939–53), v. 177.

[10] E. Gillett and K. A. MacMahon, *A History of Hull* (Oxford, 1980), 121.

[11] W. J. Petchey, 'The Borough of Maldon, Essex, 1500–1688', Leicester Ph.D. dissertation (1972), 174.

temporary incorporation as guests.[12] This pattern was common throughout our period, but obviously assumed a greater importance from the later sixteenth century onwards, as the urban and rural élites acquired closer political and social links. The generous entertainment that the Elizabethan corporation of Plymouth gave to the gentry of Devon, or the regular junketings for Cambridgeshire gentry provided by the university city, are only two examples of a routine pattern.[13] Here honour and neighbourliness were joined in a powerful expression of the interests of the town, or rather of its leading members.

Finally, similarities between noble and urban views of hospitality can be found in the expression of openness and enclosure by the latter as well as the former. The old corporate borough was able to employ urban geography rather as the nobleman employed his dwelling: the gates provided the ceremonial focus for entry and departure, the guild-hall or similar administrative centre the great hall of entertainment, the inn the individual lodging. The analogy is not perfect, but the functions of these spaces were similar, and were used both to offer welcome to outsiders and to emphasize the integrity of the community. Even when neighbouring gentry were incorporated into the town as guests, they were welcomed with some ceremoniousness, drinking with the mayor and aldermen, or perhaps being sent formal gifts of cakes and wine at their inns.[14] When important strangers were received they might, if sufficiently exalted, be greeted at the gates, or be guided to their inns and then visited by mayor and corporation bearing appropriate gifts. In a gesture that suggests the need to assimilate the guest, the mayor would often drink with the stranger at his inn, thereby underlining the honorific position which he occupied in the town.[15] It is important to note that these gestures were as carefully contrived, and as sensitive to status,

[12] Phythian-Adams, *Desolation of a City*, 263; Nathaniel Bacon, *The Annals of Ipswich*, ed. W. H. Richardson (Ipswich, 1884), 143.

[13] R. N. Worth (ed.), *Plymouth Municipal Records* (Plymouth, 1893), 121–34; C. H. Cooper (ed.), *Annals of Cambridge*, 5 vols. (Cambridge, 1842–1908), ii. 244 ff.

[14] Leicester records give particularly full details of gifts sent to inns: *HMC, App. to 8th Report*, i. fo. 428–29ᵛ.

[15] Cambridge Corporation paid a solemn visit of this kind to the Prince of Tuscany, who stayed at 'The Rose' during his 1669 visit: J. E. Foster (ed.), *The Diary of Alderman Samuel Newton* (Proc. of the Camb. Antiq. Soc., 1890), 43.

as any of those prescribed by Russell or Coleman for the great household.

Yet, like the nobleman, the town retained its authority as host: although its economic interests dictated that it should normally be physically accessible to all and sundry, it could use hospitality as a means of excluding strangers as well as incorporating them. The great religious fraternities which, in the old corporate towns, were often made up of the urban élite at prayer, were in theory often accessible to strangers who could ask for membership. However, in practice they sometimes sought to limit access to a small élite, as when the Guild of St George, Norwich, agreed with the city government in 1452 that only gentlemen by birth or persons 'set in gret worschip' should be received.[16] A century later the same guild specifically denied hospitality or alms at its feast to 'strangers of the contrith', who provided 'great . . . trowble [to] the seide feastemakers'.[17] Guild entertainments often provided this type of opportunity to differentiate sharply between types of guest: thus the triennial feast of St Antony's Guild at York was open to the gentlemen of the liberty of Ainsty, as well as city freemen, but extended its entertainment no further.[18] In a very different context, the early attempts to expel vagrants from English towns such as London and Norwich, and the insistence that inns and alehouses give them no lodging, could be seen as an assertion of the right of the corporate body to be open or closed to whom it chose, to offer hospitality only to those it selected as guests.[19]

Thus, the concerns of town-dwellers can at times be identified with those of the élites who are the primary focus of this work. But, while these concerns inform some civic activity, we must also be careful not to assimilate them too neatly to the distinctive circumstances of urban life. In the town, public and private worlds coexisted and overlapped in a variety of complex ways: it is impossible to discuss a city as though it were a well-integrated body, with ordered functioning parts analogous to those of the great household. While corporations might at times like to

---

[16] M. Grace (ed.), *Records of the Gild of St. George in Norwich, 1389–1547* (Norfolk Rec. Soc., 9, 1937), 41.
[17] W. H. Hudson and J. C. Tingey (eds.), *Selected Records of the City of Norwich*, 2 vols. (Norwich, 1906–10), ii. 403.
[18] *York Civic Records*, ii. 28–9.   [19] See below, pp. 318–19

describe their towns in this way, employing the rhetoric of wholeness and integration, the reality is far less tidy. Even if the problem of economic and social competition is set aside, there is still that of the plurality of the units that formed the early modern town. Household, ward, parish, and guild all provided alternative focuses for the activity and loyalty of the urban resident, and the primary institutions with which he or she might identify. When the issue of economic conflict is added to this mixture, it can be seen that hospitality might need to be used more dynamically, as a means of persuading the community to function co-operatively, in town than in countryside.[20] This diversified structure also makes the description of *urban* hospitality almost impossible: the nature of the records guarantees that good evidence on *civic* and guild entertainment survives, but of the behaviour of smaller groups, or of individual householders, little can be said. That little has found some place in this account, but the best that is usually possible is a prudential reminder that the experience of townsmen is not fully embodied in the minutes of their corporation act books.

II

One of the consequences of the pluralistic yet introverted nature of the early modern town is that it is often difficult to calculate who is entertaining whom at a particular municipal junket. Many of the feasts and celebrations that punctuated the corporate and guild year were not given for guests by a host or group of hosts, but were shared meals, self-financed or at least partially so, by the assembled company. This arrangement, while it undoubtedly should be described as commensality, is not always easy to identify with those ideas of hospitality as giving which have been the main theme of this analysis. A lesser difficulty also occurs in the investigation of private hospitality offered by leading citizens: many of these entertainments seem to have been official in all but venue, the corporation feasting itself in a private domus rather

---

[20] For hospitality used in this way at Coventry, see Phythian-Adams, *Desolation of a City*, 141, 263–5.

than in the council chambers.[21] In neither case would it be sensible to isolate these arrangements from assuming their place in an analysis of urban hospitality. However, it may be wise to approach our theme first via the most obvious form of entertainment: the reception of outsiders and strangers.

When the corporation of an English town thought about what its successors would call its entertainments budget, its first concern was usually the provision of sufficient resources to appear generous to visiting monarchs, foreign princes, magnates, bishops, and country gentlemen. Good behaviour was essential for 'the honour of the city', to quote the York city-house book, though it was also posited on the more materialistic assumption that favour would often be reciprocated by gifts or patronage.[22] When the auditor whom Lord Chancellor Egerton had appointed to investigate the indebtedness of Warwick corporation questioned the generosity shown to outsiders, the town clerk responded in horror. 'What would you have the corporation like stockes and stones to be miserabell of respeckts to nobell personages and to the judges and justices that come for the publicke good thereof and of the whole contrey?'[23] Since princes were (almost) always with them, and favours needed to be solicited continually, it is not surprising that towns routinely used a part of their revenues on these forms of hospitality. The York chamberlains' accounts, available from the mid-fifteenth century onwards, record a steady flow of gifts of wine, flesh, fowl, marmalade, manchpanes, and the ever-present sugar loaves, into the hands of visiting dignitaries. These were usually visitors to the city on royal or other political business, though it was also the custom to give a lavish donation of wine, fruit, and bread to those members of the élite who came to the Corpus Christi plays.[24]

Most demanding and expensive of all was, of course, a royal visit: Edward IV cost York corporation £35 in 1478, though this was very small beer compared with the cost many towns

---

[21] See the example of Bristol Christmas drinkings: E. W. W. Veale (ed.), *The Great Red Book of Bristol*, 3 vols. (Bristol Rec. Soc. 16, 1951), iii. 96; *York Civic Records*, iii. 27.

[22] R. Davies, *Walks through the City of York* (London, 1880), 267.

[23] Wa. RO, Warwick Borough MSS., W21/6, 262.

[24] R. Davies (ed.), *Records of the City of York* (London, 1843), 15, 77.

experienced in entertaining Elizabeth and her successors.[25] Monarchs did not often reside in towns, but they had to be greeted with gifts, entertainments, and various forms of banquet. Lesser mortals, like queens consort and dowager, and princes were capable of staying at high charge to the town, as Bristol discovered when Anne of Denmark took up residence for several days in 1612.[26] Beneath the throne, the judges of assize were most likely to make mandatory demands upon the hospitality of the larger towns: major food gifts towards their subsistence were always expected, as well as some appropriate 'treat' from the town authorities. The arrangements at Reading in 1625 are typical: the judges were entertained at the house of Mr Thomas Turner, 'he being at noe damage', with the provision of four barrels of beer, seven gallons of sack, two of claret, and commensurate quantities of food.[27] When hospitality was inadequate the judges complained, as James Whitelocke did about the costliness of Chester in 1620. However, they could also find the generosity of communities impressive: at Denbigh, Whitelocke and his fellow were given food and a Latin oration in the market-place, at Ruthin a banquet with the town waits, an interlude, *and* a Latin oration.[28]

Assize visits by the judges brought in their wake further mandatory expenditures as the county community flooded into their local legal centres. Although the sheriff of the county normally bore the main cost of hospitality, corporations often seem to have given something towards the charges.[29] The

---

[25] Davies, *Records of the City of York*, 69.

[26] Robert Ricart, *The Maire of Bristowe is Kalendar*, ed. L. T. Smith (Camden Soc., N.S. 5, London, 1872), 64–5. For other royal visits, see J. Nichols, *The Progresses of Queen Elizabeth*, 3 vols. (London, 1823), i. 159, 192–7, 337–9; ii, 134–50.

[27] J. M. Guilding (ed.), *Records of the Borough of Reading*, 4 vols. (London, 1892–6), ii. 241–3. Similar examples can be found for Ipswich in Bacon, *Annals of Ipswich*, 518; Leicester in *HMC, App. to 8th Rep*, pt. i, fo. 428; and York in *Records of the City of York*, 69.

[28] J. Bruce (ed.), *Liber Famelicus of Sir James Whitelocke* (Camden Soc., O.S. 70, London, 1858), 85–8.

[29] GRO, GBR, B3/1, fo. 73. At St Albans in 1579 the cost was £2. 19s. 10d., *HMC, App. to 9th Rep*, 567; in 1609 Canterbury organized dinner at an inn for £3. 16s. 0d., ibid. 161; while in 1662 Axbridge tried to limit lavish spending at sessions dinners, which had been 'to the greate exhaustinge of the annuall revenew of this Corporacion', to 13s. 4d., *HMC, App. to 3rd Rep.*, 303.

pomposity of such entertainments may have increased somewhat as towns sought to demonstrate their assimilation to cosmopolitan culture after the sixteenth century, but their essential character was unchanged. Similar actions were undertaken in those towns that were merely the focus of quarter sessions: dinners had to be offered and noblemen and gentry had to be given gifts; at Saffron Walden in 1560, for example, presents were given to the Earl of Oxford, Lady Audley, and Mr Mildmay.[30] Nevertheless, the honour of becoming an assize or quarter session town was eagerly sought as having an economic value of its own.[31]

The honour that accrued from other compulsory hospitality was apparently rather asymmetrical, but the danger was that if it was not adequate the town was liable to suffer a withdrawal of favour, a risk that few towns were willing to run. Sometimes the government felt obliged to nudge cities into generosity, not to a reigning monarch, but to more peripheral figures like ambassadors or foreign dignitaries. In 1550 the future Duke of Guise visited York *en route* to Scotland, and the Lords of the Council in London felt that it was politic to tell the Earl of Shrewsbury and the corporation that they should receive him well, 'wherein you shall both do the King our master right good service, and also win yourself therein much honour'.[32] When the Duke of Württemburg was travelling through England in 1608 he was preceded by a royal letter requesting all corporations to do him honour and courtesy, and reminding them that he had been invited everywhere 'either to dinner or a banckett'.[33] So routine were the demands of this species of official entertainment in some of the greater towns, that major inns could acquire a fixed status as the location for the lodging of corporation guests. The Angel Inn, Leicester, housed Mary, Queen of Scots and Elizabeth, daughter of James I, as well as almost every great nobleman who visited the town between the mid-sixteenth century and the Civil War.[34] York had the King's Manor as an alternative, and in a rare case like Lincoln there was, by the late sixteenth century, an official mayoral residence for accommodation, but elsewhere the

---

[30] Saffron Walden Town Muniments, Accounts of the Holy Trinity Guild, 49. I am very grateful to Mark Byford for this reference.
[31] A. Fletcher, *Reform in the Provinces* (New Haven, Conn., 1986), 165.
[32] Davies, *Walks through York*, 263. [33] Ibid. 272.
[34] C. J. Billson, *Medieval Leicester* (Leicester, 1920), 26.

corporations organized major inns almost as though they were extensions of the local guild-hall.[35]

At the apex of this system of public hospitality offered by English towns sat the Lord Mayor of London, though that title was only routinely used from the 1530s. Harrison noted with chauvinistic pride that 'there is no public officer of any city of Europe, that may compare in port and countenance with him during the time of his office', and indeed most evidence points to the maintenance of a very elaborate household by the sixteenth-century mayors.[36] Ordinances for 1502 and again for the 1590s suggest a domestic structure comparable to that of the greatest nobility, and the costliness of hospitality is indicated by the fear officially expressed in 1555 that, 'almoste all goode Cytizens flye and refuse to serve' because of the 'chargeable dyete'.[37] Some of this cost was a matter of choice by individual incumbents, or by the Common Council, as, for example, was the elaboration of the Show and Dinner from the time of Sir John Shaw in 1500 onwards.[38] However, much of it must have originated from the need to serve the Crown, since English monarchs came to regard it as a routine duty of the Lord Mayor that he should give lavish hospitality to all visiting dignitaries. The *Venetian Relation* incorporates a long description of the Mayor's feast, at which 'he is obliged to give a sumptuous entertainment to all the principal people in London, as well as to foreigners of distinction'.[39] Not only did ambassadors and foreign visitors attend the mayoral feast, but they were sometimes given separate banquets: for example, the Mayor was required to entertain Cardinal Campeggio when he first came to England as papal legate in 1514, and one of his successors had the pleasure of feeding Anjou during Elizabeth's flirtation with the idea of a French marriage. Honour may have accrued to the city from all of this, but the more general impression is that various English

---

[35] Billson, *Medieval Leicester*, 27. C. Haskins, *The Ancient Trade Guilds and Companies of Salisbury* (Salisbury, 1912), 292–3, suggests that 'The George' played a similar role in fifteenth-century Salisbury.

[36] Harrison, *Description of England*, i. 150.

[37] Masters, 'The Lord Mayor's Household, 108–9; Guildhall RO, Journal of Common Council, 16, fo. 354ᵛ.

[38] C. L. Kingsford (ed.), *Chronicles of London* (Oxford, 1905), 234.

[39] C. A. Sneyd (ed.), *A Relation of the Island of England* (Camden Soc., o.s. 37, London, 1847), 44.

governments used the city authorities as a convenient source of good meals, recognizing that they could not afford to decline the pleasure of entertainment. These arrangements were formalized in the financial burdens the Crown laid on the city, requiring it to meet the costs of accommodating ambassadors and their trains.[40]

Not all the hospitality offered by civic authorities to distinguished outsiders was as constrained as royal and judicial receptions. Nobles and gentlemen who were 'friends' of a town might choose to visit, or might be bidden, but in either case there was more likely to be some mutuality in the exchange than is suggested above. The warmth with which York greeted its patron the Duke of Gloucester in 1483 was intended to express gratitude for his assistance to the city, a gratitude that was also exemplified by its abiding loyalty to him during the following years.[41] Ipswich thought it worth providing a special banquet in 1569 for the coming of the Lord Keeper, Nicholas Bacon, who exercised much influence in East Anglian politics, though later the same year it was even more generous to the Master of the Rolls and the local magnate Sir Thomas Cornwallis, who were acting on its behalf in a suit.[42] It is often difficult to disentangle from the surviving records the reasons for hospitality to these influential men: sometimes we seem to be seeing gestures to those who happened to be passing through the town, sometimes a dinner provided at musters, or the meeting of other commisssions. In the case of Plymouth, it appears that under Elizabeth the corporation believed that it was in its interests to provide a steady stream of treats for the neighbouring gentry such as the Drakes, Hawkinses, and Champernownes.[43]

Examples of generosity to friends and patrons could be multiplied endlessly from the surviving chamberlains' accounts. However, it may be more instructive to look at one late, fully documented example of this civic interchange, made more interesting by the political tensions underlying it. John Paston, Earl of Yarmouth, was the great Tory patron of Norfolk in the 1670s and, as his title indicates, particularly concerned with the

---

[40] *LP*, II, ii. 4333. [41] *Records of the City of York*, 124-5.
[42] *HMC, App to 9th Rep.*, 249.
[43] *Plymouth Municipal Records*, 121-34.

town of Great Yarmouth. He was also profoundly at odds with the corporation of that community, because of his attempts to establish a new harbour against its wishes. Yet the town could not afford to neglect its powerful neighbour, and indeed shared with him some important political and economic interests. When, therefore, Yarmouth visited Norfolk with grand ceremony in 1675, the town was determined to receive him with all due formality. His entertainment was princely: the entire populace apparently turned out to line the streets, bells were rung, speeches made, and guns discharged. At the entrance to the town the full corporation greeted Yarmouth 'with a glass of good wine in their hands', and after the procession he received all the townsmen at the bailiff's house before the grand dinner.[44] This elaborate and expensive piece of urban theatre had, at least temporarily, the desired effect of impressing and surprising Yarmouth and his followers and creating an atmosphere more conducive to political negotiation. The long-term effects were less promising, and indeed towns must often have doubted the utility of their polite pressures. In a moment of real disillusion in 1641, the corporation of Guildford complained that it had laid out large sums on entertainment and gifts to the gentry of the area, but had received no benefit in return.[45]

Even when the most desirable rewards of clientage were not always forthcoming, there was still exchange of a more formalized kind in the social contacts between the landed élite and their urban clients. Sugar-loaves, manchpane, and local commodities of high status were given by the towns, and in return an occasional haunch of venison would be sent in to the borough.[46] This exchange would be of little relevance were it not for the solemnity with which corporations normally greeted their present. The method of eating the venison was dilated on at

---

[44] *HMC, App. to 6th Rep.*, 373–4. A similar display was mounted by Worcester for the benefit of the Duke of Beaufort in 1684, culminating in 'a very great and noble collation'. P. Borsay, '"All the Town's a Stage": Urban Ritual and Ceremony, 1660–1800', in P. Clark (ed.), *The Transformation of English Provincial Towns* (London, 1984), 232.

[45] *HMC, App. to 6th Rep.*, 374; V. J. Hodges, 'The Electoral Influence of the Aristocracy: 1604–41', Columbia Univ. Ph.D. dissertation (1977), 290.

[46] For lists of gifts given by towns, see e.g., Davies, *Walks through York*, 258–61; D. M. Livock (ed.), *City Chamberlains' Accounts for Bristol* (Bristol Rec. Soc., 24, 1966), 44–5; *Annals of Cambridge*, i. 235–6; ii. 244.

some length in corporation minutes, with precise arrangements about who had the right to participate, how the extra commodities should be provided, and what, if anything, should be paid by those involved. The most elaborate example is that of the York venison feast of 1487. The Earl of Northumberland, who was to be murdured in a tax riot two years later, expressed his goodwill to the city with the gift of eight bucks and 5 marks in cash. This was so unusual an event that the city extracted another £6 from the resources of the St Christopher Guild and organized a dinner for the aldermen, common council, gentlemen of Ainsty, and 'sex hundreth of the moost honest Commoners of the said citie'.[47] More commonly only the council and office-holders were involved, and rules determined the benefit that accrued to them in a hierarchical manner. By the seventeenth century it seems to have been considered particularly appropriate for the high steward of a town to present venison, a pattern that was well established in, for example, Oxford, Hereford, and Gloucester.[48] Venison was, of course, a high-status food, but the elaboration of the arrangements surrounding the feasts suggests that their critical aspect was participation in the beneficence of a patron or friend of the town.

Such participation was more directly expressed when the exchanges involved entertainment by the relevant magnate or gentleman. Extensive urban records of hospitality, and the relative paucity of such details for the landed élite, often make it difficult to calculate how far the banquets and treats given by corporations were reciprocated. There were, of course, practical problems: when a magnate was physically distant from his favoured community, and had no property within the walls, it might be difficult to entertain the entire magistracy. However, where such constraints did not apply, there was sometimes a formal return for meals given. Cambridge had an institutionalized exchange with the owners of Barnwell Abbey, by which the Mayor and Council of Twenty-Four each year visited the house and consumed gammons, bacon, and stewed prunes, although the city

[47] York Civic Records, ii. 28–9.
[48] *VCH, Oxford*, iv. 135; R. Johnson, *The Ancient Customs of Hereford* (Hereford, 1868), 115; GRO, GBR, B3/1, fos. 57, 249.

provided the wine.[49] More usual was the occasion when, in 1569, the Mayor and aldermen went to 'Mr. Baron Frevile . . . to make merie', and provided in return a generous gift to the value of £1. 16s. 4d.[50]

Bishops and local magnates seem routinely to have entertained leading townsmen at Christmas: in Tobie Matthews's solemn arrangements, for example, they were bidden on 29 December in 1624.[51] The Mayor of Guildford was at the Mores' house at Loseley at Christmas 1620, and gave 6s. in gratuities.[52] They could also expect to be included in any public ceremony for the county community, such as the feasts given by Matthew Parker to celebrate the rebuilding of the palace of Canterbury, to which Canterbury corporation was invited.[53] Really ostentatious generosity of the kind offered by Great Yarmouth to its patron demanded reciprocation: Lord Yarmouth entertained members of the oligarchy in 1676 to a dinner, at which he 'set a bottle at every man's trencher', so that 'we parted with that they call starke love and kindness'.[54] Nevertheless, a reading of full records for towns such as Leicester, Canterbury, and even Cambridge would suggest that corporations expected to give, rather than to receive, the treats that lubricated relations between themselves and the élite. At Bristol in the 1630s the new Bishop, George Coke, was generously entertained by the townsmen, but was assured 'that they expect not the like answerableness of my inviting them, and that they did not expect it in my predecessor, neither did he do it to them'.[55]

It is tempting to argue that the extension of sociability between townsmen and the landed élite was the product of the changing aspirations of the former, their greater desire from the mid-sixteenth century onwards to identify themselves politically and socially with their gentry neighbours. We should not, however, immediately conclude that there was a dramatic change: the burghers of Bristol seem just as eager to fraternize with the Abbot of St Augustine's or the Duke of Buckingham at the beginning of

[49] *Annals of Cambridge*, iii. 529; *Diary of Alderman Newton*, 27, 47.
[50] *Annals of Cambridge*, ii. 244.   [51] BL, Lans. MS, 973/80.
[52] Hodges, 'Electoral Influence of the Aristocracy', 291.
[53] J. Strype, *The Life and Acts of Matthew Parker*, 3 vols. (London, 1821), iii. 287.
[54] *HMC, App. to 6th Rep.*, 377.   [55] *HMC, Cowper*, ii. 29.

the period as do those of Great Yarmouth with Paston at the end.[56] Moreover, as Paston's language in the above example suggests, the social gulf between town and aristocracy remained wide even in the late seventeenth century. In strong corporations most hospitality could continue to be intramural even after the Restoration: this is shown most vividly in the diary of Alderman Newton of Cambridge.[57] Moreover, some focuses for élite interaction were in decline from the mid-Tudor period onwards. For example, the religious guilds, which before the Reformation had afforded a means of incorporating the favoured outsider either by actual membership or by invitation to specific feasts, had either vanished completely or been replaced by secularized town guilds which, as we shall see, often found it difficult to sustain a routine of entertainment.[58]

Nevertheless, social interchange with the gentry did at times modify the behaviour of the urban élites. In those communities where a sense of civic identity was not strong, oligarchies often sought to assimilate themselves into the society of their rural neighbours. This was the case at Southampton where, its historian has suggested, the merchant classes turned outwards to the county from an early date.[59] It is a pattern that can also be discerned at Leicester, where a corporation that did share some collective identity was nevertheless inordinately eager to draw the gentry into its ambit through entertainment, and gifts to visitors to bear-baitings and horse-races.[60] But in the Elizabethan period it often shows most clearly in small corporate towns, such as Banbury or Stratford-on-Avon, which were engaged in rather ambivalent exercises. On the one hand they wished to affirm their own integrity through full charters, and new civic buildings; on the other they constantly called upon the gentry to acknowledge

---

[56] *Maire of Bristowe is Kalendar*, 86.

[57] *Diary of Alderman Newton, passim*, shows constant entertainment of the aldermen by the mayor, and by each other, but only occasionally did outsiders become involved, as in the Barnwell collation.

[58] On guilds offering membership to outsiders see *The Gild of St. George in Norwich*, 41; Phythian-Adams, *Desolation of a City*, 20; J. J. Scarisbrick, *The Reformation and the English People* (Oxford, 1984), 23. On invitations, see R. S. Ferguson and W. Nanson (eds.), *Some Municipal Records of the City of Carlisle* (Cumb. and Westmors. Antiq. and Arch. Soc., E.S. 4, 1887), 94.

[59] C. Platt, *Medieval Southampton* (London, 1973), 217.

[60] *HMC, App. to 8th Rep.*, pt. i, fo. 428; Billson, *Medieval Leicester*, 28.

their triumphs.[61] building of a new town-hall at Bridport in 1576 had to be celebrated with the active participation of the neighbouring gentry.[62] After the Civil War these tentative attempts at social integration rapidly developed into that full perception of 'civilized society' that enabled townsmen to believe that they *were* part of the ruling class if they played the role of gentlemen.[63]

In political contexts civic hospitality to the landed classes was even more obviously modified by the experience of the sixteenth century. The vast extension of local-government business forced a more regular contact between town and countryside and led to regular entertainments at musters and commissions as well as the legal sessions.[64] But there were also the opportunities provided by urban offices such as the steward, and above all the lure of parliamentary seats, to draw gentry and townsmen closer together. In the seventeenth century gentry were increasingly made 'free' of the towns: Anthony Ashley Cooper, for example, was made a freeman of Tewkesbury in 1640 because at a dinner he defended his hosts against the insults of another guest, Sir Henry Spiller.[65] Country gentlemen became aldermen, and even occasionally mayors of large corporations: Cambridge for example, had a gentleman mayor in 1616.[66] Such men must certainly have entertained their fellows on roughly equal terms. In the case of elections the townsmen were usually recipients

[61] J. S. W. Gibson and E. R. C. Brinkworth (eds.), *Banbury Corporation Records: Tudor and Stuart* (Banbury Hist. Soc., 15, 1977), 19–31, 34; R. Savage and E. I. Fripp (eds.), *Minutes and Accounts of Stratford-upon-Avon Corporation*, 4 vols. (Dugdale Soc., 1, 3, 5, 10, 1921–9), i. 1–22; R. Tittler, 'The Building of Civic Halls in Dorset, ca. 1560–1640', *BIHR*, 58 (1985), 37 ff.

[62] Tittler, 'Civic Halls', 44.

[63] A. Everitt, 'The English Urban Inn, 1560–1670', in his *Perspectives in English Urban History* (London, 1973), 91–137; Borsay, 'Urban Ritual and Ceremony', 247–50. The language of some late-seventeenth-century town records is revealing here: for example, the Coronation of William and Mary in 1689 was celebrated by Leicester Corporation with a dinner at the Angel for 'persons of good quality and fashion': Billson, *Medieval Leicester*, 29.

[64] Canterbury Chamberlains' accounts, which are full from the late fifteenth century onwards, give a good view of these increased contacts: *HMC, App. to 9th Rep.*, 143–63.

[65] Hodges, 'Electoral Influence of the Aristocracy', 292; K. H. D. Haley, *The First Earl of Shaftesbury* (Oxford, 1968), 33–4.

[66] *Annals of Cambridge*, iii. 116. Sir Edward Hynde was mayor in 1616, but the experiment proved costly for him, and was not repeated.

rather than givers of hospitality, although those patrons who influenced elections were often in other contexts treated by the borough, as were the Hastings and Stanhopes in Leicester.[67] The importance of appropriate generosity in influencing electoral fortunes only gradually began to manifest itself during the seventeenth century, but long before the arrival of the Whig magnates, good hospitality was occasionally believed to have determined the outcome of a disputed poll. In 1604 Sir Thomas Puckering, owner of the Priory in Warwick, had every hope of election, but in the event the victor was Sir Thomas Lucy, who was praised for 'sheweinge more favour to the Corporation than Sir Thomas Puckreing, who was but a stranger in the contry and not so comodious . . . nor a man of such nobell hospitality as that worthey familee of the Lucyes'.[68] The clear implication is that behind the moment of the poll lay a tradition of sociable interchange between Warwick and the Lucy home at Charlecote.

III

Influential outsiders had to be treated with liberality and due deference to rank and political influence, but the rest of the populace was rarely the subject of municipal sympathy. It is worth observing that there was little 'middle ground' in urban entertainment of strangers, since ordinary country-dwellers bent on business or pleasure had inns for their convenience and probably troubled citizens only if they were friends. There is no reason to suppose that visitors were not entertained in towns much as they would have been elsewhere when they came in the name of friendship: Hollybrand's French discourse shows a London citizen of the Elizabethan period receiving several guests, and the evidence of Richard Stonley's diary reveals that he rarely ate without three or four guests present when he was at home in the city.[69] When Harrison commented on the lack of generosity of ordinary burghers, he may have had in mind the

---

[67] *HMC, App. to 8th Rep.*, pt. i, cols. 428–429b.

[68] Wa. RO, Warwick Borough MSS., W21/6, 269.

[69] M. St Clare Byrne, *The Elizabethan Home* (London, 1930), 20 ff; Folger Lib., V/a/459, fos. 81ᵛ, 86–90.

tendency to give elaborate entertainment in inns, rather than in the limited space available domestically. It has already been noted that even the greater gentry often ate in inns, or had their food prepared there, before the extension of the West End made London residence more commodious.[70] Guests of middling status were unlikely to be of much concern to the city fathers, since normally they neither conferred honour nor subverted order.

The stranger poor were altogether less welcome for all the reasons already considered in relation to the countryside, but also because they represented a peculiar threat to order in the town. As early as the 1520s London had put into operation a scheme differentiating deserving local poor, who were licensed to beg, and vagrants, who were to be expelled.[71] In 1539 Chester Corporation ordered that stranger poor could only remain within the city and beg if they were listed and assigned to one ward of the city; the schedule of licensed beggars was then to be 'sett up in every mans house . . . for knowledge to whome they shall geve their allmys' or relief.[72] The Norwich Guild of St George probably had the stranger poor in mind when it forbade its feastmakers in 1548 to make any provision for those of the country.[73] At the end of the first decade of Elizabeth's reign, the Lord Mayor of London defended his decision not to hold the marching watch on the grounds that it led to the 'callinge and confluence of moche people to the cytie out of the countreye', and hence to disorder created by rogues and vagabonds.[74] The growth and development of these urban arrangements in London, Norwich, Bristol, and Coventry is intimately linked to the general history of the poor laws, and need not be repeated in detail here.[75]

---

[70] See above, ch. 2.

[71] E. M. Leonard, *The Early History of English Poor Relief* (Cambridge, 1900), 26. Gloucester had tried a similar scheme as early as 1504: Thomas, *Town Government*, 115.

[72] R. H. Morris, *Chester in the Plantagenet and Tudor Reigns* (Chester, 1893), 363.

[73] Hudson, *Select Records of Norwich*, ii. 403.

[74] M. Berlin, 'Civic Ceremony in Early Modern London', *Urban History Yearbook* (1986), 19.

[75] J. Pound, *Poverty and Vagrancy in Tudor England* (London, 1971); P. A. Slack, *Poverty and Policy in Tudor and Stuart England* (London, 1988), ch. 6.

What is interesting in the context of openness and hospitality to the poor is the anxiety displayed by municipal authorities about the lodging of strangers and travellers. As early as 1491 the burgesses of Southampon were ordered to accept the close supervision of the mayor in the matter of lodging strangers, and in the latter half of the sixteenth century it was common to order that no outsider should be permitted to remain for more than three days without specific licence.[76] The language of the constables' returns shows that these activities were seen as 'giving hospitality' to strangers, and that innkeepers and alehouse keepers who displayed undue welcome were likely to be pursued as delinquents.[77] In practice, of course, most sixteenth-century towns found it extremely difficult to regulate the influx of poor strangers, and London found it impossible. With the assistance of the late Elizabethan legislation, local justices spent much of their time sifting the worthy from the unworthy and passing the latter onwards as soon as it could be arranged. Nevertheless, householders in cities like London still complained in the early seventeenth century that they were 'continually troubled with relieving of beggars at their doors'.[78]

One interesting question that arises from this Elizabethan and Stuart evidence is whether there had ever been a tradition of open household relief in the towns of the kind that would have attracted stranger poor. Stow offers a number of London examples of indiscriminate gate doles, but all the donors are noblemen or great men such as Cromwell.[79] Household ordinances for the establishment of Thomas Cranmer also suggest general giving, though with a preference for the known poor, while the much later ones for Lionel Cranfield's London home are quite clearly directed primarily to assisting the local

---

[76] P. Studer (ed.), *The Oak Book of Southampton*, 3 vols. (Southants. Rec. Soc., 6, 1910–11), i. 156; *HMC, App. to 3rd Rep.*, 42. Sir William Bellenden proposed even tighter controls that would permit alehouse keepers to harbour those they did not know for only one night and day: Bodl. Bankes Papers, 66/12.

[77] J. Kent, *The English Village Constable, 1580–1642* (Oxford, 1986), 147.

[78] Guildhall RO, Journal of Common Council, 25, fo. 257. On the general problem of influx into towns, see A. L. Beier, *Masterless Men: The Vagrancy Problem in England, 1560–1640* (London, 1985).

[79] John Stow, *A Survey of London*, ed. C. L. Kingsford, 2 vols. (Oxford, 1908), i. 88–9.

needy.[80] None of this, however, is of much value in gaining insight into the behaviour of the mercantile élite. A number of London wills reveal suspicion of elaborate funeral entertainments and doles at an early date, but these are matched by many that seem happy to entice all and sundry with the promise of doles.[81] Pamphlets such as *The Lamentacyon of a Christen against the Citye of London* (1548), excoriated the citizens for providing only a few scraps and bones to be sent to Newgate, but the pleading is too clearly self-serving to be of any utility as evidence.

Generosity, at least to neighbours and the known poor, seems to have been expected of townsmen, just as it was of their rural counterparts. In the church of All Saints, North Street, York, there is a fine window illustrating the Six Corporal Acts of Mercy, in which a well-dressed man, probably a merchant, performs all the works himself, including the feeding of the poor at the gates.[82] This dates from the first half of the fifteenth century, but the ordinances for the Lord Mayor of London's household in the next century indicate a similar sense of obligation, even if one that was not discharged personally.[83] Guild feasts sometimes seem to have provided open doles for the poor, since they were usually supposed to be offered the residue of the food that had been served.[84] Indeed, fifteenth-century regulations for the guilds often emphasized duty to the poor, as at Southampton, where the Guild Merchant meetings were to include the giving of four cisterns of ale to poor folk. Wills sometimes ordained funeral dinners to which rich and poor neighbours were bidden, though some, like Katherine Waddington, thought it prudent to separate the two groups and give the most substantial meal to

[80] LPL, Fulham Papers 426, fo. 31. See also Coleman's earlier orders for the household of Lord Keeper Egerton in the parish of St Martin-in-the-Fields: Bodl. Rawl D/406, fo. 170ᵛ.

[81] S. Thrupp, *The Merchant Class of Medieval London* (Ann Arbor, 1948), 154–5; I. Darlington (ed.), *London Consistory Court Wills: 1492–1547* (London Rec. Soc., 3, 1967), 69, 80, 138, 143.

[82] See plate 2. I am grateful to David Palliser for drawing this window to my attention.

[83] Masters, 'The Lord Mayor's Household', 111.

[84] *HMC, App. to 9th Rep.*, 295 (Wisbech, Holy Trinity); but at Norwich in 1531 an attempted guild economy ordered that food in hand should be sold 'to helpe to the charge of the said felawship and brethren': Hudson, *Selected Records of Norwich*, ii. 113.

the wealthy.[85] Moreover, begging seems to have survived in a partially sanctioned form in some of the smaller towns until a late date. The Oxford beggars who prayed for alms at the houses of citizens were only repressed during the Civil War.[86] Finally the readiness of townsmen to accept that they should give alms and hospitality to a fixed and known group of poor, especially in response to the Privy Council's orders of 1596 for the sharing of suppers, indicates the existence of a residual belief that this had been an appropriate mode of giving in the towns.[87]

At festival seasons we have clear evidence from Stow and from sources such as the York city books that open house was held. Stow's famous account of Londoners at the midsummer festival has the wealthy sort welcoming both 'neighbours and passengers also to sit, and be merry with them in great familiarity'.[88] In York, the celebrations in 1586 for Elizabeth's deliverance from the Babington plot involved the householders in bringing tables and their plate out into the streets to welcome all and sundry.[89] Moments such as mayor-making in Coventry or Worcester included the giving of largess to all comers, although by the seventeenth century it was becoming rare for this to be undertaken on a grand scale.[90] Changes in the nature of urban festivity, which will be considered in detail below, may have removed some of the major occasions for open giving to the poor. However, the principal agent for change in the larger towns must surely have been the pressure of population increase, which translated the problem of poverty in general, and of the mobile poor in particular, to a level beyond the remedy of individual householders. In the countryside this often led to a powerful concern for the local poor, still sufficiently manageable in number to be the focus of individual charity as well as public forms of giving. In the town this dichotomy also existed, but the nature of the communities made it more difficult to sustain the informal charitable impulses of a face-to-face society. The identification

---

[85] Archer, 'Governors and Governed', 88.

[86] Studer, *The Oak Book*, i, 87; Anthony Wood, *Life and Times* ed. A. Clark, 5 vols. (Oxford Hist. Soc., 19, 21, 26, 30, 40, 1891–1900), ii. 212.

[87] Guildhall RO, Journal of Common Council, 24, fos. 174, 204, 206ᵛ; *The Maire of Bristowe is Kalendar*, 63.

[88] Stow, *Survey*, i. 101.   [89] *York Civic Records*, viii. 123–4.

[90] Phythian-Adams, *Desolation of a City*, 264; S. M. Bond (ed.), *The Chamber Order Book of Worcester, 1602–1650* (Worcester Hist. Soc., N.S. 8, 1974), 198.

of poor neighbours as suitable subjects for hospitality sometimes continued within the city: even in London, the daughter of Lawrence Withers sought to stay in his house after his death 'for the refrrechementt of poor neighbours', and the Elizabethan writer Howes hints that the poor still had 'the revercion of meat and porrege' from wealthier households.[91] Yet it is difficult to find extensive evidence that individuals or groups in the late sixteenth-century town felt that the local poor were important beneficiaries from any species of 'open house'.[92]

IV

While much of the cost of civic entertainment seems to have derived from the need to show favour to influential outsiders, the social energies of urban oligarchies were frequently directed inwards, towards ritual and celebration that was essentially designed for the benefit of some section of the town population. This can best be demonstrated by three detailed examples, each separated by approximately a century. The importance of intramural commensality in the ceremonial life of Bristol is shown in the description of part of the urban year in the compilation of one of the fifteenth-century town clerks: *The Maire of Bristowe is Kalendar*.[93] There the ritualized activities of the councillors in the season between Michaelmas mayor-making and the end of the Christmas festivities are carefully set out. On All Hallows Even, to take one example, the whole Council assembled after dinner 'with many other gentils and worshipfull comeners', and went in procession to make their offertory at All Hallows church, and thence back to the mayor's house, 'there to have their fyres and their drynkyngs with spiced Cakebrede and sundry wynes'. Later in November they would meet again on St Katheryn's Eve, hear evensong at St Katheryn's Chapel, and be entertained by the wardens and brethren of the guild, 'the cuppes merelly filled aboute the house'. The Christmas drinkings, described in detail in *The Great Red Book of Bristol*, began in the mayor's house on or immediately after the festival, and then moved outwards

---

[91] Archer, 'Governors and Governed', 234.
[92] On alms to poor neighbours, see below, p. 384
[93] *The Maire of Bristowe is Kalendar*, 72–86.

until by Twelfth Night the council were being entertained by the abbot of St Augustine's, the only specific example of hospitality from beyond the ranks of the city fathers.[94] Although Ricart did not include the rest of the social year, we know from other sources that there were feasts at St George's and Midsummer, and drinkings on St John's and St Peter's Eves as well, of course, as at mayor-making. While strangers no doubt participated in these ceremonies on occasion, their purpose seems unquestionably to be to display power and identity within the city itself.[95]

A second example is provided by York during the reign of Mary Tudor. The economic crisis which induced the corporation to reduce the number of its feasts also offers the historian an excellent account of the range of entertainments that had previously been customary.[96] There had been banquets in Lent, on Palm Sunday, St George's Day, Whitsunday, Corpus Christi, Midsummer Eve, St Blaise's Day, St William's Day, and St Stephen's, from the sacred calendar, and at mayor-making, the three justices feast, the venison and fishing feasts, and the election to St Thomas's Hospital, from the urban calendar. This, in fact, is not exhaustive, since the sheriffs provided entertainment at their entry to office and riding, but these were not funded by the city.[97] Some of these occasions did involve outsiders—the Corpus Christi plays have already been mentioned—but most seem to have been designed for the council and their wives, with some concessions to the populace at Midsummer, Corpus Christi, and sometimes the venison dinner.

Finally we can turn to the diary of Alderman Newton of Cambridge for the 1660s and 1670s.[98] Newton is particularly useful on feasting, describing meals with the loving detail usually associated with Parson Woodforde. He reveals much informal interchange among the aldermen in private dinners at which the other guests are normally fellow-members of the oligarchy. Sometimes generosity might extend rather further, as when

[94] *Great Red Book of Bristol*, pt. iii, 95–6.

[95] *The Maire of Bristowe is Kalendar*, intro. xix; E. Ralph (ed.), *The Great White Book of Bristol* (Bristol Rec. Soc., 32, 1979), intro. xxxii.

[96] *York Civic Records*, v. 177.

[97] D. Palliser, 'Civic Mentality and the Environment in Tudor York', *Northern History*, 18 (1982), 84.

[98] *Diary of Alderman Newton, passim*.

'Mr. Crabb mayor made a feast inviting his neighbours about him', but those beyond the town were not mentioned.[99] Civic occasions like mayor-making, the elevation of new aldermen, the opening of Sturbridge Fair, and the formal elements of the Christmas celebrations were normally the monopoly of the aldermen and inner council, though the electors and minor officials were sometimes treated. Only the mayoral feast seems to have been a moment to welcome strangers, and even then Newton remarks on at least two occasions on the small number of outsiders bidden.[100]

To understand more fully the significance of intramural commensality, we need to look in some detail at the arrangement of particular feasts. It is not, of course, easy to generalize, since English towns were of their nature very diverse, and since the long chronological time-span from the mid-fifteenth to the late seventeenth century should lead us to question the reality underlying apparent continuities. Nevertheless, certain festivals and methods of celebration do seem to be widely shared among early modern towns. The most obvious moment in the urban year at which feasting was likely in provincial capitals and small corporate market-towns alike was mayor-making, often, though not always, a Michaelmas festival.[101] It is unusual to find a description of the ceremony that does not incorporate some eating and drinking, though the scale and choice of participants was extremely variable. One of the best early descriptions of the full ritual is given in the Bristol calendar, and is worth quoting in full.

Item, it hath be usid on the seide Michelmasse day, the most parte of the Counseill for to dyne with the both maires, that is to sey, a grete parte of theym with the new Maire, and a parte with the olde Maire; in especial all officers to dyne with the olde Maire. And after they dyned, to assemble all the hole Counseille at the High Crosse, and fro thens the new maire and the old maire, with alle the hole company, to walke honourably to Seint Mighels churche and there to offre. And then to retorne to the new Maires hous, there to take cake brede and wyne.[102]

[99] *Diary of Alderman Newton,* 40.
[100] Ibid. 23, 38. The ministers of the town churches were also bidden on the King's birthday: ibid. 47.
[101] For a published account, see D. H. Kennett, 'Mayor-making at Norwich, 1706', *Norfolk Archaeology,* 35 (1971), 271–4.
[102] *Maire of Bristowe is Kalendar,* 72.

Descriptions for a rather later date for cities such as Norwich and York follow a very similar pattern, though York was prone to economize and only bid the office-holders to dine.[103] Elsewhere, election dinners were often given by the newly chosen mayor, and the invitation could be extended to all freemen, or even beyond, as in the case of Coventry.[104] The election dinner was the highlight of the social calendar at Oxford, where all freemen were still bidden to it in the early seventeenth century, and at Cambridge.[105] When a wide electorate or citizen body were treated in this way it led to predictable tensions about cost: at Coventry, where the mayor had to pay, there was a complaint to Cromwell in 1539 that the money spent on this one occasion 'myght well keipp his house halfe a yeire after'.[106] In Oxford, where the city itself met the charges, the rising cost of the election dinner was a regular subject for discussion at the council board, and eventually led to its demise.[107] Nevertheless, councils felt that some commensality was a necessary part of this principal urban day. It seems that in the fifteenth century some councils were deliberately increasing their investment in mayor-making: at Canterbury, for example, the election feast only became a regular event in the 1470s.[108]

The Bristol narrative suggests that the entertainment provided on mayor-making day discharged two related functions. The first, and most interesting, was that it marked the transition of power by separation and then integration. The council divided to dine with the old and new incumbents, more honour being accorded at this moment to the old office-holder as a symbol of his residual control. Newton's diary reveals the same process in Cambridge, where some of the aldermen customarily assembled at the house of the mayor-elect, and were given sugar-cakes and wine, before moving to that of his predecessor, where normally they did not

---

[103] *York Civic Records*, vi. 74.
[104] Devizes is a good example of a small borough that had a lavish election dinner, costing £4 in 1606: B. Howard Cunnington, *Some Annals of the Borough of Devizes, 1555–1791* (Devizes, 1925), pt. ii, 27–45.
[105] W. H. Turner (ed.), *Selections from the Records of the City of Oxford* (Oxford, 1880), 102–3, 323; H. E. Salter (ed.), *Oxford Council Acts, 1583–1626* (Oxford Rec. Soc., 87, 1928), xxxiii, 113, 396; *Annals of Cambridge*, iii. 146.
[106] Phythian-Adams, *Desolation of a City*, 263.
[107] *VCH, Oxford*, iv. 134.
[108] *HMC, App. to 9th Rep.*, 144.

eat.[109] But power was fractured and the body politic had to be made whole again, a process that was accomplished by the combined procession, the offertory, and finally by eating together, this time eating food that was less substantial, but more clearly identified with urban ritual.

The second related function was that of communication: the articulation for a wider audience of the fact that authority had been transferred from one generation to the next. If such a demonstration was necessary, it was likely that it would in the first instance consist of formal public processions and worship, and these are, of course, to be found routinely in English towns. When commensality was extended beyond the inner élite we may infer that it had been designed, at least originally, to involve the wider community in acknowledgement of the transfer, and perhaps of their role within it. The Lord Mayor of London was generous in the invitations he extended to outsiders, but the main function of the great inauguration dinner was the integration of the companies who formed the basis of the freeman body into the celebration.[110] The generous election dinner at ·Oxford is likely to be related to the relatively broad franchise of the university city, while even after the Restoration the Cambridge freemen, with their residual voice in the affairs of the city, were allowed sugar-cakes and claret at the house of the new mayor.[111]

Other elections or admissions to council and guild were scarcely charged with the same importance and the same uncertainties as mayor-making. Nevertheless, there was a widespread belief that they had to be marked by more than the taking of an oath, and hospitality to one's fellow-townsmen was often perceived as the most appropriate way of gaining the honour that should accrue to office. Aldermen were frequently expected to breakfast or dine their new peers on elevation: at Kendal in 1585 it was clearly felt that new men were being unnecessarily lavish, and they were forbidden to have 'spyced meate or Accates

---

[109] *Diary of Alderman Newton*, 2–3, 23, 34. On the significance of such ritual transfers of authority, see V. Turner, *The Ritual Process* (Ithaca, 1977), 94–130; Borsay, 'All the Town's a Stage', 239–40.

[110] Stow, *Survey*, ii. 190–92; Berlin, 'Civic Ceremony in London', 18.

[111] I. Hammer, 'Anatomy of an Oligarchy: the Oxford Town Council in the Fifteenth and Sixteenth Centuries', *JBS*, 18 (1978–9), 1–27; *VCH Cambridge and Isle of Ely*, iii. 49–50.

comonlye which us called small meate' [presumably mince meat]
at their 'principall feast'.[112] The more usual problem was to
persuade newly elected aldermen, bailiffs, and sheriffs to take
their duties seriously enough. In 1516 a dispute arose at York
between William Barker, one of the current sheriffs, and the
corporation.[113] The issue here was the feast at the sheriff's
riding, which was his major moment of hospitality rather than
election day. The second sheriff, unlike Barker, was willing to
pay for a dinner, but was determined to hold it in his own home,
not the Common Hall, and to bid 'none to dynar with hym bot
a certan of the Aldermen and othure frends'. The council, on the
other hand, wanted to hold the event in the Common Hall, and
to leave open the possibility of inviting the freemen. The council
lost, probably because Barker had the ear of Wolsey to whom
the matter was referred. However, the interest of this dispute,
and of similar ones to be found later in the century, lies in the
importance that many towns continued to attach to events which
would seem to us to have a very optional social character.
Gloucester and Leicester were only two of the Elizabethan
councils that exerted themselves with surprising vigour to try to
retain election-tide or related commensality.[114] This is made
more striking by the fact that most election drinkings and similar
events do seem to have been rather small and exclusive occasions
involving the inner council. So serious was the commitment that
friends could be ordered by the corporation to perform the duty
of a sick office-holder: as at York in 1504, when the friends of
Oliver Middleton were ordered to perform his duties and pay for
the feast in his absence.[115]

This earnest offering of hospitality at entrance into office seems
to permeate far down the social system, to the drinkings that
apprentices were expected to provide at the termination of their
seven years' service.[116] Of course, these lesser junketings did not

[112] R. S. Ferguson (ed.), *A Boke off Recorde . . . within the Town of
Kirkbiekendall* (Cumbs. and Westmors. Antiq. and Arch. Soc., E.S. 7, 1892), 133.
[113] *York Civic Records*, iii. 53–4, 63.
[114] GRO, GBR, B3/1, fos. 42^v, 132; M. Bateson (ed.), *Records of the Borough
of Leicester*, 3 vols. (Cambridge, 1899–1905), iii. 186.
[115] *York Civic Records*, iii. 10.
[116] J. R. Boyle (ed.), *Records of the Merchant Adventurers of Newcastle-upon-
Tyne* (Surtees Soc., 93, 1895), i. 18.

always meet with the approval of the magistrates and guild masters, and there were a number of attempts to dissuade men from misspending their wages on convivial riot.[117] However, the cultural assumption that this rite of passage had to be celebrated among one's peers remained powerful, and no doubt the ritual involved, if we could penetrate it, sought to express the consequences of transition. The invaluable Newton, who did leave a full description of his aldermanic dinner, must stand as exemplar for many lesser men. The occasion of his election was also that of the proclamation of Sturbridge Fair; he therefore presided with the mayor at the dispensing of sugar-cakes and sack from the alderman's table in Guildhall. Thence they returned with the other aldermen to Newton's house and had an elaborate dinner at which the mayor and 'Mrs. New Elect' sat at the head of the table, and Newton himself beside his wife.[118] A variety of other ceremonies ensured that the new alderman was treated with all the respect that was due to his membership of a more elevated order.

Eating and drinking at other civic ceremonies such as the riding of the bounds, the assertion of riparian and fishing rights, and on urban court days seems broadly to have two purposes. First, it provided necessary practical sustenance for those who were engaged in civic business: chamberlains' books throughout the period are full of breakfasts, suppers, and dinners provided at the end of court sessions.[119] Secondly, it was probably designed to attract a substantial body of witnesses to the assertion of urban rights. Thus, at Oxford the sheriff's ridings were conducted in an alcoholic atmosphere that ended in drinking at the Red Lion or some similar hostelry. This was not necessarily free to the participants, who might pay a fixed sum for their entertainment, but the council also provided wine or beer, and by the seventeenth century it was customary for the High Steward to offer venison as well.[120] The York fishing dinner, when the city asserted its

---

[117] Haskins, *Trade Guilds of Salisbury*, 390.

[118] *Diary of Alderman Newton*, 29–30.

[119] On occasions court sessions were the focus for the town's main feast-day, as at Guildford, where Hock Day, 'the great law daye' included an elaborate breakfast for all the participants: E. M. Dance (ed.), *Guildford Borough Records, 1514–46* (Surrey Rec. Soc., 24, 1958), 131.

[120] Salter, *Oxford Council Acts,* intro. xxxix, 10–11; vol. ii. 7, 12, 420; *VCH Oxford*, iv. 135.

rights as conservator of the Ouse, was a similar occasion, as was the grand water feast at Yarmouth.[121] Perhaps it was assumed that as youths had to be beaten to remember the bounds, so the adult populace depended on alcohol to fix these things in the collective memory. It is certainly the case that these events continued to have active public participation until a late date, and, with the celebration of national events, to be some of the rare occasions shared by the élite and populace.

It is difficult to assess the importance of junketings such as these for the preservation of urban amity. However, in the case of law days and sessions feasts, involving many of a community's substantial citizens, there is some evidence for a shared interest in their preservation. The sharpest comment comes from Philip Wyot, town clerk of Barnstaple at the end of the sixteenth century. A small Devon town of this kind obviously did not have the elaborate ceremonial life of Bristol or Coventry, but there were dinners for distinguished visitors and an annual sessions meal for the jurors and other officials. In 1601 this was not held because the mayor, John Delbridge, was absent in Northamptonshire: an excuse which Wyot regarded with contempt. Instead, the jury were given 6*d.* each to dine out, an order, Wyot observed that 'hath no father to any man's remembrance now living, but sponge up of the infected ayr, lately amongst us'.[122] Here the main source of conflict was the town preacher, but given the factional nature of much urban government the same complaint could have been made about almost any aspect of rulership. The refusal of feast-makers to perform their duties bred acrimonious debates on a number of councils.[123]

Although mayor-making and the other secular ceremonies of the urban year were clearly important for commensality, they scarcely, in the pre-Reformation period, rivalled the opportunities for enjoyment offered by the religious calendar. In addition to the obvious festivals of Christmas, Easter, and Whitsuntide, there were the crucial urban celebrations of St George's Day and Corpus

[121] *York Civic Records*, iv. 157; v. 183; Palliser, 'Civic Mentality', 85.

[122] J. R. Chanter, *Sketches of the Literary History of Barnstaple* (Barnstaple, 1866), 110.

[123] Bacon, *Annals of Ipswich*, 412 ff; Hudson, *Selected Records of Norwich*, ii. 111–15.

Christi, and then a host of other days that might be marked because they were the principal day of a particular guild or fraternity, because they were the object of local church dedications, or because they were the days of a local or regional saint.

The Christmas season and, in lesser measure, that at Easter seem to be distinguished by individual hospitality rather than corporate celebration. There were a few Christmas civic dinners—that at Lincoln is probably the best-known—but the more usual pattern was for leading citizens to give breakfasts and to keep some measure of open house.[124] The entertainment was not necessarily 'private', or separated from the civic environment: the Bristol drinkings which took place in the homes of aldermen were heavily subsidized by the municipal purse before 1519.[125] At Chester, on the other hand, aldermen gave breakfasts at their own cost: these were lavish enough to incur the criticism of the council because they made men miss divine service on the festival and allowed them to 'pass all the daye after idelie in wyne and wantonness'.[126] However, the Chester burghers, like their gentry counterparts, were expected to make gestures of open hospitality at the Christmas season, giving 'their frinds and pore nyghbours' liberal entertainment on the other days. Such mimesis of aristocratic custom is not always easy to detect from the surviving urban records, but is suggested in sources such as Robert Herrick's letters from Leicester, or by the notes of our old friend Alderman Newton.[127] That third-rate poet and flatterer Thomas Churchyard argued that Shrewsbury was remarkable for its Christmas feasting which

        . . . compares with all I know
Save London sure, whose state is farre much more.[128]

---

[124] J. W. F. Hill, *Tudor and Stuart Lincoln* (London, 1956), 35. London also had a Christmas celebration, from which Lords of Misrule were banned in 1555: Guildhall RO, Journal of Common Council, 16, fo. 335.

[125] I. S. Leadam (ed.), *Select Cases before the King's Council in the Star Chamber*, 2 vols. (Selden Soc., 16, 25, 1903, 1911), ii. 154.

[126] Morris, *Chester*, 336.

[127] Nichols, *History of Leicester*, I. ii. 340; *Diary of Alderman Newton*, 7, 38. At least one mayor of Coventry kept open house for the Twelve Days early in the sixteenth century: Phythian-Adams, *Desolation of a City*, 141.

[128] Thomas Churchyard, *The Worthines of Wales* (Spenser Soc., 1876), 82.

The summer festivals of the Church were much more likely occasions for various forms of civic junketing. Between St George's Day on 23 April and St Peter's Day on 29 June there were many opportunities for the ritual expression of community.[129] The particular feasts favoured depended upon the cultural traditions of the city or town, on the names of its guilds and fraternities, for example, and on the strength or weakness of its trade-guild organization. St George's and Trinity were perhaps the most constant feasts for the religious guilds and subsequently for those town élites that absorbed some of the fraternities after the Reformation. Although the celebrations of these guilds might extend outwards ceremonially to embrace the whole of the town, the actual commensality was usually confined to the fraternity itself and a few selected guests. Our most detailed evidence comes from the St George's celebrations in Norwich, where the guild was secularized in 1547 and became effectively an adjunct of the council. Three days of processions and services marked the festival, and already in the mid-sixteenth century it was a local tourist attraction, with the carrying of the dragon, music of the waits, and so forth. The feasting, however, was intended principally for the brethren of the guild, and extended outwards only in that provision was made for Norwich citizens to be given drink if they came to the hall during the three days.[130]

The Norwich junketings, though more grandiose in scale than most, typify the feasting of both trade-guilds and fraternities in many English towns in the fifteenth and sixteenth centuries. Guild regulations almost always required that there should be solemn procession to church for divine service, in some cases with members clad in appropriate livery. Having made themselves visible in the public space of the town, and engaged in worship, the guild members were then free to 'make merry' within their own territory.[131] Except in those cases where an endowed feast was being kept, the sense of corporate rejoicing was reinforced by

---

[129] On the division of the sacred/secular year, see Phythian-Adams, 'Ceremony and the Citizen', 70–8.

[130] Hudson, *Selected Records of Norwich*, ii. 401–3; Benjamin Mackerell, 'History of Norwich', NRO, NNAS Safe II, shelf I, vol. 6, 727–9. I am very grateful to Victor Morgan for the latter reference.

[131] Haskins, *The Trade Guilds of Salisbury*, 101, where the fifteenth-century regulations of the Tailors' Guild are given in detail.

the obligation of each member present or absent to contribute his financial share to the proceedings. There might be feast-makers, and when there were they frequently had extraordinary difficulty in managing the provisioning with the monies available, but there was nearly always a notion of shared duty in payment.[132] Indeed, the argument can be extended to incorporate the idea that participation in guild feasts was mandatory not only because of the duty to contribute to the cost, but because absence expressed a separation from fellowship.[133] The guild articulated the urban identity of its individual members, and this must be expressed through the ritual of commensality. Guests might be bidden to these celebrations, but the primary objective was the afforcement of friendship within the guild membership.

The most visible gestures of hospitality beyond these closed circles were made to the less powerful sections of the urban community. Thus, masters of the trade-guilds sometimes used the opportunity of the principal day feast, or an equivalent occasion, to feast the journeymen and even the apprentices.[134] There is a full description of such a treat given by the Tailors' Guild at Salisbury, where the obit feast of William Swayne included the journeymen, though they had to pay 4d. for the privilege of attendance.[135] It was characteristic of the urban environment that the journeymen shared their masters' food, but were placed at a separate table, and had to serve their betters before they could eat. They in their turn were served 'by the apprentices, at the maysters assignment conveniently for their degree'. The religious fraternities took a rather broader view of their obligations beyond their own ranks. They often collected donations for 'the poor men's box', but sometimes offered gestures of a more integrative

---

[132] At Beverley, for example, the Merchants and Mercers paid 6d. for each brother and his wife, a sum that remained constant at least from the beginning of the sixteenth century to the Civil War: A. F. Leach (ed.), *Beverley Town Documents* (Selden Soc., 14, 1900), 81, 95; J. Dennett (ed.), *Beverley Borough Records, 1575–1821* (Yorks. Arch. Soc. Record Ser., 84, 1932), 56.

[133] Hudson, *Selected Records of Norwich*, ii. 296.

[134] This was done by the Weavers Guild at Coventry in the early fifteenth century: Phythian-Adams, 'Ceremony and the Citizen', 65. Occasionally similar entertainments were held in London companies even in the later sixteenth century, though the most generous provision was for all the guild above journeyman status, and a more common arrangement was for dining to be confined to the liberty: Archer, 'Governors and Governed', 134–5.

[135] Haskins, *The Trade Guilds of Salisbury*, 122.

form of giving, such as the drink given to the citizens of Norwich at St George's Feast, or even the provision of a table in the hall at which the poor might consume the remains of the meal. The Holy Trinity Guild, Wisbech, ordered that at the Trinity Sunday dinner the steward and sewer were to summon in the poor and serve them 'with such mete as shalbe lef'.[136]

Some of the festivals of the spring and summer religious calendar extended beyond enclosed forms of commensality and actively embraced the wider community of the town. Corpus Christi, Whitsun, and the midsummer festivals of St Peter and St John, were all likely to provide the opportunity for general treating and rejoicing.[137] Any eating and drinking that took place, however, was normally ancillary to the processions, plays, or marching watch at the heart of the event. Thus, a number of councils provided wine to be disbursed by the guilds who organized the Corpus Christi plays and the marching watch, but this appears merely as a gesture to the participants in these major urban dramas.[138] The small Essex town of Maldon showed an excess of civic pride when it went further than this in 1540, and fed all the spectators at its play with 'mete, drynke and brede on the Saterdaye . . . fleshe, drynke and brede on the Sunday'.[139]

Sometimes, however, there are examples of commensality playing a key role in these popular urban festivals. The London marching watch, so vividly described by Stow, ended its cresset-borne procession with a breakfast at the Lord Mayor's, a fact that no doubt contributed to its demise on grounds of cost.[140] The Lichfield Whitsun 'Green Bower Feast', which combined the elements of marching watch and religious pageant, culminated in a party in the specially erected bower where each inhabitant was called by name and treated to 'cold hanged beef, stewed prunes, cakes and ale'.[141] This had a continuous history into the

---

[136] *HMC, App. to 9th Rep.*, 295.
[137] *The Maire of Bristowe is Kalendar*, intro. xix; Phythian-Adams, *Desolation of a City*, 270-1.
[138] Phythian-Adams, 'Ceremony and the Citizen', 64.
[139] Petchey, 'The Borough of Maldon', 185.
[140] Stow, *Survey*, i. 101-2; Berlin, 'Civic Ceremony in London', 18.
[141] Borsay, 'All the Town's a Stage', 228: the food items cited here were those consumed in the eighteenth century.

eighteenth century, even though by then it had lost most of its early associations with medieval ceremonial.

The other events that could be close in type to these calendric feasts were the occasions of national rejoicing that were marked particularly strongly by urban communities. Bonfires, bell-ringing, and so on that greeted the birth of a prince or the defeat of the nation's enemies were at one level spontaneous expressions of popular excitement.[142] They were also events that involved a greater or lesser degree of orchestration from the town élites, and they readily became moments for the dramatized articulation of civic values and concerns. The usual input from the corporation was some wine, or other beverage to encourage conviviality.[143] This was not distributed at random, but was usually carefully organized to display the beneficence of the town oligarchy. In 1510, for example, the magistrates of Plymouth celebrated the birth of Henry VIII's heir by leading a procession for a thanksgiving service, and then dispensing wine in the market-place.[144] In the case of the York rejoicings at Elizabeth's escape from assassination in 1586, the whole city became a theatre. There was a sermon, and a general communion attended by the civic dignitaries in full regalia, and a day's holiday was proclaimed. The green boughs that were always a sign of urban celebration were put up in the streets and tapestries hung from the houses. The city was then made, as it were, one household, when 'everyman supped in the seyd streetes at his own doore, with all theire plaite sett forthe in the sayde streetes', and of course in the late evening the inevitable bonfires were lit.[145] During Elizabeth's reign Accession Day provided a particularly good moment to associate popular rejoicing and formal civic munificence. At Liverpool in 1576 there was a bonfire in the market-square and the mayor and corporation, having themselves banqueted *in camera*, emerged to distribute sack, white wine, and sugar, 'standing all without the dore, lawdinge and praisinge

---

[142] On these popular rituals, see D. Cressy, *Bonfires and Bells* (London, 1989).

[143] See e.g., Bridgnorth's payments for wine and sugar-cakes at the proclamation of James I, and for a bonfire at the return of Prince Charles in 1623: *HMC, App. to 10th Rep.*, 432–3.

[144] Worth, *Plymouth Municipal Records*, 89.

[145] *York Civic Records*, viii. 123–4.

God for the most prosperouse raigne of our . . . graciose sovereigne'.[146] A favourite ploy in the seventeenth century was to have the town conduits run with wine for one or two days, thereby permitting the élite to gain political kudos from a display of self-sacrificing loyalism and cornucopian generosity.[147]

V

Some of the forms of civic commensality analysed above proved remarkably durable throughout the early modern period. Feasting at the time of mayor-making, even the structure of divided and then shared feeding, survived little altered in many English towns until at least the late eighteenth century.[148] When a sessions day, or other court meeting, had been a traditional opportunity for general hospitality, it often remained so long after the Restoration.[149] Celebrations associated with national events were also tenacious survivors: indeed, they seem to have assumed a larger place in urban ritual after 1660 than before. A few other popular junketings, such as the Lichfield Bower Feast or the Salisbury Midsummer Show retained something of their early structure, even when shorn of inner meaning by religious and social change.[150] But we cannot from this scattering of examples conclude that little had altered in the ceremonial life of English townsmen. To understand the contrasts between the later fifteenth century and the period after the Civil War, we need to return to the binary model used earlier in this analysis, contrasting the experience of the élite with that of ordinary townsmen, and especially the poor.

Many of the feasts and entertainments that marked the sacred and municipal years were always designed for a limited group of leading burghers. Their purpose was presumably not inaccurately

[146] R. Strong, 'The Accession Day of Elizabeth I', *JWCI*, 21 (1958), 91.

[147] This was done at Plymouth at the proclamation of Charles II: *HMC, App. to 9th Rep.*, 278, and at Oxford at his coronation: Wood, *Life and Times*, i. 399.

[148] Borsay, 'All the Town's a Stage', 228–32.

[149] Chanter, *Literary History of Barnstaple*, 122; C. H. Mayo (ed.), *Dorchester Municipal Records* (Exeter, 1908), 446.

[150] Haskins, *The Trade Guilds of Salisbury*, 188–90. The Chester Show was not held after 1678.

described in the York decree of 1558: the securing of neighbourly amity, and the affirmation of the collective identity of the ruling oligarchy. Not all communities pursued these objectives so avidly as York, Bristol, or London, but there seem to have been few boroughs that neglected them completely.[151] Seeking amity through shared eating indicates that opportunities for the reduction and resolution of tension were valued. It was necessary that the corporation should express its solidarity by eating together, drinking together, and of course praying together.[152] The role of commensality in dispute-resolution can sometimes be seen more formally, as in the case of John Sely, alderman of Walbrook, London, who in 1382 was penalized for not wearing robes of appropriate dignity by being required to entertain the mayor and aldermen to dine at his house 'at his own proper costs'.[153] Even more explicit was the case of Edmund Penston of Salisbury who, in 1455, had to entertain the mayor to 'a good supper . . . with sufficient white wine called "Must"', because he had judgement given against him in a dispute with the Mayor.[154] Conversely, dissension in the corporation was thought serious if it led to a refusal to share tables and food: thus, post-Restoration divisions in Barnstaple were loudly proclaimed by a minority who 'refused to sit at the Mayor's table'.[155] When men complained about failures of hospitality by individual aldermen or other office-holders, it seems that they were expressing anxieties about a failure of cohesion with the élite. Thus, the sheriffs of York were fined in 1509 because they had not kept appropriate house, 'and called the Councellours of this Cite and other honest persons, ther neigburghes, . . . accordyng to the lawdable custome of this sayd Cite'.[156]

One interesting feature of this élite commensality was that wives were frequently participants. In York this arrangement often involved separation and unique events prepared for the

---

[151] The author has traced thirty references to mayor-making entertainments in the printed sources available for the sixteenth century.

[152] On the importance of this notion after the Restoration, see Borsay, 'All the Town's a Stage', 240–1.

[153] H. T. Riley (ed.), *Memorials of London and London Life* (London, 1868), 466.

[154] Haskins, *The Trade Guilds of Salisbury*, 36.

[155] Chanter, *Literary History of Barnstaple*, 122.

[156] *York Civic Records*, iii. 27.

wives of the corporation: there were ladies' feasts at Palm Sunday, Whitsunday, Corpus Christi, St Stephen's Day, and Midsummer Eve, as well as a special women's procession to the Minster on Palm Sunday.[157] But far more commonly wives were included in guild feasts and even corporation dinners alongside their husbands, and came to expect this role as of right. Exclusion bred dissent: Philip Wyot reported that 'there was much chatteringe' among the wives of Barnstaple corporation when the mayor failed to invite them to a dinner in honour of the steward, the Earl of Bath, and Alderman Newton italicized a note that he had dined with his fellows at Mr Crabb's, *'but none of their wives'*.[158] The importance of the collective role of husband and wife is indicated by a comment on Winchester's Midsummer Feast, held in honour of the Devenishes. It was given for the corporation and their wives, and was described as a 'love-feast and merry meeting'.[159] Amity in the constricted environment of the town must often have involved amity between the female as well as the male heads of household.

No doubt a number of components were involved in the calculations which urban magistrates made about the utility of shared commensality. They can, however, often be reduced to two basic concerns: the political value of conviviality, weighed against the charge to the collective and individual purse. Feasting had political utility in communities like London where some limited power extended outwards from the centre to the guilds and the freemen.[160] The anxieties displayed by York corporation in its dispute with its sheriffs in 1517 seem to indicate that the 'public' quality of their entertainment should not be undermined by transferring it to their own dwellings.[161] In the same period, Bristol's struggle with its sheriffs raised major questions about the value of occasions such as the Christmas drinkings: a Star Chamber decree made it clear that they should not be thought sufficiently important to be a drain on the city's resources.[162]

[157] Ibid. v. 177.
[158] Chanter, *Literary History of Barnstaple*, 93; *Diary of Alderman Newton*, 6.
[159] *VCH, Hampshire*, ii. 201.
[160] F. F. Foster, *The Politics of Stability: a Portrait of the Rulers of Elizabethan London* (London, 1977), 9; Archer, 'Governors and Governed', 132–4.
[161] *York Civic Records*, iii. 54.
[162] *Cases before Star Chamber*, 164–5.

Bristol apparently surrendered without a struggle, but we have already seen that some corporations showed far more determination in their maintenance of traditional conviviality. Some of those towns which were still concerned to integrate potentially troubling members of the middling sort, often represented in the common council, had reason to value junketing among a broadly defined élite. Canterbury, with its late development of mayor-making festivities, would be one example.[163]

Conversely, towns like Hull and Newcastle upon Tyne, or cities like Exeter, which had long been dominated by a mercantile oligarchy, placed little visible emphasis on feasting as a political weapon. No doubt the inner coterie in these places entertained one another, but the public face of civic hospitality is largely absent in their records.[164] MacCaffrey's portrait of the Exeter oligarchy suggests a group who were normally confident in their control of their society, and therefore did not overtly seek the reinforcement that might have derived from elaborate commensality.[165] Since so many sixteenth- and seventeenth-century corporations went the way of these early models and became more introverted and oligarchic, we might conclude that one explanation for a decline in feasting was a diminishing need to impress or persuade a wide circle of burgesses. This argument receives some corroboration of a negative kind from the case of Oxford and Cambridge. Although in the transaction of routine business Oxford and Cambridge appear as oligarchic as any other corporate town in the late Tudor period, both retained a more serious role for the freemen than, say, York or Leicester, whose common councils had become little more than ciphers. At Oxford all freemen had a voice in the election of the mayor; at Cambridge there were six common court days a year, and much business was transacted on these occasions.[166] In communities such as these, the integrative and suasive possibilities of entertainment for the middling sort of townspeople remained attractive to the élites.

---

[163] On common councils, see P. Clark and P. Slack, *English Towns in Transition, 1500–1700* (Oxford, 1976), 128–9.

[164] *VCH, Yorkshire: East Riding*, i. 84 ff.; J. Brand, *The History and Antiquities of the Town and County of the Town of Newcastle-upon-Tyne*, 2 vols. (London, 1789), ii. 178 ff.

[165] W. MacCaffrey, *Exeter: 1500–1640* (London, 1975), 270, 277–8.

[166] See above, p. 326.

Corporations needed some very positive inducements of this political kind, since the costs of hospitality inevitably strained limited municipal budgets. When entertainment was funded directly from the resources of the town, it could be one of the major items of expenditure. The Oxford election feast cost £40 in 1602 and £43 in 1607. Most of the money came directly from the council, although the accountants had to find £13 in 1602 as a penalty for greatly exceeding their budget.[167] At Worcester in the Elizabethan period entertainment was the third highest charge on the municipal purse, although this of course includes giving to outsiders.[168] Bristol's acknowledgement of the strains imposed by hospitality led to a sharp constriction on expenditure: in the mid-sixteenth century and again at the beginning of the seventeenth, the city only spent about 5 per cent of its income on hospitality.[169] Even when a town did not fund dinners and treats directly, it was often forced to do so at one remove, by providing the mayor, sheriffs, chamberlains, or bailiffs with sufficiently large allowances to meet the costs. One of the commonest causes of contention between urban officials and councils concerned the level of such allowances, with accusations of embezzlement and mismanagement flowing freely. As inflation compounded these problems in the later sixteenth century, the office of feast-maker rapidly became one of the most unpopular in the town.[170] Although the feast-maker could often compel participants in civic and guild dinners to pay some fixed cost, this rarely met the outlay. Norwich feared as early as the reign of Henry VIII that men were not entering the city because of the cost of feast-making. At Ipswich, where in the early seventeenth century the corporation made a determined effort to sustain the feast of the town guild, approximately half of those chosen as feast-makers either compounded to avoid the office or were fined for failure to offer the required dinner.[171]

[167] Salter, *Oxford Council Acts*, 383, 396.

[168] A. D. Dyer, *The City of Worcester in the Sixteenth Century* (Leicester, 1973), 220.

[169] D. M. Livock (ed.), *City Chamberlains' Accounts for Bristol* (Bristol Rec. Soc., 24, 1966), intro.

[170] On the problem of office-holding, see P. Clark, *English Provincial Society from the Reformation to the Revolution* (Hassocks, 1977), 251–5.

[171] Hudson, *Selected Records of Norwich*, ii. 111; Bacon, *Annals of Ipswich*, 407–91.

The problem was that the early modern town was rarely adequately funded for the discharge of all the functions that contemporaries thought appropriate, indeed necessary. Even before the difficulties of inflation became critical, there is ample evidence of strain, although little agreement among historians about the depth of the crisis.[172] Thereafter, while some centres began to recover economically in the later sixteenth century, corporate finance declined in real terms because inflation was rarely met by any attempt to find new sources of revenue. When it is remembered that, for example, Gloucester was only rescued from dire indebtedness in the Elizabethan period by advance loans from its chamberlains, or that Leicester was in constant deficit in the same years, it is not surprising that there was some hesitation about lavish feasting.[173] There was little general improvement before the Restoration: indeed, for some towns such as Oxford the financial crisis came as late as the eve of the Civil War.[174] The economic crisis experienced in many towns was compounded by the eagerness of the oligarchy, as private citizens, to exploit municipal property, but their corresponding reluctance to assume burdens of expenditure which the collective purse could no longer sustain.

In these circumstances feasts and other treats among the inner or outer circles of power were prime candidates for economies. Drastic solutions, like Plymouth's ban on all entertainment in 1571, were not usual, but the curtailment of the social round certainly was.[175] In 1599 Colchester Assembly ordered that 'in respect of the better spare of the revenewes of this towne' there should be no election dinner, but that the 'floore' and the electors should be paid fixed sums instead.[176] One might expect the godly of Colchester to set aside feasting, but there are plenty of similar examples, even from communities such as Oxford and Ipswich which clearly valued entertainment. Ipswich cancelled

---

[172] C. Phythian-Adams, 'Urban Decay in Late Medieval England', in P. Abrams and E. A. Wrigley (ed.), *Towns in Societies: Essays in Economic History and Historical Sociology* (Cambridge, 1978).
[173] Clark and Slack, *English Towns*, 130.
[174] Salter, *Oxford Council Acts*, ii. 406.
[175] Worth, *Plymouth Municipal Records*, 54
[176] Colchester Assembly Book, 1576–99, fo. 159. I owe this reference to the kindness of Mark Byford.

the Corpus Christi Dinner in 1511 because of cost, revived it in 1519, cancelled it in 1521, confirmed the perpetual cancellation in 1531, but by 1542 had resuscitated it in a modified form.[177] At Oxford, the chamberlain's audit dinner was curtailed in 1520, and the mayor's inaugural feast was temporarily cancelled, though it returned ten years later; while in the Elizabethan era there were a bewildering series of changes in the pattern of feast-making.[178]

There is also evidence that corporations were willing to abandon commensality when more tangible projects demanded finance. Thus, Oxford finally sacrificed the election dinner in 1629 when the 'entertainment money' was commuted for payments by the relevant officers towards increasing the navigability of the Thames.[179] Bridgnorth had decided half a century earlier that it would rather have the annual fee-farm discharged by the bailiffs than let them pay for various banquets that had traditionally been their responsibility.[180] At Windsor the capital costs of new building for a town hall led to the cancellation of feasts and the payment of fixed sums to the common purse by officials.[181] If the situation was sufficiently desperate, a corporation would settle for a cash lump sum in lieu of hospitality: this is what happened in Wycombe which, in 1647, had to agree that the mayor should pay the chamberlain £16 at Michaelmas and £20 at Christmas, and then be discharged from all entertainment.[182] Arrangements for commutation of this kind were so common further down the urban hierarchy by the 1640s that the aldermen of Canterbury appear to have forgotten that the payments they made on entry to office were in lieu of their inaugural feast.[183]

This flexibility in the face of adverse financial circumstances prompts the thought that corporations had never perhaps taken

---

[177] Bacon, *Annals of Ipswich*, 183, 186–7, 189, 194–5, 219.
[178] Turner, *Selections from Records of Oxford*, 25, 102–3, 164, 306, 311, 323, 421.
[179] *VCH, Oxfordshire*, iv. 134, though it is worth noting that by the eighteenth century a form of commensality had been revived, breakfasts being given to the freemen by the outgoing mayor.
[180] *HMC, App. to 10th Rep.*, 426.
[181] R. R. Tighe and J. E. Davis (eds.), *Annals of Windsor* (London, 1858), 179.
[182] R. W. Greaves (ed.), *The First Wycombe Ledger Book* (Bucks. Rec. Soc., 2, 1947), 136.
[183] *HMC App. to 9th Rep.*, 164

their socializing very seriously. It is, however, as well to note that most of the extensive evidence on the subject comes from minute books which always record the removal of a dinner, but have a curious habit of not always observing its reinstatement. There were pressures to maintain tradition, like those described by Wyot, and, since the care of outsiders was a political necessity, few corporations denied themselves for long the pleasure of participating in commensality. Plymouth did not maintain its ban on feasting for more than ten years, and even the Oxford election meal reappeared in a rather different form after the Civil War.[184] Even when unusual circumstances dictated that general hospitality was inappropriate, some conviviality probably continued. This was even true in some measure during the Interregnum. Robert Beake, Mayor of Coventry in 1655-6, describes a city far less convivial than Newton's Cambridge: as a magistrate his main concern was the imposition of godly discipline on delinquent alehouse keepers, and he was morbidly sensitive about taking gifts or favours that might be construed as bribes.[185] However, even Beake arranged that Major-General Whalley should dine on several occasions at the expense of the city, and he was willing enough to dine at the guild feasts of the mercers, drapers, and apothecaries. At Salisbury the Tailors' Guild, which had been responsible for the Midsummer Show and Feast, did not hold its full celebration during the Civil War, but gradually contrived to hold the dinner, even though there were restrictions on the consumption of wine and a ban on invitations to strangers.[186]

It might be more pertinent to argue that urban élites had gradually modified the forms through which they articulated status and sought honour, and that this in turn influenced their views on the centrality of intramural hospitality. There had always been a moralistic and prudential element in mercantile behaviour, which readily led to a questioning of excessive display and lavish entertainment. Extravagance was a vice that many urban magistrates thought both reprehensible and potentially dangerous, suggesting undue affluence to the interested eyes of

---

[184] In the mid-eighteenth century Plymouth was once again making orders altering the nature of its election feast: Worth, *Plymouth Municipal Records*, 65.
[185] L. Fox (ed.), *The Diary of Robert Beake* (Dugdale Soc. Misc. 1, 1977), 120-33.
[186] Haskins, *The Trade Guilds of Salisbury*, 186-8.

Crown and nobility on the one hand and of the poor within the community on the other. This suspicion of display sometimes manifested itself in response to the Corpus Christi plays: it can also be found in doubts expressed about feasting.[187] The enthusiasm towns evinced for sumptuary legislation in the 1540s and 1550s might be no more than the usual urban interest in order and hierarchy, but in difficult economic times it also seems connected with a general anxiety about excess.[188] York's retrenchment in 1558 was prompted partly by the cost of feasting, but was justified by the pious thought that in time of dearth excess in eating was 'to the displeasor of Allmyghtie God', and no doubt that of men.[189] Chester's curtailment of breakfasting at Christmas was an earlier response to similar pressures, and even in the reign of Henry VI the corporation of Bristol cancelled drinkings on Christmas Day as inappropriate to the nature of the festival.[190] In each case the decrees reflect an awareness that public junketing by an oligarchic group, when conducted too overtly and lavishly, could be destructive of good order and a threat to the collective reputation of the élite.

By the end of the sixteenth century these impulses had been afforced by the godly Puritanism of many town governments. This did not necessarily mean that public statements about status became less important: these could still be provided by the old rituals of processions and worship, and by the newer displays of corporate building. The construction of civic halls seems to have satisfied a collective desire to manifest the power of the oligarchy in more permanent ways than was possible by the old routines of ritual and gift-giving. At the same time, they provided a means by which men of power could be separated from the rest, physically contained within the clearly defined barriers of the guild-hall. If feasting continued, it was now likely to occur in this more enclosed environment, the display that it involved, therefore, being less visible to the rest of the community. The old passion for public theatre and display never wholly vanished, indeed the Restoration saw a revival of social drama within the

---

[187] James, 'Ritual', 16–17.
[188] Guildhall RO, Journal of Common Council, 16, fos. 354-4ᵛ; Hudson, *Selected Records of Norwich*, ii. 124; Morris, *Chester*, 336.
[189] *York Civic Records*, v. 177.
[190] Morris, *Chester*, 336. *Great Red Book of Bristol*, 95–6.

town, but this was counterbalanced by the enclosed world of the oligarchy, in which traditional forms of commensality were inevitably of diminished significance.

VI

The engagement of ordinary citizens in civic sociability is even more difficult to penetrate. It is the assumption of studies of the pre-Reformation period that most ordinary members of the urban community were in some measure integrated into the social and ceremonial life of the town via their participation in ritual displays and via the largess dispensed to them by the élite.[191] The Corpus Christi marching watch, the plays, guild feasts, the celebration of the summer vigils, and the Christmas season all provided moments when intramural hospitality _could_ be extended beyond the select circles of the politically important. Even the local poor, though they were unlikely to be active participants in ceremonial, could profit from the general giving that accompanied these moments in the urban year, as at Norwich where the St George's feast-makers were instructed to offer drink to any citizen (in the sense of city resident) who presented himself.[192]

It is, however, important to be cautious about the richness of the experience of the ordinary citizen in pre-Reformation England and the degree of his integration: many cities were not, as we have seen, as committed to the public ceremonial cycle as Coventry or York, and smaller towns could hardly expect to imitate this pattern. Cities which did not have an elaborate pattern of entertainment to nurture amity among the élite were hardly likely to provide such occasions specifically for the plebs. Moreover, even a city which prided itself on its hospitable traditions did not necessarily extend them routinely to ordinary citizens. A number of cases in which mayors and sheriffs or aldermen failed to give good entertainment can be found in the older corporate towns: at York, for example, a miller was in trouble in 1511 for attacking an alderman in an alehouse, and for saying that 'he would not "away" his bonnet to none

---

[191] Phythian-Adams, _Desolation of a City_, 176 ff.; Berlin, 'Civic Ceremony in London', 16–18.
[192] Hudson, _Selected Records of Norwich_, 403.

alderman except three, for . . . they gave him neither meat nor drink'.[193] Moreover, ceremonial was not unchanging even before the Reformation: the construction of urban ritual in Canterbury seems to have occurred late in the fifteenth century as a response to disorder and decay.[194]

Nevertheless, these reservations do not finally detract from the argument that in a number of communities ceremony and largess did extend outwards the élite and did form an important part of the experience of the citizen before the Reformation. It is perhaps easiest to judge its importance from an analysis of what was lost thereafter. Even before the break with Rome there are signs of strain in the old arrangements: the Ipswich Corpus Christi plays and feast were cancelled several times early in the century, presumably because of cost.[195] Salisbury found it difficult to maintain the marching array on the day of its local saint, Osmund, from at least the early 1520s: here the problem was a combination of cost and of the individual guilds showing a preference for their own feasting.[196] Such hints of a lack of communal solidarity were immediately reinforced by the experience of the 1530s: for example, the great Trinity guild feast at Coventry was not held after 1534, apparently one sign of the decline of the fraternity long before its abolition.[197] Salisbury corporation, which struggled hard in the 1530s to maintain the Osmund feast, surrendered to the pressure of the assault on local saints' days, and acknowledged it abolished 'for certayne causes' in 1545.[198]

The most evident signs of change in the area of general conviviality came with the collapse of the marching watch and the gradual disappearance of the summer vigil feasts. The association of the watch with festivals such as St Peter's Eve or St John's Eve is one reason for its disappearance, although a full explanation must also include the cost involved, and the emergence of an alternative form of military organization in the musters. Thus, the London marching watch was suspended by Henry VIII in 1539 at the request of the Lord Mayor largely

[193] *York Civic Records*, iii. 36.
[194] Clark, *English Provincial Society*, 39.
[195] Bacon, *Annals of Ipswich*, 183, 186-7, 189.
[196] Haskins, *The Trade Guilds of Salisbury*, 70-2.
[197] Phythian-Adams, *Desolation of a City*, 270.
[198] Haskins, *The Trade Guilds of Salisbury*, 72.

because of its cost. There were a number of proposals thereafter that it should be revived, but these were resisted by the authorities, partly on the grounds that disorder would ensue, but partly, it seems, because the marching watch breakfast had become a difficult and very expensive event.[199] It appears that the corporation of London was far more willing to face the cost of an elaborate show under its control than it was a popular event for which its prime duty was to provide largess.

Coventry and Bristol provide good examples of the abolition or transmutation of the drinkings that had accompanied the summer festivities and the marching watch. At Bristol, Wolsey's decrees of 1519 curtailing the spending of the sheriffs specifically allowed £20 for the continuation of the watch, but not the money for the tunne of wine that had traditionally accompanied it.[200] With the loss of the vigil celebrations, the hospitality offered by ordinary citizens in London and elsewhere also disappeared, and so integrative hospitality was doubly affected.[201] There were some attempts to keep the old patterns alive: Hull's unusual decision to maintain the midsummer festival in Elizabeth's reign was carefully distanced from any popish remnants, but was justified for neighbourly amity and the feeding of the poor.[202] When the main popular festival happened to coincide with a major church one, such as Easter or Whitsun, it might have some chance of enduring; hence the survival of the Lichfield 'Green Bower Feast'. Norwich's continuing investment in celebrating the national, and urban, saint through its secularized guild of St George is another example of the same process.

It is very difficult to estimate from the surviving records how far corporations initiated a withdrawal from general entertainment, and how far they merely accepted transitions that were consequential on religious and political change. Sometimes the old and the new coexisted happily enough under Elizabeth and James. Thus, Kendal corporation, which was much

---

[199] Though the festivals of the vigils do not seem to have disappeared completely until the Civil War: John Aubrey, *The Remaines of Gentilisme and Judaisme*, ed. J. Britten (London 1881), 26; Stow, *Survey*, i. 101; Berlin, 'Civic Ceremony in London', 19.
[200] *Cases before Star Chamber*, 164.   [201] Stow, *Survey*, i. 101.
[202] Gillett, *History of Hull*, 121. The midsummer festivities also included a fish 'treat': *VCH, East Riding*, i. 125.

concerned with the imposition of good discipline on the populace, nevertheless gave cautious blessing to the craft plays and to the celebration of All Hallows' Eve late in Elizabeth's reign.[203] We may, however, infer that, since the main interests of élites lay in maintaining good order and controlling limited financial resources, restrictions externally imposed on popular festivities were largely attractive to them. There were some attempts to compensate for the losses of plays and watches by the introduction of midsummer shows, as at York and Chester, but they seem to have been uncertain growths, heavily dependent on support from above.[204] At York the show was associated with a distribution of grain to the poor, a transmutation presumably of the old forms of largess into an arrangement more satisfactory to the Elizabethan burgesses.[205] Other forms of substitution included more lavish provision and theatrical display at national festivals, especially in the late sixteenth century at the Accession Day celebrations.[206] Peter Borsay has suggested that by the later seventeenth century these type of celebrations were a deliberate attempt to compensate for the loss of the old forms of ritual.[207]

Between Elizabeth's reign and the Restoration lies a period in which we might legitimately assume that corporations were little interested in sustaining the forms of integrative ceremonial and commensality that had marked some later medieval towns. Godly discipline left, in theory, little room for drinkings and idleness, and the attack on alehouses and other focuses of popular entertainment must have made old forms of public conviviality more difficult. It may also be that urban magistrates bent on the creation of the new Jerusalem were even less inclined than their predecessors to offer any form of open hospitality to the citizenry. If one could use Robert Beake as a paradigm this would certainly be the case: one of Beake's major concerns seems to have been the creation of distance between himself and the ordinary residents of Interregnum Coventry.[208]

---

[203] Ferguson, *A Boke Off Recorde*, 90–1: an order limiting the number of ordinary citizens at dinners etc., of 1575, allowed general eating at meetings about pageants for Corpus Christi.

[204] *York Civic Records*, viii. 70; Borsay, 'All the Town's a Stage', 247.

[205] *York Civic Records*, viii. 70, 103, 169.

[206] Strong, 'The Accession Day of Elizabeth I', 91–3.

[207] Borsay, 'All the Town's a Stage', 252.

[208] Clarke, *The English Alehouse*, 166 ff.; *Diary of Robert Beake*, 121–3.

Yet it often appears that the strains of cost and organization had more effect on the survival of urban celebrations than did ideological differentiation. Early modern towns lacked effective structures through which to organize elaborate entertainments. The guilds, which had traditionally performed these roles, continued to do so in some cases, but the religious guilds were truncated or abolished after 1547 and the craft guilds were no longer brought together in collaborative displays after the demise of the play cycles. When a festivity did survive, like the Salisbury Summer Show, it was often because it was organized by an effective guild, in this case the Tailors.[209] The parish might occasionally form an alternative focus for commensality, but, like the corporation, this was often moving in the direction of exclusivity and social privilege by the late sixteenth century.[210] Until the rise of commercial forms of organized entertainment in the late seventeenth-century town, these arrangements were all that was available, and a corporation had to be strongly committed to ceremonial if it was to breathe life into these structures. If the absence of organizers did not discourage towns, then cost often did: oligarchies that were reluctant to feast themselves on grounds of cost were far less likely to be willing to pay for bread and circuses for the masses.

It need hardly be stated that by this date such treats would have been regarded as a totally inappropriate way of assisting the local urban poor. Even the private charity that had emanated from the celebration of feasts like midsummer had gradually disappeared. One of the few circumstances in which the public feasting of the poor still acquired a certain respectability was at election time, and even there there were grave reservations about the worthiness of the enterprise. Sir Henry Slingsby complained that at Knaresborough, 'there is an ill custom at these elections to bestow wine in all the town, which cost me 16 pounds at the least and many a man a broken pate'.[211] In 1628 Edward Rainsford observed that at Warwick the very beggars expected alms, and 'the meaner sort will do much for a meal's meat'.[212]

---

[209] Haskins, *The Trade Guilds of Salisbury*, 182 ff.
[210] Archer, 'Governors and Governed', 86–7.
[211] D. Parsons (ed.), *Diary of Sir Henry Slingsby, of Scriven Bart* (London, 1836), 63–4.
[212] Hodges, 'Electoral Influence of the Aristocracy', 125.

Where there was a large constituency for corporation elections the same pattern began to develop in the early seventeenth century. Archbishop Laud was deeply offended by the mayoral election at Oxford in 1638, where Thomas Smith's canvassing consisted of distributing huge quantities of beer to all and sundry, and offering a hogshead of wine at the guildhall, 'in so much that they drank wine there in pails and kettles'.[213] No doubt such activities merely added to the unattractive image that indiscriminate hospitality to the poor already had among the urban élites.

After the Restoration it may be that the relations between the magistracy and the rest in English towns underwent further significant change. As the crisis of poverty receded, and the pressure of the poor on urban resources began to diminish, bread and circuses once more appeared acceptable in moderation. There was, moreover, a greater incentive for urban groups to draw together in defence of their collective interests after the troubled years of the mid-century. This did not mean, of course, that political stability in the towns was easily achieved, but there was the possibility that oligarchs could now rest a little more secure from internal social turbulence in a national environment that was also more stable. These circumstances bred that expansiveness in the celebration of national events already noted, and a greater extroversion in the old formalities of procession and worship. But the connection between the behaviour of the early sixteenth and the late seventeenth centuries is often tenuous. The formalities of the post-Reformation town often seem designed to affirm distance rather than integration, just as the pompous façades of contemporary town-halls speak of power and separation. A growing concern for civic circumstance, which some historians have detected as early as the Elizabethan period, was made fully manifest in the reign of Charles II.[214]

This pleasure in pomp and circumstance is often counterpoised to the diversification of more private opportunities for sociability among the élite. By the 1670s Alderman Newton's round of civic festivals, interspersed with dinner parties shared with other

---

[213] *VCH, Oxfordshire*, iv. 145.
[214] See Hill, *Tudor and Stuart Lincoln*, 93; Borsay, 'All the Town's a Stage', 232–3.

aldermen, is beginning to appear dated and unduly introverted. The pattern of an urban season, which had developed in London and a few precocious provincial capitals and spa towns before the Civil War, was by this time spreading to many smaller centres.[215] Alan Everitt's study of Northampton reveals the extent of this season by the end of the seventeenth century, and the degree of integration which it created between worlds which have been kept separate deliberately in this chapter, those of the urban oligarchy and the rural gentry.[216] This integration, expressed institutionally through the growth of race meetings, assembly rooms, and coffee-houses, also ensured that the social differentiation which had always been an aspect of urban life was now reinforced by the demands of 'polite' society. Defoe's Doncaster landlord, who was mayor of the town in the early eighteenth century, but who kept hounds and 'lived as great as any gentleman ordinarily did', was a product of this new environment.[217]

As we have seen in the case of the nobility and gentry, the desire for physical and social distance between classes proved one of the most powerful solvents of old forms of conviviality. When new forms of entertainment were conceived they were more likely to have gentry behaviour as their prototype than to emerge from a distinctive awareness of the town as community. The town feast, which enjoyed a short-lived popularity under Charles II, illustrates the point neatly. It was modelled on the equivalent feasts that had been developed for members of the gentry community of a particular county, normally held in London.[218] At Oxford, where Anthony Wood participated in a couple of feasts as a native of the town, the idea emanated from the town clerk, John Paynton, who conceived it as a deliberate response to an event organized by the men of Berkshire.[219] The town feast did retain some of the old connotations of amity and charity:

[215] P. J. Corfield, *The Impact of English Towns, 1700-1800* (Oxford, 1982), 51 ff.
[216] Everitt, 'The English Urban Inn'. [217] Ibid. 167.
[218] These are known largely through the sermons that were printed after the celebrations. See e.g., Samuel Annesley, *The First Dish at the Wil-shire Feast* (London, 1655); George Hickes, *The Moral Shechinah* (London, 1682) [the Yorkshire feast in Bowchurch]; William Bolton, *Josephs Entertainment of his Brethren* (London, 1684) [Herefordshire feast at St Mary-le-Bow].
[219] Anthony Wood, *Life and Times*, ii, 154, 193, 201, 229, 255.

it was, says Wood, undertaken 'for the continuance of our mutual society and amity', and the profits were used for the binding of local apprentices.[220] However, the tone and language of the events revealed how much closer to the world of the gentry the ordinary prosperous town-dweller was moving. When the county feast declined with the diminishing appeal of the notion of county community, the town feast also atrophied.

As for individual hospitality in the post-Restoration town, it appears to have been clearly identified as a matter of personal preference, just as the courtesy literature asserted it should be. When Parliament debated the excise in 1670–1, the idea of a tax on home-brewing was hotly contested by MPs. One ground for their objection was that hospitality would suffer, since men brewed to provide entertainment. However, a variant clause proposed that brewing should only be subject to excise 'in Corporations', thereby protecting the country gentleman. This, observed Sir Richard Temple, was a wholly sensible arrangement since 'generally they keep no hospitality in Corporations as the gentlemen do'.[221] While Sir Richard must not be taken too seriously, it would seem that a reputation for generosity and openness, always a limited commodity in the towns, was considered most uncommon in the later years of the Stuarts.

---

[220] Ibid. i. 462.
[221] Anchitell Grey, *Debates of the House of Commons from the Year 1667 to the Year 1694*, 10 vols. (London, 1763), i. 398.

9
Hospitality Among the Populace

IN a study overwhelmingly concerned with the élite as the active players in the social interactions associated with household entertainment, the mass of the English populace have thus far only appeared as the largely passive recipients of largess, or the victims of its absence. Since prosperity and a large household were necessary conditions for full openness of hospitality, the exclusion of those social groups below the gentry, clergy, and mercantile élites might be thought to be an appropriate reflection of the realities of 'good housekeeping'. Moreover, that preoccupation with the culture of honour that was so significant a feature of the aristocracy is often seen as irrelevant to the rest of the social order. Yeomen, for example, are often claimed to have distanced themselves from their gentry neighbours not so much by wealth, as by deliberate choices about modes of consumption, by a reluctance to sustain the 'port and countenance' of a gentleman.[1] Since a part of that 'port' was at least the semblance of openness in entertainment, it might well be argued that the idea of hospitality was perceived as part of a pattern of conspicuous consumption alien to the middling and lesser sort in early modern England.

However, it is unwise to dismiss the majority of the population in so cavalier a manner. The clearly expressed views of ordinary villagers and townsmen as guests have already been considered: notions of right, custom, and due behaviour deeply influenced their behaviour towards their superiors, and there is no reason to suppose that they were not equally influential when it fell to them to play an active role as hosts. Moreover, the moralists were

---

[1] J. Youings, *Sixteenth-Century England* (London, 1984), 121–3.

never wearied of arguing that all men could play a part in the reception of the needy and the poor in Christ, even if the gesture could be little more than symbolic: the offering of a cup of cold water, or the indication of where the suffering might find shelter. Custom and precept, therefore, combine to suggest that the actions of ordinary Englishmen as hosts are worth exploration.

The invaluable William Harrison once again offers an explicit guide to the activities of villagers and urban artisans as hosts. Husbandmen, he claimed:

do exceed after their manner [in feasting]; especially at bridals, purifications of women, and such odd meetings, where it is incredible to tell what meat is consumed and spent, each one bringing such a dish, or so many, as his wife and he do consult upon, but always with this consideration that the leefer friend shall have the better provision.[2]

This custom of communal celebration, in which the host was only responsible for the arrangement of the setting, and possibly for bread and drink, was not replicated in the towns, where some ordinary artisans celebrated to excess: 'yet the wiser sort can handle the matter well enough in these junketings and therefore their frugality deserveth commendation. To conclude, both the artificer and the husbandman are sufficiently liberal and very friendly at their tables.' Apart from the intermittence of entertainment by the populace, Harrison was most fascinated by the contrast between their behaviour at table and that of the élite. Country inhabitants were given to 'very much babbling (except it be here and there some odd yeoman) with whom he is thought to be the merriest that talketh most of ribaldry, or the wisest man that speaketh fastest among them'.[3] The primness of the Essex parson clearly visible, he condemned such behaviour, and the drunkenness that often accompanied it, but he also acknowledged the spontaneous generosity of 'the wealthier sort' in the countryside who, 'if the friends . . . come to their houses from afar, they are commonly so welcome till they depart, as upon the first day of their coming'. It is also at this moment that Harrison points the contrast with the town, discussed in an earlier chapter: for all the enthusiasm that townsmen might show for

---

[2] William Harrison, *The Description of England*, ed. F. J. Furnivall, 2 vols. (New Shakspere Soc., ser. 6: 1, 5, London, 1908), i. 150.
[3] Ibid. i. 151.

feasting, their daily entertainment of guests was constrained by space and habit, so that short visits and few meals were the approved modes in London and other 'good towns'.

We are here presented with an image of Elizabethan culture in which general hospitality was most commonly associated with specific celebrations of rites of passage, with town and countryside differentiated only by the method of organizing and financing entertainment. Routine generosity to friends was a feature of the countryside among those with sufficient wealth, but was not expected in the same easy manner within the towns. The few other observers who chose to reflect on the preoccupations of the populace tell a similar, if less detailed, tale. Carew in his *Survey of Cornwall* emphasized that celebrations were the main occasions of collective entertainment, though his interest was primarily in the calendric cycle of harvest feasts and dedication wakes, the latter of which offered the opportunity for 'entertaining such forrayne acquaintance, as will not fayle, when their like time cometh about, to requite them with the like kindness'.[4] Others endeavoured to separate yeomen from the rest, assimilating wealthy countrymen to Harrison's image of general beneficence to visitors, while arguing that the ordinary populace remained hostile to outsiders. Tristam Risdon in his *Chorographical Description of Devon*, written in the mid-seventeenth century, though not published until 1714, praised the freeholders for keeping up good hospitality even to strangers, while arguing that the inhabitants of the county were 'laborious, rough and unpleasant to Strangers travelling these ways'.[5]

II

There are good reasons for the historian to follow the pattern presented by Harrison and Carew, and consider first those occasions for popular hospitality sanctioned by the cycles of the calendar and by rites of passage. The principal argument here would be evidential: there is a dearth of evidence on all aspects

---

[4] Carew, *The Survey of Cornwall* (London, 1602), fo. 69.
[5] Tristam Risdon, *The Chorographical Description or Survey of the County of Devon*, 2 pts. (London, 1714), but written c.1640, 2, App., 6.

of popular entertainment, especially before the Civil War, but at least occasional feasting received some attention from contemporaries, while the normal routines of household behaviour have largely passed unobserved from the historical record. In the case of specific festivities the problem is not so much an absence of information, as the fact that most of the material derives from the comments of antiquaries far removed in time and in spirit from the celebrations themselves, or of godly divines whose impulse was one of fixed hostility to all forms of plebeian rejoicing.

The antiquaries of the late seventeenth and eighteenth centuries took an especial interest in the investigation of calendric entertainments which comprised much of the recreation of early modern Englishmen. Almost any of these junketings could be associated with hospitality or commensality, but three occasions seem more commonly linked with concern for shared feeding than others. The first was the Christmas season, at which popular and élite modes of behaviour were perhaps more closely linked than during the rest of the year. Thomas Tusser argued that Christmas was above all the season when,

> At Christmas we banket, the rich with the poore,
> who then (but the miser) but openeth [h]is doore?[6]

And in an early riposte to the Puritan attack on Christmas celebration he claimed,

> Take custome from feasting, what commeth then last,
> where one hath a dinner, a hundred shall fast.[7]

Tusser's vision may have suffered from a measure of idealization, but there is considerable supporting evidence to indicate that the Twelve Days were a period of generous entertainment according to the abilities of different ranks of society. In the 1770s Hutchinson still described Twelfth Day as distinguished in the north for its general gathering of neighbours, and in Cumberland Housman noted that the 'greatest hospitality prevails among the villagers: every family is provided with goose pies, minced

---

[6] Tusser, *Five Hundred Points of Good Husbandrie*, ed. W. Payne and S. J. Heritage (London, 1878), 62.
[7] Ibid. 64.

pies and ale'.[8] It was, as John Taylor the waterpoet remarked, a common feature of the festival that 'the rich did feast . . . the Poore rejoiced and all sorts of people in every house made me [Christmas] heartily welcome'.[9] Although public elements in the Christmas festivities were not uncommon, with mumming, sword-dancing, wassailing, and carolling all emphasizing the communal nature of the celebrations, the focus was primarily upon the household and the openness of its giving. It was this household element in the Christmas rejoicings that ensured a measure of continuity in tradition, even at the height of the Commonwealth campaign against the festival. Despite those precisians who, according to John Taylor, thought 'Plumb-Pottage was meer Popery . . . Mince-Pies were Reliques of the Whore of Babylon, and a Goose, a Turkey or a Capon, were marks of the Beast', the domestic entertainments associated with the Twelve Days proved remarkably resilient even during the Interregnum.[10]

Similar observations can be made about the second group of calendric entertainments: the feasts of the agricultural year, notably harvest home and sheep-shearing. They also provided the opportunity for licensed misrule, the obvious release from stressful demands of agricultural routine, and the excuse to be freed from labour for several days.[11] However, in the context of hospitality, they clearly have a rather different character from the Christmas rejoicings in which the attempt to act as generous hosts was apparently widely diffused through the society. The hosts on these occasions were the élite of rural society: tenant farmers and substantial yeomen, if not local gentlemen. As suggested earlier, the harvest entertainment assumed the status of a right for the participants, a right that could in certain circumstances even acquire a legal force. At Eastbourne, the occupiers of the great tithes were bound to provide a public

---

[8] Hutchinson, *The View of Northumberland*, 2 vols. (Newcastle, 1778), App., 5; J. Housman, *A Topographical Description of Cumberland, Westmorland, Lancashire and a part of the West Riding of Yorkshire* (Carlisle, 1800), 76–7.

[9] John Taylor, *The Complaint of Christmas* (1646) in *Works* (Spenser Soc., 2, 1868), 1.

[10] John Taylor, *Christmas In and Out* (1652), in *Works* (Spenser Soc., 2, 1868), 9.

[11] On the purposes of the calendric festivals, see R. W. Malcolmson, *Popular Recreations in English Society, 1700–1850* (Cambridge, 1973), 75 ff.

breakfast for local farmers and their servants on the first three Sundays in August, and when they failed in their duty Chancery upheld the farmers.[12] Such a case was unusual, but it underlines the connection between harvest feasting and the old arrangement of boon works. The residual claims to forms of boon during harvest that sometime surface as late as the seventeenth century are also of relevance here.[13]

Whatever the customary or legally binding rights that might underlie harvest home, the commentators are usually eager to emphasize the element of cornucopian generosity offered by farmers to their workers. Henry Best described in the 1640s the bidding of 'all the work folkes and their wives that helped them that harvest' to a meal of boiled beef, apple pies, hot cakes, and ale.[14] Indeed, in some parts of the country more than the immediate labourers were involved: Carew's splendid description of Cornish harvest feasts shows that the wealthy were expected to hold dinners 'whereto [they] invite . . . next neighbours and kinred; and though it beare onely the name of a dinner, yet the ghests take their supper also with them, and consume a great part of the night after in Christmas rule'.[15] Other agrarian festivals, such as the sheep-shearing sung by Tusser:

> At sheepe shearing neighbours none other thing crave,
> but good cheere and welcome like neighbours to have.[16]

or Plough Monday, might also have elements of that hospitality from farmer to labourer that affirmed the values of communal amity, while still acknowledging the ties of deference and authority that were an integral part of the culture. Neighbours expected that they would be junketed on these occasions, and any who were not bidden to share in the generosity showed vigorous resentment. When the wife of one Malter was not asked

---

[12] F. Horsfield, *The History and Antiquities of Sussex*, 2 vols. (Lewes, 1835), i. 297.

[13] See e.g., Aubrey on boons still paid at harvest and plough-time at Bishopstone, Wilts: John Aubrey, *Wiltshire: The Topographical Collections*, ed. J. E. Jackson (Devizes, 1862), 311; also some Sussex examples in *The Book of John Rowe, Steward of the Manors of Lord Bergavenny, 1597–1622*, ed. W. H. Godfrey (Sussex Rec. Soc., 34, 1928), 222, 224.

[14] C. B. Robinson (ed.), *The Rural Economy in Yorkshire 1641, being the Farming and Account Books of Henry Best* (Surtees Soc., 33, 1857), 108.

[15] Carew, *Survey*, fo. 69ᵛ.   [16] Tusser, 178.

to her neighbour's sheep-shearing dinner in 1570 she allegedly 'bewitched two of his sheep; for immediately after they were taken with sickness'.[17]

The third calendric celebration is somewhat distinct from the agrarian feasts or the Christmas season. The wake, or dedication feast or revel, was a more public articulation of community than the latter, and an event less dependent on the goodwill of the wealthy than the former.[18] It could take a variety of forms—a rush-bearing festival focused upon the parish church, a shared ale, an organized meeting for sports and/or dancing, or simply an occasion for eating and drinking in what critics invariably claimed to be excessive quantities. Although sympathetic gentlemen, clerics, and wealthy locals might participate in the wake, the evidence consistently points to this as the most widely existent example of popular revel in which élite influence was insignificant. Its hospitable elements are therefore of particular interest, and are worth considering at some length, since they are less dependent on cultural mimesis than some of the examples so far discussed. It is also fortunate that the very hostility generated by this form of popular junketing has left it rather better recorded than some of the other celebrations of the agrarian year.[19]

The tendency of godly critics in the late sixteenth century to place dedication wakes and parish ales in the same category may indicate a little more than generalized hostility to any form of popular entertainment and drinking that took place on the Sabbath. Although there is little detailed evidence for the organization of wakes in the late Middle Ages, they do appear to have been public events, often focused on the churchyard or the church itself, accompanied by general ale consumption. Churchwardens' accounts occasionally indicate the payment for ingredients designed for public brewing in advance of the

[17] Quoted by K. V. Thomas, *Religion and the Decline of Magic* (London, 1973), 664.

[18] The most useful recent analysis of wakes is in Malcolmson, 16–19, 52–6; much of the early evidence is assembled in J. Brand, *Observations on Popular Antiquities*, 3 vols. (London, 1853), ii, 1–11.

[19] Philip Stubbes, *The Anatomy of Abuses in England*, ed. F. J. Furnivall (New Shakspere Soc., London, 1877), i, 152–3; T. G. Barnes, 'County Politics and a Puritan Cause Célèbre: Somerset Churchales, 1633', *TRHS*, 5th ser., 9 (1959), 103–22.

dedication wake, as well as the church ales.[20] It seems that where church-houses existed, as they did in large numbers in the west, especially in Devon, they were used for all these communal entertainments.[21] It is probable that the form of commensality that accompanied both wakes and ales would often have been that described by John Aubrey in the case of Long Newton in Wiltshire. There an annual feast was held until the Civil War in honour of the giving of common land to the villages by King Athelstan: the beer was brewed collectively at the Haywards or Tele-house, and every commoner sent his own contribution of food to the general entertainment. The remains were distributed to the poor of the township.[22] In the absence of a focus like the church-house, the churchyard must often have proved the venue for dancing and sports, while alehouses or private homes offered appropriate sustenance. An affray at the feast in Goodrich, Hereford, in the early seventeenth century began in the alehouse of Richard Powell, who had laid in special provisions for 'banqueting the chief men' of the parish and locality. However, it spilled over into the neighbouring churchyard, where dancing and music were the centre of the revel.[23]

The Church was, by the early sixteenth century, making a sustained effort to prohibit drinking and eating within sacred precincts. One of Archbishop Warham's general monitions to his diocese at the visitation of 1511–12 was that '*parochiani non faciant aliquas potationes in ecclesiis suis quacumque ratione*'.[24] After the Reformation pressure from the bishops was increased, so that by the 1570s Archibishop Grindal's injunctions for York were attacking any form of consumption, or secular or improper behaviour in church or churchyard. These injunctions clearly were not wholly successful, and the Goodrich case is by no means the latest example of the churchyard being at the heart

[20] F. W. Weaver and G. N. Clark (eds.), *Churchwardens' Accounts of Marston, Spelsbury and Pyrton* (Oxford Rec. Soc., 6, 1925), 25; S. O. Addy, *Church and Manor* (London, 1913), 331.

[21] G. W. Copeland, 'Devonshire Church-Houses', *Transactions of the Devonshire Assoc.*, 92 (1960), 116–23.

[22] John Aubrey, *Collections for the Natural and Topographical History of Wiltshire*, ed. T. Phillips, 2 vols. (Devizes, 1821–38), i. 19.

[23] PRO, STAC 8/234/10.

[24] K. Wood-Legh (ed.), *Kentish Visitations of Archbishop Warham* (Kent Rec. Soc., 24, 1984), 55.

of the organized celebration of the feast.[25] The sorts of affray that were in consequence likely to disturb the sacred precincts were one of those aspects of the revel that tended to unite the godly and respectable in their opposition to the junketings. However, there may have been some gradual change on the issue of eating and drinking. White Kennett, who provides the earliest thorough investigation of the dedication wake, was firmly of the opinion that it had traditionally been the practice to 'adjourn . . . their eating and drinking to the more proper place of publick and private houses'.[26]

The interest of the dedication feast for the study of popular hospitality is that it was apparently seen as a particularly important moment in the year for the community to entertain outsiders. Its chief purpose, says White Kennett, was 'to maintain a Christian spirit of unity and charity, by such sociable and friendly meetings'. This could, of course, involve issues of close neighbourhood, as in Aubrey's ideal vision that wakes 'used to end many quarells between neighbour and neighbour', or the defence of the Rangeworthy revellers, when hauled before Star Chamber for disorder and riot at the wake, that they held their feast 'for preservacon of mutuall amytie . . . and allayinge of strifes, discordes and debates between neighbour and neighbour'. Bishop Piers, defending the Somerset wakes to Laud in 1633, spoke of them as composing differences by allowing the meeting of friends 'for increase of love and amity as being feasts of charity'.[27]

However, the distinctive features were the summoning of friends and relatives from far and near, and the generosity with which they had to be fed. The church ale had also fostered the idea of entertaining outsiders, but there the motive was primarily the need to make profit. As the churchwardens of St Andrew's, Plymouth, expressed it: every man was to have 'such and as many

---

[25] Frere and Kennedy (eds.), *Visitation Articles and Injunctions of the Period of the Reformation*, 3 vols. (Alcuin Club, London, 1910), iii. 291. There are even isolated cases of the church being used for celebrations at a later date, as at Berrington, Shropshire, where an Easter feast was still held as late as 1639: Addy, *Church and Manor*, 332.

[26] White Kennett, *Parochial Antiquities . . . in the Counties of Oxford and Bucks* (Oxford, 1695), 609–10.

[27] John Aubrey, *The Remaines of Gentilisme and Judaisme*, ed. J. Britten (London, 1881), 46; PRO STAC 8/239/3. *CStP Dom 1633–4*, 275.

persons estraungers as they thinke best of theyr Frends and aquaynted men and women for thencressing of the said ile'.[28] But at the wake the custom seems to have been to give food and drink as an expression of communal generosity. Philip Stubbes's bitter disapproval of the riot and licence of wakes does not negate the value of his testimony that friends and 'kynsfolks' were all bidden to these junketings. He believed the burden of entertainment on the individual householder to be 'so muche as the poore men that bear the charges of these feasts and wakesses, are the poorer and keep the Worser houses a long tyme after'.[29] Both Bishop Piers and the Rangeworthy revellers testified to the importance of bidding and feeding friends and kinsmen; but it is the evidence of Carew that is perhaps most valuable. He was clear that the holding of open house for the visitors from neighbouring parishes was an act of reciprocal giving, no doubt costly for each householder in his turn, but requited by a series of returned gifts at other dedication feasts.[30] Occasionally it is possible to confirm this image of communal interchange from other sources: for example, in the early seventeenth century the churchwardens of Mere in Wiltshire entertained 'the summer lord of Gillingham', a neighbouring parish, and his company at their revel.[31] It may be that this expectation of reciprocity between parishes and kinsfolk is one reason why many feasts were not moved to the first Sunday in October, despite the endeavours of the Henrician regime to enforce this arrangement in 1536.[32]

This pattern of hospitality to outsiders remained a deeply entrenched aspect of the wake into the eighteenth century and beyond. Henry Bourne observed in the 1720s that the people at a wake 'deck themselves in their gaudiest Clothes, and have open Doors and splendid Entertainments, for the Reception, and Treating of their Relations and Friends, who visit them on that Occasion, from each neighbouring Town'.[33] At the end of the

---

[28] Worth, *Plymouth Records*, 29. [29] Stubbes, *Anatomy*, i. 152–3.
[30] Carew, *Survey*, fos. 68ᵛ–69.
[31] T. H. Baker, 'Notes on the History of Mere', *Wilts. Arch. Magazine*, 29 (1896–7), 270.
[32] White Kennett, *Parochial Antiquities*, 611; Brand, *Popular Antiquities*, ii. 5–6.
[33] Brand, *Popular Antiquities*, ii. 5.

century Samuel Bamford's memories of his Lancashire childhood took up the same theme: 'Relations living at a distance, old friends and acquaintances, [were] generally invited to the wakes'.[34] It seems legitimate to infer that a pattern of entertainment of outsiders which had survived from the Elizabethan period to the nineteenth century could also be projected backwards in time, and claimed as a probable feature of late medieval wakes as well. It is, however, easier to observe the continuity of the phenomenon than to offer any very satisfactory explanation for it. It is conceivable that in the case of kinsfolk the custom evolved from a parish to express their devotion to the church of their origin. This would have some analogies with the annual pilgrimage to the cathedral, or with the behaviour noted by White Kennett in which dependent chapelries once a year came in procession to the mother church 'with Flags and Streamers, and other ensigns of joy and triumph'.[35] Neighbouring parishes may simply have been drawn into the pattern of hospitality by the popular desire to maximize the number of festivals that were held, reciprocal entertainment providing one legitimization for revel, although a more elaborate theory of the need to extend neighbourly amity beyond the bounds of one village is a possible alternative.

On the other hand, it does not seem possible from the surviving evidence to argue that the feasting was justified as a form of giving to the stranger and/or the poor. Bishop Piers, in his defence of Somerset revels, was eager to stress that the poor were relieved by these events, 'the richer sort keeping then open house', and it became part of the official Caroline case in favour of the wakes that they alleviated the needs of the suffering members of the community.[36] The openness of houses might in some cases, no doubt, lead to the entertainment of the poor and the outsider: Bamford claimed that in Middleton even decently clad strangers would be invited in as they passed the open doors where men were feasting their kin.[37] But, as often, these two groups seem at best the residuary legatees

---

[34] Samuel Bamford, *Autobiography, my Early Days*, ed. W. H. Chaloner (London, 1967), 155.
[35] White Kennett, *Parochial Antiquities*, 598.
[36] *C.St.P. Dom. 1633–4*, 275.   [37] Bamford, *Autobiography*, 155.

of junketing designed primarily to affirm community with neighbours and relatives.

Even the one detailed piece of evidence on the form of wake feasts in the sixteenth century indicates the importance of these occasions as a way of articulating a particular perception of community. Carew notes with approbation that, although the guests were often rustic and rude, yet they 'may for their discreete judgement in precedence and preseance, read a lesson to our civilest gentry'. At the feasts it was not wealth that determined seating or influence, but age, 'so as (save in a verie notorious disproportion of estates) the younger rich reckoneth it a shame sooner than a grace to step or sit before the elder honest'.[38] Only in circumstances where both neighbours and outsiders were reasonably well known, and their status readily determined, was such an arrangement likely to be successful. Although accounts of revels that emerge in the legal sources suggest rather less decorum than Carew's, his analysis is compatible with the formal deference given to age in the public activities of the village community, such as the provision of juries. It is also worth observing that this may have been one aspect of village behaviour easily subverted by growing social differentiation in the seventeenth century.

Wakes remained a major form of popular hospitality in many parts of the country until at least the beginning of the nineteenth century. However, unlike Christmas or Harvest Home, which seem to have been celebrated almost universally except during the crises of the mid-seventeenth century, the pattern of dedication feasts was distinctly regional. The hostility of the magistracy and many others of the 'better sort' in the early seventeenth century, led to suppression of revels as well as ales well before the outbreak of the Civil War.[39] Thereafter they were 'well laid down' for a time even in areas of strength such as Cheshire. After 'the late confusions', antiquarians such as White Kennett and Aubrey believed that they never revived in the eastern counties or in parts of the west, though they quickly regained their vitality in the north

---

[38] Carew, *Survey*, fo. 71.
[39] David Underdown, *Revel, Riot, and Rebellion: Popular Politics and Culture in England, 1603–1660* (Oxford, 1985), 44–63.

and the Midlands.[40] Gibson argued that, despite Charles I's attempts to revive wakes in the *Book of Sports*, they never fully recovered in those areas where the magistracy had been strongly opposed to their celebration.[41]

The geographical theory can be tested partially from eighteenth-century sources, such as Bridges who recorded 206 wakes for the 290 parishes of Northamptonshire, or Rawlinson, who in his survey of parochial antiquities in Oxfordshire noted ninety-four in his 193 parishes.[42] The northern antiquarians offer ample qualitative evidence of the near-universal celebrations of wakes north of the Trent.[43] Moreover, wakes certainly seem to have vanished from most of East Anglia, from Devon, and from areas around London. There are, however, two difficulties: one is the lack of detailed evidence from much of the west, even in the eighteenth century; the other, to establish how universal was the celebration of wakes *before* the beginnings of the campaign to reform manners in the late sixteenth century. Essex, for example, does not in the post-Reformation period ever appear to have had a strong tradition of holding revels, and the same may be true of Suffolk. Harrison, writing in the 1570s, noted with approval that in his county the 'superfluous number of idle wakes' was diminished.[44] In Oxfordshire in the eighteenth century there was a distinct division between the Thames Valley parishes, which had few wakes, and those of the north of the county, which almost all continued with celebrations. Was this an example of Puritan repression that had killed popular festivities in one area but not another? If so, the geography is somewhat surprising, since the north of the county was focused on the

---

[40] William Smith, *The Vale Royall of England, or County Palatine of Chester* (London, 1656), 20; White Kennett, *Parochial Antiquities*, 610.

[41] R. Burn, *Ecclesiastical Law*, 2 vols. (London, 1763), i. 277.

[42] *The History of Northamptonshire: Compiled from the MSS Collections of the Late Learned Antiquary John Bridges*, comp. P. Whalley, 2 vols. (Oxford, 1791); F. N. Davis (ed.), *Parochial Collections for Oxfordshire: Made by Wood and Rawlinson*, 3 vols. (Oxford Rec. Soc., 2, 4, 11, 1920, 1922, 1929).

[43] Hutchinson, *Northumberland*, ii. 26 n. Borlase also claimed that wakes were almost universal in Cornwall in the 1750s: W. Borlase, *The Natural History of Cornwall* (Oxford, 1758), 301.

[44] K. Wrightson, 'The Puritan Reformation of Manners, with Special Reference to the Counties of Lancashire and Essex, 1640–1660', Cambridge Ph.D. dissertation (1974), 37–8; Harrison, *Description of England*, i. 32.

radical community of Banbury and was partially clothier country, usually noted for its rejection of tradition.[45]

It may be that the godly had greater enduring effect in amending the form of revels than in wholly suppressing them in those communities and areas where they had traditionally been important. The displacement of celebration from church to churchyard and thence to individual homes and alehouses involved some transition from the sacred to the secular and from the public to the private spheres. Of course, the processions and rush-bearings always continued as public elements in the entertainments, and the account of Bamford reveals how collective the revels remained at a very late date.[46] But Bamford also shows that the church was only notionally at the heart of the festival, since the rushes were no longer brought within the precincts, and even in the seventeenth century White Kennett found it difficult to identify the festival as religious. No doubt this was in part the logical development of popular attitudes, but the attempt by the godly magistracy to separate church and revellers may also have contributed. After the promulgation of the *Book of Sports*, for example, there was a petition from the Somerset magistrates that revels should only involve 'civil feasting between neighbour and neighbour in their houses, and the orderly use of manly exercises'. It may well be that this is one of those aspects of popular culture that Wrightson is correct to argue retreated from the communal culture of the churchyard to the fragmented environment of the alehouse.[47]

III

It will be recalled that William Harrison, the Essex parson, chose to concentrate not upon wakes or ales, but upon the feasting and entertainment with which ordinary Englishmen accompanied rites of passage. Despite the very patchy evidence available to assess the behaviours of hosts and guests on these occasions, we can construct some tentative image of the significance of

---

[45] *Parochial Collections for Oxfordshire*, i. 1.
[46] Bamford, *Autobiography*, 155-6.
[47] *C.St.P. Dom. 1633-4*, 351; Wrightson, 'Puritan Reformation', 38-40.

giving and receiving hospitality at these moments of celebration. Sociability at births and churchings seems to have been widespread, especially among women; indeed, foreign commentators such as Van Meteren believed that much of the gadding and gossiping of English wives was bound up with the rituals associated with birth.[48] Much information on the subject comes from the determined attempt by a few town councils to regulate the entertainment that was customary on the grounds that it impoverished families and encouraged idleness. Long before the full flood of reformation of manners at the end of the sixteenth century, Chester was using the conventions of sumptuary legislation to limit the cost of food and drink brought to women lying in childbed, and the reciprocal giving that was customary at the churching by which 'meane persons in substance many tymes strayne themselves to such chargis more then their habilities may well sustayne'.[49] Later in the century Kendal corporation insisted as part of its programme for the reform of the poor that there should be no general drinking or 'wyffe kyrkynge' at the churching, but only a dinner for up to twelve persons. Kendal was more permissive than Chester on the subject of gifts, but 'duringe onely the tyme off beinge in Childbed', not after a wife's purification.[50] In 1568, Leicester made a similar order, insisting that there should be no feast at any churching, except for one mess of meat for the midwife and 'gosseps', so that the poor could be relieved and superfluous charge avoided.[51]

These urban orders when placed together suggest several things about the entertainment that accompanied childbirth. It would appear to be commonplace, to involve reciprocal giving (although the mention of a churching ale suggests that it could be a self-financing occasion for the hostess if she were sufficiently poor),

---

[48] W. B. Rye (ed.), *England as Seen by Foreigners in the Days of Elizabeth and James I* (London, 1865), 72.

[49] R. H. Morris, *Chester in the Plantagenet and Tudor Reigns* (Chester, 1893), 336.

[50] R. S. Ferguson (ed.), *A Boke off Recorde . . . within the Town of Kirkbiekendall* (Cumbs. and Westmors. Antiq. and Arch. Soc., E.S. 7, 1892), 89.

[51] Bateson (ed.), *Records of the Borough of Leicester*, 3 vols. (Cambridge, 1899–1905), iii. 122. There was a virtually identical order for London in 1565; Archer, 'Governors and Governed in late Sixteenth-Century London', Oxford D.Phil. thesis (1988), 64.

and to extend well down the ranks of society, since the poverty of participants was a cause for anxiety. Two of the examples drawn from the north also point to an issue that is relevant in all rites of passage: the scale of public or quasi-public celebration of births, marriages, and funerals seems greater there than in the south. The antiquary, Waldron, describing Manx christenings, gives a vivid account of the bidding of the whole country to the ceremony, who then return to the house 'and spend the whole day, and a good part of the night, in feasting'.[52] In the eighteenth century, and no doubt earlier, it was customary on the Borders and in Scotland to ask a great number of people to the christening, and then to have a collection to defray the cost of the feast if the couple were poor.[53] Although commentators believed by then that this practice was confined to the north, the notion of such contributions to entertainment was not, as Harrison reminds us, alien in the south, and certainly the custom of bride-ale was to be found very widely in the sixteenth century.[54]

The northern examples also serve to remind us of the obvious point that christening, unlike the more intimate, feminine moments of birth and churching, was an event to be celebrated publicly with the bidding of neighbours and kin, both male and female, as witnesses as well as celebrants. Exclusion from a legitimate role in these events could cause deep resentment, and the wicked fairy of the Sleeping Beauty legend found her counterpart in the occasional witchcraft allegation. In 1599, for example, Anne Kerke of Broken Wharf, London, was charged with tormenting a child because she was not invited to its christening by a hostile neighbour.[55]

Occasionally even childbirth could acquire the status of an event requiring the celebratory participation of the whole community. At Eastbourne as late as the Civil War there was a custom which required the lords of the manor, at the safe delivery of any child of a substantial member of the community, to provide 'sops and ale' for the congregation in a room next to

[52] G. Waldron, *A Description of the Isle of Man*, ed. W. Harrison (Manx Soc., 11, 1865), 60.

[53] Brand, *Popular Antiquities*, ii. 81.

[54] Harrison, *Description of England*, i. 150.

[55] *The Triall of Maister Dorrell* (London, 1599), 100.

the church.[56] This was the subject of a petition to Parliament in 1640, in which the three lords of the manor claimed that the custom offended principally because the congregation left church after the second lesson to devour the meal. This would suggest that ceremonies surrounding the birth of a child could easily become one of those areas of conflict between the godly and those elements in the populace that wished to maintain tradition. This may well be the case when public ritual was involved, though many Puritans seem to have accepted the moment of christening as entirely appropriate for the giving of hospitality. Ralph Josselin noted with pride on the occasion of the birth of his eldest child that he 'entertayned my neighbors all about it cost me 6li and 13s 4d at least'.[57] Since Josselin was not in general much given to hospitality this grand gesture of neighbourhood is particularly revealing. The cost of the occasion no doubt derived partly from the numbers bidden, but also from the fare that had to be provided both at the celebration and to take away afterwards. A character in Brathwait's *Whimzies* had to offer 'store of biskets, wafers and carewayes' to his neighbours, and allow the wives to carry away the remains in their pockets at the end of the day.[58]

The popular celebration of marriage, though marked by its own specific rites and customs, seems essentially socially analogous to christening. Kin, friends, and neighbours were the obvious recipients of hospitality, and guests performed, as they still do, the dual roles of witness and celebrant. The witnessing function is, however, seen at its most specific not at the marriage ceremony, but at the moment of marriage contract, which even after the Reformation assumed a binding importance in the eyes of the Church and in popular culture. In the north, contract was not just a matter of formal declaration before witnesses, but was accompanied by the ceremony of hand-fasting. This is vividly described in a Durham deposition of 1573: neighbours of Janet Ferry were invited to dine with her father—a large group of them since four messes were involved. Some of the guests were, in the

---

[56] Horsfield, *Sussex*, i. 297.
[57] A. Macfarlane (ed.), *The Diary of Ralph Josselin* (London, 1976), 12.
[58] Richard Brathwait, *Whimzies: Or a New Cast of Characters* (London, 1631), 192.

words of the deponent 'of the man's partie', some of Janet's. After the meal, Janet's grandfather led the young couple outside and 'dyd handfast them' before the company.[59]

While witnessing might create a need for entertainment at either marriage contract or marriage ceremony, the conviviality involved was in the main purely celebratory. A rare illustration such as Hofnaegel's painting, which is probably of a wedding in Bermondsey in Elizabeth's reign, suggests an atmosphere that is both open and informal, with the sexes mingling freely in a mixed pattern of eating, drinking, and dancing.[60] The mood of such a country wedding is also evoked by the author of *Choice, Chance and Change* (1606), who describes the squire who is father of the bride as providing a feast that was 'a great meeting for all the gallants of both genders in the Country'.[61] Yeomen fathers, and even husbandmen, seem to have endeavoured to do the same on a more modest scale. Robert Plot observed that, in the late seventeenth century, Oxfordshire weddings were still celebrated with this sort of public entertainment.[62] As with christenings, exclusion of neighbours from such public conviviality could cause animus: when Jane Milburne did not ask Dorothy Strangers to her wedding supper in Newcastle in 1663, she was subsequently plagued by cats whom she believed to be her neighbour disguised to perform *maleficium*.[63]

One aspect of the celebration that does appear to have changed with social status was the method of financing the wedding. While gentry fathers, even as lowly as the squire, were expected to reach some agreement to defray the costs between them, further down the social scale some form of bride-ale became the accepted mode.[64] A true bride-ale involved, as did other ales, some element of self-financing: it began with the right granted to the

---

[59] J. Raine (ed.), *Depositions and Other Ecclesiastical Proceedings in the Courts of Durham* (Surtees Soc., 21, 1845), 241.

[60] See Plate 6. There is some uncertainty about the occasion depicted: hence the illustration is now referred to as 'The Fête at Bermondsey'.

[61] Nicholas Breton, *Choice, Chance and Change* (London, 1606). See also Robinson, *Rural Economy*, 117.

[62] Robert Plot, *The Natural History of Oxfordshire* (Oxford, 1677), 200-1.

[63] Raine, *Depositions from the Castle of York*, 112-14.

[64] There seems to have been no firmly fixed convention among prosperous families about the payment of wedding costs: often the matter was agreed at the time the contract was drawn up.

parties involved to brew and sell a special ale as a way of raising money not only for hospitality at the wedding, but to provide initial support within marriage. This arrangement did not necessarily preclude the expenditure of considerable sums by either the father of the bride or the groom. In a Suffolk dispute on inheritance in the Court of Requests it was stated by a variety of witnesses that Joan Colby's father had paid all the wedding costs, save for one bullock and some breadcorn, presumably the bridegroom's contribution.[65] This, however, had not prevented both father and groom from procuring 'divers of his frindes to spende there money at the saide dynner'. The importance of the occasion, incidentally, is reflected in the apparent accuracy of the witnesses' memories nineteen years afterwards. The full custom was perhaps at its strongest in Wales and Scotland: hence the disapproving comments that are to be found in the literature on 'Welsh weddings' or 'penny weddings' north of the Scottish border.[66] But it was, in various forms, also commonplace in England: the court rolls of Halesowen for 1573, for example, forbade the brewing of 'above twelve strike of mault, and that the said persons so married shall not keep nor have above eight messe of persons at his dinner'.[67]

Those corporations that sought to restrict the wasteful behaviour of the populace at churchings also took a predictable interest in the extravagance of the bride-ale. Chester forbade its citizens to gad to Welsh weddings outside the city limits, or to incite others to gather for ales by holding them within the city.[68] Kendal in 1575 ordered that no wedding should be accompanied by general or public drinking, 'onlie made fframyd and devysed . . . mooste chefflye ffor takynge off moneye', though the corporation did defer to public sentiment to the extent of permitting 'offerands or bryde hawes' under licence from the mayor. There was also an attempt to limit the numbers attending the bridal feast to eighty persons, an interesting indication of the scale of customary entertainment.[69] Later attempts by Kendal to control licence and waste were predictably more severe: in the early seventeenth century, dinners were limited to twelve persons

---

[65] PRO, Req. 2/199/66.   [66] Brand, *Popular Antiquities*, ii. 145, 148.
[67] Ibid. ii. 143.   [68] Morris, *Chester*, 334–5.
[69] Ferguson, *Kirkbiekendal*, 86–8.

and no drinkings were permitted before or after the marriage.[70] However, in the long run local custom seems to have triumphed, for gift bidding and ale sales were still common in the Restoration period. Even in the eighteenth century antiquarians observed the popularity of bid-weddings not only in Scotland but in other upland zones such as the Lake District and northern Wales.[71]

The entertainment associated with rites of passage at death is a somewhat more complex phenomenon. The purpose of bidding and feeding large groups of kin, friends, and neighbours to christening or marriage seems self-evidently celebratory, that of receiving all who would attend a funeral less so. But there is no doubt that many relatively humble men and women felt themselves deeply obliged to be lavish with funeral hospitality. Some gave detailed consideration to the matter in their wills: more seem to have trusted their executors to conform to appropriate custom.[72] Adam Martindale rarely records elaborate entertainment in his diary of the 1650s and 1660s, but his father's funeral provided a notable exception. All men who came to the house 'to fetch his corpse thence (beggars not excepted) were entertained with good meat, piping hote, and strong ale in great plentie'. After the burial a great dinner was held at the tavern for as many friends and kin as the room would hold, and there was food and drink left over for the poor outside. The whole occasion filled Martindale with a justifiable pride that the family had 'done well' by his father.[73]

The categories of those who might be entertained at the burial were, as this case suggests, very diverse. Kin evidently had some right to be present, and wills sometimes refer to a 'dinner for my kinsfolk and friends', such as that ordained by George Derrington of Harlow. Elizabeth Stow, the mother of the chronicler, left 10*s.* for 'my children and fryndes to drincke withall after my buryall'. The ambiguous term 'friends' was often supplemented by that of neighbours: Robert Robinson left the large sum of £30 'to be spent uppon a dynner . . . amongst my good neighbours, that

---

[70] Ferguson, *Kirkbiekendal.* 90–1, 165.

[71] *The Gentleman's Magazine*, iv. 86; *The Cambrian Register* (1796), 430.

[72] C. Gittings, *Death, Burial and the Individual in Early Modern England* (London, 1984), 7–19.

[73] R. Parkinson (ed.), *The Life of Adam Martindale* (Chetham Soc., O.S. 4, 1845), 119–20.

accompany my body to the buryall'.[74] Neighbours, both poor and rich, were intended to be the beneficiaries of the 'solemn drinking' at the funeral of John Coult of Heydon in Essex in 1561, while the 'better sort' among the neighbours were fed according to a funeral account for Isaac Menton of Kent in 1638.[75] Sometimes the occupation of an individual served to define a particular group of friends as important: William Cowley, one of the Queen's gunners at Berwick left bread for the poor in 1580, but also 6s. 8d. for a 'banket upon my fellowes and frendes the day of my buryall'. Londoners not infrequently left sums of money for a 'recrayson' to the members of their company, usually with the stipulation that they had to attend the burial.[76]

But in addition to those who might be given hospitality for the sake of friendship we must, of course, acknowledge the abiding importance of the entertainment of the poor at funerals. Martindale indicates pride that even beggars were fed, thereby, of course, associating himself with the long history of funeral doles. In the 1590s the godly ministers of Chester, complaining about the survival of a variety of popish practices in the diocese, pointed out that at burials poor neighbours were still 'made partakers of the ded manse dowle or Banquet of Charitie'.[77] It remained far more common in mid- and late sixteenth-century wills to instruct executors to give food and alms to the poor, than to arrange a specific funeral dinner for friends. The associations of dole-giving with both Catholic theology and indiscriminate relief of the unworthy seems to have taken some considerable time to penetrate the consciousness of ordinary Englishmen. Even in godly Essex, it was still very common in the late 1570s to find gifts of bread, cheese, and drink being ordained for the poor in attendance at the funeral.[78] Sometimes a measure of

---

[74] F. G. Emmison (ed.), *Wills of the County of Essex: 1558–77*, 3 vols. (Washington, 1982–6), iii. no. 1015; John Stow, *Survey of London*, ed. C. L. Kingsford, 2 vols. (Oxford, 1908), i. xlv; M. Campbell, *The English Yeoman* (London, 1967), 312.

[75] Emmison, *Essex Wills*, ii. no. 452; Gittings, 157.

[76] J. C. Hodgson (ed.), *Durham Wills and Inventories, pt. iii* (Surtees Soc., 112, 1906), 85; I. Darlington (ed.), *London Consistory Court Wills: 1492–1547* (London Rec. Soc., 3, 1967), 80, 87–8, 137.

[77] *Chetham Miscellany V* (1875), 5.

[78] Emmison, *Essex Wills*, iii. Archer points out that the dole survived in London wills of the late Elizabethan period largely because it did not need to be linked with prayers for the dead: Archer, 'Governors and Governed', 222.

differentiation was introduced in order to protect executors from indiscriminate demands upon them: one of the funeral accounts for Berkshire differentiates between poorer neighbours who drank at the church, and the richer who were entertained at home, and it was common to specify that food doles should be given only to the poor of the parish. George Derrington of Harlow was even more precise: money dole was distributed to local householders at 4*d*. each, householders from elsewhere at 2*d*., and the rest at 1*d*. Outsiders, whether poor or rich were to be entertained 'in the church', kin and friends at home.[79] While doles seem to have been in decline in the south by the early seventeenth century, they were still mentioned in over a third of Lincolnshire accounts for the decade before the Civil War, and are to be found in parts of the north at the end of the century.[80]

The form of funeral hospitality seems essentially similar throughout the early modern period. Friends, kin, and bidden guests would come to the house of the deceased for a drinking before the burial, even consuming wine and so on in the presence of the corpse.[81] If, as in the case of Martindale's father, the 'forth coming' was self-consciously public, then men of any standing or none would be encouraged to accompany the corpse with the inducement of food and drink. In the north-east, the public entertainment associated with burial was still known in this period as the 'Arvel' dinner, and derived from the notion that there had to be an open presentation of the corpse to the community as witness by the heir that there had been no foul play in the death.[82] The drinking in which most of those present participated after the burial might be held in an appropriate public house, or at the house once more, though in the first half of the sixteenth century the churchyard or even the church was still a possible venue. There is the famous example from Stow of Margaret Atkinson, who in her will of 1544 left money for a dinner to be held in church on the Sunday after her burial, 'desiring all the parish, as well rich as poor, to take part thereof;

[79] Emmison, *Essex Wills*, iii. no. 1015.
[80] Gittings, 241. Aubrey suggests that they continued in the west of England until the Civil War: *Gentilisme and Judaisme*, 36.
[81] Gittings, 154.   [82] Hutchinson, *Northumberland*, i. App. 20.

and a table to be set up in the midst of the church'.[83] That this
was still a popular notion at this period is suggested by the
complaint of the churchwardens of Willesborough to Warham's
visitors in 1512 that parishioners would not make proper
offerings at churchings or obits, 'bicause they cannot drink in the
churche'.[84] But the retreat from church to churchyard and
thence to other secular establishments does not seem to have
diminished the commitment to funeral conviviality.

The purposes of these rituals are somewhat more difficult to
penetrate than in our earlier examples. A concern for neighbourly
reputation is perhaps one of the most visible, a reputation which
in the case of ordinary yeoman or husbandmen was no doubt to
be found in feeding the community generously. Some of the
indiscriminate dole-giving to the poor may indicate that even men
of this standing were not immune from the idea usually associated
with the nobility, that great crowds at a funeral were an indicator
of status. The unlovely impulse to affirm influence even in death
was presumably softened by the commemorative nature of the
funeral feast; Robert Jennings, a London draper, indicated this
when he left money to his company, not only for a dinner at the
time of his funeral, but for two or three thereafter.[85] Although
the tradition of the month's mind survived the Reformation less
well than dole-giving, it still indicates that feeding and drinking
had been seen as an integral part of refreshing the collective
memory of an individual.

A closer analysis suggests that there was often an implicit desire
to reaffirm the identity of the community through commensality
after it had been fractured by the death of a member. Van Gennep
argued that this was a principal objective of funeral ritual, which
sought 'to reunite all the surviving members with each other
. . . in the same way that a chain which has been broken by the
disappearance of one of its links must be rejoined'.[86] Yet this
implies too sharp a dissociation between the living and the dead
to explain fully the experience of early modern Englishmen. A
more appropriate insight can perhaps be disinterred from two

---

[83] John Strype's edn. of Stow, *Survey*, i. 259.
[84] Wood-Legh, *Kentish Visitations*, 156.
[85] Campbell, *English Yeoman*, 312; *London Consistory Wills*, 88.
[86] A. Van Gennep, *The Rites of Passage* (Chicago, 1960), 165.

diverse pieces of contemporary evidence. Anthony Wood reports a very curious funeral ritual in pre-Civil War Oxford. On the day before an academic funeral the university bellman went from college to college giving notice of the event, 'dressed in the deceased's robes and square cap', as though he were bidding men to his own funeral.[87] In the same period an Essex yeoman, Richard Meade, instructed his executors to summon his former neighbours together annually for a dinner to be held *on his behalf*.[88] Both these examples suggest that the funeral rites could be conceived as hospitality given by the dead to the living: a coda that both represented a last farewell, and affirmed the communal integration of the living and the dead. Since the Reformation, with its denial of purgatory and of the efficacy of prayers for the dead, destroyed the idea of spiritual reciprocity between the two it is tempting to argue that men sought by other ritual means to perpetuate a view of community beyond the grave.[89]

Yet while we have some evidence of this perception of unity beyond the grave, and a stronger articulation of the need for good fellowship in this world, we cannot assume that there were no changes in the concept of the utility of funeral cheer throughout three centuries of English history. The doles which had been almost universal among men of sufficient wealth before the Reformation were slowly eroded. Even before their final demise it may well be that their purpose was changing in the minds of testators. Essex wills of the 1560s and 1570s frequently spread food doles over an extended period of time, to ensure that the poor had relief on fixed occasions.[90] Even when a funeral dinner or funeral-day dole was involved, the language of the will sometimes indicates a charitable impulse distanced from the old need of the testator for prayer and praise. John Rolfe of Hornchurch asked that at his burial 'a good reasonable dinner [should be given] for the relieving of poor 13s. 4d.'[91] The gradual attrition of funeral doles no doubt had the general effect

[87] Wood, *Life and Times*, ed. A. Clark, 5 vols. (Oxford Hist. Soc., 19, 21, 26, 30, 40, 1891–1900), i. 417.

[88] Campbell, *English Yeoman*, 387.

[89] See D. G. Mandelbaum, 'Social Uses of Funeral Rites', in H. Feifel (ed.), *The Meaning of Death* (London, 1959), 212–15.

[90] Emmison, *Essex Wills*, iii. nos. 21, 114, 221, 256, 318.

[91] Ibid. ii. no. 367.

of making village burials less open and public events, maybe even curtailing their celebratory style. But this change was also made by deliberate choice in many communities at the end of the sixteenth century. The Puritan attack on funeral ritual discouraged too overt a 'public forth coming', even though practices such as the tolling of bells and the wearing of mourning garments survived the precisians' assault. The intensely private quality of the modern funeral probably has its roots in this post-Reformation retreat from publicly expressed mourning and commemoration.[92]

Where direct criticism of ritual did not effect change, economic and social upheaval might perform the same task. The tradition of public commensality at funerals remained on the whole important in much of the north, but in a proto-industrial community like the Whickham coalfield in County Durham it was in decline from the 1580s, and dead by the second decade of the seventeenth century. Instead of shared eating for all, Whickham wills now often prescribed a private dinner for family and close friends and a money dole, in this religiously conservative area, for the poor.[93] Here contempt for the 'heathenish superstition' of funerals assumes a distinctly anti-communitarian style which is congruent with other evidence of weakening social bonds in this unusual environment. One must contrast this with the tenacity of the grand wakes held even by the poor in Scotland as late as the eighteenth century: in 1681 the Scottish Parliament still felt it necessary to regulate attendance at marriages, baptisms, and burials with comprehensive sumptuary legislation.[94]

IV

If the evidence for popular entertainment at festivals and rites of passage is imperfect, any attempt to assess daily behaviour towards guests and outsiders is almost certain to founder on the silence of the records. At best we have faint hints from court procedures and from contemporary observers of specific actions

---

[92] Thomas, *Religion and Magic*, 722–3.
[93] Information from a seminar paper given in Oxford by Keith Wrightson.
[94] *The Acts of the Parliament of Scotland*, viii. 350. See also funerals of the same scale for the Isle of Man: Waldron, *Isle of Man*, 61.

that appear culturally 'normal', or conversely of failures to act that are condemned by reference to some implied code of social justice.

The image that we can construct from these inferences is one in which at least the wealthier sections of rural society were traditionally expected to be generous in hospitality, imitating the landowning classes in the openness of their houses if not in the elaboration of their service. Praise for the good hospitality of the yeoman class in the sixteenth century, and anxiety about their continued ability to entertain in the next, are common among observers. The good yeoman, as characterized by Thomas Fuller, 'is bountifull both to strangers and poore people', and keeps a table that has good honest food, 'no straggling joynt of a sheep in the midst of a pasture of grasse'.[95] However, Fuller also believed that the death of hospitality, even among the yeomen, had already been pronounced by the mid-seventeenth century, and that 'she gave her last groan among the Yeomen of Kent'. William Smith firmly believed that there were many Cheshire farmers 'that in their House-Keeping, may compare with a Lord or a Baron in some Countreys beyond the seas', a view supported by Risdon's opinion of the Devon freeholders.[96] In Norden's *Surveyor's Dialogue* (1607), the farmer argues that his 'sort' had traditionally maintained 'good houses and hospitality', though rising rents now prevented this behaviour.[97] John Taylor, in pessimistic mood, saw yeomen as grasping 'cormorants' who sought to protect what they had in the face of economic difficulty. Even so, literary commentators were on the whole disposed to claim that some of the old open ways remained visible in rural society even in the face of major social change. It was in a good old farmer's house that John Taylor's figure of Christmas found the feast being celebrated in the bleak 1650s. He brought with him his 'company' of the poor, and all were seated 'at the upper end of the Table, and . . . we had good cheer and free welcome, and we were merry without Musick'.[98] This host was said to exemplify the behaviour of all the rest of his kind in Devonshire and Cornwall.

---

[95] Thomas Fuller, *The Holy State and the Profane State* (Cambridge, 1642), 117.　　　　　　　　　　　　　　[96] Smith, *Vale Royal*, 20.
[97] John Norden, *Surveyor's Dialogue*, 13.
[98] Taylor, *Christmas In and Out*, 15.

Individual biographies often painted the same picture as these generic descriptions. The most famous example is that of Latimer's pen-portrait of his father who, from his one farm, entertained his poor neighbours as well as giving alms to the poor.[99] The Furse family of Devon, yeomen on the margins of gentility, were equally proud of a hospitable reputation. The John Furse who suceeded the ambitious Henrician head of the family, was liberal to the poor: 'he did comonly upon all solen days feaste the power and in ther companye he wold be most meryeste'. Daily entertainment was also part of the expected behaviour of the family.[100] This was in the mid-sixteenth century, but a hundred years later much the same set of values seem to have moved John Chamber of Holme Cultram in Cumberland, whose epitaph is worth quoting in full:

> John Chamber, till death brought him here,
> Maintained still the custome clear:
> The church, the wood, and parish right,
> He did defend with all his might:
> Kept constant holy sabbath daies,
> And did frequent the church alwaies:
> Gave alms truely to the poor,
> Who dayly sought it at his door;
> And purchas'd land as much and more,
> Than all his elders did before.
> He had four children with two wives,
> They died young—the one wife survives.
> None of his rank could better be
> For liberal hospitallitie.[101]

With some slight adaptation to account for specific circumstance, there is an extraordinary congruity between Latimer's vision and that to be found in the Cumberland church. Prudent generosity, allied to the sound financial calculation of a successful farmer, are the prime virtues articulated. Defence of parochial custom

---

[99] Hugh Latimer, *Sermons*, ed. G. E. Corrie (Parker Soc., Cambridge, 1845), 101.

[100] H. Carpenter (ed.), 'A History of the Furse Family of Moreshead', *Trans. of the Devon Assoc.*, 26, (1894), 177.

[101] W. Hutchinson, *The History of the County of Cumberland*, 2 vols. (Carlisle, 1794), ii. 334.

and defence of hospitable values are identified as part of the obligation of the good yeoman. They can be paralleled in the 'Advice' with which Robert Furse begins the history of his ancestors: be merciful to all men, especially the poor, 'have a delyte in good housekepynge for so shalt thow have the love of God', but avoid borrowing and usury, and exercise prudence in household management and in giving to others.[102] Platitudinous sentiments, no doubt, but ones which often seem closer to the mentality of the farming élite than to the gentry at whom, as we have seen, they were also directed. Tusser's advice on moderate housekeeping:

> Good husbands that loveth good houses to keepe
> are oftentimes careful when other doe sleepe:
> To spend as they may, or to stop at the furst,
> for running in danger, or feare of the wurst.

also seems peculiarly appropriate for this social group.[103]

Substantial farmers and freeholders were certainly the subject of some expectations from the rest of the community. This was true not only in occasional feasting like Christmas and Harvest Home, but at Rogationtide, when customary entertainment was supplied by men of standing, and assumed as a right by the recipients. Although the ecclesiastical lawyers were reluctant to support popular claims to treats at the annual procession as legally binding, they were clearly at odds on this issue with much parochial feeling.[104] Presentations for failure to give hospitality to the bound-treaders can be found in various dioceses: in Oxfordshire in the 1620s, for example, three substantial parishioners from Cropredy were presented before the ecclesiastical court, 'for that they do not allow in rogation weeke such charges by drinkings so called at the severall mylnes . . . as hath bene before accustomed'.[105] In the next century the parish register of Ashampstead, Berkshire, contains a memorandum of all those tenures that had an obligation to provide either 'Bread, Cakes, Cheese, Butter or Cheesecake' at the perambulation,

---

[102] 'Furse Family', 171.   [103] Tusser, *Five Hundred Points*, 16.
[104] Burn, *Ecclesiastical Law*, ii. 133.
[105] S. A. Peyton (ed.), *Churchwardens' Presentations for the Oxfordshire Peculiars of Dorchester, Thame and Banbury* (Oxford Rec. Soc., 60, 1928), 245.

most of them being men of some substance.[106] In that struggle to maintain traditional rights which frequently reached the courts, those held responsible most often seem to have been the men who were the leading tenants of freeholders of the community.

It may be mistaken, however, for the historian to argue that these duties were seen as the peculiar obligation of a group possessing the social label 'yeoman'. First, no such clearly identified category presided unchanging over English village life in the three centuries between 1400 and 1700. Chaucer's Franklin, for example, is often taken as the model of the hospitable freeholder, and was compared by his maker to St Julian, patron of hospitality, but the Franklin had been in Parliament and was a man of great substance and influence in the affairs of his county, more appropriately the precursor of a country gentleman.[107] At the other end of our period the yeoman as a definable social category was yielding place to the tenant farmer, while the rural élite was diversifying and coming to include men whose primary income was not necessarily derived from land. The continuous articulation of a set of apparently similar values to describe dominant members of the local community has, therefore, to be considered with some caution and subtlety. It may be that no 'natural' continuity is at work, but rather a process by which groups with changing interests sought to affirm connectedness with a constructed past. Secondly, this continuity was not necessarily to the taste of all rural élites: it is presumably no accident that the most fervent praise of yeomanly generosity comes from regions such as Devon and Kent, where prosperous freeholders had a long and proud history. Elsewhere other models, such as mimesis of the godly gentry or of the new civility that was hostile to comfortable rusticity, might well attract the middling sort more strongly.[108] The energetic participation of many parish élites in the reformation of manners at the end of the sixteenth century must have distanced

---

[106] Berkshire Record Office, Reading. D/P 8/1/1, 1.

[107] G. H. Gerould, 'The Social Status of Chaucer's Franklin', *Public. of the Modern Language Assoc. of America*, 41 (1926), 262 ff.

[108] Campbell, *English Yeoman*, 21 ff.; J. C. K. Cornwall, *Wealth and Society in Early Sixteenth Century England* (London, 1988), 9–21; K. Wrightson, *English Society: 1560–1680* (London, 1982), 225–8.

many of them from the complaisant assumptions about traditions made by outsiders such as Fuller.

It may, moreover, be a mistake to concentrate too explicitly on the parish élites merely because of the existence of a rhetorical tradition praising the yeoman as good host. In the pursuit of popular values we cannot advance very far without considering the 80 per cent or more of the population that existed below this relatively prosperous superstratum. This is less daunting than it at first seems since the most important distinction, as often in English rural culture, may be between those who could maintain an independent household and husbandry on the one hand, and those who were dependants, or whose poverty placed them below the level of autonomous house-holder, on the other hand.[109] Even observers of the social order sometimes acknowledged the identity of behaviour between rural householders, as when Thomas Gainsford remarked that yeomen and husbandmen live with 'neatnes and hospitality'.[110] The identification between 'keeping household' and 'keeping hospitality' from which this volume began, is an important linguistic indication of undifferentiated perception of the role of all householders in receiving outsiders. No doubt the practical acceptance that all entertainment had to be congruent with the resources of the host imposed major limitations on expectations at the level of ordinary village culture, but it is difficult to argue that there was any perception that ordinary husbandmen should behave in a way qualitatively different from their yeoman neighbours. In a Suffolk case before Star Chamber in the 1590s, a depopulator defended himself with the argument that he had put into his second farm an honest man who lived 'both for hospitality and other good offices in as good sorte theare . . . as any other of that degree'.[111]

It is important that the glimpses that we have of this assumption derive in the main from legal and other official records rather than external observers. In 1518, for example, the jurors of Burton Dassett, Warwickshire, informed the enclosure commissioners that the lands taken into severalty in the parish

---

[109] Youings, *Sixteenth-Century England*, 310
[110] Thomas Gainsford, *The Glory of England* (London, 1618), 250.
[111] PRO, STAC 5/A 13/18.

had been beneficial to the community for a variety of reasons, including the fact that 'wheras they were able to enterteine before the Inclosure xx strangers upon occasion now they can enterteyne lx aswell'.[112] Other aspects of the return emphasize the degree to which the whole parish has been advantaged by the changes. More than a century later a petition against enclosure makes a similar social point in a different economic context: engrossing, and the subsequent destruction of houses, means that 'noe hospitalitie ys kepte upon the same' and the poor and strangers suffer.[113] In 1591 the by-laws of the manor of Spalding ordered that a man should only retain his right to 'warestead', that is, fishing in the local rivers and meres, so long as 'he is an inhabitant and keeper of hospitality within the same Towns'.[114] A few years later a Lincolnshire man sought to defend himself against the charge that he had refused to pay his proper contributions to the fifteenth and tenth partly by arguing that he kept good hospitality 'for the releefe of the poore'.[115]

While some customary rights to entertainment might be exacted only from the 'better sort', this was probably more a matter of financial convenience than fixed principle: when modest claims were involved all householders might be brought into the web of hospitality. The parish clerk of Cropwell Bishop, Nottinghamshire, was able to claim as part of his wages a dinner worth 12*d.* from every husbandman, 'or woman with husbandry farm', and maintained his right as late as the 1660s.[116] We have seen in an earlier chapter that travellers were as likely to be entertained in humble households, especially in the remoter parts of the realm, as they were by prosperous yeomen or townsmen. Finally, one can point to the official assumption in the 1590s that all householders of 'habillitie' would provide hospitality for

[112] I. S. Leadam (ed.), *The Domesday of Inclosures, 1517–1518*, 2 vols. (London, 1897), ii. 655.

[113] PRO, SP 16/307/2: this is an undated list of grievances against enclosures, but the rhetoric, especially comments on the gentry flocking to London, suggests that the authors are utilizing the language of government proclamations of the 1620s and 1630s.

[114] Spalding Gentlemen's Society, Spalding, MS MJ/B/10: it is interesting to note that similar by-laws for the 1730s make no reference to hospitality.

[115] PRO, E134, 44/45 Eliz./Mich. 15.

[116] Peyton, *Churchwardens' Presentations*, liii–liv.

the poor as a result of abstention from suppers on Wednesday and Friday evenings.[117]

The claims of good neighbourhood, including the keeping of a generous house and giving to the local poor, were sometimes believed to be sufficiently binding to be expressed in monetary terms. A private report on individuals eligible for the payment of loans to the King in 1621 in the Hundred of Forehoe, Norfolk, differentiated them not only by wealth but by their housekeeping. Thomas Hobbs and Philip Cully, for example, were both yeomen believed to be worth approximately £100 per annum, but the latter was 'good to the pore' while the former 'liveth at a meane rate'. The author therefore suggested that Cully should pay only £30, as against the £40 that could reasonably be taken from Hobbs.[118] There are a number of examples of Exchequer cases from the early decades of the seventeenth century in which individuals endeavoured to claim some remission of taxation on the grounds of good entertainment or generosity to the poor: their success seemingly dependent primarily on a sympathetic perception of their behaviour within the local community.[119]

Yet in the same decades when rural communities apparently approved hospitable daily behaviour there is also ample evidence of the failure of this and other forms of charitable giving. The work of Thomas and Macfarlane has familiarized us with the notion that, at the level of the village, witch-accusations were most frequently associated with a failure of charity: the denial of alms or some other act of giving which then led the supposed witch to cursing and *maleficium*.[120] Many of the cases involved a refusal of household giving: for example, in a York assize deposition of 1646 Richard Wood's wife was alleged to have denied Mary Midgley alms of wool, saying she had had some three weeks before, and the day afterwards six of Wood's milch-cows fell sick.[121] Actual denial of a meal within the household was not a common aspect of witchcraft depositions, though there are the

---

[117] *APC, 1596–7*, 381.

[118] W. Hudson (ed.), 'Assessment of the Hundred Forehoe, Norfolk, in 1621', *Norfolk Archaeology*, 21 (1920–3), 287.

[119] PRO, E112/48/160; 25/348; E134/1JasI/M4.

[120] Thomas, *Religion and Magic*, 638 ff; A. Macfarlane, *Witchcraft in Tudor and Stuart Essex* (London, 1970), 147 ff.

[121] *York Depositions*, 8.

complaints at exclusion from celebrations such as weddings and christenings. It was assumed by some commentators that the boldness of the witch who asked for alms at the gate also extended to a desire for hospitality in the household. Thomas Cooper, in his *Mystery of Witchcraft* (1617), warned his audience to be 'wise in our Liberalitie, and Almes deedes, not distributing to each sort of poore, because many times Witches go under this habite'. If any suspect persons approached a householder, he or she should 'not . . . entertaine them in our houses, not to relieve them with our morsels'.[122] This suspicion of the neighbouring poor, and a failure of charity that could lead through guilt-transference to accusations of witchcraft, is obviously a common sentiment in early modern England. Its causes may lie in growing economic tension and polarization, but other explanations, such as the structure of the rural economy, or the ideological perceptions of local élites, must also have played critical parts. John Aubrey, differentiating the chalk and cheese countries of Wiltshire, was insistent that Puritanism, witchcraft beliefs, and litigiousness were all bred together in the pastoral environment of the latter.[123]

When specific anxieties about witchcraft did not perturb the charitable disposition of villagers, general fear of the poor might produce the same effect. Harman's *Caveat for Common Cursetors* (1567) graphically describes the methods beggars might use to extort alms: 'yf they aske at a stoute yeman's or farmar's house his charity, they wyll goe strong as thre or foure in a company: Where, for feare more then goodwyll, they often have reliefe.'[124] The threat was exaggerated to create a good story, but fear of the wanderer was to be found in village culture as well. These anxieties, legitimized and given weight by the Elizabethan poor laws, made open beneficence appear unrealistic, and even ungodly when it encouraged idleness and crime. Not that the ordinary villager probably closed his or her heart to need in the outsider: barns, for example, were regularly offered as resting-places—in some of the early seventeenth-century surveys as many

---

[122] Thomas Cooper, *Mystery of Witch-craft* (London, 1617), 287–8.
[123] Underdown, *Revel, Riot, and Rebellion*, 73 ff; Aubrey, *Top. Coll.*, 266.
[124] Thomas Harman, *A Caveat or Warening for Commen Cursetors* (London, 1566–7), ed. E. Viles and F. J. Furnivall, *The Rogues and Vagabonds of Shakespeare's Youth*, (New Shakspere Soc., 6th Ser. 7, London, 1880), 33.

as 20 per cent of the travellers questioned had found refuge in such outbuildings.[125] When the suffering of a wanderer was visible householders would probably respond, as did Esther Parker, who in the 1680s cared for a sick boy, making him 'some warme meate', and ordering him to stay in her barn where there was fresh straw.[126] Small gestures of this kind continued for, as Ady observed, 'no man of ability is long free from poor coming to his door'.[127] However, none of this amounted to an open welcome for the outsider, still less to any sense that honour or neighbourly reputation was to be derived from such care. The existence of parish rates, and of settlement arrangements, detached the process of giving from the household and its head and placed it firmly with public officials.

These challenges to generous behaviour are to be found even in nucleated arable communities, which supposedly fostered neighbourhood values. By the seventeenth century, the attack on popular culture and then the upheavals of the Civil War were added to economic difficulty and hostility to the vagrant as reasons for a withdrawal of giving. The decline in ceremonies such as the public forthcoming at funerals, and the failure in some areas to revive the wakes after the Restoration, are obvious indicators of the weakness of tradition. When we turn to the most powerful evocation of a late seventeenth-century agrarian community, Gough's *History of Myddle*, it appears that hospitality was no longer one of the major concerns of his traditionally minded Shropshire villagers.[128] There are only four moments in his text at which Gough pauses either to praise an individual for good household entertainment or to condemn its absence. The Jacobean rector of Myddle, Mr Ralph Kinaston, was singled out for approbation and his successor condemned for parsimony. Two gentlemen were particularly isolated as good housekeepers: Mr Baker, who was High Sheriff of Shropshire under the Commonwealth, and Mr William Watkins, a local tenant on the margins of gentility, who had been active in the early seventeenth century. The latter moved Gough to quote from the Prologue to

---

[125] A. L. Beier, *Masterless Men: The Vagrancy Problem in England, 1560–1640* (London, 1985), 223.

[126] *York Depositions*, 287.

[127] Thomas Ady, *A Perfect Discovery of Witches* (London, 1661), 129.

[128] Richard Gough, *The History of Myddle*, ed. D. Hey (London, 1981).

The Canterbury Tales the famous passage on the Franklin's hospitality.[129] All these were examples drawn from the élite, and from the period of Gough's youth or earlier. Even his niggards, James Wicherley and his son Richard, were men of the early seventeenth century.[130] This silence about his own age, from a man so frank in his comments upon neighbours, is at least suggestive. Gough subscribes to the customary image of hospitality in the rural community, as indeed one would expect of a man given to the approbation of tradition. On the other hand, he neither suggests that it was a major concern of his contemporaries, nor that his community chose to define itself in any important ways as generous with entertainment.

Yeoman and prosperous farmers, even in those upland counties where pride in hospitality was supposed traditionally to be at its strongest, often seem as little concerned with its exercise as did Gough. The farming books, diaries, and household records that become common during and after the mid-seventeenth century are almost silent about household entertainment and giving. The occasional celebration of a rite of passage or of harvest normally represent the only feasts remarked, and daily conviviality, if mentioned at all, seems only to involve a selected circle of neighbours and friends.[131] For James Jackson, a farmer in the same Cumberland community of Holme Cultram that produced the eulogy of John Chamber, hospitality consisted of the treats officials like the sheriff gave at the assizes, the dinner that accompanied the local court leet, and an occasional drinking at a neighbour's.[132] Such diarists suggest that transactional relationships within the community were perceived primarily in commercial, commodity-based terms: Jackson even recorded solemnly how much had been spent by each individual at 'a drinking att Mungo Daltons'.[133]

---

[129] Gough, *The History of Myddle*, 41, 111, 160.

[130] Ibid. 138.

[131] See e.g., H. J. Morehouse (ed.), *Adam Eyre, a Diurnal* in *Yorkshire Diaries and Autobiographies* (Surtees Soc., 65, 1877); W. L. Sachse (ed.), *The Diary of Roger Lowe* (London, 1938); N. Penney (ed.), *Household Account Book of Sarah Fell of Swarthmoor Hall, 1673–8* (Cambridge, 1920).

[132] 'The Diary of James Jackson, 1650–83', selected by F. Grainger, *Trans. of the Cumb. and Westmors. Antiq. and Arch. Soc.*, N.S. 21 (1921), 96 ff.

[133] Ibid. 111.

By the late sixteenth century, when evidence of popular behaviour begins to become available to the historian in some depth, English communities seem to demonstrate a variety of ambiguous, or even contradictory, attitudes to hospitality. There was a powerful rhetorical tradition which identified the leaders of rural society with generosity and openness, and this was in harmony with assumptions made by tenants and parishioners that they had rights to claim customary entertainments from their betters. There was also a belief, probably possessing deep roots in medieval culture, that keeping a household, even a modest establishment, involved giving and openness within one's capacities. The value of good neighbourhood, which was of great apparent importance in village culture, could be articulated effectively by a combination of celebratory entertainment and giving to the poor that was comprehended by the ideas of hospitality. On the other hand, the assumptions of the diarists seem intensely individualistic: concern for neighbourhood is rarely permitted to interfere with the pursuit of economic advantage or the interest of the nuclear family. This could be a set of concerns nurtured by the experiences of the sixteenth century, but it seems possible that economic individualism was already of importance in English culture in the later Middle Ages.[134] Moreover, the English did not possess a powerful ethic of openness to strangers, which would have defined outsiders as figures to be protected and succoured. They might be offered kindness and care if their needs were urgent, but they might equally be excluded, exploited, or at least treated with suspicion. Despite the words of the preachers, it is difficult to believe that ordinary Englishmen felt any profound sense of shame when they ignored strangers, or charged them highly for services rendered.[135]

If these were common cultural assumptions stretching back into the medieval period, it seems reasonable to conclude that the late sixteenth and seventeenth centuries would have put popular hospitality under strain. Neither the economic changes of the period, nor the ideological upheavals that preceded the Civil War,

---

[134] A. Macfarlane, *The Origins of English Individualism* (Oxford, 1978).

[135] John Aubrey, *Collections for the Natural and Topographical History of Wiltshire*, ed. T. Phillips, 2 vols. (Devizes, 1821–38), i. 19; White Kennett, *Parochial Antiquities*, 614.

favoured easy generosity by ordinary yeomen, husbandmen, and artisans. The stranger was often transmuted into the figure of the vagrant, who was either a physical threat or a charge on the tax-paying capacity of the community. The traveller's ability to pay his way could perhaps become in these circumstances the test of his honesty. Within the village economic pressures could lead to definitions of neighbours as strangers, 'others', if they became too importunate, and ideological division could create differentiation and hostility in entertainment as well as other spheres of social activity. Although both economic and ideological pressures diminished after the Restoration, there was no consistent return to public and open conviviality. There is, of course, evidence of continuity in popular festivity, a continuity attested by those antiquarians such as Aubrey and White Kennett whose impulse was to mourn the world lost by the Civil War.[136] Parochial wakes, harvest celebrations, and even quasi-public rites of passage remained important parts of the cultural nexus of many Englishmen until the eighteenth century. Nevertheless, the upheavals of the mid-seventeenth century, and the Puritan ethos which had gained a temporary dominance in the society, both contributed to a permanent weakening of some aspects of public sociability and generosity. In these circumstances hospitality perhaps became a private virtue readily practised towards kin and friends, but less routinely offered as part of a holistic view of community.

[136] Underdown, *Revel, Riot, and Rebellion*, 280–2, suggests that the survival of the Puritan ethos after the Restoration contributed to the continuing decline of aspects of popular culture, although this only became apparent after the Glorious Revolution.

10
Conclusion

AT the beginning of this volume it was suggested that five major elements might be identified in a culture that was deeply committed to the practice of open hospitality. These were: an evolved perception of the naturalness of the relationship between host and guest, which could be formulated as a law of hospitality; a belief that the outsider was deserving of special generosity because of the ambiguity of his status; an aristocratic or élite ethos in which honour accrued to acts of beneficence and shame to forms of avarice; an associated ideology of generosity to all comers; and finally a social system in which gift-exchange transactions had not been wholly superseded by those of commodity-exchange. It seems necessary to conclude a discursive examination of English hospitality by asking whether society did possess these features in the early modern period and, if so, how far they were still vital in the century that followed the grand crisis of the Civil War.

Among the five themes it is easiest to argue that the English possessed a relatively sophisticated perception of a law of hospitality that bound them to generosity to defined guests. Despite occasional allusions to the barbarousness of the lower orders from commentators such as Edward Chamberlayne, there seems to have been a collective pride in a good table and in courtesy to visitors that transcended social boundaries. The objects of this generosity may have changed over time and with circumstance, but it is relatively easy to multiply evidence for the case that the English were at ease with guests and perceived entertainment as a natural social function. The continuing comfort in the entertainment of one's peer group that is expressed in the mayoral feasting in corporate towns in the eighteenth century, or in the development of the country-house party, can also be found in more humble circumstances in Bamford's description of nineteenth-century

Lancashire wakes or in the grandness of funeral celebrations in the north.[1]

The aristocratic ethos of generosity is a more interesting phenomenon, which has been analysed at length in the text. It appears possible to argue forcefully for the existence of an honour code which obliged the landed élite to represent themselves as given to largess, and their households as open suppliers of the wants of their inferiors. Shame traditionally attached to those who failed to personate themselves as men of generosity, and by implication there was also the danger that shame led to the diminution of that natural authority that derived from land and wealth. The shaming of Sir Thomas Hoby was an attempt to force upon him a recognition of the political dangers of his conflict with the Eure clan.

Elements of this culture of honour, with its concern for reputation and the display of generosity, should be seen as continuing far beyond the early modern period, probably until the demise of the English landed classes as a political and social force. It proved ideally adaptable to the circumstances of eighteenth-century political patronage, where old ideals of largess and good lordship were dusted down and transformed into a powerful form of election treating.[2] It would, however, be mistaken to see late manifestations of these gestures only in terms of a cynical manipulation of old concepts: country liberality could be a lived experience expressing profoundly held beliefs about the nature of society, the species of behaviour that we earlier identified with Reresby in Yorkshire. Colley quotes a magnificent report on the Christmas of a Tory squire that merits repetition in this context:

His House was open to entertain the Neighbourhood all the Holidays: and particularly on Tuesday was provided a Dinner for the poor Farmers and Labourers in that Parish, where the Season was celebrated with a decent Joyfulness, and long life to their liberal Benefactor, as well as Prosperity to Old England, was drunk with the greatest Cheerfulness.[3]

---

[1] Chamberlayne was of the opinion that the ordinary Englishman was rude, boisterous, and unamiable to outsiders, *Angliae Notitia: Or the Present State of England* (London, 1700 edn.), 312.

[2] L. Colley, *In Defiance of Oligarchy: The Tory Party, 1714–60* (Cambridge, 1982), 129. There is an excellent account of an election campaign in Arundel in 1770 in which 'old-style' hospitality played a major part in 'The Tompkins Diary', ed. G. W. Eustace, *Sussex Arch. Coll.* 71 (1930), 26–30.

[3] Quoted in Colley, *Oligarchy*, 100.

The identification between the good old hospitality, the honour culture, and Tory values was a powerful combination that left behind its own artefact in the form of the funeral monument, and its own chroniclers in traditionally minded county historians such as Sir Henry Chauncy.[4] Chauncy, in his pen-portraits of the Hertfordshire gentry, regularly singles out for praise those who maintained custom and upheld what he believed to be the old values of the community. Thus Sir John Monson, described as 'a great patriot to his Country', united the virtues of the hospitable squirearchy with those of support for his monarch.[5] In this Chauncy, and the writers of the memorials, are identifying a section of the élite who, though they might spend part of their time in London or Bath, achieved their sense of purpose from an association with the countryside and what they believed to be its paternalist values.

It is, however, not congruent with our earlier analysis to argue that the aristocratic ethos of largess and openness remained a dominant social trait throughout the early modern period. Even in the fifteenth century this ethos has to be understood in a context, and to be recognized as having limitations. The openness of the great household was constrained by carefully established conventions about hierarchy, deference, and place, by prudential considerations about getting and spending, that were themselves expressed in an ethical language and by the existence of alternative sources of accommodation for outsiders. In the smaller gentry household, where preoccupation with displays of magnificence for political purposes was of limited relevance, participation in the world of gentility did not routinely require grand gestures of largess, though it is probable that they were performed when necessary.

By the later sixteenth century this image of an élite given in honour to open hospitality, but not excessively so, began to yield to alternative patterns, especially those produced by growing mobility and the growth of London. Both Court and City played an increasing role in the experience of the nobility and many of the gentry, and perceptions of a civil society encouraged new

---

[4] Henry Chauncy, *The Historical Antiquities of Hertfordshire*, 2 vols. (Bishop Stortford, 1826).
[5] Ibid. i. 566–7.

ideas of social separation. It became questionable if the honour code required even the semblance of hospitality, since no reputation was to be gained from the plaudits of the multitude.[6] The cool and calculative tone of much of the advice literature of the later seventeenth century, with its emphasis on interest and on civil discourse, did little to persuade men of the value of good housekeeping. Moreover, the social mobility of the post-Restoration world, where many struggled on the margins of gentility without land or household to sustain it, encouraged the growth of that polite culture in which to be a gentleman was to behave like one in the exterior indicators of dress and style. When the reputation was defined by the ability to use appropriate modes of civility, or gain access to the correct London circles, the traditional household would no longer so easily lie at its heart.[7]

Nevertheless, aristocratic values of generosity and largess were probably England's nearest approximation to a continuing commitment to open hospitality. The belief that generosity to all comers was required by both natural and divine law had provided the underpinning for this behaviour in the Middle Ages. To be in charity with one's fellow men was to minister to their material and spiritual needs, and since the household represented the primary unit of production and consumption, it was through the household that material needs were most logically met. Despite the availability of such specialized agencies of giving as the hospitals, most support emanated from households both lay and clerical. The giving of money alms might distance this process from the immediacy of hospitable entertainment, but the expectations of the canonists and preachers was that giving would be of and from the *domus*.

It is in this area of the duty of hospitality to the needy that it is easiest to speak with confidence of change in early modern England. The experience of economic and demographic crisis in the sixteenth century led to a reconceptualization of forms of beneficence, both of the worthiness of the recipient and of the best apportionment of resources. Notions of worth, which had

----

[6] See e.g., Francis Osborne, *Advice to a Son* (London, 1656); William Ramesey, *The Gentleman's Companion* (London, 1672). This tradition culminated, of course, in Lord Chesterfield's letters to his son.

[7] The point is made clearly in Henry Peacham, *The Art of Living in London* (London, 1642), 86.

been accepted in general terms in canonistic thought, were now refined into a systematized analysis of the poor. Household giving was not wholly eliminated, but its dominant place was taken by organized schemes of relief, based on the parish, the town, and on institutions such as the almshouse. Even personal giving tended to move outside the intimate atmosphere of the household, and emerge as more permanent forms of benevolence administered through the parish.

At the very least, this process completed the separation of hospitality to the prosperous and alms to the poor that had always been latent in household culture. Funeral sermons and memorials of the seventeenth century suggest that, while personal charitable impulses had not been surrendered, they were now very clearly separated from entertainment. Typical of the latter part of the period is the memorial of the Countess of Bridgewater, who died in 1663, of whom it was said that 'the rich at her Table daily tasted her Hospitality, the poor at her gate her Charity'.[8] Richard Herbert, esquire, who died in 1676, was said to be charitable to the poor, but not to beggars, and his preacher passed 'from his charity . . . to his hospitality' as though the two universes had nothing in common.[9] As for ordinary Englishmen, it seems likely that the advent of public relief for the poor exonerated them from much commitment to local charitable giving beyond occasional alms at the door. And, despite a continuing preoccupation with the need to be generous, few preachers and moralists of the seventeenth century suggested that this generosity had to be discharged within the household.

Beneath the practical transition from private to public relief also lay that sense of distancing the poor as the objects of beneficence: an intensification of the social gulf that existed between the needy and their benefactors. As with the association between aristocracy, honour, and open hospitality, it is possible to find examples which seem to stand against this generalization. The Tichborne dole, with a history which continues far beyond our period, is one such. Equally interesting is the commemoration of Humphrey How, who until his death in 1688, was porter to Lord Leigh:

---

[8] Chauncy, ii. 489.
[9] John Slade, *A Sermon Preached at the Funeral of Richard Herbert Esq. of Oakly Park* (London, 1676), 19.

Here lyes a faithfull Friend into the Poore,
Who dealt large Alms out of his Lordps. Store.
Weepe not Poor People, Tho' thy Servant's Dead
The Lord himselfe will Give you Daily Breade.
If Markets rise, Raile not Against their Rates,
The Price is still the same at Stone Leigh Gates.[10]

Although charity continued to possess some incorporative functions, in these cases, they must of their very nature be seen as exceptional. Beneficence, by the late seventeenth century, routinely and rationally used the mechanisms of money-exchange and institutional structures as the means of achieving its objectives.[11]

To turn from the ethos of giving to the perception of the stranger is to encounter the first of our themes in which the English always seem to have been deficient as hosts. Despite the resounding phrases from the preachers about the need to love the stranger, and ample evidence that the great and good were deeply impressed by native hospitality, there is little to suggest that the English were moved by powerful sentiments of fear, fascination, or hope of reciprocity, to be kind to ordinary outsiders. There are, once again, numbers of exceptions to such generalizations, both in the particular cases of kindness that have been analysed and in the notion that in some regions and some particular subcultures more open values did prevail.[12] And it is perhaps inaccurate to say that no gestures were expected to outsiders in the rest of the society: the continuation of petty almsgiving at the household door, or the assumption that at least a drink should be given to respectable strangers, suggest in part a propitiatory offering to the alien, some residue of that belief that he could bless or curse which retains power in many cultures.

What needs to be emphasized is that these attitudes to the outsider do not appear to change in fundamental ways during our period. George Wheler, who was one of the few English authors to reflect on these issues from a comparative perspective, was aware that his countrymen behaved in these respects very

---

[10] W. Dugdale, *The Antiquities of Warwickshire*, 2 vols., 2nd edn. (London, 1730) i. 262.
[11] G. Taylor, *The Problem of Poverty, 1660–1834* (London, 1969), 56–66.
[12] See above, ch. 5.

differently from the Greeks among whom he had travelled. This he attributed in part to the absence of inns and other public accommodation in Greece, but he penetrated the issue somewhat more profoundly when he remarked that his private hosts received him with kindness into their houses, entertaining him 'with such things as they have with much Humanity'. He saw in his reception something of the ethos of the *agape* of the early Christians.[13] This was in total contrast with his experience of late seventeenth-century England, where only the cathedral of Durham and its prebendaries impressed him with their 'generous welcome' and 'Christian freedom'.[14] Perhaps more of the great houses and ecclesiastical establishments would have impressed a Wheler travelling in the early fifteenth century, but he would have encountered a world in which the humble outsider already appeared marginal, unless his estate or function afforded him good treatment, in which much of the provision for travellers was already organized on a commercial basis, and in which prayer and praise from the stranger seem to have been little valued. Evidence of ordinary village attitudes is, of course, extraordinarily thin before the late sixteenth century, but points to a well-developed commercial sense of relating to the alien, which is in contrast with assumptions about sociability and solidarity within the neighbourhood.[15]

In cultures which perceive the stranger as both powerful threat and blessing he tends to be treated with exaggerated honour and accorded an unusual precedence. Some tenuous notion of this kind can be traced in early modern England in the arrangements made for seating strangers well at the tables of the great, and ensuring that, if doubt existed about their status, it should be resolved in favour of the outsider. The same behaviour may well have obtained in the lower ranks of society, but this was action once the outsider had been offered temporary assimilation into

---

[13] Wheler, *The Protestant Monastery: Or Christian Œconomicks* (London, 1698), 173–4.

[14] Ibid. 175.

[15] See e.g., Peter Clark's analysis of the development of the medieval alehouse, *The English Alehouse: A Social History, 1200–1830* (London, 1983), 20–34. Also, J. J. Jusserand, *English Wayfaring Life in the Middle Ages* (London, 1889), 125–38. Dalechamp believed that 'abundance of Inns and Alehouses . . . convinces the World of inhospitalitie', *Christian Hospitalitie: Handled Commonplace-wise in the Chappel of Trinity College in Cambridge* (Cambridge, 1632), 123.

the household. No constraint, other than obvious physical need, seems to have compelled Englishmen to permit the alien to take the first crucial step into the *domus*.

Why this should be so is difficult to explain. So are the related problems of why the Celtic cultures, especially those of Ireland and Scotland, did possess and retain these forms of behaviour, and why in some contexts, as for example in Virginia, English settlers did extend or develop them. It may be of some value in attempting to answer the first question to look at the second, to enquire what characteristics Ireland, Scotland, and Virginia possessed that were less visible in England. An accessible answer, already considered in several contexts, is that these were societies in which public provision for outsiders was poorly developed. The case of Virginia is most self-evident here: until after the Revolution, the focus of Tidewater Virginian society was the great estate rather than the town. Outside Williamsburg and a few similar communities which developed during the eighteenth century, inns were a rarity and accommodation had to be sought from private houses.[16] This seems at one level no more than the logic of enforced hospitality in an underdeveloped territory: the sort of behaviour that W. H. Hudson described in his account of his childhood in nineteenth-century Argentina, or was remarked of the pioneers in New South Wales, where it was common in the 1840s to enjoy 'the rough hospitality offered by the inmates of a shepherd's hut'.[17] The Highlands of Scotland and much of Celtic Ireland laboured until well into the eighteenth century under a similar lack of public accommodation, often leaving travellers little choice but dependence on the individual household.[18]

Yet, while the logic of private hospitality in New South Wales in the 1840s may have been inescapable, that of Scotland, Ireland, and Virginia in the eighteenth century was not. The issue is not

---

[16] R. Isaac, *The Transformation of Virginia, 1740–1790* (Chapel Hill, 1982); D. B. Smith, *Inside the Great House: Planter Family Life in Eighteenth-Century Chesapeake Society* (Ithaca, 1980), 196–7.

[17] R. B. Walker, *Old New England* (Sydney, 1966), 26. I am grateful to Ged Martin for this reference.

[18] J. L. Campbell (ed.), *A Collection of Highland Rites and Customs* (London, 1975), 45 ff; E. Mac-Lysaght, *Irish Life in the Seventeenth Century: After Cromwell* (London, 1939), 253–6; C. Maxwell, *Country and Town in Ireland under the Georges* (Dundalk, 1949), 296. In both countries public provision improved very rapidly during the course of the 18th century.

only the presence or absence of inns, but the expectations of private hosts and their perceptions of their duties. It appears that in the Celtic zones a belief was retained in the efficacy of unforced generosity to outsiders, which revealed both the honour of the host and a conviction that some exchange was taking place which could not, indeed must not, be articulated in money terms. Thomas Bewick, travelling on foot through Scotland in the 1770s, not only found that he was offered a free welcome by poor Highlanders, but that any suggestion of recompense caused offence. When he did manage to provide reward by giving money to the children of the house, he was always 'pursued and obliged to accept of a pocket full of Bannocks and scones'.[19] Similarly the Irish expected to share whatever meagre food they had with passing strangers: a pattern of behaviour that Pitt-Rivers noticed still obtained in mid-twentieth century Andalusia, where total strangers would be asked to share in a picnic or even a restaurant meal.[20]

The hospitality of Tidewater Virginia, focusing as it did on the great planter houses, was far more socially akin to that of late medieval England than to the behaviour of the Highlands or Ireland. But, although conducted with some of the same decorum and separation of social space that would have been approved in the mother country, it developed with an intensity that is rarely visible in English culture. Strangers could 'depend on being received with Hospitality', wrote a commentator in 1705, and any failure of generosity, even from the poorest planter, meant that he had 'a mark of Infamy set upon him, and is abhorr'd by all'.[21] It is, says Rhys Isaac, as though hospitality was not only a duty to whose failure shame attached, but also a source of gratification, 'almost an inner compulsion'.[22] Compulsion also seems an appropriate term to use of the eighteenth-century Anglo-Irish who still engaged in an obsessive round of entertainment, constantly priding themselves on the endless resort of others to their households.[23]

[19] Thomas Bewick, *A Memoir*, ed. I. Bain (Oxford, 1979), 64.
[20] J. Pitt-Rivers, 'The Law of Hospitality', in his *The Fate of Schechem* (Cambridge, 1977), 105.
[21] Robert Beverley, *The History and Present State of Virginia*, ed. L. B. Wright (Chapel Hill, 1947), 312–13.
[22] Isaac, *Transformation*, 72.   [23] Maxwell, *County and Town*, 23–4.

One common explanation of why the English were not driven by these compulsions was that they had lost them at some unspecified time. Just as Jacobean preachers and ballad-makers lamented the world they had lost, so later writers acknowledged more coolly that things had once been different. Samuel Johnson observed pithily that, 'that ancient hospitality, of which we hear so much, was in an uncommercial country, when men, being idle, were glad to be entertained at rich men's tables'. Now it was no longer a road to power, while influence was far better gained 'by lending money confidentially to your neighbours at a small interest'.[24] Or as the *Encycopédie* put it even more succinctly in its entry on hospitality, it had once been a powerful social force, but was now of little relevance, since 'toute l'Europe est devenue voyageante et commerçante'.[25]

But in the case of the English this process of the abandonment of the patterns of a previous Europe is complicated by our awareness that it did not seem to possess them in full measure even in the late medieval period. England was already 'voyageante et commerçante', as indeed were significant portions of the rest of Europe, in the fourteenth century. Yet even this need not have challenged open hospitality too directly. The crucial issue would seem to be one of the mentality and structure within which transactions were conducted, what forms of exchange were of central importance in the culture. Thus we return to the last of our five analytical categories, that of the significance of gift-transactions as against other forms of exchange. As Mauss long ago argued, societies which place gift exchange at the centre of their transactional relationships are not innocent of the force of the market, nor necessarily inimical to narrowly commercial bargains. The Trobrianders, for example, conducted ordinary inter-island trade alongside the grand gift-circulation of the *kula*.[26] By analogy, the ordinary Irishman of the eighteenth century was certainly not ignorant of the market-place, and the Virginian planter was ruthless in exploitation of the commercial worth of his land.

[24] James Boswell, *The Life of Samuel Johnson*, ed. G. B. Hill, 6 vols. (Oxford, 1934–64), ii. 167.

[25] *Encyclopédie ou Dictionaire Raisonée des Sciences, des Arts et des Metiers*, 32 vols. (Neufchatel, 1751–80), viii.

[26] M. Mauss, *The Gift: Forms and Functions of Exchange in Archaic Societies* (London, 1970), 19 ff.

Nevertheless, in both cases crucial series of transactions which expressed central social values could not be articulated in terms of money or the associated absolute rights of possession. The Virginian planter, whose control over property was in many ways so much greater than that of his English counterpart, retained a physical openness to his possessions not found on the other side of the Atlantic. Its symbol was the right of all comers to take fruit from plantation orchards.[27] The exchange of hospitality within this environment was an arrangement that gave value to possession, that surrendered some portion of wealth in order to ensure its continued vitality. The cycle of giving, receiving, and repaying sustained the internal moral and social economy of these cultures, conferring honour and influence both directly through giving to the neighbour and friend, and indirectly through the gestures of the munificence scattered liberally to all. In this environment the proffer of money for services rendered was profoundly insulting because it devalued the original gift by providing it with a direct commercial equivalence, thereby robbing it of its symbolic force.

Englishmen of the fifteenth to seventeenth centuries were no more ignorant of the power of the gift than were the Irish of the market-place. It has been the burden of much of the argument that transactions involving honour, reputation, displays of altruism, and the possibility of prayer and praise, helped to sustain a perception of open hospitality in early modern England that was far more significant than our modern understanding of the term would lead us to expect. But, whereas in the Scottish Highlands or in Virginia the fact of open hospitality seems to have been constantly visible, indeed central, to contemporaries, in England there was an equally constant sense that it risked invisibility, or at least marginalization. Preachers and moralists had to labour to remind men of their duties, especially in those fields like giving to the needy where the direct gift-rewards of generosity were not obvious. One of the North American Indian chiefs thanked his guests at the clan feast by expressing his gratitude for their blessing and that of their ancestors, concluding, 'you have helped me and that means life to me'.[28] The power of belief in intangible blessing here expressed would be difficult

---

[27] Isaac, *Transformation*, 34.   [28] Mauss, *The Gift*, 69.

to translate into an English context at any time, though we might just conceive of some analogical idea being articulated by Archbishop Warham at his enthronement feast.[29] It would certainly never have been a commonplace of the culture, and it seems impossible to think of such sentiments as part of the world of the eighteenth century.

So, we need to explain why ideas of open hospitality, which were widely accepted in early modern England, were also so vulnerable, why they seem to have possessed some of the qualities of recessive genes. It may be that the most useful explanation is simply that the English *did* possess an economic and social structure in the later Middle Ages that proved very responsive to the forces of the market. A nuclear family structure, and well-developed forms of property-right, may not indicate that the English were complete individualists, but they facilitated a pattern of economic behaviour that was not obviously communal.[30] Historians of the late medieval 'peasantry' are properly cautious about generalizing from diverse local and regional economies, but they have shown that where other circumstances were favourable, a strong market-orientation could and did develop in the fourteenth and fifteenth centuries. Havering in Essex, with its relatively free institutional structure and its proximity to the London market, shows in extreme form how far the ordinary cultivator could move from what are traditionally perceived as medieval values.[31] However, Havering is not unique: other communities within reach of the London market experienced similar incentives to commercialize, and elsewhere the upper ranks of village society were often able to consolidate their wealth and influence, and strengthen their hold on land at a time of

---

[29] T. Hearne (ed.), *Lelandi . . . Collectanea*, 6 vols. (London, 1774), 16 ff. An archiepiscopal feast when some of the guests did have the function of reminding those present of their good fortune, and of providing prayers for future prosperity, was Archbishop Parker's feast for the consecration of Grindal, when six poor men sat in the hall and were feasted: J. Strype, *The Life and Acts of Matthew Parker*, 3 vols. (London, 1821), iii. 289.

[30] A. Macfarlane, *The Origins of English Individualism* (Oxford, 1978).

[31] M. K. McIntosh, *Autonomy and Community: The Royal Manor of Havering, 1200–1500* (Cambridge, 1986), 136–78. It is interesting that McIntosh suggests some link between the market-orientation of individual Havering families, and the reluctance of the more prosperous to contribute to the ceremonial life of the community: ibid. 177.

population decline.[32] The story of the success of this 'middling' sort in the two following centuries is too well known to need reiteration: but it is worth reminding ourselves that the leading men of fifteenth-century Havering, and the yeomen farmers who left behind them diaries and farming accounts in the seventeenth century, seem to have been very similar people.

The dominance of the market and the growing engagement of men in its values did not, of course, automatically lead to the decline of hospitality. Even adverse economic circumstances, in this case the tobacco-crop crisis of the 1680s, did not prevent Tidewater Virginians from playing their accustomed roles.[33] Some of the most intensely commercialized farmers of the fifteenth and early sixteenth centuries were those Kentish yeomen who were supposed to be overwhelmingly proud of their open hospitality. But in times of economic adversity the market-orientation of such men was likely to conflict with their gift-giving instincts, and the sacrifice of the latter did not necessarily then breach powerful cultural taboos. Thus, the economic upheavals of the later sixteenth and early seventeenth centuries may have played a critical role not only in temporarily threatening the giving associated with hospitality, but in demonstrating conclusively that it was a recessive trait when compared with the commodity mentality long established among the English.

The foregoing analysis is probably most relevant for the middling sort in country and town, but, given the fluidity of the land market in the century after 1540, and the social mobility that accompanied it, there is no reason to suppose that it is not also pertinent to a substantial section of the landowning élite. We have identified *arrivistes* such as the Petres and Pagets who rapidly committed themselves not only to a noble life-style but to the ethos of generosity that accompanied it. However, if the market-orientation of English society was as powerful as has been

---

[32] See e.g., C. Dyer, *Lords and Peasants in a Changing Society* (Cambridge, 1980), 340 ff., where Worcestershire cultivators, who were not always well placed to benefit from the market in a period of population contraction, nevertheless were often able to prosper because of the general economic climate. Also A. R. Bridbury, *Economic Growth in England in the Later Middle Ages* (London, 1962), 39, 92.

[33] E. S. Morgan, *American Slavery, American Freedom* (New York, 1975), 284–8.

suggested, it would be no surprise to find that substantial numbers of the newly landed purchased the possessions of the élite, without in any profound sense understanding the forms of gift-exchange that were part of the magnificence of the late medieval nobility. Moreover, as the élite also experienced the economic pressures of the late Tudor period, even those members of the landed classes who were instinctively wedded to the old forms of prayer, praise, and open entertainment became less willing to pursue them unreflectingly. It is revealing that the forms of open entertainment that survived best among the nobility were the tenant feast, which had always had a strong transactional quality, and liberality to 'the county', where patronage and interest propelled the peer into a form of gift exchange whose rewards were supposed to be tangible.

Finally, we must note that there was one change affecting patterns of hospitality that owed less to the medieval past. The growth of the central state, though now an unfashionable historiographical theme, is inescapably visible in this social study. In two important ways it was direct intervention by the state that modified behaviour: the deliberate Tudor policy of centralizing politics deprived the great household of part of its political power, and the need for a national response to the problem of the poor also shifted the focus of local charitable behaviour. Of even greater significance was the long-term response of the élite to these changes: the pursuit of influence in London, and the world of civility and fashion that emanated from that pursuit. Slowly, but steadily, households declined in size, peers and gentry shifted to London to pursue office as well as fashion, and the calculus of reward became a more important element in entertaining. None of these processes were, of course, pursued to their logical conclusion: indeed, it was the tension created between central and localist values, so lacking in, for example, late seventeenth-century France, that permitted some tenuous survival of old traditions.

Nevertheless, a cynical conclusion might be that open hospitality was something the English always approved with their lips rather than practised in their lives. Smollett, in *Humphry Clinker*, remarked of old English hospitality: 'this is a phrase very much used by the English themselves . . . but I never heard it out of the island, except by way of irony and sarcasm.'[34] There is certainly a sense that it was a form of behaviour men *wished* to practise, but often found themselves impeded by other objectives, by the problems of the society, and by the rational calculation that early modern England was not a particularly sensible environment in which to feed and harbour all comers. It seems likely that commercial considerations, more deeply rooted here than in some other contemporary cultures, always contended with beliefs that exchange should comprehend that far more complex set of constructs called the gift, and should include altruism and the pursuit of reputation. Neither view of the world can be said to have had complete ascendancy, but the latter fared worse in the centuries between 1400 and 1700. In the end, Englishmen often found that hospitality served their purposes best when it was used as a rhetorical weapon, to challenge the dominance of the market-place in their own culture by a return to a mythical past of open generosity. Perhaps, therefore, the last word should be left to an unlikely successor to the ballad writers of the seventeenth century, William Blake, who utilized the commonplace sentiment of his age to look back satirically on the world the eighteenth century had lost:

Thus sitting at the table wide the Mayor and Aldermen
Were fit to give law to the city; each eat as much as ten:
The hungry poor enter'd the hall to eat good beef and ale—
Good English hospitality, O then it did not fail![35]

[34] Tobias Smollett, *Humphry Clinker* (London, 1967), 197.
[35] William Blake, *Complete Writings*, ed. G. Keynes (Oxford, 1966), 58: this is part of 'An Island in the Moon', which satirizes contemporary London society.

BIBLIOGRAPHY

PRINTED PRIMARY SOURCES

ABBOT, GEORGE, *A Sermon Preached . . . at the Funerall . . . of Thomas [Sackville] Earle of Dorset* (London, 1608).

ADAMS, THOMAS, 'The Gallant's Burden' and 'The White Devil', in *The Workes of Tho: Adams* (London, 1630).

ADY, THOMAS, *A Perfect Discovery of Witches* (London, 1661).

AINSWORTH, SAMUEL, *A Sermon Preached at the Funeral of Mrs. Dorothy Hanbury* (London, 1642).

ALLEN, ROBERT, *A Treatise of Christian Beneficence* (London, 1600).

—— *The Oderifferous Garden of Charity* (London, 1603).

ALLESTREE, RICHARD, *The Gentleman's Calling* (London, 1696).

ANDERSON, ANTHONY, *A Sermon of Sure Comfort, Preached at the Funerall of Master Robert Keylwey esq.* (London, 1581).

ANDREWES, LANCELOT, *Sermons* ed. J. P. Wilson and J. Bliss, 5 vols., (Library of Anglo-Catholic Theology, Oxford, 1841–3).

ANGLICUS, BARTHOLOMAEUS, *De Proprietatibus Rerum*, trans. John Trevisa, eds. M. C. Seymour *et al.* (Oxford, 1975).

ANNESLEY, SAMUEL, *The First Dish at the Wil-shire Feast* (London, 1655).

Appendix to the Second Report of the Royal Commission on Ritual (London, 1867).

ARTHINGTON, HENRY, *Provision for the Poore, now in Penurie* (London, 1597).

AUBREY, JOHN, *Collections for the Natural and Topographical History of Wiltshire*, ed. T. Phillips, 2 vols. (Devizes, 1821–38).

—— *Wiltshire: The Topographical Collections of John Aubrey*, ed. J. E. Jackson (Devizes, 1862).

—— *The Remaines of Gentilisme and Judaisme*, ed. J. Britten (London, 1881).

BACON, FRANCIS, *Works*, ed. J. Spedding, 7 vols. (London, 1857–9).

BACON, NATHANIEL, *The Annals of Ipswich*, ed. W. H. Richardson (Ipswich, 1884).

BADDILEY, JOHN, *The Life of Thomas Morton* (London, 1668).

BAGLEY, J. J. (ed.), *The Great Diurnal of Nicholas Blundell*, 2 vols. (Lancs. and Cheshire Rec. Soc., 110, 112, 1968, 1970).

BAMFORD, S., *Autobiography, My Early Days*, ed. W. H. Chaloner (London, 1967).

BARKER, EDMUND, *A Sermon Preached at the Funerall of . . . Lady Elizabeth Capell* (London, 1661).

BASSE, WILLIAM, *Sword and Buckler; Or a Serving-Man's Defence* (London, 1602).

BATEMAN, STEPHEN, *A Christall Glasse of Christian Reformation* (London, 1569).

BATESON, E., 'Notes of a Journey from Oxford to Embleton and back in 1464', *Archaeologia Aeliana*, 16 (1893–4).

BATESON, M. (ed.), *Records of the Borough of Leicester*, 3 vols. (Cambridge, 1899–1905).

BATHO, G. R. (ed.), *The Household Papers of Henry Percy, 9th Earl of Northumberland* (Camden Soc., 3rd ser. 93, London, 1962).

BECON, THOMAS, *Works*, ed. J. Ayre, 3 vols. (Parker Soc., Cambridge, 1843–4).

—— *The Sicke Mans Salve* (London, 1561).

BEDEL, HENRY, *A Sermon Exhortyng to Pitie the Poore* (London, 1572).

BEVERLEY, ROBERT, *The History and Present State of Virginia*, ed. L. B. Wright (Chapel Hill, 1947).

BEWICK, THOMAS, *A Memoir*, ed. I. Bain (Oxford, 1979).

BIRD, SAMUEL, *The Lectures . . . on the 8th and 9th Chapters of the Second Epistle to the Corinthians* (Cambridge, 1598).

BLAKE, WILLIAM, *Complete Writings*, ed. G. Keynes (Oxford, 1966).

BLOOM, J. H. (ed.), *Liber Elemosinarii: The Almoner's Book of the Priory of Worcester* (Worcester Hist. Soc., 27, 1911).

BOLTON, WILLIAM, *Josephs Entertainment of His Brethren* (London, 1684).

BOND, S. M. (ed.), *The Chamber Order Book of Worcester, 1602–1650* (Worcestershire Hist. Soc., N.S. 8, 1974).

'A Booke of Orders and Rules for Anthony, 2nd Viscount Montague', *Sussex Arch. Colls.*, 7 (1854).

BOORDE, ANDREW, *A Compendyous Regyment or a Dyetary of Helth,* ed. F. J. Furnivall (*EETS*, E.S. 10, London, 1870).

BOSWELL, JAMES, *The Life of Samuel Johnson*, ed. G. B. Hill, 6 vols. (Oxford, 1934–64).

BOWLE, JOHN, *A Sermon Preached at the Funerall of Henrie, Earle of Kent* (London, 1615).

BOYLE, J. R. (ed.), *Records of the Merchant Adventurers of Newcastle-upon-Tyne* (Surtees Soc., 93, 1895).

BRADSHAW, H. and WORDSWORTH, C. (eds.), *Lincoln Cathedral Statutes*, 3 vols. (Cambridge, 1897).

BRATHWAIT, RICHARD, *The English Gentleman* (London, 1630).

—— *Whimzies: Or, a New Cast of Characters* (London, 1631).

BRAYBROOKE, LORD (ed.), *The Private Correspondence of Jane Lady Cornwallis, 1613–44* (London, 1842).

BRERETON, WILLIAM, *Notes of a Journey through Durham and Northumberland* (Newcastle, 1844).

BRERETON, WILLIAM, *Travels in Holland, the United Provinces, England, Scotland and Ireland*, ed. E. Hawkins (Chetham Soc., o.s. 1, 1844).

BRETON, NICHOLAS, *A Merrie Dialogue betwixt the Taker and Mistaker* (London, 1603).

—— *Choice, Chance and Change* (London, 1606).

—— *The Good and the Badde* (London, 1616).

—— *The Court and Country, or a Briefe Discourse betweene a Courtier and Countryman* (London, 1618).

'A Breviate touching the Order and Government of a Nobleman's House', *Archaeologia*, 13 (1800).

BRINKELOW, HENRY, *The Lamentacon of a Christian Against the Citie of London* (Bonn, 1542).

—— *The Complaynt of Roderick Mors*, ed. J. M. Cowper (*EETS*, E.S. 22, London, 1874).

BROMYARD, THOMAS, *Summa predicantum*, 2 vols. (Venice, 1586).

BROWN, P. H. (ed.), *Early Travellers in Scotland* (Edinburgh, 1891).

BROWNING, A. (ed.), *The Memoirs of Sir John Reresby* (Glasgow, 1936).

BRUCE, J. (ed.), *Liber Famelicus of Sir James Whitelocke* (Camden Soc., O.S. 70, London, 1858).

BRYSKETT, LODOVIWK, *A Discourse of Civill Life* (London, 1606).

BUCER, MARTIN, *A Treatise How . . . Christian Mens Almose Ought to be Distributed* (1557?).

BUTLER-BOWDON, W. (ed.), *The Book of Margery Kempe* (London, 1936).

BYGOD, FRANCIS, *A Treatise Concernynge Impropriations of Benefices* (London, 1535?).

BYLES, A. T. P. (ed.), *The Book of the Ordre of Chyvalry . . .* (*EETS*, 168, London, 1926).

CAMDEN, WILLIAM, *Britannia*, ed. and trans. E. Gibson (London, 1695).

CAMPBELL, ARCHIBALD, MARQUIS OF ARGYLL, *Instructions to a Son* (London, 1661).

CAMPBELL, J. L. (ed.), *A Collection of Highland Rites and Customs* (London, 1975).

CARDWELL, E., *Documentary Annals of the Reformed Church of England*, 2 vols. (Oxford, 1839).

—— *Synodalia*, 2 vols. (Oxford, 1842).

CAREW, RICHARD, *The Survey of Cornwall* (London, 1602).

CAREW, THOMAS, *Poems*, ed. R. Dunlap (Oxford, 1949).

CARPENTER, H. (ed.), 'A History of the Furse Family of Moreshead', *Trans. of the Devon Assoc.*, 26 (1894).

CARTER, BEZALEEL, *The Wise King and the Learned Judge . . . Sir Edward Lewkenor* (Cambridge, 1618).

CASTIGLIONE, BALDASSARE, *The Courtier*, trans. T. Hoby (London, 1561).

CAVENDISH, GEORGE, *Life of Wolsey*, ed. R. S. Sylvester and D. P. Harding (New Haven, Conn., 1962).

CAVENDISH, MARGARET, DUCHESS OF NEWCASTLE, *The World's Olio* (London, 1671).

—— *The Life of William, Duke of Newcastle* (London, 1675).

CECIL, WILLIAM, *Certain Precepts . . . for Well-Ordering of a Man's Life*, in Peck, *Desiderata Curiosa*, i.

Certain Sermons or homilies appointed to be Read in Churches in the Time of Queen Elizabeth (London, 1687).

CHADERTON, LAURENCE, *An Excellent and Godly Sermon, Preached at Paules Crosse the xxvi Daye of October, 1578* (London, 1578?).

CHAMBERLAYNE, EDWARD, *Angliae Notitia: Or the Present State of England* (London, 1700 edn.).

CHAMBERS, R. W. (ed.), *A Fifteenth-Century Courtesy Book* (*EETS*, 48, London, 1914).

CHAUCER, GEOFFREY, *The Complete Works*, ed. F. N. Robinson (Oxford, 1957).

CHAUNCY, HENRY, *The Historical Antiquities of Hertfordshire*, 2 vols. (Bishop's Stortford, 1826).

CHOLMLEY, HUGH, *Memoirs* (Malton, 1870).

CHURCHYARD, THOMAS, *The Worthines of Wales* (Spenser Soc., London, 1876).

CICERO, *De Officiis*, ed. and trans. W. Miller (London, 1968).

CLARKE, SAMUEL, *Lives of Eminent Divines* (London, 1660).

CLEAVER, ROBERT, *A Godly Form of Householde Governement: for the Ordering of Private Families* (London, 1598).

CLELAND, JAMES, *Hero-Paideia, or the Institution of a Young Nobleman* (Oxford, 1607).

A Collection of Ordinances and Regulations for the Government of the Royal Household (London, 1790).

COLLIER, J. P. (ed.), *Manners and Household Expenses of England in the Thirteenth and Fifteenth Centuries* (Roxburghe Club, London, 1844).

CONWAY, WILLIAM, *An Exortacion to Charite, very Needefull at this Tyme* (London, 1551).

COOPER, C. H. (ed.), *Annals of Cambridge*, 5 vols. (Cambridge, 1842–1908).

COOPER, J. P. (ed.), *Wentworth Papers, 1597–1628* (Camden Soc., 4th ser. 12, London, 1973).

COOPER, THOMAS, *The Art of Giving* (London, 1615).

—— *The Mystery of Witch-craft* (London, 1617).

CORNWALLIS, WILLIAM, *Essays*, 2nd edn. (London, 1606).

COWPER, J. M. and FURNIVALL, F. J. (eds.), *Four Supplications* (*EETS*, E.S. 13, London, 1871).

COX, J. C. (ed.), 'The Household Book of Sir Miles Stapleton, Bt., 1656–1705', *The Ancestor* (1902).

CRAMER, J. A. (ed.), *The Travels of Nicander Nucius* (Camden Soc., O.S. 17, London, 1841).

CRANMER, THOMAS, *Remains*, ed. H. Jenkyns, 4 vols. (Oxford, 1833).

The Crie of the Poor for the Death of Henry Hastings, Earl of Huntingdon (London, 1596).

CROWLEY, ROBERT, *Select Works*, ed. J. M. Cowper (*EETS*, E.S. 15, 1872).

CURTEYS, RICHARD, *The Care of a Christian Conscience* (London, 1600).

CUST, E., *Records of the Cust Family*, 2 vols. (London, 1909).

DALECHAMP, CALEB, *Christian Hospitalitie: Handled Commonplace-wise in the Chappel of Trinity Colledge in Cambridge* (Cambridge, 1632).

DANCE, E. M. (ed.), *Guildford Borough Records, 1514–46* (Surrey Rec. Soc., 24, 1958).

DARLINGTON, I. (ed.), *London Consistory Court Wills: 1492–1547* (London Rec. Soc., 3, 1967).

DAVIES, G. (ed.) *The Autobiography of Thomas Raymond* (Camden Soc., 3rd ser. 28, London, 1917).

DAVIES, R. (ed.), *Records of the City of York* (London, 1843).

—— *The Life of Marmaduke Rawdon of York* (Camden Soc., O.S. 85, London, 1863).

DAVIS, F. N. (ed.), *Parochial Collections for Oxfordshire: Made by Wood and Rawlinson*, 3 vols. (Oxford Rec. Soc., 2, 4, 11, 1920, 1922, 1929).

DAVIS, N. (ed.), *Paston Letters and Papers of the Fifteenth Century*, 2 vols. (Oxford, 1971, 1976).

DE COURTIN, ANTOINE, *The Rules of Civility* (London, 1671).

DELLA CASA, GIOVANNI, *Galateo . . . A Treatise of Manners*, trans. R. Peterson (London, 1576).

DENNETT, J. (ed.), *Beverley Borough Records, 1575–1821* (Yorks. Arch. Soc., Record Ser. 84, 1933).

DE ROMESTIN, H. (ed.), *Some of the Principal Works of St. Ambrose, in The Nicene and Post-Nicene Fathers* (New York, 1976).

D'EVELYN, C. (ed.), *Peter Idley's Instructions to his Son* [*1445–50*] (Boston, 1935).

DEVLIN, M. A. (ed.), *The Sermons of Thomas Brinton, Bishop of Rochester*, 2 vols. (Camden Soc., 3rd ser. 85–6, London, 1954).

DE VOGUE, A. (ed.), *La Règle de St. Benoit*, 6 vols. (Sources Chrétiennes, 181–6, Paris, 1971–2).

DICKENS, A. G. (ed.), *The Register of Butley Priory Suffolk: 1510–1535* (Winchester, 1951).

DOWNAME, JOHN, *The Plea of the Poore. Or a Treatise of Beneficence and Almes-Deeds* (London, 1616).

DRANT, THOMAS, *A Fruitfull and Necessary Sermon, Specially Concernyng Almesgeving* (London, 1572).

DRAYTON, MICHAEL, *Works*, ed. J. W. Hebel, 5 vols. (Oxford, 1961).

DUDLEY, 3rd LORD NORTH, *A Forest of Varieties* (London, 1645).

DUDLEY, 4th LORD NORTH, *Observations and Advices Œconomical*, (London, 1669).

DUDLEY, EDMUND, *The Tree of the Commonwealth*, ed. D. M. Brodie (Cambridge, 1948).

DUGARD, THOMAS, *Death and the Grave Little Regarded: A Sermon Preached at the Funeral of . . . Lady Alice Lucie* (London, 1649).

DUGDALE, WILLIAM, *The Antiquities of Warwickshire*, 2 vols., 2nd edn. (London, 1730).

ELLIS, CLEMENT, *The Gentile Sinner* (Oxford, 1660).

ELYOT, THOMAS, *The Boke Named the Governor*, ed. S. E. Lehmberg (London, 1962).

EMMISON, F. G. (ed.), *Wills of the County of Essex: 1558-77*, 3 vols. (Washington, 1982-6).

ERASMUS, DESIDERIUS, *Ecclesiasticae sive de ratione concionandi* (Antwerp, 1535).

EUSTACE, G. W. (ed.), 'The Tompkins Diary', in *Sussex Arch. Coll.*, 71 (1930).

EVANS, J. A. (ed.), *Ely Chapter Visitations and Ordinances* (Camden Soc., Misc. 17, 3rd ser. 64, London, 1940).

EVELYN, JOHN, 'A Character of England', in *Harleian Miscellany*, 10 (London, 1813).

'The Expense Book of James Master, Esq., 1646-79', *Archaeologia Cantiana*, 16 (1886).

FARINDON, ANTHONY, *The Sermons of the Reverend Anthony Farindon* 4 vols. (London, 1849).

FEGAN, E. S. (ed.), *The Journal of Prior William More* (Worcestershire Hist. Soc., 32, 1914).

FELTHAM, OWEN, *Resolves Divine, Morall, Politicall* (London, 1623).

FERGUSON, R. S. (ed.), *A Boke off Recorde . . . within the Town of Kirkbiekendall* (Cumbs. and Westmors. Antiq. and Arch. Soc., E.S. 7, 1892).

—— and NANSON, W. (eds.), *Some Municipal Records of the City of Carlisle* (Cumbs. and Westmors. Antiq. and Arch. Soc., E.S. 4, 1887).

FIELDING, HENRY, *The Adventures of Joseph Andrews* (London, 1910).

FISHER, JOHN, *English Works*, ed. J. E. B. Mayor (*EETS*, E.S. 27, London, 1876).

FITZHERBERT, JOHN, *Here Begynneth a Newe Tracte or Treatyse Moost Profytable for all Husbandemen*, 2nd edn. (London, 1534).

FLEMING, ABRAHAM, *A Memoriall of the Famous Monuments and Almesdeedes of William Lambe Esq.* (London, 1580).

FLOYD, THOMAS, *The Picture of a Perfit Commonwealth* (London, 1600).

FOSTER, E. R. (ed.), *Proceedings in the Parliament of 1610*, 2 vols. (New Haven, Conn., 1966).

FOSTER, J. E. (ed.), *The Diary of Alderman Samuel Newton* (Proc. of the Camb. Antiq. Soc., 1890.

FOWLER, J. T. (ed.), *Rites of Durham* (Surtees Soc., 107, 1903).

FOX, L. (ed.), *The Diary of Robert Beake* (Dugdale Soc. Misc. 1, 1977).

FOXE, JOHN, *Acts and Monuments*, ed. S. R. Cattley and G. Townsend, 8 vols. (London, 1837–41).

FRERE, W. H. and Kennedy, W. M. (eds.), *Visitation Articles and Injunctions of the Period of the Reformation*, 3 vols. (Alcuin Club, London, 1910).

FROYSELL, THOMAS, *The Beloved Disciple: A Funeral Sermon for Sir Robert Harley* (London, 1658).

FULLER, THOMAS, *The Holy State and the Profane State* (Cambridge, 1642).

—— *The History of the Worthies of England*, ed. P. A. Nuttall, 3 vols. (London, 1840).

—— *Abel Redevivus*, 2 vols. (London, 1867)

FURNIVALL, F. J. (ed.), *Early English Treatises and Poems on Education, Precedence and Manners in Olden Time* (*EETS*, E.S. 8, London, 1869).

—— (ed.), *Manners and Meals in Olden Time* (*EETS*, 32, London, 1868).

GABEL, L. C. (ed.), *Memoirs of a Renaissance Pope* (New York, 1962).

GAILHARD, JEAN, *The Compleat Gentleman* (London, 1678).

GAINSFORD, THOMAS, *The Glory of England* (London, 1618).

GAREY, SAMUEL, *A Newe Yeares Gift for the Suole* (London, 1615).

—— *Ientaculum Iudicum or a Breake-fast for the Bench* (London, 1623).

GERARD, *A Preparation . . . to the Most Holie Ministerie,* trans. N. Becket (London, 1598).

GIBBON, CHARLES, *The Praise of a Good Name* (London, 1594).

GIBSON, J. S. W. and Brinkworth, E. R. C. (eds.), *Banbury Corporation Records: Tudor and Stuart* (Banbury Hist. Soc., 15, 1977).

GIFFORD, GEORGE, *A Briefe Discourse of Certaine Points of Religion . . .* (London, 1581).

GILL, H. and GUILFORD, E. C. (eds.), *The Rector's Book: Clayworth, Nottinghamshire* (Nottingham, 1910).

GODFREY, W. H. (ed.), *The Book of John Rowe, Steward of the Manors of Lord Bergavenny, 1597–1622* (Sussex Rec. Soc., 34, 1928).

GODWIN, FRANCIS, *A Catalogue of the Bishops of England* (London, 1601).

GOUGE, WILLIAM, *Of Domesticall Duties: Eight Treatises* (London, 1622).

—— *A Learned . . . Commentary on the whole Epistle to the Hebrewes* (London, 1655).

GOUGH, RICHARD, *The History of Myddle*, ed. D. Hey (London, 1981).

GRACE, M. (ed.), *Records of the Gild of St. George in Norwich, 1389–1547* (Norfolk Rec. Soc., 9, 1937).

GRAINGER, F. (ed.), 'The Diary of James Jackson, 1650–83', *Trans. of the Cumbs. and Westmors. Antiq. and Arch. Soc.*, NS, 21 (1921).

GREAVES, R. W. (ed.), *The First Wycombe Ledger Book* (Bucks. Rec. Soc., 2, 1947).

GREENHAM, RICHARD, 'A Treatise of the Sabbath', in *The Works*, 2nd edn. (London, 1599).

GREVILLE, FULKE, *The Life of Sir Philip Sidney* (Oxford, 1907).

GRIFFITH, MATTHEW, *Bethel: Or the Forme of Families* (London, 1633).

GUILDING, J. M. (ed.), *Records of the Borough of Reading*, 4 vols. (London, 1892–6).

GUNTHER, R. T. (ed.), *The Architecture of Sir Roger Pratt* (Oxford, 1928).

GUY, J. (ed.), *Christopher St. German on Chancery and Statute* (Selden Soc., suppl. ser. 6, London, 1985).

HACKET, JOHN, *Scrinia Reserata: A Memorial Offered to the Great Deservings of John Williams, D.D.* (London, 1693).

HALES, JOHN, *Works*, 3 vols. (Glasgow, 1765).

HALL, JOSEPH, *Works*, 12 vols. (Oxford, 1837).

HALLIWELL-PHILLIPS, J. O. (ed.), *The Boke of Curtasye* (London, 1841).

―― (ed.), *The Private Diary of John Dee* (Camden Soc., OS 19, London, 1842).

―― (ed.), *The Pleasant Conceits of Old Hobson* (Percy Soc., 9, London, 1843).

―― (ed.), *The Life of Sir Simonds D'Ewes* (London, 1845).

―― (ed.), *Books of Characters* (London, 1857).

HAMMOND, HENRY, *A Practical Catechism* (Library of Anglo-Catholic Theology, Oxford, 1847).

HARINGTON, JOHN, *Nugae Antiquae*, ed. T. Park, 2 vols. (London, 1804).

HARISON, ANTHONY, *Registrum Vagum*, ed. T. F. Barton, 2 vols. (Norfolk Rec. Soc., 32, 33, 1963–4).

HARMAN, THOMAS, *A Caveat or Warening for Common Cursetors*, ed. E. Viles and F. J. Furnivall, *The Rogues and Vagabonds of Shakespeare's Youth* (New Shakspere Soc., 6th ser. 7, London, 1880).

HARPSFIELD, NICHOLAS, *Historia Anglicana Ecclesiastica* (London, 1622).

HARRIS, ROBERT, *Abner's Funerall: Preached at the Burial of Sir Thomas Lucie*, 2nd edn. (London, 1653).

HARRISON, WILLIAM, *The Description of England*, ed. F. J. Furnivall, 2 vols. (New Shakspere Soc., 6th ser. 1, 5, London, 1908).

HARTLEY, T. E. (ed.), *Proceedings in the Parliaments of Elizabeth I: 1559–1581* (London, 1981).

412   *Bibliography*

HARVEY, J. (ed.), *The Itineraries of William de Worcestre* (Oxford, 1969).

HASLOP, G. S. (ed.), *A Selby Kitchener's Roll of the Early Fifteenth Century* (Yorks. Arch. Soc. 48, 1976).

HAWARD, NICHOLAS, *The Line of Liberalitie dulie Directinge the Wel Bestowing of Benefites* (London, 1569).

HAWARDE, JOHN, *Les Reportes del Cases in Camera Stellata, 1593 to 1609*, ed. W. P. Baildon (London, 1894).

HAZLITT, W. C., *Inedited Tracts Illustrating the Manners of Englishmen during the Sixteenth and Seventeenth Centuries* (Roxburghe Club, London, 1868).

HEALE, WILLIAM, *An Apologie for Women, or an Opposition to Mr. Dr. G[ager] his Assertion. That it was Lawfull for Husbands to Beate theire Wives* (Oxford, 1609).

A Health to the Gentlemanly Profession of Servingman (London, 1598), repr. in Hazlitt (ed.), *Inedited Tracts*.

HEARNE, T. (ed.), *Joannis Lelandi . . . Collectanea*, 6 vols. (London, 1774).

HERBERT, GEORGE, *Outlandish Proverbs* (London, 1640).

—— 'A Priest to the Temple, or the Country Parson', in *Works*, ed. F. E. Hutchinson (Oxford, 1941).

HERRICK, ROBERT, *Collected Verse*, ed. L. C. Martin (Oxford, 1956).

HEYLYN, PETER, *Cyprianus Anglicus, or the History of the Life and Death [of Laud]* (London, 1668).

HEYWOOD, OLIVER, *Autobiography and Diaries*, ed. J. H. Turner, 4 vols. (Brighouse and Bingley, 1881-5).

—— *The Life of John Angier of Denton*, ed. E. Axon (Chetham Soc., NS 97, 1937).

HICKES, GEORGE, *The Moral Shechinah* (London, 1682).

HIERON, SAMUEL, *The Life and Death of Dorcas* (London, 1612).

HIGFORD, WILLIAM, *The Institution of a Gentleman* (London, 1660).

HINDE, WILLIAM, *A Faithfull Remonstrance of the Holy Life and Happy Death of John Bruen of Bruen Stapleford* (London, 1641).

Historical Manuscripts Commission Reports:
  3rd Rept., App., Records of Axbridge.
  6th Rept., App., Paston Correspondence.
  9th Rept., App., Records of St. Albans, Canterbury, Holy Trinity Gild, Wisbech, Plymouth.
  10th Rept., App., Records of Bridgnorth.
  11th Rept., App. VII, Le Strange Household Accounts.
  Var. Coll., ii, Selections from the Household Books of Sir William Fairfax.
  Cowper, Coke correspondence.
  Gawdy, Gawdy and Knyvett correspondence.

Middleton, The Willoughby Household Books.
Rutland, iv, Selections from the Household Accounts of Sir Thomas Lovell.
Salisbury MSS, vii, x, xi.
Portland MSS, ii, Thomas Baskerville's Travel Diary, 1681-2.
De L'Isle and Dudley, vi, Orders for the Household of Robert, Earl of Leicester.
Wells, ii, Manorial Records.
HOCCLEVE, THOMAS, *Works*, ed. F. J. Furnivall (*EETS*, E.S. 72, London, 1897).
HODGSON, J. C. (ed.), *Durham Wills and Inventories, pt. iii* (Surtees Soc., 112, 1906).
HOLLES, GERVASE, *Memorials of the Holles Family, 1493-1656*, ed. A. C. Wood (Camden Soc., 3rd ser. 55, London, 1937).
HOOD, C. M. (ed.), *The Chorography of Norfolk* (Norwich, 1938).
HOULBROOKE, R. (ed), *The Letter-Book of John Parkhurst* (Norfolk Rec. Soc., 43, 1974-5).
HOWSON, JOHN, *A Sermon Preached at Paul's Cross: 24th December 1597* (London, 1597).
HUDSON, W. H. (ed.), 'Assessment of the Hundred of Forehoe, Norfolk, in 1621', *Norfolk Archaeology*, 21 (1920-3).
―― and TINGEY, J. C. (eds.), *Selected Records of the City of Norwich*, 2 vols. (Norwich, 1906-10).
HUGHES, P. L. and LARKIN, J. F. (eds.), *Tudor Royal Proclamations*, 3 vols. (New Haven, Conn., 1964-9).
HUGHEY, R. (ed.), *The Correspondence of Lady Katherine Paston, 1603-1627* (Norfolk Rec. Soc., 14, 1941).
HULL, WILLIAM, *The Harborlesse Guest, or the Third Worke of Mercy* (London, 1614).
HUMPHREY, LAURENCE, *The Nobles, or Of Nobility* (London, 1563).
I.H. *This World's Folly* (London, 1615).
The Institucion of a Gentleman (London, 1555).
ISAACSON, HENRY, *The Life of the Reverend Father in God Lancelot Andrewes*, ed. S. Isaacson (London, 1829).
JACKSON, C. (ed.), *The Diary of Abraham de La Pryme* (Surtees Soc., 54, 1870).
―― *The Autobiography of Mrs. Alice Thornton* (Surtees Soc., 62, 1875).
JAMES I, *The Workes of James . . . King of Great Britain*, ed. J. Montague (London, 1616).
―― *Poems*, ed. J. Craigie, 2 vols. (Scottish Text Soc., 3rd ser. 12, 26, Edinburgh, 1955).
JEAYES, I. H. (ed.), *The Letters of Philip Gawdy of West Harling, Norfolk* (Roxburghe Club, London, 1906).

JESSOPP, A. (ed.), Visitations of the Diocese of Norwich A.D. 1492-1532 (Camden Soc., NS 43, London, 1888).

JOHNSON, ROBERT, Lux et Lex, or The Light and the Laws of Jacobs House (London, 1647).

JONSON, BEN, Works, ed. C. H. Herford, P. and E. Simpson, 11 vols. (Oxford, 1925-52).

—— The Complete Poems, ed. G. Parfitt (London, 1975).

KEMP, T. (ed.), The Book of John Fisher, Town Clerk and Deputy Recorder of Warwick (1550-88) (Warwick, 1900).

KENNETT, WHITE, Parochial Antiquities . . . in the Counties of Oxford and Bucks (Oxford, 1695).

KING, DANIEL, The Vale Royall of England, or The County Palatine of Chester (London, 1656).

KING, P. I. (ed.), The Book of William Morton, Almoner of Peterborough, 1448-67 (Northants. Rec. Soc., 16, 1954).

KING, P. J. (ed.), Tudor Songs and Ballads (London, 1978).

KINGSFORD, C. L. (ed.), Chronicles of London (Oxford, 1905).

KIRK, THOMAS, Journeyings through Northumberland and Durham Anno Dom. mdclxxvii (Newcastle, 1845).

KNAPP, WILLIAM, Abraham's Image in One of his Sonnes [John Dethick, esq. of West Newton], (London, 1658).

KOCK, E. A. (ed.), Three Middle-English Versions of the Rule of St. Benet (EETS, 120, London, 1902).

KNOWLER, W. (ed.), The Earl of Strafford's Letters and Despatches, 2 vols. (London, 1739).

LAMBARD, WILLIAM, A Perambulation of Kent (London, 1576).

LAMOND, E. (ed.), The Discourse of the Commonweal (Cambridge, 1954).

LANGLAND, WILLIAM, Piers Plowman: The B Text, ed. W. W. Skeat (EETS, 38, London, 1869).

LARKIN, J. F. and HUGHES, P. L. (eds.), Stuart Royal Proclamations, 2 vols. (Oxford, 1973-82).

LATIMER, HUGH, Sermons, ed. G. E. Corrie (Parker Soc., Cambridge, 1845).

LEACH, A. F. (ed.), Beverley Town Documents (Selden Soc., 14, 1900).

LEADAM, I. S. (ed.), The Domesday of Inclosures, 1517-1518, 2 vols. (London, 1897).

—— (ed.), Select Cases before the King's Council in the Star Chamber, 2 vols. (Selden Soc., 16, 25, 1903, 1911).

LEE, S. (ed.), The Life of Edward, Lord Herbert of Cherbury (London, 1886).

LEGG, L. G. W. (ed.), A Relation of a Short Survey of Twenty-Six Counties Observed in a Seven Weeks Journey . . . from Norwich (London, 1904).

—— (ed.), A Description of a Journie made into the Westerne Counties, 1635 (Camden Misc. 16, 3rd ser. 52, London, 1936).

LEIGH, DOROTHY, *The Mother's Blessing, Or the Godly Counsaile of a Gentlewoman* (London, 1616).

LEIGH, EDWARD, *The Gentlemans Guide* (London, 1680).

'Le Strange Household Accounts', *Archaeologia*, 69 (1917–18).

LEVER, THOMAS, *Sermons*, ed. E. Arber (London, 1870).

LEWIS, T. T. (ed.), *Letters of the Lady Brilliana Harley* (Camden Soc., OS 58, London, 1854).

LIVOCK, D. M. (ed.), *City Chamberlains' Accounts for Bristol* (Bristol Rec. Soc., 24, 1966).

LOVELACE, RICHARD, *Poems*, ed. C. H. Wilkinson (Oxford, 1930).

LUPTON, DONALD, 'London and the Country Carbonadoed and Quartered', in *Harleian Miscellany*, 9 (1812).

LYNDWOOD, WILLIAM, *Provinciale seu constitutiones Angliae* (London, 1679).

MacCULLOCH, D. (ed.), *The Chorography of Suffolk* (Suffolk Rec. Soc., 19, 1976).

MACFARLANE, A. (ed.), *The Diary of Ralph Josselin* (London, 1976).

MALFATTI, C. V. (ed.), *Two Italian Accounts of Tudor England* (Oxford, 1954).

MANSHIP, HENRY, *A Booke of the Foundation and Antiquity of Great Yarmouth*, ed. C. Palmer, 2 vols. (Great Yarmouth 1854–6).

MARTYR, PETER VERMIGLI, *The Common Places*, Eng. trans. (London, 1583).

MAYO, C. H. (ed.), *Dorchester Municipal Records* (Exeter, 1908).

MEADS, D. M. (eds.), *The Diary of Lady Margaret Hoby* (London, 1930).

MILDMAY, WALTER, *A Memorial for a Son from his Father, 1570* (London, 1893).

MILLER, WILLIAM, *A Sermon Preached at the Funerall of G Davies Esq. . . .* (London, 1621).

MORE, THOMAS, *Utopia*, ed. E. Surtz and J. H. Hexter (New Haven, Conn., 1965).

MOREHOUSE, H. J. (ed.), *Adam Eyre, a Diurnal* in *Yorkshire Diaries and Autobiographies* (Surtees Soc., 65, 1877).

MORISON, S. E. *et al.* (eds.), *The Winthrop Papers*, 3 vols. (Massachusetts Hist. Soc., 1925).

MORRIS, C. (ed.), *The Illustrated Journeys of Celia Fiennes* (London, 1982).

MORYSON, FYNES, *An Itinerary Containing his Ten Years' Travel*, 4 vols. (Glasgow, 1907–8).

MUNBY, L. (ed.), *Early Stuart Household Accounts* (Herts. Rec. Soc., ii, 1986).

MUNDY, PETER, *A Petty Progresse through Some Part of England and Wales, 1639* (Hakluyt Soc., 55, 1925).

MYERS, A. R. (ed.), *The Household of Edward IV* (Manchester, 1959).

NEWBURY, NATHANIEL, *The Yeomans Prerogative, or the Honour of Husbandry* (London, 1652).

NICHOLS, J., *The Progresses of Queen Elizabeth*, 3 vols. (London, 1823).

—— (ed.), Life of the last Fitz-Alan, Earl of Arundel, *Gentlemans Magazine* (1833).

—— (ed.), *Narratives of the Days of the Reformation* (Camden Soc., OS 77, London, 1859).

—— (ed.), *The Autobiography of Anne, Lady Halkett* (Camden Soc., NS 13, London, 1875).

NICOLAS, N. H. (ed.), *Memoirs of Lady Fanshawe, wife of . . . Sir Richard Fanshawe . . .* (London, 1829).

NORDEN, JOHN, *The Surveyor's Dialogue* (London, 1607).

NORTH, ROGER, *The Lives of. . . Francis North, Baron Guilford . . . Sir Dudley North . . . and Dr. John North*, 3 vols. (London, 1826).

O.B., *Questions of Profitable and Pleasant Concernings* (London, 1594).

OGLANDER, JOHN, *A Royalist's Notebook: The Commonplace Book of Sir John Oglander, Knt.*, ed. F. Bamford (London, 1936).

OLDMAYNE, TIMOTHY, *God's Rebuke in taking from us Sir E Lewkenor* (London, 1619).

—— *Lifes Brevitie and Deaths Debility . . . a Sermon Preached at the Funerall of E Lewkenor* (London, 1636).

ORNSBY, G. (ed.), *Selections from the Household Books of the Lord William Howard, of Naworth Castle, 1612–40* (Surtees Soc., 68, 1878).

OSBORNE, FRANCIS, *Advice to a Son* (London, 1656).

PANTON, EDWARD, *Speculum Iuventatis: or, a True Mirror where Errors in Breeding Noble and Generous Youth . . . are Manifest* (London, 1671).

PARKER, HENRY [attrib.], *Dives and Pauper* (1536?) [1st edn., 1493].

PARKER, MATTHEW, *Correspondence*, ed. J. Bruce and T. T. Perowne (Parker Soc., Cambridge, 1853).

PARKES, WILLIAM, *The Curtaine-Drawer of the World* (London, 1612).

PARKINSON, R. (ed.), *The Life of Adam Martindale* (Chetham Soc., OS 4, 1845)

PARSONS, BARTHOLEMEW, *A Christians Remembrance or Felicity by Hope: A Sermon Preached at the Burial of Sir Francis Pile, Bart of Collingborne Kingston, Wiltshire* (Oxford, 1636).

PARSONS, D. (ed.), *Diary of Sir Henry Slingsby, of Scriven Bart* (London, 1836).

PAULE, GEORGE, *The Life of the Most Reverend Prelate John Whitgift* (London, 1612).

PEACHAM, HENRY, *The Compleat Gentleman* (London, 1622).

—— *An Aprill Shower, Shed . . . for the Death of Richard Sacvile . . . Earle of Dorset* (London, 1624).

—— *The Art of Living in London* (London, 1642).

PECK, F. *Desiderata Curiosa*, 2 vols. (London, 1732–5).

PENNEY, N. (ed.), *Household Account Book of Sarah Fell of Swarthmoor, Hall, 1673–8* (Cambridge, 1920).

'Henry Percy, 9th Earl of Northumberland's Advice to his Son' *Archaeologia*, xxvii (1838).

PERCY, T. (ed.), *Regulations and Establishment of the Household of Henry Algernon Percy* (London, 1770).

PERKINS, WILLIAM, *Christian Œconomie: Or a Short Survey of the Right Manner of Ordering a Familie According to the Scriptures* (London, 1609).

—— *Works* (London, 1626).

—— *The Whole Treatise of Cases of Conscience*, ed. T. F. Merrill (Nieuwkoop, Netherlands, 1966).

PERLIN, ETIENNE, *Description des Royaulmes d'Angleterre et d'Escosse* (London, 1755).

PEYTON, S. A. (ed.), *Churchwardens' Presentations for the Oxfordshire Peculiars of Dorchester, Thame and Banbury* (Oxford Rec. Soc., 10, 1928).

PLOT, ROBERT, *The Natural History of Oxfordshire* (Oxford, 1677).

POPE, WALTER, *The Life of the Right Reverend Seth, Lord Bishop of Salisbury* (London, 1697).

POTTER, BARNABY, *The Baronet's Buriall: A Funerall Sermon at Sir Edward Seymour's Buriall* (Oxford, 1613).

POWICKE, M. and CHENEY, C. R. (eds.), *Councils and Synods, with Other Documents Relating to the English Church (1205–1313)* (Oxford, 1964).

The Prayse and Commendacion of suche as Sought Comenwelthes (London, 1549?).

PURVIS, J. S. (ed.), 'Yorkshire Dissolution Documents', in *Miscellanea* (Yorks. Arch. Soc., Rec. Ser. 80, 1931).

RAINE, A. (ed.), *York Civic Records*, 8 vols. (Yorks. Arch. Soc., Rec. Ser. 98–119, 1939–53).

RAINE, J. (ed.), *The Durham Household Book . . . 1530–34* (Surtees Soc., 18, 1844).

—— (ed.), *Depositions and Other Ecclesiastical Proceedings in the Courts of Durham* (Surtees Soc., 21, 1845).

—— (ed.), *Depositions from the Castle of York, Relating to Offences Committed in the Northern Counties* (Surtees Soc., 40, 1861).

—— (ed.), *Testamenta Eboracensia*, 5 vols. (Surtees Soc., 4, 30, 45, 53, 79, 1836–84).

RAINES, F. R. (ed.), *The Stanley Papers, pt. ii: The Derby Household Books* (Chetham Soc., OS 31, 1853).

RALPH, E. (ed.), *The Great White Book of Bristol* (Bristol Rec. Soc., 32, 1979).

RAMESAY, WILLIAM, *The Gentleman's Companion* (London, 1672).

RAVENSHAW, T. F., *Antiente Epitaphes* (London, 1878).

REEVE, THOMAS, *Lazarus his Rest* [funeral of Mr Ephraim Udall] (London, 1647).

RICART, ROBERT, *The Maire of Bristowe is Kalendar*, ed. L. T. Smith (Camden Soc., NS 5, London, 1872).

RILEY, H. T. (ed.), *Memorials of London and London Life* (London, 1868).

—— (ed.), *Johannes Amundesham Annales Monasterii St. Albani* (Rolls Ser., 1870).

RISDON, TRISTRAM, *The Chorographical Description or Survey of the County of Devon*, 2 pts. (London, 1714).

ROBINSON, C. B. (ed.), *The Rural Economy in Yorkshire 1641, being the Farming and Account Books of Henry Best* (Surtees Soc., 33, 1857).

ROBINSON, H. (ed.), *The Zurich Letters*, 2 vols. (Parker Soc., Cambridge, 1842-5).

ROBSON, SIMON, *A New Yeeres Gift: The Courte of Civill Courtesie* (London, 1577).

ROLLINS, H. E. (ed.), *The Pepys Ballads*, 8 vols. (Cambridge, Mass., 1929-32).

Roxburghe Ballads, 9 vols. (London, 1871-97).

RUSHWORTH, J. (ed.), *Historical Collections*, 7 vols. (London, 1659-1701).

RYE, W. B. (ed.), *England as seen by Foreigners in the Days of Elizabeth and James I* (London, 1865).

SACHSE, W. L. (ed.), *The Diurnal of Thomas Rugg, 1659-61* (Camden Soc., 3rd ser. 91, London, 1961).

—— *The Diary of Roger Lowe* (London, 1938).

SACKVILLE-WEST, V., *Diary of Lady Anne Clifford* (London, 1923).

SALTER, H. E. (ed.), *Oxford Council Acts, 1583-1626* (Oxford Rec. Soc., 87, 1928).

SANDYS, EDWIN, *Sermons*, ed. J. Ayre (Parker Soc., Cambridge, 1841).

SAVAGE, R. and FRIPP, E. I. (eds.), *Minutes and Accounts of Stratford-upon-Avon Corporation*, 4 vols. (Dugdale Soc., 1, 3, 5, 10, 1921-9).

SCHOFIELD, B. (ed.), *The Knyvett Letters, 1620-44* (Norfolk Rec. Soc., 20, 1949).

SEARLE, A. (ed.), *Barrington Family Letters, 1628-32* (Camden Soc., 4th ser. 27, London, 1982).

SENECA, *De Beneficiis*, in *Moral Essays*, iii, ed. and trans. J. Basore (Cambridge, Mass., 1935).

—— *De remediis fortuitorum*, ed. and trans. R. G. Palmer (Chicago, 1953).

—— *A Fruitfull Worke of Lucius Anneus Senecae Called the Myrrour or Glasse of Maners*, trans. R. Whyttynton (London, 1547).

SHEILS, W. J. (ed.), *Archbishop Grindal's Visitation of the Diocese of York 1575* (York, 1977).

SHUCKBURGH, E. S. (ed.), *Two Biographies of William Bedell, Bishop of Kilmore* (Cambridge, 1902).

SYDNEY, PHILIP, *The Countess of Pembroke's Arcadia*, ed. M. Evans (London, 1977).

SLADE, JOHN, *A Sermon Preached at the Funeral of Richard Herbert Esq. of Oakly Park* (London, 1676).

SLINGSBY, HENRY, *A Father's Legacy* (London, 1658).

SMITH, MILES, *Sermons* (London, 1632).

SMITH, RICHARD, *An Elizabethan Recusant Household: Comprising the Life of the Lady Magdalen, Viscountess Montagu*, ed. A. C. Southern (London, 1954).

SMOLLETT, TOBIAS, *Humphry Clinker* (London, 1967).

SMYTH, JOHN, *The Lives of the Berkeleys*, ed. J. Maclean, 3 vols. (Gloucester, 1883–5).

SNEYD, C. A. (ed.), *A Relation . . . of the Island of England* (Camden Soc., OS 37, London, 1847).

SONDES, GEORGE, 'Narrative of the Death of his Two Sons', in *Harleian Miscellany*, 10 (London, 1813).

SORLIEN, R. P. (ed.), *The Diary of John Manningham* (Hanover, NH, 1976).

SPARKE, THOMAS, *A Sermon at Chenies . . . at the Buriall of . . . the Earle of Bedford* (London, 1585).

—— *A Sermon Preached at Whaddon at the Buriall of Arthur Lorde Grey of Wilton* (Oxford, 1593).

'Household Book of Edward Stafford, Duke of Buckingham', *Archaeologia*, 25 (1834).

STAPLETON, T. (ed.), *The Plumpton Correspondence* (Camden Soc., OS 4, London, 1839).

STARKEY, THOMAS, *A Dialogue of Pole and Lupset*, ed. J. M. Cowper, 2 vols. (*EETS*, E.S. 12, 32, London, 1871, 1878).

STONE, L. (ed.), 'Sir Edward Montagu's Directions to his Son', *Northants Past and Present* 2 (1958).

STOW, JOHN, *A Survey of London*, ed. C. L. Kingsford, 2 vols. (Oxford, 1908).

STUBBES, PHILIP, *The Anatomy of Abuses in England*, ed. F. J. Furnivall, pt. 1 (New Shakspere Soc., London, 1877).

STUDER, P. (ed.), *The Oak Book of Southampton*, 3 vols. (Southants. Rec. Soc., 6, 1910–11).

SUMMERSON, J. (ed.), *The Book of Architecture of John Thorpe* (Walpole Soc., 40, 1966).

TASSO, TORQUATO, *The Housholders Philosophie*, trans. T. Kyd (London, 1588).

TAYLOR, JOHN, *Works* (Spenser Soc., 2, 4, 7, 14, 21, 25, Manchester, 1868–78).

THOMPSON, A. H. (ed.), *The Statutes of the Cathedral Church of Durham* (Surtees Soc., 143, 1929).

—— (ed.), *Visitations in the Diocese of Lincoln, 1517–1531*, 3 vols. (Lincs. Rec. Soc., 33, 35, 37, 1940–7).

Three Sermons, or Homelies to Moove Compassion towards the Poore, (London, 1596).

TIGHE, R. R. and DAVIS, J. E. (eds.), *Annals of Windsor* (London, 1858).

TOPSELL, EDWARD, *The House-holder or Perfect Man* (London, 1610).

TRAHERNE, J. M. (ed.), *Stradling Correspondence* (London, 1840).

TREVOR-ROPER, H. (ed.), *Selections from the Writings of the Earl of Clarendon* (Oxford, 1978).

The Triall of Maister Dorrell (London, 1599).

TURNER, WILLIAM, *The Huntyng of the Romyshe Wolfe* (Emden, 1555?).

—— *A New Booke of Spirituall Physik for Dyverse Diseases of the Nobilite and Gentlemen of Englande* (Emden, 1555).

TURNER, W. H. (ed.), *Selections from the Records of the City of Oxford* (Oxford, 1880).

TUSSER, THOMAS, *Five Hundred Pointes of Good Husbandrie*, ed. W. Payne and S. J. Heritage (London, 1878).

Valor Ecclesiasticus, 6 vols. (London, 1825–34).

VAUGHAN, WILLIAM, *The Golden Grove, Moralized in Three Books* (London, 1600).

VEALE, E. W. W. (ed.), *The Great Red Book of Bristol*, 3 vols. (Bristol Rec. Soc., 16, 1951).

VON BULOW, G. (ed.), 'Diary of the Journey of Philip Julius, Duke of Stettin-Pomerania, through England in the Year 1602', *TRHS*, 2nd ser. 6 (1892).

WALKER, OBADIAH, *Of Education, Especially of Young Gentlemen* (Oxford, 1673).

WALKER, WILLIAM, *A Sermon Preached at the Funerall of William, Lord Russell* (London, 1613).

WANDESFORD, CHRISTOPHER, *A Book of Instructions to his Son*, ed. T. Comber (London, 1777).

WARNER, WILLIAM, *Albion's England, Or Historicall Map of the same Island* (London, 1586).

WATERHOUSE, EDWARD, *The Gentlemans Monitor* (London, 1665).

WEAVER, F. W. and CLARK, G. N. (eds.), *Churchwardens' Accounts of Marston, Spelsbury and Pyrton* (Oxford Rec. Soc., 6, 1925).

WEBB, J. (ed.), *A Roll of Household Expenses of Richard de Swinfield, Bishop of Hereford . . . 1289 and 1290*, abstract etc. (Camden Soc., OS 62, London 1855).

WESTCOTE, THOMAS, *A View of Devonshire in the Year 1630* (Exeter, 1845).

WHATELY, WILLIAM, *The Poor Mans Advocate: Or a Treatise of Liberality to the Needy* (London, 1637).

WHELER, GEORGE, *The Protestant Monastery: Or Christian Œconomicks* (London, 1698).

WHETSTONE, GEORGE, *A Heptameron of Civill Discourses* (London, 1582).

WHITE, THOMAS, *A Godlie Sermon preached . . . at the Buriall of Sir H Sidney* (London, 1586).

WHITFORD, RICHARD, *The Werke for Housholders, with the Golden Pystle and Alphabete . . .* (London, 1537).

WILKINS, DAVID, *Concilia Magnae Britanniae*, 4 vols. (Oxford, 1761).

WILLET, ANDREW, *Synopsis Papismi*, 5th edn. (London, 1634).

WILLIAMS, R. F. (ed.), *The Court and Times of James I*, 2 vols. (London, 1848).

The Wonderful Discoverie of the Witchcrafts of Margaret and Phillip Flower . . . Executed at Lincolne, March 11th, 1618 (London, 1619).

WOOD, ANTHONY, *Life and Times* ed., A. Clark, 5 vols. (Oxford Hist. Soc., 19, 21, 26, 30, 40, 1891–1900).

WOOD-LEGH, K. (ed.), *Kentish Visitations of Archbishop Warham* (Kent Rec. Soc., 24, 1984).

WORDSWORTH, C. (ed.), *Ecclesiastical Biographies*, 6 vols.

WORTH, R. N. (ed.), *Plymouth Municipal Records* (Plymouth, 1893).

WOTTON, HENRY, *The Elements of Architecture* (London, 1624).

WRIGHT, LEONARD, *A Summon for Sleepers . . . Hereunto is Annexed A Pattern for Pastors* (London, 1589).

WRIGHT, T. (ed.), *History of Fulk Warine* (Warton Club, London, 1855).

WROTH, R. N. (ed.), *Plymouth Municipal Records* (Plymouth, 1893).

XENOPHON, *Treatise of a Householde* (London, 1532).

SELECTED SECONDARY WORKS

ABOU-SEID, A. H. 'Honour and Shame among the Bedouins of Egypt' in Peristiany, J. G. (ed.), *Honour and Shame: The Values of Mediterranean Society* (London, 1965).

ADDY, S. O., *Church and Manor* (London, 1913).

BARNES, T. G., 'County Politics and a Puritan Cause Célèbre: Somerset Churchales, 1633', *TRHS*, 5th ser. 9 (1959).

BEIER, A. L. 'The Social Problems of an Elizabethan Country Town: Warwick 1580-90', in P. Clark (ed.), *Country Towns in Pre-Industrial England* (Leicester, 1981).

—— *Masterless Men: The Vagrancy Problem in England, 1560-1640* (London, 1985).

BERLIN, M., 'Civic Ceremony in Early Modern London', *Urban History Yearbook* (1986).

BILLSON, C. J., *Medieval Leicester* (Leicester, 1920).

BLOMEFIELD, F. *Topographical History of Norfolk*, 11 vols. (London, 1805-10).

BOLCHAZY, L., *Hospitality in Early Rome* (Chicago, 1977).

BORLASE, W., *The Natural History of Cornwall* (Oxford, 1758).

BORSAY, P., '"All the Town's a Stage": Urban Ritual and Ceremony, 1660-1800', in P. Clark (ed.), *The Transformation of English Provincial Towns* (London, 1984).

BOSSY, J., *The English Catholic Community, 1570-1850* (London, 1975).

—— *Christianity in the West, 1400-1700* (Oxford, 1985).

BOWKER, M., *The Secular Clergy of the Diocese of Lincoln, 1495-1520* (Cambridge, 1968).

—— *The Henrician Reformation, The Diocese of Lincoln under Bishop Longland* (Cambridge, 1981).

BRAND, J., *The History and Antiquities of the Town and the County of the Town of Newcastle-upon-Tyne*, 2 vols. (London, 1789).

—— *Observations on Popular Antiquities*, 3 vols. (London, 1853).

BRIDGES, J., *History and Antiquities of Northamptonshire*, 2 vols. (London, 1791).

BRIGDEN, S., 'Religion and Social Obligation in Early Sixteenth-Century London', *PP*, 103.

BROOKS, E. ST JOHN, *Sir Christopher Hatton* (London, 1946).

BRUCKNER, M. T., *Narrative Invention in Early Twelfth-Century Romance* (Lexington, Ky., 1980).

BUTLER, L. and GIVEN-WILSON, C., *Medieval Monasteries of Great Britain* (London, 1979).

BUTLER, M., *Theatre and Crisis 1632-1642* (Cambridge, 1987).

BYRNE, M. ST CLARE, *The Elizabethan Home* (London, 1930).

CAMPBELL, M., *The English Yeoman* (London, 1967).

CHANTER, J. R., *Sketches of the Literary History of Barnstaple* (Barnstaple, 1866).

CLARK, P. and SLACK, P. *English Towns in Transition, 1500-1700* (Oxford, 1976).

CLARK, P., *English Provincial Society from the Reformation to the Revolution* (Hassocks, 1977).

—— *The English Alehouse: A Social History, 1200-1830* (London, 1983).

CLIFFE, J. T. *The Yorkshire Gentry from the Reformation to the Civil War* (London, 1969).

COLLINSON, P., *Godly People: Essays on English Protestantism and Puritanism* (London, 1983).

COLLEY, L., *In Defiance of Oligarchy: the Tory Party, 1714-60* (Cambridge, 1982).

COOK, G. H., *English Monasteries in the Middle Ages* (London, 1961).

CORFIELD, P., *The Impact of English Towns, 1700-1800* (Oxford, 1982).

CORNWALL, J. C. K., *Wealth and Society in Early Sixteenth-Century England* (London, 1988).

COWARD, B., *The Stanleys, Lord Stanley and Earls of Derby, 1385-1672* (Chetham Soc., 3rd ser. 30, 1983).

CUST, R. and LAKE, P., 'Sir Richard Grosvenor and the Rhetoric of Magistracy', *BIHR*, 54 (1981).

DAVIES, R., *Walks Through the City of York* (London, 1880).

DOBSON, R. B., *Durham Priory: 1400-1450* (Cambridge, 1973).

DOUGLAS, M., *Natural Symbols* (London, 1973).

—— 'Deciphering a Meal', in her *Implicit Meanings* (London, 1975).

DU BOULAY, F. R., *The Lordship of Canterbury* (London, 1966).

DU BOULAY, J., *Portrait of a Greek Mountain Community* (London, 1973).

DYER, C., *Lords and Peasants in a Changing Society* (Cambridge, 1980).

—— *Standards of Living in the Later Middle Ages* (Cambridge, 1989).

ELTON, G. R., *Reform & Renewal* (Cambridge, 1973).

—— 'Reform and the "Commonwealth Men" of Edward VI's Reign', in his *Studies in Tudor and Stuart Politics and Government*, iii (Cambridge, 1983).

EMMISON, F., *Tudor Secretary: Sir William Petre at Court and Home* (London, 1961).

EVERITT, A., *The Community of Kent and the Great Rebellion* (Leicester, 1966).

—— 'The English Urban Inn, 1560-1670', in his *Perspectives in English Urban History* (London, 1973).

FINLEY, M., *The World of Odysseus* (New York, 1954).

FLETCHER, A., *A County Community in Peace and War: Sussex 1600-1660* (London, 1975).

GAVITT, P., 'Economy, Charity and Community in Florence, 1350-1450', in T. Riis (ed.), *Aspects of Poverty in Early Modern Europe* (Florence, 1981).

GEROULD, G. H., 'The Social Status of Chaucer's Franklin', *Public. of the Modern Language Assoc. of America*, 41 (1926).

GIROUARD, M., *Life in the English Country House* (New Haven, Conn., 1978).

GIROUARD, M., *Robert Smythson and the Elizabethan Country House* (London, 1983).

GITTINGS, C., *Death, Burial and the Individual in Early Modern England* (London, 1984).

GREAVES, R., *Society and Religion in Elizabethan England* (Minneapolis, Minn., 1981).

HAIGH, C., *The Last Days of the Lancashire Monasteries* (Chetham Soc., 3rd ser. 17, 1969).

HAMMER, I., 'Anatomy of an Oligarchy: The Oxford Town Council in the Fifteenth and Sixteenth Centuries', *JBS*, 18 (1978-9).

HARRIS, B., *Edward Stafford, 3rd Duke of Buckingham* (Stanford, Calif., 1986).

HASKINS, C., *The Ancient Trade Guilds and Companies of Salisbury* (Salisbury, 1912).

HASTED, E., *A History and Topographical Survey of the County of Kent*, 12 vols. (Canterbury, 1797-1801).

HEAL, F., *Of Prelates and Princes* (Cambridge, 1980).

—— 'The Idea of Hospitality in Early Modern England', *PP*, 102 (1984).

—— 'The Crown, the Gentry and London: the Enforcement of Proclamation, 1596-1640', in C. Cross *et al.* eds., *Law and Government under the Tudors* (Cambridge, 1988).

HEATH, P., *Medieval Clerical Accounts* (St Anthony's Hall Public., York, 1964).

—— *The English Parish Clergy on the Eve of the Reformation* (London, 1969).

HIBBARD, G. R., 'The Country-House Poem of the Seventeenth Century', *JWCI*, 19 (1956).

HILL, C., *Economic Problems of the Church from Archbishop Whitgift to the Long Parliament* (Oxford, 1956).

HOCART, A. M., *The Life-Giving Myth* (London, 1935).

HOLMES, C. A., 'The County Community in Stuart Historiography', *JBS*, 19 (1980).

HOMANS, G. C., *English Villagers of the Thirteenth Century* (Cambridge, Mass., 1942).

HORSFIELD, F., *The History and Antiquities of Sussex*, 2 vols. (Lewes, 1835).

HOUSMAN, J., *A Topographical Description of Cumberland, Westmorland, Lancashire and a part of the West Riding of Yorkshire* (Carlisle, 1800).

HUTCHINS, J., *The History and Antiquities of Dorset*, 2 vols. (London, 1861-74).

HUTCHINSON, W., *The View of Northumberland*, 2 vols. (Newcastle 1778).

—— *The History of the County of Cumberland*, 2 vols. (Carlisle, 1794).

HYDE, L., *The Gift: Imagination and the Erotic Life of Property* (New York, 1979).

ISAAC, R., *The Transformation of Virginia, 1740–1790* (Chapel Hill, NC, 1982).

JAMES, M. E., *English Politics and the Concept of Honour, 1485–1642*, *PP* supplement, 3 (1978).

—— 'Ritual, Drama and the Social Body in the Late Medieval English Town', *PP*, 98 (1983).

JENKINS, P., *The Making of a Ruling Class* (Cambridge, 1983).

JORDAN, W. K., *Philanthropy in England, 1480–1660* (London, 1959).

JUSSERAND, J. J., *English Wayfaring Life in the Middle Ages* (London, 1889).

KENNEDY, W. P. M., *Elizabethan Episcopal Administration*, 3 vols. (Alcuin Club, London, 1924).

KENNETT, D. H., 'Mayor-making at Norwich, 1706', *Norfolk Archaeology*, 35 (1971).

KENT, J., *The English Village Constable, 1580–1642* (Oxford, 1986).

KERSHAW, I., *Bolton Priory: 1286–1325* (Oxford, 1973).

KNOWLES, D., *The Religious Orders in England*, iii (Cambridge, 1959).

LABARGE, M. W., *A Baronial Household of the Thirteenth Century*, (London, 1980).

LEONARD, E. M., *The Early History of English Poor Relief* (Cambridge, 1900).

MACCAFFREY, W., *Exeter: 1500–1640* (London, 1975).

MCCLUNG, W., *The Country-House Poem in English Renaissance Poetry* (Berkeley, Calif., 1977).

MACCULLOCH, D., 'Catholic and Puritan in Elizabethan Suffolk', *Archiv für Reformationsgeschichte*, 72 (1981).

MACFARLANE, A., *Witchcraft in Tudor and Stuart Essex* (London, 1970).

—— *The Origins of English Individualism* (Oxford, 1978).

MCGEE, S., *The Godly Man in Stuart England* (New Haven, Conn., 1976).

MCGUIRE, M. A., 'The Cavalier Country-House Poem: Mutations on a Jonsonian Tradition', *Studies in English Literature*, 19 (1979).

MCINTOSH, K. M., *Autonomy and Community: The Royal Manor of Havering, 1200–1500* (Cambridge, 1986).

MAC-LYSAGHT, E., *Irish Life in the Seventeenth Century: After Cromwell* (London, 1939).

MALCOLMSON, R. W., *Popular Recreations in English Society, 1700–1850* (Cambridge, 1973).

MALINOWSKI, B. *Argonauts of the Western Pacific* (London, 1922).

MASTERS, B. R., 'The Lord Mayor's Household before 1600', in A. E. J. Hollaender and W. Kellaway (eds.), *Studies in London History* (London, 1969).

MAUSS, M., *The Gift: Forms and Functions of Exchange in Archaic Societies* (London, 1970).

MAXWELL, C., *Country and Town in Ireland under the Georges* (Dundalk, 1949).

MENNELL, S., *All Manners of Food* (London, 1985).

MERTES, K., *The English Noble Household, 1250–1600* (Oxford, 1988).

MOIR, E., *The Discovery of Britain* (London, 1964).

MORGAN, D. A. L., 'The House of Policy: the Political Role of the late Plantagenet Household, 1422–85', in D. Starkey (ed.), *The English Court from the Wars of the Roses to the Civil War* (London, 1987).

MORRIS, R. H., *Chester in the Plantagenet and Tudor Reigns* (Chester, 1893).

NICHOLS, J., *The History and Antiquities of the County of Leicester*, 4 vols. (London, 1795–1815).

PALLISER, D., 'Civic Mentality and the Environment in Tudor York', *Northern History*, 18 (1982).

PALMER, R. E., *French Travellers in England* (London, 1960).

PANTIN, W. A., 'Medieval Inns', in E. M. Jope (ed.), *Studies in Building History* (London, 1961).

PARKES, J., *Travel in England in the Seventeenth Century* (Oxford, 1925).

PHYTHIAN-ADAMS, C., 'Ceremony and the Citizen', in P. Slack and P. Clark (eds.), *Crisis and Order in English Towns, 1500–1700* (London, 1972).

—— *Desolation of a City: Coventry and the Urban Crisis of the Late Middle Ages* (Cambridge, 1979).

PITT-RIVERS, J., 'The Law of Hospitality', in his *The Fate of Shechem* (Cambridge, 1977).

POUND, J. F. 'An Elizabethan Census of the Poor', *Univ. of Birmingham Historical Journal*, 8 (1962).

RALPH, P. L., *Sir Humphrey Mildmay, Royalist Gentleman* (New Brunswick, 1947).

RAWCLIFFE, C., *The Staffords, Earls of Stafford and Dukes of Buckingham 1394–1521* (Cambridge, 1978).

RICHARDSON, A. E. and Eberlein, H. D., *The English Inn Past and Present* (London, 1925).

ROWLANDS, M., 'Recusant Women, 1560–1640', in M. Prior (ed.), *Women in English Society, 1500–1800* (London, 1985).

RUBIN M., *Charity and Community in Medieval Cambridge* (Cambridge, 1987).

SAHLINS, M., *Stone Age Economics* (Chicago, 1972).

SAVINE, A., 'The English Monasteries on the Eve of the Dissolution', in P. Vinogradoff (ed.), *Oxford Studies in Social and Legal History*, i (Oxford, 1909).

SCARISBRICK, J. J., *The Reformation and the English People* (Oxford, 1984).

SCHENK, W., *Reginald Pole, Cardinal of England* (London, 1950).

SHARP, R. A., 'Gift Exchange and the Economies of Spirit in *Merchant of Venice*', *Modern Philology*, 83 (1986).

SHARPE, K., 'Cavalier Critic? The Ethics and Politics of Thomas Carew's Poetry', in K. Sharpe and S. Zwicker (eds.), *The Politics of Discourse* (Berkeley, Calif., 1987).

SHAW, S., *The History and Antiquities of Staffordshire*, 2 vols. (London, 1801).

SIMMS, K., 'Guesting and Feasting in Gaelic Ireland', *Journal of the Royal Society of Antiquaries for Ireland*, 108 (1978).

SIMPSON, W. D., '"Bastard Feudalism" and the Later Castles', *Antiquaries Journal*, 26 (1946).

SLACK, P. A., *Poverty and Policy in Tudor and Stuart England* (London, 1988).

SMITH, A. HASSELL, *County and Court: Government and Politics in Norfolk, 1558–1603* (Oxford, 1974).

SMITH, P., *Houses of the Welsh Countryside* (*RHMC*, London, 1975).

SMITH, R. A. L., *Canterbury Cathedral Priory* (Cambridge, 1943).

SNAPE, R. H., *English Monastic Finances in the Later Middle Ages* (Cambridge, 1926).

SODEN, G. A., *Godfrey Goodman, Bishop of Gloucester, 1583–1656* (London, 1953).

STARKEY, D. R., 'The Age of the Household', in S. Medcalf (ed.), *The Background to English Literature: The Later Middle Ages* (London, 1981).

—— 'The Court; Castiglione's Ideal and Tudor Reality', *JWCI*, 40 (1982).

STONE, L., *The Crisis of the Aristocracy* (Oxford, 1965).

—— 'The Residential Development of the West End of London in the Seventeenth Century', in B. Malament (ed.), *After the Reformation: Essays in Honour of J. H. Hexter* (Manchester, 1980).

—— and STONE, J. F., *An Open Elite? England 1540–1880* (Oxford, 1984).

STRONG, R., 'The Accession Day of Elizabeth I', *JWCI*, 21 (1958).

STRYPE, J., *The Life and Acts of Matthew Parker*, 3 vols. (London, 1821).

SURTEES, J., *History and Antiquities of the County Palatine of Durham*, 4 vols. (London, 1816–40).

THOMAS, K. V., *Religion and the Decline of Magic* (London, 1973).

—— *The Sense of the Past in Early Modern England* (Creighton Lecture, London, 1983).

THOROTON, J., *The History of Nottinghamshire, Republished with Large Additions,* 3 vols. (London, 1790).

TIERNEY, B., *The Medieval Poor Law* (Berkeley, Calif., 1959).

TITMUSS, R., *The Gift Relationship: From Human Blood to Social Policy* (London, 1970).

TITTLER, R., 'The Building of Civic Halls in Dorset, c.1560–1640', *BIHR*, 58 (1985).

TODD, H. J., *The History of the College of Bonhommes at Ashridge* (London, 1823).

TURNER, J., *The Politics of Landscape* (London, 1979).

TURNER, V., *The Ritual Process* (Ithaca, 1977).

UNDERDOWN, D., *Revel, Riot, and Rebellion: Popular Politics and Culture in England, 1603–1660* (Oxford, 1985).

USTICK, W. L., 'Changing Ideals of Aristocratic Character in Seventeenth-Century England', *Modern Philology*, 30 (1932).

VAN GENNEP, A., *The Rites of Passage* (Chicago, 1960).

WALDRON, G., *A Description of the Isle of Man*, ed. W. Harrison (Manx Soc. 11, 1865).

WHALLEY, P. (comp.), *The History of Northamptonshire: Compiled from the MSS Collections of the Late Learned Antiquary, John Bridges*, 2 vols. (Oxford, 1791).

WHITNEY, M. P., 'Largesse: Queen of Medieval Virtues', in C. Fiske (ed.), *Vassar Medieval Studies* (New Haven, Conn., 1923).

WILLIAMS, G., *The Welsh Church from the Conquest to the Reformation* (Cardiff, 1976).

WILLIAMS, R., *The Country and the City* (London, 1973).

WILLIAMSON, G. C., *Lady Anne Clifford* (Kendal, 1922).

WRIGHTSON, K., *English Society: 1560–1680* (London, 1982).

WOOD, M. M., *The Stranger* (New York, 1934).

WOOD, M., *The English Medieval House* (London, 1965).

YOUINGS, J., *The Dissolution of the Monasteries* (London, 1971).

—— *Sixteenth-Century England* (London, 1984).

UNPUBLISHED DISSERTATIONS

ARCHER, I., 'Governors and Governed in Late Sixteenth-Century London, c.1560–1603: Studies in the Achievement of Stability', Oxford D.Phil. (1988).

BRYSON, A., 'Concepts of Civility in England c.1560–1685', Oxford D.Phil. (1984).

HODGES, V. J., 'The Electoral Influence of the Aristocracy: 1604–41', Columbia Ph.D. (1977).

KENT, J. R., 'Social Attitudes of Members of Parliament, 1590–1624', London Ph.D. (1971).

LARMINIE, V., 'The Lifestyle and Attitudes of the Seventeenth-Century Gentry, with Special Reference to the Newdigates of Arbury Hall, Warwickshire', Birmingham Ph.D. (1980).

MERTES, K. A., 'The Secular Noble Household in Medieval England, 1350–1550', Edinburgh Ph.D. (1981).

NORBROOK, D., 'Panegyric of the Monarch and its Social Context under Elizabeth I and James I', Oxford D.Phil. (1978).

O'DWYER, M., 'Catholic Recusants in Essex, *c*.1580 to *c*.1600', London MA (1960).

PETCHEY, W. J., 'The Borough of Maldon, Essex, 1500–1688', Leicester Ph.D. (1972).

PRICE, E. M., 'Ralph, Lord Cromwell and His Household', London MA (1948).

THURGOOD, J. M., 'Diet and Domestic Households of the English Lay Nobility, 1265–1531', London M.Phil. (1982).

WRIGHTSON, K., 'The Puritan Reformation of Manners, with Special Reference to the Counties of Lancashire and Essex, 1640–1660', Cambridge Ph.D. (1974).

Index

Abbot, George, Archbishop of Canterbury 6, 166, 187, 276-7, 282
Aberystwyth, Cardiganshire 214
Abraham 17
accommodation, idea of 104-6, 193-6, 208
accounts 49-52, 157, 247, 250-3, 255-6
Acle, Norfolk 278
Addington Hall, Buckinghamshire 41
Adlington Hall, Cheshire 41, 211
advice literature 25-7, 177-9, 184-5, 189-90, 379, 392
Ady, Thomas 385
Ainsty Liberty, Yorkshire 305, 313
Allen, Robert 17-18, 123, 132, 136, 220
All Hallows Eve 70, 72, 322, 347
almoner 16, 33-4, 153, 234-5, 245, 265
almonry 229, 234
alms dish 34
almshouses 115, 133, 138, 180, 393
almsgiving, funeral 12, 320, 371-3
   household 14-17, 18-19, 33-5, 68-70, 77, 83-5, 91-2, 98-9, 126-8, 129-33, 138-9, 170-4, 179-80, 189-90, 217, 225-6, 233-5, 242-3, 255, 263-4, 279, 284-5, 319-21, 378, 383-4, 393-4
   monetary 16-17, 124, 134, 172, 181, 226, 259, 273, 283, 285, 292-4, 376
alms, mandatory 234-5, 242-3
almsmen 69-70, 135-6
almstub 34, 266
Alnwick Castle, Northumberland 188, 191
Alnwick Abbey, Northumberland 208, 214
Alveston Manor, Warwickshire 26
Andrewes, Lancelot, Bishop of Winchester 138, 283-5

Angier, John 289, 296
Anne of Denmark 308
Annunciation, feast of 83
Appleton family 171
Argentina 396
Aristotle 28, 100, 119
Armada 164
Arthington, Henry 129
   Provision for the Poore 129
articles and injunctions
   episcopal 263-5, 268-9, 272-4, 287, 298-9
   royal 262-3, 272
Arundel, Sussex 390 n.
   Castle 88, 196, 209
Arundel, Earl of, *see* Fitzalan, Howard
Arundel, Thomas, Archbishop of Canterbury 248
'Arvel' dinner 373
Ashby de la Zouch, Leicestershire 37, 206
Ashampstead, Berkshire 379
Ashridge, Hertfordshire 149, 161
Aske, Robert 231, 236
assize sessions 60, 308-9, 383, 386
   feasts 271, 308, 386
   judges 171, 182, 307-8
Athelstan, King 359
Atheos 291
Atkinson, George 211
Atkinson, Margaret 373
Atwater, William, Bishop of Lincoln 244, 253
Aubrey, John 359-60, 363, 384, 388
Audley End House, Essex 163
Audley, Lady Elizabeth 309
Audley, Sir Thomas 268
Austin Canons 231
Axbridge, Somerset 308 n.
Aylmer, John, Bishop of London 279

431

Babington Plot 321
Bacon, Francis, Lord Verulam 48, 119, 162
Bacon, Sir Nathaniel 71, 143
Bacon, Sir Nicholas 311
Bacon/Townshend accounts 51, 67, 71–2
Baconsthorpe, Norfolk 75
Baddiley, John 283–4
Badminton House, Gloucestershire 188
Bagworth Park, Leicestershire 199
Baker family 74
Baker, Mr 385
Baldock, Hertfordshire 252 n.
ballads 94, 113, 137, 168, 403
Bamford, Samuel 362, 365, 389
Banbury, Oxfordshire 315, 365
Bancroft, Richard, Archbishop of Canterbury 275
Banyard, Mr and Mrs 53–4, 61
Banyster, Mr 66
Barker, William 327
Barley, Hertfordshire 293
Barnes, Richard, Bishop of Durham 273
Barnsley, Yorkshire 198
Barnstaple, Devon 329, 336–7
Mayor of 329, 336–7
Barnwell Abbey, Cambridgeshire 313
Barrington family 150
Barrington, Lady Joan 150
Barrington, John 151
Barrington, Sir Thomas 150
Bash, Edward 183
Basingstoke, Hampshire 255
Basingwerk Priory, Flintshire 230
Bath, Somerset 152, 391
Bath, Lord, see Bourchier
Bath and Wells, Bishop of 206
Baynton, Sir Edward 290
Beake, Robert, Mayor of Coventry 342, 347
Beauchamp family 54, 57
Beauchamp accounts 51, 54–5
Beaudesert, Staffordshire 145
Beaufort, Lady Margaret 15, 69
Beaufort, Thomas, Duke of Exeter 70
Beaufort, Duke of, see Somerset
Beaumaris Castle, Anglesea 214
Beaurepaire, Durham 241
Becon, Thomas 125, 130, 223, 259–60, 267, 279, 284–5
The Pathway unto Prayer 126

The General Preface 260
Bedel, William 127
Bedell, William, Bishop of Kilmore 132, 284–5, 290, 292
Bedfordshire 58
Bedford, earls of, see Russell
Bedford, John, Duke of 54
Bedingfield family 61
Bedingfield, Sir Thomas 62
Bedouin, the 7
Beere, Abbot of Glastonbury 229
Beier, A. L. 219
Belgrave, Mrs 219
Bellenden, Sir William 319 n.
Belvoir Castle, Rutlandshire 188
Benedictines 5, 229, 232, 241
Berkeley Castle, Gloucestershire 63, 66, 83
Berkeley family 58, 67, 76, 82, 166, 202
accounts of 54, 63, 66–7, 77–8, 79, 86, 159
Berkeley, Lady Elizabeth, Countess of Warwick 54–5, 62–3, 66–7, 79, 83, 86, 89, 217
Berkeley, Lady Elizabeth 51, 144, 149
Berkeley, Henry, 17th Lord 66, 74, 76, 82
Lady Jane, his 2nd wife 12
Lady Katherine, his 1st wife 82
Berkeley, Gilbert, Bishop of Bath and Wells 270
Berkeley, Maurice, 13th Lord 82, 160
Lady Isabel, his wife 82
Berkeley, Thomas, 9th. Lord 71
Berkshire 350, 373
clergy in 226
Berlin, Michael 344
Bermondsey, Surrey 369
Berrington, Shropshire 360 n.
Berry, Mr 66
Bertie family 67, 81, 84
accounts of 66–7, 69, 84
Berwick, Northumberland 372
Best, Henry 357
Beverley, Yorkshire 205
Bewdley, Worcestershire 213
Bewick, Thomas 397
Bicester, Oxfordshire 204
Bigod, Sir Francis 261
Bird, Samuel 129, 131, 134–5
Lectures on . . . the 2nd Epistle to the Corinthians 129

birth, celebration of 367–8
Bishop Auckland, Durham 207
Bishopstone, Sussex 190
Bishopthorpe, Yorkshire 280
Blake, William 403
Blanchland, Abbot of 241
Blathwayt, Mr 186
Blount, Humphrey 58
Bodiam Castle, Sussex 37
Boleyn, Lady 60
Bolton Priory, Lancashire 228
bonfires 334–5
Bonner, Edmund, Bishop of London 268
Bonye, Richard 219
Booby, Sir Thomas and Lady 167
Book of Chyvalry 11, 23
Book of Common Prayer, The 64
Book of Sports, The 364–5
boon works 52, 357
Borsay, Peter 347
Bossy, John 124
Bostock, Laurence 206–7
Boston, Lincolnshire 212
Boughey, Hugh 58
Boughton, William 219
Bourchier, Thomas, Archbishop of Canterbury 63, 67, 247
  accounts of 67, 247–8
Bourchier, William, 3rd Earl of Bath 337
Bourne, Lincolnshire 66
Bourne, Henry 361
Bourne, John 195
Bowet, Henry, Archbishop of York 41
Bowker, Margaret 254
Bowser, Mrs 213
Boxgrove Priory, Sussex 232
Bradley family 171
Bradley, Mr 172
Brampton, Yorkshire 169
Brandon, Charles, Duke of Suffolk 55
Brathwait, Richard 36, 107–8
  The English Gentleman 107
  Whimzies 36, 368
Brentwood, Essex 172
Brereton, Sir William 207–8
Brescia, Albertanus di 25
Breton, Nicholas 32, 116, 221
  A Merrie Dialogue betwixt the Taker and Mistaker 221
  Choice, Chance and Change 369
  Fantasticks 32

bride-ales 367, 369–71
Bridges, Sir John 56
Bridges, Mr 56
Bridges, J. 364
Bridgewater, earls of, *see* Egerton
Bridgnorth, Shropshire 341
Bristol 201, 308, 314, 318, 322–5, 329–30, 336, 339, 346
  Corporation 314–5, 324, 330, 343
  Mayor of 324–5
  places in: All Hallows Church 322; Christchurch 63; High Cross 324; St Augustine's Abbey 314, 323; St Katherine's Chapel 322; St Michael's Church 324
  sheriffs 338–9
Broadhinton, Wiltshire 142
Bromyard, John 3, 93
Brooke, Robert, 4th Lord 209
Brookstreet, Essex 172
Brougham Castle, Westmorland 158
Browne family, Viscounts Montagu household orders of 50
Browne, Sir Anthony 171
Browne, Edward 209
Brownlow, Richard 177
Bruen, John 137, 175–7
Bucer, Martin 98, 125, 260, 264
Buckden, Huntingdonshire 283
Buckhurst, Lord, *see* Sackville
Buckingham, dukes of, *see* Stafford, Villiers
Buildwas Abbey, Shropshire 239
Bulkeley, Thomas, Viscount 214
Bulpham, Essex 172
Burdet, Mr 56
Burgh, Elizabeth de 69
Burgoyne, Lady Anna 152
Burton Dassett, Warwickshire 381
Butley Priory, Suffolk 238, 242
Buttsbury, Essex 75

Caernarvon 215
Caesar, Thomas 152
Calthorp, Mr 61
Caludon, Warwickshire 82
Calvinism 133–8, 282–5, 295–6, 343, 347
Cambridge 304, 313–14, 323–5, 338
  Corporation 313–14, 323–4
  freemen of 326, 338
  Mayor of 316, 324, 326

Cambridge University 152, 201, 204
  Library 255
Campbell, Archibald, 7th Marquis of
  Argyll 189–91
  Instructions to a Son 189–90
Campbell, Mildred 20
Campeggio, Lorenzo, Bishop of Salisbury
  310
Campion, Mr 219
Canada 1, 399
Candlemas 72
canon law viii, 223–8, 250, 299
  canons of 1571 272, 290
  provincial decrees 225–8, 253–4,
    272, 288
Canterbury, Kent 87, 231, 237, 271,
  325, 338, 345
  Corporation 271, 314; aldermen of
    341
  places in: Chequers Inn 237–9; St
    Gregory's Priory 235
Canterbury
  archbishops of 251, 270, 282; house-
    hold of 247, 265–8, 270–1, 277
  Diocese of 251, 262, 268
Capel, Lady Elizabeth 182
  Sir Gamaliel 171
Carbery, Earl of, *see* Vaughan
Carew, John 214
Carew, Richard 20, 106, 111, 117,
  205, 213, 354, 357, 361, 363
  Survey of Cornwall 354
Carew, Thomas 108–9, 111, 113, 121
Carmarthen Priory 230, 236
Castiglione, Baldassare 102–4
  The Courtier 103
Castle Acre Priory, Norfolk 237
Castle Combe, Wiltshire 201
Castle Hedingham, Suffolk 48
Catesby Priory, Northamptonshire 231
Cave, Sir Brian 199
Cavendish family 151
Cavendish, Christiana, Countess of
  Devonshire 182
Cavendish, George 249
Cavendish, Margaret, Duchess of
  Newcastle 11, 22, 179, 188
Cavendish, William, Duke of Newcastle
  186, 188
Cawood, Yorkshire 212
Cawston, Norfolk 287
Cecil, William, Lord Burghley 83–4,
  128, 155, 157, 159, 257

Chaderton, Laurence 258
Chaloner, Sir Thomas and Lady 74
Chamber, John 378, 386
Chamberlayne, Edward 389
Champernowne family 311
Chancery, Court of 357
charity 93, 123–9, 138–9, 245–9,
    258–64, 279, 281–4, 292, 321–2,
    375, 394
  definitions of 14–16, 122–3, 136–9
  discrimination in 127–39, 170–1,
    187–8, 225–7, 373, 392
  and household 33–5, 125–8, 133,
    140, 187, 228–9
  failure of 383–4
  public provision of 97–9, 123–5,
    127–8, 132–5, 256, 263–4, 274,
    286, 318, 321, 385, 392, 402
Charlecote, Warwickshire 180, 187,
  217, 317
Charles I 6, 109, 118–21, 128, 147,
  183, 364
Charles II 186
Chaucer, Geoffrey 380
  The Canterbury Tales, the Franklin
    vii, 380, 385
Chauncy, Sir Henry 391
Cheke, Mrs 56
Cheshire 41, 92, 137, 206–7, 211,
  363, 377
Chester 308, 318, 330, 343, 347, 366,
  372
  Corporation 318, 330, 366, 370
Chester, Bishop of 78, 81
Childerditch, Essex 172
Chilldenden, Thomas, Prior of
  Canterbury 238
Cholmley, Sir Hugh 89, 117, 146, 179,
  183
Cholmley, Sir Richard 89, 146
christenings 54, 80–1, 367–8, 384
Christmas season and hospitality 44,
  50, 54, 57–8, 68, 70–7, 80, 82–3,
  87, 104, 118–19, 144, 146, 148–9,
  151, 168, 172–5, 186–7, 192, 219,
  235, 238, 240, 252, 256, 280–1,
  283, 285, 290, 291 n., 293–4, 297,
  314, 322–3, 329–30, 337, 343–4,
  355–8, 363, 377–9, 390
Church, the 124, 224–8, 246, 257,
  259–68, 272–4, 297–9, 368
  alienation of wealth of 257–8, 261,
    268–70, 274–5

church ales 358–61, 363
church houses 254, 295, 359
churching 54, 81, 353, 366–8, 370, 374
Churchyard, Thomas 330
churchyards 359, 365, 373–4
Cicero 26, 99–101
  De Officiis 26, 100
Cistercians 228–9, 232, 239
city, hospitality in 85–6, 106–7, 112, 115, 140, 149, 196–7, 300–1
  residence in 119–20, 143, 150–2
civility, ideals of 12, 20, 102–11, 115, 117, 122, 151–2, 168–9, 182, 190–1, 206–7, 215, 301, 380, 391–2, 402
  French 107
  Italian 102–3, 107, 119
Clare, Earl of, *see* Holles
Clarence, George, Duke of 46
Clarendon, Earl of, *see* Hyde
Clark, Peter 345
Clarke, Samuel 295
  Lives of Eminent Divines 294
Clayworth, Nottinghamshire 297
Cleeve Abbey, Somerset 229, 231
Cleland, James 107
  Hero-Paideia 107
clergy, income of 225–6, 250–2, 278–9, 288, 294, 296
clerks of the kitchen, books of 49–54, 62, 64–5, 67–8, 83
Cliffe, J. T. 144
Clifford family 151
Clifford, Lady Anne 157–8, 161, 182, 205, 221
Clogie, Alexander 284–5
  Speculum Episcoporum 284
Clopton, Sir William 18
Cobbett, William 299
Coke, George, Bishop of Bristol 314
Colby, Joan 370
Colchester, Essex 340
Coleman, Morgan 95, 305
Coleshill House, Berkshire 158
Colley, Linda 390
Combe, Abbot of 82
commensality 40–4, 91–2, 110, 154, 157–8, 189, 241, 303, 306–7, 322–44, 356–8, 366–7, 373–6
Common Pleas, Court of 177
Compton, Lady 81
Coningsby, Mr 61

Constable, Sir Marmaduke 56
convocation 272
cookery 115–17
  English 115–16
  Flemish 116
  French 116
Cookridge, Yorkshire 208
Cooper, Anthony Ashley, 1st Earl of Shaftesbury 116, 316
Cooper, Thomas
  The Art of Giving 101–2
  The Mystery of Witchcraft 384
Corket, Thomas 219
Cornwall 105, 111, 117, 205, 207, 213, 357, 377
Cornwallis, Lady Jane 195
Cornwallis, Sir Thomas 311
Cornwallis, Sir William 171, 198, 216
  Essays 101
Corpus Christi, feast of 302, 307, 323, 329–30, 333, 337, 341
  plays 307, 323, 333, 343–5
Corsley Hall, Wiltshire 51, 71
Cotswolds, the 212
Cottingham, Yorkshire 255
Coult, John 372
country, images of 106–22, 140–3, 151, 183–8, 300, 353–4, 390–1
  residence in 144–8, 152, 391
country-house poems 108–14, 117, 120–1
country-house viewing 208–9
Court, the, and courtiers 102–11, 113, 116, 120–1, 140, 142, 154, 169, 182, 188–9, 211, 277, 391–2
Courtenay, Katherine, Countess of Devon 47, 53
Courtenay, Thomas, 14th Earl of Devon 201
courtesy literature 33, 94, 102–8, 112, 193–8, 351, 392
Coventry, Warwickshire 74, 76, 82, 160, 166, 195, 211, 217, 243, 302, 318, 325, 329, 344, 346–7
  Carthusian Priory in 243
  Mayor of 72, 82, 304, 321, 325
Coventry and Lichfield, Diocese of 247–8
Cowley, William 372
Cox, Richard, Bishop of Ely 263, 279
Coxford, Prior of 62–3
Crabb, Mr 324, 337

Cranfield, Lionel, Earl of Middlesex 50, 95, 190, 319
Cranford, Middlesex 144-5, 149
Cranham, Essex 172
Cranmer, Margaret 181
Cranmer, Thomas, Archbishop of Canterbury 247, 262, 264-72, 319
Craven, Deanery of, Yorkshire 289
Cressener, John 61
Crompton, Dr 275
Cromwell, Ralph Lord 78, 83
Cromwell, Thomas, Earl of Essex 85, 97, 231-3, 240, 245, 252, 262-3, 325
Cropredy, Oxfordshire 379
Cropwell Bishop, Nottinghamshire 382
Crowland Abbey, Lincolnshire 243
Crowley, Robert 259, 264
Cully, Philip 383
Cumberland 355, 378, 386
Curteys, Richard 123, 127-9
    The Care of a Christian Conscience 123, 128-9
Curzon family 74
Cyvile and Uncyvile Life 61, 101, 104, 106, 117

Dafydd, Abbot of Valle Crucis 230
Dalechamp, Caleb 4, 18, 20, 119, 193-4
    Christian Hospitalitie 193
Danbury, Essex 146
Darrell, Lady 56
Day, George, Bishop of Chichester 263
Dee, John 104
Defoe, Daniel 210, 350
Delbridge, John 329
Della Casa, Giovanni 102
De Montfort, Eleanor, Countess of Leicester 57, 64 n.
Denbigh 308
Denton family 74
Derby, earls of, *see* Stanley
Dering, Edward 134
Derrington, George 371, 373
Dethick, John 136
Devenish family 337
De Vere family 78
De Vere, John, 13th Earl of Oxford 46, 48, 87

De Vere, John, 16th Earl of Oxford 309
Devizes, Wiltshire 201, 325 n.
Devon 359, 364, 377, 380
Devon, earls of, *see* Courtenay
Devonshire, Countess of, *see* Cavendish
D'Ewes, Sir Simonds 142
diaries 199-200, 206, 294-6, 371, 386-7, 401
Discourse of the Commonweal, The 258
Dives and Pauper 123
Dockery, Mr 66
Dod, John 294-5
Doddinghurst, Essex 64, 74
Doncaster, Yorkshire 211, 350
Donne, John 180
Dorindo 221
Dorset, earls of, *see* Sackville
Dorset, Marquis of, *see* Grey
Dovell, Abbot of Cleeve 229
Downame, John 123
Drake family 311
Drant, Thomas 127
Drayton, Middlesex 54, 67, 79-80, 84, 86
Drayton, Michael 132
drinkings
    in church 359, 365, 373-4
    of healths 208, 221, 300
    urban entertainments 303, 322-8, 333, 335, 337, 346, 366, 370, 372-3
Drury, Sir Robert 171
Dudley, Edmund 248-9
    Tree of Commonwealth, The 15, 249
Dudley, Mrs 74
Durham 368
Durham
    Bishopric of 240, 250, 273, 276
    Bishop of 201, 280
    Dean of 201, 207, 280, 395
    Priory 230, 239-41
    Sheriff of 241
Dutch, the 10

Earl's Colne, Essex 296
East Anglia vii, 200, 311, 364
Eastbourne, Sussex 356, 367
Easter, celebration of 50, 70, 77-8, 172, 254, 290, 329, 346
East Horndon, Essex 172

East Lulworth, Dorset 174
East Rudham, Norfolk 62
Edward II 40, 267
Edward IV 307
 Household Ordinances 24-7, 40,
 46-7
Edward VI 124, 279
Egerton, Elizabeth, Countess of
 Bridgewater 393
Egerton, John, 1st Earl of Bridgewater
 149-51, 162, 190
Egerton, Sir Thomas, 307
Elizabeth I 43, 118, 163, 270-1, 276,
 278, 287, 308, 321, 334
 Accession Day of 334, 347
Elizabeth of Bohemia 309
Ellis, Clement 16
 The Gentile Sinner 16
Elsing, Norfolk 64
Eltham Ordinances, the 43
Elvetham, Hampshire 55
Ely, Isle of 219
Ely Priory, Cambridgeshire 227 n., 244
Encyclopédie 398
England vii-viii, 2, 9-10, 19, 22, 55,
 118-20, 179, 185, 189, 192, 201-4,
 210, 226, 228, 231, 257, 279, 310,
 352, 370, 392, 394-5, 398-401
enclosure 6, 381-2
Epiphany, feast of 57, 68, 71, 73-4,
 173, 323, 355
Erasmus, Desiderius 266
Essex 77, 117, 146, 150, 172, 175,
 186, 353, 364, 372, 375
Eure family 13, 198, 390
Evelyn, John 197
 A Character of England 197
Everitt, Alan 350
Evesham, Worcestershire 213
 Abbey 236
 Abbot of 232
Exchequer, the 64, 383
excise 351
Exeter 201, 234, 285
 Corporation 338
 St Nicholas's Priory in 234
Exeter, Bishop of 206

Fanshawe, Lady Anne 120, 180, 205
Fanshawe, Sir Richard 10, 120
Farnham Castle, Hampshire 299
Fastolf, Sir John 200-1
feast-makers 329, 332, 339

feasts 16, 26-7, 31-2, 40, 49, 54,
 92, 111, 162, 191-3, 203, 230,
 241, 271, 285, 301-6, 310-3,
 320, 330-43, 355-6, 363-7,
 369-70
 aldermanic 326-8
Fell, John 293
Feltham, Owen 21
Fenner, Lady Jane 180
Ferry, Janet 368-9
Fielding, Henry
 Joseph Andrews 167-8, 212
Fielding, Mr 85
Fiennes, Bridget, Countess of Lincoln
 119
Fiennes, Celia 152, 167, 205-6,
 210
Fisher, John, Bishop of Rochester 15
Fisher, John 218
Fitzalan, Henry, 12th Earl of Arundel
 88
Fitzherbert, John 16
 Boke of Husbandry 16
Fitzwarenne, Fulk 26
Fleetwood, William 196
Fletcher, Anthony 146
Fletcher, Richard, Bishop of London
 279
Florence 17
Flower, Joan 188
food-gifts and alms 16-18, 68-70, 98,
 177, 192, 230-1, 243, 249, 267,
 290, 293, 299, 359, 371-3, 375,
 385
 lavish provision of 111-13, 248,
 371
 plainness of 116-18, 267
Forehoe Hundred, Norfolk 383
Foxe, John 266
 Book of Martyrs, The 266
Foxe, Richard, Bishop of Winchester
 248
Framlingham, Suffolk 66, 71, 84
France 10, 202-3, 402
Freke, Edmund, Bishop of Rochester
 272
Freville, George 314
Friskney, Lincolnshire 254
Froombridge Mill, Gloucestershire
 213
Fuller, Thomas 8, 15, 177, 183, 377,
 381
Fulwood, Mr 219

funeral monuments 16, 105, 114–15,
139, 180–1, 255, 391, 393–4
sermons 16, 114–15, 136–7, 139,
176–80, 295, 393
funerals 82, 88, 92, 184, 256, 371–6,
390
doles at 372–5
public 'forthcoming' at 371–3, 376,
385
Furse family 378
Furse, John 48, 89, 378
Furse, Robert 48, 89, 379

Gage, Sir John 147
Gailhard, Jean 22
Gainsford, Thomas 381
Gardiner, Stephen, Bishop of
Winchester 55, 248, 281
Garey, Samuel 127, 148
gate-doles 16–17, 34–5, 85–6, 98,
130–2, 149, 172, 176–7, 184, 187,
189–90, 228, 234–5, 243, 250,
265, 278, 284, 286, 293, 319–20,
384
Gawdy family 61, 142
Gawdy, Framlingham 148
Geneva bible
1560 edition 131
Beza-Tomson edition 131
Gershow, Friedrich 204
Gibson, E. 364
Giffard, Godfrey, Bishop of Worcester
237
Gifford, George 291
Dialogue of the Country Divinitie
291
gift-exchange and reciprocity 19–22,
62–3, 100–1, 134, 174, 184, 192–4,
209, 216, 218, 235, 237–8,
249–50, 302, 304–15, 343, 353–4,
361–2, 366, 389, 397–403
Gillingham, Wiltshire 361
Gilpin, Bernard 293
Girouard, Mark 37, 154, 157
Glamorgan 164
Glastonbury, Somerset 229–30, 239
George Inn at 239
St Benignus Church 230
Gloucester 313, 327, 340
New Inn at 239
Gloucester, Humphrey, Duke of 31
Gloucestershire 56–8
Godolphin, Mr 213

Golden Grove, Carmarthenshire 215
Golden Legend, The vii
good lordship 11–12, 21, 58, 86–9,
125, 166, 249–50, 302, 390
Goodman, Godfrey, Bishop of
Gloucester 293
Goodrich, Herefordshire 359
Goodwife Neale 172
Goodwife Wetham 172
Gosmore, Richard 255–6
Gouge, William 138
Gough, Richard 385–6
The History of Myddle 385
Gorges, Edmund 58
Grand Tour, the 153
Gratian 224, 226
The Decretals 224–5
Gray, William, Bishop of Ely 244
Great Chalfield, Wiltshire 37
Great Ilford, Essex 255
Great Malvern Priory, Worcestershire
232–3
Great North Road, the 211
Great Red Book of Bristol, The 322
Great Tew, Oxfordshire 121
Great Warley, Essex 172
Great Yarmouth, Norfolk 291 n., 312,
314–15
Corporation 312, 314
water feast 329
Greece 1, 395
Greene, Mr 172
Gregory the Great 225
Gregory, Mr 209
Greville, Sir Fulke, 1st Lord Brooke
219
Grey family 56
Grey, Annabel, Countess of Kent 180
Grey, Henry, 3rd Marquis of Dorset
202
Grimsthorpe, Lincolnshire 84
Grindal, Edmund, Archbishop of York
and Canterbury 271–3, 289, 359
Grosvenor, Sir Richard 177
Guazzo, Stephano 102
guests 32, 50–2, 100–3, 158, 167,
179, 189, 203–5, 209–13, 216,
221, 225, 228, 240–1, 244–5, 251,
280, 293, 307, 332, 366, 381–2,
399
lists of 49–55, 70, 171, 186, 280
reception of 31–2, 36, 49, 101,
195–9, 204, 208, 230–1, 389–90

role of 11, 49, 192–201, 215–16, 225, 368–9, 389
status: clergy 62–5, 171–2, 176, 186, 240–1, 247, 251, 255, 266, 271, 280–1, 285, 292; middling sort 65–8, 91–2, 160–2, 167, 186, 189, 283, 297, 318, 323, 352; nobility and gentry 32, 54–5, 58–62, 162–3, 199–200, 204, 230, 271, 276–7, 280–1, 303–4, 307–9, 311, 314–17, 329; poor 68–70, 91–2, 113, 176–7, 190, 256, 362; royal 32, 48, 56, 61, 163, 228, 230, 271, 307–8, 311
guest-houses 176–7, 229–30, 234, 244
Guildford, Surrey
Corporation 312
Mayor of 314
guilds 302, 306–7, 330–3, 347
religious 252 n., 305, 313–15, 331–3; feasts of 305, 313, 320, 331–2, 342–5
trade 331–2, 345
Guise, Francis, Duc de 309
Gundulf, Bishop of Rochester 235

Hacket, John 283
Hackness, Yorkshire 13, 135
Hackwood, Hampshire 207
Haddon Hall, Derbyshire 36
Hales, John 138
Halesowen, Worcestershire 370
Hall, Joseph, Bishop of Exeter 282
Hall, Mr 66
Halland, Sussex 146, 152, 190
Hals, John, Bishop of Coventry and Lichfield 247, 281
Hammond, Henry 138–9, 293
Practical Catechism 138
Hammond, Lieutenant 150, 195, 207, 209
Hampshire 231, 236
Hampton Court Palace 163
Hampton Gay, Oxfordshire 180
Hanbury, Dorothy 137, 178
Hanbury, Edward 137
hand-fasting 368–9
Hanwell, Oxfordshire 294
Haproole, Steward to Lord Cobham 132
Hardwick Hall, Derbyshire 159, 163

Hare, Michael 170
Harington, Lady Elizabeth 86
Harington, Sir John 276
Harison, Antony 279
Harley family 175
Harlow, Essex 371, 373
Harman, Thomas
A Caveat for Common Cursetors 384
Harpsfield, Nicholas 248
Harrison, William 91, 96, 203, 252, 290, 300–1, 310, 317, 353–4, 364–5, 367
Description of England 91
harvest festivities 70, 168, 220, 354, 356–7, 363, 379, 386, 388
Hastings family 317
Hastings, Henry, 5th Earl of Huntingdon
household ordinances 43, 202
Hastings, Henry 116–17
Hastings, Sir Hugh 52, 61, 64–5, 71, 77, 79, 89
Hatcher, Mr 66
Hatfield House, Hertfordshire 163, 188
Hatfield Priory, Essex 150–1
Hatton, Sir Christopher 155, 207
Havant, Hampshire 196
Havering, Essex 400
Hawes, Thomas 6
Hawkins family 311
Hazlewood Castle, Yorkshire 169
Heacham, Norfolk 81
Heale, William 5
Health to the Gentlemanly Profession of Servingman, A 165–6
Heath, Nicholas, Archbishop of York 263
Heath, Peter 254
Heaton, Martin, Bishop of Ely 276
Henry VII 44, 48, 56, 87–8, 251
Henry VIII 54, 72, 88, 233, 256, 261–2, 334, 345, 361
court of 55, 261
heraldic devices 30
Herbert, George 291–3, 297–8
The Country Parson 291
Herbert, Richard 393
Herbert, Lord Edward of Cherbury 180
Hereford 212, 313
Hereford, Dean of 206

Herefordshire 213
hermits 63, 217
Herrick, Robert 108-13, 168
Herrick, Robert, Alderman of Leicester 330
Hertfordshire 183, 391
Heydon, Essex 294, 372
Heydon, Sir Christopher 75
Heylyn, Peter 277, 282
Heywood, Oliver 289, 296
Hieron, Samuel 136
High Wycombe, Buckinghamshire 341
Hinchcliff, William 198
Hinde, William 175-6
Hinton Priory, Somerset 231
Hobart, Sir John 197
Hobbs, Thomas 383
Hobson, William 196
Hoby, Lady Margaret 13, 136, 196
Hoby, Sir Philip 74
Hoby, Sir Thomas Posthumous 13-14, 22, 136, 180, 196, 198, 390
Hoccleve, Thomas 25, 93
Hofnaegel, J. 369
Hogen, Robert 231
Holdenby House, Northamptonshire 155, 155 n., 207
Holford, Mr 172
Holland, Dr 211
Holles, Gervase 72, 89, 105
Holles, John, 1st Earl of Clare 105
Holles, Sir William 72, 89
Hollewman, Mr 209
Hollybrand, Claudius 317
Holme Cultram, Cumberland 378, 386
Holy Island, Northumberland 208
Holy Trinity, feast of 78, 331, 333
Homer 93
Hornsea, Yorkshire 252
homilies 128-9
Hooker, Thomas 234
Hooper, John, Bishop of Gloucester and Worcester 263, 266-7, 292
Horace 108
Hornchurch, Essex 375
Horton, Mr 56
hospitality
  abuse of 13-14, 34, 152, 197-8, 390
  of bishops vii-viii, 223-5, 246-51, 257-63, 265-86, 299
  of cathedrals 263, 274

Catholic vii, 123-5, 144, 160-75, 178, 185, 223, 260
Christian ideals of 3-6, 14-15, 17-19, 23, 33-4, 93, 122-40, 169-78, 194, 220-1, 223, 258-9, 353, 395
classical ideals of 4-5, 25, 99-102, 194
of clergy 6, 14, 128, 196, 201, 205-6, 211, 221, 225-99
by culture: English 10-11, 14, 17, 28, 91-2, 119, 153, 179, 183, 189, 194, 216, 389, 394, 398-403; Greek and Roman 1-2; Irish 26-8, 93, 192-3, 396-7; Mediterranean 10-11, 397; North-West Pacific Tribes 1-2; Provençal 1, 93; Scottish 9, 189, 203, 396-7; Virginian 396-7; Welsh 26-8, 192, 396
decay of 93-4, 112-14, 118-19, 125-6, 140-1, 168-9, 194, 214, 242-3, 336, 398
definitions of 3, 9-10, 14-19, 23, 25-6, 389
and honour 12-14, 24-5, 33, 100, 113-14, 140, 174-5, 183-4, 206, 210, 227, 229, 300-2, 307, 309, 311, 327, 389-93, 397-400
to kin 206-7, 360-1, 371-3, 388
law of 4-5, 192, 199, 215, 389
of monasteries 35, 55, 62, 200-1, 220, 222, 225-46, 253, 258
open 7-8, 12-17, 23, 35, 42-3, 48, 54, 91-3, 101, 108-13, 117, 125-6, 140, 155, 167-8, 174, 183-5, 189-91, 214, 229, 239, 249-50, 276-7, 280, 285, 293-4, 298-9, 300, 304, 319-21, 329-30, 352, 355-6, 362-3, 367, 377, 382-3, 389-93, 398-403
of peerage and gentry 6-7, 12-13, 22-92, 112-13, 123, 140-92, 194-9, 207-9, 212-15, 219, 314-15, 380, 385-6, 390-4
to the poor 14-15, 33-5, 114-5, 124-39, 170-7, 180-1, 217-20, 223-4, 227, 231-6, 240-1, 253-6, 266-7, 274, 283-6, 292-5, 303, 318-22, 332-3, 346, 348-9, 356, 362-3, 372-3, 375, 382-5, 392-4

Protestant vii, 17–19, 64, 99, 122–40, 174–8, 258–62, 284, 291–2, 295–6
  to the saints 135–7, 175–8, 294, 296
  to scholars 217–18
  of towns 300–51, 353–4, 389
  and women 178–83
  of yeoman and ordinary householders 16, 219, 221–2, 352–9, 377–86, 401, 403
hospitals 236, 392
hosts 3, 8, 12, 14, 16, 18, 45, 141, 164, 192–5, 199–205, 208–10, 215–17, 221–2, 249, 261, 266, 279–80, 296, 305–6, 352, 356, 365, 378, 395
  role of 32–5, 389, 397
Houghton, Durham 293
household ordinances 12, 27–32, 42–3, 49–50, 70, 92, 92–5, 154–8, 167, 189–90, 198, 265, 270, 310, 319, 390
households
  break-up of 83–5, 129, 149–51, 301
  conventual 240–1
  education in 165
  episcopal 246–51, 260, 262, 265–70, 277–81, 283, 285
  royal 27–30, 40, 43–4; Chamber 201; Privy Chamber 44
  secret 47
  size of 45–8, 85–6, 97, 149–50
  worship in 78–9, 117
houses, of nobles and gentry
  design of 36–41, 44, 153–64
  social geography of 29–32, 43–4, 109, 153–8, 164, 167; buttery bar 30, 33, 167; chamber 30–2, 36–42, 52, 58, 153–4, 159–60; chapel 44, 117, 176; dais 29–30, 33, 41; dining room 37, 43–4, 154, 157–8; door, gate 8–9, 15–16, 29, 32, 34, 98, 182, 190, 221, 229, 385; gallery 44; great chamber 41, 43–4, 154–5, 157, 164; hall 29–33, 35–44, 50, 66–7, 91, 104, 109, 117, 153–62, 167, 177, 190; lodgings 32, 154; parlour 43, 109, 154–7, 160; servants' hall 155, 162, 167; service rooms 30, 37, 109, 153–4, 159; study 43

houses
  royal 163
  urban 300, 305–6
Housman, J. 355
How, Humphrey 393
Howard family 60, 63, 67, 152, 202, 207
  accounts of 63, 66–7, 69, 71, 78, 83
Howard, John, 1st Duke of Norfolk 46, 85
Howard, Thomas, 3rd Duke of Norfolk 55, 63, 66, 71, 84, 217
  Elizabeth his wife 78, 84
Howard, Thomas, 14th Earl of Arundel 165
Howard, Edward, 9th Duke of Norfolk 174
Howard, Lord William of Naworth 165, 170, 205, 207
  accounts of 170
Howes, Thomas 322
Howson, John, Bishop of Durham 274
Hudson, W. H. 396
Hull, Yorkshire 322, 338
  Corporation 303, 346
  Charterhouse in 231, 233
humanists 95–6, 99, 124, 246, 249, 251
Humphrey, Laurence 130
Hungerford, Mr and Mrs 56
Hungerford, Robert, 2nd Lord Moleyns 202
Huntingdon, earls of, *see* Hastings
Huntingdonshire 58, 212
Hunstanton, Norfolk 47, 59–62, 64, 81
Hutchinson, Sir Thomas 212
Hutchinson, William 190–1, 355
Hyde, Edward, 1st Earl of Clarendon 181
Hythlodaeus, Raphael 96, 251

Idley, Peter 26
  Instructions to his Son 25
Ingatestone, Essex 52, 67, 74–5, 84, 171
Ingrave, Essex 172
Innocents, the feast of 73
inns and alehouses 55–6, 137, 201–9, 212–15, 218–19, 221, 229, 237, 255, 273, 305–6, 309, 317–18, 347, 359, 365, 395–7
  development of 202–3, 300

inns and alehouses (*cont.*)
  landlords of 203-4, 211-12, 214, 219
  monastic 236-9, 245
Inns of Court, the 146
Institucion of a Gentleman, The 10, 23, 116
inventories 41, 43
invitations 195-6, 207, 292, 314, 325, 342, 368
Ipswich, Suffolk 63, 311, 339-40, 345
  guild feast 303, 339
Ireland 137, 185, 192-3, 208, 285-6, 396-8
Isaac, Rhys 397
Isaacson, Henry 283
Italy 10, 153, 193, 260

Jackson, James 386
James I 118-21, 128, 143, 147-8, 152, 163, 183, 277
James V of Scotland 203
Jegon, John, Bishop of Norwich 278-9
Jennings, Robert 374
Jewel, John, Bishop of Salisbury 279
John of Gaunt 85
Johnson, Robert 275
Johnson, Samuel 398
Jonson, Ben 104, 108-14, 120, 291
  The Magnetick Lady 291
Jordan, W. K. 122
Josselin, Ralph 295-6, 368
Joye, George 248
Justices of the Peace 13, 132-3, 147, 169, 219

Kaye, John 114
Kelmarsh, Northamptonshire 137
Kempe, Margery 248
Kemys, Williams 58
Kendal, Westmorland 231, 326
  Corporation 346, 366, 370
  Mayor of 370
Kennett, White, Bishop of
  Peterborough 297, 360, 362-3, 365, 369, 388
Kenninghall, Norfolk 61, 74
Kent 106, 109, 113, 132, 152, 213, 271, 277, 282, 372, 377, 380, 401
Kent, Countess of, *see* Grey
Kerke, Anne 367
Kettlewell, Yorkshire 289
Kett's Rebellion 88

Kilmore, co. Galway 285
Kinaston, Ralph 385
King, Daniel 377
King's Lynn, Norfolk
  Austin Friary 62
Kingswood, Abbot of 62
Kirk, Thomas 208, 214
Kirkwood, Revd. James 9, 203
Kirmington, Lincolnshire 254
Kitchen, Anthony, Bishop of Llandaff 276
Knaresborough, Yorkshire 348
Knightley family 171
Knights Templar 37
Knole, Kent 157, 161
Knowles, David 243
Knowsley, Lancashire 53
Knyvett family 58, 61, 195
Knyvett, Thomas 195
Knyvett, Sir William 53, 58

Lake District 371
Lambeth, Surrey 63, 277
Lamentacyon of a Christian against the Citye of London 320
Lancashire 92, 211, 220, 231, 243, 362, 390
Lancaster 211
Langland, William 40-2, 63, 93
  Piers Plowman 40
Latimer, Hugh, Bishop of Worcester 16, 125, 232-3, 259, 290, 378
Laud, William, Archbishop of
  Canterbury 277, 282, 349, 360
Laudians 138
Law, William 298
Laycon, William 219
Layton, Richard 232
leases, clerical 253-4, 258, 270-3, 288-90
Legh, Sir Urian 211
Leicester 212, 317, 339-40
  Angel Inn. Cheapside 202, 309
  Corporation 315, 316 n., 327, 366
Leicester, Archdeaconry of 253
Leicester, Countess of, *see* De Montfort
Leicestershire 199, 293
Leigh, Francis Lord 393
lent 323
Le Strange family 47, 51, 54, 64, 71, 81, 89
  accounts 59-60, 62-3, 67, 77, 151, 184

Le Strange, Sir Hamon 63
Le Strange, Nicholas 206
Le Strange, Sir Thomas 46–7, 53, 59–62, 64, 74, 85
Lever, Thomas 25, 125–6, 259, 267, 285
Lewes, Sussex 209
Lewkenor family 176
Lewkenor, Sir Edward 176–7
liberality 24–7, 99–100, 141, 248, 290
Lichfield, Staffordshire
  'Green Bower Feast' 333, 335, 346
Lincoln 309, 330
  Mayor of 302, 309
Lincoln, Diocese of 244, 253, 287
  Archdeaconry of 253–4
  Cathedral 263
Lincolnshire 62, 373, 382
Little Gidding, Huntingdonshire 121
Little Warley, Essex 172
Liverpool 334
  Corporation 334
lollards 132
London 8, 13, 53, 55, 58, 68, 74, 77, 102, 115–16, 145–50, 167–8, 175, 182, 184, 196–7, 202, 206–7, 216, 237, 246, 249–50, 285, 300–302, 309, 317–20, 330, 337, 344, 354, 364, 391, 400
  companies 332 n.
  Corporation 11, 302, 310, 330 n., 336, 346, 403
  expulsion of gentry from 119–20, 144, 146–7
  freemen 337, 346
  hospitals 125
  Lord Mayor 128, 204, 302, 310, 326, 333, 336, 345–6, 403; feast and show of 310, 346; household of 310, 320
  movement of gentry to 8, 113, 118–19, 122, 129, 141–4, 146–50, 301, 402
  places in: Broken Wharf 367; Clerkenwell 146; 'The Harp Inn' 85; King St., Covent Garden 151; Newgate 320; Royal Exchange 277; St Olave's Parish 180; St Paul's 277; Savoy Palace 85; West End 147; Westminster Hall 277
  residence in 72, 85–6, 104, 111, 113, 118, 145–53, 172, 180–3, 186, 277, 301, 318
  season 144–8, 183, 391
London, Diocese of 268
Longland, John, Bishop of Lincoln 244, 253
Longleat House, Wiltshire 142, 149, 151, 209
Long Newton, Wiltshire 359
Lord Keeper, the 128
Loseley House, Surrey 314
Louth, Nicholas of 255
Lovelace, Richard 121
Lovell family 61
Lovell, Sir Thomas 47, 55
Lower Shuckburgh, Warwickshire 205
Lucy family 187
Lucy, Lady Alice 180
Lucy, Sir Thomas, the 2nd 217, 317
Lucy, Sir Thomas, the 3rd 105, 187
Ludham, Norfolk 278
Luttrell family 78
Lydgate, John 27
Lyndwood, William 224, 226, 228
Lyng, Norfolk 64

MacCaffrey, Wallace 338
Macfarlane, Alan 383–4, 400
McGee, Sears 139
magnificence 24–9, 31, 44, 48, 56–8, 95, 100, 141, 188–91, 247, 271, 391, 402
Maldon, Essex 218, 303, 333
Malter's wife 357
Man, Isle of 367
Manchester, Lancashire 211
Manners, Francis, 6th Earl of Rutland 188
Manningham, John 157 n.
Mansell, Sir Edward 164
marching watch 318, 333, 344–6
Margaretting, Essex 75
Markham, Gervase 183
marriages 52, 80–1, 104, 184, 353, 368–71, 383
  clerical 257
  Welsh 370
Martial 108
Martindale, Adam 371, 373
Martyr, Peter Vermigli 260
Marvell, Andrew 108–9
Marwood and his wife 172
Mary I 323

Mary Queen of Scots 309
Mary Tudor, sister to Henry VIII 238
Maoris 1
Master, James, 152
Matthew, Tobie, Archbishop of York 280-1, 314
Matthew, Sir Tobie 147
Maundy Thursday, ceremonies on 70, 139, 174, 235
Mauss, Marcel 398
Maynard, Mrs 54
mayor-making 322-6, 335, 338
Mead, Joseph 119
Meade, Richard 375
meals 9, 34-5, 39-42, 50-4, 65-7, 91, 96, 116-17, 153-4, 174, 181, 187, 213, 220, 243, 255-6, 266-7, 283-4, 289, 296, 308, 311, 313, 328, 333-4, 357, 360
    breakfast 43, 179, 290, 326-30, 346, 357, 367-8, 383
    dinner 52-4, 66-7, 104, 110, 116-17, 157-8, 171-2, 195, 205, 207-8, 213, 221, 234-5, 249, 251, 280, 283, 286, 292-3, 303, 308-14, 327-9, 339, 341-2, 355, 358, 368-72, 382
    hierarchical seating at 31-3, 42, 92, 96, 110, 157, 267, 302, 332, 363, 395
    messes at 31, 49, 65, 159, 366, 368, 370
    supper 52, 67, 110-11, 283, 321, 328, 336, 357
Meautys, Thomas 195
Mediterranean cultures 10
Menton, Isaac 372
Mere, Wiltshire 361
Mertes, K. 78
Middlethorpe, Yorkshire 280
Middleton, Lancashire 362
Middleton, Oliver 327
Midgley, Mary 383
Midlands, the 364
midsummer festivals 303, 323, 333, 335, 337, 342, 347
    shows 347
Milbourne Port, Somerset 185
Milburne, Jane 369
Mildmay, Mr 309
Mildmay, Sir Humphrey 117, 146-8, 185
Mildmay, Sir Thomas 171

Miles, Mr 66
Mingay, Anthony 148
Minster Lovell, Oxfordshire 37
mock beggars' hall 8, 83, 150, 221
monasteries, dissolution of 231-3, 236, 245, 258, 261-3
    commissioners for 231-2, 239
Monmouth 215
Monson, Sir John 391
Montagu, Viscount, *see* Browne
Montagu, Lady Magdalen 170, 178
Montagu, Sir Edward 177-8
Montagu, Sir Edward junior 178
Mordaunt, Sir John 56
More, Sir Thomas 95-8, 243 n., 256
    Utopia 63, 95-8, 125, 251
More, William, Prior of Worcester 240
More, Sir William 81, 314
    his daughter Elizabeth 81
Morice, Ralph 266
Mors, Roderick 258
Morton, John, Cardinal and Archbishop of Canterbury 63, 96, 251
Morton, Thomas, Bishop of Durham 207, 283-5
Moryson, Fynes 91
Mountnessing, Essex 75
Musard, John 240
Myddle, Shropshire 385

nature, images of 109-14, 121-2
Naworth Castle, Cumberland 221
neighbours and neighbourhood 20, 114-15, 117, 121, 129, 140, 143, 169, 172-3, 184-5, 187-8, 254, 256, 264, 294-5, 303-4, 321-2, 330, 336, 360, 362, 366, 368, 371-5, 378, 382-3, 386, 390, 395
Neile, Richard, Archbishop of York 212, 276
neo-Platonism 121
Netley Abbey, Hampshire 231
Neville family 87
    feast of 26, 40, 87, 271
Neville, George, Archbishop of York 87
Neville, Henry 7
Neville, Richard, Earl of Warwick 85
Newark, Nottinghamshire 211
Newcastle-upon-Tyne, Northumberland 338, 369
Newcastle, dukes of, *see* Cavendish; Pelham-Holles

Newdigate, Sir John 143, 177
Newminster, Abbot of 241
Newport family 74
New South Wales, Australia 396
Newton, Norfolk 64
Newton, Yorkshire 196
Newton, Samuel, Alderman of
    Cambridge 315, 323-5, 328, 330,
    337, 342
New Year celebrations 70, 73-6,
    148-9, 172, 219
New Year gifts 75
noble councils 53, 58-9
Norden, John
    The Surveyor's Dialogue 377
Norfolk 60-1, 89, 114-15, 142-3,
    158, 206-7, 231, 278, 312
Norfolk, dukes of, *see* Howard
North, the 204-6, 210, 214, 216, 238,
    363, 367-8, 373, 376, 390
North, Dudley, 3rd Lord 151, 209, 301
North, Sir Dudley, 4th Lord 167
Northallerton, Yorkshire 219
Northampton 231, 350
Northamptonshire 61, 232, 329, 364
Northumberland 201
Northumberland, earls and dukes of, *see*
    Percy
Norwich 92, 133, 148, 195, 204-5,
    207, 209, 318, 325, 331, 339
    Corporation 331
    St George's Guild 305, 318, 331-2,
        344
Norwich
    Bishop of 165
    Diocese of 287
    Prior of 62
Norwich, Dame Catherine de 69
Nottingham 212
Nottinghamshire 56
Nykke, Richard, Bishop of Norwich
    244, 253

Oakhampton, Devon 201
Offley, Hertfordshire 254
Oglander, Sir John 184
Oldcastle, Sir John, Lord Cobham 132
Oldham, Hugh, Bishop of Exeter 251
oration 308
'Orders of Service . . . of a Duke . . .'
    31-2
Orleans 283
Ó Ruaric 192

Osney Abbey, Oxfordshire 237, 239
Oxford 313, 321, 325, 328, 338-40
    Corporation 328, 340
    election feast 325-6, 339-42
    freemen 338
    High Steward 328
    Mayor of 341
    places in: Red Lion 328; Star Inn
        239
    Sheriff of 328
Oxford, Archdeaconry of 253
Oxford, Bishop of 206
Oxford University 152, 204, 375
    Magdalen College 217, 255
    Merton College 201
Oxford, earls of, *see* De Vere
Oxfordshire 362, 369, 379
Oxnead, Norfolk 114, 197

Paget family 51, 74, 79-80, 86, 89, 401
    accounts of 43, 51, 84, 173
Paget, Sir William, 1st Lord Paget 51,
    65, 68, 71, 79-80, 84
    Lady Anne, his wife 43, 54, 79
Paget, William, 5th Lord 144, 147
Paget, William, 7th Lord 167
Palm Sunday 323, 337
Palmer, Sir Thomas 73
Panton, Edward 20-1
Parham, Sir John 185
Parker, Esther 385
Parker, Matthew, Archbishop of
    Canterbury 270-4, 314
Parkhurst, John, Bishop of Norwich
    272, 278-9, 287
parliament 98, 275
    of 1529 274
    of 1542 268
    of 1571 131
    of 1584 274
    of 1610 275
    of 1621 146
    Long 150, 275, 368
    of 1670 351
parliamentary elections 316-17, 348,
    390
Parr, Sir William 232-3
Parson Adams 167-8
Parson Fabbin and his wife 172
Parson Palate 291
Partesoil, Robert 58
Paschall family 171
Paston family 61

Paston, Clement 114, 220
Paston, Robert, 1st Earl of Yarmouth 92–3, 158, 197, 312, 314–15
Paule, George 280
Paulet, John, 5th Marquis of Winchester 207
Paynton, John 350
Peacham, Henry 21, 198
  The Compleat Gentleman 107
Peaks, the 212
Pearson family 74
Pecham, John, Archbishop of Canterbury 226–7, 254, 272, 288
Pelham family 152
Pelham, Sir Thomas 146
Pelham-Holles, Thomas, 1st Duke of Newcastle 190
Pemberton, Sir Lewis 109–10
Penistone, Yorkshire 205
Pennines, the 205, 221
Penruddock family 142
Penshurst House, Kent 36 n., 108–11, 113, 120, 293
Penston, Edmund 336
Pentney Priory, Norfolk 231, 233
Percy family 47, 77
  household book of 27, 47, 49, 84–5
Percy, Henry, 4th Earl of Northumberland 313
Percy, Henry Algernon, 5th Earl of Northumberland 46, 49
Percy, Henry, 9th Earl of Northumberland 179
Percy, Hugh, 1st Duke of Northumberland 190
  Elizabeth his wife 190
Perkins, William 123, 127, 131, 135, 138
  Whole Treatise of Cases of Conscience 131
Perlin, Etienne 203
Pershore, Worcestershire 236
Petre family 64, 68, 74–5, 80, 89, 144, 148, 171–3, 175, 280, 401
  accounts of 67–8, 73, 75–7, 79–80, 84
Petre, John, 1st Lord Petre 147
Petre, John 81
Petre, Sir William 52, 56, 71, 75, 77, 79, 81, 88
  Lady Anne, his second wife 84
Petworth House, Sussex 188, 209, 213
Phelip, Otys 201

Phythian-Adams, Charles 344
Piccolomini, Aeneas Sylvius, Pope Pius II 201, 204
Piddington, Oxfordshire 297
Piers, John, Bishop of Bath and Wells 360–2
Pile, Sir Francis 15
pilgrimage 18, 193, 211, 217, 236–7, 362
Pilgrimage of Grace 231
pilgrims 18, 36, 66, 202, 227, 230, 235–7, 239
Pipewell Abbey, Northamptonshire 232
Pittington, Durham 241
Pitt-Rivers, Julian 397
Plough Monday 357
Plumpton correspondence 72
Plumpton, Edward 72
pluralities and non-residence 253–4, 274–5, 287–8
Plymouth, Devon 216, 334
  Corporation 304, 311, 334, 340, 342
  St Andrew's church 360
Pole, Reginald, Cardinal and Archbishop of Canterbury 268–9, 287–8
Polesworth Priory, Warwickshire 232–3
poor laws 97–8, 133–5, 263, 319, 385
  of 1536 97–8, 125, 130, 263
  of 1547 130
  of 1572 132
  of 1576 132
  of 1598 131–2
  of 1601 132
Pope, Walter 281
Porter, Endymion 121
porters 9, 30, 33, 47, 189, 393
portraits 114, 146
Pounsett family 171
poverty, problem of 16–17, 96, 118, 128–30, 132–3, 187, 256, 299, 321–2
  attitude of monasteries to 242–6
  attitude of towns to 98–9, 133, 317–19, 321–2, 366–7
Powell, Richard 359
Poyntington, Somerset 185
Poyntz, Sir Robert 58
Pratt, Sir Roger 158, 162
Presbyterianism 134–5
Prestwich, Edmund 211
Price, Sir Richard 215

privacy 42–4, 106, 157–8, 164, 376
Privy Council 13, 128–9, 274, 309, 321
proclamations 118–20, 126–8, 144, 146–7
Provence 1
prudence in giving 26–7, 100–1, 342–3, 379, 392
pseudo-Seneca 101
  The Glasse of Manners 101
Puckering, Sir Thomas 317
Pure, Philip 201

Quarr Abbey, Hampshire 231, 233
quarter-sessions 60, 276, 303, 309

Radcliffe, Robert, 1st Earl of Sussex 55, 58, 60
Raglan Castle, Monmouthshire 92, 188
Rainsford, Edward 348
Ramsey, Abbot of 62
Rangeworthy, Gloucestershire 360–1
Rant, Sir Thomas 115
Ratcliffe-on-Sower, Yorkshire 219
Rawlinson, Richard 364
Raymond, Thomas 178
Reading, Berkshire 308
  Abbey 200, 237
rectories and vicarages 253–5, 287, 289
  alehouses in 273, 289
  leasing of 254, 272, 288, 290
recusants 169–70, 173
Requests, Court of 370
Reresby, Sir John 168, 186–7, 281, 390
retainers 30, 37, 48, 66–7, 154, 164–6
Reyniere, Grimod de la 192
Ricart, Robert 323
  The Maire of Bristowe is Kalendar 322
Rich family 175
Rich, Barnabe 155 n.
Richard III 311
Richardson, Samuel 168
  Pamela 168
Ridley, Nicholas, Bishop of London 125
Risdon, Tristan 354, 377
  A Chorographical Description of Devon 354
Rites of Durham 230–1, 234
rites of passage 80, 87, 354–5, 366–8, 374–6, 386

hospitality for 80–2, 325–8, 365–76, 388
Robinson, Robert 371
Robsart family 61
Robsart, John 61
Robson, Simon 198
Rochester Priory, Kent 235
Rodney, John 58
Rogationtide 220, 290, 297, 379–80
Rolfe, John 375
Rome 1–2, 4
Rotherham, Yorkshire 186
Rouen 54
rush-bearing 365
Russell family 151
Russell, Francis, 2nd Earl of Bedford 137
Russell, John 32
  The Book of Nurture 12, 30–1
Ruthal, Thomas, Bishop of Durham 250
Ruthin, Denbighshire 308
Rutland, earls of, *see* Manners

Sacheverell, Mr 219
Sackfield, Arthur 217
Sackville, Richard, 3rd Earl of Dorset 182, 209
Sackville, Thomas, Lord Buckhurst and 1st Earl of Dorset 6, 155, 187
Sadler, Sir Thomas 8, 185
Saffron Walden, Essex 152, 309
St Alban's Abbey 200, 228, 237–8
St Ambrose 19, 135, 224
St Augustine of Canterbury 225
St Augustine of Hippo 124, 135, 224
St Benedict 225, 227, 235–6, 242, 246
  Rule of 225, 227–9, 235, 244, 246
St Benet's, Holme, Norfolk 200, 242, 244
St Blaise's Day 323
St George's Day 50, 70, 323, 329, 331, 346
St John Chrysostom 224, 226
St John's Eve 323, 333, 345
St Julian vii, 380
St Katherine's Eve 322
St Nicholas 78
St Osmund's Day 345
St Paul 14, 223, 260
  on household and hospitality 14, 135, 223, 260–1, 281, 285

St Peter's Eve and Day   323, 331, 333, 345
St Stephen's Day   323, 337
St Thomas's Day   78
St William's Day   337
St Winefride the Virgin   78
Salisbury, Wiltshire   202, 281, 322, 336, 345
  Corporation   345
  Mayor of   336
  midsummer show   342, 348
  places in: George Inn   202
  Tailors' Guild   322, 342, 348
Salveyn, Matilda   86
Sancroft, William, Archbishop of Canterbury   298
Sanderson, Robert, Bishop of Lincoln   282
Sandys, Bedfordshire   290
Sandys, Edmund, Archbishop of York   273, 279
Savage, Sir John   81
Savile, William   143
Savine, Alexander   242-3
Saxham, Suffolk   108-10, 114, 120
Scarborough, Yorkshire   146
Scory, John, Bishop of Hereford   279
Scotland   201, 203, 208, 210-11, 309, 367, 370-1, 376
  Borders of   109, 221, 367
  Highlands of   9, 203, 396, 399
  inns in   203
  parliament   203, 376
Scott, John   58
Scroby, Yorkshire   249
Selby Abbey, Yorkshire   235
Selwood, John, Abbot of Glastonbury   239
Sely, John   336
Sempringham, Abbot of   62
Seneca   99, 101-2
  De Beneficiis   25, 101
Sergeants' Feast, the   302
sermons   93-4, 127-9, 136, 138-9, 148, 176, 220, 263, 272, 274-5, 330, 334, 399
servants   13, 27, 32-6, 45-9, 51, 62, 83-4, 89, 91, 149-50, 155-70, 209, 215, 221, 247-8, 252, 256, 265-6, 278
  in chamber   29-31, 47, 164
  chaplains   209
  criticism of   95, 164-6, 267

  estate officials   53, 58, 160, 166
  female   160, 166-7, 215
  in hall   31, 42-3, 47, 190
  housekeepers   190
  in husbandry   47, 52
  'Service to the Baron-Bishop of Yorke'   40
  sessions dinners   328-9, 335
  seven works of mercy, the   123, 127, 170, 255, 281, 320
Severn, the   212
Seymour family   54, 202
  accounts of   54, 72
Seymour, Edward, Duke of Somerset   55-6, 65, 72, 83, 86, 89, 259, 262
Seymour, Sir Thomas   262, 265
Shaw, Sir John   310
sheep-shearing festivities   70, 356-8
Shelley, Sir John   147
Shenfield, Essex   172
Sheppard, William   294-5
Sherburne, Robert, Bishop of Chichester   87 n., 250
sheriffs   171, 308, 386
Shipward, Mr   66-7
Shrewsbury, Shropshire   213, 330
Shropshire   213, 385
Shuckburgh, Lady   205
Sibbes, Richard   123, 138
Sidney family   111, 113
Sidney, Sir Henry   114
Sidney, Sir Philip   4, 4 n.
  The New Arcadia   36 n.
Sir Gawain and the Green Knight   40
Skipwith, Henry   199
Slingsby, Sir Henry   116, 148, 280, 348
Slipslop, Mrs   167
Smith, Sir John, priest   255
Smith, Miles, Bishop of Gloucester   284
Smith, Peter   293
Smith, Thomas   349
Smyth, John   71, 74, 76, 82
Smollett, Tobias   402
  Humphry Clinker   402-3
Snape, R. H.   242
Snettisham, Norfolk   64
Somerset   57, 185, 231, 360, 362, 365
Somerset, Duke of, *see* Seymour
Somerset, Edward, 4th Earl of Worcester   171
  his wife   171

Somerset, Henry, 5th Earl of Worcester 92, 173, 188
Somerset, Henry, 1st Duke of Beaufort 162 n, 312 n.
Somerset, Sir Thomas 171
Sondes, Sir George 121, 183
Sotby, Lincolnshire 253
Southcote family 171
Southampton 315, 319
 Guild Merchant 320
 Mayor of 319
Southampton, Countess of, *see* Wriothesley
Southwell, Nottinghamshire 249
Southwell, Sir Richard 62, 74, 231
South Wingfield, Derbyshire 37
South Wraxall, Somerset 37
Spalding, Lincolnshire 382
Spain 10, 397
Spiller, Sir Henry 316
Stafford family 54, 78, 100
 accounts 57-9, 63, 68, 73, 100
Stafford, Edward, 3rd Duke of Buckingham 30, 44-8, 53-9, 62-3, 70-1, 86, 88, 314
Stafford, Lord Henry 54, 58
Staffordshire 58
Stanhope family 317
Stanley, Henry, 13th Earl of Derby 53, 78, 92, 104, 202
 household book of 78
Stanley, Alice, Lady Strange, wife of 14th Earl of Derby 81
Stanley, George, Lord Strange, 72
Stapleford Abbots, Essex 293
Stapleton, Sir Miles 173
Star Chamber, Court of 13, 119, 128, 198, 337, 360, 381
Starkey, Thomas 96, 267
 The Dialogue of Pole and Lupset 267
statutes
 of Dissolution (27 HVIII, c. 28) 262-3
 of Exchange (1 Eliz I, c. 19) 270
 Extinguishing First Fruits (2 & 3 P. & M, c. 4) 269
 Pluralities (21 HVIII, c. 13) 256, 275, 288
 of Westminster (3 Ed. I, c. 1) 200, 238
 see also poor laws
Stephens, John 218

Stettin-Pomerania, Duke of 204
stewards 49
Stilton, Huntingdonshire 219
Stoics and stoicism 4, 101-2, 105, 112
Stone, Lawrence 82
Stonesfield, Oxfordshire 254
Stonley, Richard 64-5, 75, 76, 171, 175, 317
Stonor family 78
Stourton, William, 7th Lord 56
Stow, Archdeacon of 253
Stow, Elizabeth 371
Stow, John 85, 320-1, 373
Strange, Lady and Lord, *see* Stanley
strangers 19, 52, 95-6, 228-30, 266, 304-5, 354, 362-3, 377, 387-8
 attitude of the English to 10-13, 17-18, 220, 362-3, 394-5
 definition of 9-10, 193
 entertainment of 30-4, 49-50, 65-8, 100, 110, 117, 150, 157, 182, 193, 197-8, 203, 260, 283, 293, 307, 322, 377, 381, 397
 foreign 204, 309-10
 poor 17-18, 226-7, 285, 317-9
Strangers, Dorothy 369
Stratford-upon-Avon, Warwickshire 315
Stratford, John de, Archbishop of Canterbury 226, 247, 253
Stroud, Gloucestershire 213
Stourmouth, Kent 288
Stubbes, Philip 360-1
Sturbridge Fair, Cambridge 324, 328
Suffolk 60, 132, 170, 176, 284, 364, 370, 381
Sulyard, Sir Edward 171
Sumner, Charles, Bishop of Winchester 299
sumptuary legislation 128, 267-8, 342-3, 376
Sunday, hospitality on 66, 79-80, 86, 150, 172, 175, 289, 292-4, 296, 373
Sussex 146, 213
 and 1549 rising 88
Sussex, Earl of, *see* Radcliffe
Swansea, Glamorgan 215
Swanton, Norfolk 64
Swayne, William 332
Swinfield, Richard de, Bishop of Hereford 200, 237

Swydardby, Elizabeth 41
Sylvius, Aeneas, *see* Piccolomini

Talbot, Francis, 8th Earl of Shrewsbury 309
Tankerd, Thomas 169
Tasso, Torquato 107
   The Householder's Philosophie 107
Tattershall Castle, Lincolnshire 83
taxation and loans 382–3
Taylor, John 210–17, 221–2, 356, 377
   Penniless Pilgrimage 211–12
Temple, Sir Richard 351
tenants 53, 92–3, 121, 144, 167–8,
   172–5, 177, 182, 184, 220, 234,
   240, 262, 280–1, 386
   feasts for 74–7, 154, 172–3, 186,
   220, 390, 402
Tewkesbury, Gloucestershire 316
Thames, the 210, 212–13, 341
Thames valley 207, 364
Theobalds, Hertfordshire 83
Thimbelthorpe, George 278
Thomas, Sir Anthony 212
Thomas, K. V. 383
Thomas, Walter, 215
Thornbury, Gloucestershire 44, 58
Thorndon, Essex 81
Thornham, Norfolk 63
Thornton, Alice 196
Thorpe, John 154–5
Thorpe Market, Norfolk 115
Throckmorton family 60
Throckmorton, Sir George 147
Thrupp, Sylvia 320
Thurlaston, Leicestershire 293
Thynne family 71, 80, 142, 149
   accounts 79, 149, 151
Thynne, Sir John 51, 79, 142, 149
Thynne, Thomas 151
Tichborne family 174
Tichborne Dole, the 174, 393
Tichborne, Sir Edward 171
Tierney, Brian 244–5
Tiptoft, John, Earl of Worcester 302
tithes 297, 356
tokens for relief 17
Topcliffe, Yorkshire 211
Topsell, Edward 17
Tories 390–1
towns
   cost of entertainment in 339–47
   feasts 350–1

gates 304, 312
guildhalls 304, 310, 315–6, 343
   indebtedness of 307, 339–41
   social geography of 304–5, 312,
   322–3, 343
town halls 315–16, 341, 343
Townshend family 195
Townshend, Sir Roger 195
travellers 226–8, 231–2, 235–7, 291,
   295, 382, 384–5, 387–8
   English 199–217
   foreign 201, 203–4
   the poor 216–22, 285, 319
Trelawny, Mr 206
Tresham family 60
Tresham, Sir Lewis 147
Trobrianders 398
Turberville, Robert 58
Turner, Mr Thomas 308
Turner, William, Dean of Wells 34–5,
   125–6, 177, 264
Tusser, Thomas 70, 355, 357, 379
   *Five Hundred Points of Good
   Husbandry* 70
Twynning, John 239
Tyrell, Catherine 81
Tyrell, Sir Henry 56
   his wife 56
Tyrell, Sir John 171
Tyrell, Mr 56

Ulverscroft Priory, Leicestershire 231,
   233, 236
ushers 16, 31–2, 43, 164

vagrancy and begging 130–5, 137–8,
   189–90, 217–20, 256, 282, 285,
   292, 299, 305, 318–21, 372–3,
   384–5, 388, 393
   Act against (1 EVI, c. 3) 130
   licences to beg/travel 285, 290, 292,
   318–19
Valle Crucis Abbey, Denbighshire 230
Valor Ecclesiasticus 242, 252
Van Gennep, A. 374
Van Meteren, Emmanuel 366
Vaughan, Richard, Earl of Carbery 215
Vaughan, William 25, 127, 135
   The Golden Grove 102, 135
Vaux family 59
Vaux, Elizabeth, Lady 178
Vavasour, John 169
Venetian Relation, The 310

venison 312–13, 323, 328
Villiers, George, 1st Duke of Buckingham 276
Villiers, George, 2nd Duke of Buckingham 190
Virginia 396–401
visitations 253–4, 272, 286–9, 359
visiting, conventions of 195–8, 206–7, 215

wakes, dedication feasts 176, 185, 354, 358–65, 385, 388, 390
Waddington, Katherine 320
Waldron, G. 367
Wales 41, 58, 192, 210, 214–15, 370
North 175, 214, 371
South 58, 215
Walker, Obadiah 197
Wallington, Norfolk 61
Walsingham, Norfolk 60, 114, 237
Prior of 62
Walter, Sir William 116
Walton, Isaac 282
Walwyn, William 58
Wandesford, Sir Christopher 4, 20, 101, 184, 196
Wandesford, Lady 185
Ward, Seth, Bishop of Salisbury 281, 285–6
Ward, William 218–9
Ware, Dr 172
Wareham, Dorset 207
Warham, William, Archbishop of Canterbury 87, 251, 265, 359
enthronement feast of 26, 87, 271, 400
Warine, John, Bishop of Rochester 280
Warner, Sir Edward and Lady 74
Warrington, Lancashire 92
Warwick 55, 133, 209, 217–20, 348
Corporation 133, 307, 317
Priory in 317
Warwick, earls of, see Neville, Rich
Warwickshire 60, 143
Warkworth, Northamptonshire 37
Waterhouse, Edward 105
Watkins, Mr William 385
Weld, Edward 174
Welles, Edward 66
Wendover, Buckinghamshire 254
Wentworth, Thomas, Earl of Strafford 101, 143

Wesley, John 298
Wessington, John, Prior of Durham 230, 241
West, Nicholas, Bishop of Ely 248
West Country, the 186, 196, 200, 206, 210, 363–4
Westfaling, Herbert, Bishop of Hereford 273
West Horndon, Essex 144, 172
West Ilsley, Berkshire 293
West Kington, Wiltshire 290
Westminster Abbey 243 n.
Westminster, Dean of 172
Westmorland 231
Weston, Richard, 1st Earl of Portland 184
Westwood, Prioress of 62
Whalley Abbey, Lancashire 243
Whalley, Edward, Major-General 342
What, Mary 172
Wheler, George 3, 17, 394–5
The Protestant Monastery 3
Whetstone, George 104
A Heptameron of Civil Discourses 104
Whickham, Durham 376
Whitby, Yorkshire 146
Whitelocke, Sir James 308
Whitgift, John, Archbishop of Canterbury 104, 128, 164, 273–6, 280
Whitmore, Sir William 213, 222
Whitsun, celebration of 70, 78, 149, 172, 235, 271, 323, 329, 333, 337, 346
Wicherley, James 386
Wicherley, Richard 386
Wisbech, Cambridgeshire
Holy Trinity Guild 333
Widow Holland 172
Widow Letton 172
widows 178, 180–2
Wight, Isle of 184–5, 231, 233
Wilbraham, Mr 176
Willet, Andrew 370
William III and Mary II 163, 316 n.
Williams, John, Bishop of Lincoln 283
Williamsburg, Virginia 396
Willis, Richard 297
Willoughby family
accounts of 67, 71, 75, 78
ordinances 36

Willoughby, Sir Francis 56, 65, 71, 78, 86
Willoughby, Catherine, Duchess of Suffolk 52, 66–7, 84
wills 245, 320, 371–6
Wilson, Thomas 131
Wiltshire 142, 384
Winchelsea, Robert de, Archbishop of Canterbury 230
Winchester, Hampshire 212, 249
Corporation 337
Winchester Cathedral 281
Winchester, Marquis of, *see* Paulet
Windrush, the 213
Windsor, Berkshire 341
Wingfield, Mr 66
Wingham, Kent 73
Winthrop, John 6
Winwood, Sir Ralph 119
witchcraft accusations 357–8, 367, 369, 383–4
Withers, Lawrence 322
Withyham, Sussex 155
wives, role of in hospitality 54, 57, 60, 68, 81, 119–20, 143–4, 178–83, 196–7, 252, 289, 337, 366
Wolfs Hall, Wiltshire 55–6, 83
Wollaton, Nottinghamshire 56
Wolsey, Thomas, Cardinal and Archbishop of York 247, 249–50, 327, 346
Wolterton, Norfolk 64
Wolvesey Palace, Winchester 281
Womburne, Staffordshire 295
Wood, Anthony 217, 350, 375
Wood, Margaret 37
Wood, Richard, wife of 383
Woodforde, James 298, 323
Woodhouse, Roger 60, 62
Woodhouse, Sir Thomas 85
Woodsome, Yorkshire 114
Worcester 312 n., 321, 339
Priory 234–5, 240, 243
Worcester, earls of, *see* Somerset, Tiptoft

Worcestre, William de 69, 200–201, 242
Itineraries 200
Worksop, Nottinghamshire 174
World's Folly, This 8
Worsley, Sir Richard 184
Wortley, Sir Francis 212
Wotton, Henry 10, 153, 159
Elements of Architecture 6
Wrest, Bedfordshire 109–11
Wrightson, Keith 365
Wriothesley, Elizabeth, Countess of Southampton 171
Wroth, Sir Robert 111
Wroughton, Mr 56
Wurtemberg, Duke of 204, 309
Wyatt, Sir Thomas 106
Wymondham, Edmund 60–1
Wymondham, Sir Thomas 61
Wye, the 213
Wyot, Philip 329, 337, 342

Yarmouth, Earl of, *see* Paston
Yaxley, Francis 195
York 182, 186–7, 204, 211, 280, 313, 320, 323, 325, 334, 336–7, 339, 343–7
assizes 383
Corporation 303, 307, 309, 311, 313, 323, 327, 336–8, 344–5
Mayor of 323
places in: All Saints Church, North St. 320; Kings Manor 309; Ouse River 329; St Thomas's Hospital 323
St Antony's Guild 305
St Christopher's Guild 313
sheriffs of 232, 327, 336–7
York, Diocese of 249, 272, 289
Yorkshire 13, 114, 117, 168, 173, 183–4, 186, 212, 231, 289, 390
Young, John, Bishop of Rochester 279
youths 77, 152

Zouche, Mr 74